Revenue Statistics in Latin America and the Caribbean

1990-2015

Estadísticas tributarias en América Latina y el Caribe

1990-2015

This work is published under the responsibility of the Secretary-General of the OECD. The opinions expressed and arguments employed herein do not necessarily reflect the official views of OECD member countries, its Development Centre or of the United Nations Economic Commission for Latin America and the Caribbean (UN-ECLAC), the Inter-American Center of Tax Administrations (CIAT) or the Inter-American Development Bank (IDB), its Board of Directors, or the countries they represent.

El presente trabajo se publica bajo la responsabilidad del Secretario General de la OCDE. Las opiniones expresadas y los argumentos utilizados en el mismo no reflejan necesariamente el punto de vista oficial de los países miembros de la OCDE, ni del Centro de Desarrollo de la OCDE, ni de la Comisión Económica para América Latina y el Caribe de las Naciones Unidas (CEPAL-UN), ni del Centro Interamericano de Administraciones Tributarias (CIAT), ni del Banco Interamericano de Desarrollo, de su Directorio Ejecutivo ni de los países que representa.

This document, as well as any data and map included herein, are without prejudice to the status of or sovereignty over any territory, to the delimitation of international frontiers and boundaries and to the name of any territory, city or area.

Tanto este documento, así como cualquier dato y cualquier mapa que se incluya en él, no conllevan perjuicio alguno respecto al estatus o la soberanía de cualquier territorio, a la delimitación de fronteras y límites internacionales, ni al nombre de cualquier territorio, ciudad o área.

Please cite this publication as:
OECD/ECLAC/CIAT/IDB (2017), *Revenue Statistics in Latin America and the Caribbean 2017*, OECD Publishing, Paris.
http://dx.doi.org/10.1787/rev_lat_car-2017-en-fr

Por favor, cite esta publicación de la siguiente manera:
OCDE/CEPAL/CIAT/BID (2017), Estadísticas tributarias en América Latina y el Caribe 2017, OECD Publishing, Paris.
http://dx.doi.org/10.1787/rev_lat_car-2017-en-fr

ISBN 978-92-64-27289-7 (print/impresa)
ISBN 978-92-64-27292-7 (PDF)

Corrigenda to OECD publications may be found on line at: *www.oecd.org/publishing/corrigenda.*
Las erratas de las publicaciones de la OCDE se encuentran en línea en *www.oecd.org/publishing/corrigenda.*

Foreword

Revenue Statistics in Latin America and the Caribbean is a joint publication by the OECD Centre for Tax Policy and Administration, the OECD Development Centre, the United Nations Economic Commission for Latin America and the Caribbean (ECLAC), the Inter-American Center of Tax Administrations (CIAT) and the Inter-American Development Bank (IDB). It presents detailed, internationally comparable data on tax revenues for 24 Latin American and Caribbean economies, two of which are OECD members. Its approach is based on the well-established methodology of the OECD Revenue Statistics database, which has become an essential reference source for OECD member countries. Comparisons are also made with the average tax indicators for OECD economies.

The term "taxes" in this publication is confined to compulsory, unrequited payments to general government. As outlined in the Interpretative guide to the Revenue Statistics, taxes are "unrequited" in the sense that benefits provided by government to taxpayers are not normally in proportion to their payments. The OECD methodology classifies a tax according to its base: income, profits and capital gains (classified under heading 1000), payroll (heading 3000), property (heading 4000), goods and services (heading 5000) and other taxes (heading 6000). Compulsory social security contributions paid to general government are treated as taxes, and classified under heading 2000. Much greater detail on the tax concept, the classification of taxes and the accrual basis of reporting is set out in the Interpretative Guide in Annex A.

Extending the OECD methodology to Latin America and the Caribbean countries enables comparisons of tax systems on a consistent basis both across this region and between them and OECD countries. However, in a few cases this methodology is different from the approach used by ECLAC, CIAT and IDB. In these cases the differences are noted in the text and in the tables, either with a footnote or an extra row.

The report provides an overview of the main taxation trends in Latin America and the Caribbean. It examines changes in both the level and the composition of taxation plus the attribution of tax collection by sub-level of government between 1990 and 2015.

Presentación

La publicación *Estadísticas tributarias en América Latina y el Caribe* ha sido elaborada conjuntamente por el Centro de Política y Administración Tributaria de la OCDE, el Centro de Desarrollo de la OCDE, la Comisión Económica de las Naciones Unidas para América Latina y el Caribe (CEPAL), el Centro Interamericano de Administraciones Tributarias (CIAT) y el Banco Interamericano de Desarrollo (BID). Esta publicación presenta datos detallados comparables a escala internacional sobre los ingresos tributarios de 24 economías latinoamericanas y caribeñas, dos de las cuales son miembros de la OCDE. Su enfoque se basa en la metodología contrastada de la base de datos "Revenue Statistics" de la OCDE, que se ha convertido en un referente esencial para los países miembros de la OCDE. Se presentan también comparaciones con la media de medidas tributarias de la OCDE.

En la presente publicación, el término "impuestos" se circunscribe exclusivamente a los pagos obligatorios sin contraprestación efectuados al gobierno general. Tal y como lo subraya la Guía de interpretación de Revenue Statistics, los impuestos carecen de contraprestación en el sentido en que, normalmente, las prestaciones proporcionadas por el gobierno a los contribuyentes no guardan relación directa con los pagos realizados por estos. La metodología de la OCDE clasifica los impuestos según la base sobre la que recaen: renta, utilidades y ganancias del capital (categoría 1000); nómina (categoría 3000); propiedad (categoría 4000); bienes y servicios (categoría 5000); y otros impuestos (categoría 6000). Las contribuciones obligatorias a la seguridad social abonadas al gobierno general se tratan aquí como impuestos (categoría 2000). Para mayor detalle sobre el concepto de impuesto, su clasificación y su registro según el criterio de devengo, véase la Guía de interpretación que figura en el Anexo A.

Aplicar la metodología de la OCDE a América Latina y el Caribe posibilita la comparación de sistemas tributarios a partir de una base coherente en la region, entre los países latinoamericanos, y con los países de la OCDE. Sin embargo, en algunas ocasiones, esta metodología difiere de la empleada por la CEPAL, el CIAT y el BID; en esos casos, las diferencias se han indicado en el texto y los cuadros, sea con una nota a pie de página, o en una línea adicional.

El informe ofrece un panorama general de las principales tendencias en materia tributaria en América Latina y en el Caribe. A tal efecto, examina los cambios registrados entre 1990 y 2015 en el nivel y la composición de la tributación, así como en la atribución de la recaudación tributaria a los diversos subsectores de gobierno.

Acknowledgements

Revenue Statistics in Latin America and the Caribbean has been jointly produced by the Organisation for Economic Co-operation and Development (OECD) Centre for Tax Policy and Administration, the OECD Development Centre, the United Nations Economic Commission for Latin America and the Caribbean (ECLAC), the Inter-American Center of Tax Administrations (CIAT) and the Inter-American Development Bank (IDB). The staff from these organisations with responsibility for producing the publication were: René Orozco and Juan Carlos Benítez of the OECD Development Centre under the supervision of the Director, Mario Pezzini and the Head of the Latin American and Caribbean Unit, Angel Melguizo; and Emmanuelle Modica of the OECD Centre for Tax Policy and Administration under the supervision of the Director, Pascal Saint-Amans, Deputy Director, Grace Perez-Navarro, the Head of the Tax Policy and Tax Statistics Division, David Bradbury and the Head of the Tax Data and Statistical Analysis Unit, Michelle Harding; Michael Hanni, Juan Pablo Jimenez, Ignacio Ruelas and Miguel Angel González of the Economic Development Division of UN-ECLAC under the supervision of the Director, Daniel Titelman, and the Chief of the Fiscal Affairs Unit, Ricardo Martner; and Julio Alberto López, Dalmiro Morán and Agnes Rojas from the CIAT Tax Studies and Research Directorate, under the supervision of Director Santiago Díaz de Sarralde and Miguel Eduardo Pecho; and Karla Hernández under the supervision of the Principal Technical Leader in Fiscal Economics, Alberto Barreix of the IDB.

The authors would like to thank other staff at the OECD Development Centre, the Centre for Tax Policy and Administration and the Ibero-American Secretariat General (SEGIB) for sponsoring the "First Technical Seminar on Revenue Statistics for Latin America and the Caribbean" and for their invaluable help in improving and completing this sixth edition of the publication. Elizabeth Nash and Delphine Grandrieux from the OECD Development Centre's Communications and Publications team and Ludivine Baudouin, statistical editor from the OECD Publications and Communications directorate ensured the production of the publication, in both paper and electronic form.

Finally, the Centre for Tax Policy and Administration and the Development Centre are also very grateful to our colleagues working in national entities with whom we have consulted regularly. These institutions include the finance ministries and national tax agencies of Argentina, Barbados, Belize, Bolivia, Brazil, Chile, Colombia, Costa Rica, Cuba, Dominican Republic, Ecuador, El Salvador, Guatemala, Honduras, Jamaica, Mexico, Nicaragua, Panama, Paraguay, Peru, Uruguay and Venezuela, the Ministry of Economy and Production of Argentina, the Central Bank of Barbados and the Central Reserve Bank of Peru. In addition, CIAT would like to thank their Network of Tax Studies and Research.

Agradecimientos

La publicación *Estadísticas tributarias en América Latina y el Caribe* ha sido elaborada conjuntamente por el Centro de Política y Administración Tributaria de la Organización para la Cooperación y el Desarrollo Económicos (OCDE), el Centro de Desarrollo de la OCDE, la Comisión Económica de las Naciones Unidas para América Latina y el Caribe (CEPAL), el Centro Interamericano de Administraciones Tributarias (CIAT) y el Banco Interamericano de Desarrollo (BID). Las personas de esas organizaciones responsables de redactar la presente publicación han sido: René Orozco y Juan Carlos Benítez del Centro de Desarrollo de la OCDE, bajo la supervisión del director, Mario Pezzini y del Jefe de la Unidad de América Latina y el Caribe Angel Melguizo; Emmanuelle Modica del Centro de Política y Administración Tributaria de la OCDE, bajo la supervisión del director, Pascal Saint-Amans, sub-directora Grace Perez-Navarro y el Jefe de la División de Políticas y Estadísticas Tributarias, David Bradbury y la Jefe de la Unidad de Análisis de Datos Tributarios y Estadísticas, Michelle Harding; Michael Hanni, Juan Pablo Jiménez, Ignacio Ruelas y Miguel Angel González de la División de Desarrollo Económico de la CEPAL, bajo la supervisión del director Daniel Titelman y del jefe de la Unidad de Asuntos Fiscales Ricardo Martner; Julio Alberto López, Dalmiro Morán y Agnes Rojas de la Dirección de Estudios e Investigaciones Tributarias del CIAT, bajo la supervisión del Director Santiago Díaz de Sarralde y Miguel Eduardo Pecho; y Karla Hernández, bajo la supervisión del Líder Técnico Principal en Economia Fiscal del BID, Alberto Barreix.

Los autores desean agradecer a otras personas del Centro de Desarrollo de la OCDE, del Centro de Política y Administración Tributaria de la OCDE y a la Secretaría General Iberoamericana (SEGIB) por el financiamiento del "Primer Seminario Técnico de Estadístcas Tributarias en América Latina y el Caribe" y su incalculable contribución a la mejora y finalización de la tercera edición de esta publicación. En particular, Elizabeth Nash y Delphine Grandrieux, del equipo de Comunicaciones y Publicaciones del Centro de Desarrollo de la OCDE, y Ludivine Baudouin, editora estadística del equipo de Publicaciones y Comunicaciones de la OCDE que aseguraron la producción de la publicación, tanto fisica como en formato electrónico.

Por último, El Centro de Política y Administración Tributaria y el Centro de Desarrollo de la OCDE hacen partícipes de nuestro agradecimiento a nuestros colegas de entidades nacionales, a los que hemos consultado con frecuencia. Entre esas instituciones, se cuentan los ministerios de finanzas y las agencias tributarias nacionales de Argentina, Barbados, Belice, Bolivia, Brasil, Chile, Colombia, Costa Rica, Cuba, Ecuador, El Salvador, Guatemala, Honduras, México, Nicaragua, Panamá, Paraguay, Perú, República Dominicana, Uruguay y Venezuela, así como el Ministerio de Economía y Producción de Argentina, el Banco Central de Barbados (CBB) y el Banco Central de Reserva del Perú. Asimismo, CIAT también desea agradecer La Red de Estudios e Investigaciones Tributarias.

Table of contents

Índice de materias

LIST OF TABLES/ÍNDICE DE CUADROS

Chapter 1/Capítulo 1
Tax revenue trends, 1990-2015/Tendencias tributarias, 1990-2015

Chapter 2/Capítulo 2
Special feature/Sección especial

Chapter 3/Capítulo 3
Special feature/Sección especial

Chapter 4/Capítulo 4
Tax levels and tax structures, 1990-2015/Niveles impositivos y estructuras tributarias, 1990-2015

LIST OF FIGURES/ÍNDICE DE GRÁFICOS

Chapter 1/Capítulo 1
Tax revenue trends, 1990-2015/Tendencias tributarias, 1990-2015

Chapter 2/Capítulo 2

Special feature/Sección especial

Chapter 3/Capítulo 3

Special feature/Sección especial

Executive summary

Revenue Statistics in Latin America and the Caribbean provides internationally comparable data on tax levels and tax structures for 24 Latin American and Caribbean (LAC) countries: Argentina, the Bahamas, Barbados, Belize, Bolivia, Brazil, Chile, Colombia, Costa Rica, Cuba, the Dominican Republic, Ecuador, El Salvador, Guatemala, Honduras, Jamaica, Mexico, Nicaragua, Panama, Paraguay, Peru, Uruguay, Trinidad and Tobago, and Venezuela. This data allows policy makers to assess tax levels and structures across LAC and OECD economies to inform policy reforms and promote public sector transparency and accountability.

In this publication, "taxes" are defined as compulsory, unrequited payments to the general government. Taxes are "unrequited" in the sense that benefits provided by government to taxpayers are not normally in proportion to their payments. Compulsory social security contributions (SSCs) paid to general government are classified as taxes. More information on the tax classification and the basis of reporting is set out in the Interpretative Guide in Annex A.

Tax-to-GDP ratios in the LAC region

The tax-to-GDP ratio is measured as tax revenues, including SSCs paid to general government, as a proportion of GDP. In 2015, the average tax-to-GDP in the LAC region was 22.8%. Tax-to-GDP ratios varied widely between countries, ranging from 12.4% in Guatemala and 13.4% in the Dominican Republic to 32.0% in Brazil, 32.1% in Argentina and 38.6% in Cuba. In fact, Cuba is the only country that had a tax-to-GDP ratio above the OECD average of 34.3%.

Since 2014, the average LAC tax-to-GDP ratio increased by 0.6 percentage points. This was driven by an increase of 0.3 percentage points in the revenue from taxes on general consumption (mainly VAT) and an increase of 0.2 percentage points in revenue from taxes on specific goods and services (mainly excises, customs and imports duties). This contrasts with the overall economic environment in the Latin American region, and the contraction of regional real GDP in 2015 by 0.5% due to a weaker global economy and lower commodity prices.

The increase in the LAC average tax-to-GDP ratio in 2015 was mirrored in 19 of the 24 countries. The Bahamas and Mexico recorded the highest increases of 2.6 and 2.3 percentage points respectively, whereas Peru experienced the largest decrease of 1.7 percentage points, with changes in all three countries driven by significant tax reforms. Peru also suffered from low corporate income tax revenues as a result of low commodity prices in the oil and mining sector.

Since 1990, the average tax-to-GDP ratio in LAC countries has risen continuously, with the exception of 2008 and 2009, increasing by more than seven percentage points from 15.8% in 1990 to 22.8% in 2015. This trend contrasts with the OECD average, which has been relatively stable and increased by 2.3 percentage points between 1990 and 2015, from 32.0% to 34.3% of GDP. The main contributor to the increase of the average LAC tax-to-GDP ratio between 1990 and 2002 was VAT due to its increasing use in LAC countries over that period. Between 2002 and 2015, revenue from taxes on income and profits was the main contributor.

Tax structures in the LAC region

In 2014, the LAC countries on average were relatively reliant on indirect taxes. Taxes on goods and services made up about half of all tax revenues compared with a third in the OECD. On average, 44% of tax revenues (9.9% of GDP) in LAC countries come from taxes on income and profits and SSCs, compared with 60% (20.6% of GDP) in the OECD.

Within taxes on income and profits, the revenue share of corporate income tax was high in the LAC region compared to the OECD whereas the personal income tax revenue share was low. In 2014, corporate and personal income tax revenue were 16.8% (3.8% of GDP) and 8.7% (2.0% of GDP) of total tax revenues respectively, compared to 8.8% (2.8% of GDP) and 24.0% (8.4% of GDP) in the OECD. The low revenue share from personal income tax is partly explained by generous tax reliefs and high standard allowances as well as tax evasion by wealthy taxpayers. Similarly, the share of SSCs (as defined in the Interpretative Guide in Annex A) in total tax revenues was about 10 percentage points lower in the LAC average than in the OECD average (16.3% compared with 26.2%, or 3.6% and 9.1% of GDP). The privately-oriented provision of social security in many countries in the LAC region may explain some of this difference.

VAT revenue ratios

The VAT revenue ratio (VRR) has been included for the first time in this publication. A VRR of 100% suggests no loss of VAT revenue due to exemptions, reduced rates, fraud, evasion or tax planning. In the LAC region, VRRs in 2014 ranged from 25% in Jamaica and 32% in Mexico to Bolivia at 101% and Paraguay at 93%. The design of VAT partly explains this variation: Mexico and Jamaica have exemptions and a zero-rate for a large number of goods and services, whereas Bolivia does not apply any reduced rates and has a broad VAT base. Bolivia and Paraguay also have implemented policies to address VAT evasion, although high informality in the trade sector (as in Paraguay) may also contribute to the high VRR ratios in these countries. Better evidence on VAT non-compliance and informality are needed to provide more conclusive findings.

Tax revenues by level of government

For the 15 LAC countries with available sub-national data in 2014, the share of sub-national tax revenues as a proportion of total tax revenue was lower than 8%, except in Argentina, Brazil and Colombia, where they reached more than 15% of total tax revenue (and over 30% in Brazil). These figures reflect that sub-national governments in LAC countries tend to have a relatively narrow range of taxes under their jurisdiction compared to OECD member countries.

Special features

The first special feature describes trends in non-renewable natural resource-related public revenues in the LAC region in 2015 and 2016. The substantial decline in the international price of crude oil that started in 2014 resulted in a sharp fall in hydrocarbons public revenues in the region, which fell on average from 6.8% of GDP in 2014 to 4.4% in 2015 for the ten countries included in the analysis, and are estimated to have fallen to 2.6% of GDP in 2016. Similarly, the decline in mineral and metal prices reduced public revenues from mining, which fell from 0.5% of GDP in 2014 to 0.4% in 2015, with a further fall to 0.3% estimated for 2016.

The second special feature analyses the financing structure of sub-national governments in nine countries in Latin America and measures the tax autonomy of sub-national governments in Argentina, Brazil, Chile and Mexico. In the nine countries studied, the sub-national tax revenues come principally from recurrent taxes on immovable property, taxes on consumption and taxes on business and motor vehicle licences. Payroll tax was an important source of sub-national tax revenue in Mexico and amounted to 41% of total sub-national tax revenue. Sub-national governments in Argentina, Brazil and Mexico were found to have a high level of tax autonomy, whereas in Chile 58% of sub-national tax revenue is subject to a tax-sharing agreement.

Resumen ejecutivo

Estadísticas tributarias en América Latina y el Caribe proporciona datos internacionalmente comparables sobre los niveles y estructuras de recaudo tributario para 24 países de América Latina y el Caribe (ALC): Argentina, Las Bahamas, Barbados, Belice, Bolivia, Brasil, Chile, Colombia, Costa Rica, Cuba, República Dominicana, Ecuador, El Salvador, Guatemala, Honduras, Jamaica, México, Nicaragua, Panamá, Paraguay, Perú, Uruguay, Trinidad y Tobago y Venezuela. Esta data permite a los tomadores de decisiones evaluar los niveles y estructuras del recaudo tributario en economías de OCDE y América Latina y el Caribe, informar reformas y contribuir a la transparencia y responsabilidad del sector público.

En esta publicación, el término "impuestos" se refiere a pagos obligatorios sin contraprestación efectuados al gobierno general. Los impuestos carecen de contraprestación en el sentido que normalmente las contribuciones brindadas por los gobiernos a los contribuyentes no guardan relación directa con los pagos efectuados por estos. Las contribuciones a la seguridad social (CSS) pagadas al gobierno general se clasifican como impuestos. Se proveen mayores detalles sobre la clasificación de los impuestos y su criterio de registro en la Guía en el Anexo A.

Ratios de recaudo tributario y PIB en la región de ALC

El ratio de recaudo tributario y PIB se mide como los ingresos tributarios, incluyendo CSS pagadas al gobierno general, como proporción del PIB. En 2015, el promedio del ratio entre recaudo tributario y PIB para la región de ALC fue de 22.8%. Los ratios de ingresos tributarios y PIB varían extensamente entre los países, desde 12.4% en Guatemala y 13.4% en República Dominicana hasta 32% en Brasil, 32.1% en Argentina y 38.6% en Cuba. Es notable, que Cuba sea el único país cuyo recaudo tributario como proporción del PIB haya superado el promedio de 34.3% de la OCDE.

Desde 2014, el promedio del recaudo tributario, como proporción del PIB, en ALC aumentó 0.6 puntos porcentuales. Esto fue posibilitado por un incremento de 0.3 puntos porcentuales en el recaudo proveniente de los impuestos sobre bienes y servicios específicos (principalmente, impuestos específicos, e impuestos sobre importaciones y aduanas). Esto contrasta con la coyuntura económica de la región de América Latina y la contracción de 0.5% del PIB real en 2015 debido a una economía global más débil y precios más bajos de las materias primas.

El aumento en el promedio del recaudo tributario, como porcentaje del PIB, de ALC en 2015 fue el reflejo del aumento observado en 19 de los 24 países. Las Bahamas y México registraron los incrementos más altos de 2.6 y 2.3 puntos porcentuales respectivamente; mientras que Perú experimentó la caída más pronunciada en 1.7 puntos porcentuales. Las variaciones en estos países fueron impulsadas por reformas fiscales significativas. Perú también registró menor recaudo del impuesto sobre la renta de sociedades, como resultado del bajo precio de las materias primas en los sectores de hidrocarburos y la minería.

El promedio del ratio de ingresos tributarios y PIB en los países de ALC ha crecido desde 1990, con la excepción de los años 2008 y 2009, aumentando más de siete puntos porcentuales de 15.8% en 1990 hasta 22.8% en 2015. Esta tendencia contrasta con el promedio de la OCDE, el cual ha sido relativamente estable y aumentó en 2.3 puntos porcentuales entre 1990 y 2015, pasando de 32.0% a 34.3%. El IVA fue el principal causante del aumento en el promedio de los ingresos tributarios en ALC durante 1990-2002. En tanto que, el impuesto sobre la renta, utilidades y ganancias de capital lo fue entre 2002-2015.

Estructuras tributarias en la región

En 2014, el promedio de los países de ALC dependió mayoritariamente de impuestos indirectos. Los impuestos sobre bienes y servicios comprendieron cerca de la mitad de todos los ingresos tributarios, comparados con un tercio en OCDE. En promedio, 44% de todos los ingresos tributarios (9.9% del PIB) en los países de ALC provino de impuestos sobre la renta y utilidades y las CCS, comparado con 60% (20.6% del PIB) en la OCDE.

Centrándonos en el impuesto sobre la renta y utilidades, la proporción del impuesto sobre la renta de sociedades fue alta en la región de ALC comparado con la OCDE, mientras que la proporción del impuesto sobre la renta de personas físicas fue bajo. En 2014, los ingresos del impuesto sobre la renta de sociedades e individuos fue 16.8% (3.8% del PIB) y 8.7% (2.0% del PIB) del recaudo tributario total respectivamente comparado con 8.8% (2.8% del PIB) y 24.0% (8.4% del PIB) en la OCDE. El bajo recaudo del impuesto sobre la renta en ALC se explica parcialmente por las generosas exenciones fiscales y los altos desgravámenes fiscales, así como también por la evasión fiscal de los contribuyentes de ingresos más altos. De igual forma, las SSC (definidas en la Guía en el Anexo A) como proporción de los ingresos tributarios totales fue 10 puntos porcentuales más baja que el promedio de la OCDE (16.3% comparado con 26.2% ó 3.6% y 9.1% del PIB). La provisión-privada de la seguridad social en varios países en la región de ALC puede explicar esta diferencia en alguna medida.

Ratio de recaudo del IVA

La medida del ratio de recaudo del IVA (VRR por sus siglas en inglés) ha sido incluida por vez primera en esta publicación. Un VRR de 100% sugiere que no existe pérdida en el recaudo del IVA por exenciones, tasas reducidas diferenciadas, fraude, evasión o planificación fiscal. En la región de ALC, las medidas de VRR en 2014 variaron desde 25% en Jamaica y 32% en México hasta 101% en Bolivia y 93% en Paraguay. El diseño del IVA explica parcialmente estas diferencias: México y Jamaica tienen exenciones y gravan con tasa cero un número amplio de bienes y servicios, mientras que Bolivia no aplica tasas reducidas y tiene una base amplia. Bolivia y Paraguay también han implementado reformas dirigidas hacia la reducción de la evasión, aunque los altos niveles de informalidad in el sector de comercio (como en Paraguay) pueden haber contribuido a un alto índice del VRR. Se requiere de más evidencia respecto al no-cumplimiento e informalidad en el IVA para proveer conclusiones más definitivas.

Ingresos tributarios por nivel de gobierno

Para los 15 países de ALC con información subnacional disponible en 2014, los ingresos tributarios subnacionales, como proporción de los ingresos totales, fueron menores al 8% excepto en Argentina, Brasil y Colombia, países en los cuales alcanzaron 15% del recaudo total (30% en el caso de Brasil). Estas cifras reflejan que los gobiernos subnacionales en ALC tienden a contar con un escaso número de impuestos bajo su jurisdicción comparado a lo observado en los países miembros de la OCDE.

Secciones especiales

La primera sección especial describe las tendencias de los ingresos fiscales de recursos naturales no-renovables en la región de ALC en 2015 y 2016. La significativa caída en los precios internacionales del petróleo crudo que inició en 2014 resultó en una marcada disminución en los ingresos públicos provenientes de hidrocarburos en la región, los cuales cayeron en promedio desde 6.8% del PIB en 2014 hasta 4.4% en 2015 para los diez países analizados. Se estima que la caída fue de 2.6% del PIB en 2016. Asimismo, la caída en los precios de los minerales y metales redujo los ingresos públicos provenientes de estas fuentes, reduciéndose de 0.5% del PIB en 2014 hasta 0.4% en 2015, continuando su caída estimada hasta 0.3% en 2016.

La segunda sección especial analiza la estructura del financiamiento de los gobiernos subnacionales en nueve países de América Latina y mide la autonomía fiscal de los gobiernos subnacionales de Argentina, Brasil, Chile y México. En los nueve países estudiados, los ingresos tributarios subnacionales provienen principalmente de los impuestos sobre la propiedad inmueble, impuestos sobre el consumo, impuestos sobre negocios y licencias de vehículos. Los impuestos sobre la nómina son una fuente importante de ingresos subnacionales en México y representaron el 41% del recaudo tributario subnacional total. Los gobiernos subnacionales de Argentina, Brasil y México tienen altos niveles de autonomía tributaria mientras que en Chile el 58% de los ingresos subnacionales están sujetos a los acuerdos de coparticipación tributaria.

CHAPTER 1

TAX REVENUE TRENDS, 1990-2015

CAPÍTULO 1

TENDENCIAS TRIBUTARIAS, 1990-2015

CHAPTER 1

TAX REVENUE TRENDS, 1990-2015

1.1. Tax ratios

The tax-to-GDP ratio reflects the collection of taxation revenue by governments to finance public goods and services and to invest in infrastructure. Raising revenue through taxes is important to ensure a country's economic emergence (OECD, 2014a). Taxation provides a predictable and sustainable source of government revenue, in contrast with declining development assistance and the volatility of non-tax revenues with respect to commodity prices.

This report presents internationally comparable data on the tax revenues of 24 Latin American and Caribbean countries. This chapter discusses the trends in these countries of several key tax indicators: the tax-to-GDP ratio, the tax structure and the share of tax revenue by level of government. The discussion supplements the detailed country information found in Chapter 5.

Tax ratios in 2015

The average tax-to-GDP ratio in Latin America and the Caribbean (LAC) amounted to 22.8% in 2015 (Figure 1.1). The tax-to-GDP ratio is measured as tax revenues (including social security contributions paid to the general government) as a proportion of gross domestic product (GDP). Tax-to-GDP ratios varied widely in the region and ranged from 12.4% in Guatemala to 38.6% in Cuba. All LAC countries had a tax-to-GDP ratio below the OECD average[1] of 34.3% except for Cuba. Figures for Venezuela in 2015 should be interpreted with caution as they have been affected by the high rate of inflation from the previous year. Excluding Venezuela, the average tax-to-GDP ratio for the remaining LAC countries was 22.9% in 2015.

Figure 1.1. **Tax-to-GDP ratios (total tax revenue as % of GDP), 2015**

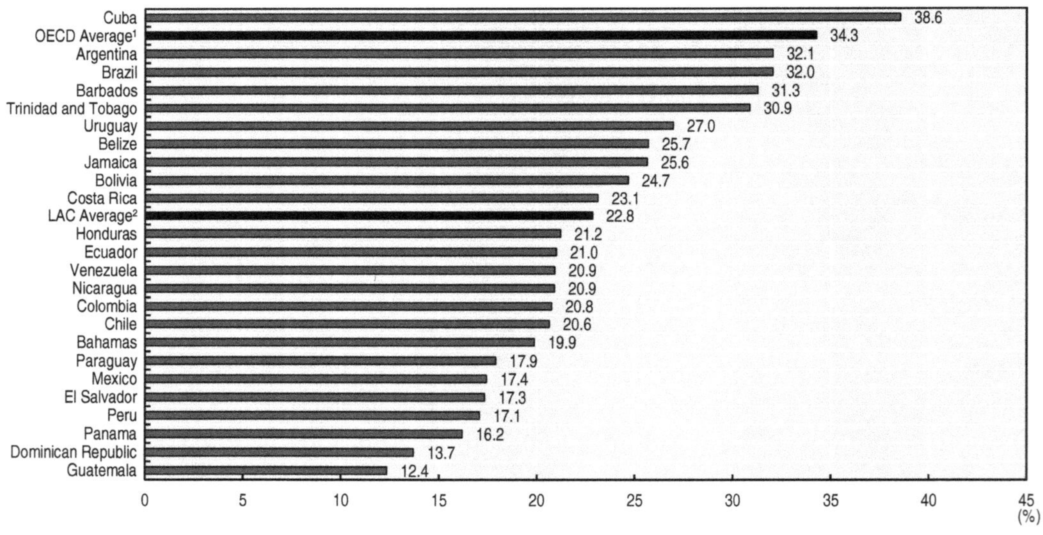

Note: The figures exclude local government revenues for Argentina (but include provincial revenues), the Bahamas, Barbados, the Dominican Republic, Nicaragua and Venezuela as the data are not available.

1. Represents OECD member countries. Chile and Mexico are also part of the OECD (35) group.
2. Represents the unweighted average of the 24 Latin American and Caribbean countries.

Source: Table 4.1.

StatLink http://dx.doi.org/10.1787/888933462250

The highest tax-to-GDP ratios were seen in Cuba (38.6%), Argentina (32.1%) and Brazil (32.0%). The other seven countries above the LAC average were Barbados, Trinidad and Tobago, Uruguay, Belize, Jamaica, Bolivia and Costa Rica. The countries with the lowest tax-to-GDP ratios below were Guatemala (12.4%) and the Dominican Republic (13.7%).

In 2015, the average LAC tax-to-GDP ratio was 0.6 percentage points higher than the previous year (Figure 1.2).[2] This contrasts with the overall economic environment in the Latin America and Caribbean region. On average, the real GDP growth rate in Latin America has been slowing down since 2012 and continued to do so in 2015 (OECD/CAF/ECLAC, 2015). GDP growth amounted to 1% in 2014 whereas it reached 5% per year in the mid-2000s. OECD/CAF/ECLAC (2015) explains that Latin America has started to suffer from a weaker growth in the global economy, lower commodity prices as well as a reduction of capital flows since 2012.

There is a range of different situations across LAC countries as 19 countries out of 24 recorded an increase and five countries recorded a decrease in their tax-to-GDP ratio in 2015. The Bahamas recorded the highest increase of 2.6 percentage points in 2015. Another large increase occurred in Mexico (2.3 percentage points) due to increases in revenue as a percentage of GDP from taxes on income and profits (1.1 percentage points) and from taxes on specific goods and services (1.2 percentage points) (Figure 1.3). In contrast, Peru experienced the largest decrease of 1.7 percentage points principally due to a decrease of 1.4 percentage points in revenue from taxes on income and profits.

Figure 1.2. **Change in tax-to-GDP ratios in 2015 (percentage points of GDP)**

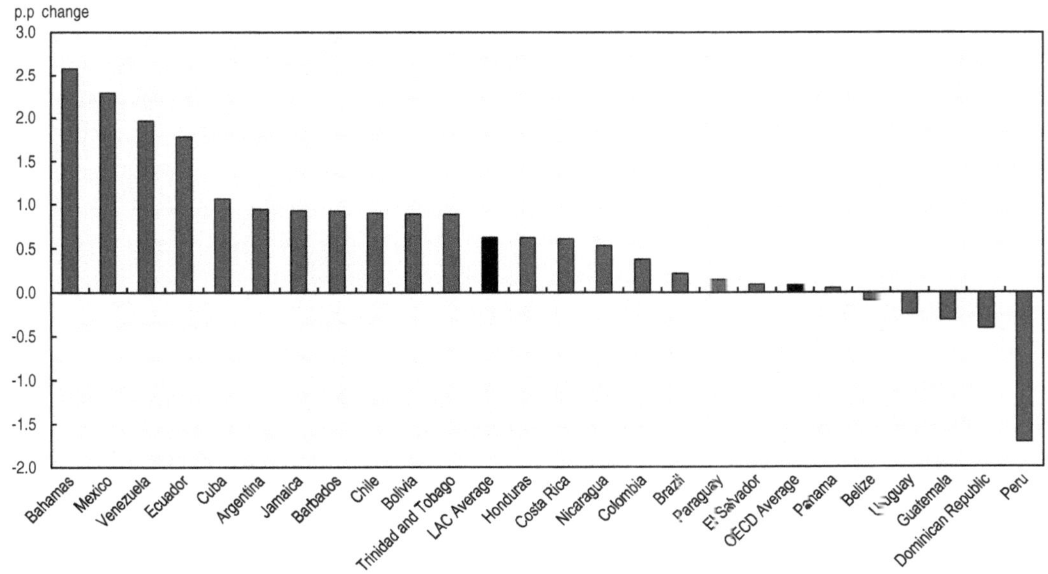

Source: Authors' calculations based on Table 4.1.

StatLink http://dx.doi.org/10.1787/888933462265

Significant tax reforms and the economic context have driven the increases in the Bahamas, Mexico and the decrease in Peru in 2015. The Bahamas introduced VAT in January 2015 (IMF, 2016a). In 2014, Mexico implemented a major tax reform which included changes to the special tax on production and services (an excise tax) that led to greater tax revenues from gasoline and diesel (OECD, 2017a), an increase of personal income tax rates, limitations of personal deductions as well as the broadening of the corporate income tax base through the elimination of certain deductions (International Tax Review, 2014). There were two major reasons underpinning the decrease for Peru in 2015: the end-of the commodity cycle that affected tax revenue from the oil and mining sector in 2015 which dropped by 0.5 p.p. compared to 2014 (see the special feature in Chapter 2 of this publication) and a major tax reform in 2014 that included the reduction of corporate income tax rate from 30% to 28% (PWC, 2015).

The main driver for the increase in the tax-to-GDP ratio for LAC countries on average in 2015 was an increase in the revenue from taxes on general consumption. The annual change of this category was 0.3 p.p. followed by an increase of 0.2 percentage points in revenue from taxes on specific goods and services as a percentage of GDP (Figure 1.3).

Figure 1.3. **Change in tax-to-GDP ratios by type of tax categories in 2015 (percentage points of GDP)**

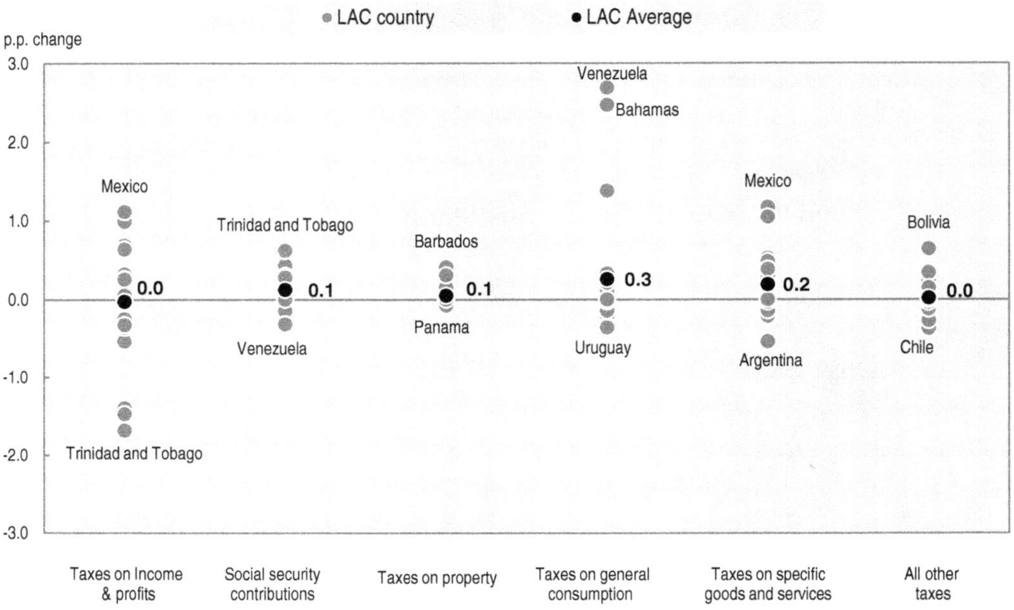

Note: The annual changes in revenue from taxes on general consumption and on specific goods and services for Venezuela should be interpreted with caution as they have been affected by the high rate of inflation.
Source: Authors' calculations based on tables in Chapter 4.

StatLink http://dx.doi.org/10.1787/888933462271

There is great heterogeneity among countries in respect to the annual changes in 2015. Changes in revenue from taxes on general consumption and from taxes on income and profits showed the largest variations among countries (Figure 1.3). Changes to the revenue from taxes on goods and services were the main driver for the changes in the tax-to-GDP ratios in nine countries, increasing in all cases except for Uruguay. Changes to the revenue from taxes on income and profits were the main driver for the changes in tax-to-GDP ratios for eight countries (Figure 1.4).

Figure 1.4. **Changes in tax revenues by category of largest change, as % of GDP, 2014-15 (percentage points)**

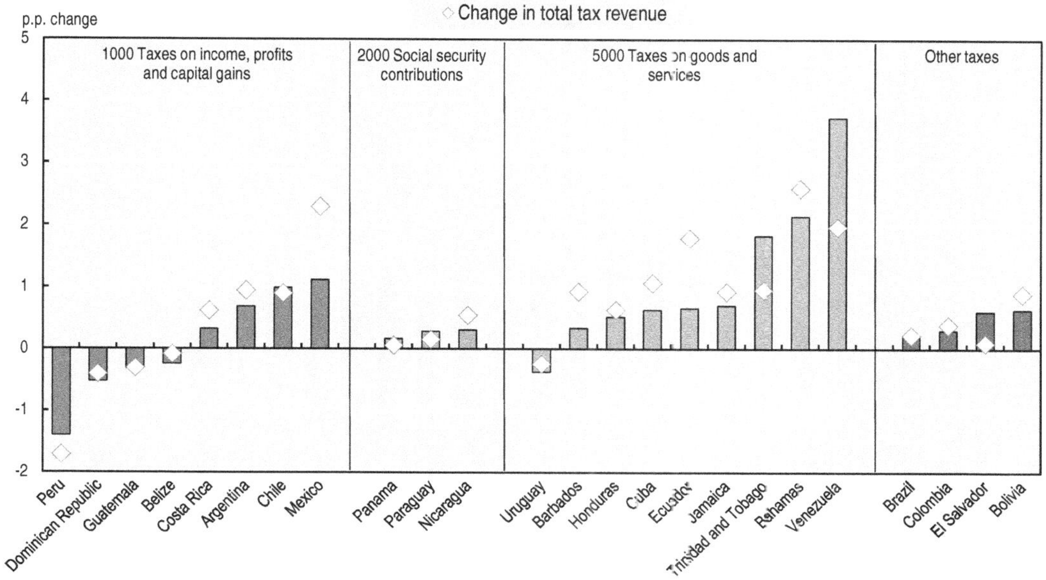

Note: The annual changes in revenue from taxes on goods and services for Venezuela should be interpreted with caution as they have been affected by the high rate of inflation.

Source: Authors' calculations based on tables in Chapter 4.

StatLink http://dx.doi.org/10.1787/888933462281

Evolution of tax ratios since 2000

The average tax-to-GDP ratio in LAC countries has, with the exception of 2008 and 2009, risen continuously between 1990 and 2015 (Figure 1.5). It increased by more than seven percentage points from 15.8% in 1990 to 22.8% in 2015. This growth reflects favourable macroeconomic conditions, changes in tax system design and strengthening of tax administrations. This trend contrasts with that in the OECD area where the ratio has been relatively stable, reaching 34.3% in 2015, 2.3 percentage points above its corresponding level in 1990.

The global financial crisis briefly interrupted the steady growth of the LAC tax-to-GDP ratio. The crisis resulted in a decrease of the LAC average of 0.5 percentage points between 2008 and 2010 due to the fall in economic activity and commodity prices. In contrast, the OECD average was mainly affected by the crisis between 2007 and 2009. Over this period, the OECD tax-to-GDP ratio registered a decrease of 1.3 percentage points. The OECD area recovered to its pre-crisis tax-to-GDP level of 33.8% in 2013 whereas the LAC region reached its 2008 level (21.3%) two years earlier, in 2011.

The difference between the LAC and OECD average tax-to-GDP ratios reduced between 1990 and 2008. It then remained relatively steady until 2014 before decreasing again in 2015 (Figure 1.5). The tax-to-GDP ratio gap between LAC and the OECD averages decreased from 16 percentage points in 1990 to about 12 percentage points in 2008 and stayed stable at that level until 2014. The gap decreased again in 2015 to stand at 11.4 percentage points, its lowest point since 1990.

Figure 1.5. **Tax-to-GDP ratios, 1990-2015**

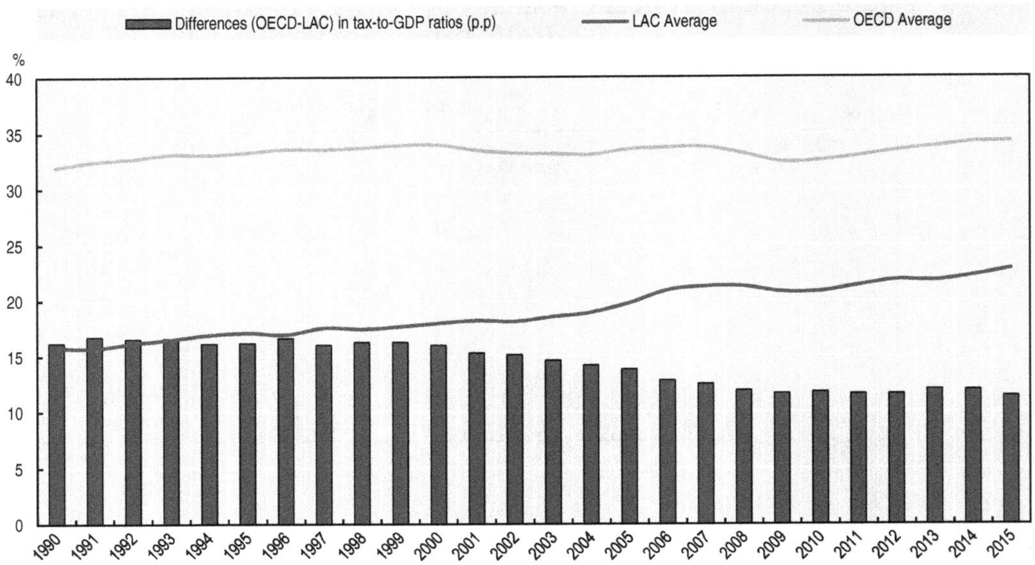

Source: Table 4.1.

StatLink http://dx.doi.org/10.1787/888933462315

The tax-to-GDP ratios in LAC countries increased in the early 1990s after a period of macroeconomic instability during the previous decade. During the 1980s, countries ran large fiscal imbalances and at the same time some recoursed to alternative ways to finance their spending (borrowing or printing money). This caused rapid inflation across the region, which eroded the real value of their tax revenues. As a result, the reforms in the 1990s focused on fighting inflation, opening trade and imposing fiscal discipline. Most LAC governments responded by both cutting public expenditure and implementing policies aimed at increasing tax revenues with budget management and fiscal balance improving considerably. The impact of inflation on revenues forced policy makers to identify tax policy and tax administrations reforms to render tax systems less vulnerable to inflationary episodes by shortening collection lags and indexing tax liabilities.

Significant efforts were undertaken to modernise tax administrations and tax systems over the last two decades. Over that period, new information technology systems were implemented, the structures of tax administrations were rationalised, tax collection systems became more efficient and staff gained in expertise (IDB, 2013). In addition LAC countries made significant changes to simplify their tax systems by broadening their tax bases. They reduced the number of exemptions and tax incentives granted to certain activities and sectors principally to incentivise foreign investment that did – however – not always prove successful. Tax reforms included the introduction or development of simplified regimes for small taxpayers and the taxation of property based on presumed incomes. During the past half-decade various income tax reforms were introduced in LAC countries, which have included rate hikes and broadening of the tax base. These measures have had a positive effect on revenues thanks to the expansion of taxation to all labour and capital income, including dividends (Colombia, Dominican Republic, Guatemala, El Salvador, Nicaragua, Panama, Peru). Tax reforms have also included the establishment of minimum taxes and taxes on financial transactions and the gradual reduction in the real income level taxed at the top marginal rate and additional controls on transfer prices (ECLAC, 2013).

The introduction of VAT was the most significant tax reform in Latin America and the Caribbean in the 1980s and early 1990s. Subsequent reforms relating to VAT have concentrated on extending and strengthening it by increasing the tax rate and widening the tax base. Between 1990 and 2015, the revenue as a percentage of GDP has more than doubled from 2.4% of GDP in 1990 to 6.0% in 2015 (Figure 1.6). Over the same period, Latin America and Caribbean countries have reduced their revenues from the other taxes on goods and services as a percentage of GDP (essentially excises, customs and import duties). This decline is associated with the trade liberalisation that resulted in changes in LAC countries in the taxation of imported and exported goods as well as of specific goods and services. These changes included the reduction of import tariffs, the narrowing of the base of products and services subject to excises (for example focusing on products such as alcoholic beverages, fuel and derivatives and tobacco) and the elimination of taxes on exports. One important exception is Argentina where taxes on exports were re-established in 2002; however the current government established in December 2015 has abolished export taxes on certain almost all agricultural products (World Grain, 2016 and IMF, 2016b).

Figure 1.6. **Revenue from taxes on income and profits, VAT and other taxes on goods and services as a percentage of GDP in the Latin America and Caribbean region, 1990-2015**

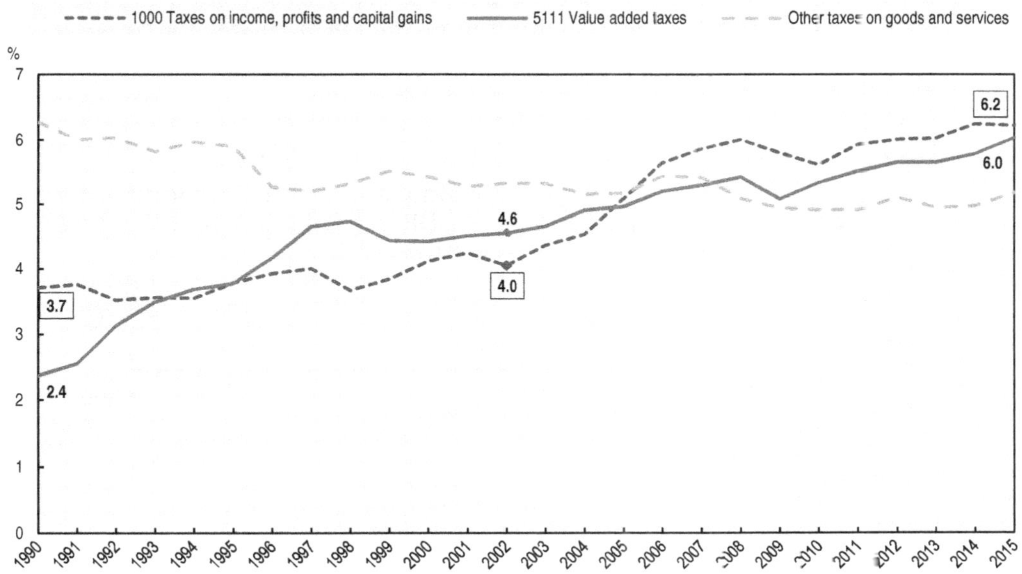

Source: OECD (2017), "Revenue Statistics in Latin America: Comparative tables", *OECD Tax Statistics* (database), http://dx.doi.org/10.1787/ctpa-revlat-data-en.

StatLink http://dx.doi.org/10.1787/888933462292

The main contributor to the increase of the average LAC tax-to-GDP ratio was VAT between 1990 and 2002 and taxes on income and profits between 2002 and 2015. The VAT revenue as a percentage of GDP increased by 2.2 percentage points between 1990 and 2002 whereas revenue from taxes on income and profits only increased by 0.3 percentage points over the period (Figure 1.6). In contrast, revenue from taxes on income and profits as a percentage of GDP increased by 2.2 percentage points against 1.5 percentage points for VAT revenue between 2002 and 2015. One of the elements that contributed to this result was the recovery of LAC economic activity (ECLAC-OECD, 2012) and the commodity prices' boom period following 2003 that increased corporate income tax revenue (Barreix et al, 2017). After the global financial crisis, changes in revenue from taxes on goods and services, taxes on income and profits and social security contributions have contributed to the recovery in the LAC tax-to-GDP ratio.

Since 2007, revenue from taxes on incomes and profits as a percentage of GDP has been increasing with an interruption during the financial crisis (Figure 1.7). The increase of revenue from taxes on income and profits was driven by corporate income tax revenues. ECLAC 2014 explains that corporate income tax revenue grew faster than personal income tax revenue over the past 25 years and this growth reflected the sizeable increase in tax revenues from companies in the natural resources sector. It was also the result of tax policies reducing tax incentives in free-trade zones, the introduction of minimum taxes for corporations, reforms in international taxation and agreements between countries to fight tax evasion.

During the financial crisis, the average LAC corporate income tax revenue as a percentage of GDP decreased whereas the average LAC personal income tax revenue as a percentage of GDP stayed steady over this period (Figure 1.7). Between 2008 and 2010, corporate income tax revenue as a percentage of GDP dropped sharply (by 0.4 percentage points). It stayed steady at 3.8% from 2011 and recorded its first decrease of 0.2 percentage points in 2015. The latter decrease may be partly explained by the drop of corporate income tax revenue from non-renewable commodities (see the special feature in Chapter 2 of this publication). In contrast, personal income tax revenue as a percentage of GDP has been increasing steadily since 2011 and reached its highest-ever level in 2015 (2.1%). From 2012, the growth rate of personal income tax revenue as a percentage of GDP was higher than that of corporate income tax revenue partially due to the slowing down of the LAC economic environment and lower commodity prices. The LAC averages for corporate income tax revenue and personal income tax revenue as a percentage of GDP should be interpreted with caution as Ecuador, Nicaragua and Venezuela are excluded from the calculation as more than a third of their revenue from taxes on income and profits cannot be allocated to corporate income tax revenue (1200) or personal income tax revenue (1100).

Figure 1.7. **Revenue from taxes on income and profits, corporate income tax and personal income as a percentage of GDP in the Latin American and Caribbean region, 2007-15**

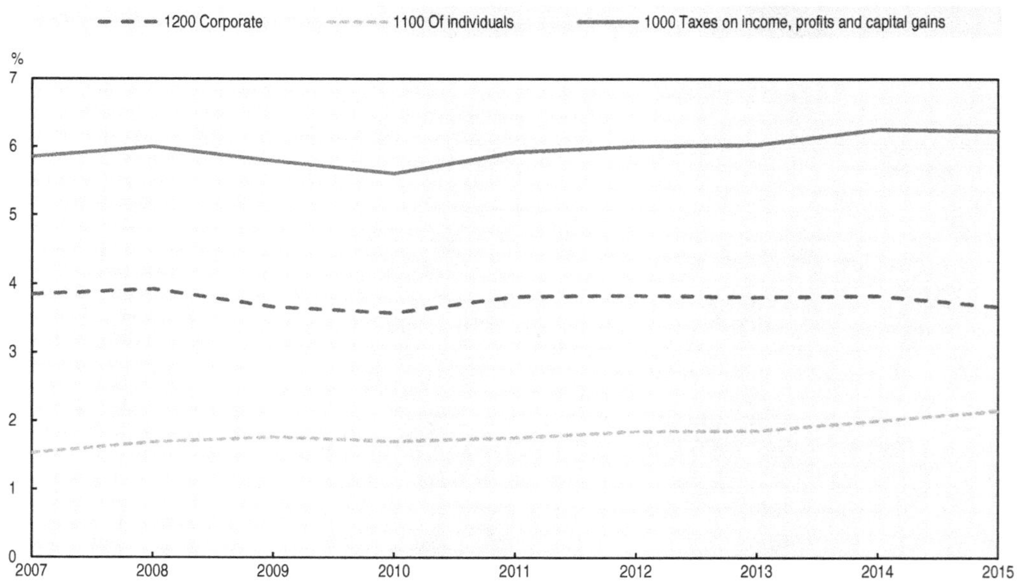

Note: Ecuador, Nicaragua and Venezuela are excluded from the LAC averages for corporate income tax revenue as a percentage of GDP and personal income tax revenue as a percentage of GDP as more than a third of their revenue from taxes on income and profits cannot be allocated to corporate income tax revenue (1200) or personal income tax revenue (1100).

Source: OECD (2017), "Revenue Statistics in Latin America: Comparative tables", *OECD Tax Statistics* (database), http://dx.doi.org/10.1787/ctpa-revlat-data-en.

StatLink http://dx.doi.org/10.1787/888933462306

The changes in corporate income tax revenue as a percentage of GDP between 2014 and 2015 show large variations across countries (Figure 1.8). In 2015, Trinidad and Tobago recorded a decrease of 1.7 percentage points in revenue from income and profits as a percentage of GDP due to the substantial decline in corporate income tax receipts (2.8 percentage points). This is mainly explained by the decrease of revenue from hydrocarbons (see the special feature in Chapter 2 of this publication). Other countries dependent on commodities revenue such as Peru and the Dominican Republic also recorded important decreases in corporate tax receipts in 2015.

Figure 1.8. **Annual change in revenue from taxes on income and profits, corporate income tax and personal income tax, 2015 (percentage points of GDP)**

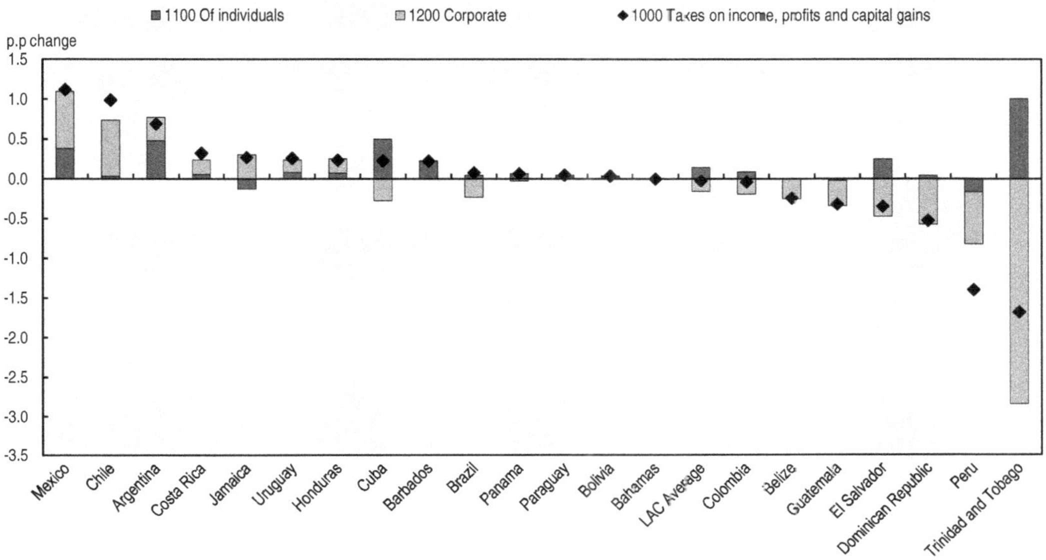

Note: Ecuador, Nicaragua and Venezuela are excluded as more than a third of their revenue from taxes on income and profits cannot be allocated to corporate income tax revenue (1200) or personal income tax revenue (1100).
Source: OECD (2017), "Revenue Statistics in Latin America: Comparative tables", *OECD Tax Statistics* (database), http://dx.doi.org/10.1787/ctpa-revlat-data-en.

StatLink http://dx.doi.org/10.1787/888933462321

Factors influencing tax-to-GDP ratios

The differences between the LAC and OECD average tax-to-GDP ratios reflect the fact that higher income countries tend to have higher tax-to-GDP ratios. The data implies a positive correlation between GDP per capita (a measure of the level of income of a country or its level of development) and tax-to-GDP ratios (Figure 1.9). In general, OECD countries have higher average incomes than the LAC countries and collect higher tax revenues. Argentina, Barbados, Brazil, Trinidad and Tobago and Uruguay show similar tax-to-GDP ratios and levels of income to the less wealthy OECD countries.

Tax-to-GDP ratios are influenced by economic and structural factors. GDP per capita, openness to trade, the extent of the informal economy, natural resource endowments and the importance of agriculture in the economy are all factors that can influence tax-to-GDP ratios. Socio-demographic determinants are also key, such as the level of education or the level of female participation in the labour force. The power of tax administrations, the levels of corruption and tax morale (or willingness of people to pay taxes) are also strongly linked to the level of tax revenues (OECD, 2014a). Finally, geographic location and historical factors can also influence tax-to-GDP ratios: for example landlocked countries are less able to impose taxes on goods and services at the port of entry than coastal countries. In addition, international factors, including the tax policies of other countries, can impact tax-to-GDP ratios.

Figure 1.9. **GDP per capita in PPP (USD) and tax-to-GDP ratios for countries in Latin America and the Caribbean, the OECD and a group of African and Asian countries**

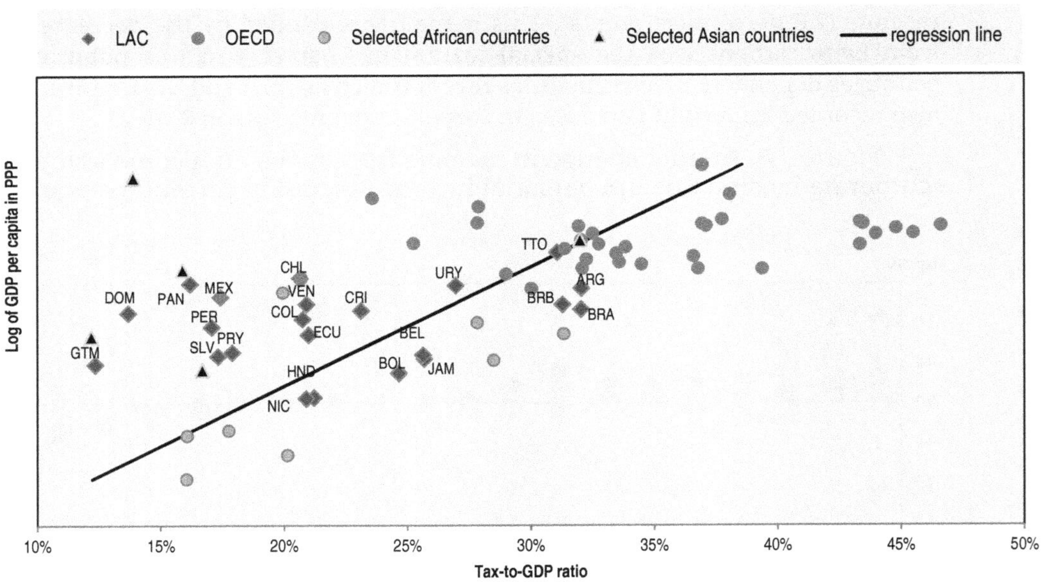

Note: The purchasing-power-parity (PPP) between two countries is the rate at which the currency of one country needs to be converted into that of a second country to ensure that a given amount of the first country's currency will purchase the same volume of goods and services in the second country as it does in the first. The implied PPP conversion rate is expressed as national currency per current international dollar. An international dollar has the same purchasing power as the U.S. dollar has in the United States. An international dollar is a hypothetical currency that is used as a means of translating and comparing costs from one country to the other using a common reference point, the US dollar (Definitions derived from IMF, 2016c and WHO, 2015).

Source: IMF (2016c), *World Economic Outlook*, October 2016, International Monetary Fund for figures of GDP per capita. Tax-to-GDP ratios are sourced from the regional Revenue Statistics publications (www.oecd.org/tax/tax-policy/revenue-statistics-comparable-tax-revenue-data.htm).

StatLink http://dx.doi.org/10.1787/888933462334

The extent of the state participation in financing social security is another important factor underlying the level of tax ratios in the LAC region. From the 1980s onwards, many LAC countries have privatised healthcare, pension and social security to greater or lesser degrees (ECLAC, 2010). Chile, El Salvador and Mexico for example have shifted their public pension programme to a mostly privately fully funded pension system. In Colombia and Peru, the private and public programmes compete and employees opt for one of them (OECD, 2015). On the other hand, Argentina, Brazil and Uruguay follow a model where the public and private systems are complementary. In these three countries substantial reforms were undertaken to extend the coverage of social security systems to those previously excluded. This has also been instrumental in the increase of tax revenues (ECLAC, 2014).

Informality levels hinder tax revenue collected in LAC countries as they significantly reduce the taxable base (OECD, 2008 and Gómez Sabaini et al. 2010). In Latin America[3] the rate of informality[4] was around 55% on average in 2013 (IDB, 2013). Bolivia, Guatemala, Honduras, Nicaragua, Paraguay and Peru have the highest rates of informality exceeding 65% and Brazil, Chile, Costa Rica and Uruguay have rates of informality of less than 40%. These levels were higher in the 1990s, prompting governments to introduce simplified tax systems for small taxpayers that were to some extent successful in integrating informal workers into the formal sector. These simplified systems varied greatly in success depending on the type of taxpayers covered and the actual capacity of tax administrations (ECLAC 2014).

1.2. Tax structures

The tax structure depicts the composition of tax revenues by different tax types. This is a second important indicator, since different taxes have different economic and social effects. Across the 24 countries in this publication, the composition of taxes varies widely, reflecting their different policy choices, economic structures and conditions, tax administration capabilities and historical factors.

Evolution of tax structures

The average LAC tax mix (defined as the share of major tax types in total tax revenue) shifted towards greater revenue shares from taxes on general consumption, taxes on income and profits and social security contributions between 1990 and 2015. The share of revenues from taxes from incomes and profits grew from 22.3% to 27.2% of total tax revenues between 1990 and 2015, mainly as a result of much higher collection levels in the late 2000s. The share of social security contributions in total tax revenues increased by 3.4 percentage points over the last 25 years reaching 15.4% in 2015. The proportion of revenue from taxes on goods and services in the total tax revenue increased by 5 percentage points over the same period. The revenue share of general consumption taxes (mainly VAT) increased by 10 percentage points between 1990 and 2015, while the revenue share of taxes on specific goods and services (excises, customs and import duties) declined by 16 percentage points over the same period (Figure 1.10).

Figure 1.10. **Average tax structure in the Latin America and Caribbean region, 1990 and 2015**

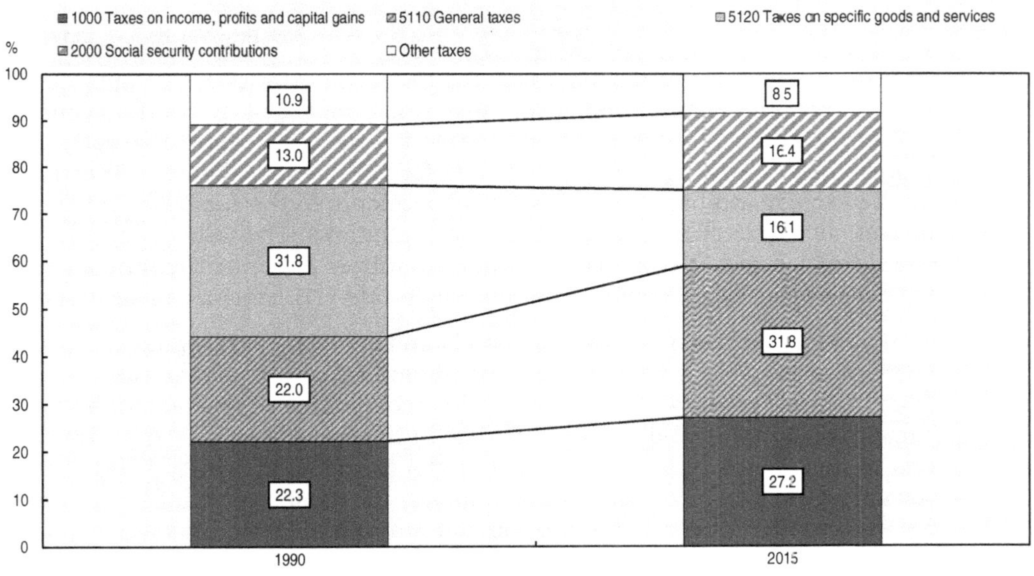

Source: Authors' calculations based on tables in Chapter 4.

StatLink http://dx.doi.org/10.1787/888933462347

The average LAC revenue share of taxes from specific goods and services (essentially excises, customs and import duties) became lower than the revenue share from general consumption (mainly VAT) in 1995 and has remained lower ever since. This hides a wide disparity across countries as in 1995 the revenue share from specific consumption was higher in 11 countries. By 2005 it was higher in only five countries, principally in the Caribbean countries (the Bahamas, Belize, the Dominican Republic and Jamaica) and in 2015 only in two (the Bahamas and Jamaica). The Bahamas introduced VAT in 2015 and its revenue share from specific consumption is expected to decrease in future years. In Jamaica, tariffs and other trade duties are their main trade policy instrument (US mission Geneva, 2011).

Figure 1.11. **Average tax structure in the Latin America and Caribbean region, 1990-2015**

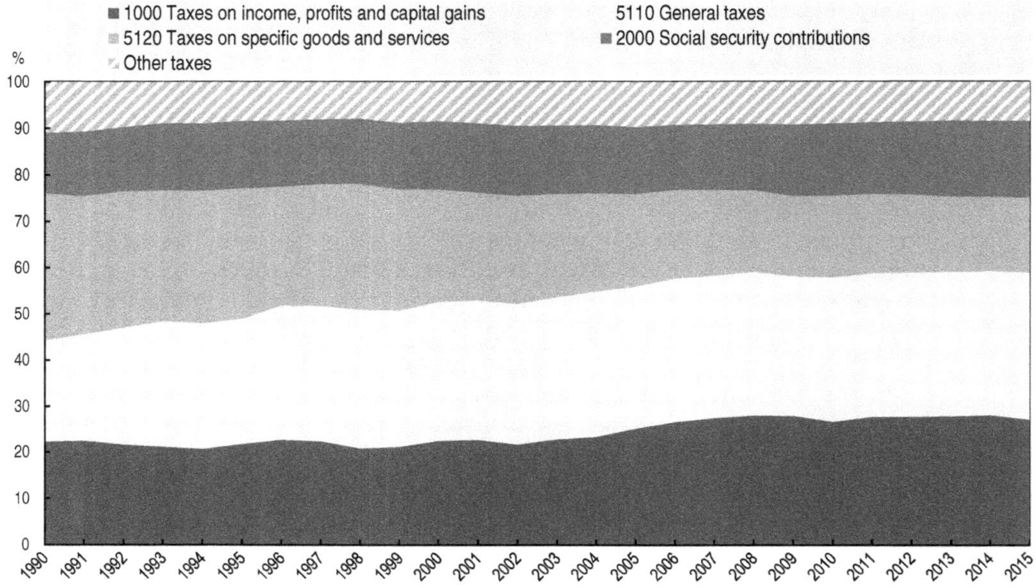

Source: Authors' calculations based on tables in Chapter 4.

StatLink http://dx.doi.org/10.1787/888933462356

These two opposing trends reflect the rising importance of VAT and the diminishing role of specific consumption taxes. VAT was adopted early by the economies of the region (twelve[5] countries had implemented it by 1980). From the early 1990s, it has represented a growing source of revenue for LAC countries and has been consolidated by the implementation of cumulative adjustments to the tax base and statutory rates, as well as the strengthening of tax administrations. The reforms also focused on the simplification of tax systems, with most countries reducing the number of items with zero or reduced rates, moving towards single-rate VAT schemes in several cases.

In 2015, revenue from taxes on goods and services represented the largest revenue share on average for LAC countries and amounted to 50% of total tax revenue. Revenue from taxes on goods and services are the main source of revenue for all LAC countries except for Trinidad and Tobago, Mexico and Panama. Revenue from taxes on income and profits represented the largest share for Mexico and Trinidad and Tobago whereas revenue from social security contributions is the most important source of tax revenue for Panama. Trinidad and Tobago sourced more than 60% of its tax revenue from taxes on income and profits in 2015.

In 2015, 28% of the total tax revenues in LAC countries on average came from VAT. However there is wide heterogeneity within the region. The shares of VAT revenue in these countries range from 12.4% in the Bahamas to 55.8% in Venezuela. There is no VAT in Belize as it was abolished in 1999 and replaced by a sales tax (Peters and Bristol, 2006). The wide variation across countries is also the result of differences in the design of the VAT: the rates and tax bases vary widely in the region. For example Mexico does not apply VAT on food, medicines or numerous other products, resulting in a relatively narrow tax base. ECLAC 2014 suggests that the tax loss from these particular exemptions could range between 1.1% and 2.5% of GDP.

Figure 1.12. **Tax structure in Latin America and the Caribbean countries, 2015**

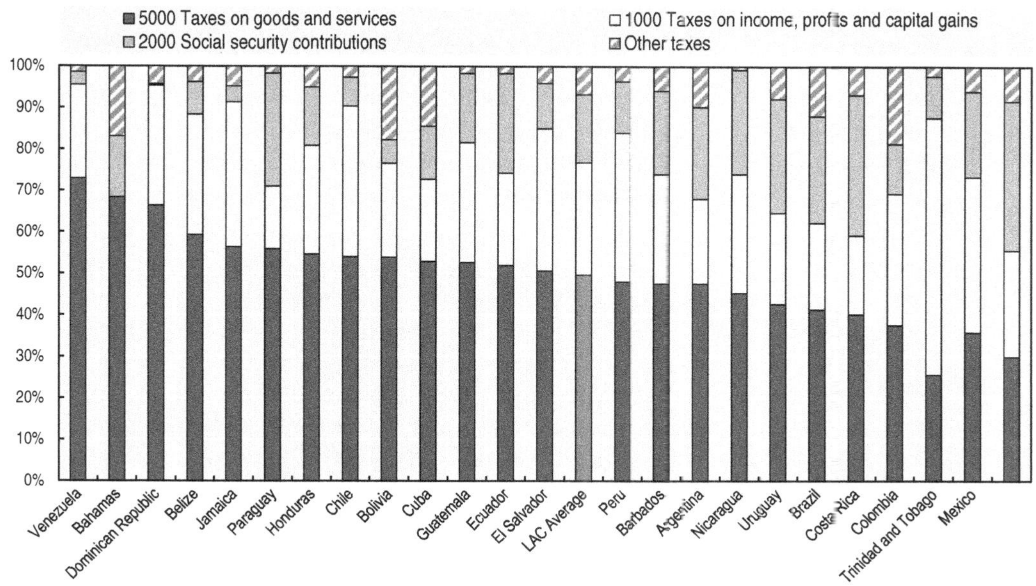

Note: The revenue shares of the different tax categories for Venezuela should be interpreted with caution as they have been affected by the high rate of inflation.

Source: Authors' calculations based on tables in Chapter 4.

StatLink http://dx.doi.org/10.1787/888933462364

Figure 1.13. **Revenue from VAT as a proportion of total tax revenue in LAC countries, 2015**

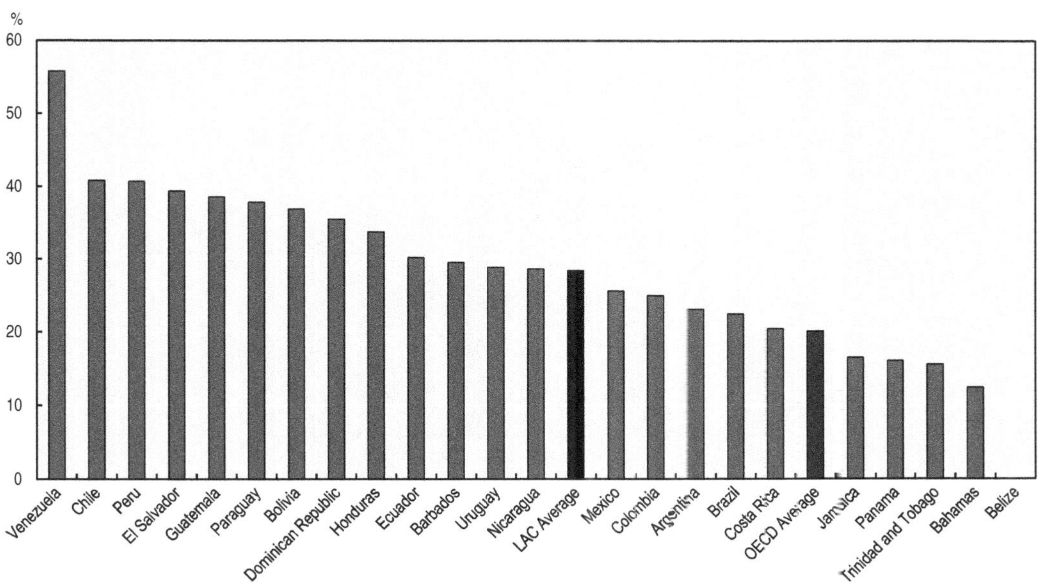

Note: Cuba is excluded as the information is not available.

Source: OECD (2017), "Revenue Statistics in Latin America: Comparative tables", *OECD Tax Statistics* (database), http://dx.doi.org/10.1787/ctpa-revlat-data-en.

StatLink http://dx.doi.org/10.1787/888933462377

1.3. VAT revenue ratio

The VAT revenue ratio (VRR) measure for selected[6] LAC countries has been calculated for the first time and included in this publication. OECD (2016) explains that "the VRR measures the difference between the VAT revenue actually collected and what would theoretically be raised if VAT was applied at the standard rate to the entire potential tax base in a "pure" VAT regime and all revenue was collected". This section describes the VRR levels in Latin American and the Caribbean countries in 2014 and focuses on analysing in more depth three countries, Bolivia, Paraguay and Panama.

There was a wide disparity of VRRs in Latin American and the Caribbean countries in 2014 (Figure 1.14). Jamaica and Mexico have the lowest VRR ratios at 25% and 32% respectively whereas Bolivia and Paraguay have the highest at 101% and 93% respectively. The low level of VRR in Jamaica may be explained by the application of exemptions or a zero-rate to a large number of goods and services. In addition, certain goods (e.g. petroleum products, cigarettes, spirits and beer) are not subject to VAT but to a special consumption tax akin to an excise tax (PKF, 2013). For Mexico, OECD (2016) explains that several factors may explain the low VRR, for example the scope of VAT exemptions, the application of a domestic zero rate to numerous goods and services, a reduced VAT rate (11%) at the border areas as well as a low compliance rate. A VAT reform was implemented in January 2014 that replaced the reduced rate of 11% with the standard rate of 16%. The reform also removed the zero rate on hotel and related services to foreigners, now taxed at the standard rate, and adjusted the regime of inward processing arrangements (maquiladores) to reduce the risk of fraud. The VRR in Mexico increased by 0.3 points between 2013 and 2014.

Figure 1.14. **VAT revenue ratio (VRR) in LAC countries, 2014**

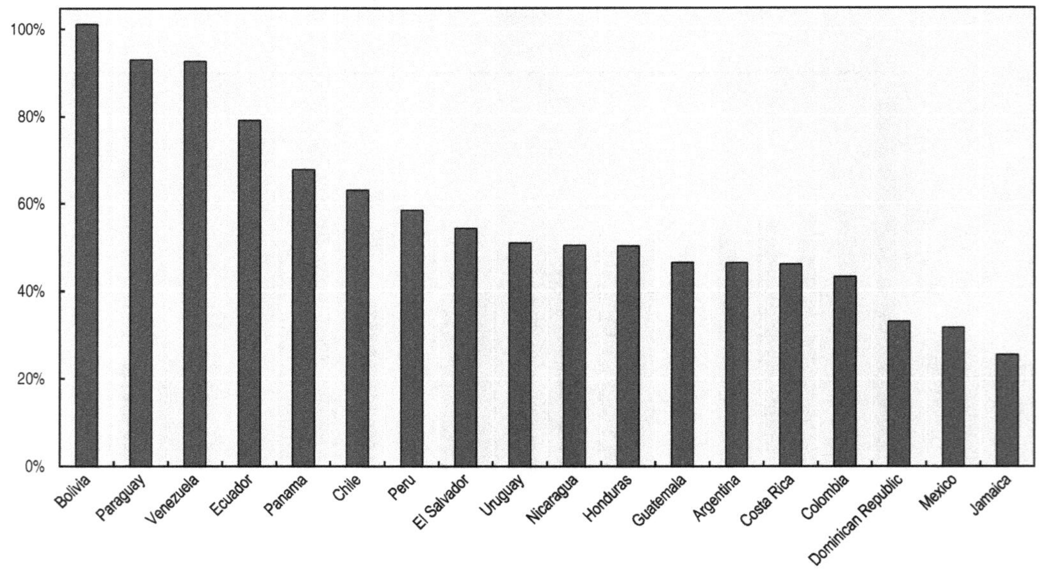

Note: Brazil, Belize, The Bahamas, Barbados, Cuba and Trinidad & Tobago are excluded. Brazil operates a multiple-rate system with tax levied at different rates for each sub-national level. Some underlying information was not available for Barbados, Cuba, Trinidad and Tobago; Belize and the Bahamas did not operate a VAT system in 2014.

Source: The VAT rates are sourced from CIAT, Trading Economics and Deloitte websites, the final expenditure consumption figures from the United Nations Statistics Division website and VAT revenues from the country tables in Chapter 5.

StatLink http://dx.doi.org/10.1787/888933462385

In 2014, the VRR in Bolivia exceeded 100%. The figures need to be interpreted with caution as a VRR of 100% suggests no loss of VAT revenue as a consequence of exemptions, reduced rates, fraud, evasion or tax planning. The high level of VRR may be partly explained by different factors. Firstly, Bolivia applies a standard VAT rate of 13% to the final price of a good or services (including VAT) leading to a VAT effective rate (14.94%) higher than the standard rate. The VRR measure is reduced from 101% to 88% in 2014 when the VAT effective rate is used rather than the standard rate. Secondly Bolivia applies VAT to a wide range of goods and products and does not have reduced rates (EY, 2014). High levels of informality can also affect VRR ratios, although it is unclear if this is the case in Bolivia.

The VRR in Bolivia has been increasing since 1990 although this growth was interrupted between 1997 and 2000. A wide public sector reform adopted in 2000 that included the strengthening of the inspection, control process and procedures for VAT refunds may have contributed to the recovery in 2000. According to Zuleta (2008) "the changes in processes and procedures for VAT refunds have had a significant positive impact during the institutional reform". This was evident in the decrease in VAT evasion of 23 percentage points from 42%[7] in 2001 to 29% in 2004, and decreases in VAT refunds as a percentage of exports and of VAT revenue (Zuleta, 2008). Zuleta (2008) suggests that these results indicate that the corruption in the process of VAT refunds had been reduced. Over the same period, the VRR improved by 15 percentage points from 51% to 64%. Between 2004 and 2013, the VRR continued to increase (except during the financial crisis period). However little evidence is available to explain the reasons behind this: measurement of VAT non-compliance over-time or of the level informality affecting the VAT sector may be useful information to provide more conclusive findings.

Paraguay has the second highest VRR at 93% in 2014 in the selected group of LAC countries. The figures need to be interpreted with caution as Paraguay has a reduced tax rate of 5% for certain products and services (e.g. basic family products, pharmaceutical, goods, real estate, leasing and interest on loans or debts) as well as exemptions (EY, 2014) that make it unlikely that only 7% of VAT revenue is not recovered. According to the IMF (2010), the "high VAT productivity[8] reflects in large part the high revenues from re-exports (about two percent of GDP). Much of the re-export trade is informal, with payments of VAT on the imports that are not deducted when the goods are re-exported".

The VRR has been increasing steadily in Paraguay since 2002. The increase in 2004 may be partly explained by tax policy and tax administrations reforms undertaken by the Paraguayan government. A comprehensive tax reform which included VAT base broadening measures and a new legal framework for tax and customs which enabled the modernisation of controls, procedures and revenue collection systems, was implemented in 2004 with the objective to make the tax system simpler and more efficient (IMF, 2010). At the same time, the Paraguayan government addressed the endemic corruption which had hindered the tax revenue collection (Franks et al, 2005).

In 2014, Panama had the fifth highest VRR at 64% and has had a VRR above 60% since 2008. Panama recorded a substantial rise in the VRR in one year from 28% in 2007 to 63% to 2008. This followed an extensive audit in 2008 from the Direction General of Taxes to end VAT revenue loss from businesses failing to report the VAT charged to customers to the tax authorities. Following this audit, in the first quarter 2008, VAT revenue increased by 22% compared to the whole year in 2007 (The Panama Investor Blog, 2008). As a percentage of GDP, the VAT revenue more than doubled between 2007 and 2008 from 1% to 2.1%.

Figure 1.15. **VAT revenue ratio (VRR) in Bolivia, Paraguay and Panama, 1990-2014**

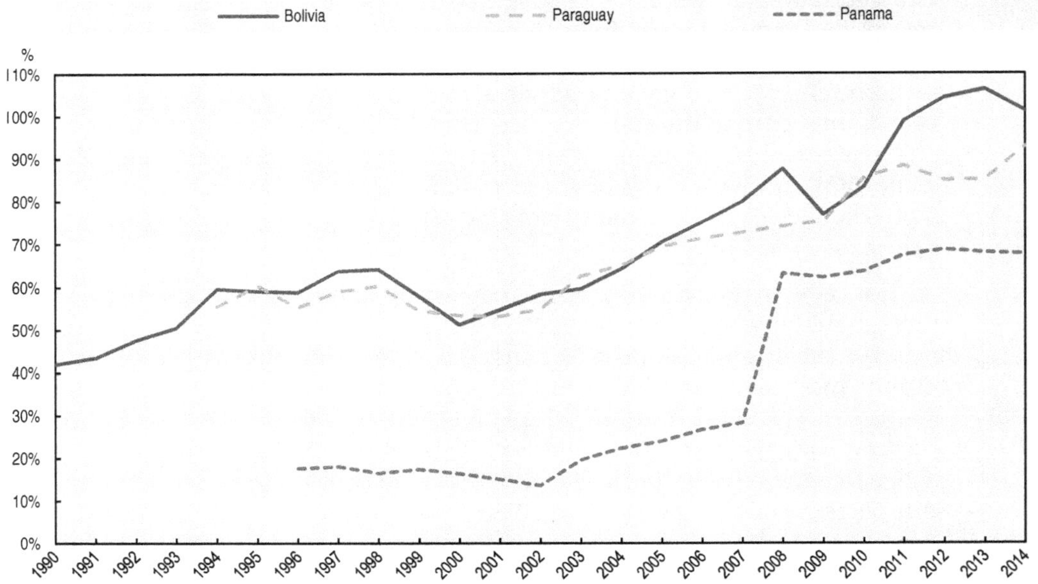

Note: Final consumption expenditure figures to compile the VRR were not available for Panama prior to 1996. There is no VRR between 1990 and 1993 for Paraguay as VAT was implemented in mid-1993.

Source: The VAT rates are sourced from the CIAT, Trading Economics and Deloitte websites, the final expenditure consumption figures from the United Nations Statistics Division website and VAT revenues from the country tables in Chapter 5.

StatLink http://dx.doi.org/10.1787/888933462395

Taxes on income and profits and social security contributions

In 2015, the share of revenues from taxes on incomes and profits amounted to 27.2% of total tax revenues. The corporate income revenue represented the main share of revenue from taxes on incomes and profits at 15.8% whereas personal income tax revenue share amounted to 9.1% of total tax revenue (Figure 1.16).[9] While the share of revenues from taxes on incomes and profits was 27% in 2007 and 2015, the LAC average tax structure shifted towards a greater revenue share from personal income taxes and a lower revenue share from corporate income taxes.

Corporate income tax is an important source of revenue in LAC countries. Trinidad and Tobago has the highest share of corporate income tax with 44% of tax revenues being generated from this source, most of it being collected from oil and gas companies (see the special feature in chapter 2 of this publication). In the other LAC countries, the share of corporate income tax revenues ranges from 8% (Barbados) to 25% (Colombia) (Figure 1.17). The Bahamas is the only country covered in this report not to operate an income tax (corporate or personal) regime.

Figure 1.16. **Average tax structure in the Latin America and Caribbean region, 2007 and 2015**

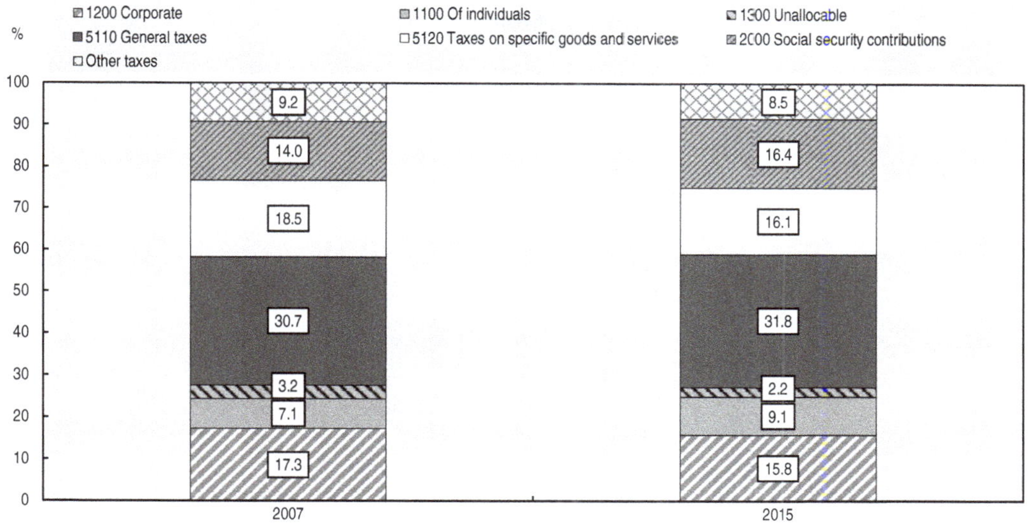

Note: The LAC corporate income tax revenue and personal income tax revenue as a percentage of GDP should be interpreted with caution as Ecuador, Nicaragua and Venezuela are excluded in the calculation. For these countries, more than a third of their revenue from taxes on income and profits cannot be allocated to corporate income tax revenue (1200) or personal income tax revenue (1100). Excluding these countries, a small proportion from revenue from taxes on income and profits remains unallocable.

Source: OECD (2017), "Revenue Statistics in Latin America: Comparative tables", *OECD Tax Statistics* (database), http://dx.doi.org/10.1787/ctpa-revlat-data-en.

StatLink http://dx.doi.org/10.1787/888933462402

The share of personal income tax revenue remains low in LAC countries despite some countries having implemented reforms to expand their tax base. After the crisis several countries established flat rates on capital income previously exempt and implemented progressive rates on labour income (ECLAC 2014), however the share of personal income tax in LAC countries remains modest as more than half of the countries generate less than 10% of their tax revenue from this source. The personal income tax revenue shares range from 0.9% (Bolivia) to 19.7% (Mexico) of total tax revenue excluding the Bahamas which does not operate a personal income tax system (Figure 1.17). Previous OECD studies (OECD, 2008 and Daude et al., 2010) suggest that the share of labour income in GDP is low in LAC countries: there are relatively few taxpayers, given the concentration of income earners at low income levels: 10% of the population in Latin America are registered taxpayers (IDB, 2013). Moreover, several studies (Barreix et al, 2017, IDB, 2015, ECLAC, 2014, ECLAC, 2010 and Gómez Sabaini et al., 2010) mention additional factors: a limited taxable base that is comprised primarily of wages, as tax privileges are granted to returns on capital, and high levels of evasion. IDB, 2013 explains that in Latin American countries "about half of potential revenue from personal income tax is lost through evasion".

Figure 1.17. **Revenue from corporate income tax and personal income tax as a proportion of total tax revenue in some LAC countries, 2015**

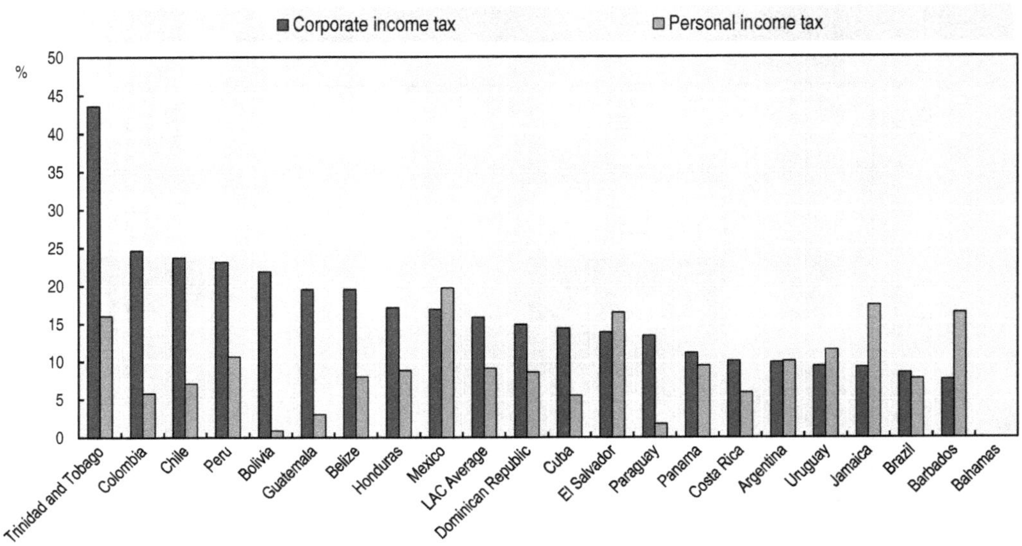

Note: The share of corporate income tax and the share of personal income tax may not add up to the total share of taxes on incomes and profits due to unallocable revenue. Only countries that could allocate two-thirds or more of revenue of taxes on incomes and profits into corporate income tax and personal income tax are shown in the figure above. Ecuador, Nicaragua and Venezuela are excluded for this reason.

Source: OECD (2017), "Revenue Statistics in Latin America: Comparative tables", *OECD Tax Statistics* (database), http://dx.doi.org/10.1787/ctpa-revlat-data-en.

StatLink http://dx.doi.org/10.1787/888933462410

The share of social security contributions in total tax revenues increased by 3.4 percentage points over the last 25 years reaching 16.4% in 2015 (Figure 1.10). This reflects two major factors working simultaneously. Firstly, rising personal incomes have had an upward impact on the amounts collected. But this is counter-balanced or off-set by the varying processes of full or partial privatisation that occurred in many countries in the region. In countries with public or mixed social security schemes, including Argentina, Barbados, Brazil, Costa Rica, Mexico, Panama, Paraguay, Uruguay, social security contributions still have a significant weight (more than 20% of total tax revenues). In Colombia and Peru, where the private and public programmes compete, social security contributions as a share of total tax revenue amount to around 12%. In Argentina, the figures reflect the introduction of funded schemes in 1994 and their subsequent nationalisation in 2008.

Comparison with the OECD

Relative to the OECD average, the LAC average tax mix exhibits a relatively low direct-tax take, counterbalanced by high indirect-tax receipts (see Figure 1.18). In particular, LAC countries on average rely heavily on taxes on goods and services, which make up about half of overall tax revenues compared with around 33% in OECD economies on average. On average, 44% of tax revenues in LAC countries come from the combination of taxes on income and profits and social security contributions compared with 60% in the OECD region. As a result, these taxes play a secondary role as a source of revenue in LAC countries compared with the OECD area. The share of social security contributions in total tax revenues was about 10 percentage points lower in the LAC average than in the OECD average (16.3% compared with 26.2%). The tendency towards the privately-oriented provision of social security in many countries in the LAC region explains some of the differences for this category. The corresponding figures for taxes on income and profits were 6 percentage points lower than the OECD average (23.3% compared with 33.7%).

Corporate income tax revenue as a share of total tax revenue is 16.8% in the LAC region compared to 8.8% in the OECD area (Figure 1.18). Revenue from personal income taxes contributed 24% of the average tax collection in the OECD area in 2014, while this category has a considerably lower share in LAC countries on average (8.7%).

Figure 1.18. **Tax structures in LAC and the OECD, 2014**

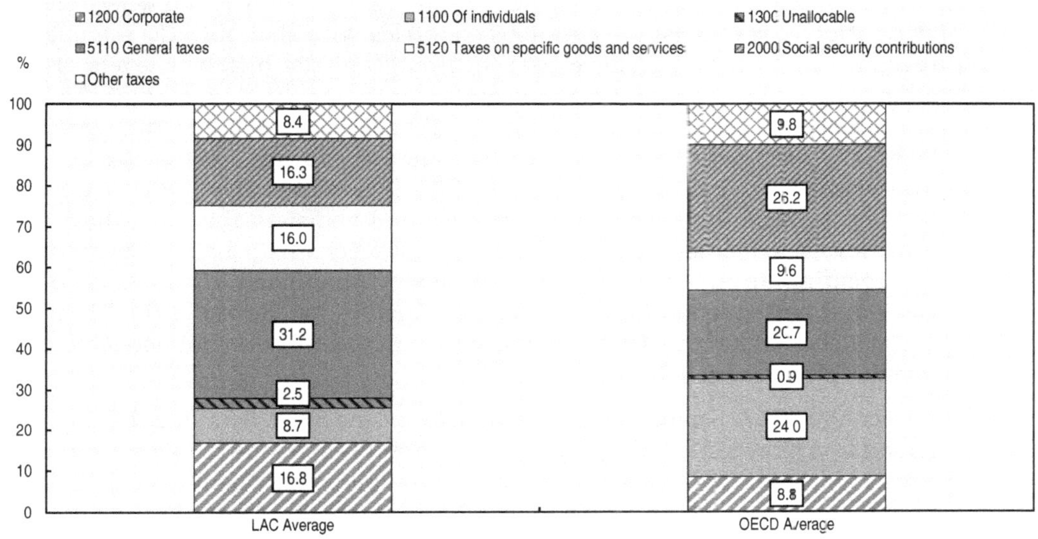

Source: OECD (2017), "Revenue Statistics in Latin America: Comparative tables", *OECD Tax Statistics* (database), http://dx.doi.org/10.1787/ctpa-revlat-data-en.

StatLink http://dx.doi.org/10.1787/888933462422

As a counterpart to the lower share of direct taxes, general consumption taxes represent a higher proportion of total tax collection in the LAC region than in the OECD. In 2014, this category accounted for 31.2% of the total tax revenues in the region whereas the corresponding figure in the OECD area is 20.7%. Similarly the revenue share of taxes on specific goods and services is higher in LAC countries, amounting to 16.0% on average compared to 9.6% in the OECD area.

Finally, taxes on immovable property and payroll (comprised within the category "Other taxes" in Figure 1.18) are less important sources of revenues for LAC countries. The difficulties that sub-national governments have in collecting their own taxes are exemplified by the low revenue-generating capacity of property taxes, which are generally the main source of revenue for local governments in the region (Brossio and Jiménez, 2012), although missing data at the sub-national level makes the analysis of this category difficult. The share of payroll taxes is negligible over the whole period. The revenue shares of property and payroll taxes as a proportion of total tax revenue in the LAC region are similar to the OECD average.

1.4. Taxes by level of government

Since the mid-1980s the LAC countries have transferred some government functions from the central government to sub-national entities. In the first stage, this wave of decentralisation mainly focused on strengthening the democratic role of local authorities.

This has been followed by a gradually increasing trend towards a higher share of public expenditure being executed at sub-national level. Not-withstanding these points, tax revenues appear to be essentially collected by the central or federal entities, with sub-national activities relying more heavily on a system of transfers from upper to lower levels of administration compared with OECD countries. In all LAC countries where sub-national data is available, receipts by central governments accounted for two thirds or more of the total collected whereas the corresponding figure for the OECD countries was about 60%. Brazil is a notable exception as the central government collection amounted to 42% in 2014 (Table 1.1).

There are two statistical issues to be taken into account when comparing the attribution of revenues for these LAC countries with that of OECD members. First, the revenues of both groups have been attributed to the different levels of government according to the revised guidelines set out in to the final version of the 2008 System of National Accounts (SNA). This means that revenues are generally attributed to the level of government that exercises the authority to impose the tax or has the final discretion to set and vary the tax rate. This has implications for situations where one level of government collects tax revenues and transfers them in whole or in part to other levels. Regional examples of this type of mechanism are the Co-participation Law in Argentina, federal participations in Mexico (mandated in the Fiscal Co-ordination Law), and participation funds in Brazil (defined in Article 159 of the Constitution). The second issue is that the data for some of the LAC countries are affected by the lack of tax revenue statistics at sub-national level.

For the 15 LAC countries with available sub-national data in 2014, the share of sub-national tax revenues as a proportion of total tax revenue is lower than 8% except in Argentina, Brazil and Colombia. In Brazil, states and municipalities collect more than 30% of total tax revenues, indicating a significant degree of decentralisation of tax collection powers at the sub-national level. A large part of the VAT (ICMS – imposto sobre operações relativas à circulação de mercadorias e prestação de serviços de transporte interestadual e intermunicipal e de comunicação) is collected at the sub-national state level. Sub-national tax revenue governments in Argentina and Colombia represent more than 15% of total tax revenue. Argentina has a significant collection at state level, which is explained in part by the provincial sales tax (impuesto sobre los ingresos brutos). Between 2000 and 2014, the share of revenue raised by sub-national levels of government declined in seven countries and rose in eight countries. The highest decline was in Uruguay by 3.5 percentage points and the highest increase was in Brazil (3.7 percentage points).

These figures reflect the fact that sub-national governments in LAC countries tend to have a relatively narrow range of taxes under their jurisdiction. The taxes most frequently assigned to sub-national entities are property taxes, motor-vehicle licenses, taxes on specific services and municipal fees and the revenue generation potential of these instruments is relatively limited compared with the tax bases under central jurisdiction, such as VAT and income taxes. In 2014, the entire subnational tax revenue in Belize, Guatemala, Jamaica, Trinidad and Tobago and more than 50% of the tax revenue collected at the sub-national level in Peru and Paraguay was sourced from property taxes. All other countries rely principally on revenue from general and specific consumption. Brazil and Mexico are the only two countries that also collected revenue from different tax bases. In 2014, 5% of the sub-national tax revenue in Brazil and 41% of the sub-national tax revenue in Mexico came respectively from income taxes and from payroll taxes. In OECD member countries, sub-national entities tend to have much broader potential tax bases. A substantial proportion of the revenue collection for sub-national governments in OECD countries is through income taxes and profits (representing more than a third of the total collected amount at sub-national level on average).

Figure 1.19. **Tax mix of the sub-national tax revenue in LAC countries, 2014**

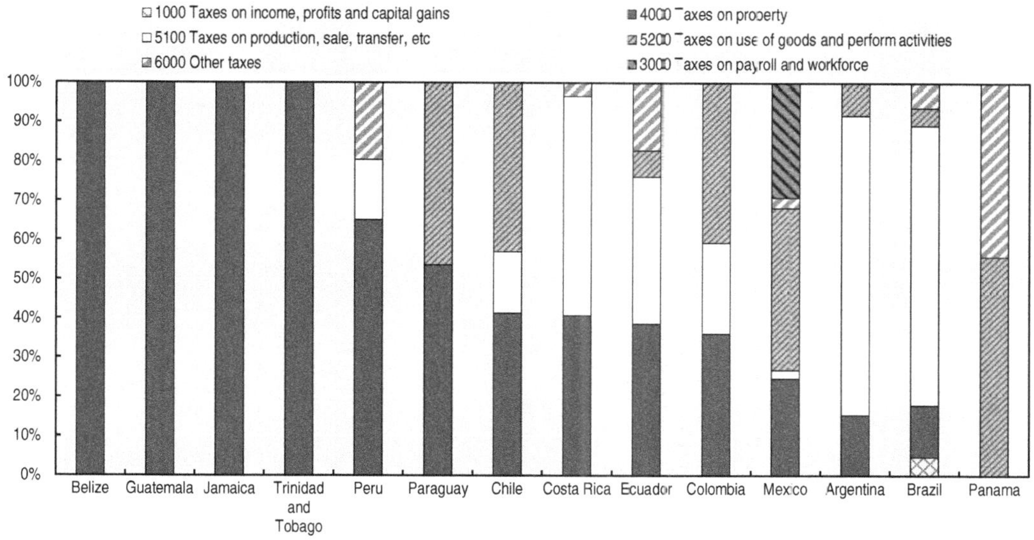

Note: The Bahamas, Barbados, Bolivia, Cuba, the Dominican Republic, El Salvador, Honduras, Nicaragua, Paraguay and Venezuela are excluded as either the sub-national tax revenue data or the breakdown of sub-national tax revenue data by the main type of tax category are not available. The figures exclude local government revenues for Argentina (but include provincial revenues).

Source: Authors' calculations based on tables in Chapter 6.

StatLink http://dx.doi.org/10.1787/888933462438

Low tax revenues at the sub-national level in LAC countries may also result from a lack of administrative and technical capacity to collect high level of tax revenues. For example property taxes – a common source of sub-national revenue – require sophisticated systems and information since the collection of this revenue is expensive. In addition appropriate property registers are lacking in many countries and when they exist they are rarely updated (IDB, 2012). As a result, tax authorities have little access to accurate valuations of lands and buildings and real estate registries are often reluctant to share this information. Property tax also suffers from other characteristics of developing countries such as a high level of informality. Buildings are constructed without permits, properties are not registered and reported prices of some real estate transactions are falsified. As property tax is one of the most controversial taxes with citizens and has high political costs, local tax officials are often unwilling to invest the appropriate resources to levy this revenue (IDB, 2015).

Between 1995 and 2000 the share of revenue raised by social security funds fell in ten LAC countries sometimes due to full or partial privatisation. The largest decreases were in Argentina and Ecuador (by around 7.6 and 13.4 percentage points respectively). Argentina adopted a model in 1994 in which some compulsory contributions were directed to individual capital accounts run by privately managed pension funds. Between 2000 and 2014, the share of social security funds increased in 15 LAC countries out of the 24. The two countries that experienced the largest decreases between 1995 and 2000 were also the countries which recorded the largest increases in the share of social security funds between 2000 and 2014 (Table 1.1). In Argentina, the compulsory model adopted in 1994 was reversed in 2008 and the compulsory contributions previously collected by privately managed pension funds were moved to public pension funds.

Table 1.1. Attribution of tax revenues to sub-sectors of general government as percentage of total tax revenue[1]

	Central government			State or regional government			Local government			Social security funds		
	1995	2000	2014	1995	2000	2014	1995	2000	2014	1995	2000	2014
Federal countries												
Argentina	59.0	66.4	61.5	17.5	17.8	16.9				23.4	15.8	21.6
Brazil	44.7	47.8	41.6	26.8	25.3	26.0	3.7	3.4	6.4	24.8	23.5	26.0
Mexico	73.9	76.5	73.3	2.8	2.5	4.4	1.5	1.0	1.6	21.8	20.1	20.6
Venezuela	94.6	94.6	95.0							5.4	5.4	5.0
OECD[2,3]	52.5	55.9	53.4	16.0	15.4	16.7	7.7	6.9	7.6	23.6	21.5	22.2
Regional countries												
Colombia[4]	63.2	68.6	71.9	5.5	5.6	4.5	8.6	9.4	11.1	22.7	16.4	12.5
OECD[5]	50.4	49.0	42.3	4.8	7.7	13.6	8.5	9.1	10.0	35.8	33.8	33.6
Unitary countries												
Bahamas	89.1	88.1	83.5							10.9	11.9	16.5
Barbados	85.3	84.3	79.9							14.7	15.7	20.1
Belize	93.2	93.5	91.7	0.0	0.0	0.0	0.5	0.7	0.6	6.3	5.8	7.7
Bolivia	95.0	86.4	90.1	0.0	0.0	0.0	5.0	6.3	4.0	0.0	7.3	5.9
Chile	89.9	87.8	86.7	0.0	0.0	0.0	6.5	7.9	7.6	3.6	4.4	5.8
Costa Rica	68.6	67.4	59.3					2.1	3.2	31.4	30.6	37.5
Cuba	88.7	89.6	88.0							11.3	10.4	12.0
Dominican Republic	99.3	98.9	99.6							0.7	1.1	0.4
Ecuador	70.5	86.1	73.6				4.0	1.8	2.4	25.5	12.1	24.0
El Salvador	85.9	83.4	89.3						0.0	14.1	16.6	10.7
Guatemala	83.8	83.6	84.4				0.6	0.9	1.4	15.6	15.5	14.2
Honduras	86.1	84.5	82.0				4.4	5.5	3.1	9.5	10.0	14.9
Jamaica	100.0	99.3	94.2					0.7	1.6	0.0	0.0	4.2
Nicaragua	84.1	80.1	75.7							15.9	19.9	24.3
Panama	62.0	61.1	63.3					2.1	1.5	38.0	36.8	35.2
Paraguay	100.0	82.7	80.6						3.0	0.0	17.3	16.4
Peru	88.2	87.8	86.2						2.8	11.8	12.2	11.0
Trinidad and Tobago	94.4	91.6	90.3				2.4	2.0	1.5	3.2	6.5	8.2
Uruguay	61.4	62.0	67.2				8.4	8.4	4.9	30.1	29.6	27.9
OECD[2,6]	65.5	66.4	63.5	0	0	0	10.7	10.8	11.7	23.5	22.6	24.5

1. The figures exclude local government revenues for Argentina (but include provincial revenues), the Bahamas, Barbados, Bolivia (prior to 1994), Costa Rica (prior to 1998), Cuba, the Dominican Republic, El Salvador (prior to 2015), Jamaica (prior to 1998), Nicaragua, Panama (prior to 1998), Paraguay (prior to 2004), Peru (prior to 2001) and Venezuela as the data are not available.
2. Chile and Mexico are also part of the OECD group.
3. Represents the unweighted average for OECD federal member countries.
4. Colombia is constitutionally a unitary country with high autonomy of its territorial entities.
5. Represents Spain, which is constitutionally a non-federal country with a highly decentralised political structure.
6. Represents the unweighted average for OECD unitary countries.

StatLink http://dx.doi.org/10.1787/888933463000

1.5. Comparative figures / 1.5. Gráficos comparativos

Figure 1.20. **Tax-to-GDP ratios in Latin American and Caribbean countries, 1990 and 2015**

Gráfico 1.20. **Recaudación tributaria como porcentaje de PIB en países de América Latina y el Caribe, 1990 y 2015**

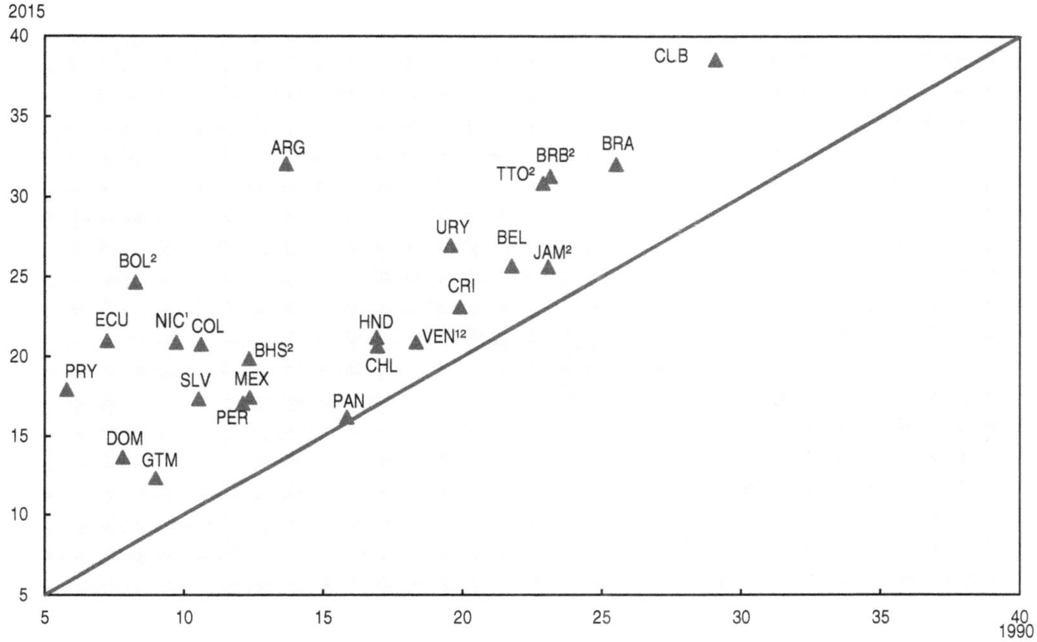

Note: The figures exclude local government revenues for Argentina (but include provincial revenues), Bahamas, Barbados, Bolivia (prior to 1994), Costa Rica (prior to 1998), Cuba, Dominican Republic, El Salvador (prior to 2015), Jamaica (prior to 1998), Nicaragua, Panama (prior to 1998), Paraguay (prior to 2004), Peru (prior to 2001) and Venezuela as the data are not available.

Nota: Las cifras excluyen los ingresos de gobiernos locales en Argentina (pero incluye ingresos de las provincias), Bahamas, Barbados, Bolivia (previo a 1994), Costa Rica (previo a 1998), Cuba, República Dominicana, El Salvador (previo a 2015), Jamaica (previo a 1998), Nicaragua, Panamá (previo a 1998), Paraguay (previo a 2004), Perú (previo a 2001) y Venezuela dado que los datos no están disponibles.

1. Figures for 1991 are used.

1. Se utilizan datos para el 1991.

2. The data are estimated for the following countries: Bahamas (social security contributions for 2015), Barbados (social security contributions for 2015), Belize (social security contributions from 2013 onward), Bolivia (social security contributions from 2013 onward), Jamaica (environmental levy for years 2014 and 2015),Trinidad and Tobago (local property taxes for 2015) and Venezuela (social security contributions from 2011 onward). See the corresponding country tables in Chapter 5 for more information

2. Datos estimados para los siguientes países: Bahamas (contribuciones a la seguridad social para 2015), Barbados (contribuciones a la seguridad social para 2015), Belice (contribuciones a la seguridad social desde 2013), Bolivia (contribuciones a la seguridad social desde 2013), Jamaica (impuesto ambiental para los años 2014 y 2015), Trinidad y Tobago (impuestos sobre la propiedad municipales) y Venezuela (contribuciones a la seguridad social desde 2011). Véanse los cuadros de país en el capítulo 5 para mayor información.

Source: Table 4.1 in Chapter 4/Cuadro 4.1 en el capítulo 4.

StatLink http //dx.doi.org/10.1787/888933462449

Figure 1.21. **Tax-to-GDP ratios in Latin American and Caribbean countries, 1990 and 2000**

Gráfico 1.21. **Recaudación tributaria como porcentaje del PIB en países de América Latina y el Caribe, 1990 y 2000**

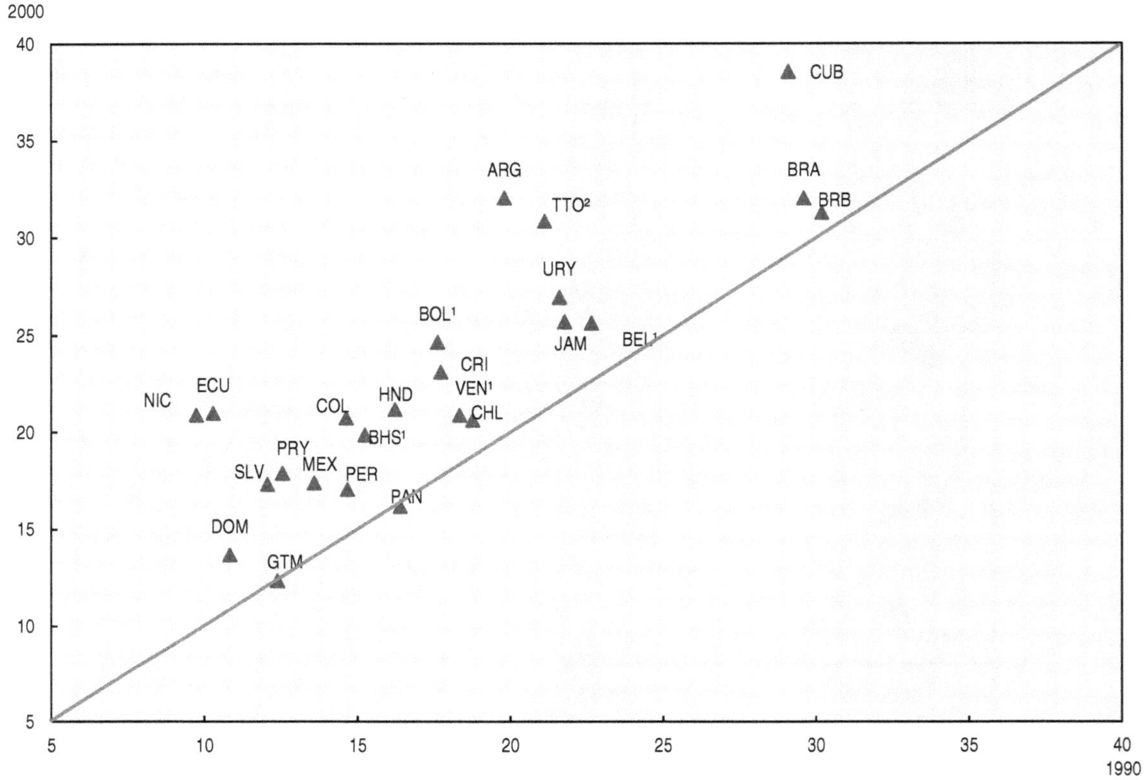

Note: The figures exclude local government revenues for Argentina (but include provincial revenues), Bahamas, Barbados, Bolivia (prior to 1994), Costa Rica (prior to 1998), Cuba, Dominican Republic, El Salvador (prior to 2015), Jamaica (prior to 1998), Nicaragua, Panama (prior to 1998), Paraguay (prior to 2004), Peru (prior to 2001) and Venezuela as the data are not available.

Nota: Las cifras excluyen los ingresos de gobiernos locales en Argentina (pero incluye ingresos de las provincias), Bahamas, Barbados, Bolivia (previo a 1994), Costa Rica (previo a 1998), Cuba, República Dominicana, El Salvador (previo a 2015), Jamaica (previo a 1998), Nicaragua, Panamá (previo a 1998), Paraguay (previo a 2004), Perú (previo a 2001) y Venezuela dado que los datos no están disponibles.

1. Figures for 1991 are used.

1. Se utilizan datos para el 1991.

2. The data are estimated for the following countries: Bahamas (social security contributions for 2015), Barbados (social security contributions for 2015), Belize (social security contributions from 2013 onward), Bolivia (social security contributions from 2013 onward), Jamaica (environmental levy for years 2014 and 2015),Trinidad and Tobago (local property taxes for 2015) and Venezuela (social security contributions from 2011 onward). See the corresponding country tables in Chapter 5 for more information

2. Datos estimados para los siguientes países: Bahamas (contribuciones a la seguridad social para 2015), Barbados (contribuciones a la seguridad social para 2015), Belice (contribuciones a la seguridad social desde 2013), Bolivia (contribuciones a la seguridad social desde 2013), Jamaica (impuesto ambiental para los años 2014 y 2015), Trinidad y Tobago (impuestos sobre la propiedad municipales) y Venezuela (contribuciones a la seguridad social desde 2011). Véanse los cuadros de país en el capítulo 5 para mayor información.

Source: Table 4.1 in Chapter 4/Cuadro 4.1 en el capítulo 4.

StatLink http://dx.doi.org/10.1787/888933462457

Figure 1.22. **Tax-to-GDP ratios in Latin American and Caribbean countries, 2000 and 2015**

Gráfico 1.22. **Recaudación tributaria como porcentaje del PIB en países de América Latina y el Caribe, 2000 y 2015**

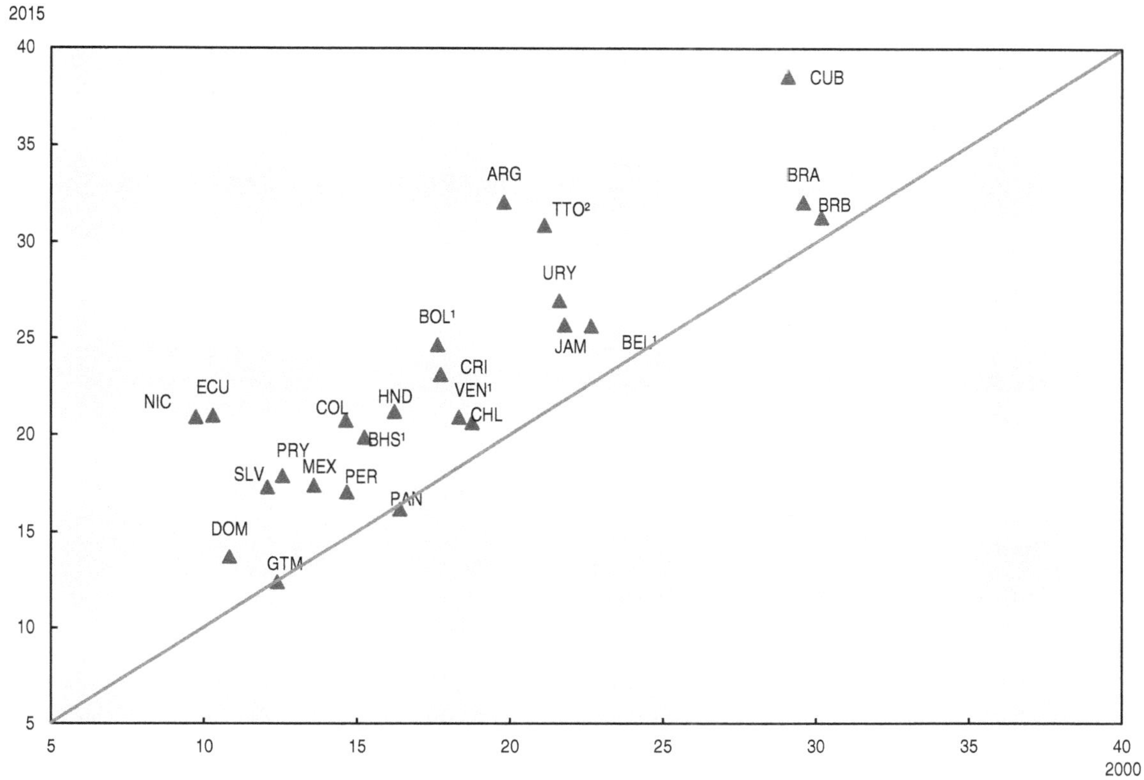

Note: The figures exclude local government revenues for Argentina (but include provincial revenues), Bahamas, Barbados, Bolivia (prior to 1994), Costa Rica (prior to 1998), Cuba, Dominican Republic, El Salvador (prior to 2015), Jamaica (prior to 1998), Nicaragua, Panama (prior to 1998), Paraguay (prior to 2004), Peru (prior to 2001) and Venezuela as the data are not available.

Nota: Las cifras excluyen los ingresos de gobiernos locales en Argentina (pero incluye ingresos de las provincias), Bahamas, Barbados, Bolivia (previo a 1994), Costa Rica (previo a 1998), Cuba, República Dominicana, El Salvador (previo a 2015), Jamaica (previo a 1998), Nicaragua, Panamá (previo a 1998), Paraguay (previo a 2004), Perú (previo a 2001) y Venezuela dado que los datos no están disponibles.

1. The data are estimated for the following countries: Bahamas (social security contributions for 2015), Barbados (social security contributions for 2015), Belize (social security contributions from 2013 onward), Bolivia (social security contributions from 2013 onward), Jamaica (environmental levy for years 2014 and 2015),Trinidad and Tobago (local property taxes for 2015) and Venezuela (social security contributions from 2011 onward). See the corresponding country tables for more information

1. Datos estimados para los siguientes países: Bahamas (contribuciones a la seguridad social para 2015), Barbados (contribuciones a la seguridad social para 2015), Belice (contribuciones a la seguridad social desde 2013), Bolivia (contribuciones a la seguridad social desde 2013), Jamaica (impuesto ambiental para los años 2014 y 2015), Trinidad y Tobago (impuestos sobre la propiedad municipales) y Venezuela (contribuciones a la seguridad social desde 2011). Véanse los cuadros de país en el capítulo 5 para mayor información.

Source: Table 4.1 in Chapter 4/Cuadro 4.1 en el capítulo 4.

StatLink http://dx.doi.org/10.1787/888933462463

Notes

1. The figure is provisional and has been calculated by applying the unweighted average percentage change for 2015 in the 32 countries providing data for that year to the overall average tax to GDP ratio in 2014.
2. The year-on-year change remains 0.6 percentage points if the LAC average for both years is calculated excluding Venezuela where high inflation affected both tax revenues and GDP in 2015.
3. In the IDB publication, the Latin America average represents the average of 19 countries Argentina, Bolivia, Brazil, Chile, Colombia, Costa Rica, Dominican Republic, Ecuador, Guatemala, Honduras, Jamaica, Mexico, Nicaragua, Panama, Peru, Paraguay, El Salvador, Uruguay and Venezuela.
4. Informality is defined as the percentage of non-contributors to pension systems over total employed in Latin America and the Caribbean.
5. This includes Argentina; Brazil, Bolivia, Chile, Colombia, Costa Rica, Ecuador, Honduras, Mexico, Nicaragua, Panama and Peru.
6. The VRR could not be compiled or was not applicable for Brazil, Belize, the Bahamas, Barbados, Cuba and Trinidad & Tobago.
7. VAT evasion is compiled as the loss of VAT revenue as a percentage of expected VAT revenue.
8. The IMF compiled a c-efficiency measure. The C-efficiency aimed to measure the same thing as the VRR, however their measurement differs slightly. More information on the differences is available on OECD (2016).
9. Around 2% of total tax revenue is revenue from taxes on income and profits that cannot be allocated between corporate income tax and personal income tax.

References

Barreix A., J.C. Benitez and M. Pecho (forthcoming – 2017), "Revisiting Personal Income Tax", *OECD Development Centre Working Papers*, OECD Publishing, Paris.

Brossio, G. and J.P. Jiménez (2012), *Decentralization and Reform in Latin America: Improving Intergovernmental Relations*, Edward Elgar, in press, Cheltenham, UK and Northampton, MA.

Daude, C., A. Melguizo and A. Neut (2010), "Fiscal Policy in Latin America: Countercyclical and Sustainable at Last?", *OECD Development Centre Working Paper* No. 291, OECD Development Centre, Paris.

ECLAC (2014), *Tax policy in Latin America. Assessment and guidelines for a second generation of reforms*, Santiago, Chile, ECLAC.

ECLAC (2013), *Fiscal Panorama of Latin America and the Caribbean: Tax reform and renewal of the fiscal covenant*, ECLAC, Santiago de Chile

ECLAC (2010), "La Hora de la igualdad. Brechas por cerrar, caminos por abrir", (LC/G.2432(SES.33/3)), Santiago, Chile, ECLAC.

EY 2014, "Worldwide VAT GST and sales tax guide 2014", Ernst & Young Global Limited, www.ey.com/Publication/vwLUAssets/Worldwide-VAT-GST-and-sales-tax-guide-2014/$FILE/Worldwide-VAT-GST-and-sales-tax-guide-2014.pdf.

IDB (2015), "Decentralizing Revenue in Latin America Why and How", Inter-American Development Bank, Washington, DC.

IDB (2013), "More than revenues, Taxation as a development tool", Inter-American Development Bank, Washington, DC.

IDB (2012), "Sub-national Revenue Mobilization in Peru" *IDB Working Paper Series* No. IDB-WP-299, Inter-American Development Bank, Washington, DC.

IMF (2016a), "The Bahamas: 2016 article IV consultation—press release; staff report; and statement by the executive director for the Bahamas", *IMF Country Report* No. 16/224, International Monetary Fund, Washington, DC, https://www.imf.org/external/pubs/ft/scr/2016/cr16224.pdf.

IMF (2016b). "Argentina 2016 Article IV Consultation", *IMF Country Report* No. 16/346, International Monetary Fund, Washington, DC.

IMF (2016c), *World Economic Outlook Database*, October 2016 Edition, International Monetary Fund, Washington, DC.

IMF (2010), "Paraguay: Selected Issues", *IMF Country Report* No. 10/170, International Monetary Fund, Washington, DC, https://www.imf.org/external/pubs/ft/scr/2010/cr10170.pdf.

Franks J. R., R. Benelli, V. Mercer-Blackman and R. SabParaguay (2005), "Corruption, Reform, and the Financial System", International Monetary Fund, Washington, DC.

International Tax Review (2014), "Mexico 2014 income tax-reform, Considerations for the financial-sector", www.internationaltaxreview.com/Article/3352686/Mexico-2014-income-tax-reform-Considerations-for-the-financial-sector.html.

Gómez Sabaini, J.C., J.P. Jiménez and A. Podestá (2010), "Evasión y equidad en América Latina", *Project documents*, No. 309 (LC/W.309/ Rev.1), Santiago, Chile, ECLAC.

The Panama Investor Blog (2008), "Audit uncovers millions in unpaid sales taxes", http://primapanama.blogs.com/_panama_residential_devel/2008/06/audit-uncovers.html.

Peters, A.C and M.A Bristol (2006), "VAT: Is it Suitable for the Caribbean Community?", *MPRA Paper* No. 8, https://mpra.ub.uni-muenchen.de/8/1/MPRA_paper_8.pdf.

OECD (2017, forthcoming), *Tax Policy Reforms in the OECD*, OECD Publishing, Paris.

OECD (2016), *Consumption Tax Trends 2016: VAT/GST and Excise Rates, Trends and Policy Issues*, OECD Publishing, Paris, http://dx.doi.org/10.1787/ctt-2016-en.

OECD (2014a), *Development Co-operation Report 2014: Mobilising Resources for Sustainable Development*, OECD Publishing, Paris, http://dx.doi.org/10.1787/dcr-2014-en.

OECD (2014b), *Revenue Statistics 1965-2014*, OECD Publishing, Paris, http://dx.doi.org/10.1787/rev_stats-2014-en-fr.

OECD (2008), *Latin American Economic Outlook 2009*, OECD Publishing, Paris, http://dx.doi.org/10.1787/leo-2009-en.

OECD/ECLAC (2012), *Latin American Economic Outlook 2013: SME Policies for Structural Change*, ECLAC and OECD Publishing, http://dx.doi.org/10.1787/leo-2013-en.

OECD/CAF/ECLAC (2015), *Latin American Economic Outlook 2016: Towards a New Partnership with China*, OECD Publishing, Paris, http://dx.doi.org/10.1787/9789264246218-en.

OECD/ECLAC/CIAT/IDB (2015), *Revenue Statistics in Latin America and the Caribbean 2015*, OECD Publishing, Paris, http://dx.doi.org/10.1787/rev_lat-2015-en-fr.

PKF (2013), *PKF Worldwide Tax Guide 2013*, PKF International Limited, www.pkf.com/publications/tax-guides/pkf-international-worldwide-tax-guide-2013.

PWC (2015), "Peru's major tax reform include rate changes and a new tax ruling request procedure 2015", www.pwc.com/us/en/tax-services/publications/insights/assets/pwc-perus-major-tax-reform-includes-rate-changes.pdf.

US mission Geneva (2011), Mission of the United States of America to the United Nations and Other International Organizations in Geneva, Geneva, https://geneva.usmission.gov/2011/01/18/tpr-jamaica/.

World Grain (2016), "Reforms boost Argentine grain industry", www.world-grain.com/articles/news_home/Features/2016/05/Reforms_boost_Argentine_grain.aspx?ID=%7BAE4EE339-0D46-43EF-A962-5ED9DEF72B53%7D.

Zuleta J.C (2008), "Combating corruption in the revenue service: the case of VAT refunds in Bolivia", Anti-Corruption Resource Centre, www.U4.no/themes/pfm.

CAPÍTULO 1

TENDENCIAS TRIBUTARIAS, 1990-2015

1.1. Proporciones de ingresos tributarios

La relación de impuestos y el PIB refleja el recaudo tributario de los gobiernos para financiar la provisión de bienes y servicios públicos y la inversión en infraestructura. La movilización de recursos fiscales mediante impuestos es importante para asegurar el desarrollo económico de los países (OCDE, 2014a). Los impuestos constituyen una fuente predecible y sostenible de ingresos para los gobiernos, en contraste con la disminución de la asistencia al desarrollo y la volatilidad de los ingresos no-tributarios con respecto a los precios de las materias primas.

Este reporte presenta data internacional comparable sobre recaudo tributario para 24 países de América Latina y el Caribe. Este capítulo describe las tendencias en estos países y varios indicadores tributarios claves: el recaudo tributario total en relación al PIB, la estructura impositiva y la proporción de ingresos tributarios por nivel de gobierno. Esta discusión suplementa la información detallada de países que se encuentra en el capítulo 5.

Proporciones de ingresos tributarios en 2015

El promedio del recaudo tributario como proporción del PIB en América Latina y el Caribe (ALC) fue de 22.8% en 2015 (gráfico 1.1). La proporción tributaria en relación al PIB se mide como el recaudo tributario (incluidas las contribuciones a la seguridad social) como proporción del Producto Interno Bruto (PIB). La razón de impuestos y PIB varió ampliamente en la región, desde 12.4% en Guatemala a 38.6% en Cuba. Todos los países de ALC tuvieron ingresos tributarios como proporción del PIB inferiores al promedio de la OCDE[1] de 34.3%, con la excepción de Cuba. Las cifras presentadas para Venezuela en 2015 deben ser manejadas con precaución dado que han sido afectadas por altos niveles de inflación. Excluyendo a Venezuela, la proporción de ingresos tributarios en relación al PIB para los países de ALC fue de 22.9% en 2015.

Gráfico 1.1. **Relación de ingresos tributarios y el PIB (Ingresos tributarios totales como % del PIB), 2015**

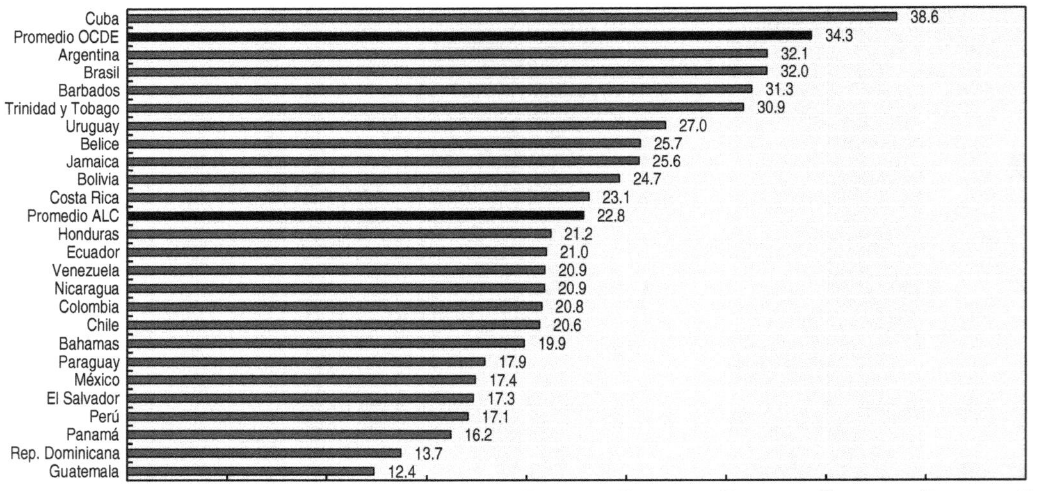

Nota: Las cifras excluyen los ingresos subnacionales de Argentina (aunque se incluyen los ingresos de las provincias), Las Bahamas, Barbados, República Dominicana, Nicaragua y Venezuela dado que los datos no se encuentran disponibles.

1. Representa el promedio de los países miembros de la OCDE. Chile y México forman también parte del promedio del grupo de la OCDE (35).

2. Representa el promedio no ponderado de 24 países de América Latina y el Caribe.

Fuente: Cuadro 4.1.

StatLink http://dx.doi.org/10.1787/888933462499

Las proporciones más altas de ingresos tributarios respecto al PIB se dieron en Cuba (38.6%), Argentina (32.1%), y Brasil (32.0%). Los otros países cuyo recaudo tributario estuvo por encima del promedio fueron Barbadas, Trinidad y Tobago, Uruguay, Belice, Jamaica, Bolivia y Costa Rica. Los países con los ingresos tributarios como proporción del PIB más bajos fueron Guatemala (12.4%) y República Dominicana (13.7%).

En 2015, el promedio del recaudo tributario sobre PIB de ALC fue 0.6[2] puntos más alto que en el año previo (gráfico 1.2). Lo anterior contrasta con la coyuntura económica global de la región de América Latina y el Caribe. En promedio, las tasas de crecimiento del PIB para la América Latina han experimentado una desaceleración desde 2012, la cual ha continuó en 2015 (OCDE/CAF/CEPAL, 2015). La tasa de crecimiento fue de 1% en 2014 mientras que alcanzó 5% a mediados de la década del 2000. OCDE/CAF/CEPAL (2015) explican que América Latina ha experimentado un bajo crecimiento debido a la fragilidad de la economía mundial, precios más bajos de las materias primas y la reducción de los flujos de capital desde 2012.

Existe una amplia gama de situaciones en los países de ALC, puesto que 19 de los 24 países registraron un incremento y 5 países registraron una disminución en sus ingresos tributarios como proporción del PIB en 2015. Las Bahamas tuvieron el incremento más alto en 2015. Otro aumento pronunciado se dio en México (2.3 puntos porcentuales) debido al alza que tuvieron los impuestos sobre la renta y las utilidades (1.1 puntos porcentuales) y los impuestos específicos sobre bienes y servicios (1.2 puntos porcentuales) (gráfico 1.3). Por el contrario, Perú experimentó la mayor caída de 1.7 p.p., principalmente debido a una caída significativa de 1.4 puntos porcentuales en el recaudo del impuesto sobre la renta y utilidades.

Gráfico 1.2. **Cambio en los ratios de ingresos tributarios y PIB en 2015 (puntos porcentuales del PIB)**

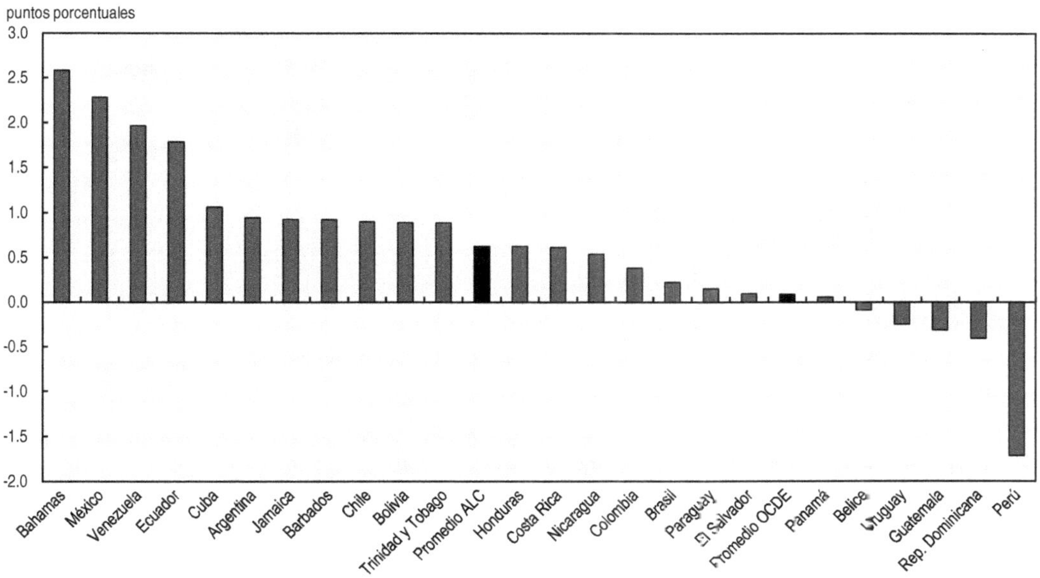

Fuente: Elaboración propia con base en la cuadro 4.1.

StatLink http://dx.doi.org/10.1787/888933462503

Reformas tributarias significativas aunadas a la coyuntura económica han llevado a los incrementos observados en las Bahamas, México y la caída en Perú en 2015. Las Bahamas introdujo un impuesto al valor agregado (IVA) en enero de 2015 (FMI, 2016). En 2014, México implementó una senda reforma tributaria mediante la cual se modificó el impuesto especial sobre la producción y servicios (un impuesto específico) lo que llevó a un mayor recaudo proveniente de gasolinas y diésel (OCDE, 2017a), un aumento en las tasas del impuesto sobre la renta de personas físicas, limitaciones sobre las deducciones personales y la ampliación de la base tributaria del impuesto al renta de sociedades a través de la eliminación de ciertas deducciones (International Tax Review, 2014). Hubo dos grades razones que explican la caída en Perú en 2015: a) el fin del ciclo de las materias primas afectó el ingreso tributario proveniente del sector minero en 2015, el cual disminuyó en 0.5 puntos porcentuales comparado a 2014 (véase el capítulo 2 de esta publicación) y b) Perú implementó una reforma tributaria en 2014 que incluyó la reducción de la tasa del impuesto a la renta corporativa de 30% a 28% (PWC, 2015).

El factor principal que impulsó el incremento en los ingresos tributarios como proporción del PIB en los países de ALC en 2015 fue el aumento en el recaudo de los impuestos generales sobre el consumo. La variación anual de estos impuestos fue de 0.3 puntos porcentuales, seguido de un alza de 0.2 puntos porcentuales en el recaudo de los tributos sobre bienes y servicios específicos, ambos como porcentaje del PIB (gráfico 1.3).

Gráfico 1.3. **Variación anual los ingresos tributarios en relación al PIB por tipo de impuesto en 2015 (puntos porcentuales de PIB)**

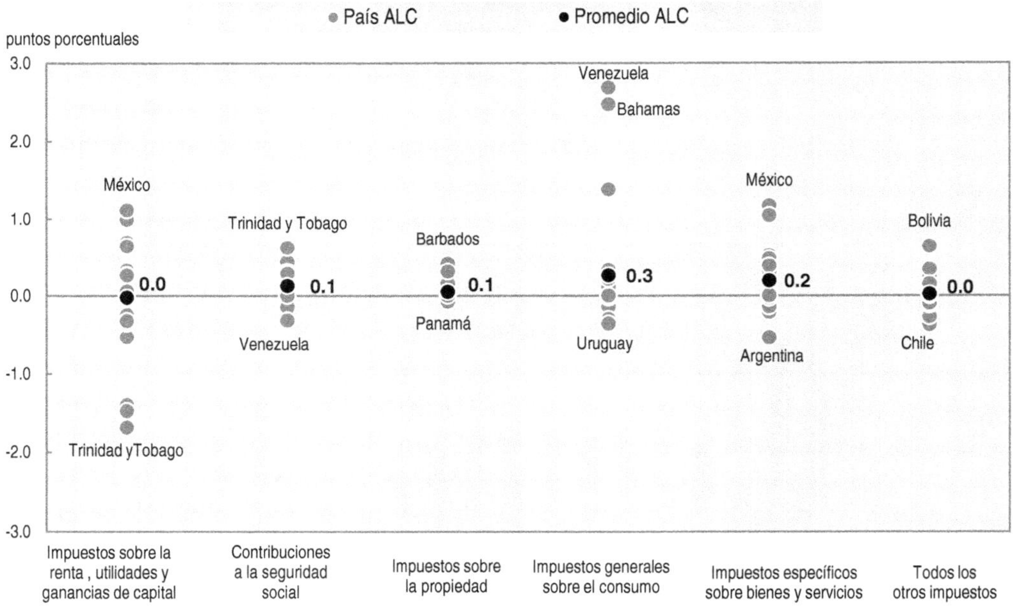

Nota: El cambio interanual en el recaudo de los impuestos generales sobre el consumo y sobre bienes y servicios específicos de Venezuela debe ser interpretado con cautela dado los altos índices de inflación que los han afectado.

Fuente: Cálculos del autor con base en las cuadros del capítulo 4.

StatLink http://dx.doi.org/10.1787/888933462511

Existe gran heterogeneidad entre los países con respecto a los cambios anuales en 2015. Las variaciones en el recaudo de los impuestos generales sobre el consumo y los impuestos sobre la renta y las utilidades mostraron las mayores variaciones entre los países (gráfico 1.3). Los cambios en los impuestos sobre bienes y servicios fueron el factor principal en los cambios del recaudo total de nueve países. Mientras que los cambios en los impuestos sobre la renta y las utilidades fueron el factor principal que impulsaron el aumento en ocho países (gráfico 1.4).

Gráfico 1.4. **Cambios en el recaudo tributario total y en el recaudo de las principales categorías de impuestos como % del PIB en 2015**

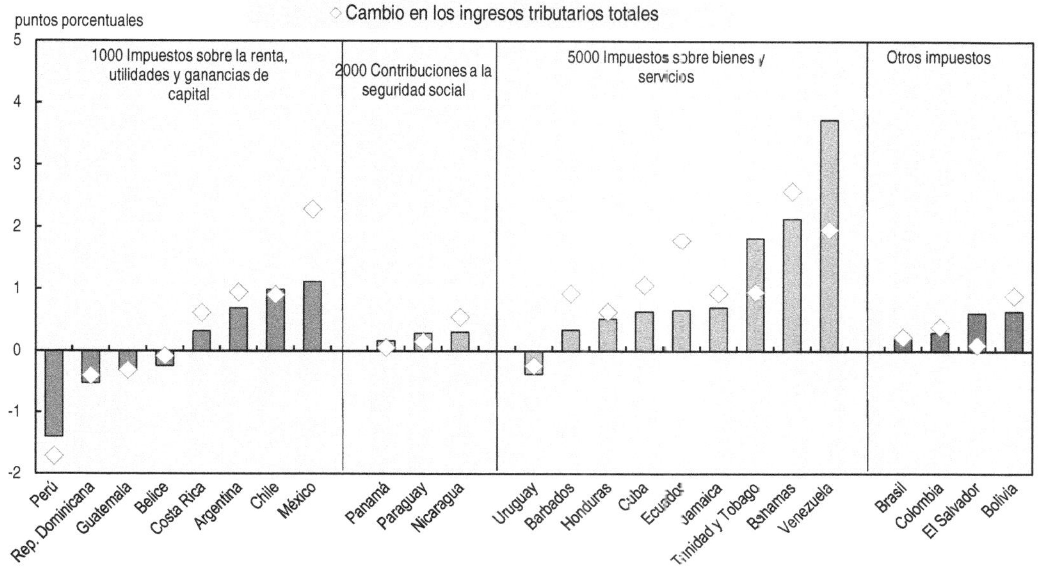

Nota: El cambio interanual en el recaudo de los impuestos sobre bienes y servicios de Venezuela debe ser interpretado con cautela dado los altos índices de inflación que los han afectado.

Fuente: Elaboración propia con base en las cuadros del capítulo 4.

StatLink http://dx.doi.org/10.1787/888933462525

Evolución del recaudo tributario desde el 2000

El promedio del recaudo tributario como proporción del PIB en los países de ALC ha aumentado, con excepción de 2008 y 2009, de forma continua entre 1990 y 2015 (gráfico 1.5). Durante este lapso ha incrementado en más desde siete puntos porcentuales desde 15.8% en 1990. Este crecimiento refleja las condiciones macroeconómicas favorables, cambios en el diseño del sistema tributario y el fortalecimiento de las administraciones tributarias. Esta tendencia se contrasta con la de los países de la OCDE dónde el recaudo tributario se ha mantenido relativamente estable alcanzando 34.3% del PIB en 2015, 2.3 puntos porcentuales por encima del nivel de 1990.

La crisis financiera global interrumpió el crecimiento sostenido del recaudo tributario como porcentaje del PIB en ALC. La crisis resultó en el descenso del promedio de ALC en 0.5 puntos porcentuales durante 2008 y 2010 debido a la caída en la actividad económica y los precios de las materias primas. De igual forma, el promedio de los países de la OCDE fue afectado principalmente por la crisis entre los años 2007 y 2009. Durante este periodo, el ratio de impuestos en relación al PIB registró una caída de 1.3 puntos porcentuales. El área de la OCDE recuperó sus niveles de recaudo tributario pre-crisis de 33.8% en 2013. Mientras que la región de ALC recuperó sus niveles de 2008 (21.3%) dos años antes, en 2011.

La diferencia entre los promedios del recaudo tributario como porcentaje del PIB de ALC y OCDE se redujo entre 1990 y 2008. Luego permaneció estable hasta 2014 previo a su nueva disminución en 2015 (gráfico 1.5). La brecha en el recaudo tributario como proporción del PIB entre ALC y OECD disminuyó de 16 puntos porcentuales en 1990 a cerca de 12 puntos puntuales en 2008, manteniéndose estable hasta 2014. La brecha disminuyó nuevamente en 2015 y se mantiene en 11.4 puntos porcentuales, la menor brecha desde 1990.

Gráfico 1.5. **Brechas en el recaudo tributario como proporción del PIB, 1990-2015**

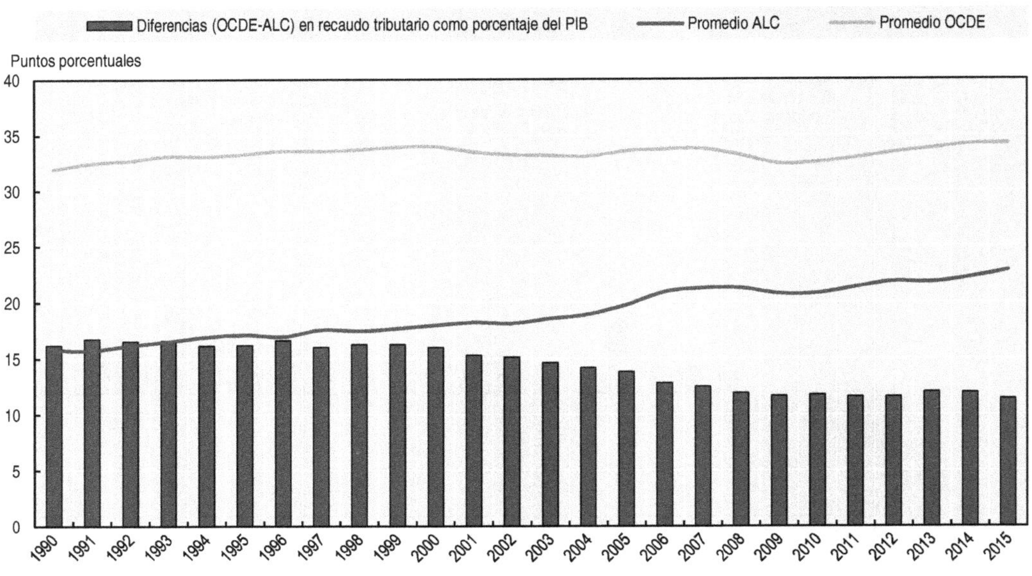

Fuente: Cuadro 4.1.

StatLink http://dx.doi.org/10.1787/888933462535

Los ratios del recaudo tributario en los países de ALC aumentaron a principios de los noventas luego de un período de inestabilidad macroeconómica experimentado en la década anterior. Durante los años ochenta, los países mantuvieron grandes desbalances fiscales y al mismo tiempo recurrieron a métodos alternativos para financiar su gasto (vía deuda y emisión de moneda). Lo anterior conllevó a un proceso inflacionario acelerado en la región, lo cual erosionó el valor real de sus ingresos tributarios. Como resultado, las reformas de los años 90s estuvieron enfocadas al combate a la inflación y a recobrar la disciplina fiscal. La mayoría de gobiernos de ALC respondieron mediante una disminución en el gasto público y la implementación de políticas con miras al incremento del recaudo tributario lo que derivó en una mejora del manejo presupuestario y de los balances fiscales. El impacto de la inflación en los ingresos tributarios obligó a las autoridades a identificar reformas de política y administración tributaria que resultaran en sistemas tributarios menos vulnerables a episodios inflacionarios. Esto se logró disminuyendo los tiempos de recaudo y mediante la indexación de las obligaciones tributarias.

Durante las últimas dos décadas se llevaron a cabo esfuerzos significativos para modernizar las administraciones y los sistemas tributarios. Durante ese lapso, se implementaron nuevos sistemas de tecnologías de información, se racionalizó la estructura de las administraciones tributarias y los sistemas de recaudo tributario se tornaron más eficientes mientras que el personal adquirió mayor experiencia (BID, 2013). Aunado a ello, los países de ALC hicieron cambios significativos para la simplificación de sus sistemas tributarios y la ampliación de sus bases impositivas. Redujeron los números de las exenciones e incentivos tributarios otorgados a ciertas actividades y sectores, especialmente orientados hacia la atracción de inversión extranjera que no siempre fue exitosa. Las reformas incluyeron la introducción o el desarrollo de regímenes simplificados para pequeños contribuyentes y la imposición sobre la propiedad basada en criterios de rentas presuntas. Durante la última mitad de la década, varias reformas sobre el impuesto a la renta se implementaron en los países de ALC, las cuales han incluido aumentos de las tasas y la ampliación de la base tributaria. Estas medidas han tenido un efecto positivo gracias a la expansión del impuesto para que abarque todas las rentas del trabajo y del capital, incluyendo dividendos (Colombia, República Dominicana, Guatemala, El Salvador, Nicaragua, Panamá y Perú). Las reformas también han establecido impuestos mínimos, impuestos sobre las transacciones financieras, la reducción gradual del nivel de renta real gravado al tipo máximo marginal y controles adicionales sobre los precios de transferencia (CEPAL, 2013).

La introducción del IVA fue la reforma más significativa en los países de América Latina y el Caribe en los años ochentas y principios de los noventas. Las reformas subsecuentes relacionadas al IVA se han centrado en su extensión y fortalecimiento, mediante el aumento de la tasa y la ampliación de su base. De 1990 a 2015, el IVA como proporción del PIB se ha más que duplicado, pasando de 2.4% del PIB en 1990 a 6.0% del PIB en 2015 (gráfico 1.6). Durante el mismo período, los países de América Latina y el Caribe han reducido sus ingresos tributarios, como porcentaje del PIB, provenientes de otros impuestos sobre los bienes y servicios (esencialmente, los impuestos específicos y los derechos sobre las aduanas y las importaciones). Esta caída está asociada a la liberalización del comercio que trajo consigo un cambio en la forma en la que se gravan los bienes importados y exportados y también los productos y servicios específicos. Estos cambios incluyeron la reducción de los aranceles a la importación, la reducción de la base y de los productos y servicios sujetos a impuestos específicos (por ejemplo, focalizándose en productos como bebidas alcohólicas, tabaco, petróleo y sus derivados) y la eliminación de los impuestos sobre las exportaciones. Una importante excepción es en Argentina, país en el cual los impuestos sobre las exportaciones fueron re-establecidos en 2002. No obstante, el gobierno actual abolió este impuesto sobre ciertos productos agropecuarios en 2015 (World Grain, 2016).

Gráfico 1.6. **Recaudo de los impuestos sobre la renta y las utilidades, el IVA y otros impuestos sobre bienes y servicios como porcentaje del PIB en América Latina y el Caribe, 1990–2015**

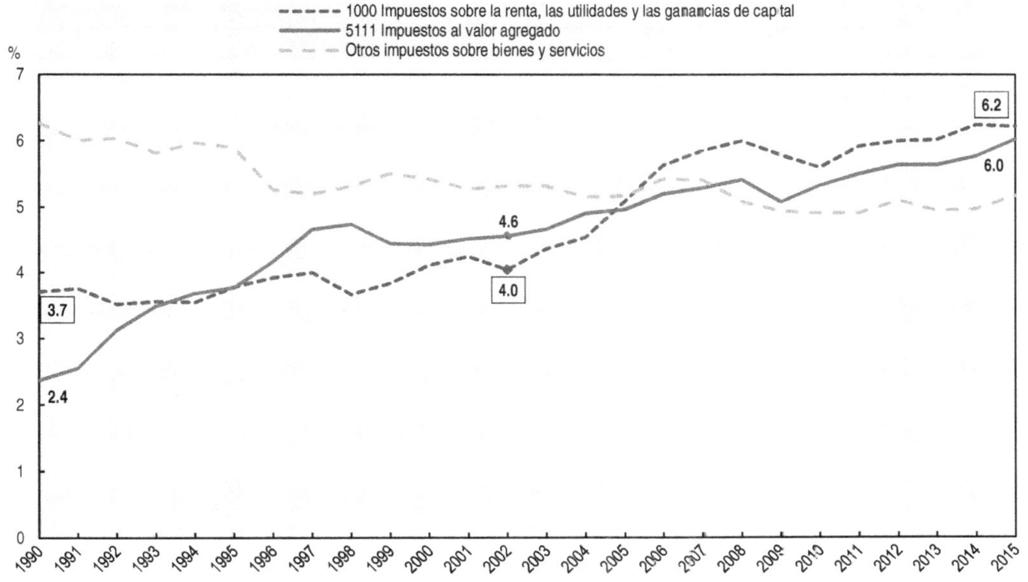

Fuente: OCDE (2017), "Estadísticas tributarias en América Latina: tablas comparativas", *OCDE Estadísticas tributarias* (base de datos), http://dx.doi.org/10.1787/ctpa-revlat-data-en.

StatLink http://dx.doi.org/10.1787/888933462545

Los principales contribuyentes al incremento en el recaudo tributario en ALC fueron el IVA desde 1990 hasta 2002 y los impuestos sobre las rentas y utilidades entre 2002 y 2015. Los ingresos tributarios provenientes del IVA aumentaron en 2.2 puntos porcentuales del PIB desde 1990 hasta 2012, mientras que los ingresos del impuesto a las rentas y utilidades aumentaron 0.3 puntos porcentuales durante el mismo periodo (gráfico 1.6). En contraste, los ingresos del impuesto sobre la renta y utilidades aumentaron 2.2 puntos porcentuales del PIB mientras que el IVA lo hizo en 1.5 puntos porcentuales durante el lapso de 2002 a 2015. Uno de los elementos que contribuyó a esta tendencia es la recuperación de la actividad económica en ALC (CEPAL-OCDE, 2012) y el boom en el precio de las materias primas luego de 2003, que contribuyó al aumento en el recaudo del impuesto sobre las rentas y utilidades de sociedades (Barreix et al, 2017). Luego de la crisis financiera, el incremento en los ingresos provenientes de los impuestos sobre bienes y servicios, impuestos sobre las rentas y utilidades y las contribuciones a la seguridad social han contribuido a la recuperación en el promedio de los ingresos tributarios para la región.

Desde 2007, los ingresos tributarios, como porcentaje del PIB, del impuesto a las rentas y utilidades han incrementado con una interrupción durante la crisis financiera (gráfico 1.7). Este incremento se explica por el aumento en los ingresos del impuesto sobre sociedades. CEPAL (2014), expone como el impuesto a la renta de sociedades creció mucho más rápido que el impuesto sobre la renta de personas físicas durante los últimos 25 años y que este incremento refleja los aumentos en los ingresos tributarios derivados de compañías en los sectores de recursos naturales. También fue el resultado de políticas tributarias que redujeron los incentivos en zonas de libre-comercio, la introducción de impuestos mínimos a las empresas y reformas en el ámbito de la imposición internacional y acuerdos entre países para combatir la evasión.

Gráfico 1.7. **Recaudo de impuesto sobre la renta y utilidades, el impuesto sobre la renta de empresas y el impuesto sobre la renta de personas, como porcentaje del PIB en América Latina y el Caribe, 2007-15**

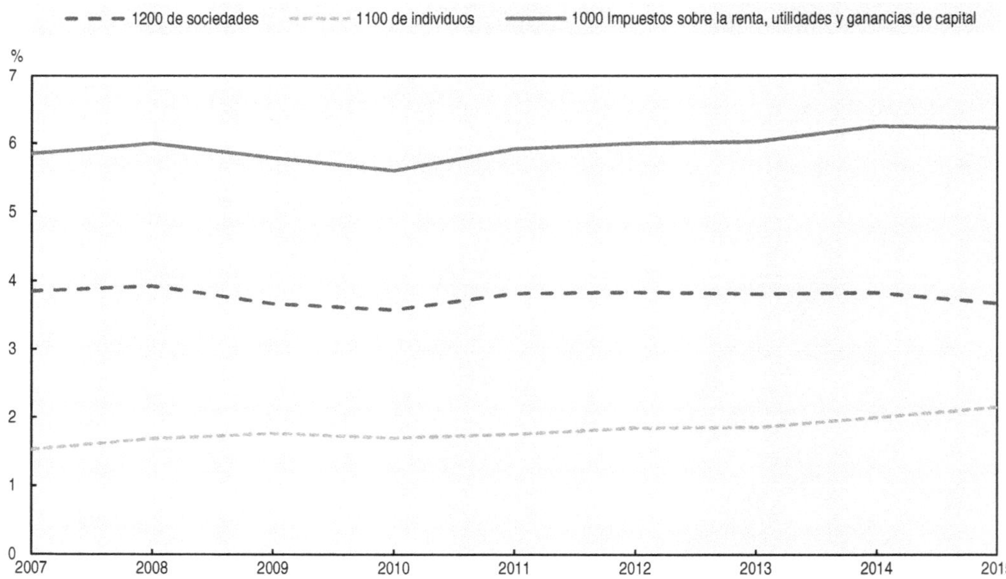

Nota: Ecuador, Nicaragua y Venezuela han sido excluidos de los promedios de los impuestos sobre la renta de empresas y personas físicas dado que más de un tercio de su recaudo no puedo ser atribuido a las categorías de renta de empresas (1200) o impuesto sobre la renta de personas (1100).

Fuente: OCDE (2017), "Estadísticas tributarias en América Latina: tablas comparativas", *OCDE Estadísticas tributarias* (base de datos), http://dx.doi.org/10.1787/ctpa-revlat-data-en.

StatLink http://dx.doi.org/10.1787/888933462552

Durante la crisis financiera, el promedio del impuesto sobre la renta y utilidades de empresas se redujo mientras que el promedio del impuesto sobre la renta y utilidades de personas físicas se mantuvo estable durante este período, ambos como porcentaje del PIB (gráfico 1.7). Entre 2008 y 2010, el recaudo del impuesto sobre la renta de empresas cayó fuertemente (0.4 puntos porcentuales). Se mantuvo estable a un nivel de 3.8% desde 2011 hasta que en 2015 experimentó una nueva caída de 0.2 puntos porcentuales. Esta disminución puede ser explicada parcialmente por la caída en el recaudo de las materias primas no renovables (véase el capítulo 2 de esta publicación). Por el contrario, el recaudo del impuesto a la renta de personas, como porcentaje del PIB, ha estado incrementando continuamente desde 2011 y alcanzó su máximo nivel en 2015 (2.1%). Desde 2012, la tasa de crecimiento del impuesto sobre la renta de personas físicas ha sido mayor que la del impuesto que recae sobre las empresas, especialmente debido a la coyuntura de desaceleración económica y los bajos precios de las materias primas. Los promedios del recaudo de los impuestos sobre la renta y utilidades de empresas y personas físicas deben ser interpretados con cautela dado que Ecuador, Nicaragua y Venezuela ha sido excluidos de la estimación en vista que más de un tercio de todo el recaudo no puede ser atribuido al impuesto a la renta de empresas (1200) o al impuesto sobre la renta de personas físicas (1100).

Los cambios en el recaudo del impuesto sobre la renta de empresas experimentados entre 2014 y 2015 muestran amplias variaciones entre los países (gráfico 1.8) En 2015, Trinidad y Tobago registró una caída de 1.7 puntos porcentuales en el recaudo del impuesto sobre la renta y utilidades, explicado principalmente por el desplome del recaudo del impuesto sobre la renta de empresas (2.8 puntos porcentuales), que tiene su raíz en la disminución del recaudo sobre hidrocarburos (véase el capítulo 2 de esta publicación). Otros países que también dependen de materias primas, como Perú y República Dominicana también vieron disminuidos sus recaudos del impuesto a la renta de empresas en 2015.

Gráfico 1.8. **Tasa de cambio anual de los impuestos sobre la renta y utilidades, impuesto sobre la renta de empresas y sobre la renta de personas, 2015 (puntos porcentuales del PIB)**

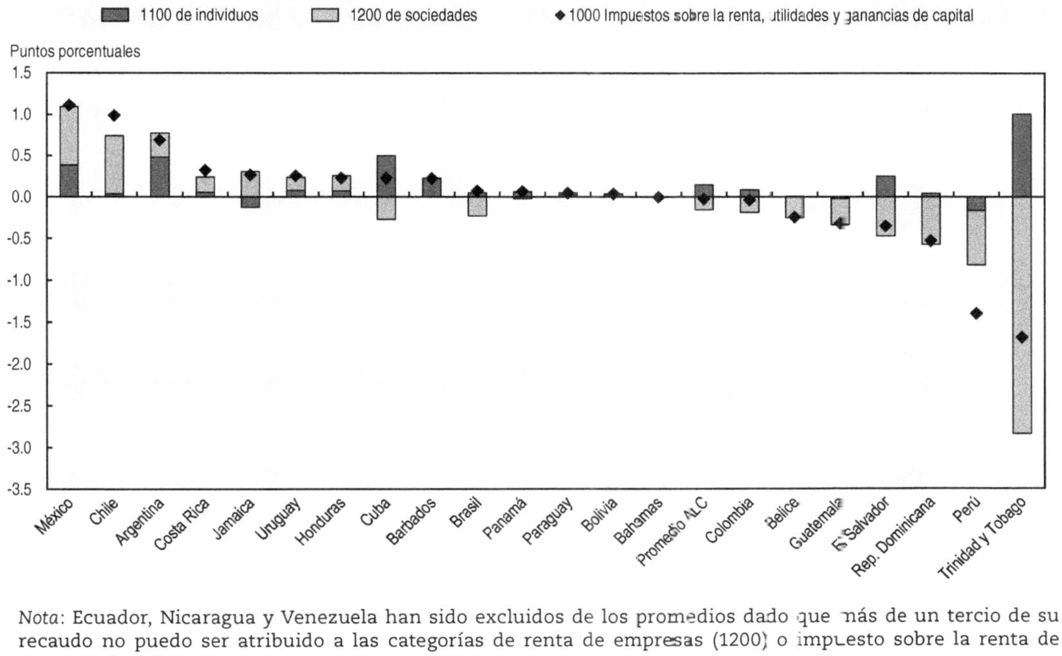

Nota: Ecuador, Nicaragua y Venezuela han sido excluidos de los promedios dado que más de un tercio de su recaudo no puedo ser atribuido a las categorías de renta de empresas (1200) o impuesto sobre la renta de personas (1100).

Fuente: OCDE (2017), "Estadísticas tributarias en América Latina: tablas comparativas", *OCDE Estadísticas tributarias* (base de datos), http://dx.doi.org/10.1787/ctpa-revlat-data-en.

StatLink http://dx.doi.org/10.1787/888933462567

Factores que han influenciado los niveles de recaudo tributario

La diferencia entre los promedios de recaudo tributario, como porcentaje del PIB, entre ALC y la OCDE reflejan el hecho que países con una mayor renta per cápita tienen mayores niveles de recaudo tributario. La data muestra una correlación positiva entre el PIB per cápita (una medida del nivel de ingreso de los países o su grado de desarrollo) y las relaciones entre los ingresos tributarios y el PIB (gráfico 1.9). En general, los países de la OCDE tienen ingresos más altos que los países de ALC y también recaudan más en impuestos. Argentina, Barbados, Brasil, Trinidad y Tobago y Uruguay muestran niveles de recaudo tributario similares los de la OCDE pese a niveles de ingreso por debajo del promedio de países de la OCDE.

Gráfico 1.9. **PIB per cápita en PPP (USD) y recaudo tributario (como porcentaje del PIB) en países de América Latina y el Caribe, la OCDE y un grupo de países de África y Asia**

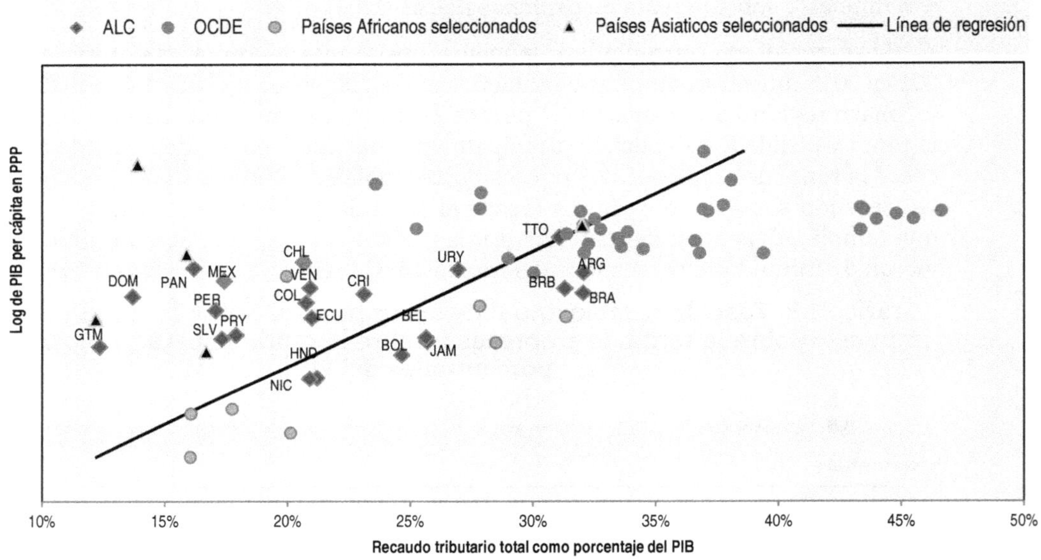

Nota: La paridad de poder de compra (PPP) entre dos países es la tasa a la cual la moneda de un país necesita ser convertida en la de un segundo país para asegurar que el mismo volumen de bienes y servicios puedan ser adquiridos en ambos países. El tipo de conversión PPP implícito se expresa como moneda nacional por dólar internacional actual. Un dólar internacional tiene el mismo poder adquisitivo que el dólar estadounidense en los Estados Unidos. Un dólar internacional es una moneda hipotética que se utiliza como medio para convertir y comparar los costos de un país a otro utilizando un punto de referencia común, el dólar estadounidense (Definiciones derivadas del FMI, 2016c y OMS, 2015).

Fuente: FMI (2016c), *Perspectivas de la economía mundial*, octubre de 2016, Fondo Monetario Internacional para cifras del PIB per cápita. Las proporciones entre los ingresos tributarios y el PIB se obtienen de las publicaciones regionales de estadísticas de tributarias (www.oecd.org/tax/tax-policy/revenue-statistics-comparable-tax-revenue-data.htm).

StatLink http://dx.doi.org/10.1787/888933462579

El recaudo tributario, como porcentaje del PIB, es influenciado por factores económicos y estructurales. El PIB per cápita, la apertura comercial, el tamaño de la economía informal, la dotación de recursos naturales y la importancia del sector agrícola en la economía son todos factores que pueden influenciar el nivel de recaudo tributario. Los determinantes socio-demográficos son también claves, por ejemplo el nivel de educación o el grado de participación femenina en la fuerza de trabajo. El poder de las administraciones tributarias, el nivel de corrupción y la moral fiscal (o la disposición de la gente para pagar impuestos) son todos factores que están fuertemente vinculados al nivel de recaudo (OCDE, 2014a). Finalmente, la ubicación geográfica y factores históricos también inciden en la recaudación. Por ejemplo, la posibilidad de gravar bienes y servicios en el puerto de entrada es menor en países sin costa marítima. Adicionalmente, factores internacionales, incluyendo las políticas tributarias adoptadas por otros países pueden tener un impacto en los niveles de recaudo tributario.

El grado de participación del estado en el financiamiento de la seguridad social es otro factor importante para explicar los niveles de recaudo tributario en la región de ALC. Desde 1980 en adelante, muchos países de ALC privatizaron sus sistemas sanitarios, previsionales y de seguridad social en mayor o menor medida (CEPAL, 2010). Chile, El Salvador y México son ejemplos de países que han migrado sus esquemas previsionales a programas de cuentas individuales administrados por el sector privado. En Colombia y Perú, los sistemas públicos y privados compiten y los empleados pueden determinar su afiliación a uno u otro (OCDE/CEPAL/CIAT/BID, 2015). Por otra parte, Argentina, Brasil y Uruguay siguen un modelo en los cuales los sistemas públicos y privados son complementarios. En estos tres países se han llevado a cabo sendas reformas para expandir la cobertura de los sistemas de seguridad social e incluir a los excluidos. Esto ha sido también un factor importante en el aumento del recaudo tributario (CEPAL, 2014).

Los niveles de informalidad erosionan el recaudo tributario en los países de ALC dado que reducen la base impositiva significativamente (OCDE, 2008 y Gómez Sabaini et al. 2010). En América Latina[3] la tasa de informalidad[4] fue alrededor de 55% en promedio en 2014 (BID, 2013). Bolivia, Guatemala, Honduras, Nicaragua, Paraguay y Perú tienen las tasas de informalidad más altas, excediendo el 65%. Brasil, Chile, Costa Rica y Uruguay tienen tasas de informalidad inferiores al 40$. Estos niveles eran aún más elevados en los años noventa, lo que llevó a algunos gobiernos introducir impuestos simplificados para pequeños contribuyentes que fueron en alguna medida exitosos en integrar a trabajadores informales dentro del sector formal. Estos sistemas simplificados variaron en cuanto al nivel de éxito alcanzado dependiendo del tipo de contribuyentes cubiertos y la capacidad de las administraciones tributarias (CEPAL, 2014).

1.2. Estructuras tributarias

La estructura impositiva muestra la composición del recaudo tributario por sus diferentes impuestos. Este es un indicador importante dado que los impuestos tienen efectos económicos y sociales diferentes. Las estructuras tributarias varían en los 24 países incluidos en esta publicación, lo que refleja diferentes opciones de política, estructuras económicas, coyunturas, capacidades de las administraciones tributarias y factores históricos.

Evolución de las estructuras tributarias

El promedio del tax mix (definido como la proporción de los agregados tributarios más importantes en América Latina dentro de los ingresos tributarios totales) aumentó la proporción de impuestos generales sobre el consumo, los impuestos sobre la renta y utilidades y las contribuciones a la seguridad social entre 1990 y 2015. La proporción de impuestos sobre las rentas y utilidades creció de 22.3% a 27.2% del recaudo tributario total entre 1990 y 2015, como resultado de los mayores niveles de recaudo experimentado en la segunda mitad de los años 2000. Las contribuciones a la seguridad social como porcentaje del recaudo tributario total aumentó en 3.4 puntos porcentuales durante los últimos 25 años, alcanzando un 16.4% en 2015. La proporción de impuestos sobre bienes y servicios también cayó 5 puntos porcentuales durante el mismo período. El recaudo de los impuestos generales sobre el consumo (principalmente el IVA) incrementó 10 puntos porcentuales entre 1990 y 2015, mientras que la proporción de los impuestos específicos sobre bienes y servicios (impuestos específicos, impuestos en aduanas y sobre importaciones) cayeron en 16 puntos porcentuales durante este lapso (gráfico 1.10).

Gráfico 1.10. Estructura tributaria promedio en América Latina y el Caribe, 1990 y 2015

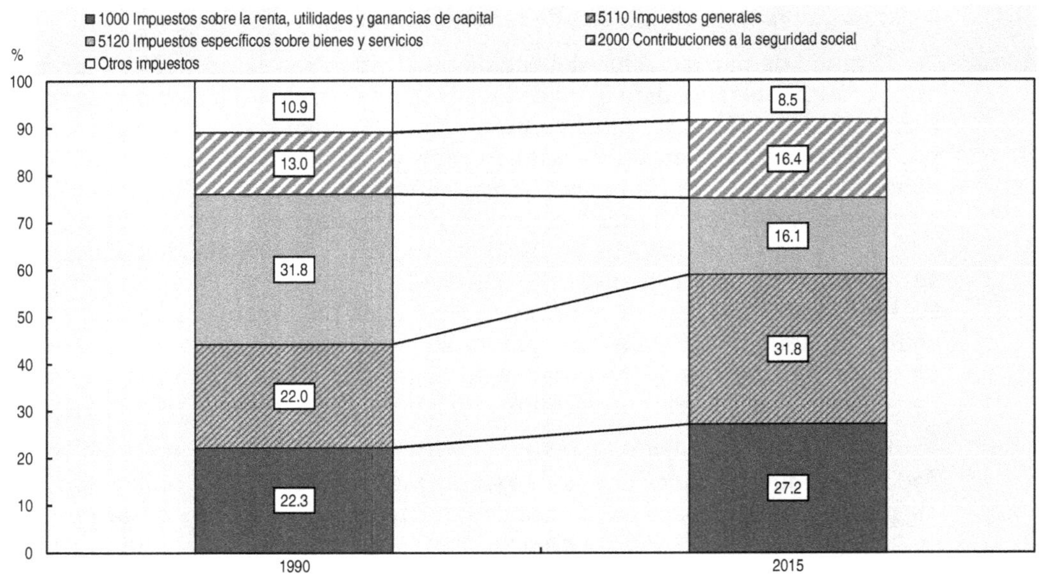

Fuente: Elaboración propia con base en las cuadros presentadas en el capítulo 4.

StatLink http://dx.doi.org/10.1787/888933462588

El recaudo de los impuestos específicos sobre bienes y servicios e impuestos sobre las exportaciones se tornó más bajo que el recaudo de los impuestos generales sobre el consumo (principalmente el IVA) en 1995 y ha permanecido más bajo desde entonces. Esto esconde una gran disparidad entre los países ya que en 11 países la razón de impuestos específicos e impuestos sobre las importaciones sobre el recaudo total seguía siendo más alto en 11 países en 1995. Para el año de 2005 esta proporción continuaba siendo más alta únicamente en cinco países, principalmente países del Caribe (Las Bahamas, Belice, Jamaica y la República Dominicana) y en 2015 únicamente en dos países (Las Bahamas y Jamaica). Las Bahamas introdujeron el IVA dentro de su estructura impositiva en 2015 y se espera que su recaudo supere al derivado de los impuestos específicos en los años venideros. En Jamaica, los aranceles y otros impuestos sobre el comercio internacional constituyen su principal instrumento de política comercial (US misión Ginebra, 2011).

Las tendencias opuestas experimentadas dentro de los impuestos a los bienes y servicios evidencian la importancia cada vez mayor del IVA y la caída en el papel que juegan los impuestos específicos sobre el consumo. El IVA fue adoptado de forma temprana por las economías de la región en los años ochentas (Doce[5] países lo habían implementado para el año 1980). Desde los años noventa significó una fuente creciente de recaudo tributario para la región de ALC, rol que ha sido consolidado mediante la implementación de ajustes a la base del impuesto y a sus tasas, así como al fortalecimiento de las administraciones tributarias. Las reformas también se focalizaron en la simplificación del sistema tributario, en la medida que muchos países redujeron el número de productos gravados a tasa cero y a tasas reducidas, avanzando hacia sistemas de una sola tasa del IVA en muchos casos.

Gráfico 1.11. **Evolución de la estructura tributaria promedio en la región de América Latina y el Caribe, 1990-2015**

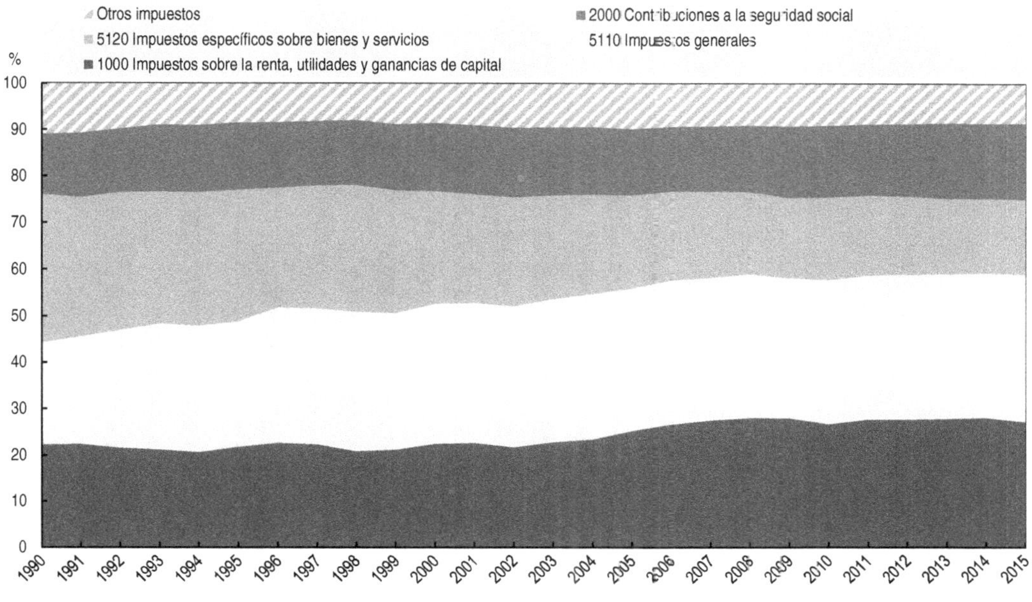

Fuente: Elaboración propia con base en las cuadros presentadas en el capítulo 4.

StatLink http://dx.doi.org/10.1787/888933462593

En 2015, el recaudo de los impuestos sobre bienes y servicio representó la mayor proporción del recaudo tributario en la región de ALC, representando el 50% de todos los ingresos tributarios. El recaudo de los impuestos sobre los bienes y servicios fue la principal fuente de recaudo en todos los países de ALC con la excepción de Trinidad y Tobago, México y Panamá. Los ingresos provenientes de impuestos sobre la renta y utilidades fueron la principalmente fuente de recaudo para México y Trinidad y Tobago. Mientras que las contribuciones a la seguridad social fueron la fuente más importante para Panamá.

En 2015, el 28% del recaudo total procedió del IVA en los países de América Latina. Aunque existe mucha heterogeneidad en la región. El IVA, como porcentaje del recaudo total, varía de 12.4% en Bahamas hasta 55.8% en Venezuela. No existe IVA en Belice desde su derogación en 1999 y su reemplazo por un impuesto sobre las ventas (Peters y Bristol, 2006). La amplia variación entre los países es también un resultado de los diferentes diseños del IVA: las tasas y bases varían ampliamente en la región. Por ejemplo, México no grava los alimentos, medicinas y números otros productos lo que se traduce en una base estrecha. CEPAL (2014) sugiere que las pérdidas tributarias de estas exenciones pueden ir desde 1.1% hasta 2.5% del PIB.

Gráfico 1.12. **Estructura tributaria por país en América Latina y el Caribe, 2015**

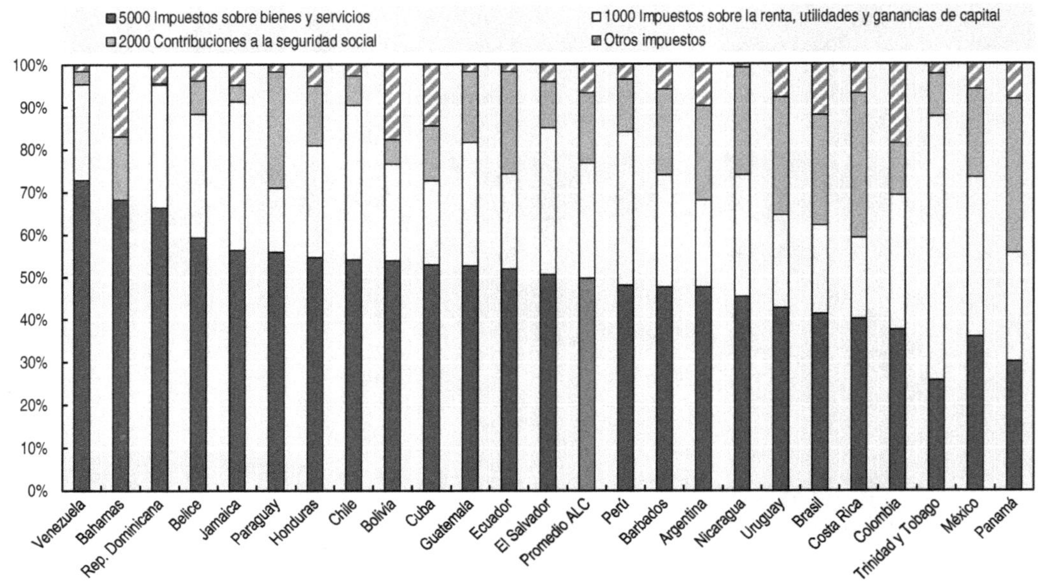

Nota: Las proporciones tributarias de las distintas categorías impositivas deben ser interpretadas con cautela en Venezuela dado que los altos índices de inflación las han afectado.

Fuente: Elaboración propia con base en las tablas del Capítulo 4.

StatLink http://dx.doi.org/10.1787/888933462607

Gráfico 1.13. **Recaudo del IVA como proporción del ingreso tributario total en ALC, 2015**

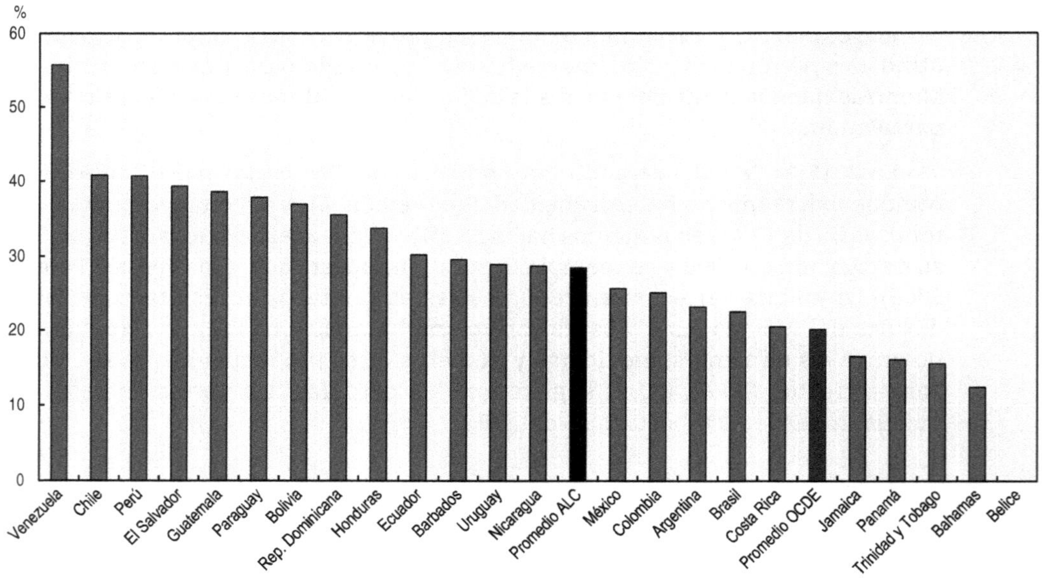

Nota: Cuba se ha excluido ante la falta de información.

Fuente: OCDE (2017), "Estadísticas tributarias en América Latina: tablas comparativas", *OCDE Estadísticas tributarias* (base de datos), http://dx.doi.org/10.1787/ctpa-revlat-data-en.

StatLink http://dx.doi.org/10.1787/888933462616

1.3. Ratio de recaudo del IVA

La medida del ratio de recaudo del IVA (VRR por sus siglas en inglés) para los países seleccionados de América Latina[6] ha sido estimada e incluida por primera vez dentro de esta publicación. OCDE (2016) explica que el VRR mide la diferencia entre el recaudo observado del IVA y el recaudo teórico o potencial del IVA si este fuese aplicado a una tasa única a toda la base impositiva en un régimen de IVA "puro". Esta sección muestra los niveles del VRR en América Latina y el Caribe en 2014 y se centra en el análisis a mayor profundidad de tres países, Bolivia, Paraguay y Panamá.

Hubo disparidad en los VRRs de los países de América Latina y el Caribe en 2014 (gráfico 1.14). Jamaica y México tuvieron los índices más bajos de VRR en 25% y 32% respectivamente. Mientras que Bolivia y Paraguay tuvieron los niveles más altos en 101% y 93% respectivamente. El bajo nivel del VRR en Jamaica puede explicarse por la aplicación de tasa cero a una amplia gama de productos y servicios. Adicionalmente, ciertos productos (por ejemplo, productos derivados del petróleo, cigarrillos, licores y cervezas) no están gravados con IVA sino con un impuesto especial al consumo similar a un impuesto específicos (PKF, 2013). Para México, OCDE (2016) señala que existen varios elementos que explican un bajo VRR, por ejemplo el alcance de las exenciones al IVA, la aplicación de una tasa cero a un gran número de bienes y servicios, una tasa reducida del 11% en zonas fronterizas y también un bajo nivel de cumplimiento. Una reforma al IVA se implementó en enero de 2014 que extendió la tasa estándar de 16% a las zonas fronterizas, eliminando las tasas diferenciadas. La reforma también eliminó la tasa cero sobre hoteles y sobre los servicios provistos a extranjeros, que ahora se encuentran gravados a la tasa estándar y se ajustó el régimen de los maquiladores para reducir el riesgo al fraude. El VRR en México se incrementó 0.3 puntos entre 2013 y 2014.

Gráfico 1.14. **Ratio de recaudo del IVA (VRR) en países de ALC, 2014**

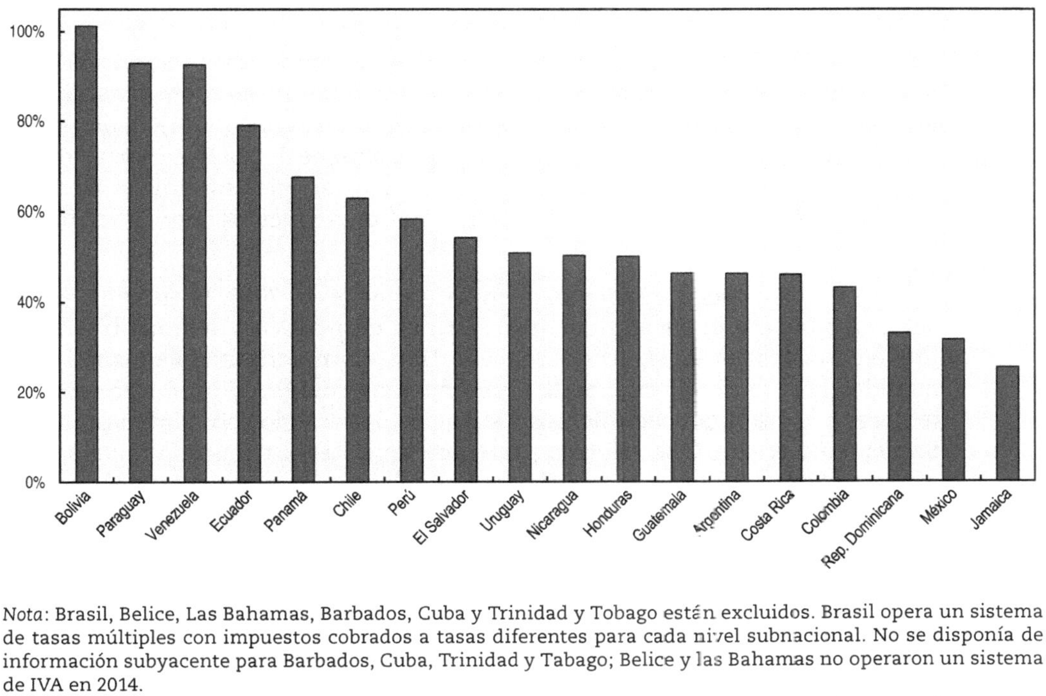

Nota: Brasil, Belice, Las Bahamas, Barbados, Cuba y Trinidad y Tobago están excluidos. Brasil opera un sistema de tasas múltiples con impuestos cobrados a tasas diferentes para cada nivel subnacional. No se disponía de información subyacente para Barbados, Cuba, Trinidad y Tabago; Belice y las Bahamas no operaron un sistema de IVA en 2014.

Fuente: Las tasas de IVA provienen de los sitios web CIAT, Trading Economics y Deloitte, las cifras de consumo final de gastos del sitio web de la División de Estadística de las Naciones Unidas y los ingresos del IVA de las tablas de países del capítulo 5.

StatLink http://dx.doi.org/10.1787/888933462628

En 2014, el VRR de Bolivia excedió el 100%. Las cifras deben interpretarse con cuidado ya que la tasa del VRR de un 100% sugiere que no existe pérdida en el IVA como consecuencia de exenciones, tasas diferenciadas reducidas, fraude, evasión o planificación fiscal. El alto nivel del VRR puede ser parcialmente explicado por distintos factores. Primero, Bolivia aplica una tasa estándar de 13% al producto final de los bienes y servicios que ya incluyen el IVA, lo que lleva a una tasa efectiva de 14.94%, más alta que la tasa nominal. Al utilizar la tasa efectiva la medida del VRR cae de 101% hasta 88% en 2014. Segundo, Bolivia no tiene tasas reducidas y aplica el IVA a una amplia gama de productos y servicios. Los altos índices de informalidad pueden afectar los niveles del VRR, pero es claro si este es el caso en Bolivia.

El VRR de Bolivia ha estado aumentando desde 1990 aunque este crecimiento fue interrumpido entre 1997 y el 2000. Una amplia reforma del sector público en 2000 incluyó el fortalecimiento de los procesos de inspección y control de las devoluciones del IVA puede haber contribuido a la mejora del indicador a partir del año 2000. De acuerdo a Zuleta (2008), "los cambios en los procesos y los procedimientos para la devolución del IVA han tenido un impacto positivo durante la reforma institucional". Esto se evidenció en la caída en la evasión del IVA en 23 puntos porcentuales, pasando de 42%[7] en 2001 a 29% en 2004. También disminuyeron las devoluciones del IVA como porcentaje de las exportaciones y del recaudo total del IVA (Zuleta, 2008). Estas tendencias muestran que la corrupción en los procesos de devolución del IVA han sido reducidos (Zuleta, 2008). Dentro del mismo período, el VRR mejoró 15 puntos porcentuales, pasando de 51% a 64%. Por otra parte, entre 2004 y 2013, el VRR continuó incrementado (excepto durante el período de la crisis fiscal). No obstante, existe poca evidencia para explicar las razones de ello. La medición del incumplimiento en el pago del IVA durante el tiempo o los niveles de informalidad que afectan al IVA pueden ser información útil para llegar a conclusiones más robustas.

Paraguay tiene el segundo VRR más alto, puntuando 93% en 2014 dentro del grupo de países seleccionados de ALC. Las cifras deben interpretarse con cautela dado que Paraguay tiene tasas reducidas del 5% para algunos productos y servicios (productos de la canasta básica, medicamentos, bienes raíces e intereses sobre préstamos o deudas) así como también exenciones (EY, 2014). De acuerdo al FMI (2010), la alta productividad del IVA[8] refleja, en parte, el alto recaudo que se obtiene de las re-exportaciones (cercanas a 2% del PIB). Mucho del comercio de las re-exportaciones son informales, razón por la cual los pagos al IVA en las importaciones no son deducidos cuando los bienes vuelven a ser exportados.

El VRR ha estado incrementado en Paraguay desde 2002. El aumento en 2004 puede ser parcialmente explicado por las reformas de política y administración tributarias implementadas por el gobierno Paraguayo. Una reforma tributaria exhaustiva que incluyó medidas para la ampliación de la base impositiva del IVA y un nuevo marco legal para mejorar el control, procedimientos y sistemas de recaudo sobre impuestos y aduanas se implementó en 2004. La reforma perseguía un sistema tributario mucho más simple y eficiente (FMI, 2010). Al mismo tiempo, el gobierno paraguayo atacó la corrupción que había estado obstaculizando una mayor recaudación tributaria (Franks, et al., 2005).

En 2014, Panamá tuvo el quinto porcentaje más alto de VRR en 64% y ha tenido un VRR sobre el 60% desde 2008. Panamá tuvo un alza significativa en el VRR de un año a otro, pasando de 28% en 2007 hasta 63% en 2008. Esto fue precedido de una amplia auditoría realizada a la Dirección General de Impuestos en 2008 con la finalidad de detener las pérdidas en el IVA por la falta de cumplimiento de las empresas en declarar el IVA cobrado a clientes. Luego de esta auditoría, llevada a cabo en el primer trimestre de 2008, el IVA aumentó en 22% comparado con todo el año de 2007 (The Panama Investor Blog, 2008). El IVA, como porcentaje del PIB, se duplicó en más del doble entre 2007 y 2008, pasando de 1% a 2.1%.

Gráfico 1.15. **Ratio de recaudo del IVA (VRR) en Bolivia, Paraguay y Panamá, 1990 –2014**

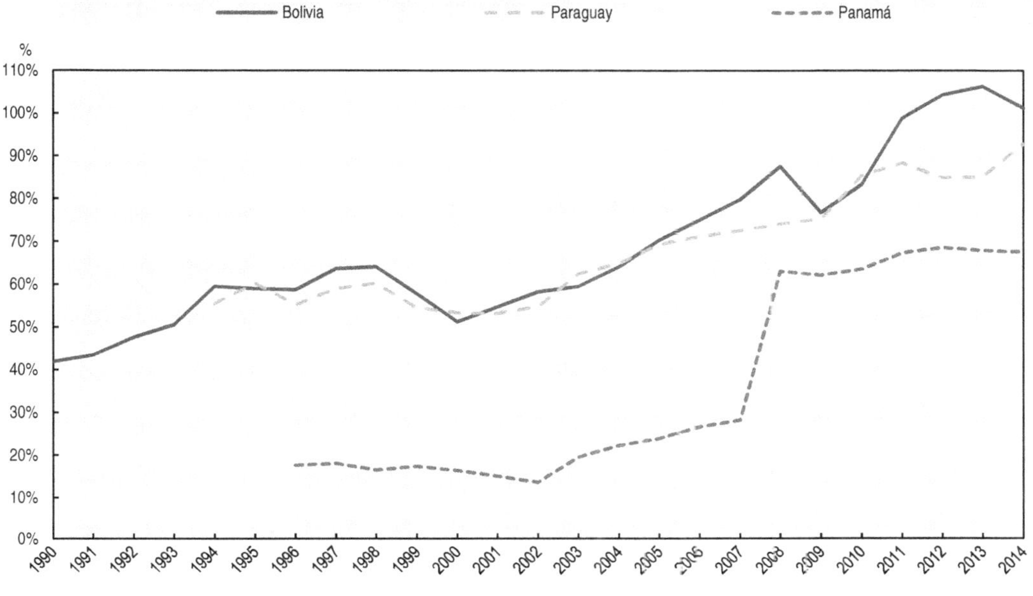

Nota: Las cifras del gasto de consumo final utilizadas para compilar el VRR no estaban disponibles para Panamá antes de 1996. En Paraguay, el IVA fue implementado a mediados de 1993, por lo que no hay VRR entre 1990 y 1993.

Fuente: Las tasas de IVA provienen de los sitios web CIAT, Trading Economics y Deloitte, las cifras de consumo final del sitio web de la División de Estadística de las Naciones Unidas y los ingresos por IVA de las cuadros de países del capítulo 5.

StatLink http://dx.doi.org/10.1787/888933462634

Impuestos sobre las rentas y utilidades y contribuciones a la seguridad social

En 2015, los ingresos provenientes de los impuestos sobre las rentas y utilidades se situaron en 27.2% como proporción de todos los ingresos. El impuesto sobre la renta de empresas representó la proporción más grande de los impuestos sobre la renta y utilidades en 15.8 puntos porcentuales, mientras que el impuesto sobre la renta de personas representó 9.1 puntos porcentuales[9] (gráfico 1.16). Si bien, la proporción de impuestos sobre la renta y utilidades fue alrededor de 27% en 2007 y 2015, la estructura impositiva en ALC incluye una mayor participación del impuesto sobre la renta de personas y una menor del impuesto sobre la renta de empresas.

Los impuestos sobre la renta de sociedades son una fuente importante de ingresos en los países de ALC. Trinidad y Tobago tuvo los ingresos del impuesto sobre la renta de sociedades más altos con 44% como porcentaje del ingreso total. La mayoría del recaudo provino de las compañías de petróleo y gas (véase el capítulo especial en el capítulo 2 de esta publicación). En los otros países de ALC, el porcentaje de ingresos, como porcentaje del recaudo total, del impuesto sobre la renta de sociedades varía entre 8% (Barbados) y 25% (Colombia) (gráfico 1.17). Las Bahamas es el único país en este reporte que no opera un impuesto sobre la renta (de personas o sociedades).

Gráfico 1.16. **Promedio la estructura tributaria en América Latina y el Caribe, 2007 y 2015**

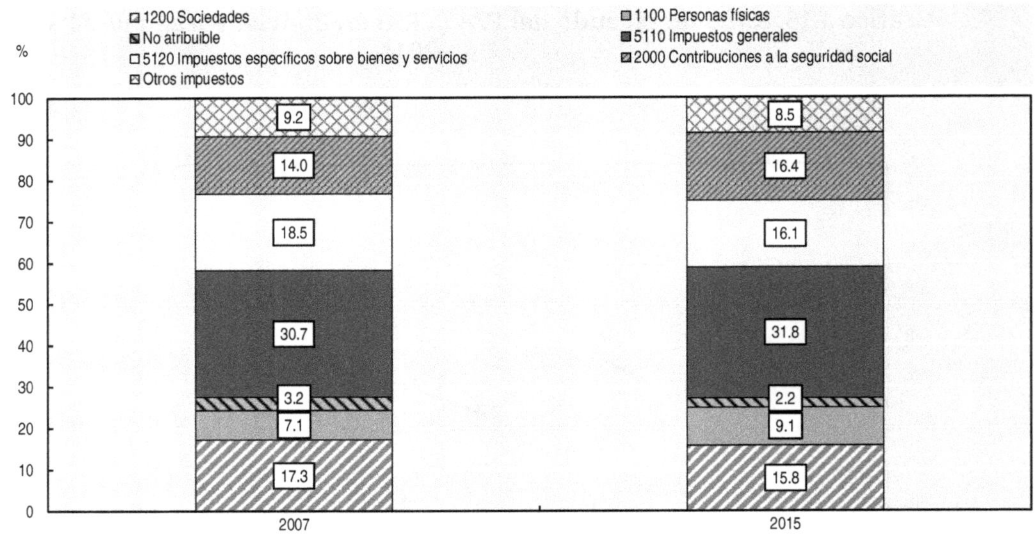

Nota: Los ingresos del Impuesto sobre la Renta de las Personas Físicas de ALC y los ingresos del impuesto sobre la renta de las personas físicas como porcentaje del PIB deben ser interpretados con cautela ya que Ecuador, Nicaragua y Venezuela están excluidos en el cálculo. Para estos países, más de un tercio de sus ingresos provenientes de los impuestos sobre la renta y utilidades no pueden ser atribuidos a los ingresos del impuesto sobre la renta de las sociedades (1200) ni a los ingresos del impuesto sobre la renta de las personas físicas (1100). Excluyendo a estos países, una pequeña proporción de los ingresos procedentes de los impuestos sobre la renta y las utilidades sigue sin poder atribuirse.

Fuente: OCDE (2017), "Estadísticas Tributarias en América Latina: tablas comparativas", *Estadísticas tributarias de la OCDE* (base de datos), http://dx.doi.org/10.1787/ctpa-revlat-data-en.

StatLink http://dx.doi.org/10.1787/888933462642

La proporción de ingresos del impuesto sobre la renta de personas sigue siendo baja en ALC a pesar de las reformas implementadas por algunos países para expandir su base tributaria. Luego de la crisis financiera varios países implementaron tasas proporcionales al capital, que previamente no se gravaban, e introdujeron esquemas progresivos para gravar las rentas del trabajo (CEPAL, 2014). No obstante, la proporción de ingresos provenientes de impuestos sobre la renta de personas físicas sigue siendo modesta en ALC, donde más de la mitad de los países generan menos del 10% de su recaudo total de esta fuente. El recaudo del impuesto a la renta de personas físicas, como proporción de los ingresos tributarios totales, varía desde 0.9% (Bolivia) hasta 19.7% (México) (gráfico 1.17). Estudios anteriores de la OCDE (OCDE, 2008 y Daude et al., 2010) sugieren que la proporción de rentas del trabajo en el PIB es baja en los países de ALC. La cantidad de contribuyentes con obligación tributaria es baja en vista de los niveles de ingresos relativamente bajos de la región. Únicamente 10% de la población en América Latina es un contribuyente tributario registrado (BID, 2013). Muchos otros estudios (Barreix, et al., 2017; BID, 2015; CEPAL, 2014; CEPAL, 2010 y Gómez Sabaini et al., 2010) atribuyen el bajo recaudo del impuesto a la renta de personas físicas a factores adicionales: un base imponible limitada de salarios, dados algunos beneficios otorgados a las rentas del capital, y altos niveles de evasión. BID (2013) estima que "más de la mitad del potencial de recaudación del impuesto se pierde a través de la evasión" en América Latina.

Gráfico 1.17. **Recaudo del impuesto sobre la renta de sociedades e impuesto sobre la renta de personas físicas, como proporción del recaudo total en ALC, 2015**

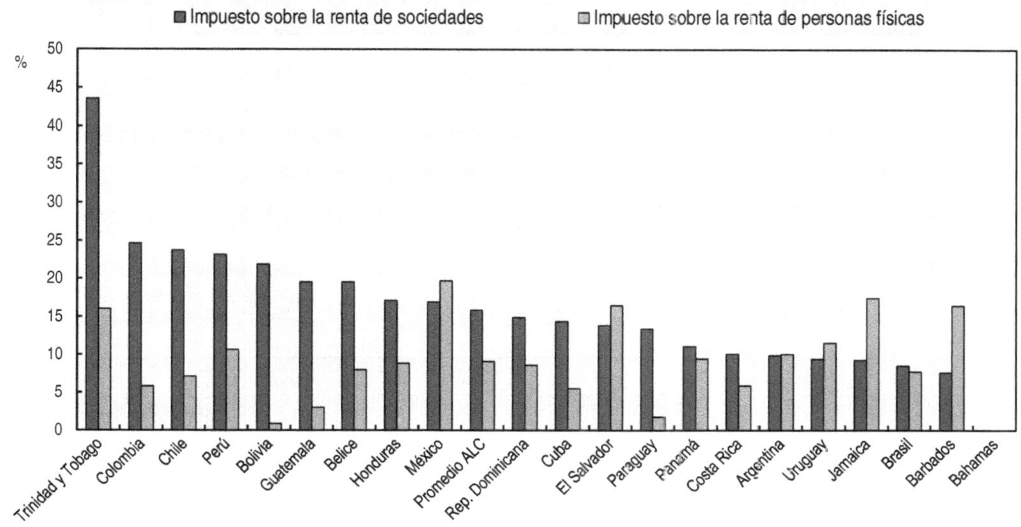

Nota: Las proporciones de impuestos sobre la renta de sociedades e impuestos sobre la renta de individuos pueden no sumar el total de impuestos sobre la renta, utilidades y capital debido a la existencia de ingresos no atribuibles. Solamente aquellos países para los cuales fue posible clasificar más de dos tercios de los ingresos de los impuestos sobre la renta, utilidades y ganancias de capital en impuesto sobre la renta de sociedades e impuestos sobre la renta de individuos han sido considerados en el gráfico. Ecuador, Nicaragua y Venezuela han sido excluidos por esta razón.

Fuente: OCDE (2017), "Estadísticas tributarias en América Latina: tablas comparativas", *OCDE Estadísticas tributarias* (base de datos), http://dx.doi.org/10.1787/ctpa-revlat-data-en.

StatLink http://dx.doi.org/10.1787/888933462657

La participación de las contribuciones a la seguridad social dentro de los ingresos tributarios totales aumentó 3.4 puntos porcentuales durante los últimos 25 años, alcanzando 16.4% en 205 (gráfico 1.10). Esto refleja dos factores trabajando de forma paralela. Primero, el aumento en la renta per cápita ha tenido un impacto positivo sobre el recaudo. Pero esto tiene como contrapeso los distintos procesos de privatización total o parcial de los sistemas de seguridad social en la región. Aquellos países con sistemas públicos o mixtos, incluidos Argentina, Barbados, Brasil, Costa Rica, México, Panamá, Paraguay, y Uruguay, las contribuciones a la seguridad social continúan teniendo un peso significativo (más del 20% del recaudo total). En Colombia y en Perú, dónde los sistemas previsionales público y privado compiten, el recaudo tributario del sistema público se sitúa en torno al 12%. En Argentina, las cifras muestran la introducción de cuentas de capitalización privadas en 1994 y su subsiguiente nacionalización en 2008.

Comparaciones con la OCDE

La mezcla tributaria (tax-mix) en los países de ALC muestra un recaudo bajo a partir de impuestos directos, con un recaudo muy alto de impuestos indirectos relativo al promedio observado en OCDE (véase el gráfico 1.18). En particular, los países de ALC dependen fuertemente de los impuestos sobre bienes y servicios, los cuales constituyen cerca de la mitad de todos los ingresos tributarios, comparado a cerca del 33% en promedio para economías de la OCDE. En promedio, menos del 44% del recaudo tributario total proviene de la suma de impuestos sobre la renta y utilidades y contribuciones a la seguridad social, comparado con 60% para el grupo OCDE. De lo que se desprende que los impuestos directos juegan un papel secundario en el recaudo en los países de la región de ALC en comparación con las economías de la OCDE. La participación de las contribuciones a la seguridad social dentro del recaudo total fue 10 puntos porcentuales más baja en ALC que el promedio de la OCDE (16.3 comparado con 26.2%). La existencia de esquemas previsionales y sanitarios privados en la región de ALC explica en alguna medida esta disparidad. Para los ingresos tributarios de los impuestos sobre la renta y las utilidades la diferencia fue de 6 puntos porcentuales más bajos que en OCDE (28.3% comparado con 33.7%).

La participación del impuesto sobre la renta y utilidades sociedades dentro del recaudo total es 16.8% en ALC comparado a 8.8% en el grupo de la OCDE (gráfico 1.18). El recaudo del impuesto sobre la renta de personas representó el 24% del recaudo total en la OCDE en 2014, mientras que esta proporción es considerablemente más baja en los países de ALC (8.7%).

Gráfico 1.18. **Estructura impositiva en ALC y en la OCDE, 2014**

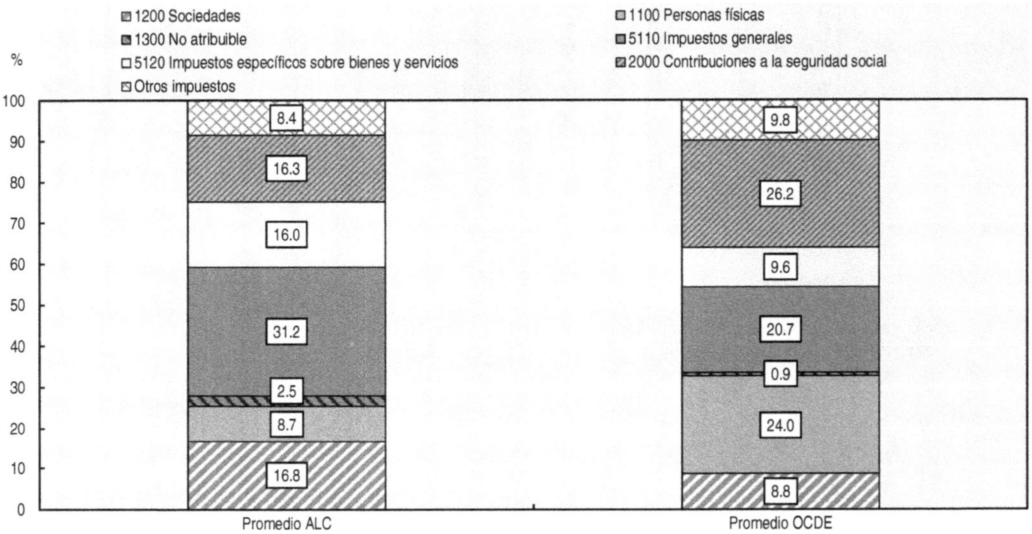

Fuente: OCDE (2017), "Estadísticas Tributarias en América Latina: tablas comparativas", *Estadísticas tributarias de la OCDE* (base de datos), http://dx.doi.org/10.1787/ctpa-revlat-data-en.

StatLink http://dx.doi.org/10.1787/888933462664

Los impuestos generales sobre el consumo representan una proporción más grande del recaudo total en los países de ALC que en la OCDE, para compensar por un bajo recaudo de los impuestos directos. En 2014, esta categoría representó el 31.2% del recaudo total en los países de la región, mientras que la cifra correspondiente para los países de la OCDE es 20.7%. De forma similar, la proporción de ingresos provenientes de los impuestos específicos sobre bienes y servicios es más alta en los países de ALC situándose en un promedio de 16.0% comparado al promedio de 9.6% en países de la OCDE.

Finalmente los impuestos sobre la propiedad inmueble y sobre la nómina (agrupados en la categoría "Otros impuestos" en el gráfico 1.18) son una fuente de ingresos poco importante en los países de ALC. Las dificultades que tienen los gobiernos subnacionales en el recaudo de sus propios impuestos queda patentado en el bajo recaudo de los impuestos sobre la propiedad, los cuales son por lo general la fuente principal de los gobiernos subnacionales en la región (Brossio y Jiménez, 2012). No obstante, debe reconocerse que la falta de datos a nivel subnacional dificulta el análisis. Por otra parte la participación de los impuestos sobre la nómina es insignificante para todo el período. El recaudo de los impuestos a la propiedad y sobre la nómina, como porcentaje del recaudo total, es similar entre la región de ALC y la OCDE.

1.4. Impuestos por nivel de gobierno

Desde mediados de los años ochentas, los gobiernos centrales en países de ALC han transferido algunas funciones hacia los gobiernos subnacionales. En una primera etapa, la ola de descentralización se centró en el fortalecimiento del rol democrático de las autoridades locales. Esto fue seguido por el aumento gradual en la ejecución de una mayor proporción del gasto público a nivel subnacional. No obstante lo anterior, el recaudo tributario es recolectado a nivel del gobierno central o federal, siendo las transferencias el principal mecanismo del cual dependen los gobiernos subnacionales a diferencia de lo registrado en los países de la OCDE. Para los países en los cuales se dispone de datos de recaudo subnacional en ALC, los ingresos tributarios a nivel del gobierno central constituyen dos tercios o más de todo el recaudo. El monto correspondiente en países de la OCDE es de 60%. Brasil es una excepción notable dado que el gobierno central recaudó un 42% de todos los ingresos totales en 2014 (cuadro 1.1)

Existen dos elementos estadísticos que deben tenerse en cuenta cuando se compara la atribución del recaudo para los países de ALC y el de países miembro de la OCDE. Primero, los ingresos tributarios de ambos grupos han sido atribuidos a diferentes niveles de gobierno de acuerdo a las guías revisadas en la versión final del Sistema de Cuentas Nacionales (SCN). Esto implica que los ingresos son generalmente atribuidos al nivel del gobierno que ejerce la potestad de aplicar el impuesto o tiene la potestad de imponer o modificar la tasa del impuesto. Esto tiene implicaciones en situaciones en las que un nivel del gobierno recauda el impuesto y transfiere lo recaudado parcial o totalmente a otros niveles de gobierno. Algunos ejemplos de este tipo de mecanismos son la Ley de Coparticipaciones en Argentina, y las Participaciones Federales en México (regida por la Ley de Coordinación Fiscal), y la participación de los fondos en Brasil (definida en el artículo 159 de la constitución). El segundo elemento es que los promedios en ALC pueden verse afectados por la falta de datos a nivel subnacional en algunos países.

El porcentaje de ingresos tributarios totales recaudado por los gobiernos subnacionales es inferior al 8%, exceptuando a Argentina, Brasil y Colombia, para los 15 países de ALC para los que se dispone datos en 2014. En Brasil, los estados y las municipalidades recaudan más de un 30% de todos los ingresos tributarios, lo que indica un alto grado de descentralización tributaria en favor de los gobiernos sub-nacionales. Una gran parte del IVA (ICMS – imposto sobre operações relativas à circulação de mercadorias e prestação de serviços de transporte interestadual e intermunicipal e de comunicação) es recaudado a nivel de gobierno estadual. El recaudo de los gobiernos subnacionales en Argentina y Colombia representa más del 15% del recaudo nacional total. Argentina tiene un recaudo sustancial a nivel provincial, el cual se explica en gran parte por el impuesto sobre los ingresos brutos. Entre 2000 y 2014, el recaudo tributario a nivel subnacional disminuyó en 7 países y aumentó en 8. La mayor caída de 3.5 puntos se dio en Uruguay y el incremento más grande fue en Brasil (3.7 puntos porcentuales).

Estas cifras reflejan el hecho que los gobiernos subnacionales en los países de ALC tienden a tener bajo su jurisdicción impuestos de bases estrechas. Los impuestos que con mayor frecuencia son asignados a los gobiernos subnacionales son los impuestos sobre la propiedad, sobre vehículos automotores e impuestos sobre servicios específicos y tasas municipales. El potencial de los ingresos tributarios de estos impuestos es mucho más limitado si se compara con los impuestos bajo la jurisdicción de gobiernos centrales o federales, tales como el IVA o los impuestos sobre la renta. En 2014, todo el recaudo subnacional de Belice, Guatemala, Jamaica y Trinidad y Tobago y más del 50% del recaudo subnacional en Perú y Paraguay provino de los impuestos sobre la propiedad. Todos los otros países dependen del recaudo proveniente de los impuestos generales y específicos sobre el consumo. Brasil y México son los únicos dos países que utilizan bases tributarias diferentes a las descritas anteriormente. En 2014, el 5% de los ingresos subnacionales en Brasil y el 41% del recaudo subnacional en México procedió de impuestos sobre la renta y de impuestos sobre la nómina. En los países miembros de la OCDE, las entidades subnacionales tienden a tener impuestos cuyas bases son mucho más amplias. Una proporción significativa del recaudo de los gobiernos subnacionales en los países de la OCDE tuvo origen en los impuestos sobre la renta y utilidades (representó más de un tercio del recaudo promedio total a nivel subnacional).

Gráfico 1.19. **Estructura de los ingresos tributarios subnacionales en países de ALC, 2014**

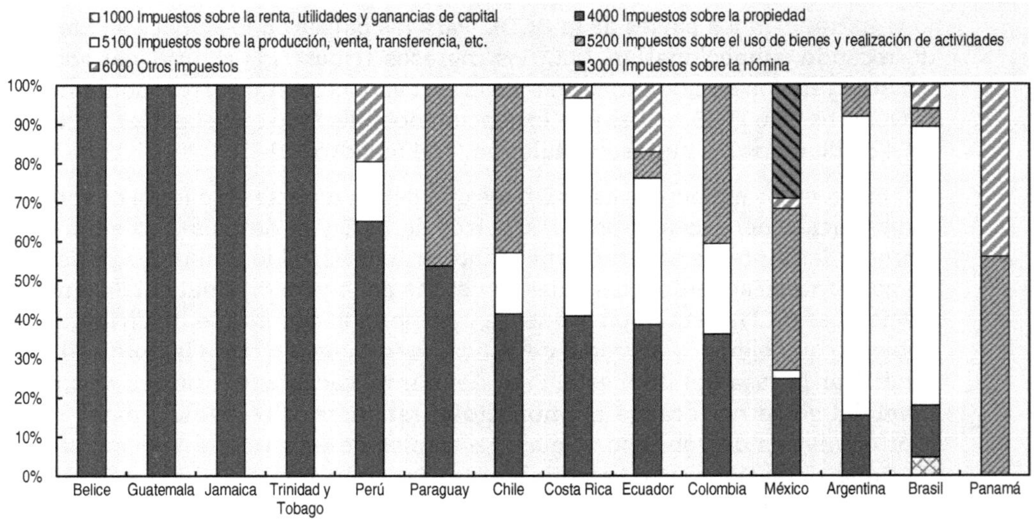

Nota: Las Bahamas, Barbados, Bolivia, Cuba, República Dominicana, El Salvador, Honduras, Nicaragua, Paraguay y Venezuela no se encuentran incluidos dado que los datos de los ingresos impositivos subnacionales o el desglose de los mismos por tipos de categorías tributarias principales no están disponibles. Las cifras excluyen los ingresos del gobierno local para Argentina (pero incluyen ingresos provinciales).

Fuente: Elaboración propia con base en cuadros del capítulo 6.

StatLink http://dx.doi.org/10.1787/888933462670

Los bajos niveles de recaudo subnacional en ALC puden también ser el resultado de una reducida capacidad administrativa y técnica. Por ejemplo, los impuestos sobre la propiedad requieren sistemas sofisticados de información, lo que aumenta el costo de recaudo de este impuesto. Adicionalmente, los registros catastrales en algunos países están ausentes en varios países y cuando existen rara vez se actualizan (BID, 2012). Como resultado, las autoridades tributarias no pueden acceder a valoraciones precisas de tierras y edificios, aunado a ello, las agencias de bienes y raíces no siempre están dispuestas a compartir esta información. Los impuestos sobre la propiedad también son susceptibles a sufrir de altos niveles de informalidad en países en desarrollo. Los edificios son muchas veces construidos sin los permisos adecuados, muchas propiedades no se encuentran registradas y los precios de venta de los bienes inmuebles son muchas veces falsificados. El impuesto a la propiedad es uno de los impuestos más controversiales a los ojos del ciudadano y conlleva altos costos políticos, por lo que las administraciones de gobiernos locales rara vez están dispuestas a invertir los recursos necesarios para recaudar este impuesto (BID, 2015).

La proporción del recaudo realizada por los sistemas de seguridad social cayó en diez países debido a la privatización de estos esquemas entre los años de 1995 y el 2000. Las caídas más grandes tuvieron lugar en Argentina y en Ecuador (7.6 y 13.4 puntos porcentuales respectivamente). Argentina adoptó un modelo mixto en 1994 en el cual una parte de las contribuciones obligatorias a los sistemas previsionales se destinaban a cuentas de capitalización individuales administradas por fondos de pensiones privadas. Entre los años 2000 y 2014, la proporción de ingresos derivados de la seguridad social incrementaron en 15 de los 24 países de ALC. Los dos países que experimentaron la caída más abrupta en la proporción de ingresos de la seguridad social también registraron las mayores alzas entre 2000 y 2014 (cuadro 1.1). En Argentina, el modelo mixto adoptado en 1994 fue abolido en 2008 y las contribuciones obligatorias a los sistemas privados fueron trasladadas a los sistemas previsionales públicos.

Cuadro 1.1. **Atribución de los ingresos tributarios por subsector del gobierno general, como porcentaje del recaudo tributario total[1]**

	Gobierno central			Gobierno estatal o regional			Gobierno local			Fondos de seguridad social		
	1995	2000	2014	1995	2000	2014	1995	2000	2014	1995	2000	2014
Países federales												
Argentina	59.0	66.4	61.5	17.5	17.8	16.9				23.4	15.8	21.6
Brasil	44.7	47.8	41.6	26.8	25.3	26.0	3.7	3.4	6.4	24.8	23.5	26.0
México	73.9	76.5	73.3	2.8	2.5	4.4	1.5	1.0	1.6	21.8	20.1	20.6
Venezuela	94.6	94.6	95.0							[illegible]	5.4	5.0
OCDE[2,3]	52.5	55.9	53.4	16.0	15.4	16.7	7.7	6.9	7.6	23.5	21.5	22.2
Países regionales												
Colombia[4]	63.2	68.6	71.9	5.5	5.6	4.5	8.6	9.4	11.7	22.7	16.4	12.5
OCDE[5]	50.4	49.0	42.3	4.8	7.7	13.6	8.5	9.1	10.0	35.1	33.8	33.6
Países unitarios												
Las Bahamas	89.1	88.1	83.5							10.9	11.9	16.5
Barbados	85.3	84.3	79.9							14.7	15.7	20.1
Belice	93.2	93.5	91.7	0.0	0.0	0.0	0.5	0.7	0.6	6.3	5.8	7.7
Bolivia	95.0	86.4	90.1	0.0	0.0	0.0	5.0	6.3	4.0	0.0	7.3	5.9
Chile	89.9	87.8	86.7	0.0	0.0	0.0	6.5	7.9	7.6	3.6	4.4	5.8
Costa Rica	68.6	67.4	59.3					2.1	3.2	31.4	30.6	37.5
Cuba	88.7	89.6	88.0							11.3	10.4	12.0
Ecuador	70.5	86.1	73.6				4.0	1.8	2.4	25.5	12.1	24.0
El Salvador	85.9	83.4	89.3						0.0	14.1	16.6	10.7
Guatemala	83.8	83.6	84.4				0.6	0.9	1.4	15.6	15.5	14.2
Honduras	86.1	84.5	82.0				4.4	5.5	3.1	9.5	10.0	14.9
Jamaica	100.0	99.3	94.2					0.7	1.6	0.0	0.0	4.2
Nicaragua	84.1	80.1	75.7							15.9	19.9	24.3
Panamá	62.0	61.1	63.3					[illegible]	1.5	38.0	36.8	35.2
Paraguay	100.0	82.7	80.6						3.0	0.0	17.3	16.4
Perú	88.2	87.8	86.2						2.8	11.8	12.2	11.0
República Dominicana	99.3	98.9	99.6							0.7	1.1	0.4
Trinidad y Tobago	94.4	91.6	90.3				2.4	2.0	1.5	3.2	6.5	8.2
Uruguay	61.4	62.0	67.2				8.4	8.4	4.9	30.1	29.6	27.9
OCDE[2,6]	65.5	66.4	63.5	0	0	0	10.7	10.8	11.7	23.5	22.6	24.5

1. Las cifras excluyen los ingresos del gobierno local para Argentina (pero incluyen ingresos provinciales), Las Bahamas, Barbados, Bolivia (antes de 1994), Costa Rica (antes de 1998), Cuba, República Dominicana, El Salvador (antes de 2015), Jamaica (antes de 1998), Nicaragua, Panamá (antes de 1998), Paraguay (antes de 2004), Perú (antes de 2001) y Venezuela dado que los datos no se encuentran disponibles.
2. Chile y México también forman parte del grupo de la OCDE.
3. Representa el promedio no ponderado de los países federales miembros de la OCDE.
4. Colombia es constitucionalmente un país unitario con alta autonomía de sus entidades territoriales.
5. Representa a España, constitucionalmente un país no federal con una estructura política altamente descentralizada.
6. Representa el promedio no ponderado de los países unitarios de la OCDE.

StatLink http://dx.doi.org/10.1787/888933463018

Notas

1. Esta cifra es provisional y ha sido estimada aplicando el promedio no ponderado del cambio porcentual para 2015 en los 32 países que han provisto información para ese año. Esta tasa de cambio se aplicó posteriormente al promedio de ingresos tributarios sobre el PIB de 2014.
2. La variación interanual en ALC se mantiene en 0.6 puntos porcentuales aún y cuando se excluye a Venezuela del cálculo, dada la alta inflación que afectó tanto a los ingresos tributarios como al PIB en 2015.
3. En la publicación del BID, el promedio de América Latina incluye 19 países: Argentina, Bolivia, Brasil, Chile, Colombia, Costa Rica, El Salvador, Ecuador, Guatemala, Honduras, Jamaica, México, Nicaragua, Panamá, Perú, Paraguay, República Dominicana, Uruguay y Venezuela.
4. La informalidad se define como el porcentaje de individuos que no contribuyen a sistemas previsionales sobre el total de la fuerza de trabajo en ALC.
5. Estos países son Argentina, Brasil, Bolivia, Chile, Colombia, Costa Rica, Ecuador, Honduras, México, Nicaragua, Panamá y Perú.
6. El VRR no pudo ser estimado para Brasil, Belice, Las Bahamas, Cuba y Trinidad y Tobago.
7. La evasión del IVA se compila como la pérdida de IVA en términos del recaudo esperado del IVA.
8. El FMI estima una medida de eficiencia sobre el consumo, que busca medir lo mismo que el VRR, aunque el método de estimación varía ligeramente. Un detalle más amplio sobre las diferencias se presenta en OECD (2016).
9. Aproximadamente 2% de todos los ingresos tributarios provenientes de impuestos sobre la renta y utilidades no pueden ser atribuidos al impuesto a la renta de empresas o de personas físicas.

Referencias

Barreix A., J.C. Benitez and M. Pecho (forthcoming – 2017), "Revisiting Personal Income Tax", *OECD Development Centre Working Papers*, OECD Publishing, Paris.

BID (2015), "Decentralizing Revenue in Latin America Why and How", Banco Interamericano de Desarrollo, Washington, DC.

BID (2013), "More than revenues, Taxation as a development tool", Banco Interamericano de Desarrollo, Washington, DC.

BID (2012), "Sub-national Revenue Mobilization in Peru", *IDB Working Paper Series* No. IDB-WP-299, Banco Interamericano de Desarrollo, Washington, DC.

Brossio, G. and J.P. Jiménez (2012), *Decentralization and Reform in Latin America: Improving Intergovernmental Relations*, Edward Elgar, in press, Cheltenham, UK and Northampton, MA.

Daude, C., A. Melguizo and A. Neut (2010), "Fiscal Policy in Latin America: Countercyclical and Sustainable at Last?", *OECD Development Centre Working Paper* No. 291, OECD Publishing, Paris.

CEPAL (2014), *Tax policy in Latin America. Assessment and guidelines for a second generation of reforms*, CEPAL, Santiago de Chile.

CEPAL (2013), *Fiscal Panorama of Latin America and the Caribbean: Tax reform and renewal of the fiscal covenant*, CEPAL, Santiago de Chile.

CEPAL (2010), "La Hora de la igualdad. Brechas por cerrar, caminos por abrir", (LC/G.2432(SES.33/3)), CEPAL, Santiago de Chile.

EY 2014, "Worldwide VAT GST and sales tax guide 2014", Ernst & Young Global Limited, www.ey.com/Publication/vwLUAssets/Worldwide-VAT-GST-and-sales-tax-guide-2014/$FILE/Worldwide-VAT-GST-and-sales-tax-guide-2014.pdf.

FMI (2016a), "The Bahamas: 2016 article IV consultation—press release; staff report; and statement by the executive director for the Bahamas", *IMF Country Report* No. 16/224, Fondo Monetario Internacional, Washington, DC, https://www.imf.org/external/pubs/ft/scr/2016/cr16224.pdf.

FMI (2016b). "Argentina 2016 Article IV Consultation", *IMF country report* No. 16/346, Fondo Monetario Internacional, Washington, DC.

IMF (2016c), *World Economic Outlook Database*, October 2016 Edition, Fondo Monetario Internacional, Washington, DC.

FMI (2010), "Paraguay: Selected Issues", *IMF Country Report* No. 10/170, Fondo Monetario Internacional, Washington, DC, https://www.imf.org/external/pubs/ft/scr/2010/cr10170.pdf.

Franks J. R., R. Benelli, V. Mercer-Blackman and R. SabParaguay (2005), "Corruption, Reform, and the Financial System", Fondo Monetario Internacional, Washington, DC.

International Tax Review (2014), "Mexico 2014 income tax-reform, Considerations for the financial-sector", www.internationaltaxreview.com/Article/3352686/Mexico-2014-income-tax-reform-Considerations-for-the-financial-sector.html.

Gómez Sabaini, J.C., J.P. Jiménez and A. Podestá (2010), "Evasión y equidad en América Latina", *Project documents*, No. 309 (LC/W.309/ Rev.1), CEPAL, Santiago de Chile.

The Panama Investor Blog (2008), "Audit uncovers millions in unpaid sales taxes", http://primapanama.blogs.com/_panama_residential_devel/2008/06/audit-uncovers.html.

Peters, A.C and M.A Bristol (2006), "VAT: Is it Suitable for the Caribbean Community?", MPRA Paper No. 8, https://mpra.ub.uni-muenchen.de/8/1/MPRA_paper_8.pdf.

OCDE (2017, forthcoming), *Tax Policy Reforms in the OECD*, OECD Publishing, Paris.

OCDE (2016), *Consumption Tax Trends 2016: VAT/GST and excise rates, trends and policy issues*, OECD Publishing, Paris, http://dx.doi.org/10.1787/ctt-2016-en.

OCDE (2014a), *Development Co-operation Report 2014: Mobilising Resources for Sustainable Development*, OECD Publishing, Paris, http://dx.doi.org/10.1787/dcr-2014-en.

OECD (2014b), *Revenue Statistics 1965-2014*, OECD Publishing, Paris, http://dx.doi.org/10.1787/rev_stats-2014-en-fr.

OECD (2008), *Perspectivas Económicas de América Latina 2009*, OECD Publishing, Paris, http://dx.doi.org/10.1787/leo-2009-es.

OCDE/CEPAL (2012), *Perspectivas económicas de América Latina 2013: Políticas de pymes para el cambio estructural*, CEPAL and OECD Publishing, http://dx.doi.org/10.1787/leo-2013-es.

OCDE/CAF/CEPAL (2015), *Perspectivas económicas de América Latina 2016: Hacia una nueva asociación con China*, OECD Publishing, Paris, http://dx.doi.org/10.1787/9789264246348-es.

OCDE/CEPAL/CIAT/BID (2015), *Estadísticas tributarias en América Latina y el Caribe 1990-2013*, OECD Publishing, Paris, http://dx.doi.org/10.1787/rev_lat_car-2016-en-fr.

PKF (2013), *PKF Worldwide Tax Guide 2013*, PKF international limited, www.pkf.com/publications/tax-guides/pkf-international-worldwide-tax-guide-2013.

PWC (2015), "Peru's major tax reform include rate changes and a new tax ruling request procedure 2015", www.pwc.com/us/en/tax-services/publications/insights/assets/pwc-perus-major-tax-reform-includes-rate-changes.pdf.

US mission Geneva (2011), Mission of the United States of America to the United Nations and Other International Organizations in Geneva, Geneva, https://geneva.usmission.gov/2011/01/18/tpr-jamaica/.

World Grain (2016), "Reforms boost Argentine grain industry", www.world-grain.com/articles/news_home/Features/2016/05/Reforms_boost_Argentine_grain.aspx?ID=%7BAE4EE339-0D46-43EF-A962-5ED9DEF72B53%7D.

Zuleta J.C (2008), "Combating corruption in the revenue service: the case of VAT refunds in Bolivia", Anti-Corruption Resource Centre, www.U4.no/themes/pfm.

CHAPTER 2

SPECIAL FEATURE

Fiscal revenues from non-renewable natural resources in Latin America and the Caribbean

CAPÍTULO 2

SECCIÓN ESPECIAL

Ingresos fiscales provenientes de recursos naturales no renovables en América Latina y el Caribe

CHAPTER 2

SPECIAL FEATURE

Fiscal revenues from non-renewable natural resources in Latin America and the Caribbean

SPECIAL FEATURE
Fiscal revenues from non-renewable natural resources in Latin America and the Caribbean

Principal findings

Non-renewable natural resource-related public revenues in Latin America and the Caribbean fell sharply in 2015

- The dramatic decline in the international price of crude oil, which began in 2014, intensified in 2015, resulting in a sharp fall in fiscal revenues related to the production and commercialisation of hydrocarbons in the region. These revenues fell on average from 6.8% of GDP in 2014 to 4.4% of GDP in 2015 for the ten countries included in this analysis, representing their lowest level since the series began in 2000.
- Public revenues from mining continued to decline in 2015, falling from 0.52% of GDP in 2014 to 0.37% of GDP. Of particular note was the decline in tax revenues associated with the sector, principally in the form of corporate tax receipts, due to sliding prices and mounting financial losses.

Despite an uptick in commodities prices, non-renewable natural resource revenues are estimated to have retreated further in 2016

- International commodities prices appear to have bottomed out in 2016. Although they are still estimated to register a decline for the year on average, this mainly reflects their evolution during the first months of the year. Prices for the majority of the region's major non-renewable natural resources began to rise in the second half of the year. Nevertheless, this change in trend offered little relief to fiscal accounts given the difficult financial situation that many of the region's major producers are facing.
- Hydrocarbons related revenues are estimated to have fallen to 2.6% of GDP in 2016. Notably, oil revenues fell sharply in Colombia (2.5% of GDP to an estimated 0.7% of GDP) – aggravated by the loss recorded by Ecopetrol – and in Trinidad and Tobago (7.7% of GDP to 2.0% of GDP) – where corporate tax receipts from oil companies, which make up the majority of oil revenues, fell 90%.
- Mining revenues are estimated to have continued their downward trend, reaching a regional average of 0.3% of GDP. In particular, these revenues plummeted in Chile, falling from 1.3% of GDP to 0.4% of GDP, as the result of a collapse in corporate income tax payments by private mining companies.

Non-renewable natural resource revenues in this Special Feature refer to tax (income tax, sector specific taxes, and certain excise taxes) and non-tax revenues (royalties, dividends) deriving from hydrocarbons production and commercialization and from mining. They do not include tax withholdings or payments made by companies on behalf of their employees or investors, nor do they include payments of consumption taxes (namely the value-added tax, where applicable).

2.1. Non-renewable natural resource-related public revenues in Latin America and the Caribbean fell sharply in 2015

Public revenues from hydrocarbons collapsed in line with the price of crude oil

Trends in fiscal revenues associated with the production and commercialisation of hydrocarbons in Latin America and the Caribbean followed in step with the dramatic decline in the international reference prices for crude oil – principally the spot prices of West Texas Intermediate (WTI) and of Brent. It is estimated that the price of crude oil on average fell 47.2% during 2015, which surpassed the decline registered during the economic and financial crisis of 2008-2009 (-36.3%) (Figure 2.1). A further decoupling of the demand and the supply of oil in the international market was the key driver of this downturn.

Figure 2.1. **International reference price for crude, 2000-15**

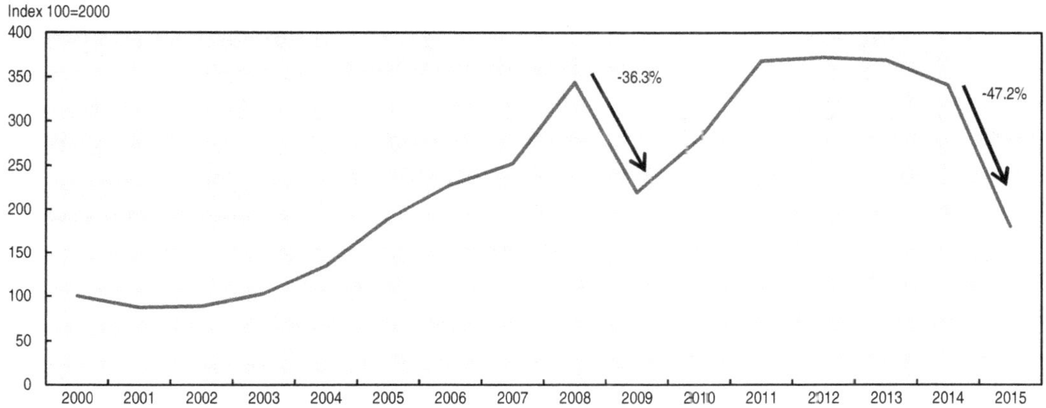

Note: The price corresponds to the simple average of the spot prices for Brent, West Texas Intermediate and Dubai.

Source: Economic Commission for Latin America and the Caribbean (ECLAC), on the basis of figures from CEPALstat.

StatLink http://dx.doi.org/10.1787/888933462682

According to estimates by the International Energy Agency (IEA), global daily crude oil production rose 3.0% in 2015, bolstered by important increases in the United States, Saudi Arabia, Iraq and Brazil (IEA, 2016). Rising production in the United States, as a result of the extraction of natural gas and crude oil from shale deposits (shale revolution), has significantly modified international market dynamics in recent years. This has been apparent in the action of the members of the Organization of Oil Producing Countries (OPEC), who maintained their production levels in 2015, despite the fall in price, in an effort to defend their market share.

Growth in the global demand for oil, in contrast, remained modest, though it rose at a faster pace in 2015 (1.9%) than in 2014 (1.0%) (IEA, 2016). In particular, oil consumption among OECD countries rebounded (1.2%), after having registered a decline of 0.6% in the previous year. There was, however, a deceleration in demand among non-OECD countries, with growth of 2.7% in 2015 compared to 3.3% in 2014, although with significant differences among regions. Oil demand accelerated in Asia (5.2%), while it declined in the Commonwealth of Independent States (-1.3%) and in Latin America (-1.0%).

The continued divergence in the growth rates of supply and demand undermined oil prices at the international level and resulted in a substantial increase in crude oil stocks. This was especially evident among OECD countries, where oil stocks increased by 287 million barrels (from 4 285 million barrels to 4 572 million barrels) between the end of 2014 and the end of 2015 (IEA, 2016). More than half of this increase (55%) occurred in the United States, where oil stocks rose by 158 million barrels, reaching 1 987 million barrels (including the Strategic Petroleum Reserve of the federal government) by year's end.

These trends in the international market resulted in an important reduction in public revenues from hydrocarbons for the countries of the region. As Table 2.1 highlights, fiscal revenues deriving from the production and commercialization of hydrocarbons plummeted in 2015, falling 31.6% in current dollar terms. Revenues solely associated with the extraction of hydrocarbons registered a 44.4% decline for the region as a whole (compared to the 47.2% decline in the international price for crude oil). Weakening currencies softened these declines when revenues are expressed in national currency terms. For example, Argentina, Brazil, Colombia and Mexico all saw their currencies fall by 10% or more relative to the US dollar.

Table 2.1. **Year-on-year change in fiscal revenues from hydrocarbons and production of hydrocarbons, 2014-15**

Country	Fiscal revenues from hydrocarbons		Production of hydrocarbons	
	% change in national currency	% change in USD	% change in the production of crude oil (thousand barrels daily)	% change in production of marketed natural gas (billion cubic meters)
Argentina	20.1	8.7	0.0	2.7
Bolivia	-20.9	-20.9	n.a.	7.1
Brazil	-8.7	-33.9	8.1	13.5
Colombia	-38.5	-57.1	1.5	1.0
Ecuador	-41.8	-41.8	-2.4	-14.0
Mexico	-12.0	-25.2	-6.7	-9.0
Peru	-38.8	-43.9	-16.3	3.6
Suriname	-90.7	-91.0	1.0	n.a.
Trinidad and Tobago	-36.4	-35.9	-3.1	-2.9
Venezuela	24.5	-62.3	-1.1	18.9
Latin America and the Caribbean	**n.a.**	**-31.6**	**-0.3**	**1.9**

Source: Economic Commission for Latin America and the Caribbean (ECLAC), on the basis of figures from the Organization of Petroleum Exporting Countries (OPEC, 2016) and Staatsoile (2014, 2015, 2016).

StatLink http://dx.doi.org/10.1787/888933462784

While the movement in the price of crude oil predominated, fiscal revenues from hydrocarbons in the region were also impacted by changes in production levels. Although statistics published by OPEC (2016) show that the production of crude oil fell slightly in Latin America and the Caribbean (-0.3%), there were significant differences between countries. For example, among the largest producers oil production rose in Brazil (8.1%) and Colombia (1.5%), while Mexico (-6.7%) and Venezuela (-1.1%) registered declines (Table 2.1). The production of natural gas in the region increased (1.9%), after two consecutive years of growth rates near zero.

Significant differences in hydrocarbons revenues trends are apparent at the level of countries when analysed these revenues are analysed relative to nominal GDP. This reflects not only differences between the relative weight of the sector among countries, but also the differing fiscal frameworks employed to appropriate rent from hydrocarbons, as well as changes in exchange rates and production levels. As Table 2.2 shows, fiscal revenues from hydrocarbons, for the average of the ten countries considered, fell from 6.8% of GDP in 2014 to 4.4% of GDP in 2015. This represents their lowest level since the beginning of the series in 2000. There were important reductions in both tax revenues (-0.7 percentage points) and non-tax revenues (-1.7 percentage points), although in the first case a sharp decline in corporate income tax receipts was offset in part by relatively strong revenues from selective taxes on the consumption of hydrocarbons.

Table 2.2. **Public revenues from hydrocarbons, by country and type of revenue, 2014-15**

Percentage of GDP

Country	Total			Tax revenues			Non-tax revenues		
	2014 (r)	2015 (p)	Δ	2014 (r)	2015 (p)	Δ	2014 (r)	2015 (p)	Δ
Argentina	1.8	1.7	-0.1	1.3	1.3	-0.1	0.4	0.4	0.0
Bolivia	13.1	10.4	-2.7	2.3	2.4	0.1	10.8	7.9	-2.9
Brazil	1.5	1.3	-0.2	0.9	0.9	0.0	0.7	0.4	-0.2
Colombia	4.3	2.5	-1.8	1.8	1.3	-0.4	2.5	1.1	-1.4
Ecuador	10.7	6.3	-4.3	0.0	0.0	0.0	10.7	6.3	-4.3
Mexico	7.0	5.9	-1.2	0.0	1.3	1.3	7.1	4.6	-2.5
Peru	1.6	0.9	-0.7	0.8	0.5	-0.2	0.8	0.4	-0.4
Suriname	5.2	0.5	-4.8	2.3	0.3	-2.1	2.9	0.2	-2.7
Trinidad and Tobago	12.3	7.7	-4.7	10.9	6.7	-4.2	1.4	0.9	-0.5
Venezuela	10.7	6.7	-4.0	2.5	0.8	-1.7	8.2	6.0	-2.3
Simple average	**6.8**	**4.4**	**-2.4**	**2.3**	**1.5**	**-0.7**	**4.6**	**2.8**	**-1.7**

Notes: (r) revised; (p) preliminary.
Tax revenues refer to corporate income taxes (Argentina, Bolivia , Brazil (Petrobras), Colombia, Peru, Suriname (Staatsolie), Trinidad and Tobago and Venezuela), export duties (Argentina), excise taxes on hydrocarbons production (Bolivia and Mexico) and excise taxes on hydrocarbons products (Argentina, Bolivia, Brazil, Colombia, Mexico and Peru). Non-tax revenues principally refer to production levies and dividends (Argentina: national and subnational royalties; Bolivia: royalties and special transfers of "Yacimientos Petrolíferos Fiscales Bolivianos" (YPFB); Brazil: royalties, special state participation, signing bonuses, occupation and retention fees and dividends from Petrobras; Colombia: royalties and dividends from EcoPetrol; Ecuador: non-financial public sector revenues from export sales of petroleum; Mexico: PEMEX revenues Peru: royalties; Suriname: dividends from Staatsolie; Trinidad and Tobago: royalties; and Venezuela : royalties, dividends from PDVSA and extraordinary non-tax petroleum revenues.) Figures may not add due to rounding.

Source: Economic Commission for Latin America and the Caribbean (ECLAC).

StatLink http://dx.doi.org/10.1787/888933462794

Hydrocarbons revenues in Argentina held relatively stable with respect to GDP in 2015, registering a 0.1 percentage point decline to 1.7% of GDP. Tax revenues associated with hydrocarbons fell marginally due to a pronounced decline in revenues from hydrocarbons export duties as a result of the reduction in rates and the introduction of a new sliding scale for specified products that the government decreed at the end of 2014. This was largely offset by a strong increase in revenues from the selective tax on liquid fuels and gas, due mainly to a sharp rise in prices in nominal terms, which also contributed to the overall increase in hydrocarbons revenues expressed in current dollar terms (Figure 2.1).

In the Plurinational State of Bolivia, hereafter Bolivia, the reduction in hydrocarbons revenues (from 13.1% of GDP to 10.4% of GDP) was entirely due to a decline in non-tax revenues (from 10.8% of GDP to 7.9% of GDP). In particular, receipts from the direct tax on hydrocarbons (IDH, for its initials in Spanish) and from royalties and participations of the State in production fell around 30%. While production increased, this more moderate decline relative to the decline in the price of oil was largely due to the pricing structure embedded in the long-term export contracts for natural gas the country has with Argentina and Brazil. These contracts generally establish the price of natural gas relative to a basket of hydrocarbons products for a period of three months. This mechanism offers some respite in times when prices are falling, though the reverse is true when prices rise. At the general government level hydrocarbons revenues were also bolstered by the transfer of Bs676 million (0.3% of GDP) by "Yacimientos Petrolíferos Fiscales Bolivianos" (YPFB) – the state-owned energy producer – to the central government in line with the Law 550 of July 2014 (YPBF, 2016). This law authorized public enterprises to transfer resources to the national treasury to finance investment projects or programs of social interest.

Falling non-tax revenues – principally of royalties and the special participation of the State in production – weighed on overall hydrocarbons revenues in Brazil, which fell from 1.5% of GDP in 2014 to 1.3% of GDP in 2015. These declines were compounded by the fact that Petrobras did not pay a dividend to the federal government for the first time since the series began in 2000, reflecting the difficult financial situation the company currently faces. Tax revenues, in contrast, held stable at 0.9% of GDP, boosted by strong receipts from taxes on the consumption of fuels as well as the reintroduction of the Cide Combustíveis – a federal tax on gasoline and diesel – whose revenues in 2014 were nearly nil.

In Colombia the downward trend in oil revenues (from 4.3% of GDP to 2.5% of GDP) has largely followed the deterioration of the financial situation of EcoPetrol, the country's principal producer. The company's profits have fallen significantly from their recent highs resulting in a significant impact on public revenues. In particular, dividend payments to the central government – which are considered non-tax revenues – have plummeted, falling from 1.4% of GDP in 2014 to 0.5% of GDP in 2015. Unsurprisingly, corporate tax receipts for the sector as a whole retreated 0.4 percentage points of GDP, from 1.4% of GDP to 0.9% of GDP. It is important to note that while Ecopetrol reported a loss for 2015 this will more significantly impact government revenues in 2016 (Ecopetrol, 2016).

The fall in hydrocarbons revenues in Ecuador – from 10.7% of GDP to 6.3% of GDP – was the result of the collapse in the price of oil as well as a reduction in oil production (-2.4% in 2015). Oil revenues in Ecuador are nearly entirely composed of revenues from exports by EP Petroecuador, the state-owned producer, and from private contractors. While private oil contractors pay corporate income tax, these receipts are negligible.

In Mexico the reduction in oil revenues (from 7.0% of GDP to 5.9% of GDP) was softened by a surge in receipts of the special tax on production and services (IEPS) as applied to gasoline and diesel, which registered a positive value (that is to say it ceased to function as a subsidy), rising from -0.1% of GDP in 2014 to 1.2% of GDP in 2015. Tax revenues were also bolstered marginally by the introduction of two new sources whose genesis stems from the energy reform adopted in 2013: the tax on hydrocarbons exploration and extraction as well as the payment of corporate income tax by contractors and assignation holders. Non-tax revenues – composed principally of operating revenues of PEMEX and transfers from the Mexican Petroleum for Stabilization and Development to the federal government – reduced in line with the price of crude oil and, to a lesser extent, the reduction in production.

In Peru the impact of falling prices was aggravated by a decline in production (16% for crude oil and 3% for natural gas), resulting in a 0.7 percentage point reduction (from 1.6% of GDP to 0.9% of GDP) in public revenues from hydrocarbons. Corporate tax receipts from the sector fell sharply (from 0.4% of GDP to 0.2% of GDP), reflecting reduced profit margins as well as the reduction in the corporate tax rate – from 30% to 28% – which the government approved at the end of 2014 as part of a package of measure to stimulate the domestic economy.

Suriname experienced the most pronounced decline in hydrocarbons revenues in the region as a result of a slump in profits of the state-owned producer Staatsoile (Staatsoile, 2016). The company's fiscal contribution to the national budget fell 91% in dollar terms, or 4.8 percentage points of GDP. Tax revenues – composed of corporate income tax receipts – and non-tax revenues – derived from dividend payments to the government – registered similar sized reductions.

In Trinidad and Tobago the fall in hydrocarbons revenues (from 12.3% of GDP to 7.7% of GDP) was principally due to a sharp reduction in corporate income tax payments by companies operating in the sector (-38%). Non-tax revenues, mainly composed of royalties, fell in line with crude oil and natural gas prices as well as a drop in production of both products during the year.

Oil revenues in the Bolivarian Republic of Venezuela, hereafter Venezuela, are estimated to have registered a significant decline in 2015 (from 10.7% of GDP to 6.7% of GDP). Tax revenues, principally corporate income tax payments by PDVSA, fell from 2.5% of GDP to 0.8% of GDP as a result of the decline in PDVSA's profits as well as the high base of comparison. Profits in 2014 were exceptionally strong due to the sale of stake in an affiliate of PDVSA to the Central Bank (PDVSA, 2016). Non-tax revenues fell sharply (8.2% of GDP to 6.0% of GDP) reflecting lower royalty payments and a reduction in extraordinary non-tax oil revenues, although in the second case updated figures have not yet been released.[1]

Mining revenues continued to trend downwards in 2015

Fiscal revenues from mining in the region continued to follow their downward trajectory that began in 2012. As in the case of hydrocarbons, movements in market prices for minerals and metals were the principal factor behind the trends observed in the region. ECLAC estimates the weighted price of minerals and metals for the region, based on their share in the region's exports of mining products, fell 23% in 2015 and were down 45% from their high in 2011. Nevertheless, there were significant differences in the evolution of prices for individual mining products during the year. Those for lead (-8%), gold (-8%) and zinc (-11%) posted modest declines, while that of iron ore plunged (-42%) (Figure 2.2).

Figure 2.2. **Year-on-year change in minerals and metals prices**

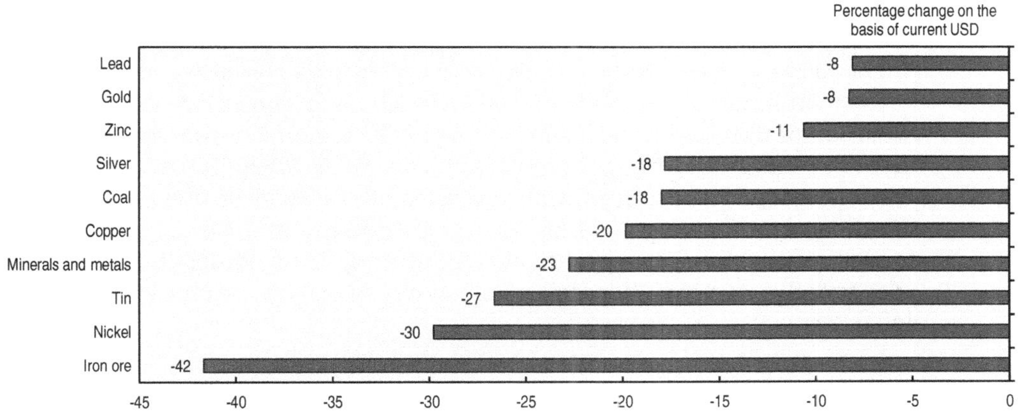

Source: Economic Commission for Latin America and the Caribbean (ECLAC), on the basis of figures from CEPALstat.

StatLink http://dx.doi.org/10.1787/888933462690

As was highlighted in last year's special feature, the variation in minerals and metals price has largely correlated with economic growth in East Asia (OECD-ECLAC-CIAT-IDB, 2016). Rapid double-digit growth in China during the lead-up to the global economic financial crisis of 2008-09, as well as the surge in investment in the direct aftermath supported by unprecedented fiscal and monetary stimulus, supported historically high prices for a wide spectrum of commodities. As a result China is now estimated to account for half of global base metal demand (IMF, 2015). However, as the country's economy slows – with growth at single digit rates and continuing to decelerate – demand has weakened and commodities prices have retreated.

As prices have fallen so too has the financial position of the principal firms who operate in the sector at the global level. According to PriceWaterhouseCooper (2016) the 40 largest mining companies in the world recorded a combined loss, for the first time in a decade, of USD 105 billion in 2015 (Figure 2.3). While plunging revenues undermined profitability among the largest firms, a surge in impairment charges as firms wrote down the value of their assets in light of lower commodities prices also played a key role. Unsurprisingly, the income tax expense of this group of companies fell 81.8%, from USD 22 billion in 2014 to USD 4 billion in 2015.

Figure 2.3. **Net income and income tax expense of the 40 principal mining firms in the world, 2006-15**

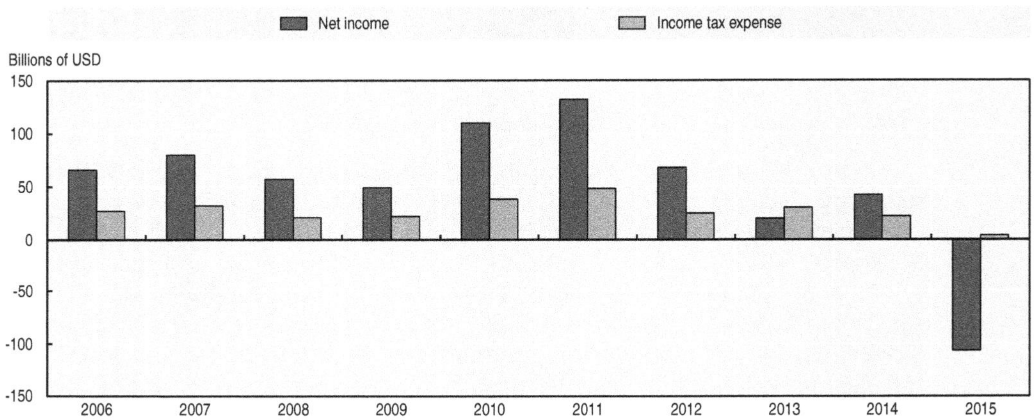

Source: Economic Commission for Latin America and the Caribbean (ECLAC), on the basis of figures from PriceWaterhouseCoopers (2016).

StatLink http://dx.doi.org/10.1787/888933462709

These trends in the international prices of minerals and metals as well as of the financial situation of the largest firms that dominate the sector at the global level – and in Latin America and the Caribbean through their subsidiaries – are apparent in the evolution of fiscal revenues from mining in the region. For the ten countries considered these revenues fell 33% in current dollar terms in 2015 (Table 2.3). Nevertheless, the year-on-year variation in mining revenues at the level of individual countries varied significantly, reflecting differences in their mineral and metals product specialisation as well as in the relative profitability of mining firms associated with these products. Additionally, currency depreciations served to soften declines registered in current dollar terms.

Table 2.3. **Year-on-year change in fiscal revenues from mining, 2014-15**

In percentages

Country	Fiscal revenues from mining	
	% change in national currency	% change in USD
Argentina	-16.3	-24.3
Bolivia	-24.7	-24.7
Brazil	-30.9	-50.0
Chile	-25.9	-34.6
Colombia	-7.1	-30.6
Dominican Republic	-23.9	-26.1
Jamaica	353.9	334.4
Mexico	-4.6	-18.9
Peru	-39.2	-44.3
Suriname	-48.0	-49.8
Latin America and the Caribbean	**n.a.**	**-33.2**

Source: Economic Commission for Latin America and the Caribbean (ECLAC).

StatLink http://dx.doi.org/10.1787/888933462804

As Table 2.4 shows, fiscal revenues from mining in the region fell from 0.52% of GDP in 2014 to 0.37% of GDP in 2015. Declining tax revenues – principally from instruments whose tax bases are based on mining firms' profits – accounted for the majority of this decline (falling from 0.33% of GDP to 0.22% of GDP). This marks a significant retreat from the average of 1.0% of GDP registered in 2011. Non-tax revenues, which largely correspond to royalty payments, dipped 0.04 percentage points of GDP, in line with the variation observed in prices; though this was offset to some extent by production increases in some countries.

Table 2.4. **Public revenues from mining, by country and type of revenue, 2013-14**

Percentage of GDP

Country	Total			Tax revenues			Non-tax revenues		
	2014 (r)	2015 (p)	Δ	2014 (r)	2015 (p)	Δ	2014 (r)	2015 (p)	Δ
Argentina	0.08	0.05	-0.03	0.08	0.05	-0.03	0.00	0.00	0.00
Bolivia (Plur. State of)	0.66	0.50	-0.16	0.09	0.07	-0.03	0.57	0.43	-0.14
Brazil	0.08	0.05	-0.03	0.04	0.02	-0.02	0.04	0.03	0.00
Chile	1.83	1.27	-0.56	1.57	1.27	-0.30	0.26	0.00	-0.26
Colombia	0.30	0.26	-0.04	0.09	0.05	-0.04	0.21	0.21	0.00
Dominican Republic	0.50	0.35	-0.15	0.42	0.29	-0.13	0.07	0.06	-0.01
Jamaica	0.04	0.17	0.13	0.00	0.00	0.00	0.04	0.17	0.13
Mexico	0.21	0.19	-0.02	0.20	0.16	-0.03	0.01	0.03	0.01
Peru	0.67	0.38	-0.28	0.46	0.24	-0.22	0.21	0.15	-0.06
Suriname	0.85	0.43	-0.42	0.38	0.06	-0.32	0.48	0.37	-0.10
Simple average	**0.52**	**0.37**	**-0.16**	**0.33**	**0.22**	**-0.11**	**0.19**	**0.14**	**-0.04**

Notes: (r) revised; (p) preliminary.

Tax revenues refer to corporate income taxes (Argentina, Bolivia Brazil (Vale), Chile, Colombia, Dominican Republic, Mexico, Jamaica, Peru and Suriname (IAMGOLD)), export duties (Argentina; Chile: Impuesto Ley N°13.196) and other sector specific taxes (Chile: specific tax on mining; Dominican Republic: annual minimum mining tax and net mining profits tax; Peru: special mining tax (IEM)). Non-tax revenues principally refers to production levies (Bolivia: royalties; Brazil: CFEM (Financial Compensation for the Exploration of Mineral Resources), TAH (Taxa Anual por Hectare) and the TFRM (Taxa de fiscalizacao de recursos minerarios) in Minas Gerais; Chile: dividends from CODELCO; Colombia: royalties; Dominican Republic: net smelter royalty; Jamaica: bauxite levy and bauxite royalties; Mexico: mining duties; Peru: royalties and GEM (Gravámen Especial a la Minería); Suriname: royalties (IAMGOLD)). Figures may not add due to rounding.

Source: Economic Commission for Latin America and the Caribbean (ECLAC).

StatLink http://dx.doi.org/10.1787/888933462818

In Argentina the fall in mining revenues (from 0.08% of GDP to 0.05% of GDP) was due to a decline the receipts from export duties on mining products (-42.1%), reflecting lower export volumes for metallic ores (-29.7%) and reduced unit prices (-19.2%). The decline in revenues in the Bolivia (from 0.66% of GDP to 0.50% of GDP) is largely explained by a reduction in mining royalty receipts (-24.2%), which have accounted for more than 80% of total mining revenues in the last two years.

The collapse in the price of iron ore (-42%) was the principal driver of the slump in mining revenues in Brazil (from 0.08% of GDP to 0.05% of GDP). Tax revenues bore the brunt of this decline as corporate income tax payments by Vale S.A. fell 49.2%. In Chile, mining revenues dipped (from 1.83% of GDP to 1.27% of GDP) as payments by Codelco, the state-owned producer, to the central government declined as a result of the company declaring a loss for the year (CODELCO, 2016). This impacted both tax revenues – as the company's payment of income taxes fell sharply – and non-tax revenues – with the transfer of after-tax profits to the central government falling to zero for the first time since 2002.

Mining revenues in Colombia – which are principally associated with the production of coal – fell marginally (or from 0.30% of GDP to 0.26% of GDP) as a result of a 39.0% decline in corporate income tax payments by the sector. In contrast, non-tax revenues rose 7.2% – leaving them stable at 0.21% of GDP – as royalty payments rose on higher production. Jamaica was the only country in the region to register an increase in its mining revenues in 2015 (from 0.04% of GDP to 0.17% of GDP), as the government reinstated the bauxite levy, which had been suspended in 2014 in an effort to support the sector.

In Mexico, mining revenues also fell modestly (from 0.21% of GDP to 0.19% of GDP) as a result of a decline in corporate income tax payments (-12.8%). This was offset to some extent by a jump in receipts from mining duties, which more than doubled from their 2014 level. In Peru corporate income tax receipts from the sector nearly halved (-46.2%) leading to a significant reduction in mining revenues (from 0.67% of GDP to 0.38% of GDP). While this reflected shrinking profit margins of mining firms operating in the country, it was also compounded by the reduction in the corporate income tax rate (from 30% to 28% for 2015 and 2016) enacted by the government at the end of 2014.

In the Dominican Republic a sharp decline in corporate income tax receipts (-39.2%) was offset in part by a rise in revenues from the minimum annual mining tax (64.1%) – which rises when income tax payments fall – and from the mining profits tax (13.9%). It should be noted that these last two instruments seek to ensure a minimum participation of the State in mining rents.

The fall in mining revenues in Suriname (from 0.85% of GDP to 0.43% of GDP) was largely due to a reduction in tax revenues as corporate income tax payments by IAMGOLD fell sharply compared to their 2014 levels. Non-tax revenues – composed of royalty payments by the same company – fell 19.8%, due to the combination of the falling price of gold and a cut in production (-11.7%) (IAMGOLD, 2016).

2.2. Despite an uptick in commodities prices, non-renewable natural resource revenues are estimated to have retreated further in 2016

During 2016 there were signs that the imbalances between supply and demand for commodities in international markets were beginning to subside. The oversupply of crude oil in the market reduced somewhat as demand continued to growth (1.1% for the first three quarters of the year) while growth in supply moderated considerably (0.0% over the same period) (IEA, 2016). In particular, production in the United States dipped as some shale production became economically unviable. OPEC supply was also set to decline as member States agreed their first cut in production quotas in eight years in November 2016.

Similar trends were observed in markets for minerals and metals, with a strengthening of demand and a reduction in supply. In China, efforts by the government to support the infrastructure and construction sectors boosted global demand in 2016 (World Bank, 2016). At the same time global supply has declined as mining firms cut production and closed high-cost mines. Nevertheless, this has not been uniform across mining products. For example, while there was a significant reduction in the supply of zinc, that of copper continued to grow (including in the region).

As a result of these trends in supply and demand, the fall in the international prices for non-renewable natural resources attenuated in 2016 (Table 2.5). Although the International Monetary Fund (IMF, 2016) estimates additional declines in the price of crude oil (-15%) and metals (-8%), quarterly data suggest the existence of an inflection point mid-year. This was especially apparent in the case of mining products, in particular for iron ore, tin, zinc and coal. The price of crude oil also posted a year-on-year increase in the fourth quarter of the year.

Table 2.5. **Year-on-year change in selected international commodities prices, 2015-16**

In percentages

Product	2015	2016				
	Year	Q1	Q2	Q3	Q4	Year
Metals	-23	n.a.	n.a.	n.a.	n.a.	-8
Copper	-20	-20	-22	-8	-2	-14
Iron ore	-43	-24	-5	6	20	-2
Tin	-27	-16	8	19	22	7
Zinc	-11	-19	-13	22	42	5
Lead	-15	-4	-12	8	13	1
Crude oil	-47	-37	-26	-6	15	-15
Coal	**-19**	**-17**	**-12**	**15**	**29**	**3**

Source: Economic Commission for Latin America and the Caribbean (ECLAC), based on figures from IMF (2016).

StatLink http://dx.doi.org/10.1787/888933462823

The rebound in commodities prices in the second-half of 2016, however, offered little relief for fiscal revenues from non-renewable natural resources. This is largely due to the grave financial situation of many of the principal producers in the region. As Figure 2.4 shows, net income has trended lower in recent years, with a significant negative impact on tax revenues – corporate tax receipts and revenues from other instruments whose tax base is profits – and non-tax revenues – mainly dividends. There have been an increasing number of firms that have booked losses. For example, among hydrocarbons producers: Petrobras (Brazil), Ecopetrol (Colombia) and Petrotrin (Trinidad and Tobago). Likewise, losses have mounted for mining firms, including that of Codelco (Chile) in 2015.

In this context ECLAC estimates that fiscal revenues from non-renewable natural resources declined further in 2016. In the case of revenues associated with the production and commercialisation of hydrocarbons, these are estimated to have dropped from 4.4% of GDP in 2015 to 2.6% of GDP in 2016; their lowest level since the beginning of the series in 2000 (Figure 2.5). Significant declines are estimated for the Bolivia (from 10.4% of GDP to 6.8% of GDP), Colombia (2.5% of GDP to 0.7% of GDP) and Trinidad and Tobago (from 7.7% of GDP to 2.0% of GDP). In this last country preliminary data for the fiscal year point to a 90% decline in corporate income tax receipts from oil companies (which represent the majority of oil revenues). In contrast, there were modest declines in Mexico (5.9% of GDP to 5.6% of GDP) and Brazil (1.3% of GDP to 1.2% of GDP).

Figure 2.4. **Net income of selected petroleum producers, 2010-15**

Index 100 = 2005

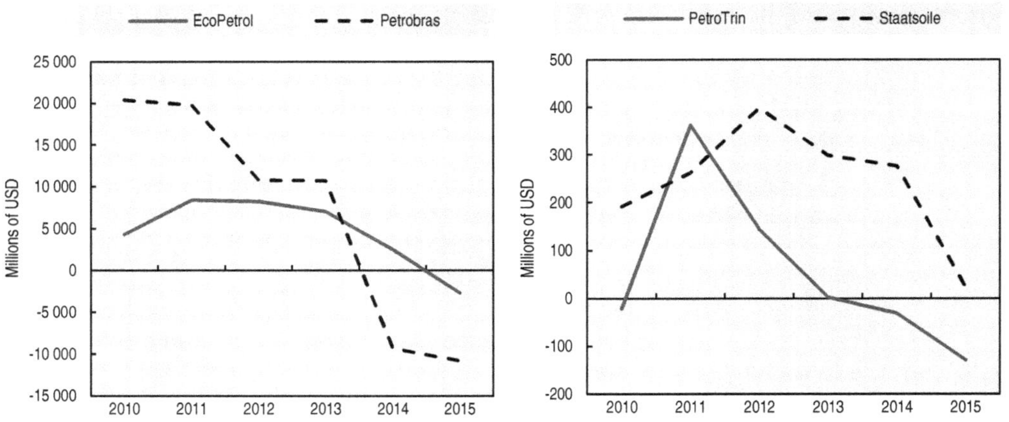

Source: Economic Commission for Latin America and the Caribbean (ECLAC), based on figures from Bloomberg and financial statements.

StatLink http://dx.doi.org/10.1787/888933462719

Mining revenues are also estimated to have declined in 2016, falling on average from 0.4% of GDP to 0.3% of GDP. In Chile, these revenues dropped sharply – from 1.3% of GDP to 0.4% of GDP – as a tax receipts from private mining firms collapsed, with corporate tax payments falling to a net devolution for the year. Preliminary figures for Peru point to a moderate decline (from 0.4% of GDP to 0.3% of GDP) as the result of a further reduction in corporate income tax payments from the sector. Nevertheless, mining revenues could increase in some countries, reflecting improvements in prices for some products. For example, in Brazil revenues from the Financial Compensation for Mineral Resources Exploitation (CFEM, for its initials in Portuguese) – a royalty – rose 20.1% in 2016 as production rose and iron ore prices began to recover.

Figure 2.5. **Public revenues from non-renewable natural resources, 2000-16**

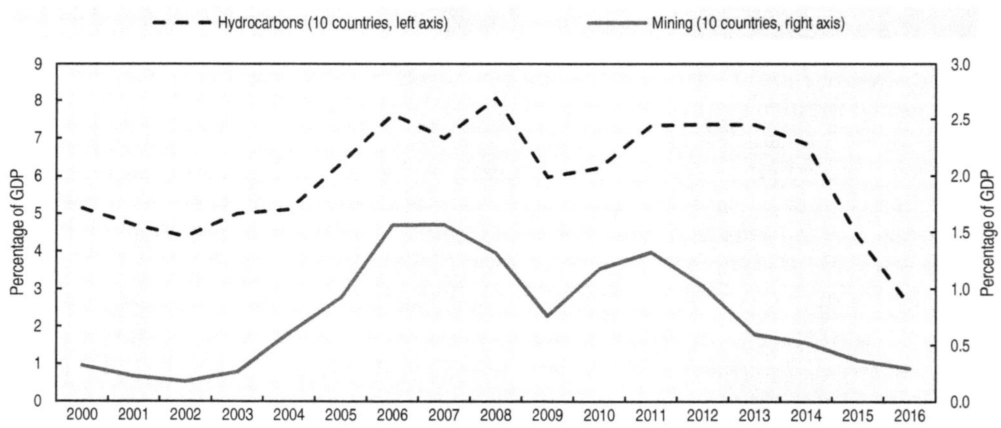

Note: Mining includes: Argentina, Bolivia , Brazil, Chile, Colombia, Jamaica, Mexico, Peru, Dominican Republic and Suriname. Hydrocarbons include: Argentina, Bolivia , Brazil, Colombia, Ecuador, Mexico, Peru, Suriname, Trinidad and Tobago and Venezuela . Values for 2016 are based on official government estimates from 2017 budget documents or from preliminary annual figures. When figures for 2016 were not available they were estimated using monthly data (typically for the first three quarters of the year). When monthly data was not available revenues were estimated by applying the year-on-year change in the price for the most representative product – or basket of products in the case of mining – for the country, expressed in national currency terms, to 2015 revenues.

Source: Economic Commission for Latin America and the Caribbean (ECLAC).

StatLink http://dx.doi.org/10.1787/888933462729

Notes

1. The principal source for this information is the explanatory memorandum that accompanies the national budget document; the 2017 edition has not yet been released.

References

Codelco (2016), *Memoria anual 2015*, Corporación Nacional del Cobre de Chile.

Ecopetrol (2016), *Reporte Integrado de Gestión Sostenible*, 2015, Bogota.

IEA (2016), *Oil Market Report* [online], International Energy Agency, https://www.iea.org/oilmarketreport/omrpublic/.

IMF (2016), "Prices & Forecasts", *IMF Primary Commodity Prices Forecasts* [online], International Monetary Fund, www.imf.org/external/np/res/commod/index.aspx.

IMF (2015), "Special feature: commodity market developments and forecasts, with a focus on metals in the world economy", *World Economic Outlook*, International Monetory Fund, October.

IAMGOLD Corporation (2016), *Annual Report 2015*.

MEM (2016), *Reporte Anual Producción Minera 2015*, Ministerio de Energía y Minas de la República del Perú, Lima.

OECD-ECLAC-CIAT-IDB (2016), *Revenue Statistics in Latin America and the Caribbean 1990-2014*, OECD Publishing, Paris, http://dx.doi.org/10.1787/rev_lat_car-2016-en-fr.

OPEC (2016), *Annual Statistical Bulletin 2016*, Organization of Petroleum Exporting Countries.

PriceWaterhouseCoopers (2016), "Mine 2016: slower, lower, weaker... but not defeated".

PDVSA (2016), *Informe de Gestión Anual 2015*, Petróleos de Venezuela, S.A.

Staatsolie (2016), *Annual Report 2015*.

Staatsolie (2015), *Annual Report 2014*.

Staatsolie (2014), *Annual Report 2013*.

Vale (2016), *Annual Report 2015* (20-F).

World Bank (2016), "Commodity Markets Outlook: OPEC in Historical Context", World Bank, October.

YPBF (2016), *Notas a los estados financieros 2015*, Yacimientos Petrolíferos Fiscales Bolivianos.

CAPÍTULO 2

SECCIÓN ESPECIAL

Ingresos fiscales provenientes de recursos naturales no renovables en América Latina y el Caribe

SECCIÓN ESPECIAL
Ingresos fiscales provenientes de recursos naturales no renovables en América Latina y el Caribe

Principales conclusiones

Los ingresos fiscales provenientes de recursos naturales no renovables cayeron fuertemente en 2015

- La caída en los precios internacionales del petróleo, que empezó en 2014, intensificó en 2015 resultando en un desplome en los ingresos fiscales relacionados con la explotación y la comercialización de hidrocarburos en la región. Los mismos se redujeron de 6.8% del PIB en 2014 a 4.4% del PIB en 2015 en el promedio de los diez países abarcados, lo cual representa el valor más bajo desde el comienzo de la serie en 2000.
- Los ingresos fiscales provenientes de la minería continuaron su descenso en 2015, cayendo de 0.52% del PIB en 2014 a 0.37% del PIB en 2015. Destaca la reducción en los ingresos tributarios asociados con el sector, principalmente en los pagos del impuesto sobre la renta, debido a la menor rentabilidad de la actividad minera.

A pesar de una mejora en los precios de materia primas, se estima que los ingresos provenientes de recursos naturales no renovables han bajado aún más en 2016

- En 2016 se observa un punto de inflexión en la evolución de los precios internacionales de recursos naturales no renovables. Aunque se estima que ellos todavía mostrarían una caída por el año, esto refleja mayormente su comportamiento en los primeros meses del año. A partir del segundo semestre se nota un repunte en los precios para la mayoría de estos productos. No obstante, este cambio de tendencia ofrece poco alivio a las cuentas fiscales para 2016, especialmente dada la grave situación financiera de los principales productores de la región.
- En este contexto se estima que los ingresos provenientes de los hidrocarburos han bajado a 2.6% del PIB en 2016. Destacan las caídas en Colombia (2.5% del PIB a 0.7% del PIB) – agravado por la pérdida declarada de Ecopetrol – y Trinidad y Tobago (de 7.7% del PIB a 2.0% del PIB) – donde el pago del impuesto sobre la renta de empresas petroleras (que representan la mayoría de los ingresos petroleros en este país) ha caído 90%.
- Por su parte, los ingresos mineros han mantenido su tendencia a la baja, llegando a un promedio de 0.3% del PIB. Destaca el caso de Chile donde estos ingresos cayeron fuertemente, de 1.3% del PIB en 2015 a 0.4% del PIB en 2016, debido al desplome en la recaudación del impuesto sobre la renta de la minería privada.

Los ingresos fiscales provenientes de recursos naturales no renovables analizados en esta Sección Especial se refieren a ingresos tributarios (impuesto sobre la renta, impuestos específicos del sector y ciertos impuestos indirectos) e ingresos no tributarios (regalías y dividendos) derivados de la producción y comercialización de hidrocarburos y de la minería. No incluyen retenciones impositivas ni pagos realizados por empresas en nombre de sus empleados o inversionistas, y tampoco incluyen pagos de impuestos sobre el consumo (específicamente el impuesto sobre el valor agregado, cuando corresponda).

2.1. Los ingresos fiscales provenientes de recursos naturales no renovables cayeron fuertemente en 2015

Se desplomaron los ingresos fiscales provenientes de los hidrocarburos

La evolución de los ingresos fiscales provenientes de la explotación y la comercialización de hidrocarburos en América Latina y el Caribe obedeció la caída continua de los precios referenciales para el petróleo crudo – principalmente los precios spot de West Texas Intermediate (WTI) y de Brent. Se estima que el precio promedio del petróleo crudo bajó 47.2% durante el año 2015, que a su vez superó la reducción observada durante la crisis económica y financiera de 2008-09 (-36.3%) (véase el grafico 2.1). Esto se debe mayormente por el desacoplamiento entre la demanda y la oferta de petróleo crudo en el mercado internacional.

Gráfico 2.1. **Precio referencial internacional del petróleo crudo, 2000-15**

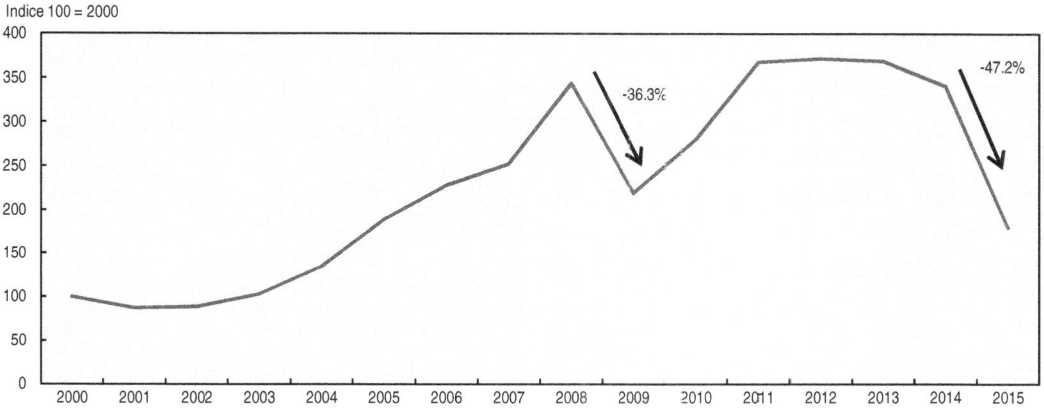

Nota: El precio corresponde al promedio simple del Brent, el West Texas Intermediate (WTI) y el Dubai.
Fuente: Comisión Económica para América Latina y el Caribe (CEPAL), sobre la base de cifras de CEPALstat.

StatLink http://dx.doi.org/10.1787/888933462730

Según estimaciones de la Agencia Internacional de la Energía (IEA, por sus siglas en ingles), la producción diaria de petróleo crudo al nivel mundial aumentó 3.0% en 2015, impulsado por alzas importantes en los Estados Unidos, Arabia Saudita, Iraq y Brasil (AIE, 2016). Es importante resaltar que el ascenso de la producción en los Estados Unidos, como resultado de la revolución de la producción de gas natural y petróleo crudo de esquistos bituminosos (shale revolution), ha modificado significativamente la dinámica del mercado internacional últimamente. Esto se ve en las acciones de los países miembros de la Organización de los Países Exportadores de Petróleo (OPEP), que mantuvieron sus niveles de producción en 2015, a pesar de la caída en el precio, en un intento de defender su cuota de mercado.

Por su parte, el crecimiento en la demanda se mantuvo moderado, aunque se aceleró en 2015 (1.9%) en comparación con 2014 (1.0%) (AIE, 2016). Destaca el alza en el consumo de petróleo crudo entre los países miembros de la OCDE (1.2%), después de registrar una caída de 0.6% el año anterior. Por su parte, se observa una desaceleración de la demanda entre los países no miembros de la OCDE (2.7% en 2015 comparado con 3.3% en 2014) aunque con tendencias opuestas entre regiones: con un alza de 5.2% para los países asiáticos, y reducciones en la Comunidad de Estados Independientes (-1.3%) y en América Latina (-1.0%).

La divergencia entre las tasas de crecimiento de la oferta y de la demanda socavó el precio internacional y resultó en un aumento substancial en las existencias de petróleo crudo. Esto fue especialmente notable entre los países de la OCDE, donde el aumento de estas existencias alcanzó 287 millones de barriles (de 4.285 millones a 4.572 millones) entre finales de 2014 y finales de 2015 (AIE, 2016). Cabe mencionar que más de la mitad de este aumento (55%) ocurrió en los Estados Unidos, donde las existencias incrementaron en 158 millones de barriles para llegar a 1.987 millones de barriles (incluyendo la reserva estratégica de petróleo crudo del gobierno federal).

Las tendencias del mercado internacional se tradujeron en una reducción importante en los ingresos públicos percibidos por los países de la región. Como se aprecia en el cuadro 2.1, los ingresos fiscales provenientes de la explotación y la comercialización de hidrocarburos se desplomaron en 2015, cayendo 31.6% en términos de dólares corrientes. Cabe mencionar que si consideran solamente los ingresos fiscales provenientes de la explotación de los hidrocarburos la reducción es de 44.4% en dólares para la región en su conjunto (en comparación con una caída de 47.2% en el precio internacional de petróleo crudo). Sin embargo, resulta importante subrayar que a nivel de los países la variación en los ingresos fiscales provenientes de hidrocarburos en términos de moneda nacional fue suavizada por una depreciación del tipo de cambio. Destacan los casos de la Argentina, Brasil, Colombia y México donde se registraron depreciaciones de más de 10% frente al dólar.

Cuadro 2.1. **Variación inter-anual de los ingresos fiscales provenientes de hidrocarburos y la producción de hidrocarburos, 2014-15**

País	Ingresos fiscales de hidrocarburos		Producción de hidrocarburos	
	% de variación en moneda nacional	% de variación en USD	% de variación en la producción de petróleo crudo (Miles barriles por día)	% de variación en la producción de gas natural comercializado (Mil millones de metros cúbicos)
Argentina	20.1	8.7	0.0	2.7
Bolivia	-20.9	-20.9	n.a.	7.1
Brasil	-8.7	-33.9	8.1	13.5
Colombia	-38.5	-57.1	1.5	1.0
Ecuador	-41.8	-41.8	-2.4	-14.0
México	-12.0	-25.2	-6.7	-9.0
Perú	-38.8	-43.9	-16.3	3.6
Surinam	-90.7	-91.0	1.0	n.a.
Trinidad y Tobago	-36.4	-35.9	-3.1	-2.9
Venezuela	24.5	-62.3	-1.1	18.9
América latina y el Caribe	**n.a.**	**-31.6**	**-0.3**	**1.9**

Fuente: Comisión Económica para América Latina y el Caribe (CEPAL), sobre la base de cifras de Organización de Países Exportadores de Petróleo (OPEP, 2016) y Staatsolie (2014, 2015, 2016).

StatLink http://dx.doi.org/10.1787/888933462838

Aunque el efecto de la caída en el precio del petróleo crudo fue el principal factor detrás de la evolución en los ingresos provenientes de hidrocarburos en la región, también se vieron efectuados por la variación en la producción. Aunque cifras de la OPEP (2016) muestran que la producción de petróleo crudo cayó levemente en América Latina y el Caribe (-0.3%), se notan importantes diferencias en tendencias entre países. Por ejemplo, entre los grandes productores destacan los aumentos en Brasil (8.1%) y Colombia (1.5%) que fueron contrarrestados por reducciones en México (-6.7%) y Venezuela (República Bolivariana de) (-1.1%) (véase el cuadro 2.1). En cambio, la producción de gas natural en la región registró un aumento (1.9%), después de dos años consecutivos con tasas de crecimiento cercanas a cero.

Se observa una alta heterogeneidad en resultados a nivel de los países cuando se analiza estos ingresos relativos al producto, reflejando el peso relativo de la actividad en cada país y los diferentes marcos fiscales empleados para apropiar la renta que derivada de los hidrocarburos, así como las tendencias cambiarias y de producción. Como se aprecia en el cuadro 2.2, en el promedio de los diez países abarcados los ingresos fiscales provenientes de los hidrocarburos se redujeron de 6.8% del PIB a 4.4% del PIB en 2015. Esto representa el valor más bajo desde el comienzo de la serie en 2000. Se observan reducciones importantes tanto en los ingresos tributarios (-0.7 puntos porcentuales) como los ingresos no tributarios (-1.7 puntos porcentuales), aunque en el primer caso la caída en el pago del impuesto sobre la renta de las actividades de explotación fue suavizada en general por el comportamiento positivo de la recaudación de los impuestos selectivos sobre el consumo de hidrocarburos.

Cuadro 2.2. **Ingresos públicos provenientes de los hidrocarburos, por país y tipo de ingreso, 2014-15**

En porcentajes del PIB

País	Total			Ingresos tributarios			Ingresos no tributarios		
	2014 (r)	2015 (p)	Δ	2014 (r)	2015 (p)	Δ	2014 (r)	2015 (p)	Δ
Argentina	1.8	1.7	-0.1	1.3	1.3	-0.1	0.4	0.4	0.0
Bolivia	13.1	10.4	-2.7	2.3	2.4	0.1	10.8	7.9	-2.9
Brasil	1.5	1.3	-0.2	0.9	0.9	0.0	0.7	0.4	-0.2
Colombia	4.3	2.5	-1.8	1.8	1.3	-0.4	2.5	1.1	-1.4
Ecuador	10.7	6.3	-4.3	0.0	0.0	0.0	10.7	6.3	-4.3
México	7.0	5.9	-1.2	0.0	1.3	1.3	7.1	4.6	-2.5
Perú	1.6	0.9	-0.7	0.8	0.5	-0.2	0.8	0.4	-0.4
Surinam	5.2	0.5	-4.8	2.3	0.3	-2.1	2.9	0.2	-2.7
Trinidad y Tobago	12.3	7.7	-4.7	10.9	6.7	-4.2	1.4	0.9	-0.5
Venezuela	10.7	6.7	-4.0	2.5	0.8	-1.7	8.2	6.0	-2.3
Promedio simple	**6.8**	**4.4**	**-2.4**	**2.3**	**1.5**	**-0.7**	**4.6**	**2.8**	**-1.7**

Notas: (r) revisados; (p) preliminares.

Los ingresos tributarios se refieren a impuestos de sociedades (Argentina, Bolivia, Brasil (Petrobras), Colombia, Perú, Suriname (Staatsolie), Trinidad y Tobago y Venezuela, derechos de exportación (Argentina), impuestos indirectos sobre la producción de hidrocarburos (Bolivia y México) e impuestos indirectos sobre los productos de hidrocarburos (Argentina, Bolivia, Brasil, Colombia, México y Perú). Los ingresos no tributarios se refieren principalmente a dividendos y gravámenes sobre la producción (Argentina: regalías nacionales y subnacionales; Bolivia: regalías y transferencias especiales de Yacimientos Petrolíferos Fiscales Bolivianos (YPFB); Brasil: regalías, participación especial del Estado, bonos de suscripción, tasas de ocupación y retención, y dividendos de Petrobras; Colombia: regalías y dividendos de EcoPetrol; Ecuador: ingresos del sector público no financiero derivados de las ventas de exportación del petróleo; México: ingresos de Petróleos Mexicanos (PEMEX); Perú: regalías; Suriname: dividendos de Staatsolie; Trinidad y Tobago: regalías, y Venezuela: regalías, dividendos de Petróleos de Venezuela, S.A. (PDVSA) e ingresos no tributarios extraordinarios derivados del petróleo.) Las cifras pueden no sumar exactamente debido al redondeo.

Fuente: Comisión Económica para América Latina y el Caribe (CEPAL).

StatLink http://dx.doi.org/10.1787/888933462840

En la Argentina los ingresos provenientes de los hidrocarburos se mantuvieron relativamente estables en 2015, con una reducción de 0.1 puntos porcentuales del PIB a 1.7% del PIB. Los ingresos tributarios bajaron moderadamente debido a la caída pronunciada en la recaudación de los derechos de exportación de productos de hidrocarburos como resultado de la reducción de tasas y la introducción de una nueva escala móvil para determinados productos que el gobierno argentino decretó a fines de 2014. Esto fue compensado en gran medida por el fuerte aumento en la recaudación del impuesto selectivo sobre combustibles líquidos y gas por el alza en los precios en términos nominales; lo que también contribuyó al aumento en estos ingresos expresados en dólares.

En el Estado Plurinacional de Bolivia, de aquí en adelante Bolivia, la caída en los ingresos por hidrocarburos (de 13.1% del PIB a 10.4% del PIB) se debe principalmente una caída en los ingresos no tributarios (de 10.8% del PIB a 7.9% del PIB). En particular, la recaudación del impuesto directo a los hidrocarburos (IDH) y las regalías y participaciones del Estado en la producción cayeron alrededor 30%. Aunque la producción aumentó, se explica este menor descenso relativo a la evolución del precio del petróleo crudo por la manera en que se fija el precio de gas natural en los contratos de largo-plazo con Argentina y Brasil. En general estos contratos fijan el precio de gas natural relativo a los precios de una canasta de productos de hidrocarburos por un periodo de tres meses. Este mecanismo brinda un respiro cuando los precios de hidrocarburos están cayendo, aunque lo mismo se aplica cuando los precios aumentan. Resulta interesante destacar la transferencia de Bs676 millones (0.3% del PIB) efectuada por Yacimientos Petrolíferos Fiscales Bolivianos (YPFB) – una empresa estatal – al fisco en septiembre 2015, dentro del marco de la ley 550 de julio de 2014 (YPBF, 2016). Dicha ley autorizó que las empresas públicas transfirieran recursos al Tesoro General de la Nación para financiar proyectos de inversión o programas de interés social.

Una reducción en los ingresos no tributarios – principalmente de regalías y de la participación especial del Estado en la producción – incidió en la disminución de estos ingresos en Brasil, los cuales cayeron de 1.5% del PIB a 1.3% del PIB en el año. Además, cabe mencionar que en 2015 el gobierno federal no percibió un dividendo de Petrobras, reflejando la difícil situación financiera de esta empresa. Por su parte los ingresos tributarios se mantuvieron estables en 0.9% del PIB, apoyado por la evolución favorable de la recaudación de los impuestos sobre el consumo de combustibles así como por la reintroducción de la Cide Combustíveis – un impuesto federal sobre gasolina y diesel – cuya recaudación en 2014 fue casi nula.

En Colombia la tendencia a la baja de los ingresos petroleros (de 4.3% del PIB a 2.5% del PIB) se ha seguido del deterioro de la situación financiera de EcoPetrol, el principal productor en el país. Últimamente sus utilidades se han reducido cada año, con un impacto significativo sobre su aporte al fisco. En particular, los pagos de dividendos al gobierno – que figuran prominentemente en los ingresos no tributarios – se han reducido fuertemente de de 1.4% del PIB en 2014 a 0.5% del PIB en 2015. Análogamente la recaudación del impuesto sobre la renta de empresas en el sector cayó 0.4 puntos del PIB, de 1.4% del PIB a 0.9% del PIB. Resulta importante destacar que en 2015 EcoPetrol declaró una perdida financiera, aunque esto afectará más los ingresos que el gobierno percibirá en 2016 (Ecopetrol, 2016).

La caída en los ingresos provenientes de los hidrocarburos en el Ecuador – de 10.7% del PIB a 6.3% del PIB – se debe al desplome del precio de petróleo crudo así como la reducción de la producción (-2.4% en 2015). Resulta importante resaltar que la mayoría de los ingresos petroleros corresponden a los ingresos obtenidos por la venta al exterior del petróleo crudo por parte de EP Petroecuador – una empresa estatal – y de contratistas privadas. Aunque estas contratistas privadas deben pagar el impuesto sobre la renta, su recaudo es insignificante.

En México la reducción en los ingresos petroleros (de 7.0% del PIB a 5.9% del PIB) fue suavizada por un alza de la recaudación del impuesto especial sobre producción y servicios (IEPS) de gasolina y diesel que registró un valor positivo (es decir se dejó de funcionar como un subsidio), pasando de -0.1% del PIB en 2014 a 1.2% del PIB en 2015. Los ingresos tributarios también fueron apoyados por la introducción de dos nuevas fuentes que tuvieron su génesis con la reforma energética aprobada en a fines de 2013: el impuesto por la actividad de exploración y extracción de hidrocarburos así como el pago del impuesto sobre la renta de contratistas y asignatarios. Por otro lado, los ingresos no tributarios – compuestos por los ingresos propios de PEMEX y las transferencias del Fondo Mexicano del Petróleo para la Estabilización y el Desarrollo al gobierno federal – redujeron en línea con el precio de petróleo crudo y, en menor medida, la baja en el volumen producido.

En el Perú la baja en la producción de hidrocarburos (de 16% para petróleo crudo y de 3% para gas natural) incidió en la caída de 0.7 puntos del producto (de 1.6% del PIB a 0.9% del PIB) en los ingresos públicos asociados con los hidrocarburos. Destaca la caída en la recaudación del impuesto sobre la renta del sector (de 0.4% del PIB a 0.2% del PIB), la cual refleja la menor rentabilidad de la actividad así como la reducción de la tasa del mismo impuesto – de 30% a 28% – que el gobierno aprobó a fines de 2014 como parte de un paquete de medidas para impulsar la economía nacional.

Surinam experimentó la reducción más pronunciada en los ingresos provenientes de hidrocarburos en la región como resultado del desplome de los beneficios de la empresa petrolera estatal Staatsoile (Staatsoile, 2016). El aporte de la misma empresa al presupuesto nacional cayó 91% en términos de dólares, o 4.8 puntos del PIB. Se observa una reducción parecida entre los ingresos tributarios – compuestos por el pago del impuesto sobre la renta – y los ingresos no tributarios – derivados de los dividendos remitidos al gobierno.

En Trinidad y Tobago la caída de los ingresos provenientes de hidrocarburos (de 12.3% del PIB a 7.7% del PIB) se explica principalmente por la fuerte reducción en los pagos por el impuesto sobre la renta de empresas operando en el sector (-38%). Por su parte, los ingresos no tributarios – principalmente compuestos por el pago de regalías – disminuyeron en línea con la evolución del precio de petróleo crudo y gas natural así como una caída en la producción de ambos productos durante el año.

Se estima que los ingresos petroleros en la República Bolivariana de Venezuela, de aquí en adelante Venezuela, registraron una caída importante en 2015 (de 10.7% del PIB a 6.7% del PIB). Los ingresos tributarios, compuestos principalmente por los pagos del impuesto sobre la renta de PDVSA, cayeron de 2.5% del PIB a 0.8% del PIB, reflejando la bajada en los beneficios de dicha empresa así como el alto base de comparación. Las utilidades de PDVSA en 2014 fueron excepcionalmente elevadas debido a la venta de una participación en una filial de la empresa al Banco Central (PDVSA, 2016). Por otro lado, los ingresos no tributarios cayeron fuertemente (de 8.2% del PIB a 6.0% del PIB) debido a la reducción en el pago de regalías así como en los ingresos extraordinarios no tributarios petroleros, aunque en el segundo caso no se cuenta con cifras actualizadas.[1]

El descenso de los ingresos fiscales provenientes de la minería siguió en 2015

Los ingresos fiscales provenientes de la minería en la región siguieron su tendencia a la baja en 2015 que empezó en 2012. Como en el caso de los hidrocarburos, la evolución de los precios del mercado para los minerales y metales fue el factor principal detrás de las tendencias observadas en la región. La CEPAL estima que el precio ponderado de la cesta de minerales y metales de la región cayó 23% en 2015. Cabe resaltar que esto representa una reducción de 45.1% con respecto a su valor máximo alcanzado en 2011. Se observa una variedad de tendencias entre los diferentes productos al nivel mundial, con caídas menores para plomo (-8%), oro (-8%) y cinc (-11%), que contrastan con el desplome en el precio de mineral de hierro (-42%) (véase el gráfico 2.2).

Gráfico 2.2. **Variación inter-anual en los precios de minerales y metales**

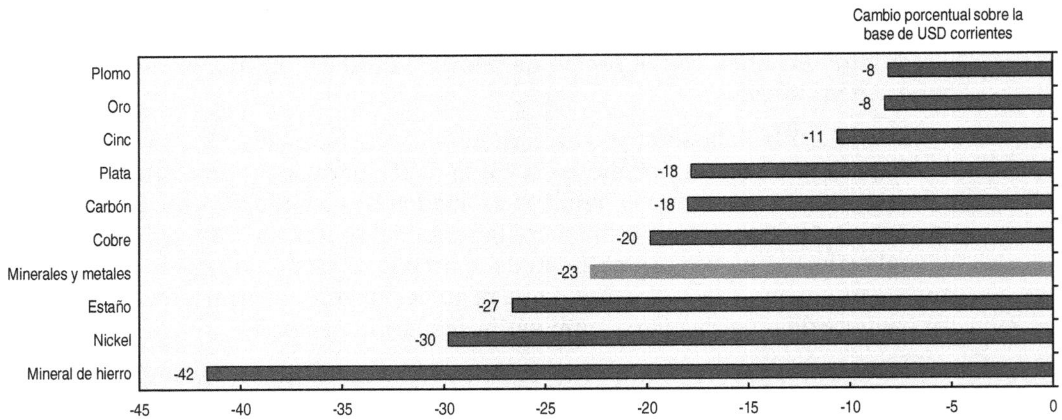

Fuente: Comisión Económica para América Latina y el Caribe (CEPAL), sobre la base de cifras de CEPALstat.

StatLink http://dx.doi.org/10.1787/888933462749

Como se reveló en la sección especial del año pasado, la variación en los precios de minerales y metales se ha correlacionado con el crecimiento económico en Asia del Este (OCDE/CEPAL/CIAT/BID, 2016). El alto crecimiento de dos dígitos en China en el periodo antes de la crisis económica y financiera mundial de 2008-09, así como el alza en inversión en el periodo anterior apoyado por estímulos fiscales y monetarios sin precedentes, sostuvo los precios de materias primas en niveles históricos. Como resultado se estima que China abarca ahora la mitad de la demanda global para los metales básicos (FMI, 2015). Sin embargo, con la desaceleración de la economía de China – ahora con tasas de crecimiento de un digito y cuya desaceleración continua – se ha debilitado la demanda y se han reducido los precios de las materias primas.

A medida que bajan los precios de materias primas, se nota un deterioro también en la situación financiera de las principales empresas que operan en el sector. Según PriceWaterhouseCooper (2016) las 40 empresas más grandes del sector al nivel mundial, en su conjunto, registraron pérdidas, por la primera vez en una década, de USD 105 000 millones en 2015 (véase el gráfico 2.3). Aunque el desplome en ingresos perjudicó la rentabilidad de las empresas más grandes, resulta importante subrayar el papel del alza en los cargos por deterioro de activos como resultado de la caída en los precios internacionales en este resultado. No se extraña que el gasto financiero para el pago del impuesto sobre la renta de estas empresas cayera 81.8%, de USD 22 000 millones en 2014 a USD 4 000 millones en 2015.

Gráfico 2.3. **Utilidades netas y gasto por el impuesto sobre la renta de las 40 principales empresas mineras en el mundo, 2006-15**

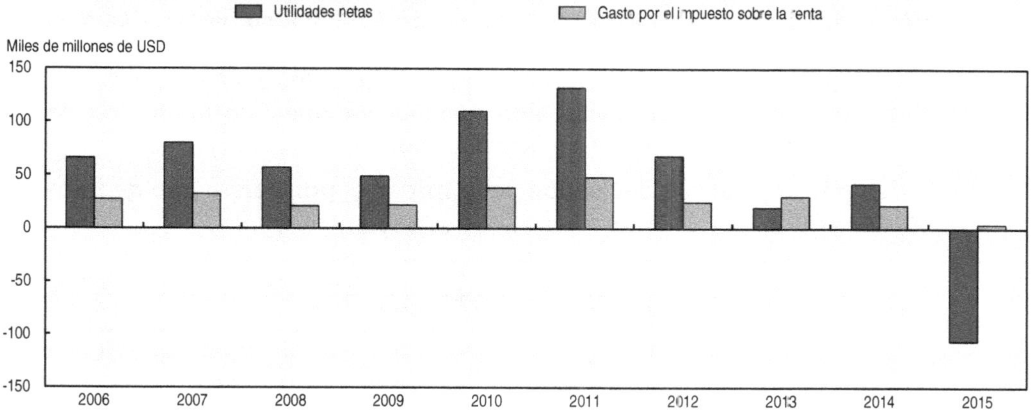

Fuente: Comisión Económica para América Latina y el Caribe (CEPAL), sobre la base de cifras de PriceWaterhouseCoopers (2016).

StatLink http://dx.doi.org/10.1787/888933462750

Las tendencias de los precios internacionales de minerales y metales así como la situación financiera de las grandes empresas que dominan el sector mundialmente – y en la región a través de sus filiales – se ven en la evolución de los ingresos fiscales provenientes de la minería para el conjunto de los diez países considerados, los cuales cayeron 33% expresados en dólares corrientes (véase el cuadro 2.3). Cabe mencionar que la heterogeneidad de variaciones observadas a nivel de los países refleja tanto las diferentes canastas de producción y de exportación de cada país así como la rentabilidad relativa entre empresas mineras asociado con estos productos. También no se puede descartar el impacto de la deprecación de algunas monedas nacionales, los cuales sirvieron de suavizar en parte las caídas registradas en términos de dólares.

Cuadro 2.3. **Variación inter-anual de los ingresos fiscales provenientes de la minería, 2014-15**

En porcentajes

País	Ingresos fiscales provenientes de la minería	
	% de variación en moneda nacional	% de variación en USD
Argentina	-16.3	-24.3
Bolivia	-24.7	-24.7
Brasil	-30.9	-50.0
Chile	-25.9	-34.6
Colombia	-7.1	-30.6
Jamaica	353.9	334.4
México	-4.6	-18.9
Perú	-39.2	-44.3
República Dominicana	-23.9	-26.1
Surinam	-48.0	-49.8
Latin America and the Caribbean	**n.a.**	**-33.2**

Fuente: Comisión Económica para América Latina y el Caribe (CEPAL).

StatLink http://dx.doi.org/10.1787/888933462853

Como el cuadro 2.4 ilustra, los ingresos fiscales provenientes de la minería, relativos al producto, se redujeron de 0.52% del PIB en 2014 a 0.36% del PIB en 2015. Este descenso se explica principalmente por la caída en los ingresos tributarios, compuestos principalmente por el pago de impuestos que gravan las utilidades de empresas mineras, los cuales se redujeron de 0.33% del PIB a 0.22% del PIB. Esto representa una reducción significativa del promedio de 1.0% del PIB en 2011. Por su parte, la baja en los ingresos no tributarios – que corresponden principalmente a los pagos de regalías que gravan el valor comercial de la producción – fue menor (de 0.19% del PIB a 0.14% del PIB), en línea con la evolución de los precios referenciales; aunque esto fue suavizado en parte en algunos países por aumentos en la producción.

Cuadro 2.4. **Ingresos públicos derivados de la minería, por país y tipo de ingreso, 2014-15**

En porcentajes del PIB

País	Total			Ingresos tributarios			Ingresos no tributarios		
	2014 (r)	2015 (p)	Δ	2014 (r)	2015 (p)	Δ	2014 (r)	2015 (p)	Δ
Argentina	0.08	0.05	-0.03	0.08	0.05	-0.03	0.00	0.00	0.00
Bolivia	0.66	0.50	-0.16	0.09	0.07	-0.03	0.57	0.43	-0.14
Brasil	0.08	0.05	-0.03	0.04	0.02	-0.02	0.04	0.03	0.00
Chile	1.83	1.27	-0.56	1.57	1.27	-0.30	0.26	0.00	-0.26
Colombia	0.30	0.26	-0.04	0.09	0.05	-0.04	0.21	0.21	0.00
Jamaica	0.04	0.17	0.13	0.00	0.00	0.00	0.04	0.17	0.13
México	0.21	0.19	-0.02	0.20	0.16	-0.03	0.01	0.03	0.01
Perú	0.67	0.38	-0.28	0.46	0.24	-0.22	0.21	0.15	-0.06
República Dominicana	0.50	0.35	-0.15	0.42	0.29	-0.13	0.07	0.06	-0.01
Surinam	0.85	0.43	-0.42	0.38	0.06	-0.32	0.48	0.37	-0.10
Promedio simple	**0.52**	**0.37**	**-0.16**	**0.52**	**0.37**	**-0.16**	**0.19**	**0.14**	**-0.04**

Notas:(r) revisados; (p) preliminares.
Los ingresos tributarios se refieren a impuestos de sociedades (Argentina, Bolivia, Brasil (Vale), Chile, Colombia, México, Jamaica, Perú, República Dominicana y Surinam (IAMGOLD)), derechos de exportación (Argentina; Chile: Impuesto Ley N°13.196) y otros impuestos específicos del sector (Chile: impuesto específico a la minería; Perú: impuesto especial a la minería (IEM); República Dominicana: impuesto mínimo anual minero e impuesto a los beneficios netos de la minería).
Los ingresos no tributarios se refieren principalmente a gravámenes sobre la producción (Bolivia: regalías; Brasil: Compensación Financiera por la Exploración de Recursos Minerales (CFEM), Tasa Anual por Hectárea (TAH) y tasa de fiscalización de recursos minerales (TFRM) en Minas Gerais; Chile: dividendos de CODELCO; Colombia: regalías; República Dominicana: neto regalía de retorno de fundición; Jamaica: gravamen sobre la bauxita y regalías sobre la bauxita; México: derechos de minería; Perú: regalías y Gravamen Especial a la Minería (GEM); Surinam: regalías (IAMGOLD)). Las cifras pueden no sumar exactamente debido al redondeo.
Fuente: Comisión Económica para América Latina y el Caribe (CEPAL).

StatLink http://dx.doi.org/10.1787/888933462864

En la Argentina la reducción en estos ingresos (de 0.08% del PIB a 0.05% del PIB) se debe a la caída en la recaudación de los derechos de exportación por productos mineros (-42.1%), reflejando una reducción de 29.7% en el volumen exportado de minerales metalíferos, escorias y cenizas así como la baja de 19.2% en el precio unitario de ellos. El descenso en los ingresos por minería en el Estado Plurinacional de Bolivia (de 0.66% del PIB a 0.50% del PIB) se explica por una reducción en los ingresos por regalías mineras (-24.2%), las cuales han representado más de 80% del total en los últimos dos años.

El desplome del precio del mineral de hierro (-42%) incidió fuertemente en la reducción de los ingresos mineros en Brasil (de 0.08% del PIB a 0.05% del PIB). En particular, se registró una baja importante en el pago del impuesto sobre la renta de Vale S.A., que cayó 49.2% en moneda nacional, lo que rebajó los ingresos tributarios. En Chile la caída en los ingresos mineros (de 1.83% del PIB a 1.27% del PIB) se explica mayormente por la reducción en los traspasos de Codelco, el productor estatal, al fisco como resultado de la perdida que dicha empresa declaró para el año (CODELCO, 2016). Esto repercutió tanto en los ingresos tributarios – su pago del impuesto sobre la renta cayó fuertemente – como en los ingresos no tributarios – por el primer año desde 2002 su traspaso de excedente al gobierno central bajó a cero.

En Colombia los ingresos mineros – que corresponden mayormente a la producción de carbón – cayeron ligeramente (de 0.30% del PIB a 0.26% del PIB), producto de un descenso de 39.0% en el pago del impuesto sobre la renta. En cambio, los ingresos no tributarios aumentaron 7.2% – permaneciendo estables relativo al producto en 0.21% del PIB – reflejando un incremento en el pago de regalías. Jamaica fue el único país de la región que registró un aumento en sus ingresos mineros en 2015 (de 0.04% del PIB a 0.17% del PIB). Esto se debe a la reintroducción del gravamen sobre la bauxita (bauxite levy) que se había suprimido en 2014 como medida de apoyo para el sector.

En México los ingresos mineros también cayeron ligeramente (de 0.21% del PIB a 0.19% del PIB) como resultado de una reducción en el pago del impuesto sobre la renta de empresas mineras (-12.8%). Esto fue compensado en parte por un alza en la recaudación de los derechos mineros que más que duplicó su nivel de 2014. En el Perú los ingresos tributarios provenientes del pago del impuesto sobre la renta se redujeron por casi la mitad (-46.2%), lo que explica fundamentalmente la reducción de los ingresos mineros (de 0.67% del PIB a 0.38% del PIB). Cabe mencionar que este resultado refleja también el hecho de que el gobierno peruano aprobó a finales de 2014 una reducción en la tasa del impuesto sobre la renta de empresas (de 30% a 28% para los años 2015 y 2016).

En la República Dominicana la fuerte reducción en el pago del impuesto sobre la renta (-39.2%) se vio suavizado por aumentos en la recaudación del impuesto mínimo anual minero (64.1%) – que aumenta cuando el pago del impuesto sobre la renta baja – y de la participación sobre utilidades netas (el impuesto sobre utilidades mineras) (13.9%). Cabe mencionar que los últimos dos instrumentos buscan a asegurar una participación mínima del Estado en la renta minera.

La caída en los ingresos mineros en Surinam (de 0.85% del PIB a 0.43% del PIB) se debe a la reducción en el pago del impuesto sobre la renta de IAMGOLD, lo que había disparado en 2014. Los ingresos no tributarios – los pagos de regalías de la misma empresa – bajaron 19.8% en moneda nacional, producto de la reducción en el precio de oro y un recorte en la producción (-11.7%) (IAMGOLD, 2016).

2.2. A pesar de una mejora en los precios de materia primas, se estima que los ingresos provenientes de recursos naturales no renovables han bajado aún más en 2016

Durante 2016 se ha observado una cierta reducción en los desequilibrios entre la oferta y la demanda de materias primas en el mercado internacional. La sobreoferta en el mercado de petróleo crudo se ha reducido parcialmente, producto de un aumento en la demanda (de 1.1% para el promedio de los primeros tres trimestre de 2016 sobre el valor de 2015) y una considerable moderación en el crecimiento de la oferta (de 0.0% sobre el mismo periodo) (AIE, 2016). En particular, se registró una reducción de la producción en los Estados Unidos, producto de la caída del precio. También se prevé que disminuya la oferta de los países miembros de la OPEP, los cuales adoptaron el primer recorte en ocho años en sus cuotas de producción en noviembre 2016.

En el caso de los minerales y metales se observan tendencias parecidas, con un fortalecimiento de la demanda y una restricción en la oferta. En China, los esfuerzos del gobierno para apoyar los sectores de infraestructura y construcción ha impulsado la demanda global para estos productos en 2016 (BM, 2016). Al mismo tiempo, la oferta de varios productos mineros se ha reducido producto de recortes de producción y por el cierre de minas con altos costos. Sin embargo, esto no ha sido uniforme sobre todos los productos. Por ejemplo, se observan reducciones importantes en el caso de cinc, pero la oferta de cobre sigue creciendo.

Como producto de las tendencias observadas en los mercados internacionales, el ritmo del desplome en los precios internacional de recursos naturales no renovables se atenuó en 2016 (véase el cuadro 2.5). Aunque las estimaciones del Fondo Monetario Internacional (FMI) apuntan a reducciones adicionales de los precios de petróleo crudo (-15%) y de la cesta de metales (-8%), se puede apreciar la existencia de un punto de inflexión a mitad del año en las tendencias registradas. Esto es especialmente obvio entre los productos mineros, en particular en los casos de mineral de hierro, estaño, cinc y carbón. No obstante, se espera también un repunte del precio de petróleo crudo en el cuarto trimestre del año.

Cuadro 2.5. **Variación inter-anual de los precios internacionales de materias primas seleccionadas, 2015-16**

En porcentajes

Producto	2015	2016				
	Año	T1	T2	T3	T4	Año
Metales	-23	n.a.	n.a.	n.a.	n.a.	-8
Cobre	-20	-20	-22	-8	-2	-14
Mineral de hierro	-43	-24	-5	6	20	-2
Estaño	-27	-16	8	19	22	7
Cinc	-11	-19	-13	22	42	5
Plomo	-15	-4	-12	8	13	1
Petróleo crudo	-47	-37	-26	-6	15	-15
Carbón	**-19**	**-17**	**-12**	**15**	**29**	**3**

Fuente: Comisión Económica para América Latina y el Caribe (CEPAL), sobre la base de FMI (2016).

StatLink http://dx.doi.org/10.1787/888933462879

Sin embargo, el repunte en los precios del mercado en el segundo semestre de 2016 ofrece poco alivio para los ingresos fiscales provenientes de recursos naturales no renovables. Esto se debe en parte a la grave situación financiera de las principales empresas que operan en el sector extractivo en la región. Como el gráfico 2.4 ilustra, las utilidades netas registradas en los últimos años han tendido a la baja con un efecto negativo sobre los ingresos tributarios – en términos de los pagos del impuesto sobre la renta y por otros instrumentos que gravan las utilidades operativas resultantes de la producción – y los ingresos no tributarios – como dividendos. Resulta importante destacar el número creciente de empresas que han declarado perdidas últimamente. Por ejemplo, entre los productores de hidrocarburos: Petrobras (Brasil), EcoPetrol (Colombia) y Petrotrin (Trinidad y Tobago). Esto se ve también en el ámbito de los mineros, como se mencionó anteriormente Codelco (Chile) declaró una perdida en 2015.

En este contexto la CEPAL estima que los ingresos fiscales provenientes de recursos naturales no renovables han bajado nuevamente en 2016. En el caso de los ingresos asociados con la producción y la comercialización de hidrocarburos, se espera que estos se hayan reducido de 4.4% del PIB en 2015 a 2.6% del PIB en 2016, el nivel más bajo desde el comienzo de la serie en 2000 (véase el gráfico 2.5). Destacan las reducciones estimadas en los casos de Bolivia (de 10.4% del PIB a 6.8% del PIB en 2016), Colombia (2.5% del PIB a 0.7% del PIB) y Trinidad y Tobago (de 7.7% del PIB a 2.0% del PIB). En este último país resulta importante señalar que el gobierno ha estimado que el pago del impuesto sobre la renta de empresas petroleras (que representan la mayoría de los ingresos petroleros) han caído 90% en 2016. En cambio, se prevé reducciones menores en México (de 5.9% del PIB a 5.6% del PIB) y Brasil (1.3% del PIB a 1.2% del PIB).

Gráfico 2.4. **Evolución de las utilidades netas de productores petroleros seleccionados, 2010-15**

Index 100 = 2005

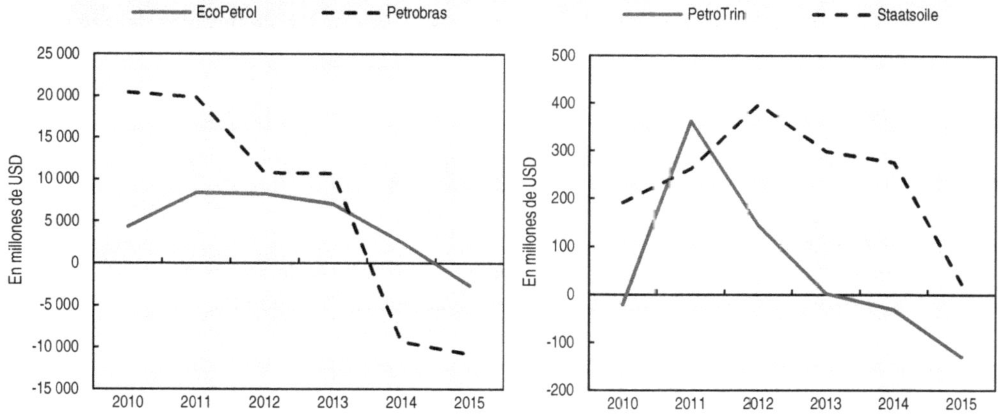

Fuente: Comisión Económica para América Latina y el Caribe (CEPAL), sobre la base de Bloomberg e informes financieros oficiales.

StatLink http://dx.doi.org/10.1787/888933462760

Por su parte, se estima que los ingresos provenientes de la minería también han disminuido en 2016, cayendo en promedio de 0.4% del PIB a 0.3% del PIB. Estos ingresos cayeron significativamente en Chile, de 1.3% del PIB a 0.4% del PIB, debido al desplome en la recaudación proveniente de la minería privada. Cifras preliminares también apuntan a una reducción en los ingresos mineros en el Perú, de 0.4% del PIB a 0.3% del PIB, como resultado de una caída adicional en el pago del impuesto sobre la renta de empresas mineras. A pesar de estas tendencias, los ingresos mineros en algunos países podrían aumentar en 2016, en línea con los alzas en los precios registrados para algunos productos. Por ejemplo, en Brasil se estima que la recaudación de la compensación financiera por la explotación de recursos minerales (CFEM) – una regalía – aumentó 20.1% en 2016, reflejando el aumento en la producción y la mejora del precio de mineral de hierro.

Gráfico 2.5. **Ingresos provenientes de recursos naturales no renovables, 2000-16**

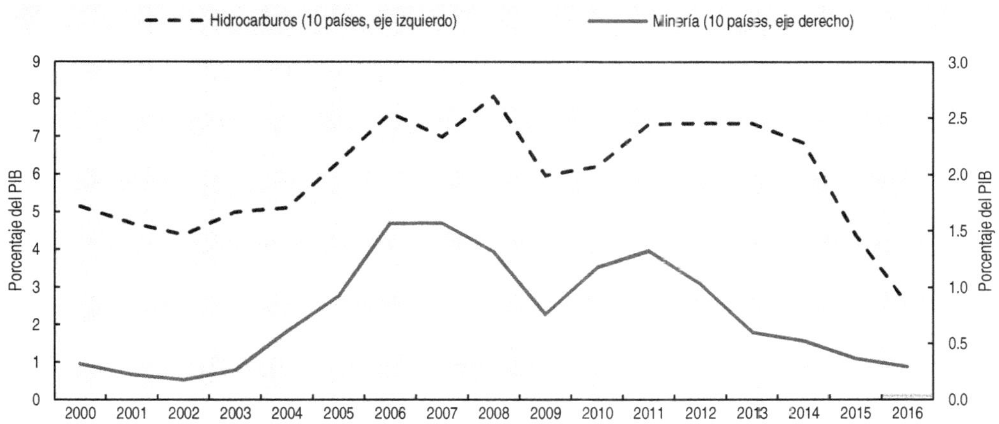

Nota: La minería incluye: Argentina, Bolivia (Estado Plurinacional de), Brasil, Chile, Colombia, Jamaica, México, Perú, República Dominicana y Surinam. Hidrocarburos incluye: Argentina, Bolivia, Brasil, Colombia, Ecuador, México, Perú, Surinam, Trinidad y Tobago y Venezuela. Los valores de 2016 se basan en estimaciones oficiales disponibles de los gobiernos registrados en los informes de presupuesto público de 2017. En los casos en que no hay estimaciones oficiales disponibles, los ingresos anuales por instrumento se estiman usando datos mensuales (para los primeros tres trimestres del año). Cuando no se dispone de datos mensuales, para los pagos de impuesto de sociedades por sector, por lo general los ingresos se estiman aplicando el cambio interanual para el precio del producto básico más representativo para el instrumento de ingreso en cuestión, expresado en moneda nacional a ingresos de 2015.

Fuente: Comisión Económica para América Latina y el Caribe (CEPAL).

StatLink http://dx.doi.org/10.1787/888933462774

Notas

1. La principal fuente de esta información es la exposición de motivos del presupuesto nacional, cuya edición para el año 2017 no se ha difundido.

Referencias

AIE (2016), *Oil Market Report* [en línea], Agencia Internacional de la Energía, https://www.iea.org/oilmarketreport/omrpublic/.

Banco Mundial (2016), "Commodity Markets Outlook: OPEC in Historical Context", Banco Mundial, octubre.

Codelco (2016), *Memoria anual 2015*, Corporación Nacional del Cobre de Chile.

Ecopetrol (2016), *Reporte Integrado de Gestión Sostenible*, 2015, Bogotá.

FMI (2016), "Prices & Forecasts", *IMF Primary Commodity Prices Forecasts* [en línea], Fondo Monetario Internacional, www.imf.org/external/np/res/commod/index.aspx.

FMI (2015), "Special feature: commodity market developments and forecasts, with a focus on metals in the world economy", *World Economic Outlook*, Fondo Monetario Internacional, octubre.

IAMGOLD Corporation (2016), *Annual Report 2015*.

MEM (2016), *Reporte Anual Producción Minera 2015*, Ministerio de Energía y Minas de la República del Perú, Lima.

OCDE-CEPAL-CIAT-BID (2016), *Revenue Statistics in Latin America and the Caribbean 1990-2014*, OECD Publishing, París, http://dx.doi.org/10.1787/rev_lat_car-2016-en-fr.

OPEP (2016), *Annual Statistical Bulletin 2016*, Organización de Países Exportadores de Petróleo.

PriceWaterhouseCoopers (2016), "Mine 2016: slower, lower, weaker... but not defeated".

PDVSA (2016), *Informe de Gestión Anual 2015*, Petróleos de Venezuela, S.A.

Staatsolie (2016), *Annual Report 2015*.

Staatsolie (2015), *Annual Report 2014*.

Staatsolie (2014), *Annual Report 2013*.

Vale (2016), *Annual Report 2015* (20-F).

YPBF (2016), *Notas a los estados financieros 2015*, Yacimientos Petrolíferos Fiscales Bolivianos.

CHAPTER 3

SPECIAL FEATURE

Tax revenue and tax autonomy of sub-national governments in Latin America

CAPÍTULO 3

SECCIÓN ESPECIAL

La tributación y la autonomía fiscal en los gobiernos subnacionales de América Latina

CHAPTER 3

SPECIAL FEATURE

Tax revenue and tax autonomy of sub-national governments in Latin America

SPECIAL FEATURE
Tax revenue and tax autonomy of sub-national governments in Latin America[1]

Introduction

The way in which the provision of public services and goods is funded, and their allocation between levels of government, is a central theme for achieving a sound and stable intergovernmental system and a sustainable decentralisation process. Since sub-national governments often have different instruments to finance their public expenditure responsibilities, the level of funding and the way in which these different instruments are combined will largely determine the outcome of these processes.

In order to analyse one aspect of this problem, this chapter describes and analyses the financing structure of sub-national governments in Latin America and the Caribbean, stressing the evolution and composition of their own resources, specifically the tributary ones. The analysis of a series of cases aims to show the financing options available to these jurisdictions (whether intermediate and/or local), beyond the predominance of central government transfers in this sense.[2] Subsequently, in order to explore the institutional and fiscal capacity determinants of sub-national governments an analysis of the tax autonomy is performed for some selected countries,[3] following the methodology proposed by OECD (1999), Jounard and Kongsrud (2003), Blöchliger and King (2006), Blöchliger and Petzold (2009), Blöchliger and Nettley (2015).

3.1. Sub-national tax revenues performance in the recent decentralisation processes

In recent decades, Latin America has witnessed the consolidation of a gradual and clear trend toward fiscal decentralisation from the central government to its lower levels. It is worth mentioning that this phenomenon has been reflected in both traditional federal countries like Argentina or Brazil, which transferred part of the functions of the federal government to their lower levels, as well as in unitary countries where – according to the case – a significant transfer of functions to local governments took place or new intermediate levels of government were created, which were entrusted with the formulation and execution of important public policies.

This process, in its different periods, occurred mainly through public expenditure (instead of income); however, the situation is quite heterogeneous between countries. In addition, the way sub-national governments finance their (allocated) spending responsibilities is a key concern. This is achieved through three modalities: a) generation of own resources, whether taxes or other non-tax revenues (royalties, municipal taxes, rights, etc.); b) intergovernmental transfers, and c) through debt, or a combination of the three alternatives.

It should be clarified that, in a strict sense that own sub-national revenues are defined as those taxes in which sub-national governments have discretionary powers to determine the tax burden on citizens (Brosio and Jiménez, 2012). However, in some cases, some tax sharing arrangements, i.e. the German one, are considered as true own sub-national revenue too. This power can be exercised by three different instruments: tax administration, tax rate setting and tax base determination.

In the case of Latin America, we have been working with a laxer definition of own resources since we can observe a combination of these three dimensions, without having the necessary information in all cases (Gómez Sabaini and Jiménez, 2011). However, as discussed above, in the last section of this chapter, an analysis of the fiscal autonomy of some countries of the region will be presented, taking into account the capacity of the sub-national governments of Argentina, Brazil, Chile and Mexico to establish taxable bases and rates. This is an incipient development, with the aim of being able to expand it in future publications to other countries of the region.

As can be seen in Figure 3.1, the total fiscal revenues of these governments have grown quite steadily in the last fifteen years, on an unweighted average basis. This is mainly due to the growing importance of transfers from central governments and not so much because of the increase in tax resources at intermediate and local levels. On average, total transfers increased from 2.3% of GDP in 2000 to 4% in 2014, while own resources only increased from 2.6% of GDP to 3.2 % in the same period.

Figure 3.1. **Evolution of the total revenue structure in sub-national governments, Latin America average, 2000-14**

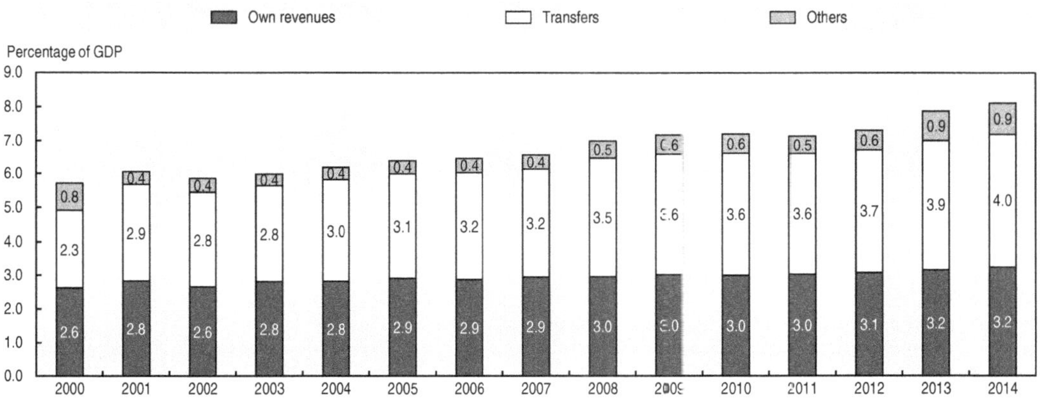

Note: Throughout the paper, it is assumed in the statistical analysis that the concept of sub-national governments will refer to the provinces in the case of Argentina; Prefectures and municipalities in Bolivia; States and municipalities in Brazil; Municipalities in Chile; Departments and municipalities in Colombia; Local governments (cantons) in Costa Rica; Provincial councils and municipalities in Ecuador; States and municipalities in Mexico.

Source: Economic Commission for Latin America and the Caribbean (ECLAC), on the basis of official statistics.

StatLink http://dx.doi.org/10.1787/888933462881

Table 3.1 shows the current financing structure of sub-national governments of the Latin American countries included in the descriptive part of this report. The first salient fact is the differences found in the relative weight of own resources (tax and non-tax) within the total income received by these levels of government. In this regard, it can be seen that the states and municipalities of Brazil earn more than half of their income (75.1%) from their own resources, representing 11.1% in terms of GDP (more than 90% corresponding to tax revenues).[4] Costa Rica's own resources – despite their low level relative to GDP – have a significant weight within the structure of their total revenues (99.8%), although it is recognised that the process of fiscal decentralisation has not experienced any significant progress in terms of an adequate delegation of spending responsibilities or tax powers to lower levels of government. The same happens in Uruguay where own resources account to almost 64% of the total resources of local governments.

A similar situation is observed in Chile, where municipal resources represent 60.5% of their total income (Table 3.1). However, it is worth noting that in this country the preponderance of own resources as the main source of sub-national income has two components: permanent own revenues and revenues from the Municipal Common Fund (FCM). Since this mechanism of horizontal equalisation between municipalities is practically nourished entirely (99%) of the same tax resources collected by these jurisdictions,[5] this report considers its influence before being distributed, that is, within the set of own resources available to better reflect their potential in sub-national financing.[6]

Table 3.1. **Total revenue structure of sub-national governments, 2014**

Percentage of GDP and percentage of total resources

Country	Own revenues		Transfers		Others		Total revenues
	% GDP	% Total	% GDP	% Total	% GDP	% Total	% GDP
Argentina	6.3	41.7	8.8	58	0.1	0.4	15.2
Brazil*	11.1	75.1	3.7	24.8	0	0.1	14.8
Chile	2.1	60.5	1.4	39.1	0	0.4	3.5
Colombia	3.7	31.6	5	42.8	3	25.6	11.8
Costa Rica	1.15	99.78	0.001	0.09	0.00	0.13	1.15
Ecuador*	1.0	21.6	3.6	77	0.1	1.3	4.6
Mexico*	1.4	13.8	8.7	86.2	0	0	10.1
Peru	1.1	27.3	2.6	66.7	0.23	6	3.9
Uruguay	**1.99**	**63.8**	**1.1**	**36.2**	**0**	**0**	**3.1**

a / As "own resources" is taken into account own tax revenues and own non-tax revenues.
b/ "Other Income" may include different forms of indebtedness, investments, asset sales, loan recovery, capital transfers, etc.
The data for countries marked with an asterisk corresponds to 2013.
Source: Economic Commission for Latin America and the Caribbean (ECLAC), on the basis of official numbers.

StatLink http://dx.doi.org/10.1787/888933462940

On the contrary, in the rest of the countries of the region, the main source of public resources of sub-national governments comes from the transfer system that each central government implements to complement the financing of its spending responsibilities, that is, the provision of public goods to its citizens. Central governments of countries such as Argentina and Mexico contribute more than 8% of GDP to transfers directed to lower levels of government. In the case of Colombia and Ecuador, this source of sub-national income represents 5.0% and 3.6% of GDP respectively, while in Brazil these resources represent 3.7% of its GDP.[7] In Peru and Uruguay, transfers amounted to 2.6% and 1.1% of GDP respectively with a relative weight greater than 66% and 36% with respect to their fiscal revenue structures.

When going deeper by type of tax, it can be seen that the revenue of taxes on goods and services (general and specific taxes) has been the highest, exceeding 1% of GDP, and near 2% over the last two years on an unweighted average basis. Revenue from recurrent taxes on immovable property (4100), mostly considering the property tax has remained stable reaching 0.4% of GDP during all the period analysed.

Figure 3.2. **Evolution of sub-national government tax revenues, by type of tax, Latin America average, 2000-15**

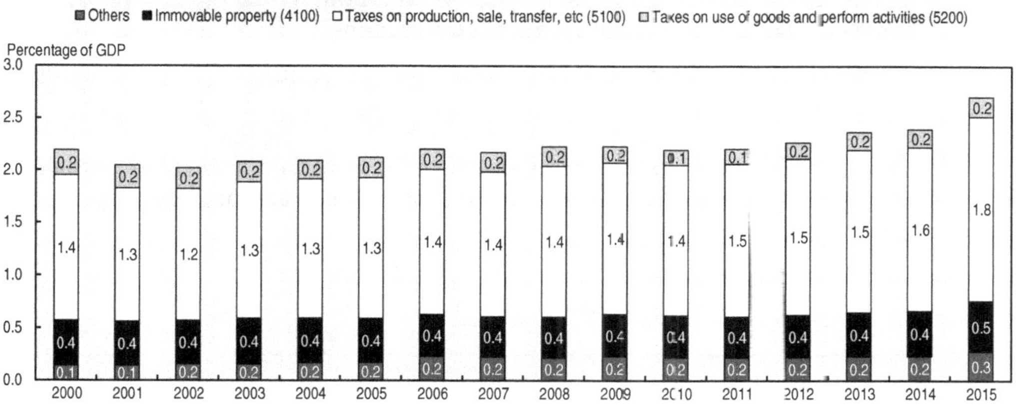

Source: Authors' elaboration based on data presented in Chapter 6.

StatLink http://dx.doi.org/10.1787/888933462898

3.2. Tax revenues of sub-national governments: Structure and evolution

As has been emphasised in the relevant literature, the decentralisation of tax powers to sub-national governments has been relatively weak in most countries, although subject to the particularities of each country. Figure 3.3 evidences the disparity and mostly low participation of sub-national governments in the total revenue of Latin American countries. The exception is Brazil, where states and municipalities jointly own more than 30% of total revenues, denoting a significant degree of decentralisation of tax powers to these levels of government. In a second tier of countries are Argentina and Colombia, in which the sub-national levels contribute approximately 15% of the total collection.

However, in the rest of the countries, central governments have not made significant progress in the decentralisation of tax resources. Thus, in these countries, the sub-national tax collection is on average, about 2-5% of the total tax revenues of each country.

Figure 3.3. **Tax revenue by level of government, 2014**

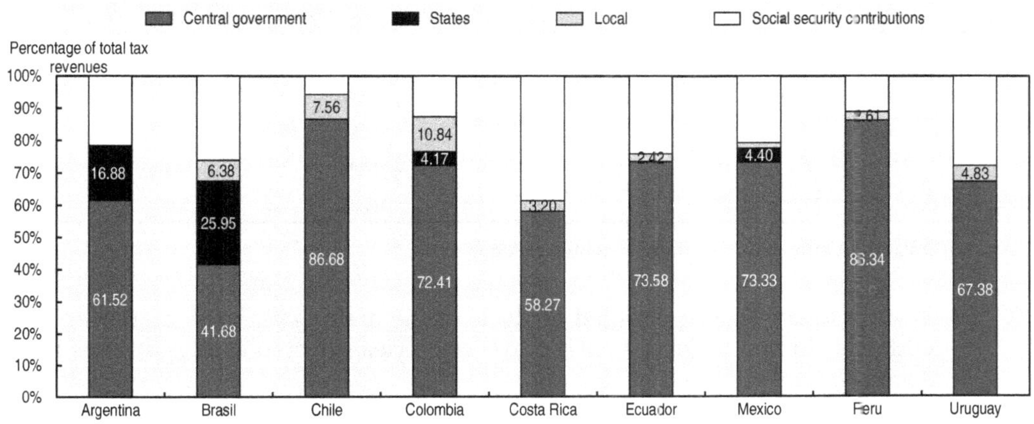

Source: Authors' elaboration based on data presented in Chapter 6.

StatLink http://dx.doi.org/10.1787/888933462906

It is also noted that tax collection of sub-national governments in the countries of the region has grown very little during the last ten years (which contrasts with fiscal revenues at central government level) and this poor evolution is related to the weakness in the level and structure of sub-national taxation, which in turn has to do with the tax bases available to the lower levels of government.

While low own tax revenue is a problem, it should be noted that when assessing the amount of expenditures that intermediate and local governments have to fund, there does not appear to be much scope for reassigning tax powers. In this regard, what comes into view is that sub-national governments find it difficult to take advantage of existing tax powers, as observed in the low income generated by property taxes of Latin American countries.

Table 3.2. **Structure of the main taxes of subnational governments – intermediate and local governments – in Latin America, 2014**

Country	Recurrent taxes on immovable property (4100)	Taxes on production, sale, transfer, etc (5100)	Taxes on use of goods and perform activities (5200)	Others	Total
	Percentage of GDP				
Argentina	0.38	4.02	0.26	0.59	5.25
Brazil	0.48	7.61	0.00	2.21	10.30
Chile	0.62	0.23	0.64	0.00	1.49
Colombia	0.73	1.39	0.00	1.06	3.18
Costa Rica	0.29	0.40	0.00	0.02	0.72
Ecuador	0.11	0.17	0.03	0.15	0.46
Mexico	0.22	0.03	0.12	0.55	0.91
Peru	0.21	0.08	0.00	0.24	0.53
Uruguay	0.81	0.00	0.51	0.00	1.32

Country	Recurrent taxes on immovable property (4100)	Taxes on production, sale, transfer, etc (5100)	Taxes on use of goods and perform activities (5200)	Others	Total
	Percentage of total tax revenue				
Argentina	7.30	76.48	4.99	11.23	100
Brazil	4.68	73.83	0.00	21.49	100
Chile	41.33	15.72	42.94	0.00	100
Colombia	23.06	43.67	0.00	33.27	100
Costa Rica	40.76	55.88	0.00	3.37	100
Ecuador	24.11	37.56	6.66	31.68	100
Mexico	23.95	3.04	12.97	60.04	100
Peru	40.07	15.33	0.00	44.60	100
Uruguay	61.35	0.00	38.65	0.00	100

Source: Author's elaboration based on data presented on Chapter 6.

StatLink http://dx.doi.org/10.1787/888933462951

The following is a detailed analysis of the main taxes presented in the table above, with the characteristics of each of the countries selected as case studies in the present document.

a) Recurrent taxes on immovable property (4100)

The most recent research papers together with the statistical information available confirm that the relevance of equity taxation in terms of GDP and in relation to total collected (excluding taxes on financial transactions from this category) it is not significant in any of the Latin American tax systems. Even so, taxes affecting wealth are the main instrument for generating own resources with which sub-national governments of the region have to fund their spending responsibilities.

Simultaneously, within the broad range of taxation that usually falls on the taxpayer's estate, the tax on immovable property is the commonly accepted and exploited instrument as a source of fiscal resources at lower levels of government, even with a low relative weight, below 0.7% of GDP in most Latin American and Caribbean countries (except in Colombia and Uruguay).[8]

Notwithstanding the above, the tax on immovable property acquires a very unequal relative importance with respect to the totality of sub-national tax resources depending on the country analysed. Thus it can be seen in Table 3.2 that in some countries the recurrent taxes on immovable property provides a significant part of tax revenues, e.g. in Chile, Costa Rica Ecuador, Peru and Uruguay.

In the case of Mexico, each state is autonomous in the attributions assigned by the Constitution, including in the creation of taxes. The recurrent taxes on immovable property are a predominantly municipal tax[9] and represents more than 23% of sub-national revenues.[10] Cadastral registration and tax valuation is the responsibility of each of the municipalities, so that the unification of criteria at the national level can only be achieved through agreements between jurisdictions.

For example, the Chilean Territorial Tax (IT), which is a real estate tax, represents the main component of municipal tax revenues. Currently, this tax contributes revenues equivalent to 0.6% of GDP, which corresponds to more than 41% of total sub-national tax resources.[11] Both the tax base and its exemptions are fixed by national law, and municipalities, in practice, are only the beneficiaries of the collected resources. The base of the territorial tax is determined by the tax valuation of the property made by the Internal Revenue Service (SII) and the tax rate is fixed by law. This leads to a recurrent tax on immovable property that is not related to the payment for local goods and services that the municipality provides to the area where the real estate is located.

In Colombia, although originally under departmental jurisdiction, revenues from the Unified Property Tax were assigned by the 1991 Constitution to municipalities, which are empowered to determine rates (within a pre-established range), exemptions, preferential treatment, and the specific uses of what is collected by the tax. As might be expected, there may exist (and indeed exist) as many regulatory frameworks for the imposition of real estate property as the existing municipalities, reflecting the particular needs of each of these. Thus, the Colombian recurrent taxes on immovable property, which collects about 0.7% of GDP, is imposed on all real estate properties, urban and rural, with or without buildings, located within the geographical limits of each municipality. In addition, this tax in Colombia is the second highest collected at lower levels of government with a relative share of almost 23% in relation to the total income of these jurisdictions (Table 2).

The taxable base in this case is determined by cadastral valuation carried out by decentralised cadastre offices in Bogota, Antioquia, Cali and Medellín, and by the "Geographic Institute Agustín Codazzi" (IGAC) in the other departments. Although real estate values are updated annually by applying a ratio that takes into account the consumer price index, in several municipalities of Colombia there have been problems with the updating of cadastral values with respect to market values, turning to the mechanism of self-determined valuation or "self-valuation". As for the tax rates, these can be established by the municipal authorities within a certain range with respect to the cadastral valuation, using a differentiated and progressive structure depending on the type of social stratification and land use in the urban areas that determine, ultimately, the fiscal value of the buildings affected by the tax on immovable property .

In Ecuador, recurrent taxes on immovable property account for approximately 24% of sub-national tax revenues (0.11% of GDP). The tax base corresponds to the total value of the property determined and updated every two years by the municipal cadastre office based on: the value of the land, the value of the buildings and the replacement value, provided by the Municipal Council. Notwithstanding, the cadastral valuation method combines information provided directly by the owner together with the deed data due to the logistical difficulties observed in most jurisdictions. The tax rates for urban properties vary between 0.25 and 5 points per thousand of the value of the property, while for rural areas they are between 0.25 and 3 per thousand.

As mentioned, the contribution of tax collection from the cantons in Costa Rica is insignificant with respect to the national total. The main reason for this is that municipalities have only the responsibility of tax administration for some taxes on property and on sales. In this regard, local levels of government must make the valuations, collect and demand the payment of taxes in their jurisdictions. In particular, tax on immovable property in this country accounts for a large part (40% in 2014) of sub-national tax resources, which is equivalent to 0.3% of GDP (Table 3.2). The current tax rate, decided by the central government, is 0.25% on the value of the property and is applicable throughout the national territory.

In Argentina and Brazil, the two countries with the highest sub-national participation in total tax revenues, lower levels of government also levy recurrent taxes on immovable property, although these are subordinated to other taxes that generate higher resources, such as taxes on economic activity (which will be analysed in the next section).

In Argentina, the immovable property tax is the third largest source of provincial revenues (intermediate level of government), now surpassed by the taxes on economic activity (gross income) and other taxes, representing just under one-tenth of the total obtained by these jurisdictions (7.3% in 2015).[12] In addition, 88% of the resources generated by this tax are concentrated in five of the 24 provinces and especially between the Federal Capital (32.8%) (GCBA) and the province of Buenos Aires (32.2%), which together account for more than 65% of the collection of this tax.

The most widely-used valuation method in Argentina takes into account both the value of land and improvements, that is, that the base is determined by the complete real estate. Another method used in the province of Buenos Aires is to separately appraise the land and the construction or improvements of the same property to apply different rates, where rates on improvements are lower than those on land.

In Brazil, there are two taxes that tax real property, depending on whether it is urban or rural. On the one hand, the Tax on Urban Property and Land (IPTU) is assigned as an exclusive power of the municipalities and the Federal District, and, therefore, the legal basis of the tax depends on rules established by each jurisdiction. The IPTU,[13] which provides tax revenues equivalent to 0.48% of GDP for 2014, taxes the ownership or possession of real estate in urban areas and the tax base is determined by the market value of the same, applying rates fixed for each particular municipality. Within the structure of municipal tax revenues, the relative weight of this tax is around 20%, while compared to all sub-national tax revenues, the importance is reduced to 4.7% (Table 3.2).

The IPTU is distinguished from the Rural Territorial Property Tax (ITR), which is a tax assigned to the central government and whose taxable base is land exclusive of improvements and buildings in rural areas.

In Peru, the rates of this tax are set by the Central Government maintaining a progressive structure. Also, part of the revenue collected from this tax is used to finance cadastral and appraisal activities. However, the municipalities obtain revenue from the collection of this tax which is close to 0.21% of GDP, and represents about 40% of the tax revenues of local governments.

In Uruguay, for its part, the real estate contribution is a tax that is charged in relation to the real value of the record (padrón), at progressive rates. The rates are set by the municipalities. By 2014, this tax amounted to 0.81% of GDP, which is equivalent to more than 61% of subnational tax revenues in this country.

b) Taxes on production, sale, transfer (5100)

Consumption taxes

The taxes on production, sale and transfer imply greater risks of tax co-ordination in the sense that the differences between rates applied in neighbouring regions may induce taxpayers to "export" consumption and production/marketing decisions to those areas with a lower relative tax burden within the same country. Lack of co-ordination can also lead sub-national governments to compete for the localisation of production or consumption (tax wars) through the modification of rates or taxable bases.[14]

In general, countries typically use two differentiated types of sales tax or consumption taxes: a) single stage, non-cumulative, such as the general sales taxes on final consumers used in the United States, and selective taxes on certain goods and/or services and b) non-cumulative multiple stages, such as the value added tax used in all Latin American countries. Less frequent, but existing in the region at the sub-national level, are the cumulative or "cascade" taxes imposed on each production, distribution and commercialisation stage, which manage to generate significant revenue with a low tax rate due to taxation of the same base.

Likewise, specific or selective taxes are potentially a good source of income for these levels of government thanks to the relative ease of administering them and the possibility of differentiation of rates between regions, although the aspect that should be highlighted is related to the jurisdictional principle applied.

To the extent that both general sales taxes and excise taxes are levied at the place where consumers reside (destination principle) and not at the place where goods and services are produced or lent (origin principle), these taxes minimise distorting effects in the economic decisions of the taxpayers (see Larios et al., 2004).

It is clear that even if the destination principle is applied to the same good, but with different levels of rates between jurisdictions, an incentive is created to make purchases outside the jurisdiction itself and therefore distortionary effects will be generated in the allocation of resources, which will be very difficult to avoid unless harmonisation of levels of taxation is achieved.

The various technical alternatives used to solve the problem of double taxation at the local level range from establishing clearing houses between jurisdictions, to deferring the payment of the tax at the time of sale, or forming an integrated system involving both the central and local governments to avoid duplication of the levy. However, the experience of the European Union indicates that these arrangements are not free of complexities and technical questions.

Among the countries analysed, four of them stand out for assigning exclusive power over certain sales taxes to their sub-national governments, making them in all cases the main source of tax resources at their respective levels.

In the case of Argentina, the main source of tax revenue in the provinces is the Gross Income Tax (which is also allocated, in much lower percentages, to some municipalities). By 2014, as already mentioned, this tax contributed 76% of the total provincial revenue, equivalent to 4% of GDP. The rates applied are differentiated between provinces and activities, and there are also differences in the relative weight of the tax in each province (ranging from 57.7% to 86.5%), although in all cases it is the highest revenue. Despite being criticised for the inefficiencies it generates as a "cascade" tax[15] (it distorts the allocation of resources by changing the structure of relative prices and harms domestic producers with respect to international competition), this tax has shown a high return contributing to provincial autonomy in terms of financing needs (see Gómez Sabaíni and Jiménez, 2011).

In Brazil, sales taxes were adopted by the three levels of government, which implies difficulties arising from interjurisdictional co-ordination. In addition to the Tax on Industrialized Products (IPI), collected by the federal government on an extensive list of goods produced and whose amount is determined following a value-added levy, state governments have full tax authority on the Tax on the Circulation of Merchandise and Services (ICMS), which also taxes goods and services at all stages but in a general way that allow it to cover a much broader base than the IPI. In addition, municipalities administer and collect the Service Tax (ISS) that taxes all service provision stipulated in legislation within the geographical limits of each municipality. By being the exclusive authority, each municipality can establish the rate that considers suitable with a maximum of 5% on the billing.

If the ICMS and the ISS are considered jointly, Brazilian sub-national governments have collected almost 74% of their tax resources from sales taxation or, seen otherwise, have fiscal resources equivalent to 7.6% of GDP (Table 3.2) corresponding to that tribute, which transforms these taxes, and especially the state ICMS, in the main and fundamental source of income of the lower levels of government.

With regard to Colombia, this country also assigns taxes on sales of goods and services a preponderant role in the set of tax resources of sub-national jurisdiction. From Table 3.2 it can be seen that the collection of these taxes in 2014 was 1.4% of the product, representing almost 44% of total sub-national tax revenues.

It is highlighted that the mentioned resources can be divided into two distinct groups. On the one hand, departmental governments contribute 29% of sub-national tax revenues and concentrate 57% of their income from the application of three selective taxes on the consumption of liquors, beers and cigarettes. On the other hand, municipalities, which contribute more than 71% of the consolidated collection of the Colombian territorial entities, have as their main source of tax revenues the Industry and Commerce Tax (ICA), which exceeds the property tax as the main source of revenue, with the latter accounting for a 38% of the total municipal revenues (and 27% of the sub-national consolidated) in 2014.

Tax on commercial patents[16]

In the case of Ecuador, a large part of the revenue from taxation on economic activity is concentrated in the Tax on Patents, which is a municipal tax and which taxes the exercise of any economic activity of a commercial or industrial nature within the jurisdiction of the municipality. This tax levies the activity of natural or legal persons who have the status of merchants or industrialists operating in each canton, as well as those who exercise any economic activity. In aggregate terms, tax revenue from economic activity reached 0.17 product points in 2014, equivalent to 36.7% of total sub-national tax revenues in this country.

In Chile, sub-national governments also have the resources generated from the collection of commercial patents, which are applied by the respective municipality to the exercise of any profession, trade, industry, commerce, art or other lucrative secondary or tertiary activity regardless of their nature or designation (including patents for alcohols). This tax contributed 15.07% of municipal tax revenues in 2014, and was equivalent to 0.23% of GDP.

Finally, Costa Rica's patent tax is the main tax levied by local governments, accounting for more than half of their tax revenues in 2014 (56% of the total and 0.4% of GDP). In this case, the taxable income is the net taxable income and the annual gross sales or income received by the natural or legal persons engaged in the exercise of lucrative activities.[17,18]

c) Tax on use of goods and perform activities

In the countries of the region there are several alternatives to taxing the use of goods and performance of activities. Thus it may be that the taxable event is a partial manifestation of the taxpayer's wealth tax that stands out in this area is the one that falls on motor vehicles. Another option is constituted if the tax falls on those who use this property to circulate on the public highway (also known as "rights of circulation"). Finally, almost all Latin American countries, through their sub-national governments, impose a tax on the transfer of vehicles among their citizens.

Taking into account the range of variants for its application and use as a source of fiscal resources at the lower levels of government, the tax on motor vehicles is present in several Latin American countries, although in some cases it is moderately significant in the sub-national tax revenues.

The justification for its use lies mainly in the fact that this tax is easy to administer and is a permanent and stable source of revenue, especially in sub-national governments with a high degree of urbanisation. On the other hand, the information on the stock of cars in a city is useful to raise ecological taxes that limit the use of vehicles and to combat environmental pollution, that is to say that the tax can be used for other objectives, not necessarily revenue.

Some countries have tried to use the vehicle tax as part of a redistributive policy, although this objective is of greater responsibility and weight at the central level, it can partially be admitted a progressive tax with a rate that taxes the purchase of new vehicles. In Argentina, the province of San Juan has a "progressive" tax on vehicles; the tax rate is 3% but the value that is applied is a function of the model, age and weight of the vehicle. This way of taxing vehicles is administratively complex and can penalise new vehicles that are more efficient and pollute less than older vehicles.

In Mexico there is the Tax over Tenancy or Use of Vehicles (ISTUV), which has been the exclusive power, since 2012, of the States and Mexico City.[19] This tax offers several advantages from a revenue and equitable point of view. The tax base is usually relatively stable as the number of cars tends to grow at a rate similar to or above the population growth rate and income level. In addition, the base is relatively difficult to hide and the burden falls on those individuals with higher purchasing power. In total, the revenue of taxes on the use of goods and perform activities in Mexico amounts to 0.12% of GDP, which is almost 13% of sub-national revenues.

In Chile, the revenue from these taxes represents almost 43% of local tax revenues (0.64% of GDP). The main source of these revenues is the owners of motor vehicles (which include both the purchase and the annual permit). In this respect, the value of the circulation permit is determined in most cases on the basis of the assessment made by the Internal Revenue Service of motor vehicles and, on this appraisal; the Municipal Revenue Law sets the different rates. It is worth noting that this tax constitutes one of the main municipal revenues, even though 62.5% of its revenue must be delivered to the Municipal Common Fund.

The Uruguay Round Filing Fee is the main (only) source of income within this classification. Its revenue amounts to 0.51% of GDP and is 38.6% of total sub-national revenues. The collection of this tax establishes its legal basis in the Constitution and its rules are published annually. The rates are set according to the year of registration of the vehicle.

d) Other relevant sub-national taxes in the countries of the region

In addition to the typical taxes used by the sub-national governments analysed here, it is essential to mention some examples of taxes that extend the vast range of fiscal instruments from which they obtain their financing.

In this sense, the payroll tax (3000) is assigned to the state governments of Mexico, which contributed 41% of sub-national revenue (equivalent to 0.37% of Mexican GDP) in 2014. This type of tax has advantages and disadvantages. On the one hand, it is easy to administer, especially if it is applied on large enterprises, and also when the economy has a high degree of formalisation of labour, with relatively low rates, significant resources can be raised for regional governments. On the other hand, its main disadvantage is that this tax acts as a barrier to the generation of employment in the formal sector, and may also constitute a covert way of exporting taxes to other jurisdictions by taxing on the principle of origin if it affects production costs (see Larios et al., 2004).

In Argentina, the Stamp Tax (4400) is an important source of tax resources for provincial governments. This tribute, from the point of view of economic efficiency, is detrimental in that it conspires against economic growth by establishing a tax burden so that onerous legal acts by individuals and companies fall under the legal regime. However, stamp duty is the second highest tax revenue for these jurisdictions with a share of 8.0% of the total in 2014, which is equivalent to 0.42% of GDP.

In the case of Brazil, the sub-national tax resources already explained above are complemented by taxes related to the free transfer of assets. On the one hand, the free transmission of goods is taxed by the "Inter-Vivo" Transmission Tax (ITBI), applied at municipal level; on the other hand, by the Tax on Transfers of Assets due to Death (inheritance) and Donations (ITCD) that is assigned to the states and to the Federal District.

In Peru, an important part of local government tax revenues are in the collection of taxes on financial transactions (4400), as well as other charges that are merely local powers (6200). In all, the sum of these revenues amounts to 0.24% of GDP, as 44.6% of local revenues.

3.3. Approaches to the measurement of tax autonomy

One of the most relevant methodological challenges presented by the debate on intergovernmental fiscal relations and fiscal decentralisation is the measurement of the tax autonomy of sub-national governments. A common way of measuring this autonomy is through the sum of own income, defined as own sub-national revenues, to the extent that it is that level of government which administers it and has the resources that the tax can generate. However, this type of measurement leaves out of the analysis the power and discretion that these governments could have to set tax rates and bases without any intervention by the central government.

For purposes of this section, tax autonomy is understood as the measurement that assesses the degree of freedom with which sub-national governments can create or abolish new local taxes, define tax bases or even grant tax exemptions to natural persons and companies. Thus, the measure of fiscal autonomy proposed in this chapter seeks to take care of the previous point. To do this, the methodology developed by the *OECD Fiscal Federalism Network* is used, and whose taxonomy is presented below:

Table 3.3. **Tax autonomy**

a.1	The recipient SCG sets the tax rate and any tax reliefs without needing to consult a higher level government.
a.2	The recipient SCG sets the rate and any reliefs after consulting a higher level government.
b.1	The recipient SCG sets the tax rate, and a higher level government does not set upper or lower limits on the rate chosen.
b.2	The recipient SCG sets the tax rate, and a higher level government does sets upper and/or lower limits on the rate chosen.
c.1	The recipient SCG sets tax reliefs – but it sets tax allowances only.
c.2	The recipient SCG sets tax reliefs – but it sets tax credits only.
c.3	The recipient SCG sets tax reliefs – and it sets both tax allowances and tax credits.
d.1	There is a tax-sharing arrangement in which the SCGs determine the revenue split.
d.2	There is a tax-sharing arrangement in which the revenue split can be changed only with the consent of SCGs.
d.3	There is a tax-sharing arrangement in which the revenue split is determined in legislation, and where it may be changed unilaterally by a higher level government, but less frequently than once a year.
d.4	There is a tax-sharing arrangement in which the revenue split is determined annually by a higher level government.
e	Other cases in which the central government sets the rate and base of the SCG tax.
f	None of the above categories a, b, c, d or e applies

Source: Author's elaboration based on the taxonomy proposed by OECD (Fiscal Descentralisation Database).

For this work, the approximation to tax autonomy was made by reference to the different legislative provisions that refer to the tax authorities, in terms of rates and taxable bases. In the annexes is the detail by country.

The governments of the provinces of Argentina have the power granted them by the Constitution of the Nation to set direct taxes, with regard to their rate and taxable base. The provincial taxes in this matter are real estate property taxes (4100) and stamp duty (4400), whose operation was detailed in the earlier part of this chapter.[20] The main restriction imposed by the law is in the Federal Tax Co-participation Law, where the provinces that adhere to this agreement are enforced to not apply analogous taxes to the national ones whose distribution is established in this Law. The power to fix the taxes on gross income (5100) and on the use of motor vehicles (5211) are also established in the Constitution, under the explicit proviso that indirect contributions remain as concurrent power between the Nation and the Provinces. The characteristics of all provincial taxes are established in the Tax Codes and Tax Laws of the Jurisdictions, with which it can be affirmed that the provincial governments have a wide fiscal autonomy in their own revenue, based mainly on the Constitution of this country, although they maintain a high dependence on intergovernmental transfers, mainly through the federal co-participation regime of taxes.

Brazil's state governments have autonomy over 93% of their tax revenues, consisting of inheritance and property tax (4310), ownership of motor vehicles (4600), and the circulation of goods and services ICMS (5111). The Constitution establishes the competence of the States and the Federal District in this matter, with the particularity that for taxes on inheritance and vehicles it is established that the Senate will set the maximum limits of the rates. The remaining 7% of state tax revenues are social contributions on net profits (1110) whose legal basis is found in Law 7,869, and in which the federal power of this tax is explicitly stated.

With respect to the municipalities of Brazil, the fiscal autonomy of sub-national governments reaches 90% of their tax revenues. These are composed of taxes on real estate IPTU (4100), translation of real estate (4400) as well as other taxes on goods and services ISS (5113). The power of the municipal governments on these taxes is guaranteed by the Constitution of this country.

From the first part of this chapter the operation of the territorial tax in Chile was explained; nevertheless it is worth to emphasise that an important part of the revenue of this tax finances the "Fondo Común Municipal" (FCM), whose distribution is determined by the Constitutional Organic Law of Municipalities. Any change to this Law must come from or be sponsored by the Central Government. Greater fiscal autonomy is observed in the municipal patents (5100), detailed in the second part of this chapter; however, the rates are fixed in the aforementioned law and between 55% and 65% of the collection of the four municipalities with greater fiscal capacity relative to others will finance the FCM. As with the territorial tax, taxes levied on the circulation of motor vehicles (5210) are subject to the allocation agreement of the FCM. Finally, the greatest fiscal autonomy of the municipalities of Chile is found in the taxes to obtain concessions, permits or services of the local administration (5213), which are regulated in the same way in the Law on Municipal Income. Urbanisation and construction permits are highlighted, whose maximum rate is regulated by the general law of the branch. For its part, the Law also allows that the corresponding rights to services, concessions or permits whose rates are not fixed in the law relative to new services that are created by the municipalities, are determined by local ordinances. In sum, nearly 58% of Chilean municipalities' tax revenues form part of a tax co-participation agreement established by law (FCM), while the remaining 42% are taxed powers regulated by Law with established limits regarding rates and taxable bases

In Mexico, the Constitution of the United States of Mexico empowers all state governments to handle rates and taxable bases for payroll taxes (3000), property tax (4100), translation (4400) and services (5126). In addition to these powers, it should be noted that by mandate of the Decree 21/12/2007 the Law on the Tax on Tenancy or Use of Vehicles was repealed, since 2012, thus leaving the power of this tax in the state governments too. As a result, by 2014, at least ten state governments have eliminated this tax or, in default, have subsidised it.

Likewise, the Constitution establishes that municipalities will receive the revenue-including additional taxes established by the States on real estate property-from their fragmentation, division, consolidation, relocation and improvement as well as those based on the change in real estate value. However, municipalities may conclude agreements with the State to take over certain functions related to the administration of these contributions. Thus, for example, with the 2014 plantation reform, the criteria for the allocation of the Municipal Development Fund were modified, which is constituted from 1% of the federal revenues from participations, forcing the municipality to have an agreement with the state government in which the devolution, by the municipality, of the administrative responsibility of the property tax to the state government is explicit. With this, the incentive for municipalities to grant to the state governments the power over the property tax is regulated, so as not to lose part of their financing via the units. This change would potentially leave more than 83% of municipal tax revenues under the authority of state governments.

Table 3.4. **Latin American tax autonomy, 2015**

Country	Revenues as % of total tax revenue	Tax autonomy of Subnational Government												
		a.1.	a.2	b.1	b.2	c.1	c.2	c.3	d.1	d.2	d.3	d.4	e	f
Argentina														
Provinces	16.9	100.0	..	..	..	..	..	..	..	..	..	..	..	..
Brazil														
States	25.9	93.9	..	..	..	..	..	..	..	..	..	..	6.1	..
Local	6.4	90.4	..	..	..	..	..	..	..	..	..	..	..	9.6
Chile														
Local	7.6	..	..	26.4	15.7	..	..	..	..	..	57.9	..	..	..
Mexico														
States	3.9	100.0	..	..	..	..	..	..	..	..	..	..	..	..
Local	1.4	16.5	83.5	..	..	..	..	..	..	..	..	..	..	..

Source: ECLAC's elaboration on the basis of the methodology proposed by OECD (1999). The figures presented above may differ from those published by the OECD. Fiscal Decentralisation Database due to minor differences in classifications and sources between ECLAC and OECD.

StatLink http://dx.doi.org/10.1787/888933462962

In general terms, the intermediate governments of the countries analysed have an important level of fiscal autonomy derived from the power – founded in the Constitution of each of the countries – with which governments have to set rates and modify taxable bases within their jurisdiction, although, as emphasised in the first part of this chapter, on average the level of vertical asymmetry is high. The main difference is observed in Chile, where most sub-national tax revenues are regulated in a distribution agreement established by Law, while the rest are subject to limits and restrictions also established in the Municipal Revenue Law. In this sense, and in both cases, any modification of the law is attributed to the central government.

In order to deepen the discussion, Box 3.1 shows the analysis including the different tax co-participation agreements. In summary, this aggregate allows the analysis to be expanded and to show the different levels of autonomy, differentiating by the capacities that the sub-national governments have to modify the distribution systems of taxes. As was seen in the initial part of the chapter, with the exception of Brazil, fiscal revenues from different co-participation agreements have a greater relative weight within the fiscal structures of sub-national governments.

Box 3.1. Tax autonomy including tax co-participation agreements

From what has been explored in the legal frameworks, it is observed that intermediate governments have an important level of tax autonomy, derived from the power with which governments count to set rates and modify taxable bases within the jurisdiction, although in a context of high vertical asymmetry. A lower level of autonomy is observed in local governments. However, a more detailed analysis is achieved by including the mechanisms of tax co-participation in the calculation of sub-national fiscal autonomy. These systems, with their particularities, are of vital importance to sub-national finance and, although they originate in taxes collected at the level of the central government, their different regulatory frameworks determine different degrees of autonomy, related to the ability of sub-national governments to modify the distribution system.

For this analysis, it is worth noting that in the case of Argentina, any modification of the co-participation regime requires the approval of the provincial legislatures (law-agreement); While in the case of the states and municipalities of Mexico, these agreements make them beneficiaries and even oblige them to create agreements of collaboration and devolution of powers and tax responsibilities (specifically real estate), without giving them any negotiation space in the formation and Distribution of participating federal revenue. On the other hand, in the case of Chile the particularity is that the Municipal Common Fund (instrument of co-participation) is financed for the most part with the own resources of the municipalities, although any modification is attributed solely by the Central Government. The exception would be Brazil, where it is shown that both state and local governments (the latter to a lesser extent) have a capacity and fiscal autonomy reflected both in the collection and tax powers that the Constitution grants them.

In sum, considering the different co-participation agreements, the results would be the following:

Country	Tax autonomy of subnational governments												
	a.1.	a.2	b.1	b.2	c.1	c.2	c.3	d.1	d.2	d.3	d.4	e	f
Argentina													
Provinces	44.2	..	..	..	..	..	..	..	55.8	..	..	..	..
Brazil													
States	81.5	..	..	..	..	..	..	..	..	13.2	..	5.3	..
Local	58.5	..	..	..	..	..	..	..	..	35.3	..	..	6.2
Chile													
Local	..	..	26.4	15.7	..	..	..	..	..	57.9	..	..	..
Mexico													
States	18.2	..	..	..	..	..	..	..	..	81.8	..	..	..
Local	4.2	21.4	..	..	..	..	..	..	..	74.4	..	..	..

Source: Own elaboration on the basis of the methodology proposed by OECD (1999). Co-participation agreements are not included in the OECD tax autonomy definition, which includes only tax revenues. Co-participation agreements are derived from revenue collected at the central level and then shared with states and municipalities through transfers.

Notes

1. Many of the developments presented in this chapter are based on an article named "La tributación de los gobiernos subnacionales" from Gomez Sabaíni and Jiménez (2016), in print. The chapter uses data from this publication and from the Economic Commission for Latin America and the Caribbean (ECLAC) as the analysis includes non-tax revenue and transfers that do not fall within the scope of the data presented in this publication. However, the classification terminology in this chapter uses the OECD classification in the Interpretative Guide (shown in Annex A) and refers to the main categories in which each tax occurs.
2. Despite the existence of intergovernmental transfers of remarkable relevance in sub-national government finance among Latin-American countries, this chapter focuses in own resources (tax and non-tax). For a complete analysis of the problems related to intergovernmental transfers in the region, see the works of Martinez Vazquez and Sepúlveda (2012a), Rezende and Veloso (2012) and Jiménez and Podestá (2009).
3. Only some countries were selected because of a minimum amount of information requirement to perform the analysis.
4. Afonso (2016) provides an actualised analysis about the weight of sub-national resources in Brazil.
5. For a detailed analysis about the functioning, composition and distribution of the FCM, the "Sistema Nacional de Información Municipal" from SUBDERE, Chile, www.sinim.gov.cl/desarrollo_local/selfcm.htm can be consulted.
6. The last part of this chapter deepens the analysis about the importance of the FCM in the determination of the fiscal autonomy that currently reaches the municipalities of Chile.
7. The work that gave rise to this chapter (Gómez Sabaini y Jiménez, 2011) shows the structure of the total revenues of the sub-national governments to the year 2008, including the case of Brazil where transfers are close to 8% of the Gross Domestic Product. The remarkable differences with the data presented here (Table 3.1) – whose source is the Brazilian National Treasury – have a methodological explanation, which is related to the weighing of the transfers made between sub-national governments that are constituted mainly by 25% of the collection of ICMS from the states to the municipalities. The inclusion or not of this concept within the total amount of transfers would explain the differences indicated with the official data.
8. For more details about its performance in Latin America see Martínez Vázquez and Sepúlveda (2012b).
9. Although De Cesare and Lazo Marín (2008) clarify that the municipalities propose annually their prices and tables of unit values of land and construction before their State Congresses.
10. Even in Ruelas Ávila (2015) it is shown that the relative importance of this tax averaged 55% municipal tax revenues in the period 1989-2013, although it has been historically low – about 7% – when it is compared with the total revenues of the municipalities. On the other hand, it is also shown that this tax distorts the territorial equity since 90% of the tax collection is concentrated in only 12% of the municipalities.
11. In the calculations of the sub-national tax burden for the Chilean case, the DIPRES methodology was followed in which the duplications originated in the application of the Municipal Common Fund (FCM) were eliminated. Thus, adding the residual difference to the respective taxes which form it, it is possible to visualise exactly what has been collected for each concept of operating income, although information on what is received by each municipality is lost through participation in this Fund.
12. Some municipalities can fix rates and exemptions relative to the tribute.
13. For a detailed analysis of this tax, it is recommended to consult the work of Bruno de Carvalho, P.H. (2006), "IPTU in Brazil: Progressivity, Collection and Extra-Fiscal Aspects", IPEA.
14. For more detail on the problems of co-ordination between government levels of consumption taxes, see Arroyo, Jiménez and Mussi (2012).
15. For more information about the inefficiencies of "cascading' see Keen (2013).
16. There are classification differences between ECLAC and the OECD regarding the tax on patents. ECLAC classify this tax as a tax on production, sale, transfer, etc (5100) whereas the OECD classify this tax as a tax on use of goods or perform activities.
17. According to the Constitution and the Municipal Code, each municipality has its own law of patents.
18. In the case of Ecuador, Chile and Costa Rica, the classification of these taxes was recently changed from 5126 to 5213. For this special feature, the former classification was used.

19. Starting in 2012, the tax on the possession and use of vehicles became the power of state governments, a tax on which they could not previously modify taxes or eliminate surcharges; they were only beneficiaries of the revenue. Given this change, some states eliminated this tax, creating an incentive for other states to reduce rates and the taxable base, while increasing the payroll tax.
20. The most relevant direct tax in terms of tax revenue is the income tax, which is a delegated authority of the provinces to the federal government and which forms part of the Federal Tax Co-participation Regime.

References

Afonso, J.R. (2016); "Carga tributaria en Brasil: redimensionada y repensada", *Revista de Administración Tributaria*, 40 (February), CIAT/AEAT/IEF, pp. 1-16.

Arroyo, J.M., J.P. Jiménez and C. Mussi (2012), "Revenue Sharing: The case of Brazil's ICMS", *Serie Macroeconomía del desarrollo* No. 121, División de Desarrollo Económico, CEPAL.

Blöchliger, H. and M. Nettley (2015), "Sub-central Tax Autonomy: 2011 Update", *OECD Working Papers on Fiscal Federalism*, No. 20, OECD Publishing, http://dx.doi.org/10.1787/5js4t79sbshd-en.

Blöchliger, H. and J. Rabesona (2009), "The Fiscal Autonomy of Sub-Central Governments: An Update", *OECD Working Papers on Fiscal Federalism*, No. 9, OECD Publishing, http://dx.doi.org/10.1787/5k97b111wb0t-en.

Blöchliger, H. and D. King (2006), "Fiscal Autonomy of Sub-Central Governments", *OECD Working Papers on Fiscal Federalism*, No. 2, OECD Publishing, http://dx.doi.org/10.1787/5k97b127pc0t-en.

Brosio, G. (2015); "Step on the Gas: Bolivia's Reliance on Natural Resource Revenue", en Fretes Cibils, V. y T. Ter Minassian (Eds.), *Decentralizing Revenue in Latin America – Why and How*, Inter-American Development Bank, Washington DC., pp. 79-116.

Brosio, G. and J.P. Jiménez (2012), "The intergovernmental allocation of revenue from natural resources: finding a balance between centripetal and centrifugal pressure", in Brosio, G. and J.P. Jiménez (eds.), *Decentralization and Reform in Latin America – Improving Intergovernmental Relations*, Elgar Publishing, Cheltenham, pp. 290-320.

Bruno de Carvalho (Jr.), P. (2006), "IPTU no Brasil: Progressividade, Arrecadação E Aspectos Extra-Fiscais", *Texto para Discussão* N° 1251 del Instituto de Pesquisa Econômica Aplicada -IPEA-, Brasilia, December, www.ipea.gov.br.

CEPAL (2014), "Pactos para la igualdad: Hacia un futuro sostenible". Trigésimo quinto período de sesiones de la CEPAL, documento oficial del 35° período de sesiones de la CEPAL (Lima, Perú), LC/G.2586 (SES.35/3), Santiago de Chile, April.

De Cesare, C. and J.F. Lazo Marín (2008), "Impuestos a los patrimonios en América Latina", *Serie Macroeconomía del Desarrollo* N° 66, ECLAC, Santiago de Chile.

Del Valle, M. (2013); "Ingresos Fiscales por Explotación de Recursos Mineros e Hidrocarburos en Perú", *Resumen de políticas del BID* N° 197, Inter-American Development Bank, Washington, DC, September.

Gómez Sabaini J.C. and J.P. Jiménez (2011), "El financiamiento de los gobiernos subnacionales en América Latina: un análisis de casos", *Serie macroeconomía del desarrollo* No. 111. División de Desarrollo Económico, ECLAC.

Horst, B. (2010), "Fuentes de financiamiento para gobiernos subnacionales y descentralización fiscal", *Serie Informe Económico* N° 202, Libertad y Desarrollo, Santiago de Chile.

Jiménez, J.P. and A. Podestá (2009), "Las relaciones fiscales intergubernamentales y las finanzas subnacionales ante la crisis", LC/R.2155, CEPAL, Santiago de Chile.

Jiménez, J.P. and J. Viñuela (2004), "Marco institucional para la gestión del gasto público en países descentralizados", Departamento de Finanzas Públicas, Fondo Monetario Internacional.

Keen, M. (2013), "Targeting, Cascading and Indirect Tax Design", *IMF Working Paper*, WP/13/57, Fiscal Affairs Department, International Monetary Fund.

Larios, J., B. Alvarado and E. Conterno (eds.) (2004), "Descentralización Fiscal. Análisis Conceptual y Revisión de Experiencias de Nueve Países", *Documento Técnico* N° 7, USAID, Lima.

Martínez-Vázquez, J. and C. Sepúlveda (2012a), "Intergovernmental transfers: a policy reform perspective", in Brosio, G. and J.P. Jiménez (eds.), *Decentralization and Reform in Latin America – Improving Intergovernmental Relations*, Elgar Publishing, Cheltenham pp. 260-289.

Martínez-Vázquez, J. and C. Sepúlveda (2012b), "Explaining property tax collections in developing countries: the case of Latin America", in Brosio, G. and J.P. Jiménez (eds.), *Decentralization and Reform in Latin America – Improving Intergovernmental Relations*, Elgar Publishing, Cheltenham, pp. 172-222.

OECD (2017), *Fiscal Decentralisation Database*, OECD Publishing, Paris, www.oecd.org/ctp/federalism/oecdfiscaldecentralisationdatabase.htm.

OECD (1999), "Taxing powers of state and local government", *Tax Policy Studies* No 1, Paris.

Rezende, F. and J. Veloso (2012), "Intergovernmental transfers in sub-national finances", in Brosio, G. and J.P. Jiménez (eds.), *Decentralization and Reform in Latin America – Improving Intergovernmental Relations*, Edward Elgar Publishing, Cheltenham, pp. 223-259.

Ruelas Ávila, I. (2015), "Evaluación de las características del impuesto predial en México", *Revista Iberoamericana de Estudios Municipales (RIEM)*, N° 12, Año VI, pp. 67-102.

Sánchez Torres, F., I. España Eljaiek and J. Zenteno (2015), "Fiscal Cumbia: Colombia's Revenue Dynamism", in Fretes Cibils, V. and T. Ter Minassian (eds.), *Decentralizing Revenue in Latin America – Why and How*, Inter-American Development Bank, Washington DC, pp. 155-198.

Ter Minassian, T. (2015), "Elusive Goal: Brazil's Subnational Revenue System Reform", in Fretes Cibils, V. and T. Ter Minassian (eds.), *Decentralizing Revenue in Latin America – Why and How*, Inter-American Development Bank, Washington DC., pp. 117-154.

CAPÍTULO 3

SECCIÓN ESPECIAL

La tributación y la autonomía fiscal en los gobiernos subnacionales de América Latina

SECCIÓN ESPECIAL
La tributación y la autonomía fiscal en los gobiernos subnacionales de América Latina[1]

Introducción

La forma en que se financia la provisión de servicios y bienes públicos y su asignación entre niveles de gobierno es un tema central para lograr un sistema intergubernamental sano y estable y un proceso de descentralización sostenible. Dado que los gobiernos subnacionales suelen contar con distintos instrumentos para financiar sus responsabilidades de gasto público, el nivel de financiamiento y la forma en que se combinen estos diferentes instrumentos va a determinar en gran parte el resultado de estos procesos.

Con el propósito de analizar un aspecto de esta problemática, en este capítulo se describe y analiza la estructura de financiamiento de los gobiernos subnacionales, haciendo referencia a la evolución y la composición de los recursos propios, específicamente los tributarios. A través del análisis de una serie de casos se pretende mostrar las opciones de financiamiento propio de que disponen estas jurisdicciones (ya sean intermedias y/o locales), más allá de la predominancia de las transferencias del gobierno central en ese sentido[2]. Posteriormente, con el fin de explorar los determinantes institucionales y de capacidad fiscal de los gobiernos subnacionales, se analiza la autonomía fiscal de algunos países seleccionados,[3] siguiendo para ello la metodología propuesta por OECD (1999), Jounard y Kongsrud (2003), Blochliger y King (2006), Blochliger y Petzold (2009), Blochliger y Nettley (2015).

3.1. El desempeño de los ingresos tributarios subnacionales en los procesos de descentralización recientes

En las últimas décadas, se ha observado en América Latina el afianzamiento de una gradual y clara tendencia hacia la descentralización fiscal desde el gobierno central hacia niveles inferiores de gobierno. Vale señalar que este fenómeno se ha visto reflejado tanto en los países federales tradicionales como Argentina o Brasil, los cuales traspasaron parte de las funciones del gobierno federal hacia los niveles inferiores de gobierno, así como en países unitarios donde – según el caso – se produjo una transferencia importante de funciones hacia los gobiernos locales o bien se crearon nuevos niveles intermedios de gobierno a los que se encomendó la formulación y ejecución – o exclusivamente la gestión – de importantes políticas públicas.

Este proceso, en sus diferentes períodos, se dio principalmente vía gasto público (en lugar de los ingresos); no obstante la situación es bastante heterogénea entre países. Aunado a esto, la forma en cómo los gobiernos subnacionales financien sus responsabilidades (asignadas) de gasto es una preocupación clave. Este financiamiento es logrado mediante tres modalidades: a) generación de recursos propios, ya sean tributos u otros ingresos no tributarios (regalías, tasas municipales, derechos, etc.); b) las transferencias intergubernamentales; y c) mediante endeudamiento, o una combinación de las tres alternativas.

Debe aclararse que, en sentido estricto, se define a los ingresos subnacionales propios como aquellos tributos en que los gobiernos subnacionales tienen potestades discrecionales para determinar la carga impositiva sobre los ciudadanos (Brosio y Jiménez, 2012). Sin embargo, en algunos casos los acuerdos existentes de coparticipación, por ejemplo en el caso de Alemania, se consideran como ingresos tributarios también. Esta potestad puede ser ejercida por tres instrumentos diferentes: administración tributaria, fijación de alícuota impositiva y determinación de la base imponible.

Para el caso de América Latina, se ha venido trabajando con una definición más laxa de recursos propios ya que se observa una combinación de estas tres dimensiones, no contando con la información necesaria en todos los casos (Gómez Sabaini y Jiménez, 2011). Ahora bien, tal como se señaló anteriormente, en la última sección de este capítulo, se presentará un análisis de la autonomía fiscal de algunos países de la región, tomando en cuenta la capacidad de los gobiernos subnacionales de Argentina, Brasil, Chile y México para fijar bases imponibles y alícuotas. Se trata de un desarrollo incipiente, con el objetivo de poder ampliarlo en futuros trabajos a otros países de la región.

Como se puede observar en el siguiente gráfico, los ingresos fiscales totales de estos gobiernos han crecido sostenidamente en los últimos quince años. Sin embargo, esto se debe fundamentalmente a la importancia creciente que han tenido las transferencias provenientes desde los gobiernos centrales y no tanto por el más limitado incremento de los recursos tributarios propios de los niveles intermedios y locales. En promedio, las transferencias totales aumentaron del 2.3% del PIB en el año 2000 a un 3.9% en 2014, en tanto que los recursos propios apenas pasaron del 2.6% del PIB a 3.2% en ese mismo período.

Gráfico 3.1. **Evolución de la estructura de los ingresos totales en gobiernos subnacionales, países seleccionados, 2000-14**

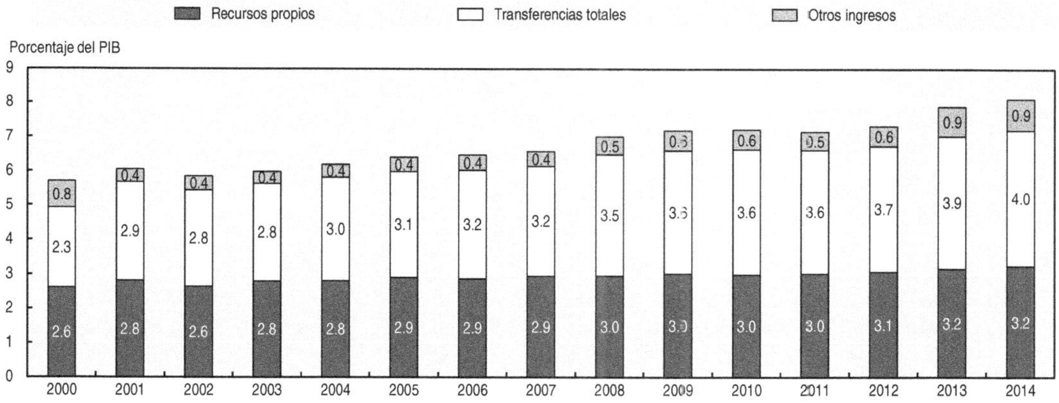

Nota: A lo largo del trabajo, se asume que en el análisis estadístico, el concepto de gobiernos subnacionales se referirá a las provincias en el caso de Argentina; estados y municipios en Brasil; municipios en Chile; departamentos y municipios en Colombia; gobiernos locales en Costa Rica; consejos provinciales y municipios en Ecuador; estados y municipios en México, gobiernos locales de Perú y gobiernos locales de Uruguay.

Fuente: Comisión Económica para América Latina y el Caribe (CEPAL), sobre la base de cifras oficiales.

StatLink http://dx.doi.org/10.1787/888933462919

En este sentido, en el cuadro 3.1 puede observarse la estructura actual de financiamiento de los gobiernos subnacionales en los países latinoamericanos incluidos en la parte descriptiva de este informe. El primer hecho saliente lo constituyen las diferencias encontradas en el peso relativo que poseen los recursos propios (tributarios y no tributarios) dentro del total de ingresos percibidos por estos niveles de gobierno. Al respecto puede comprobarse que los estados y municipios de Brasil obtienen más de la mitad de sus ingresos (75.1%) a partir de sus recursos propios, lo que representa el 11.1% en términos del PIB (más del 90% de los cuales corresponden a ingresos tributarios)[4]. Por su parte, los recursos propios en Costa Rica -pese a su bajo nivel respecto al PIB- tienen un peso importante dentro de la estructura de sus ingresos totales (99.8%), si bien se reconoce que el proceso de descentralización fiscal no ha experimentado avances significativos a partir de una adecuada delegación de responsabilidades de gasto ni de potestades tributarias hacia niveles inferiores de gobierno. Lo mismo sucede en Uruguay, donde los recursos propios representan casi el 64% de los recursos totales de los gobiernos locales.

Resulta particular el caso de Chile, donde los recursos propios de los municipios representan el 60.5% de sus ingresos totales (cuadro 3.1). Sin embargo, vale notar que en este país la preponderancia de los recursos propios como fuente principal de ingresos subnacionales posee dos componentes: los ingresos propios permanentes y los ingresos provenientes del Fondo Común Municipal (FCM). Dado que este mecanismo de igualación horizontal solidaria entre municipios se nutre prácticamente en su totalidad (99%) de los mismos recursos tributarios recaudados por estas jurisdicciones[5], en este informe se considera su influencia antes de ser distribuido, o sea dentro del conjunto de recursos propios disponibles para reflejar mejor la potencialidad de los mismos en materia de financiamiento subnacional[6].

Cuadro 3.1. **Estructura de los ingresos totales de los gobiernos subnacionales, 2014**

Como porcentaje del PIB y de los ingresos totales

País	Recursos propios		Transferencias		Otros Ingresos		Ingresos Totales
	% PIB	% Total	% PIB	% Total	% PIB	% Total	% PIB
Argentina	6.3	41.7	8.8	58	0.1	0.4	15.2
Brasil*	11.1	75.1	3.7	24.8	0	0.1	14.8
Chile	2.1	60.5	1.4	39.1	0	0.4	3.5
Colombia	3.7	31.6	5	42.8	3	25.6	11.8
Costa Rica	1.15	99.78	0.001	0.09	0.00	0.13	1.15
Ecuador*	1.0	21.6	3.6	77	0.1	1.3	4.6
México*	1.4	13.8	8.7	86.2	0	0	10.1
Perú	1.1	27.3	2.6	66.7	0.23	6	3.9
Uruguay	**1.99**	**63.8**	**1.1**	**36.2**	**0**	**0**	**3.1**

a/ Como "recursos propios" se toma en cuenta a los ingresos tributarios propios y no tributarios.
b/ "Otros Ingresos" puede incluir distintas formas de endeudamiento, inversiones, recursos por ventas de activos, recuperación de préstamos, transferencias de capital, etc.
Los datos para los países marcados con asterisco corresponden a 2013.
Fuente: Comisión Económica para América Latina y el Caribe (CEPAL), sobre la base de cifras oficiales.

StatLink http://dx.doi.org/10.1787/888933462972

Por el contrario, en el resto de los países de la región la principal fuente de recursos públicos de los gobiernos subnacionales proviene del sistema de transferencias que cada gobierno central implementa para complementar el financiamiento de sus responsabilidades de gastos, es decir la provisión de bienes públicos a sus ciudadanos. Las administraciones centrales de gobierno de países tales como Argentina y México aportan más de 8% del PIB en concepto de transferencias hacia los niveles inferiores de gobierno. En los caso de Colombia y Ecuador, esta fuente de ingresos subnacionales representa 5.0% y un 3.6% del PIB respectivamente, mientras que en Brasil estos recursos equivalen a 3.7 puntos porcentuales del producto de dicho país[7]. En lo que corresponde a Perú y Uruguay, las transferencias ascienden a 2.6% y 1.1% del PIB respectivamente con un peso relativo superior al 66% y al 36% dentro cada una de sus respectivas estructuras de ingresos fiscales.

Al profundizar por tipo de impuestos, se puede observar que la recaudación de los impuestos a la actividad económica (cuya clave es 5100 dentro de la clasificación utilizada) ha sido la más alta, superando en la mayor parte del periodo el 1% del PIB, incluso acercándose a los 2 puntos del producto durante los últimos dos años. La recaudación de los impuestos a la propiedad (4100), en donde se consideran principalmente el impuesto a la propiedad inmobiliaria, se ha mantenido estable alcanzando un 0.4% del PIB durante todo el periodo analizado.

Gráfico 3.2. **Evolución de los ingresos tributarios de los gobiernos subnacionales, por tipo de impuesto, países seleccionados, 2000-15**

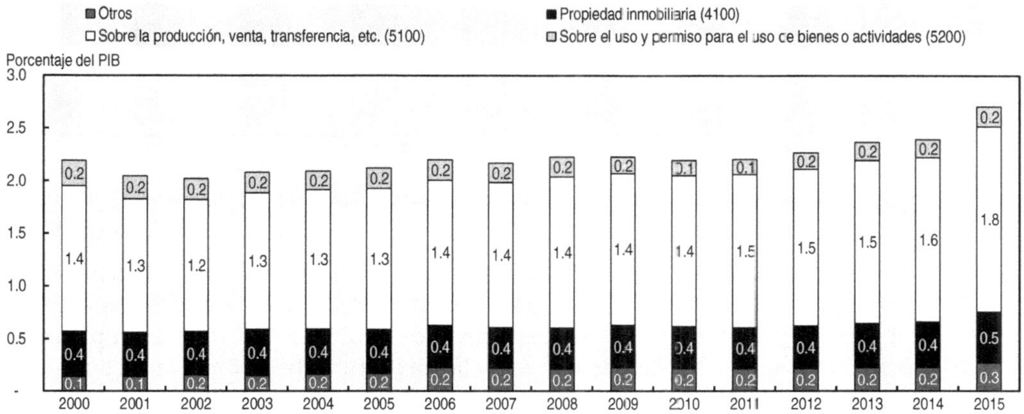

Fuente: Elaboración propia con base en los datos presentados en el capítulo 6.

StatLink http://dx.doi.org/10.1787/888933462922

3.2. Los ingresos tributarios de los gobiernos subnacionales: estructura y evolución

Como se ha enfatizado en la literatura relevante, la descentralización de potestades tributarias a los gobiernos subnacionales ha sido relativamente débil en la mayoría de los países, si bien ha estado sujeta a las particularidades propias de cada país. El gráfico 3.3 pone en evidencia la dispar y mayoritariamente escasa participación de los gobiernos subnacionales en la recaudación total de los países latinoamericanos. La excepción la constituye Brasil, en el que los estados y los municipios poseen conjuntamente más del 30% de la recaudación total, denotando un importante grado de descentralización de potestades tributarias hacia dichos niveles de gobierno, acompañado de un aumento significativo en las capacidades fiscales de los gobiernos subnacionales de este país (punto respaldado en el ejercicio de autonomía fiscal que se realiza en la última parte). En un segundo escalafón de países se encuentran Argentina y Colombia, en los cuales los niveles subnacionales aportan aproximadamente más del 15% de la recaudación total.

Sin embargo, en el resto de los países, los gobiernos centrales no han avanzado de manera significativa en la descentralización de los recursos tributarios. De este modo, en estos países la recaudación tributaria subnacional representa, en promedio, entre el 2% y el 5% de los ingresos tributarios totales de cada país.

Gráfico 3.3. **Ingresos tributarios según nivel de gobierno, 2014**

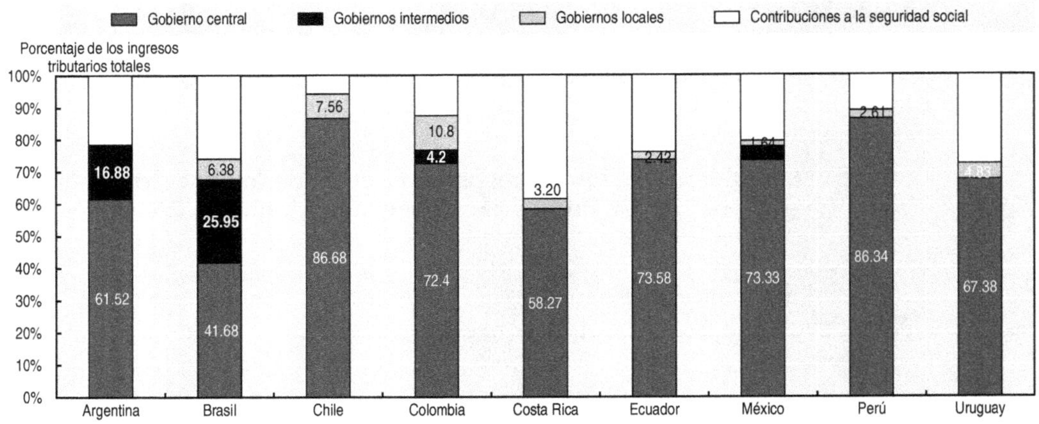

Fuente: Elaboración propia con base en los datos presentados en el capítulo 6.

StatLink http://dx.doi.org/10.1787/888933462939

Se observa además que la recaudación tributaria de los gobiernos subnacionales en los países de la región ha crecido muy poco durante los últimos diez años (lo que contrasta con los ingresos fiscales a nivel de gobierno central) y esta pobre evolución se relaciona con la debilidad en el nivel y la estructura de la imposición subnacional, lo que a su vez tiene relación con las bases tributarias disponibles por parte de estos niveles de gobierno.

Si bien la baja recaudación de impuestos propios es un problema, debe señalarse que cuando se evalúa la cantidad de gastos que los gobiernos intermedios y locales tienen que financiar, no parece que haya mucho margen adicional para reasignar potestades tributarias. Al respecto, lo que surge claramente es que a los gobiernos subnacionales les resulta difícil aprovechar las potestades tributarias ya disponibles, como por ejemplo se observa en los magros ingresos generados por el impuesto predial en los países de América Latina.

Cuadro 3.2. **Estructura de los principales impuestos de los gobiernos subnacionales – gobiernos intermedios y locales- en América Latina, 2014**

	En % del PIB				
País	Propiedad inmobiliaria (4100)	Sobre la actividad económica (5100)	Sobre el uso de bienes y contribuciones de mejora (5200)	Otros	Total
Argentina	0.38	4.02	0.26	0.59	5.25
Brazil	0.48	7.61	0.00	2.21	10.30
Chile	0.62	0.23	0.64	0.00	1.49
Colombia	0.73	1.39	0.00	1.06	3.18
Costa Rica	0.29	0.40	0.00	0.02	0.72
Ecuador	0.11	0.17	0.03	0.15	0.46
Mexico	0.22	0.03	0.12	0.55	0.91
Peru	0.21	0.08	0.00	0.24	0.53
Uruguay	0.81	0.00	0.51	0.00	1.32

País	En % de los ingresos totales				
	Propiedad inmobiliaria (4100)	Sobre la actividad económica (5100)	Sobre el uso de bienes y contribuciones de mejora (5200)	Otros	Total
Argentina	7.3	76.5	5.0	11.2	100
Brasil	4.7	73.8	0.0	21.5	100
Chile	41.3	15.7	42.9	0.0	100
Colombia	23.1	43.7	0.0	33.3	100
Costa Rica	40.8	55.9	0.0	3.4	100
Ecuador	24.1	37.6	6.7	31.7	100
México	24.0	3.0	13.0	60.0	100
Perú	40.1	15.3	0.0	44.6	100
Uruguay	61.4	0.0	38.6	0.0	100

Fuente: Elaboración propia con base a los datos presentados en el capítulo 6.

StatLink http://dx.doi.org/10.1787/888933462983

A continuación, se expone un análisis detallado de los principales impuestos presentados en el cuadro precedente, con las características propias de cada uno de los países seleccionados como casos de estudio en el presente trabajo.

a) Imposición sobre la propiedad inmobiliaria (4100)

Los trabajos de investigación más recientes junto con la información estadística disponible confirman que la relevancia de la imposición patrimonial en términos del PIB y en relación con total recaudado (si se excluyen de esta categoría a los impuestos que gravan las transacciones financieras) no resulta significativa en ninguno de los sistemas tributarios latinoamericanos. Aún así, los tributos que afectan el patrimonio constituyen el principal instrumento de generación de recursos propios con que los gobiernos subnacionales de la región cuentan para financiar sus responsabilidades de gasto.

Simultáneamente, dentro de la amplia gama de impuestos que suelen recaer sobre el patrimonio de los contribuyentes, el impuesto a la propiedad inmueble o predial es el instrumento más comúnmente aceptado y explotado como fuente de recursos fiscales en las instancias subnacionales de gobierno, aún con un escaso peso relativo que se ubica por debajo del 0.7% del PIB en la mayoría de los casos (a excepción de Colombia y Uruguay)[8].

No obstante lo anterior, el impuesto predial adquiere una muy desigual importancia relativa respecto de la totalidad de recursos tributarios subnacionales según el país analizado. Así puede observarse en el cuadro 3.2 que en algunos países el impuesto a la propiedad inmueble aporta una parte relevante de la recaudación propia, como sucede en Chile, Costa Rica, Perú y Uruguay.

En el caso de México, cada estado es autónomo en las atribuciones asignadas en la Constitución, inclusive en la creación de impuestos. En lo que respecta al impuesto a la propiedad inmueble, el mismo es un tributo eminentemente municipal[9] y representa más del 23% de los ingresos subnacionales[10]. El registro catastral y la valuación fiscal es responsabilidad de cada uno de los municipios, por lo cual la unificación de criterios sólo puede ser alcanzada a través de acuerdos entre jurisdicciones.

Por ejemplo, el impuesto territorial chileno (IT), que fija el pago de contribuciones de bienes raíces, representa el principal componente de los ingresos tributarios municipales. Actualmente este impuesto contribuye con ingresos equivalentes a 0.6% del PIB, lo cual corresponde a más del 41% del total de recursos tributarios subnacionales[11]. Para este impuesto, tanto la tasa como la base imponible y las exenciones a su pago se encuentran fijadas por ley (nacional) y los municipios, en la práctica, sólo son los beneficiarios de los recursos que se recaudan. La base del impuesto territorial está determinada por la valuación fiscal de la propiedad realizada por el Servicio de Impuestos Internos (SII) y la tasa del impuesto está fijada por ley. Ello lleva a que se trate de un impuesto patrimonial que no tiene relación con el pago por bienes y servicios locales que el municipio entrega al entorno donde se encuentra emplazado el bien inmueble.

En Colombia, aunque originalmente fue de jurisdicción departamental, el Impuesto Predial Unificado está asignado por la Constitución de 1991 a los municipios, los cuales fueron dotados del poder para determinar las tasas (dentro de un rango preestablecido), las exenciones, los tratamientos preferenciales y los usos específicos de lo recaudado por el tributo. Como podría esperarse, pueden existir (y de hecho, existen) tantos marcos regulatorios para la imposición a la propiedad inmueble como los municipios existentes, reflejando las necesidades particulares de cada uno de estos. Así, el impuesto predial colombiano, que recauda cerca de 0.7% del PIB, se impone sobre todas las propiedades inmuebles, urbanas y rurales, con o sin edificaciones, ubicadas dentro de los límites geográficos de cada municipio. Además, el impuesto predial en Colombia constituye el segundo impuesto que mayor recaudación reporta a los niveles inferiores de gobierno con una participación relativa superior al 23% respecto de los ingresos totales de estas jurisdicciones (cuadro 3.2).

La base imponible en este caso está determinada por la valuación catastral, la cual es realizada por oficinas de catastro descentralizadas en el caso de Bogotá, Antioquia, Cali y Medellín y por el Instituto Geográfico Agustín Codazzi (IGAC) en el resto de las jurisdicciones. Si bien los valores de los inmuebles son actualizados anualmente aplicando un ratio que toma en cuenta el índice de precios al consumidor, en varios municipios de Colombia se han evidenciado problemas con la actualización de los valores catastrales respecto de los valores de mercado, recurriéndose al mecanismo de valuación auto determinada o "auto-valuación" catastral. En cuanto a las alícuotas del impuesto, éstas pueden ser establecidas por las autoridades municipales dentro de cierto rango respecto de la valuación catastral, con una estructura diferenciada y progresiva en función del tipo de estratificación social y de utilización de las tierras en las áreas urbanas que determinan, en última instancia, el valor fiscal de los inmuebles afectados por el impuesto predial.

En Ecuador, el impuesto predial aporta aproximadamente el 24% de los ingresos tributarios subnacionales (0.11% del PIB). La base gravable del tributo corresponde al valor global del predio determinado y actualizado cada dos años por la oficina de catastro municipal con base en: el valor del suelo, el valor de las edificaciones y el valor de reposición, conforme a lo dispuesto por el Concejo Municipal. No obstante lo anterior, el método de valuación catastral conjuga información provista directamente por el propietario junto con los datos de escrituración debido a dificultades logísticas observadas en la mayoría de las jurisdicciones. Las tasas del impuesto para propiedades urbanas varían entre 0.25 y 5 puntos por mil del valor del inmueble, mientras que para las áreas rurales se ubican entre 0.25 y 3 por mil.

Como se mencionó, el aporte de recaudación tributaria de los cantones en Costa Rica resulta poco significativo respecto del total nacional. La razón principal de esto consiste en que los municipios tienen sólo la responsabilidad de administración tributaria de algunos impuestos sobre la propiedad y sobre las ventas. Al respecto, los niveles locales de gobierno deben realizar las valuaciones, recaudar y exigir el pago de los tributos en sus jurisdicciones. En particular, el impuesto predial en este país aporta gran parte (más del 40% en 2014) de los recursos tributarios subnacionales, lo que equivale a casi el 0.3% del PIB (cuadro 3.2). La alícuota vigente, decidida por el gobierno central, es de 0.25% sobre el valor del inmueble y es de aplicación en todo el territorio nacional.

En Argentina y Brasil, los dos países de la región con mayor participación subnacional dentro de los ingresos tributarios totales, los niveles inferiores de gobierno también recaudan el impuesto a la propiedad inmueble, aunque éste se encuentra subordinado a otro tipo de impuestos que reportan mayores recursos tributarios como los impuestos que gravan la actividad económica (que serán analizados en el próximo apartado).

En Argentina, el Impuesto Inmobiliario es el tercer impuesto en importancia de la recaudación provincial (nivel intermedio de gobierno), superado actualmente por los impuestos que gravan a la actividad económica (ingresos brutos) y otros impuestos (como a los sellos), representando poco menos de la décima parte del total obtenido por estas jurisdicciones (7.3% en 2014)[12]. Además, el 88% de los recursos que genera este tributo se concentra en 5 de las 24 provincias y especialmente entre la Capital Federal (32.8%) (GCBA) y la provincia de Buenos Aires (32.2%), las cuales explican, a su vez, más del 65% de la recaudación de este impuesto.

La forma de valuación más utilizada en Argentina tiene en cuenta tanto el suelo como la construcción, o sea que la base se determina por el inmueble completo. Otro método utilizado, puntualmente en la provincia de Buenos Aires, consiste en valuar por separado el suelo y la construcción o mejoras de un mismo inmueble para aplicarle tasas diferentes, donde las tarifas de las mejoras son más bajas que las del suelo.

En Brasil, existen dos impuestos que gravan la propiedad inmueble, según sea urbana o rural. Por un lado, el Impuesto a la Propiedad Predial y Territorial Urbana (IPTU) está asignado como potestad exclusiva de los municipios y del Distrito Federal y, por ende, la base legal del impuesto depende de normas directamente establecidas por cada jurisdicción. El IPTU[13], que aporta ingresos tributarios por un monto equivalente a 0.48% del PIB para 2014, grava la propiedad o posesión de bienes inmuebles en las zonas urbanas y la base del impuesto está determinada por el valor de mercado de los mismos, aplicándose tasas fijadas por cada municipio en particular. Dentro de la estructura de los ingresos tributarios municipales, el peso relativo de este impuesto ronda el 20%, mientras que comparado con todos los ingresos tributarios subnacionales la importancia se reduce al 4.7% (cuadro 3.2). El IPTU se distingue del Impuesto a la Propiedad Territorial Rural (ITR), el cual es un impuesto asignado al gobierno central y cuya base imponible es la tierra libre de mejoras y edificaciones en zonas rurales.

En Perú, las tasas de este impuesto son fijadas por el Gobierno Central manteniendo una estructura progresiva. Asimismo, parte de los ingresos recaudados de este impuesto se utilizan para financiar las propias actividades catastrales y de avalúo. Con todo, las municipalidades obtienen ingresos provenientes del cobro de este impuesto cercanos a los 0.21% del producto, lo que representa cerca del 40% de los ingresos tributarios de los gobiernos locales.

En Uruguay, por su parte, la contribución inmobiliaria es un impuesto que se cobra en relación al valor real del padrón con tasas progresivas. Las tasas son fijadas por las municipalidades. Para el 2014, la recaudación de este impuesto ascendió a 0.81% del PIB, cifra equivalente a más del 61% de los ingresos tributarios subnacionales de este país.

b) Imposición sobre la producción, venta y transferencia de bienes (5100)

Impuestos sobre el consumo

Los tributos sobre la producción, venta y transferencia de bienes implican mayores riesgos de coordinación tributaria en la medida que las diferencias entre las tasas aplicadas en regiones vecinas pueden inducir a los contribuyentes a "exportar" decisiones de consumo y de producción/comercialización hacia aquellas áreas de menor carga tributaria relativa dentro de un mismo país. La falta de coordinación también puede llevar a los gobiernos subnacionales a competir por la localización de producción o consumo (guerras tributarias) a través de la modificación de alícuotas o bases gravables[14].

En general, los países suelen utilizar dos tipos diferenciados de impuestos sobre las ventas o consumos: a) de única etapa, no acumulativos, tal como es el impuesto general a las ventas al consumidor final utilizados en los Estados Unidos, y como suelen ser los impuestos selectivos sobre determinados bienes y servicios y b) de etapas múltiples no acumulativos, tal como es el impuesto al valor agregado utilizado en todos los países de América Latina. Menos frecuentes, pero existentes en la región a nivel subnacional, son los impuestos acumulativos o "en cascada" que gravan cada una de las etapas de producción, distribución y comercialización, los cuales logran generar una significativa recaudación con una baja alícuota en razón de gravar reiteradamente la misma base imponible.

Asimismo, los impuestos específicos o selectivos son potencialmente una buena fuente de ingresos para estos niveles de gobierno gracias a la relativa facilidad de administrarlos y la posibilidad de diferenciación por alícuotas entre regiones, aunque el aspecto que debe ser destacado está relacionado con el principio jurisdiccional aplicado.

En la medida que, tanto los impuestos generales a las ventas o consumos como los impuestos específicos, son cobrados en el lugar en donde residen los consumidores (principio de destino) y no en el lugar donde se producen o prestan los bienes y servicios (principio de origen), estos tributos no generan efectos distorsivos sobre las decisiones económicas de los contribuyentes (Larios et al., 2004) .

Resulta evidente que aunque se aplique para un mismo bien el principio del destino, pero con distintos niveles de tasas entre las jurisdicciones, se estará creando un incentivo a efectuar compras fuera de la propia jurisdicción y por lo tanto se generarán efectos distorsivos en la asignación de los recursos, que resultarán muy difíciles de evitar a menos que se logre una armonización de los niveles de imposición entre las mismas.

Las diversas alternativas técnicas utilizadas para dar solución al problema de la doble imposición a nivel local van desde establecer cajas compensadoras entre las jurisdicciones, diferir el pago del gravamen en el momento de la venta, o conformar un sistema integrado donde participe tanto el gobierno central como los locales para evitar la duplicación del gravamen. No obstante la experiencia de la Unión Europea señala que las mismas no están libres de complejidades y cuestionamientos técnicos.

Entre los países analizados, cuatro de ellos se destacan por asignar la potestad exclusiva sobre determinados impuestos sobre las ventas a sus gobiernos subnacionales, constituyéndolos en todos los casos en la principal fuente de recursos tributarios propios de su respectivo nivel de gobierno.

En el caso de Argentina, la fuente principal de ingresos tributarios de las provincias es el Impuesto a los Ingresos Brutos (el cual también está asignado, en porcentajes mucho menores, a algunos municipios). Para el año 2014, este tributo contribuyó con casi un 76% de la recaudación total provincial lo que equivale a 4 puntos porcentuales del PIB. Las tasas aplicadas son diferenciadas entre provincias y entre actividades, y también existen diferencias en el peso relativo del impuesto en cada provincia (oscilando entre

57.7% y 86.5%) aunque en todas resulta el tributo de mayor recaudación. A pesar de ser criticado por las ineficiencias que genera como impuesto "en cascada"[15] (distorsiona la asignación de recursos al cambiar la estructura de precios relativos y perjudica a los productores internos respecto de la competencia internacional), este tributo ha mostrado un elevado rendimiento tributario contribuyendo a la autonomía provincial en cuanto a necesidades de financiamiento (Gómez Sabaini and Jiménez, 2011).

En Brasil, los impuestos sobre las ventas fueron adoptados por los tres niveles de gobierno lo cual implica dificultades de coordinación interjurisdiccional. Además del Impuesto sobre Productos Industrializados (IPI), recaudado por el gobierno federal sobre una extensa lista de bienes producidos y cuyo monto se determina siguiendo el de un gravamen al valor agregado, los gobiernos estatales poseen potestad tributaria plena sobre el Impuesto a la Circulación de Mercaderías y Servicios (ICMS), que también grava a los bienes y servicios en todas las etapas pero de manera general, es decir que cubre una base de imposición mucho más amplia que el IPI. Asimismo, los municipios administran y recaudan el Impuesto sobre Servicios (ISS) que grava toda prestación de servicios estipulada en la legislación que se desarrolle dentro de los límites geográficos de cada municipio. Al ser potestad exclusiva, cada municipio puede establecer la alícuota que considere oportuna con un máximo de 5% sobre la facturación.

Si se consideran conjuntamente el ICMS y el ISS, se tiene que los gobiernos subnacionales brasileños recaudan casi el 74% de sus recursos tributarios a partir de la imposición sobre las ventas o, visto de otra manera, disponen de recursos fiscales equivalentes a 7.6% del PIB merced a ese tipo de tributación (cuadro 3.2), lo cual transforma a estos impuestos, sobre todo el ICMS estadual, en la principal y fundamental fuente de ingresos de los niveles inferiores de gobierno en dicho país.

En lo que respecta a Colombia, este país también asigna a los impuestos sobre las ventas de bienes y servicios un rol preponderante en el conjunto de recursos tributarios de jurisdicción subnacional. A partir del cuadro 3.2 puede observarse que la recaudación de estos tributos en 2014 fue de casi 1.4% del producto, lo que equivale a casi el 44% del total de ingresos tributarios subnacionales.

Se destaca que los recursos mencionados se pueden dividir en dos grupos diferenciados. Por un lado, los gobiernos departamentales aportan el 29% de la recaudación tributaria subnacional y concentran un 57% de sus ingresos a partir de la aplicación de tres impuestos selectivos a los consumos de licores, cervezas y cigarrillos. Por otro lado, los municipios, que contribuyen con más del 71% de la recaudación consolidada de las entidades territoriales colombianas, poseen como principal fuente de ingresos tributarios propios al Impuesto de Industria y Comercio (ICA), el cual supera al impuesto predial como principal tributo subnacional en cuanto a recaudación generada, representando este último un 38% del total de la recaudación municipal (y un 27% del consolidado subnacional) en el año 2014.

Impuestos sobre las patentes comerciales[16]

En el caso de Ecuador, gran parte de los ingresos por imposición a la actividad económica se concentran en el Impuesto a las Patentes, el cual es de potestad municipal y grava el ejercicio de cualquier actividad económica de carácter comercial o industrial dentro de la jurisdicción del municipio. Este tributo grava la actividad de las personas naturales o jurídicas que tengan la calidad de comerciantes o industriales que operen en cada cantón, así como a quienes ejerzan cualquier actividad de orden económico. En términos agregados, la recaudación de impuestos a la actividad económica alcanzó 0.17 puntos del producto para el 2014, lo que equivale al 37.6% del total de los ingresos tributarios subnacionales en este país.

En Chile, los gobiernos subnacionales también disponen de los recursos generados a partir del cobro de patentes comerciales, las cuales se aplican por la municipalidad respectiva al ejercicio de toda profesión, oficio, industria, comercio, arte u otra actividad lucrativa secundaria o terciaria – sea cual fuere su naturaleza o denominación (incluidas las patentes de alcoholes). Este tributo aportó en 2014 el 15.7% de los ingresos tributarios municipales, lo que equivale a 0.23% del PIB.

Finalmente, el impuesto de patentes en Costa Rica constituye el principal tributo recaudado por los gobiernos locales de ese país, aportando más de la mitad de la recaudación tributaria de los mismos en el año 2014 (56% del total y 0.4% del PIB). En este caso, la base imponible es la actividad económica realizada o la renta líquida gravable y las ventas o ingresos brutos anuales que perciban las personas físicas o jurídicas que se dediquen al ejercicio de actividades lucrativas[17,18].

c) Imposición sobre el uso de bienes y contribuciones de mejora (5200)

En los países de la región existen diversas alternativas para gravar el uso de bienes y contribuciones de mejora. Así puede ser que el hecho imponible del tributo sea directamente una manifestación parcial del patrimonio del contribuyente. El impuesto que más se destaca en este rubro es el que recae sobre los vehículos automotores. Otra opción se constituye si el impuesto recae sobre aquellos que utilizan este bien para circular en la vía pública (también conocidos como "derechos de circulación"). Por último, casi todos los países, a través de sus gobiernos subnacionales, imponen un tributo sobre la transferencia de los vehículos entre sus ciudadanos.

Tomando en consideración la gama de variantes para su aplicación y aprovechamiento como fuente de recursos fiscales en los niveles inferiores de gobierno, el impuesto sobre automotores está presente en varios países latinoamericanos aunque sólo en algunos resulte moderadamente significativo en la recaudación tributaria subnacional.

La justificación de su utilización radica principalmente en que este tributo es fácil de administrar, de llevar sus registros y es una fuente permanente y estable de ingresos, especialmente en gobiernos subnacionales con un alto grado de urbanización. Por otra parte, la información sobre el stock de automóviles en una ciudad es útil para poner impuestos ecológicos que limiten el uso de vehículos y combatir la contaminación ambiental, es decir que el gravamen puede ser utilizado para otros objetivos no necesariamente recaudatorios.

En algunos países se ha tratado de utilizar el impuesto a los vehículos como parte de una política redistributiva, si bien este objetivo es de mayor responsabilidad y peso a nivel central, aunque parcialmente se puede admitir un impuesto progresivo cuya tasa grave la compra de vehículos nuevos. En Argentina, la provincia de San Juan tiene un impuesto "progresivo" a los vehículos; la tasa del impuesto es 3% pero el valor que se aplica es función del modelo, antigüedad y peso del vehículo. Esta forma de gravar a los vehículos es administrativamente compleja y puede penalizar a vehículos nuevos que son más eficientes y contaminan menos que los vehículos más antiguos.

De modo similar, en México existe el Impuesto sobre Tenencia o Uso de Vehículos (ISTUV), el cual se encuadra como potestad exclusiva, desde el año 2012, de los estados y la Ciudad de México[19]. Este tributo ofrece varias ventajas desde el punto de vista recaudatorio y equitativo. La base del impuesto suele ser relativamente estable en la medida en que el número de automóviles tiende a crecer a un ritmo similar o superior a la tasa de crecimiento poblacional y su nivel de ingresos. Adicionalmente, la base es relativamente difícil de ocultar y el gravamen recae sobre aquellos individuos de mayor poder adquisitivo. En total, la recaudación de los impuestos sobre el uso de bienes y contribuciones de mejora en México asciende a 0.12% del PIB, lo cual significa casi el 13% de los ingresos subnacionales.

En Chile, la recaudación de estos impuestos representan casi el 43% de los ingresos tributarios locales (0.64% del PIB). Principalmente, la principal fuente de estos recursos recae sobre los propietarios de vehículos automotores (y que comprende tanto la compra como el permiso anual para circular con el mismo). Al respecto, el valor del permiso de circulación se determina en la mayoría de los casos sobre la base de la tasación que realiza el Servicio de Impuestos Internos de los vehículos motorizados y, sobre esta tasación, la Ley de Rentas Municipales fija las diferentes tasas. Vale señalar que este tributo constituye uno de los principales ingresos municipales, destacándose que el 62.5% de su recaudación debe ser entregada al Fondo Común Municipal.

El cobro de Patente de Rodados en Uruguay es la principal (única) fuente de ingresos dentro de esta clasificación. Su recaudación asciende a 0.51% del PIB y su peso relativo es del 38.6% dentro de los ingresos totales subnacionales. El cobro de este impuesto sienta sus bases legales en la Constitución y sus normas se publican anualmente. Las alícuotas se fijan según el año de empadronamiento del vehículo.

d) Otros impuestos subnacionales relevantes en los países de la región

Además de los típicos impuestos utilizados por los gobiernos subnacionales que aquí se han analizado resulta indispensable comentar algunos ejemplos de tributos que amplían la vasta gama de instrumentos fiscales a partir de los cuales obtienen su financiamiento.

En este sentido, el impuesto sobre nóminas (3000) es un tributo asignado a los gobiernos estatales de México que contribuyó en el año 2014 con el 41% de la recaudación subnacional (monto equivalente al 0.37% del PIB mexicano). Este tipo de impuesto tiene ventajas y desventajas. Por una parte, resulta fácil de administrar, especialmente si se aplica sobre empresas grandes, y asimismo cuando la economía tiene un alto grado de formalización laboral, con tasas relativamente bajas, se pueden recaudar recursos significativos para gobiernos regionales. Por la otra, se argumenta que su principal desventaja es que este impuesto actúa como una barrera a la generación de empleo en el sector formal, y además puede constituir una forma encubierta de exportar impuestos a otras jurisdicciones al gravar en base al principio del origen en el supuesto de que el mismo afecte los costos de producción (Larios et al., 2004).

En Argentina, no debe dejar de mencionarse el Impuesto a los Sellos (4400) como una importante fuente de recursos tributarios para los gobiernos provinciales. Este tributo, desde el punto de vista de la eficiencia económica, resulta cuestionable al establecer una carga fiscal para que los actos jurídicos onerosos realizados por las personas y las empresas queden encuadrados dentro del régimen legal. Sin embargo, el Impuesto a los Sellos constituye el segundo gravamen de mayor recaudación para estas jurisdicciones con una porción de 8.0% del total para el año 2014, lo cual equivale a 0.42 puntos porcentuales del producto.

En el caso de Brasil, los recursos tributarios subnacionales ya explicitados anteriormente se complementan con los impuestos relacionados con la transmisión gratuita de bienes en todas sus variantes. Por un lado, la transmisión gratuita de bienes es gravada por el Impuesto a la Transmisión "inter-vivos" (ITBI), de potestad municipal; por el otro lado, el Impuesto sobre Transmisiones de Bienes por Causa de Muerte (herencias) y Donaciones (ITCD) que es asignado a los estados y al Distrito Federal.

En Perú, parte importante de los ingresos tributarios de los gobiernos locales se encuentran en el cobro de los impuestos a las transacciones financieras (4400), así como otras cargas que son facultades meramente locales (6200). En total, la suma de estos ingresos asciende a 0.24% del PIB, lo que corresponde al 44.6% de los ingresos de los gobiernos locales.

3.3. Aproximaciones a la medición de la autonomía fiscal

Uno de los desafíos metodológicos más relevantes que ha presentado el debate sobre las relaciones fiscales intergubernamentales y la descentralización fiscal, es la medición de la autonomía fiscal de los gobiernos subnacionales. Una forma habitual de medir esta autonomía es a través de la suma de los ingresos propios, definido como propio subnacional en la medida en que sea ese nivel de gobierno quien lo administre y disponga de los recursos que el tributo pueda generar. Sin embargo, este tipo de mediciones dejan fuera del análisis la potestad y la discrecionalidad que estos gobiernos pudiesen tener para fijar tasas y bases gravables sin intervención alguna del gobierno central.

Para efectos de esta sección, la autonomía fiscal se entiende como la medición que evalúa el grado de libertad con el que los gobiernos subnacionales pueden crear o abolir nuevos impuestos locales, definir bases fiscales o incluso otorgar exenciones tributarias a personas naturales y empresas. Es así que la medición de autonomía fiscal que en este trabajo se propone, busca hacerse cargo del punto anterior. Para ello, se utiliza la metodología desarrollada por la OCDE en el *Fiscal Federalism Network*, cuya taxonomía se presenta a continuación:

Cuadro 3.3. **Taxonomía de la autonomía fiscal**

a.1	El GSN fija las tasa impositiva y cualquier exención sin necesidad de consultar a un nivel superior de gobierno
a.2	El GSN fija las tasas y exenciones después de consultar al nivel superior de gobierno
b.1	El GSN fijas las tasas sin límites (máximo y mínimo) impuestos por el nivel superior
b.2	El GSN fija las tasas considerando los límites (máximo y mínimo) impuestos por el nivel superior de gobierno
c.1	EL GSN establece las exenciones, pero únicamente fija las deducciones fiscales
c.2	El GSN establece las exenciones, pero únicamente fija los créditos fiscales
c.3	El GSN establece las exenciones y fija tanto las deducciones y los créditos fiscales
d.1	Existe un sistema de coordinación fiscal de distribución de impuestos en el cual el GSN determina el reparto de los ingresos
d.2	Existe un sistema de coordinación fiscal de distribución de impuestos en el cual el reparto de los ingresos recaudados pueden cambiarse únicamente con el consentimiento de los GSN
d.3	Existe un sistema de coordinación fiscal en el cual el reparto de los ingresos recaudados es determinado por Ley y además puede ser cambiado unilateralmente por el nivel superior de gobierno, pero de manera poco frecuente (más de un año)
d.4	Existe un sistema de coordinación fiscal en el cual el reparto de los ingresos recaudados es determinado anualmente por el nivel superior de gobierno
e	Otros casos en el que el GC fija la tasa y la base del impuesto subnacional
f	Ninguna de las anteriores categorías (a,b,c y e)

Fuente: elaboración sobre la base de la taxonomía propuesta por OCDE (Fiscal Decentralisation Database).

Para este trabajo, la aproximación a la autonomía fiscal se realizó a través de la revisión de las distintas legislaciones que hacen referencia a las potestades tributarias, en cuanto a tasas y bases gravables. En los anexos se encuentra el detalle por país analizado.

Los gobiernos de las provincias de Argentina tienen la potestad que les otorga la Constitución de la Nación para fijar impuestos directos, en cuanto a su tasa y base gravable. Los impuestos provinciales en esta materia son a la propiedad inmobiliaria (4100) y el impuesto a los sellos (4400), cuyo funcionamiento ya fue detallado en la parte anterior de este capítulo[20]. La principal restricción que existe por ley se encuentra en la Ley de Coparticipación Federal de Impuestos, en donde las provincias que se adhieran a este convenio quedan obligadas a no aplicar gravámenes análogos a los nacionales cuya distribución queda establecida en esta Ley. La potestad para fijar los impuestos a los ingresos brutos (5100) y sobre el uso de vehículos automotores (5211) también queda establecida en la Constitución, bajo la salvedad explícita de que las contribuciones indirectas quedan como facultad concurrente entre la Nación y las Provincias. Las características de todos los impuestos provinciales quedan establecidas en los Códigos Fiscales y las Leyes impositivas de las Jurisdicciones, con lo cual se puede afirmar que los gobiernos provinciales cuentan con una amplia autonomía fiscal en sus ingresos propios, fundada principalmente en la Constitución de este país, si bien mantienen una alta dependencia de las transferencias intergubernamentales, fundamentalmente a través del régimen de coparticipación federal de impuestos.

Los gobiernos estaduales de Brasil cuentan con autonomía fiscal que supera el 93% de sus ingresos tributarios, constituidos por los impuestos a la herencia y donación de propiedad (4310), a la propiedad de vehículos automotores (4600) y sobre la circulación de bienes y servicios ICMS (5111). La Constitución establece la competencia de los Estados y del Distrito Federal en esta materia, con la particularidad de que para los impuestos a las herencias y a los vehículos se establece que el Senado fijará los límites máximos de las alícuotas. El restante 7% de los ingresos tributarios estatales son contribuciones sociales sobre las ganancias netas (1110) cuya base legal se encuentra en la Ley 7,869, y en la cual queda explícita la potestad federal de este impuesto.

Respecto a los municipios de este país, la autonomía fiscal de los gobiernos alcanza el 90% de sus ingresos tributarios; éstos se componen por los impuestos a los bienes inmuebles IPTU (4100), a la traslación de bienes inmuebles (4400) así como a otros impuestos sobre bienes y servicios ISS (5113). La potestad de los gobiernos municipales sobre estos impuestos tiene origen en la Constitución de este país.

Desde la primera parte de este capítulo se explicó el funcionamiento del impuesto territorial en Chile; no obstante vale profundizar que parte importante de la recaudación de este impuesto financia el FCM, cuyo reparto está determinado por la Ley Orgánica Constitucional de Municipalidades. Cualquier cambio a esta Ley debe provenir o contar con el patrocinio del Gobierno Central. Mayor autonomía fiscal se observa en las patentes municipales (5100), cuyo hecho generador queda detallado en la segunda parte de este capítulo; no obstante, las tasas quedan fijadas en la ley citada, además que entre el 55% y 65% de la recaudación de los cuatro municipios con mayor capacidad fiscal va a financiar el FCM. Al igual como sucede con el impuesto territorial, los impuestos que gravan la circulación de vehículos automotores (5210) quedan supeditados al acuerdo de repartición del FCM. Por último, la mayor autonomía fiscal de las municipalidades de Chile se encuentra en las contribuciones por obtener concesiones permisos o servicios de la administración local (5213), las cuales están normadas de igual forma en la Ley sobre Rentas Municipales. Se destacan los permisos de urbanización y construcción cuya tasa máxima está regulada en la ley general del ramo. Por su parte, la Ley también permite que los derechos correspondientes a servicios, concesiones o permisos cuyas tasas no estén fijadas en la ley relativos a nuevos servicios que se creen por las municipalidades, se determinen mediante ordenanzas locales. En resumen, aproximadamente el 58% de los ingresos tributarios de las municipalidades de Chile forman parte de un acuerdo de coparticipación de impuestos establecido por ley (FCM), mientras que el restante 42% son potestades tributarias reglamentadas por Ley con límites establecidos en cuanto a las tasas y bases gravables.

En México, la Constitución de los Estados Unidos Mexicanos faculta en su totalidad a los gobiernos estatales en cuanto al manejo de las tasas y bases gravables de los impuestos sobre nómina (3000), predial (4100), traslación (4400) y servicios (5126). Aunado a estas potestades, cabe resaltar que a través del Decreto 21/12/2007 quedó derogada, a partir del año 2012, la Ley del Impuesto Sobre la Tenencia o uso de Vehículos, quedando así la potestad de este impuesto, también, en los gobiernos de las entidades federativas. Como resultado, al año 2014, al menos diez gobiernos estatales han eliminado este impuesto o en su defecto lo han subsidiado.

Asimismo, la Constitución establece que los municipios percibirán las contribuciones, incluyendo tasas adicionales, que establezcan los Estados sobre la propiedad inmobiliaria, de su fraccionamiento, división, consolidación, traslación y mejora así como las que tengan por base el cambio de valor de los inmuebles. Sin embargo, también se señala que los municipios podrán celebrar convenios con el Estado para que éste se haga cargo de algunas funciones relacionadas con la administración de estas contribuciones. Es así que, por ejemplo, con la reforma hacendaria del 2014, se modificaron los criterios para la asignación del Fondo de Fomento Municipal, el cual se constituye con el 1% de la recaudación federal participable (participaciones), obligando a que el municipio tenga un acuerdo con el gobierno estatal en el cual quede explícita la devolución, por parte del municipio, de la responsabilidad administrativa del impuesto predial al gobierno estatal. Con esto queda normado el incentivo para que los municipios cedan a los gobiernos estatales la potestad sobre el impuesto predial, de forma tal de no perder parte de su financiamiento vía las participaciones. Esta modificación dejaría potencialmente más del 83% de los ingresos tributarios municipales bajo la potestad de los gobiernos estatales.

Cuadro 3.4. **América Latina: Autonomía fiscal, 2015**

País	Recaudación de los gobiernos subnacionales, como porcentaje de los ingresos tributarios totales	Recaudación tributaria de los gobiernos subnacionales, por tipo de autonomía fiscal												
		a.1.	a.2	b.1	b.2	c.1	c.2	c.3	d.1	d.2	d.3	d.4	e	f
Argentina														
Gobiernos Provinciales	16.9	100.0	..	..	..	..	..	..	..	..	..	..	..	..
Brasil														
Estados	25.9	93.9	..	..	..	..	..	..	..	..	..	..	6.1	..
Municipios	6.4	90.4	..	..	..	..	..	..	..	..	..	..	..	9.6
Chile														
Municipios	7.6	..	..	26.4	15.7	..	..	..	..	..	57.9	..	..	..
México														
Estados	3.9	100.0	..	..	..	..	..	..	..	..	..	..	..	..
Municipios	1.4	16.5	83.5	..	..	..	..	..	..	..	..	..	..	..

Fuente: Elaboración basada en la metodología propuesta en OCDE (1999). Las cifras presentadas en el cuadro pueden diferir de las publicadas por la OCDE en la base de datos de descentralización fiscal debido a pequeñas diferencias en la clasificación y en las fuentes consultadas entre CEPAL y la OCDE.

StatLink http://dx.doi.org/10.1787/888933462997

En términos generales, los gobiernos intermedios de los países analizados cuentan con un nivel importante de autonomía fiscal derivado esto de la potestad – fundada en la Constitución de cada uno de los países – con la que los gobiernos cuentan para fijar tasas y modificar bases gravables dentro de la jurisdicción, si bien, como se enfatizó en la primera parte de este capítulo, en promedio el nivel de asimetría vertical es alto. La principal diferencia se observa en Chile, en donde la mayor parte de los ingresos tributarios están normados en un acuerdo de repartición establecido por Ley, mientras que el restante mantiene límites y restricciones también establecidas en la Ley de Rentas Municipales. En este sentido, y en ambos casos, cualquier modificación es atribución del gobierno central.

Con fines de profundizar en la discusión, en el siguiente cuadro se muestra el análisis incluyendo los distintos acuerdos de coparticipación de impuestos. En resumen, este agregado permite ampliar el análisis y mostrar los diferentes niveles de autonomía, diferenciando por las capacidades que tengan los gobiernos subnacionales de modificar los sistemas de distribución de impuestos. Como se vió en la parte inicial del capítulo, a excepción de Brasil, los ingresos fiscales provenientes de los distintos acuerdos de coparticipación mantienen un mayor peso relativo dentro de las estructuras fiscales de los gobiernos subnacionales.

Cuadro 3.1. Autonomía fiscal incluyendo los acuerdos de coparticipación de impuestos

A partir de lo explorado en los marcos legales, se observa que los gobiernos intermedios cuentan con un nivel importante de autonomía fiscal, derivado esto de la potestad con la que los gobiernos cuentan para fijar tasas y modificar bases gravables dentro de la jurisdicción, si bien en un contexto de alta asimetría vertical. Un menor nivel de autonomía se observa en los gobiernos locales. No obstante, un análisis más detallado se logra si se incluyen los mecanismos de coparticipación de impuestos en el cálculo de la autonomía fiscal subnacional. Estos sistemas, con sus particularidades, resultan de vital importancia para las finanzas subnacionales y, si bien se originan en impuestos recaudados por el gobierno central, sus diferentes marcos regulatorios determinan distintos grados de autonomía, relacionada con la capacidad que pueden tener los gobiernos subnacionales de modificar el sistema de reparto.

Para este análisis, vale destacar que en el caso de Argentina, cualquier modificación del régimen de coparticipación requiere de la aprobación de las legislaturas provinciales (ley-convenio); mientras que en el caso de los estados y municipios de México, estos acuerdos los hace beneficiarios e incluso los obliga a crear convenios de colaboración y devolución de potestades y responsabilidades tributarias (específicamente el predial), sin darles espacio alguno de negociación en la conformación y distribución de la recaudación federal participable. Por su parte, en el caso de Chile la particularidad se encuentra en que el Fondo Común Municipal (instrumento de coparticipación) se financia en su mayor parte con los recursos propios de los municipios, no obstante que cualquier modificación es atribución únicamente del Gobierno Central. La excepción vendría a ser Brasil, en donde se demuestra que tanto los gobiernos estatales como los locales (estos últimos en menor medida) cuentan con una capacidad y autonomía fiscal reflejadas ambas en la recaudación y las potestades tributarias que la Constitución les otorga.

En suma, considerando los diferentes acuerdos de coparticipación los resultados serían los siguientes:

País	Recaudación tributaria de los gobiernos subnacionales incluyendo acuerdos de reparticion de impuestos, por tipo de autonomia												
	a.1.	a.2	b.1	b.2	c.1	c.2	c.3	d.1	d.2	d.3	d.4	e	f
Argentina													
Gobiernos Provinciales	44.2	..	..	..	..	..	..	..	55.8	..	..	..	..
Brasil													
Estados	81.5	..	..	..	..	..	..	..	..	13.2	..	5.3	..
Municipios	58.5	..	..	..	..	..	..	..	..	35.3	..	..	6.2
Chile													
Municipios	..	..	26.4	15.7	..	..	..	..	..	57.9	..	..	..
México													
Estados	18.2	..	..	..	..	..	..	..	..	81.8	..	..	..
Municipios	4.2	21.4	..	..	..	..	..	..	..	74.4	..	..	..

Fuente: Elaboración propia sobre la metodología propuesta en OCDE (1999) y la revisión de los distintos marcos legales. Los acuerdos de co-participación no están incluidos en la definición de autonomía fiscal de la OCDE, la cual únicamente incluye ingresos tributarios. Los acuerdos de co-participación se derivan de los tributos recaudados al nivel del gobierno central y luego compartidos con los estados y las municipalidades a través de transferencias.

Notas

1. Muchos de los desarrollos presentados en este capítulo se basan en el artículo "La tributación en los gobiernos subnacionales" de Gomez Sabaini y Jiménez (2016), en imprenta. Parte del análisis que se realiza en este capítulo considera los ingresos no tributarios y las transferencias, por lo cual los datos usados para ello provienen de la CEPAL. Los datos usados para el análisis de los ingresos tributarios provienen de esta publicación y respetan la terminología de la OCDE (presentada en mayor detalle en el Anexo A) y hacen referencia a las categorías principales en las que cada impuesto se clasifica.
2. A pesar de que en la mayoría de los países latinoamericanos existen sistemas de transferencias intergubernamentales que adquieren notable relevancia en cuanto al financiamiento de los gobiernos subnacionales, el presente trabajo se concentra en las fuentes de recursos propios (específicamente tributarios). Para un análisis exhaustivo de la problemática de las transferencias intergubernamentales en América Latina, véanse los trabajos de Martínez Vázquez y Sepúlveda (2012a), Rezende y Veloso (2012) y Jiménez y Podestá (2009).
3. Se seleccionaron únicamente algunos países por cuestiones de accesibilidad a la información mínima necesaria para realizar el análisis.
4. Afonso (2016) provee un análisis actualizado acerca del peso de los recursos subnacionales en Brasil.
5. Para un análisis detallado del funcionamiento, composición y distribución del FCM, consultar el Sistema Nacional de Información Municipal (SINIM) del SUBDERE, Chile, www.sinim.gov.cl/desarrollo_local/selfcm.htm.
6. En la última parte de este capítulo se profundiza en lo determinante que resulta el FCM en la autonomía fiscal que actualmente alcanza los municipios de Chile.
7. En (Gómez Sabaini y Jiménez, 2011) se muestra la estructura de los ingresos totales de los gobiernos subnacionales al año 2008, incluyéndose el caso de Brasil en donde las transferencias se acercan al 8% del Producto Interno Bruto. Las notables diferencias con los datos aquí presentados (cuadro 3.1) -cuya fuente es el Tesoro Nacional brasilero- cuentan con una explicación metodológica, la cual se relaciona con la ponderación de las transferencias realizadas entre gobiernos subnacionales que se constituyen principalmente por el 25% de la recaudación del ICMS de los estados hacia los municipios. La inclusión o no de este concepto dentro del monto total de transferencias explicaría las diferencias señaladas con los datos oficiales.
8. Para más detalle sobre el desempeño de los impuestos sobre la propiedad inmueble en América Latina, véase Martínez Vázquez y Sepúlveda (2012b).
9. Aunque De Cesare y Lazo Marín (2008) aclaran que los municipios deben proponer anualmente sus tarifas y tablas de valores unitarios de terreno y construcción ante sus Congresos Estatales.
10. Incluso, en Ruelas Ávila (2015) se muestra que la importancia relativa de este impuesto promedió el 55% los ingresos tributarios municipales en el período 1989-2013, no obstante que la misma ha sido históricamente baja – alrededor del 7% – cuando se le compara con los ingresos totales de los municipios. Por otro lado, también se muestra que este impuesto distorsiona la equidad territorial ya que el 90% de la recaudación del tributo se concentra solamente en el 12% de los municipios.
11. En los cálculos de carga tributaria subnacional para el caso chileno, se siguió la metodología de la DIPRES en la cual se eliminan las duplicaciones originadas en la aplicación del Fondo Común Municipal (FCM), De este modo, sumando la diferencia residual a los respectivos tributos que lo forman, es posible visualizar exactamente lo recaudado por cada concepto de ingresos de operación aunque se pierde información de lo recibido por cada municipio a través de la participación en este Fondo.
12. Algunos municipios pueden fijar tasas y excepciones relativas al tributo.
13. Para un análisis detallado de este impuesto, se recomienda consultar el trabajo de Bruno de Carvalho, P.H. (2006), "IPTU no Brasil: Progressividade, Arrecadação E Aspectos Extra-Fiscais", IPEA.
14. Para más detalle acerca de los problemas de coordinación entre niveles de gobierno de los impuestos al consumo, véase Arroyo, Jiménez y Mussi (2012).
15. Para mayor información respecto a las ineficiencias derivadas de los impuestos "en cascadas", véase Keen (2013).
16. Existen diferencias entre la clasificación de CEPAL y la OCDE respecto a las patentes comerciales. CEPAL las clasifica como impuestos a la producción, venta, transferencia, arrendamiento y entrega de bienes, y la prestación de servicios (5100), mientras que la OCDE lo clasifica como un impuesto sobre el uso de bienes y sobre el permiso para usar bienes o realizar actividades.

17. De acuerdo con la Constitución de este país, así como con el Código Municipal, cada municipio tiene su propia ley de impuestos de patentes.
18. Para el caso de Ecuador, Chile y Costa Rica, la clasificación de este tipo de impuestos fue cambiada recientemente del 5126 al 5213, no obstante para este capítulo permanecen en esta parte conservando su clasificación original.
19. A partir del 2012, el impuesto sobre tenencia y uso de vehículos pasó a ser potestad de los gobiernos estatales, impuesto sobre el cual antes no podían modificar tasas ni eliminar recargos, sólo eran beneficiarios de la recaudación. Dado este cambio, algunos estados eliminaron este impuesto, lo que generó un incentivo a que los demás estados redujeran las tasas y la base gravable, y por otro lado aumentaran el impuesto sobre nómina.
20. El impuesto directo más relevante en términos recaudatorios, es el impuesto a las ganancias, que es una facultad delegada de las provincias al gobierno federal y que forma parte del Régimen de Coparticipación Federal de Impuestos.

Referencias

Afonso, J.R. (2016); "Carga tributaria en Brasil: redimensionada y repensada", *Revista de Administración Tributaria*, 40 (febrero), CIAT/AEAT/IEF, pp. 1-16.

Arroyo, J.M., J.P. Jiménez y C. Mussi (2012), "Revenue Sharing: The case of Brazil's ICMS", *Serie Macroeconomía del desarrollo* No. 121, División de Desarrollo Económico, CEPAL.

Blöchliger, H. y M. Nettley (2015), "Sub-central Tax Autonomy: 2011 Update", *OECD Working Papers on Fiscal Federalism*, No. 20, OECD Publishing, http://dx.doi.org/10.1787/5js4t79sbshd-en.

Blöchliger, H. y J. Rabesona (2009), "The Fiscal Autonomy of Sub-Central Governments: An Update", *OECD Working Papers on Fiscal Federalism*, No. 9, OECD Publishing, http://dx.doi.org/10.1787/5k97b111wb0t-en.

Blöchliger, H. y D. King (2006), "Fiscal Autonomy of Sub-Central Governments", *OECD Working Papers on Fiscal Federalism*, No. 2, OECD Publishing, http://dx.doi.org/10.1787/5k97b127pc0t-en.

Brosio, G. (2015); "Step on the Gas: Bolivia's Reliance on Natural Resource Revenue", en Fretes Cibils, V. y T. Ter Minassian (eds.), *Decentralizing Revenue in Latin America – Why and How*, Banco Interamericano de Desarrollo, Washington DC., pp. 79-116.

Brosio, G. y J.P. Jiménez (2012), "The intergovernmental allocation of revenue from natural resources: finding a balance between centripetal and centrifugal pressure", en Brosio, G. y J.P. Jiménez (eds.), *Decentralization and Reform in Latin America – Improving Intergovernmental Relations*, Elgar Publishing, Cheltenham, pp. 290-320.

Bruno de Carvalho (Jr.), P. (2006), "IPTU no Brasil: Progressividade, Arrecadação E Aspectos Extra-Fiscais", *Texto para Discussão* N° 1251 del Instituto de Pesquisa Econômica Aplicada -IPEA-, Brasilia, diciembre, www.ipea.gov.br.

CEPAL (2014), "Pactos para la igualdad: Hacia un futuro sostenible". Trigésimo quinto período de sesiones de la CEPAL, documento oficial del 35° período de sesiones de la CEPAL (Lima, Perú), LC/G.2586 (SES.35/3), Santiago de Chile, abril.

De Cesare, C. y J.F. Lazo Marín (2008), "Impuestos a los patrimonios en América Latina", *Serie Macroeconomía del Desarrollo* N° 66, CEPAL, Santiago de Chile.

Del Valle, M. (2013); "Ingresos Fiscales por Explotación de Recursos Mineros e Hidrocarburos en Perú", *Resumen de políticas del BID* N° 197, Banco Interamericano de Desarrollo, Washington, DC, septiembre.

Gómez Sabaini J.C. y J.P. Jiménez (2011), "El financiamiento de los gobiernos subnacionales en América Latina: un análisis de casos", *Serie macroeconomía del desarrollo* No. 111. División de Desarrollo Económico, CEPAL.

Horst, B. (2010), "Fuentes de financiamiento para gobiernos subnacionales y descentralización fiscal", *Serie Informe Económico* N° 202, Libertad y Desarrollo, Santiago de Chile.

Jiménez, J.P. y A. Podestá (2009), "Las relaciones fiscales intergubernamentales y las finanzas subnacionales ante la crisis", LC/R.2155, CEPAL, Santiago de Chile.

Jiménez, J.P. y J. Viñuela (2004), "Marco institucional para la gestión del gasto público en países descentralizados", Departamento de Finanzas Públicas, Fondo Monetario Internacional.

Keen, M. (2013), "Targeting, Cascading and Indirect Tax Design", *IMF Working Paper*, WP/13/57, Departamento de Finanzas Públicas, Fondo Monetario Internacional.

Larios, J., B. Alvarado y E. Conterno (eds.) (2004), "Descentralización Fiscal. Análisis Conceptual y Revisión de Experiencias de Nueve Países", *Documento Técnico* N° 7, USAID, Lima.

Martínez-Vázquez, J. y C. Sepúlveda (2012a), "Intergovernmental transfers: a policy reform perspective", en Brosio, G. y J.P. Jiménez (eds.), *Decentralization and Reform in Latin America – Improving Intergovernmental Relations*, Elgar Publishing, Cheltenham pp. 260-289.

Martínez-Vázquez, J. y C. Sepúlveda (2012b), "Explaining property tax collections in developing countries: The case of Latin America", en Brosio, G. y J.P. Jiménez (eds.), *Decentralization and Reform in Latin America – Improving Intergovernmental Relations*, Elgar Publishing, Cheltenham, pp. 172-222.

OCDE (2017), *Fiscal Decentralisation Database*, OECD Publishing, París, www.oecd.org/ctp/federalism/oecdfiscaldecentralisationdatabase.htm.

OCDE (1999), "Taxing powers of state and local government", *Tax Policy Studies* No 1, París.

Rezende, F. y J. Veloso (2012), "Intergovernmental transfers in sub-national finances", en Brosio, G. y J.P. Jiménez (eds.), *Decentralization and Reform in Latin America – Improving Intergovernmental Relations*, Edward Elgar Publishing, Cheltenham, pp. 223-259.

Ruelas Ávila, I. (2015), "Evaluación de las características del impuesto predial en México", *Revista Iberoamericana de Estudios Municipales (RIEM)*, N° 12, Año VI, pp. 67-102.

Sánchez Torres, F., I. España Eljaiek y J. Zenteno (2015), "Fiscal Cumbia: Colombia's Revenue Dynamism", en Fretes Cibils, V. y T. Ter Minassian (eds.), *Decentralizing Revenue in Latin America – Why and How*, Banco Interamericano de Desarrollo, Washington DC, pp. 155-198.

Ter Minassian, T. (2015), "Elusive Goal: Brazil's Subnational Revenue System Reform", en Fretes Cibils, V. y T. Ter Minassian (eds.), *Decentralizing Revenue in Latin America – Why and How*, Banco Interamericano de Desarrollo, Washington DC., pp. 117-154.

CHAPTER 4

TAX LEVELS AND TAX STRUCTURES, 1990-2015

CAPÍTULO 4

NIVELES IMPOSITIVOS Y ESTRUCTURAS TRIBUTARIAS, 1990-2015

Chapter 4 / Capítulo 4

4.1. Comparative tables, 1990-2015

In all of the following tables a (..) indicates not available or not applicable. The main series in this volume cover the years 1990 to 2015.

Figures referring to 1991-94 and 1996-97 in Table 4.1 and figures relating to 1991-99, 2001-04 and 2006-08 in Tables 4.4 to 4.16 have been omitted because of lack of space. Complete series are, however, available on line at www.latameconomy.org and on the OECD iLibrary.

4.1. Cuadros comparativos, 1990-2015

En todos los cuadros siguientes, (..) indica no aplicable o dato indisponible. Las principales series de datos de esta sección cubren el periodo que va de 1990 a 2015.

Las cifras relativas a 1991-94 y a 1996-97 en Cuadro 4.1 y las cifras relativas a 1991-99, 2001-04 y 2006-08 en Cuadros 4.4 hasta 4.16 a se han omitido por falta de espacio. Sin embargo, las series completas están disponibles en línea en www.latameconomy.org y en OECD iLibrary.

Table 4.1. Total tax revenue as percentage of GDP, 1990-2015
Cuadro 4.1. Total de ingresos tributarios en porcentaje del PIB, 1990-2015

	1990	1995	1998	1999	2000	2001	2002	2003	2004	2005
Argentina	13.7	18.7	19.4	19.5	19.8	19.3	18.4	21.6	24.3	24.5
Bahamas[1]	12.3	14.4	14.5	13.8	15.2	14.9	12.8	13.5	13.5	13.8
Barbados[1]	23.2	27.2	29.0	28.9	30.2	31.2	29.6	31.2	31.2	29.5
Belize / Belice[1]	21.8	19.6	20.6	18.9	19.1	20.7	21.7	22.4	21.7	22.3
Bolivia[1,2]	8.3	13.8	15.7	14.9	17.6	16.6	16.9	16.4	18.7	20.0
Brazil / Brasil	25.5	26.6	26.8	28.1	29.6	30.7	31.4	30.9	31.8	32.8
Chile	17.0	18.4	18.8	18.1	18.8	19.0	19.0	18.7	19.1	20.7
Colombia	10.6	15.0	15.3	15.2	14.6	16.3	16.2	16.7	17.5	18.1
Costa Rica	19.9	15.9	17.9	17.2	17.7	18.8	19.3	19.3	19.1	19.6
Cuba	29.1	33.5	35.9	37.1	37.2	36.0	36.6	36.6	35.6	41.1
Dominican Republic / República Dominicana	7.8	10.0	11.0	11.1	10.8	12.2	12.4	10.8	10.2	11.9
Ecuador	7.3	8.1	9.0	9.0	10.3	11.8	12.7	11.8	11.8	12.1
El Salvador	10.5	13.0	12.1	12.0	12.1	12.1	12.9	13.1	13.0	13.9
Guatemala	9.0	10.4	11.5	12.3	12.4	12.7	13.7	13.5	13.4	13.1
Honduras	16.9	18.9	19.7	20.5	16.2	16.3	16.6	17.3	18.0	17.9
Jamaica[1]	23.1	21.8	21.0	22.1	22.7	21.6	22.1	25.0	24.7	23.3
Mexico / México[3,4]	12.4	11.4	12.8	13.6	13.6	14.4	14.6	14.1	12.9	12.6
Nicaragua	..	10.9	13.0	12.8	13.0	12.6	13.3	14.7	15.3	16.1
Panama / Panamá	15.9	18.4	15.5	16.3	16.4	15.4	14.9	14.7	14.5	14.4
Paraguay	5.8	12.1	11.1	12.4	12.6	11.9	10.8	11.6	13.1	13.8
Peru / Perú	12.1	15.9	16.6	15.2	14.7	15.0	14.8	15.6	15.8	16.5
Trinidad and Tobago / Trinidad y Tobago[1]	22.9	22.9	16.3	19.6	21.1	23.2	21.6	22.0	22.5	26.5
Uruguay	19.6	21.0	22.0	21.7	21.6	22.0	21.1	21.5	22.7	23.9
Venezuela[1]	18.1	12.8	12.9	13.8	13.6	12.2	11.2	11.9	13.3	15.9
Unweighted average / Promedio no ponderado										
LAC / ALC[5]	**15.8**	**17.1**	**17.4**	**17.7**	**18.0**	**18.2**	**18.1**	**18.5**	**18.9**	**19.8**
OECD / OCDE[6]	**32.0**	**33.3**	**33.7**	**33.9**	**34.0**	**33.5**	**33.2**	**33.2**	**33.1**	**33.6**

	2006	2007	2008	2009	2010	2011	2012	2013	2014	2015
Argentina	25.1	26.4	27.6	28.9	29.1	29.3	30.6	31.2	31.1	32.1
Bahamas[1]	15.6	16.3	17.2	16.5	16.1	18.9	17.6	17.0	17.3	19.9
Barbados[1]	30.5	30.2	31.1	30.5	30.6	32.4	33.1	29.5	30.4	31.3
Belize / Belice[1]	22.5	25.4	24.1	25.4	26.6	25.1	25.0	25.7	25.8	25.7
Bolivia[1,2]	19.3	19.8	21.2	21.7	20.3	22.1	22.5	23.3	23.8	24.7
Brazil / Brasil	34.8	35.1	33.7	32.1	32.3	33.2	32.5	32.5	31.8	32.0
Chile	22.0	22.8	21.4	17.4	19.7	21.2	21.5	20.0	19.8	20.6
Colombia	19.1	19.1	18.8	18.6	18.0	18.8	19.7	20.1	20.4	20.8
Costa Rica	20.1	21.4	22.1	20.6	20.3	20.8	20.7	22.5	22.5	23.1
Cuba	45.5	44.6	41.7	41.1	37.6	38.4	39.7	37.3	37.5	38.6
Dominican Republic / República Dominicana	13.6	15.0	14.2	12.7	12.3	12.3	13.1	13.9	14.1	13.7
Ecuador	12.7	13.2	14.3	15.2	16.6	17.7	19.8	19.6	19.2	21.0
El Salvador	15.1	15.2	15.1	14.4	15.1	15.4	16.1	17.0	17.2	17.3
Guatemala	13.8	13.9	12.9	12.2	12.4	12.8	12.9	13.0	12.7	12.4
Honduras	18.3	19.6	19.6	17.8	18.1	17.5	18.4	19.0	20.6	21.2
Jamaica[1]	24.1	24.8	25.1	24.9	24.9	24.5	24.5	24.9	24.7	25.6
Mexico / México[3,4]	12.8	13.2	13.8	13.6	14.1	14.0	13.9	14.6	15.2	17.4
Nicaragua	17.1	17.3	16.8	16.9	18.0	18.8	19.6	19.9	20.4	20.9
Panama / Panamá	15.9	16.5	16.4	16.4	17.3	17.0	17.4	17.4	16.1	16.2
Paraguay	14.2	13.9	14.6	16.1	16.5	16.9	17.7	16.4	17.8	17.9
Peru / Perú	18.0	18.5	18.8	17.0	17.9	18.6	19.3	18.8	18.8	17.1
Trinidad and Tobago / Trinidad y Tobago[1]	30.2	26.2	29.4	28.2	27.3	26.6	27.4	27.6	30.0	30.9
Uruguay	25.1	24.9	26.0	25.7	26.1	26.5	26.8	27.4	27.2	27.0
Venezuela[1]	16.3	16.8	14.1	14.3	11.8	13.5	14.2	14.5	19.0	20.9
Unweighted average / Promedio no ponderado										
LAC / ALC[5]	**20.9**	**21.3**	**21.3**	**20.8**	**20.8**	**21.3**	**21.8**	**21.8**	**22.2**	**22.8**
OECD / OCDE[6]	**33.7**	**33.8**	**33.2**	**32.4**	**32.6**	**33.0**	**33.4**	**33.8**	**34.2**	**34.3**

Note: The figures exclude local government revenues for Argentina (but include provincial revenues), Bahamas Barbados, Bolivia (prior to 1994), Costa Rica (prior to 1998), Cuba, Dominican Republic, El Salvador (prior to 2015), Jamaica (prior to 1998), Nicaragua, Panama (prior to 1998), Paraguay (prior to 2004), Peru (prior to 2001) and Venezuela as the data are not available.

1. The data are estimated for the following countries: Bahamas (social security contributions for 2015), Barbados (social security contributions for 2015), Belize (social security contributions from 2013 onward), Bolivia (social security contributions from 2013 onward), Jamaica (environmental levy for years 2014 and 2015), Trinidad and Tobago (local property taxes for 2015) and Venezuela (social security contributions from 2011 onward). See the corresponding country tables for more information.
2. Previous editions of Revenue Statistics in Latin America and the Caribbean included fees levied on hydrocarbon production as tax revenue. For this publication, revenues from hydrocarbon production have been excluded from tax revenues and are instead treated as non-tax revenues.

3. Revenue Statistics in Latin America and the Caribbean and Revenue Statistics in OECD countries included fees levied on hydrocarbon production at the federal level. From the data provided for Revenue Statistics in OECD countries (2016) and for this publication, revenues from hydrocarbon production have been excluded from tax revenues and are instead treated as non-tax revenues.
4. The data are estimated for 2015 including expected revenues for state and local governments.
5. Represents a group of 24 Latin American and Caribbean countries, the average is calculated using calendar year data, except for Bahamas and Trinidad and Tobago where fiscal year data are used. Chile and Mexico are also part of the OECD (35) group.
6. Calculated by applying the unweighted average percentage change for 2015 in the 32 countries providing data for that year to the overall average tax to GDP ratio in 2014.

Nota : Las cifras excluyen los ingresos de gobiernos locales en Argentina (pero incluye ingresos de las provincias), Bahamas, Barbados, Bolivia (previo a 1994), Costa Rica (previo a 1998), Cuba, República Dominicana, El Salvador (previo a 2015), Jamaica (previo a 1998), Nicaragua, Panamá (previo a 1998), Paraguay (previo a 2004), Perú (previo a 2001) y Venezuela dado que los datos no están disponibles.

1. Datos estimados para los siguientes países: Bahamas (contribuciones a la seguridad social para 2015), Barbados (contribuciones a la seguridad social para 2015), Belice (contribuciones a la seguridad social desde 2013), Bolivia (contribuciones a la seguridad social desde 2013), Jamaica (impuesto ambiental para los años 2014 y 2015), Trinidad y Tobago (impuestos sobre la propiedad municipales) y Venezuela (contribuciones a la seguridad social desde 2011). Véanse las tablas de país para mayor información.
2. Las ediciones anteriores de Estadísticas Tributarias en América Latina y el Caribe incluyeron las sobretasas sobre la producción de hidrocarburos como ingresos tributarios. En esta edición, el recaudo proveniente de la producción de hidrocarburos ha sido excluido de los ingresos tributarios y tratado como ingresos no tributarios.
3. Estadísticas Tributarias en América Latina y el Caribe y Estadísticas Tributarias en países de la OCDE incluían tasas sobre la producción de hidrocarburos al nivel federal. A partir de los datos provistos, para Estadísticas Tributarias en países de la OCDE (2016) y para esta publicación, el recaudo de la producción de hidrocarburos ha sido separado de los ingresos tributarios y tratados como ingresos no tributarios.
4. Los datos estimados incluyen ingresos esperados a nivel estatal y local para el 2015.
5. Representa un grupo de 24 países de América Latina y el Caribe. Para la estimación del promedio se utiliza el año calendario, excepto para Barbados y Trinidad y Tobago donde se utiliza el año fiscal. Chile y México son también parte del grupo OCDE (35).
6. Calculado aplicando el promedio no ponderado en el cambio porcentual para el 2015 en los 32 países con datos disponibles para ese año en el total de ingreso tributario en porcentaje del PIB.

StatLink http://dx.doi.org/10.1787/888933463027

Table 4.2. Tax revenue of main headings as percentage of GDP, 2015
Cuadro 4.2. Ingresos tributarios en las principales partidas en porcentaje del PIB, 2015

	1000 Income & profits / Renta y utilidades	2000 Social security / Seguridad social	3000 Payroll / Nómina	4000 Property / Patrimonio	5000 Goods and services / Bienes y servicios	6000 Others / Otros
Argentina	6.6	7.1	0.0	2.8	15.2	0.3
Bahamas[1]	0.0	2.9	0.0	1.2	13.6	2.2
Barbados[1]	8.3	6.3	0.0	1.7	14.9	0.1
Belize / Belice[1]	7.5	2.0	0.0	1.0	15.2	0.0
Bolivia[1]	5.6	1.4	0.0	0.2	13.3	4.2
Brazil / Brasil	6.7	8.3	0.8	2.0	13.2	1.0
Chile	7.5	1.4	0.0	0.9	11.2	-0.3
Colombia	6.6	2.5	0.3	2.3	7.8	1.2
Costa Rica	4.4	7.8	1.0	0.4	9.3	0.2
Cuba	7.7	5.0	3.2	0.0	20.4	2.4
Dominican Republic / República Dominicana	4.0	0.0	0.0	0.6	9.1	0.0
Ecuador	4.7	5.0	0.0	0.2	10.9	0.1
El Salvador	6.0	1.9	0.0	0.4	8.8	0.3
Guatemala	3.6	2.1	0.0	0.1	6.5	0.1
Honduras	5.6	3.0	0.0	0.5	11.6	0.6
Jamaica[1]	9.0	1.0	0.0	0.4	14.4	0.8
Mexico / México[2]	6.8	3.3	0.4	0.3	6.2	0.2
Nicaragua	6.0	5.3	0.0	0.1	9.5	0.0
Panama / Panamá	4.1	5.8	0.2	0.6	4.9	0.5
Paraguay	2.7	4.9	0.0	0.3	10.0	0.0
Peru / Perú	6.2	2.1	0.0	0.4	8.2	0.2
Trinidad and Tobago / Trinidad y Tobago[1]	19.1	3.1	0.0	0.5	7.9	0.3
Uruguay	5.9	7.4	0.0	2.1	11.5	0.0
Venezuela[1]	4.7	0.6	0.0	0.0	15.2	0.3
Unweighted average / Promedio no ponderado						
LAC / ALC[3]	**6.2**	**3.8**	**0.2**	**0.8**	**11.2**	**0.6**
OECD / OCDE[4]	**11.6**	**9.1**	**0.4**	**1.9**	**11.0**	**0.2**

Note: The figures exclude local government revenues for Argentina (but include provincial revenues), Bahamas, Barbados, Bolivia (prior to 1994), Costa Rica (prior to 1998), Cuba, Dominican Republic, El Salvador (prior to 2015), Jamaica (prior to 1998), Nicaragua, Panama (prior to 1998), Paraguay (prior to 2004), Peru (prior to 2001) and Venezuela as the data are not available.

1. The data are estimated for the following countries: Bahamas (social security contributions), Barbados (social security contributions), Belize (social security contributions), Bolivia (social security contributions), Jamaica (environmental levy), Trinidad and Tobago (local property taxes) and Venezuela (social security contributions).
2. Data for 2014 are used for 3000 and 4000. Federal government data are used for 5000 and 6000.
3. Represents a group of 24 Latin American and Caribbean countries. Chile and Mexico are also part of the OECD (35) group.
4. Represents the unweighted average for OECD member countries. Data for 2014 are used for 2000, 3000, 4000, 5000 and 6000.

Nota : Las cifras excluyen los ingresos de gobiernos locales en Argentina (pero incluye ingresos de las provincias), Bahamas, Barbados, Bolivia (previo a 1994), Costa Rica (previo a 1998), Cuba, República Dominicana, El Salvador (previo a 2015), Jamaica (previo a 1998), Nicaragua, Panamá (previo a 1998), Paraguay (previo a 2004), Perú (previo a 2001) y Venezuela dado que los datos no están disponibles.

1. Datos estimados para los siguientes países: Bahamas (contribuciones a la seguridad social) Barbados (contribuciones a la seguridad social), Belice (contribuciones a la seguridad), Bolivia (contribuciones a la seguridad), Jamaica (impuesto ambiental), Trinidad y Tobago (impuesto sobre la propiedad municipal) y Venezuela (contribuciones a la seguridad social).
2. Se utilizan los datos de 2014 en 3000 y 4000. Datos del nivel federal se utilizan para 5000 y 6000.
3. Representa un grupo de 24 países de América Latina y el Caribe. Chile y México son también parte del grupo OCDE (35).
4. Representa el promedio no ponderado para los países miembros de la OCDE. Los datos de 2014 se utilizan para 2000, 3000, 4000, 5000 y 6000.

StatLink http://dx.doi.org/10.1787/888933463038

Table 4.3. Tax revenue of main headings as percentage of total taxation, 2015
Cuadro 4.3. Ingresos tributarios en las principales partidas en porcentaje del total de ingresos tributarios, 2015

	1000 Income & profits / Renta y utilidades	2000 Social security / Seguridad social	3000 Payroll / Nómina	4000 Property / Patrimonio	5000 Goods and services / Bienes y servicios	6000 Others / Otros
Argentina	20.5	22.2	0.0	8.9	47.5	0.9
Bahamas[1]	0.0	14.8	0.0	6.1	68.3	10.8
Barbados[1]	26.5	20.1	0.0	5.5	47.5	0.4
Belize / Belice[1]	29.1	7.8	0.0	3.8	59.3	0.0
Bolivia[1]	22.8	5.7	0.0	0.8	53.8	16.9
Brazil / Brasil	20.9	25.9	2.6	6.3	41.3	3.1
Chile	36.4	6.9	0.0	4.4	54.0	-1.7
Colombia	31.7	12.1	1.7	11.0	37.5	6.0
Costa Rica	19.1	33.9	4.1	1.9	40.1	0.9
Cuba	19.9	12.9	8.2	0.0	52.8	6.2
Dominican Republic / República Dominicana	28.9	0.4	0.0	4.4	66.3	0.0
Ecuador	22.4	24.0	0.0	1.1	51.9	0.6
El Salvador	34.5	10.9	0.0	2.4	50.5	1.7
Guatemala	29.1	16.6	0.0	1.2	52.6	0.6
Honduras	26.3	14.1	0.0	2.4	54.6	2.6
Jamaica[1]	35.0	3.8	0.0	1.7	56.3	3.1
Mexico / México[2]	37.6	20.6	2.5	2.1	35.8	1.4
Nicaragua	28.8	25.2	0.0	0.7	45.2	0.1
Panama / Panamá	25.5	36.1	1.3	3.8	30.1	3.2
Paraguay	15.2	27.3	0.0	1.7	55.8	0.1
Peru / Perú	36.1	12.4	0.0	2.3	47.9	1.3
Trinidad and Tobago / Trinidad y Tobago[1]	61.9	10.0	0.0	1.5	25.7	0.9
Uruguay	21.9	27.6	0.0	7.7	42.6	0.1
Venezuela[1]	22.6	3.0	0.0	0.2	72.9	1.3
Unweighted average / Promedio no ponderado						
LAC / ALC[3]	**27.2**	**16.4**	**0.9**	**3.4**	**49.6**	**2.5**
OECD / OCDE[2,4]	**33.7**	**26.2**	**1.1**	**5.6**	**32.6**	**0.7**

Note: The figures exclude local government revenues for Argentina (but include provincial revenues), Bahamas, Barbados, Bolivia (prior to 1994), Costa Rica (prior to 1998), Cuba, Dominican Republic, El Salvador (prior to 2015), Jamaica (prior to 1998), Nicaragua, Panama (prior to 1998), Paraguay (prior to 2004), Peru (prior to 2001) and Venezuela as the data are not available.

1. The data are estimated for the following countries: Bahamas (social security contributions), Barbados (social security contributions), Belize (social security contributions), Bolivia (social security contributions), Jamaica (environmental levy), Trinidad and Tobago (local property taxes) and Venezuela (social security contributions).
2. Data for 2014 are used.
3. Represents a group of 24 Latin American and Caribbean countries. Chile and Mexico are also part of the OECD (35) group.
4. Represents the unweighted average for OECD member countries.

Nota : Las cifras excluyen los ingresos de gobiernos locales en Argentina (pero incluye ingresos de las provincias), Bahamas, Barbados, Bolivia (previo a 1994), Costa Rica (previo a 1998), Cuba, República Dominicana, El Salvador (previo a 2015), Jamaica (previo a 1998), Nicaragua, Panamá (previo a 1998), Paraguay (previo a 2004), Perú (previo a 2001) y Venezuela dado que los datos no están disponibles.

1. Datos estimados para los siguientes países: Bahamas (contribuciones a la seguridad social), Barbados (contribuciones a la seguridad social), Belice (contribuciones a la seguridad), Bolivia (contribuciones a la seguridad), Jamaica (impuesto ambiental), Trinidad y Tobago (impuesto sobre la propiedad municipal) y Venezuela (contribuciones a la seguridad social).
2. Se utilizan los datos de 2014.
3. Representa un grupo de 24 países de América Latina y el Caribe. Chile y México son también parte del grupo OCDE (35).
4. Representa el promedio no ponderado para los países miembros de la OCDE.

StatLink http://dx.doi.org/10.1787/888933463043

Table 4.4. Taxes on income and profits (1000) as percentage of GDP
Cuadro 4.4. Impuestos sobre la renta y las utilidades (1000) en porcentaje del PIB

	1990	2000	2005	2009	2010	2011	2012	2013	2014	2015
Argentina	0.7	3.7	5.0	4.6	4.7	5.1	5.3	5.5	5.9	6.6
Bahamas	0.0	0.0	0.0	0.0	0.0	0.0	0.0	0.0	0.0	0.0
Barbados	6.2	9.2	8.2	10.2	8.6	9.0	8.6	7.0	8.1	8.3
Belize / Belice	4.5	4.6	5.8	7.9	8.9	8.5	7.4	7.6	7.7	7.5
Bolivia	0.4	2.3	3.1	5.4	4.6	4.8	5.2	5.5	5.6	5.6
Brazil / Brasil	4.6	5.7	6.9	7.0	6.7	7.2	6.7	6.8	6.6	6.7
Chile	3.9	4.4	7.5	5.4	7.5	8.5	8.4	6.9	6.5	7.5
Colombia	3.2	3.4	5.1	5.6	4.8	5.4	6.6	6.7	6.6	6.6
Costa Rica	2.2	2.6	3.3	4.0	3.8	3.9	3.8	4.1	4.1	4.4
Cuba	0.1	6.0	5.7	5.1	5.6	6.5	6.2	6.9	7.4	7.7
Dominican Republic / República Dominicana	2.0	2.6	2.8	3.1	2.7	3.0	3.9	4.3	4.5	4.0
Ecuador	0.9	1.6	2.3	4.0	3.4	3.8	3.8	4.0	4.1	4.7
El Salvador	2.0	3.1	3.7	4.6	4.6	4.9	5.2	6.1	6.3	6.0
Guatemala	1.6	2.5	2.9	3.2	3.1	3.5	3.5	3.8	3.9	3.6
Honduras	3.4	2.8	4.1	4.6	4.7	5.1	4.9	5.2	5.3	5.6
Jamaica	11.7	10.1	10.0	11.7	10.3	9.9	9.6	9.1	8.7	9.0
Mexico / México	4.2	4.5	4.3	4.9	5.2	5.3	5.1	6.0	5.7	6.8
Nicaragua	..	1.8	3.7	4.6	4.5	5.1	5.3	5.4	5.8	6.0
Panama / Panamá	3.9	3.9	3.4	4.8	4.6	3.9	5.0	4.9	4.1	4.1
Paraguay	1.2	1.6	1.7	2.8	2.2	2.5	2.7	2.5	2.7	2.7
Peru / Perú	0.7	2.9	4.8	6.0	6.5	7.6	8.0	7.4	7.6	6.2
Trinidad and Tobago / Trinidad y Tobago	11.6	11.5	18.8	18.7	18.4	19.3	18.9	18.6	20.8	19.1
Uruguay	0.9	2.0	2.8	5.3	5.5	5.4	5.5	6.0	5.7	5.9
Venezuela	15.1	5.9	6.1	5.5	3.6	3.9	4.3	4.2	6.2	4.7
Unweighted average / Promedio no ponderado										
LAC / ALC[1]	**3.7**	**4.1**	**5.1**	**5.8**	**5.6**	**5.9**	**6.0**	**6.0**	**6.2**	**6.2**
OECD / OCDE[2]	**12.2**	**12.0**	**11.7**	**10.9**	**10.8**	**11.0**	**11.2**	**11.4**	**11.5**	**11.6**

Note: The figures exclude local government revenues for Argentina (but include provincial revenues), Bahamas, Barbados, Bolivia (prior to 1994), Costa Rica (prior to 1998), Cuba, Dominican Republic, El Salvador (prior to 2015), Jamaica (prior to 1998), Nicaragua, Panama (prior to 1998), Paraguay (prior to 2004), Peru (prior to 2001) and Venezuela as the data are not available.

1. Represents a group of 24 Latin American and Caribbean countries. Chile and Mexico are also part of the OECD (35) group.
2. Represents the unweighted average for OECD member countries. The OECD average for 2015 is estimated by applying the unweighted average percentage change for 2015 in the 33 countries providing data for that year to the OECD average for 2014.

Nota : Las cifras excluyen los ingresos de gobiernos locales en Argentina (pero incluye ingresos de las provincias), Bahamas, Barbados, Bolivia (previo a 1994), Costa Rica (previo a 1998), Cuba, República Dominicana, El Salvador (previo a 2015), Jamaica (previo a 1998), Nicaragua, Panamá (previo a 1998), Paraguay (previo a 2004), Perú (previo a 2001) y Venezuela dado que los datos no están disponibles.

1. Representa un grupo de 24 países de América Latina y el Caribe. Chile y México son también parte del grupo OCDE (35).
2. Representa el promedio no ponderado para los países miembros de la OCDE. El promedio OCDE del 2015 es calculado aplicando el promedio no ponderado del cambio porcentual para el 2015 en los 33 países con datos disponibles para ese año al promedio OCDE del 2014.

StatLink http://dx.doi.org/10.1787/888933463053

Table 4.5. Taxes on income and profits (1000) as percentage of total taxation
Cuadro 4.5. Impuestos sobre la renta y las utilidades (1000) en porcentaje del total de ingresos tributarios

	1990	2000	2005	2009	2010	2011	2012	2013	2014	2015
Argentina	5.3	18.5	20.4	15.8	16.2	17.2	17.3	17.8	18.9	20.5
Bahamas	0.0	0.0	0.0	0.0	0.0	0.0	0.0	0.0	0.0	0.0
Barbados	27.0	30.5	27.8	33.2	28.0	27.7	25.9	23.9	26.6	26.5
Belize / Belice	20.8	23.9	26.1	31.1	33.4	33.8	29.6	29.6	29.9	29.1
Bolivia	5.3	13.2	15.5	24.8	22.5	21.6	23.0	23.6	23.5	22.8
Brazil / Brasil	18.1	19.4	21.0	21.9	20.6	21.6	20.5	20.8	20.8	20.9
Chile	23.2	23.3	36.3	30.8	38.1	40.1	39.0	34.8	33.0	36.4
Colombia	29.9	23.3	28.2	29.9	26.8	28.7	33.3	33.5	32.4	31.7
Costa Rica	11.1	14.4	16.9	19.3	18.8	18.7	18.4	18.2	18.2	19.1
Cuba	0.2	16.1	14.0	12.5	14.9	17.0	15.6	18.4	19.8	19.9
Dominican Republic / República Dominicana	25.9	24.0	23.2	24.6	22.0	24.0	29.7	30.6	31.8	28.9
Ecuador	12.4	15.6	18.6	26.4	20.3	21.6	19.0	20.6	21.1	22.4
El Salvador	18.9	25.7	26.7	32.0	30.8	31.7	32.6	35.7	36.7	34.5
Guatemala	18.1	19.9	22.2	25.8	25.1	27.6	27.3	29.3	30.9	29.1
Honduras	20.3	17.2	22.7	25.8	25.8	28.9	26.4	27.4	26.0	26.3
Jamaica	50.9	44.8	42.8	47.0	41.3	40.4	39.2	36.4	35.2	35.0
Mexico / México[1]	34.0	33.2	33.7	36.1	36.5	37.9	37.0	40.7	37.6	37.6
Nicaragua	..	13.6	22.9	27.1	24.8	27.1	27.2	27.1	28.3	28.8
Panama / Panamá	24.3	24.0	23.9	29.5	26.3	23.1	28.5	28.1	25.2	25.5
Paraguay	21.1	13.1	12.6	17.2	13.4	14.7	15.1	15.1	15.0	15.2
Peru / Perú	5.7	19.5	29.3	35.0	36.5	40.8	41.4	39.1	40.2	36.1
Trinidad and Tobago / Trinidad y Tobago	50.6	54.5	70.8	66.3	67.4	72.5	69.1	67.5	69.4	61.9
Uruguay	4.8	9.4	11.8	20.7	20.9	20.5	20.6	21.8	20.8	21.9
Venezuela	83.7	43.2	38.4	38.6	30.6	29.0	30.5	28.8	32.7	22.6
Unweighted average / Promedio no ponderado										
LAC / ALC[2]	**22.3**	**22.5**	**25.3**	**28.0**	**26.7**	**27.8**	**27.8**	**27.9**	**28.1**	**27.2**
OECD / OCDE[3]	**37.5**	**34.9**	**34.5**	**33.5**	**33.2**	**33.5**	**33.7**	**33.8**	**33.7**	..

Note: The figures exclude local government revenues for Argentina (but include provincial revenues), Bahamas, Barbados, Bolivia (prior to 1994), Costa Rica (prior to 1998), Cuba, Dominican Republic, El Salvador (prior to 2015), Jamaica (prior to 1998), Nicaragua, Panama (prior to 1998), Paraguay (prior to 2004), Peru (prior to 2001) and Venezuela as the data are not available.

1. Data for 2014 are used in 2015.
2. Represents a group of 24 Latin American and Caribbean countries. Chile and Mexico are also part of the OECD (35) group.
3. Represents the unweighted average for OECD member countries.

Nota : Las cifras excluyen los ingresos de gobiernos locales en Argentina (pero incluye ingresos de las provincias), Bahamas, Barbados, Bolivia (previo a 1994), Costa Rica (previo a 1998), Cuba, República Dominicana, El Salvador (previo a 2015), Jamaica (previo a 1998), Nicaragua, Panamá (previo a 1998), Paraguay (previo a 2004), Perú (previo a 2001) y Venezuela dado que los datos no están disponibles.

1. Se utilizan los datos de 2014 en 2015.
2. Representa un grupo de 24 países de América Latina y el Caribe. Chile y México son también parte del grupo OCDE (35).
3. Representa el promedio no ponderado para los países miembros de la OCDE.

StatLink http://dx.doi.org/10.1787/888933463066

Table 4.6. Social security contributions (2000) as percentage of GDP
Cuadro 4.6. Contribuciones a la seguridad social (2000) en porcentaje del PIB

	1990	2000	2005	2009	2010	2011	2012	2013	2014	2015
Argentina	3.5	3.1	3.0	6.2	6.2	6.3	6.3	7.1	6.7	7.1
Bahamas[1]	1.6	1.8	1.8	2.0	2.1	2.4	2.4	2.7	2.8	2.9
Barbados[1]	3.3	4.7	5.2	5.7	5.9	6.0	6.1	5.9	6.1	6.3
Belize / Belice[1]	1.2	1.1	2.3	2.2	2.2	2.1	2.1	2.1	2.0	2.0
Bolivia[1,2]	0.0	1.3	1.2	1.2	1.2	1.6	1.5	1.5	1.4	1.4
Brazil / Brasil	6.1	7.0	7.8	8.1	8.1	8.2	8.4	8.3	8.3	8.3
Chile	1.5	1.4	1.4	1.4	1.3	1.3	1.4	1.4	1.4	1.4
Colombia	0.8	2.4	2.3	2.0	2.1	1.7	1.8	2.3	2.5	2.5
Costa Rica	5.4	5.0	5.4	6.0	6.2	6.3	6.3	7.6	7.7	7.8
Cuba	3.2	3.9	4.2	4.5	4.6	4.3	4.2	4.0	4.5	5.0
Dominican Republic / República Dominicana	0.1	0.1	0.0	0.1	0.1	0.1	0.1	0.1	0.1	0.0
Ecuador	1.6	1.2	2.7	3.3	3.7	5.0	5.4	4.8	4.6	5.0
El Salvador	1.4	2.0	1.7	1.7	1.7	1.7	1.7	1.7	1.8	1.9
Guatemala	1.4	1.9	2.0	1.9	1.9	1.9	2.0	2.0	1.8	2.1
Honduras	1.4	1.6	2.4	2.9	2.9	2.1	3.0	3.3	3.1	3.0
Jamaica	0.0	0.0	0.7	0.7	0.7	0.9	0.9	1.0	1.0	1.0
Mexico / México	2.1	2.7	2.8	2.9	2.8	2.8	2.9	3.1	3.1	3.3
Nicaragua	..	2.6	3.2	4.0	4.3	4.3	4.5	4.8	5.0	5.3
Panama / Panamá	4.8	6.0	5.1	5.2	5.7	5.9	5.4	6.0	5.7	5.8
Paraguay	0.5	3.2	3.0	3.9	3.7	3.8	4.5	4.1	4.6	4.9
Peru / Perú	0.9	1.8	1.6	2.0	1.9	1.9	2.0	2.1	2.1	2.1
Trinidad and Tobago / Trinidad y Tobago	0.9	1.4	1.2	2.1	1.9	1.7	1.9	2.1	2.5	3.1
Uruguay[3]	6.0	6.4	5.0	6.0	6.2	6.5	7.0	7.3	7.6	7.4
Venezuela[1]	0.9	0.7	0.6	1.0	1.0	1.0	1.0	1.0	0.9	0.6
Unweighted average / Promedio no ponderado										
LAC / ALC[4]	**2.1**	**2.6**	**2.8**	**3.2**	**3.3**	**3.3**	**3.5**	**3.6**	**3.6**	**3.8**
OECD / OCDE[5]	**7.4**	**8.6**	**8.5**	**8.9**	**8.8**	**8.9**	**9.0**	**9.1**	**9.1**	..

Note: The figures exclude local government revenues for Argentina (but include provincial revenues), Bahamas, Barbados, Bolivia (prior to 1994), Costa Rica (prior to 1998), Cuba, Dominican Republic, El Salvador (prior to 2015), Jamaica (prior to 1998), Nicaragua, Panama (prior to 1998), Paraguay (prior to 2004), Peru (prior to 2001) and Venezuela as the data are not available.

1. The data are estimated in the following countries: Bahamas (2015), Barbados (2015), Belize (from 2013 onward), Bolivia (from 2013 onward), and Venezuela (from 2011 onward).
2. Data for 1990 are not available.
3. Figures for 1990-98 are estimated by the Direction General of Taxes as the methodology they use to calculate social security contributions was not employed until 1999.
4. Represents a group of 24 Latin American and Caribbean countries. Chile and Mexico are also part of the OECD (35) group.
5. Represents the unweighted average for OECD member countries.

Nota : Las cifras excluyen los ingresos de gobiernos locales en Argentina (pero incluye ingresos de las provincias), Bahamas, Barbados, Bolivia (previo a 1994), Costa Rica (previo a 1998), Cuba, República Dominicana, El Salvador (previo a 2015), Jamaica (previo a 1998), Nicaragua, Panamá (previo a 1998), Paraguay (previo a 2004), Perú (previo a 2001) y Venezuela dado que los datos no están disponibles.

1. Datos estimados para esta partida en los siguientes países: Bahamas (2015), Barbados (2015), Belice (desde 2013), Bolivia (desde 2013) y Venezuela (desde 2011).
2. Los datos de 1990 no están disponibles.
3. Las cifras de 1990-98 son estimaciones dado que el empleo de la metodología actual utilizada para calcular las contribuciones a la seguridad social tuvo lugar en 1999.
4. Representa un grupo de 24 países de América Latina y el Caribe. Chile y México son también parte del grupo OCDE (35).
5. Representa el promedio no ponderado para los países miembros de la OCDE.

StatLink http://dx.doi.org/10.1787/888933463079

Table 4.7. Social security contributions (2000) as percentage of total taxation
Cuadro 4.7. Contribuciones a la seguridad social (2000) en porcentaje del total de ingresos tributarios

	1990	2000	2005	2009	2010	2011	2012	2013	2014	2015
Argentina	25.3	15.8	12.2	21.4	21.2	21.5	22.2	22.6	21.6	22.2
Bahamas[1]	13.2	11.9	12.8	12.4	13.1	12.8	13.7	15.9	16.5	14.8
Barbados[1]	14.2	15.7	17.8	18.6	19.3	18.6	18.4	19.9	20.1	20.1
Belize / Belice[1]	5.7	5.8	10.1	8.8	8.1	8.2	8.2	8.0	7.7	7.8
Bolivia[1,2]	0.0	7.3	6.1	5.7	5.9	7.3	6.8	6.3	5.9	5.7
Brazil / Brasil	24.0	23.5	23.7	25.2	25.0	24.8	25.7	25.5	26.0	25.9
Chile	9.0	7.3	6.5	8.2	6.8	6.3	6.5	7.2	7.2	6.9
Colombia	7.9	16.4	12.8	11.0	11.7	8.8	9.0	11.7	12.5	12.1
Costa Rica	27.2	28.0	27.6	29.3	30.3	30.5	30.6	33.7	34.0	33.9
Cuba	11.0	10.4	10.1	10.9	12.3	11.3	10.5	10.8	12.0	12.9
Dominican Republic / República Dominicana	0.8	1.1	0.0	0.5	0.8	0.5	0.4	0.4	0.4	0.4
Ecuador	21.9	12.1	22.1	21.7	22.0	28.3	27.3	24.4	24.0	24.0
El Salvador	13.3	16.6	11.9	12.1	11.4	10.8	10.5	10.3	10.7	10.9
Guatemala	15.6	15.5	15.0	15.4	15.6	15.0	15.4	15.7	14.2	16.6
Honduras	8.4	10.0	13.4	16.6	16.0	11.8	16.4	17.5	14.9	14.1
Jamaica	0.0	0.0	3.0	2.8	2.9	3.8	3.5	3.9	4.2	3.8
Mexico / México[3]	16.8	20.1	22.0	21.1	20.2	20.2	20.9	20.9	20.6	20.6
Nicaragua	..	19.9	19.8	23.6	24.1	22.9	22.9	23.9	24.3	25.2
Panama / Panamá	30.4	36.8	35.1	31.8	32.7	35.0	31.1	34.2	35.2	36.1
Paraguay	8.3	25.6	21.4	24.5	22.7	22.4	25.1	25.1	25.9	27.3
Peru / Perú	7.7	12.2	9.9	11.7	10.6	10.4	10.6	11.2	11.0	12.4
Trinidad and Tobago / Trinidad y Tobago	3.7	6.5	4.4	7.5	6.9	6.3	6.8	7.5	8.2	10.0
Uruguay[4]	30.5	29.6	21.1	23.3	23.6	24.5	26.0	26.7	27.9	27.6
Venezuela[1]	4.9	5.4	3.9	6.7	8.0	7.0	6.7	6.6	5.0	3.0
Unweighted average / Promedio no ponderado										
LAC / ALC[5]	**13.0**	**14.7**	**14.3**	**15.4**	**15.5**	**15.4**	**15.7**	**16.2**	**16.3**	**16.4**
OECD / OCDE[6]	**22.0**	**24.8**	**25.3**	**26.8**	**26.6**	**26.4**	**26.4**	**26.3**	**26.2**	..

Note: The figures exclude local government revenues for Argentina (but include provincial revenues), Bahamas, Barbados, Bolivia (prior to 1994), Costa Rica (prior to 1998), Cuba, Dominican Republic, El Salvador (prior to 2015), Jamaica (prior to 1998), Nicaragua, Panama (prior to 1998), Paraguay (prior to 2004), Peru (prior to 2001) and Venezuela as the data are not available.

1. The data are estimated in the following countries: Bahamas (2015), Barbados (2015), Belize (from 2013 onward), Bolivia (from 2013 onward), and Venezuela (from 2011 onward).
2. Data for 1990 are not available.
3. Data for 2014 are used in 2015.
4. Figures for 1990-98 are estimated by the Direction General of Taxes as the methodology they use to calculate social security contributions was not employed until 1999.
5. Represents a group of 24 Latin American and Caribbean countries. Chile and Mexico are also part of the OECD (35) group.
6. Represents the unweighted average for OECD member countries.

Nota : Las cifras excluyen los ingresos de gobiernos locales en Argentina (pero incluye ingresos de las provincias), Bahamas, Barbados, Bolivia (previo a 1994), Costa Rica (previo a 1998), Cuba, República Dominicana, El Salvador (previo a 2015), Jamaica (previo a 1998), Nicaragua, Panamá (previo a 1998), Paraguay (previo a 2004), Perú (previo a 2001) y Venezuela dado que los datos no están disponibles.

1. Datos estimados para esta partida en los siguientes países: Bahamas (2015), Barbados (2015), Belice (desde 2013), Bolivia (desde 2013) y Venezuela (desde 2011).
2. Los datos de 1990 no están disponibles.
3. Se utilizan los datos de 2014 en 2015.
4. Las cifras de 1990-98 son estimaciones dado que el empleo de la metodología actual utilizada para calcular las contribuciones a la seguridad social tuvo lugar en 1999.
5. Representa un grupo de 24 países de América Latina y el Caribe. Chile y México son también parte del grupo OCDE (35).
6. Representa el promedio no ponderado para los países miembros de la OCDE.

StatLink http://dx.doi.org/10.1787/888933463082

Table 4.8. Taxes on property (4000) as percentage of GDP
Cuadro 4.8. Impuestos sobre la propiedad (4000) en porcentaje del PIB

	1990	2000	2005	2009	2010	2011	2012	2013	2014	2015
Argentina	1.6	1.3	2.7	2.7	2.6	2.6	2.7	2.9	2.8	2.8
Bahamas	0.5	0.5	0.7	1.1	1.2	1.2	1.1	1.4	1.2	1.2
Barbados	1.0	1.5	1.6	1.7	1.3	1.3	1.7	1.4	1.3	1.7
Belize / Belice	0.8	0.8	1.2	0.9	0.8	0.9	0.9	1.0	1.0	1.0
Bolivia	0.0	0.0	0.8	0.3	0.3	0.2	0.2	0.2	0.2	0.2
Brazil / Brasil	1.7	2.4	2.6	1.8	1.9	2.0	1.9	1.8	1.8	2.0
Chile	1.0	1.3	1.3	0.9	0.8	0.8	0.9	0.8	0.8	0.9
Colombia	0.2	1.0	1.4	1.6	1.6	2.1	2.1	2.1	2.1	2.3
Costa Rica	0.1	0.3	0.3	0.3	0.3	0.3	0.4	0.4	0.4	0.4
Cuba	0.0	0.0	0.0	0.0	0.0	0.0	0.0	0.0	0.0	0.0
Dominican Republic / República Dominicana	0.1	0.1	0.6	0.6	0.6	0.7	0.8	0.9	0.6	0.6
Ecuador	0.1	0.1	0.1	0.1	0.1	0.1	0.2	0.2	0.2	0.2
El Salvador	0.5	0.1	0.1	0.1	0.1	0.1	0.1	0.1	0.1	0.4
Guatemala	0.1	0.1	0.2	0.2	0.2	0.2	0.2	0.2	0.2	0.1
Honduras	0.1	0.2	0.1	0.1	0.1	0.1	0.3	0.3	0.5	0.5
Jamaica	0.2	0.2	0.2	0.2	0.2	0.2	0.2	0.4	0.4	0.4
Mexico / México[1]	0.2	0.2	0.3	0.3	0.3	0.3	0.3	0.3	0.3	0.3
Nicaragua	..	0.0	0.0	0.0	0.1	0.1	0.1	0.1	0.1	0.1
Panama / Panamá	0.8	0.5	0.7	0.7	0.7	0.7	0.7	0.8	0.7	0.6
Paraguay	0.3	0.0	0.0	0.3	0.3	0.3	0.3	0.3	0.3	0.3
Peru / Perú	1.9	0.0	0.5	0.6	0.5	0.4	0.4	0.4	0.4	0.4
Trinidad and Tobago / Trinidad y Tobago	0.7	0.5	0.4	0.4	0.3	0.3	0.3	0.4	0.4	0.5
Uruguay	1.6	2.2	2.9	2.3	2.2	2.2	2.1	2.1	2.1	2.1
Venezuela	0.1	0.5	0.9	0.0	0.0	0.0	0.0	0.0	0.0	0.0
Unweighted average / Promedio no ponderado										
LAC / ALC[2]	**0.6**	**0.6**	**0.8**	**0.7**	**0.7**	**0.7**	**0.7**	**0.8**	**0.8**	**0.8**
OECD / OCDE[3]	**1.8**	**1.8**	**1.8**	**1.7**	**1.7**	**1.8**	**1.8**	**1.9**	**1.9**	..

Note: The figures exclude local government revenues for Argentina (but include provincial revenues), Bahamas, Barbados, Bolivia (prior to 1994), Costa Rica (prior to 1998), Cuba, Dominican Republic, El Salvador (prior to 2015), Jamaica (prior to 1998), Nicaragua, Panama (prior to 1998), Paraguay (prior to 2004), Peru (prior to 2001) and Venezuela as the data are not available.

1. In 2015, federal government data are used.
2. Represents a group of 24 Latin American and Caribbean countries. Chile and Mexico are also part of the OECD (35) group.
3. Represents the unweighted average for OECD member countries.

Nota : Las cifras excluyen los ingresos de gobiernos locales en Argentina (pero incluye ingresos de las provincias), Bahamas, Barbados, Bolivia (previo a 1994), Costa Rica (previo a 1998), Cuba, República Dominicana, El Salvador (previo a 2015), Jamaica (previo a 1998), Nicaragua, Panamá (previo a 1998), Paraguay (previo a 2004), Perú (previo a 2001) y Venezuela dado que los datos no están disponibles.

1. En 2015 se utilizan datos federales.
2. Representa un grupo de 24 países de América Latina y el Caribe. Chile y México son también parte del grupo OCDE (35).
3. Representa el promedio no ponderado para los países miembros de la OCDE.

StatLink http://dx.doi.org/10.1787/888933463094

Table 4.9. Taxes on property (4000) as percentage of total taxation
Cuadro 4.9. Impuestos sobre la propiedad (4000) en porcentaje del total de ingresos tributarios

	1990	2000	2005	2009	2010	2011	2012	2013	2014	2015
Argentina	11.4	6.3	11.2	9.2	9.0	9.0	9.0	9.3	9.1	8.9
Bahamas	3.8	3.3	5.1	6.6	7.2	6.2	6.4	8.0	7.0	6.1
Barbados	4.2	4.9	5.5	5.5	4.2	4.0	5.2	4.9	4.3	5.5
Belize / Belice	3.5	4.2	5.5	3.5	3.0	3.4	3.5	3.8	3.8	3.8
Bolivia	0.1	0.0	4.2	1.4	1.3	1.1	1.0	0.8	0.8	0.8
Brazil / Brasil	6.5	8.1	7.9	5.7	5.9	6.0	5.9	5.6	5.8	6.3
Chile	6.2	7.0	6.3	5.4	4.1	4.0	4.3	4.1	4.2	4.4
Colombia	2.2	6.6	7.9	8.8	8.7	11.2	10.4	10.5	10.4	11.0
Costa Rica	0.3	1.4	1.3	1.3	1.6	1.6	1.7	1.8	1.9	1.9
Cuba	0.0	0.0	0.0	0.0	0.0	0.0	0.0	0.0	0.0	0.0
Dominican Republic / República Dominicana	0.9	1.2	5.1	5.1	5.2	5.6	6.1	6.2	4.4	4.4
Ecuador	1.2	0.6	0.9	0.7	0.7	0.7	0.9	0.9	1.0	1.1
El Salvador	5.1	0.7	0.7	0.5	0.5	0.5	0.5	0.5	0.6	2.4
Guatemala	1.6	1.0	1.3	1.5	1.5	1.4	1.5	1.4	1.5	1.2
Honduras	0.8	1.1	0.5	0.5	0.5	0.5	1.5	1.7	2.3	2.4
Jamaica	0.9	0.7	1.0	0.7	0.9	0.9	0.8	1.6	1.6	1.7
Mexico / México[1]	1.9	1.7	2.2	2.2	2.1	2.0	2.1	2.0	2.1	2.1
Nicaragua	..	0.0	0.0	0.2	0.4	0.5	0.5	0.6	0.6	0.7
Panama / Panamá	4.9	3.1	4.6	4.0	4.2	3.9	3.7	4.3	4.2	3.8
Paraguay	4.9	0.0	0.0	2.0	1.7	1.6	1.6	1.7	1.6	1.7
Peru / Perú	15.3	0.0	3.3	3.3	3.0	2.2	2.0	2.1	2.0	2.3
Trinidad and Tobago / Trinidad y Tobago	3.0	2.6	1.5	1.5	1.1	1.1	1.0	1.4	1.5	1.5
Uruguay	8.4	10.3	12.0	8.9	8.6	8.2	7.9	7.5	7.6	7.7
Venezuela	0.3	3.7	5.9	0.2	0.2	0.1	0.1	0.2	0.2	0.2
Unweighted average / Promedio no ponderado										
LAC / ALC[2]	**3.8**	**2.9**	**3.9**	**3.3**	**3.2**	**3.2**	**3.2**	**3.4**	**3.3**	**3.4**
OECD / OCDE[3]	**5.7**	**5.5**	**5.5**	**5.5**	**5.5**	**5.5**	**5.5**	**5.6**	**5.6**	..

Note: The figures exclude local government revenues for Argentina (but include provincial revenues), Bahamas, Barbados, Bolivia (prior to 1994), Costa Rica (prior to 1998), Cuba, Dominican Republic, El Salvador (prior to 2015), Jamaica (prior to 1998), Nicaragua, Panama (prior to 1998), Paraguay (prior to 2004), Peru (prior to 2001) and Venezuela as the data are not available.

1. Data for 2014 are used in 2015.
2. Represents a group of 24 Latin American and Caribbean countries. Chile and Mexico are also part of the OECD (35) group.
3. Represents the unweighted average for OECD member countries.

Nota : Las cifras excluyen los ingresos de gobiernos locales en Argentina (pero incluye ingresos de las provincias), Bahamas, Barbados, Bolivia (previo a 1994), Costa Rica (previo a 1998), Cuba, República Dominicana, El Salvador (previo a 2015), Jamaica (previo a 1998), Nicaragua, Panamá (previo a 1998), Paraguay (previo a 2004), Perú (previo a 2001) y Venezuela dado que los datos no están disponibles.

1. Se utilizan los datos de 2014 en 2015.
2. Representa un grupo de 24 países de América Latina y el Caribe. Chile y México son también parte del grupo OCDE (35).
3. Representa el promedio no ponderado para los países miembros de la OCDE.

StatLink http://dx.doi.org/10.1787/888933463108

Table 4.10. Taxes on goods and services (5000) as percentage of GDP
Cuadro 4.10. Impuestos sobre bienes y servicios (5000) en porcentaje del PIB

	1990	2000	2005	2009	2010	2011	2012	2013	2014	2015
Argentina	7.5	11.2	13.4	15.1	15.2	15.0	15.5	15.5	15.4	15.2
Bahamas	9.4	11.4	9.5	10.5	10.0	12.0	12.1	11.2	11.4	13.6
Barbados	10.4	14.4	14.1	12.2	14.0	15.7	16.4	14.8	14.5	14.9
Belize / Belice	15.3	12.7	13.0	14.4	14.8	13.7	14.7	15.1	15.1	15.2
Bolivia	5.7	10.9	11.4	11.2	11.2	12.5	12.5	12.9	13.1	13.3
Brazil / Brasil	12.2	13.7	14.6	13.5	14.0	14.1	13.8	13.8	13.3	13.2
Chile	10.7	12.0	10.7	9.7	10.1	10.5	10.8	10.8	10.9	11.2
Colombia	5.7	6.4	7.6	7.5	7.7	8.0	7.7	7.4	7.6	7.8
Costa Rica	9.8	9.1	9.7	9.3	9.0	9.2	9.1	9.2	9.1	9.3
Cuba	25.3	22.0	23.1	23.1	19.1	19.9	22.2	20.2	19.7	20.4
Dominican Republic / República Dominicana	5.5	7.9	8.4	8.9	8.9	8.6	8.4	8.7	8.9	9.1
Ecuador	4.5	7.4	7.0	7.4	9.1	8.7	10.3	10.5	10.2	10.9
El Salvador	5.4	6.9	8.5	8.0	8.7	8.8	9.0	9.1	9.0	8.8
Guatemala	5.5	7.7	7.9	6.8	7.0	7.0	7.0	6.9	6.7	6.5
Honduras	11.2	10.7	10.4	9.5	9.7	9.6	9.6	9.5	11.1	11.6
Jamaica	9.8	11.5	11.2	11.4	12.9	12.6	13.0	13.6	13.7	14.4
Mexico / México[1]	5.4	5.8	5.0	5.0	5.3	5.1	5.0	4.7	5.4	6.2
Nicaragua	..	8.6	9.2	8.3	9.1	9.3	9.7	9.6	9.5	9.5
Panama / Panamá	6.0	4.7	4.2	4.7	5.2	5.5	5.3	5.0	4.8	4.9
Paraguay	3.0	7.3	8.0	8.9	10.0	10.2	10.2	9.4	10.1	10.0
Peru / Perú	7.9	9.0	9.0	8.0	8.4	8.3	8.4	8.5	8.5	8.2
Trinidad and Tobago / Trinidad y Tobago	9.5	7.5	5.9	6.8	6.6	6.2	6.2	6.4	6.1	7.9
Uruguay	11.1	11.2	13.1	12.1	12.2	12.4	12.2	12.0	11.9	11.5
Venezuela	2.0	6.5	8.2	7.8	7.2	8.0	8.7	9.1	11.5	15.2
Unweighted average / Promedio no ponderado										
LAC / ALC[2]	**8.6**	**9.8**	**10.1**	**10.0**	**10.2**	**10.4**	**10.7**	**10.6**	**10.7**	**11.2**
OECD / OCDE[3]	**10.0**	**10.9**	**10.8**	**10.3**	**10.6**	**10.6**	**10.8**	**10.8**	**11.0**	..

Note: The figures exclude local government revenues for Argentina (but include provincial revenues), Bahamas, Barbados, Bolivia (prior to 1994), Costa Rica (prior to 1998), Cuba, Dominican Republic, El Salvador (prior to 2015), Jamaica (prior to 1998), Nicaragua, Panama (prior to 1998), Paraguay (prior to 2004), Peru (prior to 2001) and Venezuela as the data are not available.

1. In 2015, federal government data are used.
2. Represents a group of 24 Latin American and Caribbean countries. Chile and Mexico are also part of the OECD (35) group.
3. Represents the unweighted average for OECD member countries.

Nota : Las cifras excluyen los ingresos de gobiernos locales en Argentina (pero incluye ingresos de las provincias), Bahamas, Barbados, Bolivia (previo a 1994), Costa Rica (previo a 1998), Cuba, República Dominicana, El Salvador (previo a 2015), Jamaica (previo a 1998), Nicaragua, Panamá (previo a 1998), Paraguay (previo a 2004), Perú (previo a 2001) y Venezuela dado que los datos no están disponibles.

1. En 2015, se utilizan datos del nivel federal.
2. Representa un grupo de 24 países de América Latina y el Caribe. Chile y México son también parte del grupo OCDE (35).
3. Representa el promedio no ponderado para los países miembros de la OCDE.

StatLink http://dx.doi.org/10.1787/888933463110

Table 4.11. Taxes on goods and services (5000) as percentage of total taxation
Cuadro 4.11. Impuestos sobre bienes y servicios (5000) en porcentaje del total de ingresos tributarios

	1990	2000	2005	2009	2010	2011	2012	2013	2014	2015
Argentina	55.2	56.5	54.6	52.2	52.4	51.2	50.5	49.6	49.5	47.5
Bahamas	76.4	74.9	69.4	63.9	62.3	63.4	68.8	66.1	66.1	68.3
Barbados	44.8	47.6	47.9	40.0	45.7	48.4	49.5	50.2	47.8	47.5
Belize / Belice	70.0	66.1	58.3	56.5	55.5	54.6	58.8	58.7	58.6	59.3
Bolivia	68.5	61.7	56.9	51.6	55.5	56.6	55.4	55.3	54.9	53.8
Brazil / Brasil	47.7	46.3	44.7	41.9	43.2	42.5	42.5	42.5	41.8	41.3
Chile	62.9	63.8	51.5	55.6	51.2	49.3	50.1	54.0	55.3	54.0
Colombia	53.8	43.8	42.1	40.6	43.0	42.3	38.8	36.7	37.5	37.5
Costa Rica	49.0	51.1	49.4	45.1	44.3	44.2	43.8	40.8	40.3	40.1
Cuba	86.9	59.2	56.2	56.2	50.8	51.7	55.8	54.1	52.6	52.8
Dominican Republic / República Dominicana	69.9	72.6	70.4	69.9	72.0	69.9	63.8	62.7	63.4	66.3
Ecuador	61.7	71.6	57.4	48.8	54.4	49.1	52.1	53.4	53.2	51.9
El Salvador	51.3	57.0	60.7	55.5	57.3	57.1	56.3	53.5	52.0	50.5
Guatemala	61.0	62.4	60.3	55.7	56.5	54.6	54.1	52.9	52.9	52.6
Honduras	66.2	66.1	57.7	53.3	53.5	54.9	52.4	50.1	53.7	54.6
Jamaica	42.5	50.9	47.9	46.0	51.9	51.4	53.2	54.6	55.6	56.3
Mexico / México[1]	44.0	42.8	39.4	37.0	37.8	36.2	36.1	32.4	35.8	35.8
Nicaragua	..	66.3	57.2	49.1	50.7	49.5	49.4	48.2	46.6	45.2
Panama / Panamá	37.6	28.4	29.4	29.0	30.2	32.5	30.5	28.8	30.0	30.1
Paraguay	51.4	58.0	58.0	55.5	60.5	60.6	57.5	57.5	56.9	55.8
Peru / Perú	65.6	61.1	54.5	47.0	47.3	44.6	43.4	45.1	45.1	47.9
Trinidad and Tobago / Trinidad y Tobago	41.7	35.5	22.4	24.1	24.2	19.7	22.6	23.2	20.4	25.7
Uruguay	56.7	51.7	55.0	47.0	46.9	46.8	45.5	44.0	43.6	42.6
Venezuela	11.1	47.7	51.8	54.6	61.2	58.9	61.0	63.1	60.7	72.9
Unweighted average / Promedio no ponderado										
LAC / ALC[2]	**55.5**	**56.0**	**52.2**	**49.0**	**50.3**	**49.6**	**49.6**	**49.1**	**48.9**	**49.6**
OECD / OCDE[3]	**32.5**	**33.0**	**32.9**	**32.3**	**32.9**	**32.7**	**32.6**	**32.4**	**32.6**	..

Note: The figures exclude local government revenues for Argentina (but include provincial revenues), Bahamas, Barbados, Bolivia (prior to 1994), Costa Rica (prior to 1998), Cuba, Dominican Republic, El Salvador (prior to 2015), Jamaica (prior to 1998), Nicaragua, Panama (prior to 1998), Paraguay (prior to 2004), Peru (prior to 2001) and Venezuela as the data are not available.

1. Data for 2014 are used in 2015.
2. Represents a group of 24 Latin American and Caribbean countries. Chile and Mexico are also part of the OECD (35) group.
3. Represents the unweighted average for OECD member countries.

Nota : Las cifras excluyen los ingresos de gobiernos locales en Argentina (pero incluye ingresos de las provincias), Bahamas, Barbados, Bolivia (previo a 1994), Costa Rica (previo a 1998), Cuba, República Dominicana, El Salvador (previo a 2015), Jamaica (previo a 1998), Nicaragua, Panamá (previo a 1998), Paraguay (previo a 2004), Perú (previo a 2001) y Venezuela dado que los datos no están disponibles.

1. Se utilizan los datos de 2014 en 2015.
2. Representa un grupo de 24 países de América Latina y el Caribe. Chile y México son también parte del grupo OCDE (35).
3. Representa el promedio no ponderado para los países miembros de la OCDE.

StatLink http://dx.doi.org/10.1787/888933463127

Table 4.12. Taxes on general consumption (5110) as percentage of GDP
Cuadro 4.12. Impuestos generales sobre el consumo (5110) en porcentaje del PIB

	1990	2000	2005	2009	2010	2011	2012	2013	2014	2015
Argentina	3.2	8.1	8.8	10.2	10.1	10.3	10.7	11.4	11.2	11.5
Bahamas	0.0	0.0	0.0	0.0	0.0	0.0	0.0	0.0	0.0	2.5
Barbados	4.8	8.0	7.8	7.4	8.5	10.3	10.5	10.0	9.5	9.2
Belize / Belice	0.0	4.9	5.9	5.9	7.1	5.9	6.8	7.3	7.5	7.5
Bolivia	3.6	5.7	6.9	7.3	7.4	8.5	8.7	9.0	9.0	9.1
Brazil / Brasil	12.1	12.9	13.6	12.5	12.8	12.9	12.8	12.8	12.3	12.2
Chile	6.3	7.9	7.8	7.3	7.6	7.9	8.1	8.1	8.2	8.4
Colombia	2.8	4.6	5.9	6.0	6.1	6.5	6.3	5.7	6.0	6.1
Costa Rica	4.0	4.4	5.0	4.8	4.7	4.8	4.8	4.7	4.7	4.7
Cuba	23.3	20.1	21.2	20.6	16.4	17.1	19.8	18.2	17.6	17.9
Dominican Republic / República Dominicana	1.2	2.4	3.8	4.0	4.1	4.0	3.9	4.4	4.7	4.9
Ecuador	2.0	4.6	4.8	4.9	5.6	5.4	6.2	6.4	6.3	6.4
El Salvador	2.8	5.4	6.5	6.1	6.7	6.8	7.0	7.1	7.2	6.8
Guatemala	2.4	4.7	5.2	4.9	5.1	5.2	5.3	5.2	5.1	4.8
Honduras	2.7	4.8	5.2	5.2	5.4	5.7	5.6	5.5	6.8	7.2
Jamaica	0.0	3.4	3.9	3.8	3.9	3.9	3.9	4.0	4.0	4.2
Mexico / México	3.2	3.1	3.4	3.4	3.8	3.7	3.7	3.5	3.9	3.9
Nicaragua	..	4.5	5.3	5.2	5.5	5.9	6.2	6.2	6.3	6.0
Panama / Panamá	1.4	0.6	0.8	2.1	2.6	3.0	3.0	2.8	2.7	2.6
Paraguay	0.0	4.0	4.6	5.6	6.3	6.5	6.5	6.3	6.8	6.8
Peru / Perú	1.5	5.4	6.1	6.5	7.0	7.0	7.0	7.1	7.2	7.0
Trinidad and Tobago / Trinidad y Tobago	4.6	3.7	2.9	4.2	4.3	3.0	3.8	3.9	3.4	4.8
Uruguay	5.5	6.5	8.2	8.6	8.6	8.6	8.5	8.4	8.1	7.8
Venezuela	0.0	4.1	6.4	5.9	5.5	5.2	6.8	7.3	9.0	11.7
Unweighted average / Promedio no ponderado										
LAC / ALC[1]	**3.8**	**5.6**	**6.2**	**6.3**	**6.5**	**6.6**	**6.9**	**6.9**	**7.0**	**7.2**
OECD / OCDE[2]	**5.7**	**6.7**	**6.8**	**6.4**	**6.7**	**6.7**	**6.8**	**6.8**	**7.0**	..

Note: The figures exclude local government revenues for Argentina (but include provincial revenues), Bahamas, Barbados, Bolivia (prior to 1994), Costa Rica (prior to 1998), Cuba, Dominican Republic, El Salvador (prior to 2015), Jamaica (prior to 1998), Nicaragua, Panama (prior to 1998), Paraguay (prior to 2004), Peru (prior to 2001) and Venezuela as the data are not available.

1. Represents a group of 24 Latin American and Caribbean countries. Chile and Mexico are also part of the OECD (35) group.
2. Represents the unweighted average for OECD member countries.

Nota : Las cifras excluyen los ingresos de gobiernos locales en Argentina (pero incluye ingresos de las provincias), Bahamas, Barbados, Bolivia (previo a 1994), Costa Rica (previo a 1998), Cuba, República Dominicana, El Salvador (previo a 2015), Jamaica (previo a 1998), Nicaragua, Panamá (previo a 1998), Paraguay (previo a 2004), Perú (previo a 2001) y Venezuela dado que los datos no están disponibles.

1. Representa un grupo de 24 países de América Latina y el Caribe. Chile y México son también parte del grupo OCDE (35).
2. Representa el promedio no ponderado para los países miembros de la OCDE.

StatLink http://dx.doi.org/10.1787/888933463130

Table 4.13. Taxes on general consumption (5110) as percentage of total taxation
Cuadro 4.13. Impuestos generales sobre el consumo (5110) en porcentaje del total de ingresos tributarios

	1990	2000	2005	2009	2010	2011	2012	2013	2014	2015
Argentina	23.3	41.1	36.0	35.1	34.7	35.2	34.8	36.6	36.2	35.8
Bahamas	0.0	0.0	0.0	0.0	0.0	0.0	0.0	0.0	0.0	12.4
Barbados	20.9	26.6	26.6	24.1	27.7	31.8	31.6	33.8	31.1	29.5
Belize / Belice	0.0	25.8	26.4	23.4	26.8	23.5	27.2	28.6	29.1	29.4
Bolivia	43.2	32.2	34.6	33.6	36.7	38.4	38.7	38.5	38.0	36.9
Brazil / Brasil	47.4	43.4	41.4	39.0	39.7	38.8	39.2	39.3	38.7	38.1
Chile	37.4	41.8	37.8	42.1	38.5	37.0	37.7	40.8	41.6	40.8
Colombia	26.1	31.4	32.4	32.1	34.0	34.4	31.9	28.5	29.4	29.3
Costa Rica	20.0	24.9	25.3	23.3	23.1	23.2	23.2	21.2	21.1	20.4
Cuba	80.1	53.9	51.6	50.1	43.5	44.6	49.9	48.8	46.9	46.5
Dominican Republic / República Dominicana	15.1	22.1	31.6	31.5	33.3	32.5	29.5	31.7	33.2	35.5
Ecuador	27.7	44.6	39.6	32.1	33.9	30.3	31.5	32.8	32.8	30.6
El Salvador	26.2	45.1	46.3	42.2	44.3	44.3	43.8	41.8	41.5	39.3
Guatemala	27.2	37.9	39.6	39.9	41.2	41.1	41.1	39.8	40.3	38.6
Honduras	16.2	29.7	29.0	29.4	29.7	32.3	30.4	28.8	33.1	33.7
Jamaica	0.1	14.9	16.7	15.4	15.7	15.7	15.8	16.1	16.3	16.5
Mexico / México[1]	26.1	22.8	26.7	24.9	26.9	26.4	26.7	23.7	25.6	25.6
Nicaragua	..	34.8	32.9	30.7	30.8	31.3	31.5	31.3	31.1	28.6
Panama / Panamá	9.0	3.4	5.8	12.8	15.3	17.9	17.0	16.2	17.0	16.1
Paraguay	0.0	32.1	33.3	34.6	38.3	38.9	37.0	38.2	38.3	37.8
Peru / Perú	12.1	37.1	37.2	38.5	38.9	37.5	36.6	37.7	38.6	40.7
Trinidad and Tobago / Trinidad y Tobago	19.9	17.4	11.1	15.0	15.6	11.3	14.0	14.2	11.4	15.6
Uruguay	28.1	30.2	34.1	33.4	32.9	32.5	31.7	30.6	29.9	28.9
Venezuela	0.0	30.2	40.4	41.2	46.6	45.9	47.9	50.6	47.4	55.8
Unweighted average / Promedio no ponderado										
LAC / ALC[2]	**22.0**	**30.1**	**30.7**	**30.2**	**31.2**	**31.0**	**31.2**	**31.2**	**31.2**	**31.8**
OECD / OCDE[3]	**18.2**	**19.9**	**20.6**	**20.1**	**20.7**	**20.6**	**20.5**	**20.5**	**20.7**	..

Note: The figures exclude local government revenues for Argentina (but include provincial revenues), Bahamas, Barbados, Bolivia (prior to 1994), Costa Rica (prior to 1998), Cuba, Dominican Republic, El Salvador (prior to 2015), Jamaica (prior to 1998), Nicaragua, Panama (prior to 1998), Paraguay (prior to 2004), Peru (prior to 2001) and Venezuela as the data are not available.

1. Data for 2014 are used in 2015.
2. Represents a group of 24 Latin American and Caribbean countries. Chile and Mexico are also part of the OECD (35) group.
3. Represents the unweighted average for OECD member countries.

Nota : Las cifras excluyen los ingresos de gobiernos locales en Argentina (pero incluye ingresos de las provincias), Bahamas, Barbados, Bolivia (previo a 1994), Costa Rica (previo a 1998), Cuba, República Dominicana, El Salvador (previo a 2015), Jamaica (previo a 1998), Nicaragua, Panamá (previo a 1998), Paraguay (previo a 2004), Perú (previo a 2001) y Venezuela dado que los datos no están disponibles.

1. Se utilizan los datos de 2014 en 2015.
2. Representa un grupo de 24 países de América Latina y el Caribe. Chile y México son también parte del grupo OCDE (35).
3. Representa el promedio no ponderado para los países miembros de la OCDE.

StatLink http://dx.doi.org/10.1787/888933463148

Table 4.14. Taxes on specific goods and services (5120) as percentage of GDP
Cuadro 4.14. Impuestos específicos sobre bienes y servicios (5120) en porcentaje del PIB

	1990	2000	2005	2009	2010	2011	2012	2013	2014	2015
Argentina	4.1	3.0	4.7	4.9	5.1	4.7	4.6	4.0	4.1	3.6
Bahamas	8.7	10.3	8.5	9.0	8.5	10.1	10.3	9.5	9.0	8.7
Barbados	5.5	4.7	4.7	3.6	3.8	3.9	3.9	3.6	3.8	4.2
Belize / Belice	14.8	7.5	6.8	7.8	7.2	7.4	7.3	7.2	7.3	7.4
Bolivia	2.1	5.2	4.5	3.9	3.8	4.0	3.8	3.9	4.0	4.2
Brazil / Brasil	0.0	0.7	0.8	0.9	1.1	1.2	1.1	1.0	1.0	1.0
Chile	3.9	3.5	2.3	1.8	1.9	2.0	2.0	2.0	2.0	2.0
Colombia	2.9	1.8	1.7	1.6	1.6	1.5	1.3	1.7	1.7	1.7
Costa Rica	5.3	4.2	4.3	4.0	3.8	3.9	3.5	3.6	3.4	3.6
Cuba	2.0	2.0	1.9	2.5	2.7	2.7	2.4	2.0	2.2	2.4
Dominican Republic / República Dominicana	4.2	5.3	4.5	4.8	4.7	4.5	4.4	4.2	4.2	4.1
Ecuador	2.4	2.7	1.9	2.3	3.1	3.0	3.8	3.7	3.6	4.1
El Salvador	2.6	1.4	2.0	1.9	2.0	2.0	2.0	2.0	1.8	1.9
Guatemala	2.9	2.9	2.6	1.8	1.7	1.6	1.4	1.3	1.3	1.4
Honduras	8.5	5.9	5.2	4.3	4.3	4.0	4.0	4.1	4.2	4.4
Jamaica	9.6	8.0	7.1	7.4	8.8	8.6	9.0	9.4	9.5	10.0
Mexico / México[1]	2.1	2.0	0.9	1.0	0.9	0.8	0.9	0.9	1.1	2.3
Nicaragua	..	4.1	3.9	3.1	3.6	3.4	3.5	3.4	3.2	3.5
Panama / Panamá	2.5	3.7	3.1	2.4	2.4	2.3	2.2	2.1	2.0	2.1
Paraguay[1]	3.0	3.3	3.4	3.2	3.4	3.4	3.4	2.9	3.1	2.9
Peru / Perú	6.5	3.5	2.9	1.4	1.5	1.3	1.3	1.4	1.2	1.2
Trinidad and Tobago / Trinidad y Tobago	4.4	3.2	2.7	2.3	2.0	1.9	2.0	2.1	2.3	2.7
Uruguay	5.1	3.7	4.3	3.0	3.2	3.3	3.3	3.2	3.2	3.2
Venezuela	2.0	2.4	1.8	1.9	1.7	1.8	1.9	1.8	2.5	3.6
Unweighted average / Promedio no ponderado										
LAC / ALC[2]	**4.6**	**4.0**	**3.6**	**3.4**	**3.5**	**3.5**	**3.5**	**3.4**	**3.4**	**3.6**
OECD / OCDE[3]	**3.8**	**3.6**	**3.4**	**3.2**	**3.3**	**3.3**	**3.3**	**3.3**	**3.3**	..

Note: The figures exclude local government revenues for Argentina (but include provincial revenues), Bahamas, Barbados, Bolivia (prior to 1994), Costa Rica (prior to 1998), Cuba, Dominican Republic, El Salvador (prior to 2015), Jamaica (prior to 1998), Nicaragua, Panama (prior to 1998), Paraguay (prior to 2004), Peru (prior to 2001) and Venezuela as the data are not available.

1. In 2015, federal government data are used.
2. Represents a group of 24 Latin American and Caribbean countries. Chile and Mexico are also part of the OECD (35) group.
3. Represents the unweighted average for OECD member countries.

Nota : Las cifras excluyen los ingresos de gobiernos locales en Argentina (pero incluye ingresos de las provincias), Bahamas, Barbados, Bolivia (previo a 1994), Costa Rica (previo a 1998), Cuba, República Dominicana, El Salvador (previo a 2015), Jamaica (previo a 1998), Nicaragua, Panamá (previo a 1998), Paraguay (previo a 2004), Perú (previo a 2001) y Venezuela dado que los datos no están disponibles.

1. En 2015, se utilizan datos del nivel federal.
2. Representa un grupo de 24 países de América Latina y el Caribe. Chile y México son también parte del grupo OCDE (35).
3. Representa el promedio no ponderado para los países miembros de la OCDE.

StatLink http://dx.doi.org/10.1787/888933463155

Table 4.15. Taxes on specific goods and services (5120) as percentage of total taxation
Cuadro 4.15. Impuestos específicos sobre bienes y servicios (5120) en porcentaje del total de ingresos tributarios

	1990	2000	2005	2009	2010	2011	2012	2013	2014	2015
Argentina	30.1	15.0	19.0	16.8	17.6	16.0	15.1	12.7	13.3	11.2
Bahamas	70.1	67.8	62.0	54.6	52.6	53.7	58.7	55.8	51.8	44.0
Barbados	23.9	15.5	15.8	11.7	12.5	12.2	11.8	12.3	12.6	13.4
Belize / Belice	67.9	39.1	30.5	30.5	26.9	29.7	29.1	28.0	28.3	28.8
Bolivia	25.3	29.5	22.4	18.0	18.8	18.2	16.7	16.7	17.0	16.9
Brazil / Brasil	0.0	2.4	2.6	2.9	3.5	3.7	3.2	3.2	3.1	3.2
Chile	23.0	18.8	10.9	10.1	9.8	9.4	9.4	9.9	10.3	9.9
Colombia	27.8	12.4	9.7	8.4	9.0	7.9	6.8	8.3	8.1	8.2
Costa Rica	26.8	23.9	22.1	19.3	18.6	18.9	16.8	15.8	15.3	15.6
Cuba	6.8	5.3	4.6	6.1	7.3	7.1	5.9	5.3	5.8	6.3
Dominican Republic / República Dominicana	53.8	48.9	37.5	37.4	37.8	36.5	33.4	30.2	29.4	30.0
Ecuador	33.0	26.0	15.8	14.8	18.6	17.1	19.0	18.9	18.7	19.6
El Salvador	25.0	11.9	14.4	13.3	13.0	12.7	12.5	11.7	10.5	10.9
Guatemala	32.8	23.4	19.6	14.6	14.0	12.3	11.2	10.3	10.3	11.3
Honduras	50.0	36.4	28.7	24.0	23.8	22.6	22.0	21.3	20.6	20.8
Jamaica	41.6	35.1	30.5	29.8	35.4	35.0	36.6	37.7	38.6	39.1
Mexico / México[1]	17.2	14.5	7.1	7.4	6.7	6.0	6.5	5.9	7.2	7.2
Nicaragua	..	31.5	24.3	18.4	19.9	18.3	17.9	16.9	15.5	16.6
Panama / Panamá	15.5	22.9	21.4	14.6	14.1	13.8	12.7	11.8	12.2	13.1
Paraguay[1]	51.4	25.9	24.6	19.9	20.8	20.4	19.3	17.9	17.2	16.3
Peru / Perú	53.5	24.0	17.3	8.5	8.3	7.1	6.9	7.4	6.5	7.2
Trinidad and Tobago / Trinidad y Tobago	19.2	15.4	10.2	8.0	7.5	7.3	7.3	7.7	7.7	8.7
Uruguay	26.0	17.2	17.8	11.5	12.2	12.6	12.2	11.6	11.8	11.8
Venezuela	11.1	17.5	11.4	13.4	14.6	13.0	13.1	12.5	13.4	17.1
Unweighted average / Promedio no ponderado										
LAC / ALC[2]	**31.8**	**24.2**	**20.0**	**17.3**	**17.6**	**17.1**	**16.8**	**16.2**	**16.0**	**16.1**
OECD / OCDE[3]	**12.6**	**11.1**	**10.4**	**10.1**	**10.2**	**10.0**	**10.0**	**9.8**	**9.6**	..

Note: The figures exclude local government revenues for Argentina (but include provincial revenues), Bahamas, Barbados, Bolivia (prior to 1994), Costa Rica (prior to 1998), Cuba, Dominican Republic, El Salvador (prior to 2015), Jamaica (prior to 1998), Nicaragua, Panama (prior to 1998), Paraguay (prior to 2004), Peru (prior to 2001) and Venezuela as the data are not available.

1. Data for 2014 are used in 2015.
2. Represents a group of 24 Latin American and Caribbean countries. Chile and Mexico are also part of the OECD (35) group.
3. Represents the unweighted average for OECD member countries.

Nota : Las cifras excluyen los ingresos de gobiernos locales en Argentina (pero incluye ingresos de las provincias), Bahamas, Barbados, Bolivia (previo a 1994), Costa Rica (previo a 1998), Cuba, República Dominicana, El Salvador (previo a 2015), Jamaica (previo a 1998), Nicaragua, Panamá (previo a 1998), Paraguay (previo a 2004), Perú (previo a 2001) y Venezuela dado que los datos no están disponibles.

1. Se utilizan los datos de 2014 en 2015.
2. Representa un grupo de 24 países de América Latina y el Caribe. Chile y México son también parte del grupo OCDE (35).
3. Representa el promedio no ponderado para los países miembros de la OCDE.

StatLink http://dx.doi.org/10.1787/888933463167

Table 4.16. Gross domestic product for tax reporting years at market prices, in billions of national currency units
Cuadro 4.16. Producto interno bruto para los años fiscales a precios de mercado, en millardos de moneda local

	1990	2000	2005	2009	2010	2011	2012	2013	2014	2015
Argentina	75	308	583	1 248	1 662	2 179	2 638	3 348	4 579	5 843
Bahamas	4	6	8	8	8	8	8	9	9	9
Barbados	4	6	8	9	9	9	9	9	9	9
Belize / Belice	1	2	2	3	3	3	3	3	3	3
Bolivia	15	52	77	122	138	166	187	212	228	228
Brazil / Brasil	0	1 199	2 171	3 333	3 886	4 376	4 815	5 332	5 779	6 001
Chile	10 482	42 095	68 883	96 444	110 999	121 319	129 028	137 230	147 568	157 511
Colombia	24 295	208 531	340 156	504 647	544 924	619 894	664 240	710 497	757 506	800 849
Costa Rica	536	5 042	9 786	17 281	19 581	21 392	23 371	24 781	26 703	28 279
Cuba	22	31	43	62	64	69	73	77	81	87
Dominican Republic / República Dominicana	82	414	1 088	1 729	1 979	2 218	2 378	2 559	2 786	3 023
Ecuador	15	18	42	63	70	79	88	95	102	100
El Salvador	5	13	17	21	21	23	24	24	24	26
Guatemala	31	133	208	308	333	371	395	423	454	488
Honduras	13	107	184	276	299	335	361	377	407	451
Jamaica	34	387	700	1 065	1 153	1 240	1 314	1 431	1 542	1 667
Mexico / México	825	6 132	9 425	12 073	13 267	14 527	15 599	16 079	17 217	18 195
Nicaragua	1	65	106	170	187	219	246	269	306	346
Panama / Panamá	6	12	16	27	29	34	40	45	49	52
Paraguay	6 031	28 574	53 962	79 117	94 934	105 203	108 832	125 152	137 798	144 249
Peru / Perú	5	178	247	364	418	465	499	535	576	613
Trinidad and Tobago / Trinidad y Tobago	22	51	101	121	141	163	165	170	168	150
Uruguay	12	276	425	715	808	926	1 041	1 178	1 331	1 460
Venezuela	2	80	304	707	1 017	1 357	1 635	2 246	3 031	6 025

Source: OECD National Accounts data for Chile and Mexico and official National Accounts data for the other countries. CEPALSTAT (ECLAC) for Cuba, The World Economic Outlook (IMF) was used for Argentina, Bahamas, Panama, Paraguay and Venezuela.

Fuente : Datos de Cuentas Nacionales de la OCDE para Chile y México y estadísticas oficiales de Cuentas Nacionales para el resto de países. CEPALSTAT (CEPAL) para Cuba y para Argentina, Bahamas, Panamá, Paraguay y Venezuela se utilizó el World Economic Outlook (FMI).

StatLink http://dx.doi.org/10.1787/888933463173

4.2. Comparative charts / 4.2. Gráficos comparativos

Figure 4.1. Tax revenue of main headings as percentage of total tax revenue, 2015
Gráfico 4.1. Ingresos tributarios de categorías principales como porcentaje del ingreso tributario total, 2015

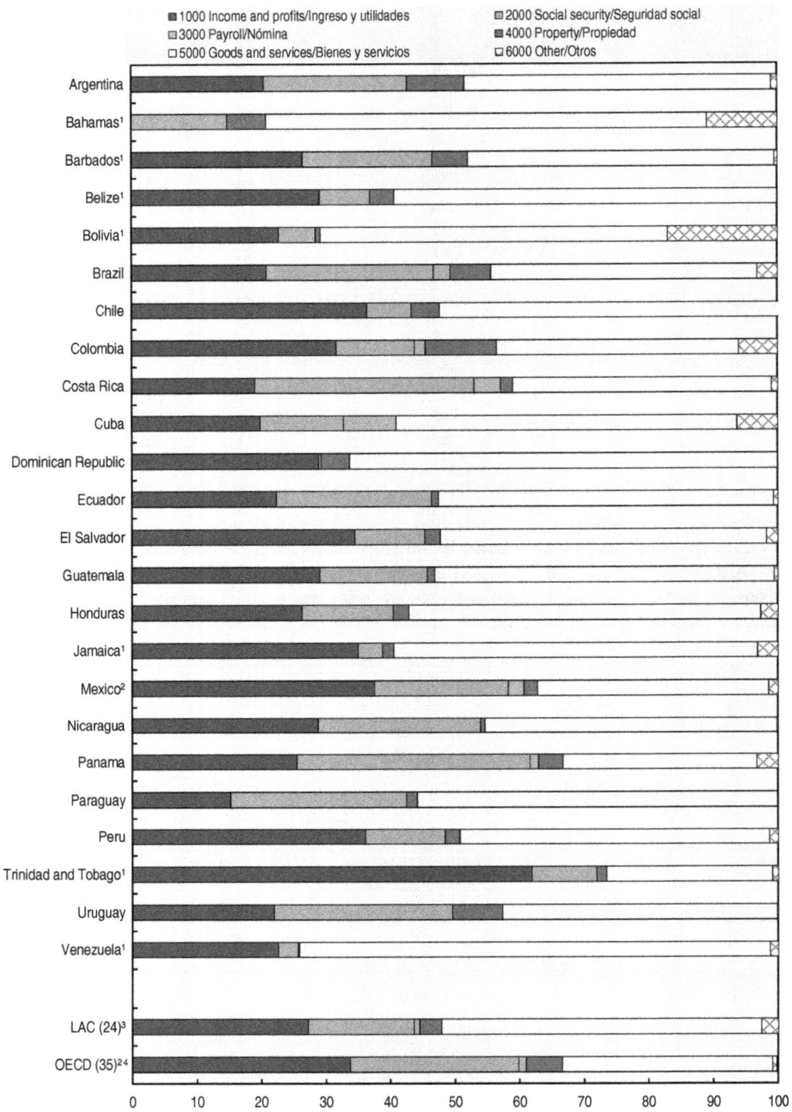

1. The data are estimated for the following countries: Bahamas (social security contributions for 2015), Barbados (social security contributions for 2015), Belize (social security contributions from 2013 onward), Bolivia (social security contributions from 2013 onward), Jamaica (environmental levy for years 2014 and 2015),Trinidad and Tobago (local property taxes for 2015) and Venezuela (social security contributions from 2011 onward). See the corresponding country tables for more information.

1. Datos estimados para los siguientes países: Bahamas (contribuciones a la seguridad social para 2015), Barbados (contribuciones a la seguridad social para 2015), Belice (contribuciones a la seguridad social desde 2013), Bolivia (contribuciones a la seguridad social desde 2013), Jamaica (impuesto ambiental para los años 2014 y 2015), Trinidad y Tobago (impuestos sobre la propiedad municipales) y Venezuela (contribuciones a la seguridad social desde 2011). Véanse las tablas de país para mayor información.

2. Data for 2014 are used.

2. Se utilizan datos del 2014.

3. Represents the unweighted average of the 24 Latin American and Caribbean countries.

3. Representa el promedio no ponderado de 24 países de América Latina y el Caribe.

4. Represents the unweighted average for OECD member countries. Chile and Mexico are also part of the OECD (35) group.

4. Representa el promedio no ponderado para los países miembros de la OCDE. Chile y México también forman parte del grupo (35) OCDE.

StatLink http://dx.doi.org/10.1787/888933462472

Figure 4.2. **Tax structures in Latin American and Caribbean countries, 1990-2015**

Receipts as percentage of total tax revenues

Gráfico 4.2. **Estructuras impositivas en países de América Latina y el Caribe, 1990-2015**

Ingresos como porcentaje de los ingresos tributarios totales

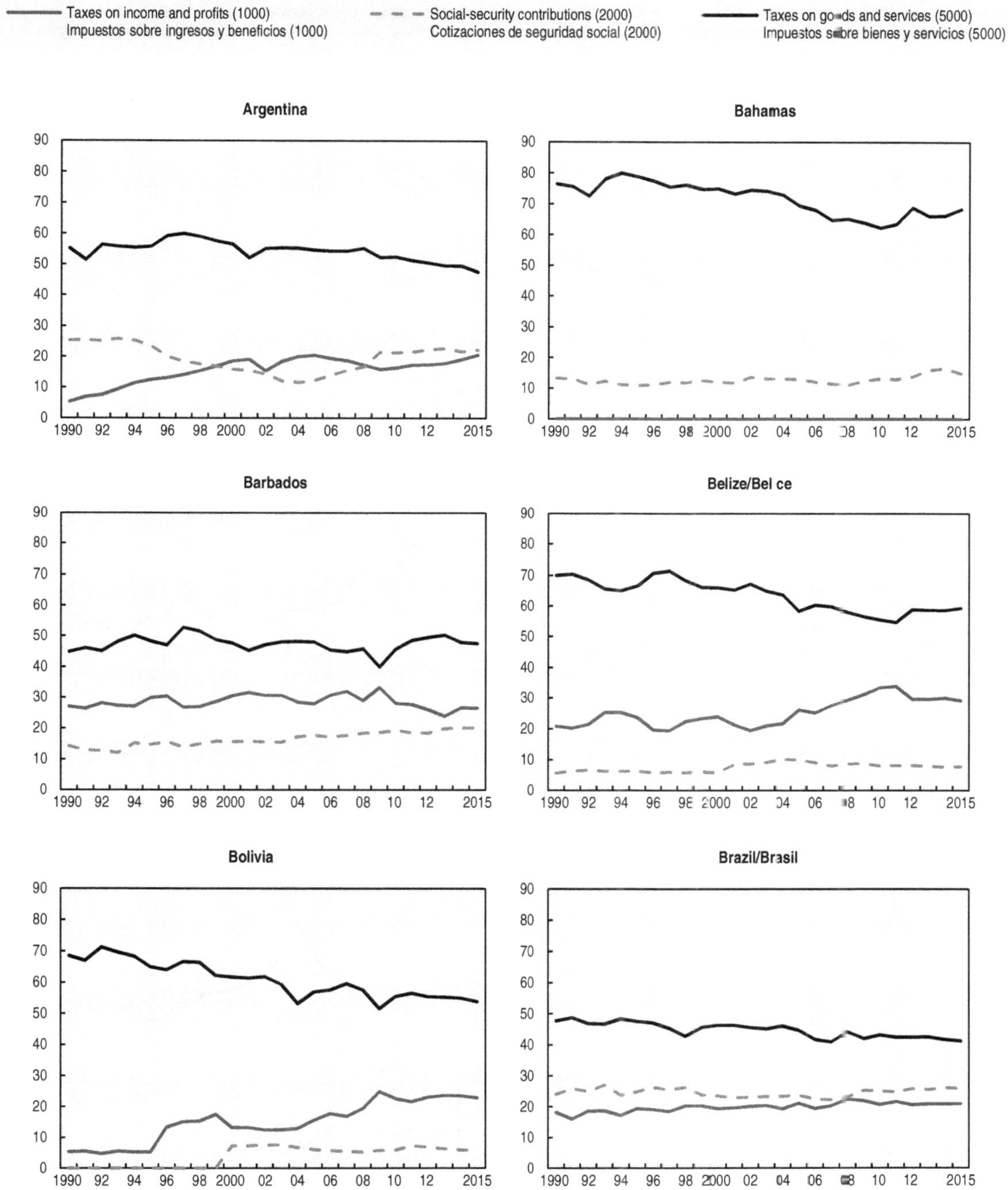

Figure 4.2. **Tax structures in Latin American and Caribbean countries, 1990-2015** *(cont.)*

Receipts as percentage of total tax revenues

Gráfico 4.2. **Estructuras impositivas en países de América Latina y el Caribe, 1990-2015** *(cont.)*

Ingresos como porcentaje de los ingresos tributarios totales

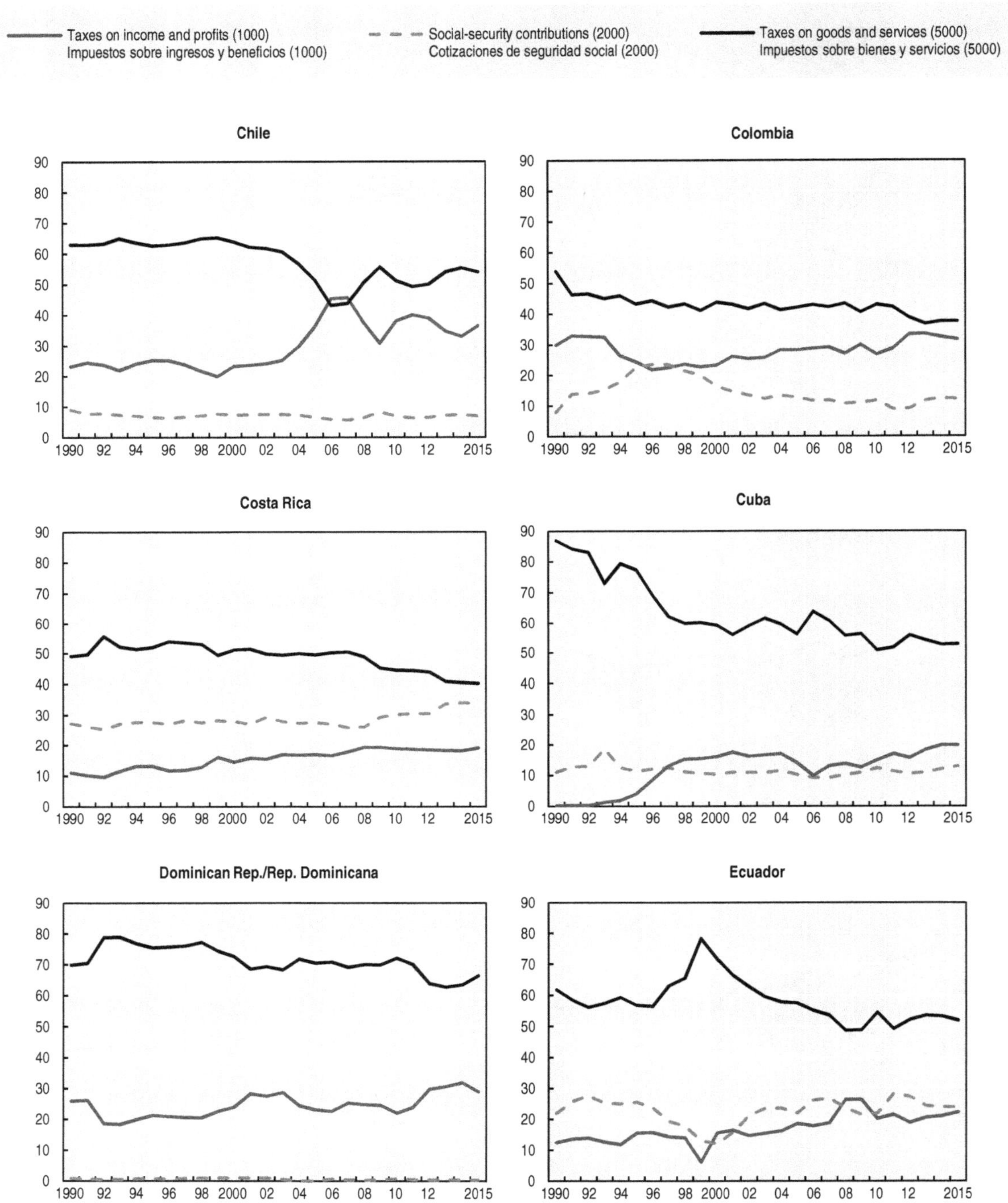

Figure 4.2. **Tax structures in Latin American and Caribbean countries, 1990-2015** *(cont.)*

Receipts as percentage of total tax revenues

Gráfico 4.2. **Estructuras impositivas en países de América Latina y el Caribe, 1990-2015** *(cont.)*

Ingresos como porcentaje de los ingresos tributarios totales

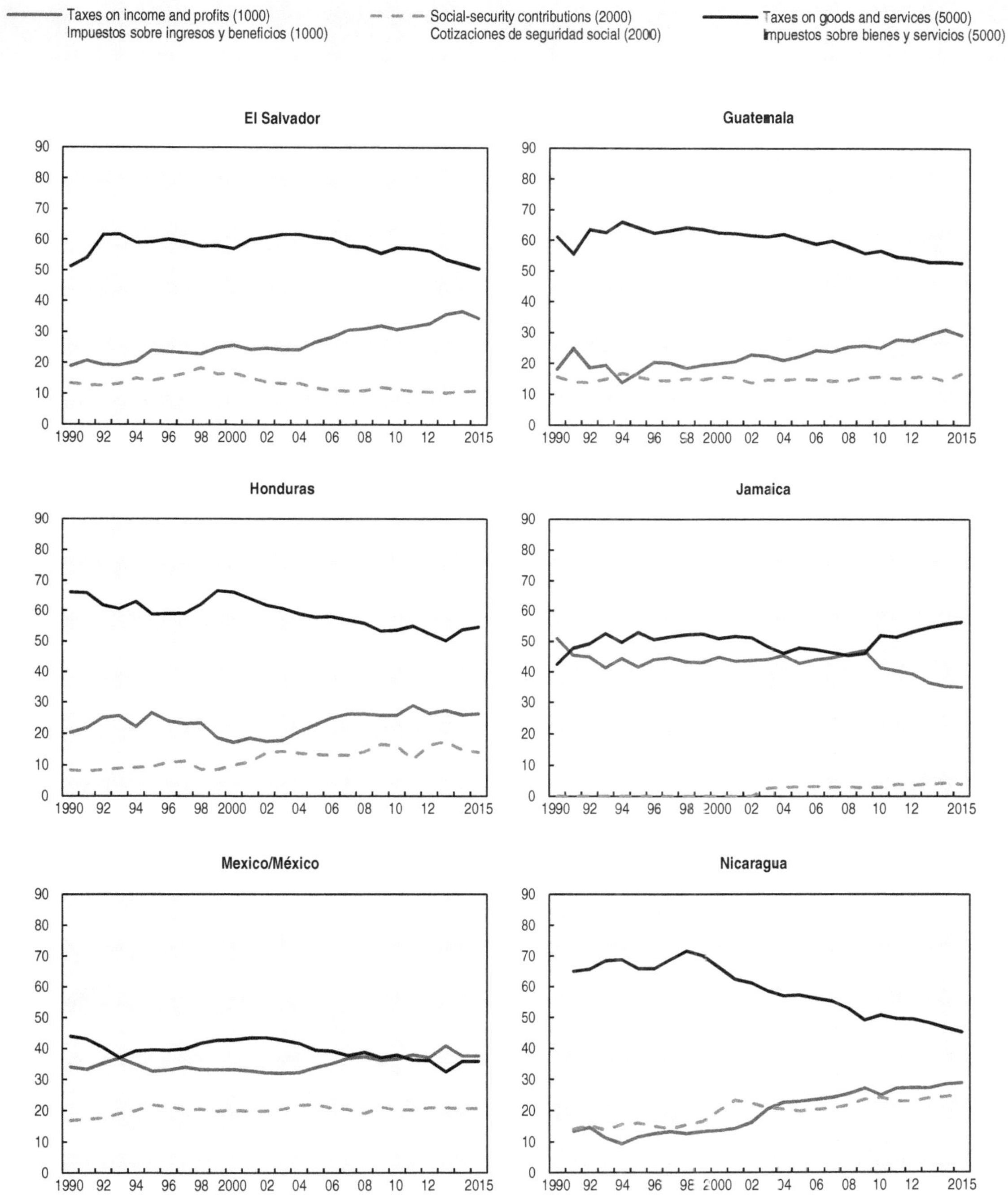

Figure 4.2. **Tax structures in Latin American and Caribbean countries, 1990-2015** *(cont.)*

Receipts as percentage of total tax revenues

Gráfico 4.2. **Estructuras impositivas en países de América Latina y el Caribe, 1990-2015** *(cont.)*

Ingresos como porcentaje de los ingresos tributarios totales

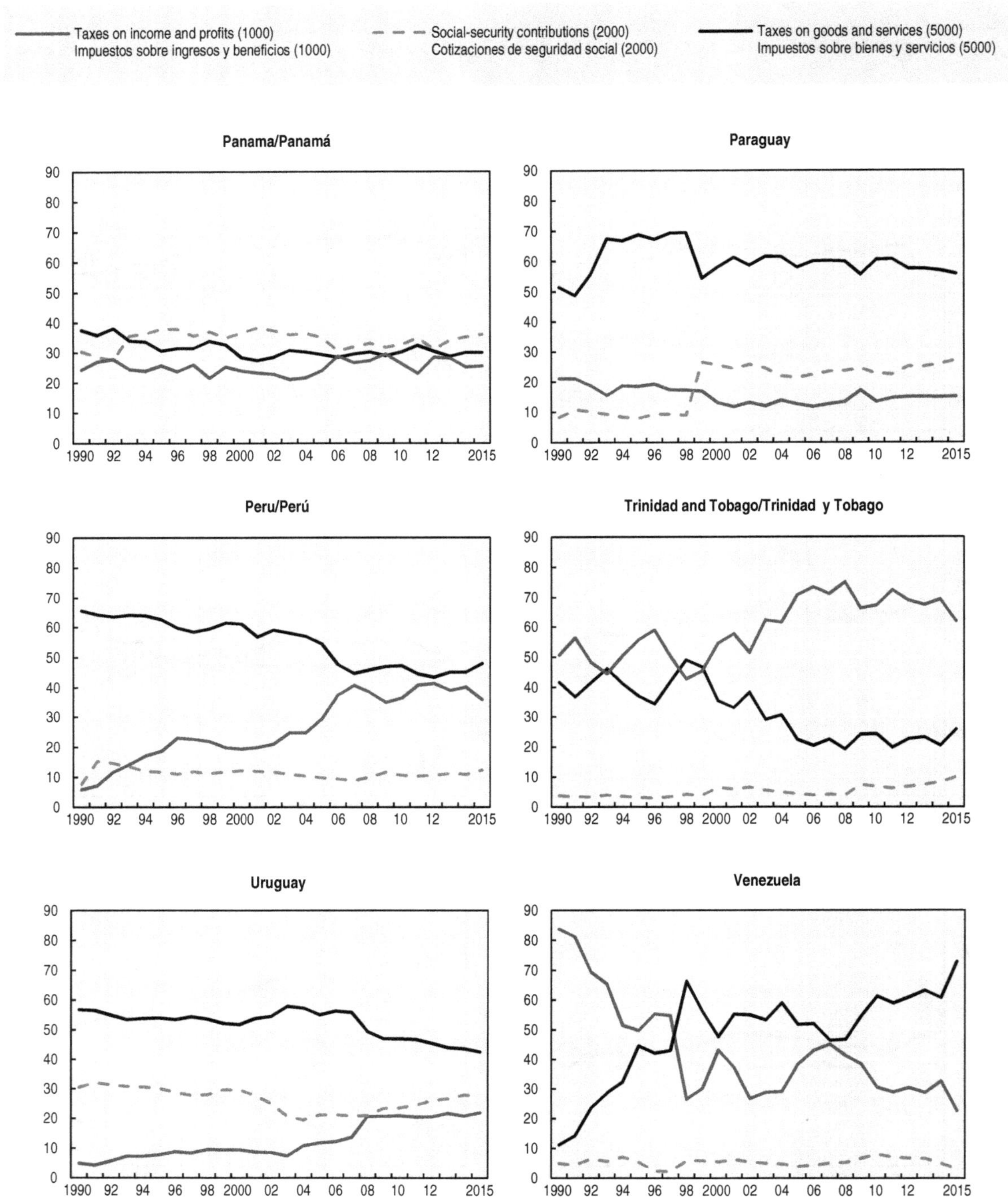

StatLink http://dx.doi.org/10.1787/888933462483

CHAPTER 5

COUNTRY TABLES, 1990-2015 – TAX REVENUES

CAPÍTULO 5

CUADROS PAÍS, 1990-2015 – INGRESOS TRIBUTARIOS

Table 5.1. Argentina

Details of tax revenue / Ingresos tributarios detallados

Million ARS

	1990	2000	2005	2009	2010	2011	2012	2013	2014	2015
Total tax revenue	**10 217**	**61 084**	**142 906**	**360 951**	**483 014**	**638 429**	**808 131**	**1 043 967**	**1 424 523**	**1 872 915**
1000 Taxes on income, profits and capital gains	**542**	**11 303**	**29 203**	**56 887**	**78 427**	**110 118**	**140 108**	**185 688**	**269 809**	**384 536**
1100 Of individuals	141	3 937	8 192	19 573	23 980	36 870	54 494	79 803	125 503	188 218
1110 On income and profits	130	3 854	8 151	19 460	23 858	36 713	54 279	79 449	125 067	187 663
1120 On capital gains	11	82	41	114	122	157	215	354	436	555
1200 Corporate	357	6 575	19 602	33 921	50 664	68 127	81 938	99 346	132 178	185 725
1210 On profits	357	6 575	19 602	33 921	50 664	68 127	81 938	99 346	132 178	185 725
Corporate income taxes	198	5 956	18 494	32 702	49 012	66 767	80 490	97 614	129 881	183 207
Tax on assets	160	19	5	6	4	4	5	3	6	4
Tax on assumed minimum income	0	600	1 102	1 213	1 648	1 357	1 443	1 728	2 291	2 513
1220 On capital gains	..	..	..	..	..	..	..	..	..	..
1300 Unallocable between 1100 and 1200	43	792	1 409	3 392	3 783	5 121	3 676	6 539	12 128	10 593
Non resident taxpayers	11	792	1 409	3 392	3 783	5 121	3 676	6 539	12 128	10 593
Other	33	0	0	0	0	0	0	0	0	0
2000 Social security contributions	**2 583**	**9 670**	**17 400**	**77 231**	**102 460**	**137 186**	**179 777**	**236 072**	**307 656**	**415 410**
2100 Employees	0	2 486	3 690	28 871	37 990	49 587	69 159	91 779	121 276	163 590
2110 On a payroll basis	..	2 486	3 690	28 871	37 990	49 587	69 159	91 779	121 276	163 590
2120 On an income tax basis	..	0	0	0	0	0	0	0	0	0
2200 Employers	0	6 069	12 557	40 473	54 713	77 596	101 114	132 999	174 965	235 610
2210 On a payroll basis	..	6 069	12 557	40 473	54 713	77 596	101 114	132 999	174 965	235 610
2220 On an income tax basis	..	0	0	0	0	0	0	0	0	0
2300 Self-employed or non-employed	98	1 115	1 153	7 886	9 757	10 003	9 504	11 293	11 416	16 210
2310 On a payroll basis	98	1 115	1 153	7 886	9 757	10 003	9 504	11 293	11 416	16 210
2320 On an income tax basis	0	0	0	0	0	0	0	0	0	0
2400 Unallocable between 2100, 2200 and 2300	2 485	0	0	0	0	0	0	0	0	0
2410 On a payroll basis	2 485	..	..	..	..	..	..	..	..	..
2420 On an income tax basis	0	..	..	..	..	..	..	..	..	..
3000 Taxes on payroll and workforce	**0**	**0**	**0**	**0**	**0**	**0**	**0**	**0**	**0**	**0**
4000 Taxes on property	**1 164**	**3 867**	**15 997**	**33 167**	**43 538**	**57 537**	**72 374**	**96 679**	**129 065**	**166 182**
4100 Recurrent taxes on immovable property	419	1 809	2 837	4 170	5 035	6 099	9 921	14 097	17 547	21 738
4110 Households	0	0	0	0	0	0	0	0	0	0
4120 Others	419	1 809	2 837	4 170	5 035	6 099	9 921	14 097	17 547	21 738
4200 Recurrent taxes on net wealth	246	1 084	1 867	4 123	5 248	6 018	7 408	10 471	14 575	18 538
4210 Individual	3	1 024	1 813	4 041	5 147	5 892	7 263	10 296	14 356	18 210
Personal assets	0	1 024	1 813	4 041	5 147	5 892	7 263	10 296	14 356	18 210
Recurrent taxes on net wealth	3	0	0	0	0	0	0	0	0	0
4220 Corporate	242	60	55	82	101	126	145	175	220	327
4300 Estate, inheritance and gift taxes	0	0	0	0	0	0	0	0	0	0
4310 Estate and inheritance taxes	..	..	..	..	..	..	..	..	..	..
4320 Gift taxes	..	..	..	..	..	..	..	..	..	..
4400 Taxes on financial and capital transactions	459	904	11 272	24 871	33 252	45 420	55 044	72 111	96 943	125 906
Immovable property transfers	0	54	116	372	539	775	721	734	912	1 256
Movable property transfers	44	0	0	0	0	0	0	0	0	0
Bank accounts' credits and debits	205	0	9 434	20 561	26 885	36 179	43 931	56 515	76 740	97 480
Provincial taxes on financial and capital transactions	0	0	0	0	0	0	0	0	0	0
Stamp taxes	211	850	1 722	3 937	5 829	8 466	10 392	14 862	19 291	27 170
4500 Non-recurrent taxes	40	70	21	4	3	0	1	0	0	0
4510 On net wealth	0	0	0	0	0	0	0	0	0	0
4520 Other non-recurrent taxes	40	70	21	4	3	0	1	0	0	0
4600 Other recurrent taxes on property	0	0	0	0	0	0	0	0	0	0
5000 Taxes on goods and services	**5 636**	**34 539**	**77 959**	**188 344**	**253 092**	**327 059**	**407 716**	**517 591**	**704 677**	**889 323**
5100 Taxes on production, sale, transfer, etc	5 462	34 288	78 555	187 568	252 550	326 822	403 294	513 926	703 883	881 120
5110 General taxes	2 384	25 123	51 467	126 858	167 534	224 813	281 589	381 630	515 090	671 297
5111 Value added taxes	1 594	19 009	36 853	87 386	116 386	154 237	190 496	249 006	331 203	433 076
5112 Sales tax	0	0	0	0	0	0	0	0	0	0
5113 Other	791	6 114	14 613	39 472	51 148	70 576	91 093	132 624	183 887	238 221
5120 Taxes on specific goods and services	3 077	9 166	27 088	60 709	85 016	102 009	121 704	132 296	188 793	209 822
5121 Excises	1 866	5 850	10 609	19 523	26 208	30 851	40 800	49 680	69 977	92 349
Alcoholic beverages	25	36	73	169	238	322	422	525	673	985
Non alcoholic beverages	25	90	189	441	501	654	912	1 195	1 586	2 168
Beers	0	50	131	226	212	210	332	650	879	1 384
Tobacco products	425	1 875	3 460	5 751	6 884	8 620	10 310	12 343	17 432	26 152
Liquid fuel and gas	1 073	3 478	6 017	11 593	15 269	18 131	25 785	31 010	44 490	56 478
Electricity	72	205	283	559	591	616	610	547	607	590
Motor vehicles	59	20	0	36	27	24	153	185	121	88
Other	189	96	456	747	2 485	2 274	2 275	3 225	4 189	4 503
5122 Profits of fiscal monopolies	0	0	0	0	0	0	0	0	0	0

Table 5.1. Argentina *(cont.)*
Details of tax revenue / Ingresos tributarios detallados

Million ARS

	1990	2000	2005	2009	2010	2011	2012	2013	2014	2015
5123 Customs and import duties	219	1 976	3 877	7 700	11 428	14 678	16 640	23 551	30 058	35 512
Import duties	166	1 938	3 780	7 526	11 183	14 373	16 313	23 134	29 482	34 822
Import fees	53	38	96	174	246	305	327	416	576	691
5124 Taxes on exports	724	32	12 323	32 042	45 547	54 163	61 316	55 465	84 088	75 939
5125 Taxes on investment goods	0	0	0	0	0	0	0	0	0	0
5126 Taxes on specific services	163	1 233	150	1 190	1 429	1 820	2 227	2 677	3 533	4 420
Insurance services	42	194	8	17	21	27	35	46	65	88
Financial services	32	855	2	0	0	0	0	0	0	0
Telephone services	82	33	110	779	936	1 163	1 391	1 605	1 983	2 301
Other specific services	7	151	31	395	472	629	801	1 026	1 486	2 031
5127 Other taxes on internat. trade and transactions	98	74	129	255	404	497	721	924	1 136	1 601
5128 Other taxes	8	0	0	0	0	0	0	0	0	0
5130 Unallocable between 5110 and 5120	0	0	0	0	0	0	0	0	0	0
5200 Taxes on use of goods and perform activities	177	833	1 289	3 228	3 598	4 928	6 409	9 059	12 010	17 035
5210 Recurrent taxes	177	833	1 289	3 228	3 598	4 928	6 409	9 059	12 010	17 035
5211 Paid by households: motor vehicles	177	833	1 289	3 228	3 598	4 928	6 409	9 059	12 010	17 035
5212 Paid by others: motor vehicles	0	0	0	0	0	0	0	0	0	0
5213 Paid in respect of other goods	0	0	0	0	0	0	0	0	0	0
5220 Non-recurrent taxes	0	0	0	0	0	0	0	0	0	0
5300 Unallocable between 5100 and 5200	-3	-583	-1 885	-2 451	-3 056	-4 690	-1 987	-5 394	-11 215	-8 831
6000 Other taxes	**292**	**1 704**	**2 347**	**5 322**	**5 497**	**6 527**	**8 157**	**7 937**	**13 316**	**17 463**
6100 Paid solely by business	0	354	757	1 550	2 093	2 983	3 825	4 423	4 259	5 624
Simplified system for small taxpayers	0	354	757	1 550	2 093	2 983	3 825	4 423	4 259	5 624
6200 Other	292	1 351	1 590	3 772	3 404	3 544	4 332	3 514	9 056	11 839
Tax debt payments	135	24	112	1 629	293	710	934	-1 313	1 340	1 306
Special payments	79	6	1	0	0	0	0	0	0	0
Other national level	0	12	7	0	0	0	0	0	0	0
Other provincial level	78	1 309	1 469	2 143	3 110	2 833	3 398	4 827	7 716	10 533

Note: Year ending 31st December.
The data are on a cash basis.
The figures exclude local government tax revenues as the data are not available (but include provincial revenues).
Heading 4400: The sub-category stamp taxes includes data classified as provincial taxes on financial transactions in previous editions.
Heading 5211: The data have been reclassified as the revenue is sourced principally from households. Previous editions classified this revenue as 5212.
Heading 5212: In ECLAC data, property tax on motor vehicles is classified in category 4000.
Heading 5300: The figures are negative as they represent general reimbursements of exports and specific taxes on goods and services. The data was accounted for in 5111 (value added taxes) in previous editions.

Source: Subsecretaría de Ingresos Públicos, Dirección Nacional de Investigaciones y Análisis Fiscal, Ministerio de Hacienda y Finanzas Públicas (Undersecretary of Public Revenue, National Direction of Research and Fiscal Analysis, Ministry of Finance).

StatLink http://dx.doi.org/10.1787/888933463186

Table 5.2. Bahamas
Details of tax revenue / Ingresos tributarios detallados

Million BSD

	1990	2000	2005	2009	2010	2011	2012	2013	2014	2015
Total tax revenue	**505**	**965**	**1 060**	**1 290**	**1 277**	**1 487**	**1 480**	**1 445**	**1 491**	**1 760**
1000 Taxes on income, profits and capital gains	**0**	**0**	**0**	**0**	**0**	**0**	**0**	**0**	**0**	**0**
1100 Of individuals	0	0	0	0	0	0	0	0	0	0
1110 On income and profits	..	..	..	..	..	..	..	..	..	..
1120 On capital gains	..	..	..	..	..	..	..	..	..	..
1200 Corporate	0	0	0	0	0	0	0	0	0	0
1210 On profits	..	..	..	..	..	..	..	..	..	..
1220 On capital gains	..	..	..	..	..	..	..	..	..	..
1300 Unallocable between 1100 and 1200	..	..	..	..	..	..	..	..	..	..
2000 Social security contributions	**66**	**115**	**136**	**160**	**167**	**190**	**203**	**229**	**246**	**260**
2100 Employees	..	..	..	..	..	..	..	..	..	..
2110 On a payroll basis	..	..	..	..	..	..	..	..	..	..
2120 On an income tax basis	..	..	..	..	..	..	..	..	..	..
2200 Employers	..	..	..	..	..	..	..	..	..	..
2210 On a payroll basis	..	..	..	..	..	..	..	..	..	..
2220 On an income tax basis	..	..	..	..	..	..	..	..	..	..
2300 Self-employed or non-employed	..	..	..	..	..	..	..	..	..	..
2310 On a payroll basis	..	..	..	..	..	..	..	..	..	..
2320 On an income tax basis	..	..	..	..	..	..	..	..	..	..
2400 Unallocable between 2100, 2200 and 2300	66	115	136	160	167	190	203	229	246	260
2410 On a payroll basis	..	..	..	..	..	..	..	..	..	..
2420 On an income tax basis	..	..	..	..	..	..	..	..	..	..
3000 Taxes on payroll and workforce	**0**	**0**	**0**	**0**	**0**	**0**	**0**	**0**	**0**	**0**
4000 Taxes on property	**19**	**32**	**54**	**85**	**92**	**92**	**95**	**115**	**104**	**107**
4100 Recurrent taxes on immovable property	19	32	54	85	92	92	95	115	104	107
4110 Households	0	0	0	0	0	0	0	0	0	0
4120 Others	19	32	54	85	92	92	95	115	104	107
4200 Recurrent taxes on net wealth	0	0	0	0	0	0	0	0	0	0
4210 Individual	..	..	..	..	..	..	..	..	..	..
4220 Corporate	..	..	..	..	..	..	..	..	..	..
4300 Estate, inheritance and gift taxes	0	0	0	0	0	0	0	0	0	0
4310 Estate and inheritance taxes	..	..	..	..	..	..	..	..	..	..
4320 Gift taxes	..	..	..	..	..	..	..	..	..	..
4400 Taxes on financial and capital transactions	0	0	0	0	0	0	0	0	0	0
4500 Non-recurrent taxes	0	0	0	0	0	0	0	0	0	0
4510 On net wealth	..	..	..	..	..	..	..	..	..	..
4520 Other non-recurrent taxes	..	..	..	..	..	..	..	..	..	..
4600 Other recurrent taxes on property	0	0	0	0	0	0	0	0	0	0
5000 Taxes on goods and services	**386**	**723**	**736**	**824**	**795**	**944**	**1 018**	**955**	**986**	**1 203**
5100 Taxes on production, sale, transfer, etc	354	654	657	704	672	799	868	806	772	993
5110 General taxes	0	0	0	0	0	0	0	0	0	219
5111 Value added taxes	0	0	0	0	0	0	0	0	0	219
5112 Sales tax	..	..	..	..	..	..	..	..	..	0
5113 Other	..	..	..	..	..	..	..	..	..	0
5120 Taxes on specific goods and services	354	654	657	704	672	799	868	806	772	775
5121 Excises	0	0	0	187	188	254	331	246	249	262
5122 Profits of fiscal monopolies	0	0	0	0	0	0	0	0	0	0
5123 Customs and import duties	289	537	525	395	364	370	366	350	336	307
Import tax	289	435	413	379	348	354	348	332	336	307
Stamp tax from imports duties	0	102	112	15	15	16	18	18	0	0
5124 Taxes on exports	6	13	13	13	14	13	15	14	10	9
Export tax	6	13	13	13	14	13	15	14	10	9
Stamp tax from exports	0	0	0	0	0	0	0	0	0	0
5125 Taxes on investment goods	0	0	0	0	0	0	0	0	0	0
5126 Taxes on specific services	59	104	119	110	106	162	156	196	178	197
Departure tax	27	64	69	70	70	103	102	144	125	147
Gaming tax	27	20	25	13	10	18	11	10	8	25
Hotel occupancy tax	5	20	25	26	25	41	43	42	45	25
5127 Other taxes on internat. trade and transactions	0	0	0	0	0	0	0	0	0	0
5128 Other taxes	0	0	0	0	0	0	0	0	0	0
5130 Unallocable between 5110 and 5120	0	0	0	0	0	0	0	0	0	0
5200 Taxes on use of goods and perform activities	32	69	78	120	123	145	150	149	214	209
5210 Recurrent taxes	32	69	78	120	123	145	150	149	214	209
Motor vehicle tax	10	14	18	23	21	27	29	28	29	29
5211 Paid by households: motor vehicles	..	..	..	..	..	..	..	..	..	..
5212 Paid by others: motor vehicles	..	..	..	..	..	..	..	..	..	..

Table 5.2. Bahamas *(cont.)*
Details of tax revenue / Ingresos tributarios detallados

Million BSD

	1990	2000	2005	2009	2010	2011	2012	2013	2014	2015
5213 Paid in respect of other goods	22	55	61	97	102	118	121	121	185	180
Company fees and registration	0	5	5	6	5	5	5	5	5	5
International business companies	0	17	15	20	19	17	17	17	17	16
Others	22	33	40	71	78	95	99	99	163	159
5220 Non-recurrent taxes	0	0	0	0	0	0	0	0	0	0
5300 Unallocable between 5100 and 5200	0	0	0	0	0	0	0	0	0	0
6000 Other taxes	**33**	**95**	**135**	**221**	**223**	**261**	**163**	**145**	**155**	**191**
6100 Paid solely by business	0	0	0	0	0	0	0	0	0	0
6200 Other	33	95	135	221	223	261	163	145	155	191
All other stamp taxes	37	74	135	194	162	258	174	160	164	191
Incentive acts and other refunds	-8	14	-15	5	11	-9	-11	-15	-8	0
Other taxes	4	7	15	22	49	12	0	0	0	0

Note: Fiscal year ending on 30th June.
The data are on a cash basis.
The figures exclude local government tax revenues as the data are not available.
Heading 2000: The data are estimated for 2015.
Heading 5111: A value added tax was enforced on 1st January 2015.

Source: Ministry of Finance, BID-CIAT (2015), *Equivalent Fiscal Pressure for Latin America and the Caribbean* and the Central Bank of the Bahamas.

StatLink http://dx.doi.org/10.1787/888933463198

Table 5.3. Barbados
Details of tax revenue / Ingresos tributarios detallados

Thousand BAR

	1990	2000	2005	2009	2010	2011	2012	2013	2014	2015
Total tax revenue	**942 335**	**1 884 313**	**2 297 009**	**2 810 305**	**2 719 302**	**2 821 723**	**2 869 093**	**2 576 301**	**2 643 446**	**2 744 363**
1000 Taxes on income, profits and capital gains	**254 016**	**573 920**	**639 432**	**934 345**	**762 340**	**781 866**	**744 289**	**615 036**	**702 017**	**727 047**
1100 Of individuals	128 857	288 692	295 737	410 348	388 177	419 468	379 969	343 828	428 599	451 578
1110 On income and profits	128 857	288 692	295 737	410 348	388 177	419 468	379 969	343 828	428 599	451 578
1120 On capital gains	..	..	..	..	..	..	..	..	..	..
1200 Corporate	111 111	252 291	294 320	457 825	327 471	298 535	276 296	191 636	208 087	209 959
1210 On profits	111 111	252 291	294 320	457 825	327 471	298 535	276 296	191 636	208 087	209 959
1220 On capital gains	..	..	..	..	..	..	..	..	..	..
1300 Unallocable between 1100 and 1200	14 048	32 937	49 375	66 172	46 692	63 863	88 024	79 572	65 331	65 510
2000 Social security contributions	**133 866**	**295 268**	**408 109**	**523 444**	**525 467**	**525 706**	**529 263**	**512 521**	**532 084**	**552 000**
2100 Employees	..	..	..	..	..	..	..	..	..	..
2110 On a payroll basis	..	..	..	..	..	..	..	..	..	..
2120 On an income tax basis	..	..	..	..	..	..	..	..	..	..
2200 Employers	..	..	..	..	..	..	..	..	..	..
2210 On a payroll basis	..	..	..	..	..	..	..	..	..	..
2220 On an income tax basis	..	..	..	..	..	..	..	..	..	..
2300 Self-employed or non-employed	..	..	..	..	..	..	..	..	..	..
2310 On a payroll basis	..	..	..	..	..	..	..	..	..	..
2320 On an income tax basis	..	..	..	..	..	..	..	..	..	..
2400 Unallocable between 2100, 2200 and 2300	133 866	295 268	408 109	523 444	525 467	525 706	529 263	512 521	532 084	552 000
2410 On a payroll basis	..	..	..	..	..	..	..	..	..	..
2420 On an income tax basis	..	..	..	..	..	..	..	..	..	..
3000 Taxes on payroll and workforce	**0**	**0**	**0**	**0**	**0**	**0**	**0**	**0**	**0**	**0**
4000 Taxes on property	**39 117**	**91 928**	**127 362**	**154 772**	**113 533**	**111 726**	**148 176**	**124 972**	**112 998**	**149 963**
4100 Recurrent taxes on immovable property	25 991	60 216	76 247	137 649	97 595	95 149	133 321	109 436	94 059	134 424
Land tax	25 991	60 216	76 247	137 649	97 595	95 149	133 321	109 436	94 059	134 424
4110 Households	..	..	..	..	..	..	..	..	..	..
4120 Others	..	..	..	..	..	..	..	..	..	..
4200 Recurrent taxes on net wealth	0	0	0	0	0	0	0	0	0	0
4210 Individual	..	..	..	..	..	..	..	..	..	..
4220 Corporate	..	..	..	..	..	..	..	..	..	..
4300 Estate, inheritance and gift taxes	0	0	0	0	0	0	0	0	0	0
4310 Estate and inheritance taxes	..	..	..	..	..	..	..	..	..	..
4320 Gift taxes	..	..	..	..	..	..	..	..	..	..
4400 Taxes on financial and capital transactions	0	0	0	0	0	0	0	0	0	0
4500 Non-recurrent taxes	13 126	31 712	51 115	17 123	15 938	16 577	14 855	15 536	18 939	15 539
4510 On net wealth	..	..	..	..	..	..	..	..	..	..
4520 Other non-recurrent taxes	..	..	..	..	..	..	..	..	..	..
4600 Other recurrent taxes on property	0	0	0	0	0	0	0	0	0	0
5000 Taxes on goods and services	**422 259**	**897 092**	**1 101 319**	**1 124 028**	**1 242 416**	**1 366 659**	**1 420 525**	**1 292 470**	**1 264 115**	**1 303 210**
5100 Taxes on production, sale, transfer, etc	422 259	793 469	973 944	1 005 599	1 092 106	1 240 429	1 244 945	1 187 410	1 156 128	1 177 680
5110 General taxes	196 817	501 399	609 915	677 415	753 003	897 020	907 255	870 692	823 208	810 593
5111 Value added taxes	0	500 951	609 915	677 415	753 003	897 020	907 255	870 692	823 208	810 593
5112 Sales tax	196 817	448	0	0	0	0	0	0	0	0
5113 Other	0	0	0	0	0	0	0	0	0	0
5120 Taxes on specific goods and services	225 442	292 069	364 029	328 184	339 103	343 409	337 690	316 718	332 920	367 087
5121 Excises	4 767	158 803	172 377	144 895	148 191	158 864	137 286	128 730	121 905	146 468
5122 Profits of fiscal monopolies	0	0	0	0	0	0	0	0	0	0
5123 Customs and import duties	202 731	132 668	191 652	183 289	190 912	184 545	200 404	187 988	211 015	220 619
Import duties	112 315	132 668	191 652	183 289	190 912	184 545	200 404	187 988	211 015	220 619
Stamp duties	90 416	0	0	0	0	0	0	0	0	0
5124 Taxes on exports	0	0	0	0	0	0	0	0	0	0
5125 Taxes on investment goods	0	0	0	0	0	0	0	0	0	0
5126 Taxes on specific services	17 944	598	0	0	0	0	0	0	0	0
Hotel and restaurant tax	17 944	598	0	0	0	0	0	0	0	0
5127 Other taxes on internat. trade and transactions	0	0	0	0	0	0	0	0	0	0
5128 Other taxes	0	0	0	0	0	0	0	0	0	0
5130 Unallocable between 5110 and 5120	0	0	0	0	0	0	0	0	0	0
5200 Taxes on use of goods and perform activities	0	103 623	127 375	118 429	150 310	126 230	175 580	105 060	107 987	125 530
5210 Recurrent taxes	..	103 623	127 375	118 429	150 310	126 230	175 580	105 060	107 987	125 530
5211 Paid by households: motor vehicles	..	0	0	0	0	0	0	0	0	0
5212 Paid by others: motor vehicles	..	0	0	0	0	0	0	0	0	0
5213 Paid in respect of other goods	..	0	0	0	0	0	0	0	0	0
5220 Non-recurrent taxes	..	0	0	0	0	0	0	0	0	0
5300 Unallocable between 5100 and 5200	0	0	0	0	0	0	0	0	0	0
6000 Other taxes	**93 077**	**26 105**	**20 787**	**73 716**	**75 546**	**35 766**	**26 840**	**31 302**	**32 232**	**12 143**
6100 Paid solely by business	0	0	0	0	0	0	0	0	0	0

Table 5.3. Barbados *(cont.)*
Details of tax revenue / Ingresos tributarios detallados

Thousand BAR

	1990	2000	2005	2009	2010	2011	2012	2013	2014	2015
6200 Other	93 077	26 105	20 787	73 716	75 546	35 766	26 840	31 302	32 232	12 143
Levies	85 937	13 993	0	60 589	61 015	23 824	15 669	21 027	19 711	1 238
Stamp duties	7 140	12 112	20 787	13 127	14 531	11 942	11 171	10 275	12 521	10 905

Note: Year ending 31st December.
The data are on a cash basis.
The figures exclude local government tax revenues as the data are not available.
Heading 2000: The data are estimated for 2015.
Source: The Central Bank of Barbados and the Inland Revenue Department.

StatLink http://dx.doi.org/10.1787/888933463204

Table 5.4. Belize / Belice

Details of tax revenue / Ingresos tributarios detallados

Million BZD

	1990	2000	2005	2009	2010	2011	2012	2013	2014	2015
Total tax revenue	**179**	**318**	**496**	**679**	**744**	**745**	**786**	**829**	**880**	**895**
1000 Taxes on income, profits and capital gains	**37**	**76**	**129**	**211**	**248**	**252**	**232**	**245**	**263**	**261**
1100 Of individuals	21	19	35	55	52	51	60	64	70	71
1110 On income and profits	21	19	35	55	52	51	60	64	70	71
Income tax (PAYE)	20	19	35	55	52	51	60	64	70	71
Income tax on individuals	1	0	0	0	0	0	0	0	0	0
1120 On capital gains	0	0	0	0	0	0	0	0	0	0
1200 Corporate	12	51	90	151	189	194	164	172	180	175
Income tax (companies)	12	1	0	27	51	48	27	18	21	8
Income tax (business tax)	0	51	90	124	138	133	132	150	159	168
Income tax (supplemental petroleum tax)	0	0	0	0	0	14	6	4	1	0
1210 On profits	..	..	..	..	..	..	..	..	..	..
1220 On capital gains	..	..	..	..	..	..	..	..	..	..
1300 Unallocable between 1100 and 1200	4	6	4	5	7	6	8	10	14	14
Income tax (arrears)	4	3	1	1	1	1	2	2	2	2
Income tax (withholding)	0	3	2	4	6	5	7	8	12	12
2000 Social security contributions	**10**	**18**	**50**	**60**	**60**	**61**	**65**	**66**	**68**	**70**
2100 Employees	..	..	..	..	..	..	..	..	..	..
2110 On a payroll basis	..	..	..	..	..	..	..	..	..	..
2120 On an income tax basis	..	..	..	..	..	..	..	..	..	..
2200 Employers	..	..	..	..	..	..	..	..	..	..
2210 On a payroll basis	..	..	..	..	..	..	..	..	..	..
2220 On an income tax basis	..	..	..	..	..	..	..	..	..	..
2300 Self-employed or non-employed	..	..	..	..	..	..	..	..	..	..
2310 On a payroll basis	..	..	..	..	..	..	..	..	..	..
2320 On an income tax basis	..	..	..	..	..	..	..	..	..	..
2400 Unallocable between 2100, 2200 and 2300	10	18	50	60	60	61	65	66	68	70
2410 On a payroll basis	..	..	..	..	..	..	..	..	..	..
2420 On an income tax basis	..	..	..	..	..	..	..	..	..	..
3000 Taxes on payroll and workforce	**0**	**0**	**0**	**0**	**0**	**0**	**0**	**0**	**0**	**0**
4000 Taxes on property	**6**	**13**	**27**	**24**	**23**	**26**	**27**	**31**	**33**	**34**
4100 Recurrent taxes on immovable property	1	2	6	5	7	7	5	6	5	5
4110 Households	1	2	6	5	7	7	5	6	5	5
4120 Others	..	..	..	..	..	..	..	..	..	..
4200 Recurrent taxes on net wealth	0	0	0	0	0	0	0	0	0	0
4210 Individual	..	..	..	..	..	..	..	..	..	..
4220 Corporate	..	..	..	..	..	..	..	..	..	..
4300 Estate, inheritance and gift taxes	0	0	0	0	0	0	0	0	0	0
4310 Estate and inheritance taxes	0	0	0	0	0	0	0	0	0	0
4320 Gift taxes	0	0	0	0	0	0	0	0	0	0
4400 Taxes on financial and capital transactions	5	11	22	19	16	19	22	25	28	29
4500 Non-recurrent taxes	0	0	0	0	0	0	0	0	0	0
4510 On net wealth	..	..	..	..	..	..	..	..	..	..
4520 Other non-recurrent taxes	..	..	..	..	..	..	..	..	..	..
4600 Other recurrent taxes on property	0	0	0	0	0	0	0	0	0	0
5000 Taxes on goods and services	**126**	**211**	**289**	**384**	**412**	**406**	**462**	**486**	**515**	**531**
5100 Taxes on production, sale, transfer, etc.	122	207	282	366	400	396	443	469	505	521
5110 General taxes	0	82	131	159	199	175	214	237	256	263
5111 Value added taxes	0	0	0	0	0	0	0	0	0	0
5112 Sales tax	..	82	131	1	0	0	0	0	0	0
5113 Other	..	0	0	158	199	175	214	237	256	263
5120 Taxes on specific goods and services	122	124	151	208	200	221	229	232	249	258
5121 Excises	35	47	57	34	31	33	34	35	38	36
Revenue replacement duty	18	39	57	9	7	9	12	13	14	12
Excise duties	17	8	0	23	22	21	20	21	22	22
Excise on locally refined petroleum products	0	0	0	3	0	1	0	0	0	0
Excise on locally extracted crude oil	0	0	0	0	1	2	2	2	1	1
5122 Profits of fiscal monopolies	0	0	0	0	0	0	0	0	0	0
5123 Customs and import duties	78	64	80	152	144	160	165	165	177	186
Import duties	50	64	80	130	123	138	141	140	151	159
Environmental tax	0	0	0	22	21	22	24	25	26	27
Imports into EPZs	0	0	0	0	0	0	0	0	0	0
Stamps duties on customs	28	0	0	0	0	0	0	0	0	0
5124 Taxes on exports	0	0	0	0	0	0	0	0	0	0
5125 Taxes on investment goods	0	0	0	0	0	0	0	0	0	0
5126 Taxes on specific services	0	0	0	0	0	0	0	0	0	0

Table 5.4. Belize / Belice *(cont.)*
Details of tax revenue / Ingresos tributarios detallados

Million BZD

	1990	2000	2005	2009	2010	2011	2012	2013	2014	2015
5127 Other taxes on internat. trade and transactions	8	14	15	22	25	28	30	32	34	35
Goods in transit - administration charge	3	1	1	1	1	1	1	1	1	1
Goods in transit - social fee	0	5	4	4	8	10	11	11	12	12
Taxes on foreign currency transactions	6	8	9	17	16	16	18	20	21	22
5128 Other taxes	0	0	0	0	0	0	0	0	0	0
5130 Unallocable between 5110 and 5120	0	0	0	0	0	0	0	0	0	0
5200 Taxes on use of goods and perform activities	4	4	7	18	13	10	19	18	10	10
5210 Recurrent taxes	4	4	7	18	13	10	19	18	10	10
5211 Paid by households: motor vehicles	2	3	5	3	3	3	3	4	4	4
5212 Paid by others: motor vehicles	0	0	0	0	0	0	0	0	0	0
5213 Paid in respect of other goods	2	1	3	15	10	7	16	14	6	7
5220 Non-recurrent taxes	0	0	0	0	0	0	0	0	0	0
5300 Unallocable between 5100 and 5200	0	0	0	0	0	0	0	0	0	0
6000 Other taxes	**0**	**0**	**0**	**0**	**0**	**0**	**0**	**0**	**0**	**0**
6100 Paid solely by business	..	..	..	..	..	..	..	..	..	..
6200 Other	..	..	..	..	..	..	..	..	..	..

Note: Year ending 31st March. Data are on a April(n-1)/March(n) fiscal year basis. For example, the data for 2015 represent March 2015 to April 2016.
The data are on a cash basis.
Heading 2000: The data for social security contributions are estimated for the period 2013 - 2015.

Source: Ministry of Finance of Belize and BID-CIAT (2015) *Equivalent Fiscal Pressure for Latin America and the Caribbean.*

StatLink http://dx.doi.org/10.1787/888933463213

Table 5.5. Bolivia
Details of tax revenue / Ingresos tributarios detallados

Million BOB

	1990	2000	2005	2009	2010	2011	2012	2013	2014	2015
Total tax revenue	**1 277**	**9 155**	**15 369**	**26 379**	**27 929**	**36 722**	**42 115**	**49 395**	**54 195**	**56 229**
1000 Taxes on income, profits and capital gains	**68**	**1 209**	**2 383**	**6 532**	**6 294**	**7 926**	**9 679**	**11 644**	**12 723**	**12 809**
1100 Of individuals	68	214	214	289	263	277	279	364	439	508
1110 On income and profits	68	214	214	289	263	277	279	364	439	508
Fiscal notes on individual income and profits	6	53	28	34	26	18	19	31	38	47
1120 On capital gains	..	..	..	..	..	..	..	..	..	..
1200 Corporate	0	995	2 169	6 243	6 031	7 649	9 400	11 280	12 284	12 302
1210 On profits	0	995	2 169	6 243	6 031	7 649	9 400	11 280	12 284	12 302
Mining profits	0	0	75	61	473	616	322	283	82	67
Tax regularisation	0	0	0	0	0	0	0	0	0	0
Corporate tax	0	546	1 481	3 761	3 874	4 724	6 256	6 824	8 026	9 235
Corporate tax remittances	0	258	315	623	742	732	718	806	954	959
Fiscal notes on corporate tax	0	192	286	1 786	768	1 451	1 773	3 137	3 150	1 898
Fiscal notes on mining profits	0	0	11	12	174	127	331	229	72	143
1220 On capital gains	..	..	..	..	..	..	..	..	..	..
1300 Unallocable between 1100 and 1200	0	0	0	0	0	0	0	0	0	0
2000 Social security contributions	**0**	**666**	**936**	**1 515**	**1 645**	**2 665**	**2 878**	**3 100**	**3 200**	**3 200**
2100 Employees	..	..	..	..	..	..	..	..	..	..
2110 On a payroll basis	..	..	..	..	..	..	..	..	..	..
2120 On an income tax basis	..	..	..	..	..	..	..	..	..	..
2200 Employers	..	..	..	..	..	..	..	..	..	..
2210 On a payroll basis	..	..	..	..	..	..	..	..	..	..
2220 On an income tax basis	..	..	..	..	..	..	..	..	..	..
2300 Self-employed or non-employed	..	..	..	..	..	..	..	..	..	..
2310 On a payroll basis	..	..	..	..	..	..	..	..	..	..
2320 On an income tax basis	..	..	..	..	..	..	..	..	..	..
2400 Unallocable between 2100, 2200 and 2300	..	666	936	1 515	1 645	2 665	2 878	3 100	3 200	3 200
2410 On a payroll basis	..	666	936	1 515	1 645	2 665	2 878	3 100	3 200	3 200
2420 On an income tax basis	..	0	0	0	0	0	0	0	0	0
2430 Unallocable	..	0	0	0	0	0	0	0	0	0
3000 Taxes on payroll and workforce	**0**	**0**	**0**	**0**	**0**	**0**	**0**	**0**	**0**	**0**
4000 Taxes on property	**1**	**3**	**640**	**357**	**367**	**401**	**401**	**412**	**433**	**424**
4100 Recurrent taxes on immovable property	0	0	0	0	0	0	0	0	0	0
4110 Households	..	..	..	..	..	..	..	..	..	..
4120 Others	..	..	..	..	..	..	..	..	..	..
4200 Recurrent taxes on net wealth	0	0	0	0	0	0	0	0	0	0
4210 Individual	..	..	..	..	..	..	..	..	..	..
4220 Corporate	..	..	..	..	..	..	..	..	..	..
4300 Estate, inheritance and gift taxes	1	3	7	18	20	22	23	28	32	36
4310 Estate and inheritance taxes	1	3	7	18	20	22	23	28	32	36
4320 Gift taxes	0	0	0	0	0	0	0	0	0	0
4400 Taxes on financial and capital transactions	0	0	633	339	347	380	378	384	401	388
4500 Non-recurrent taxes	0	0	0	0	0	0	0	0	0	0
4510 On net wealth	..	..	..	..	..	..	..	..	..	..
4520 Other non-recurrent taxes	..	..	..	..	..	..	..	..	..	..
4600 Other recurrent taxes on property	0	0	0	0	0	0	0	0	0	0
5000 Taxes on goods and services	**875**	**5 651**	**8 753**	**13 603**	**15 509**	**20 768**	**23 326**	**27 291**	**29 777**	**30 268**
5100 Taxes on production, sale, transfer, etc.	875	5 651	8 753	13 603	15 509	20 768	23 326	27 291	29 777	30 268
5110 General taxes	551	2 949	5 314	8 862	10 259	14 092	16 306	19 033	20 581	20 757
5111 Value added taxes	551	2 949	5 314	8 862	10 259	14 092	16 306	19 033	20 581	20 757
Value added taxes fiscal notes	76	299	740	1 157	967	1 983	2 061	2 519	1 918	1 104
5112 Sales tax	0	0	0	0	0	0	0	0	0	0
5113 Other	0	0	0	0	0	0	0	0	0	0
5120 Taxes on specific goods and services	324	2 702	3 439	4 741	5 250	6 676	7 020	8 258	9 196	9 511
5121 Excises	118	2 047	2 604	3 533	3 658	4 393	4 475	5 012	5 663	5 853
Excises (Internal)	61	245	209	739	933	1 204	1 157	1 468	1 365	1 487
Excises (Imports)	22	298	208	367	379	642	580	719	1 051	1 109
Special tax on hydrocarbons and derivatives	0	1 348	1 529	650	1 070	2 236	1 144	1 681	1 998	2 581
Fiscal notes on excises	35	118	309	200	155	115	290	47	328	262
Fiscal notes on special tax on hydrocarb. and deriv.	0	40	350	1 578	1 121	196	1 304	1 098	921	415
5122 Profits of fiscal monopolies	0	0	0	0	0	0	0	0	0	0
5123 Customs and import duties	204	640	803	1 170	1 545	2 218	2 485	2 850	3 102	3 254
Fiscal notes on customs and import duties	41	24	26	27	41	144	207	186	223	198
5124 Taxes on exports	0	0	0	0	0	0	0	0	0	0
5125 Taxes on investment goods	0	0	0	0	0	0	0	0	0	0
5126 Taxes on specific services	2	15	32	38	47	65	60	91	120	127
Air departure tax	2	15	32	38	47	52	51	71	90	102
Tax on gambling	0	0	0	0	0	13	9	20	30	25

Table 5.5. Bolivia *(cont.)*

Details of tax revenue / Ingresos tributarios detallados

Million BOB

	1990	2000	2005	2009	2010	2011	2012	2013	2014	2015
5127 Other taxes on internat. trade and transactions	0	0	0	0	0	0	0	306	311	277
5128 Other taxes	0	0	0	0	0	0	0	0	0	0
5130 Unallocable between 5110 and 5120	0	0	0	0	0	0	0	0	0	0
5200 Taxes on use of goods and perform activities	0	0	0	0	0	0	0	0	0	0
5210 Recurrent taxes	..	..	..	..	..	..	..	..	..	..
5211 Paid by households: motor vehicles	..	..	..	..	..	..	..	..	..	..
5212 Paid by others: motor vehicles	..	..	..	..	..	..	..	..	..	..
5213 Paid in respect of other goods	..	..	..	..	..	..	..	..	..	..
5220 Non-recurrent taxes	..	..	..	..	..	..	..	..	..	..
5300 Unallocable between 5100 and 5200	0	0	0	0	0	0	0	0	0	0
6000 Other taxes	**334**	**1 625**	**2 658**	**4 373**	**4 113**	**4 961**	**5 832**	**6 948**	**8 063**	**9 528**
6100 Paid solely by business	4	6	5	12	12	13	14	17	20	26
Simplified tax regime	3	6	4	12	12	13	14	17	20	25
Integrated tax system	1	0	0	0	0	0	0	0	0	0
6200 Other	330	1 619	2 653	4 361	4 101	4 948	5 818	6 931	8 042	9 503
Rural property tax	0	1	5	12	14	17	22	23	23	26
Transactions	157	943	1 455	2 003	2 174	2 772	3 202	3 587	4 081	4 463
Fiscal notes on transactions	15	64	250	190	108	94	56	116	53	28
Other	154	37	178	510	422	556	860	1 241	1 716	2 378
Fiscal notes on other taxes	3	0	5	478	3	5	2	9	25	23

Note: Year ending 31st December.

The data are on a cash basis.

This edition includes for the first time local government tax revenues which affects headings 6000 and 6200.

Heading 1200: Data have been revised and updated according to the criteria presented by the Ministerio de Economía and Finanzas Públicas.

Heading 2000: The data for social security contributions are only available from the year 2000 and are estimated from 2013 onward.

Heading 5111: The data have been revised.

Heading 5121: Previous editions of Revenue Statistics in Latin America and the Caribbean included fees levied on hydrocarbon production under this heading. For this publication, revenues from hydrocarbon production have been excluded from tax revenues and are instead treated as non-tax revenues.

Source: Ministerio de Economía y Finanzas Públicas, Ministry of Economy and Public Finance.

Unidad de Análisis de Políticas Sociales y Económicas, Social and Economic Policy Analysis Unit.

StatLink http://dx.doi.org/10.1787/888933463224

Table 5.6. Brazil / Brasil
Details of tax revenue / Ingresos tributarios detallados

Million BRL

	1990	2000	2005	2009	2010	2011	2012	2013	2014	2015
Total tax revenue	**3**	**354 760**	**711 145**	**1 071 319**	**1 255 454**	**1 454 751**	**1 566 449**	**1 732 142**	**1 838 983**	**1 922 868**
1000 Taxes on income, profits and capital gains	**1**	**68 667**	**149 309**	**234 400**	**258 738**	**314 299**	**321 463**	**360 549**	**381 870**	**401 048**
1100 Of individuals	0	3 406	6 981	73 962	87 828	104 336	116 342	126 006	140 446	148 795
1110 On income and profits	0	3 406	6 981	73 962	87 828	104 336	116 342	126 006	140 446	148 795
Withholding taxes on income and profits	..	..	..	60 337	71 580	83 821	93 843	101 818	114 664	121 596
1120 On capital gains	..	..	..	..	..	..	..	..	..	..
1200 Corporate	0	25 430	73 071	120 767	128 255	153 652	148 423	171 003	171 352	164 057
1210 On profits	0	25 430	73 071	120 767	128 255	153 652	148 423	171 003	171 352	164 057
Corporate income tax	0	16 680	47 832	77 343	82 474	94 958	92 589	109 316	109 020	104 910
Social contribution on net profits (CSLL)	0	8 750	25 239	43 424	45 780	58 694	55 834	61 687	62 332	59 147
1220 On capital gains	..	..	..	..	..	..	..	..	..	..
1300 Unallocable between 1100 and 1200	0	39 831	69 257	39 670	42 656	56 311	56 697	63 540	70 072	88 196
Withholding taxes	0	39 831	69 257	39 670	42 656	56 311	56 697	63 540	70 072	88 196
2000 Social security contributions	**1**	**83 469**	**168 226**	**270 302**	**313 949**	**360 277**	**402 437**	**441 880**	**478 642**	**497 791**
2100 Employees	..	..	..	..	..	..	..	..	..	..
2110 On a payroll basis	..	..	..	..	..	..	..	..	..	..
2120 On an income tax basis	..	..	..	..	..	..	..	..	..	..
2200 Employers	0	18 709	32 248	57 183	64 271	74 979	85 813	98 045	108 782	118 323
2210 On a payroll basis	0	18 709	32 248	57 183	64 271	74 979	85 813	98 045	108 782	118 323
2220 On an income tax basis	0	0	0	0	0	0	0	0	0	0
2300 Self-employed or non-employed	..	..	..	..	..	..	..	..	..	..
2310 On a payroll basis	..	..	..	..	..	..	..	..	..	..
2320 On an income tax basis	..	..	..	..	..	..	..	..	..	..
2400 Unallocable between 2100, 2200 and 2300	1	64 760	135 978	213 118	249 679	285 298	316 625	343 836	369 860	379 469
2410 On a payroll basis	1	64 760	135 978	213 118	249 679	285 298	316 625	343 836	369 860	379 469
Social security contributions (Federal)	1	59 334	118 869	197 256	231 903	266 169	294 578	319 566	341 992	349 787
Social security contributions (State)	0	4 423	14 682	11 489	12 635	13 294	15 551	16 499	19 529	20 797
Social security contributions (Municipal)	0	1 003	2 427	4 374	5 141	5 835	6 496	7 771	8 339	8 885
2420 On an income tax basis	0	0	0	0	0	0	0	0	0	0
3000 Taxes on payroll and workforce	**0**	**6 749**	**14 468**	**25 246**	**33 090**	**34 399**	**39 206**	**43 391**	**47 724**	**50 399**
PASEP contributions	0	1 312	2 863	5 137	9 880	6 958	8 398	8 775	9 491	9 958
Payroll-based contribution to education	0	2 791	5 906	9 589	11 049	13 115	14 775	16 561	18 411	19 039
"S" System contributions	0	2 646	4 397	8 524	9 925	11 858	13 557	15 351	16 884	18 153
Other	0	0	1 302	1 996	2 236	2 467	2 477	2 704	2 938	3 248
4000 Taxes on property	**0**	**28 818**	**56 274**	**61 203**	**74 377**	**86 700**	**92 085**	**97 817**	**106 597**	**120 378**
4100 Recurrent taxes on immovable property	0	4 753	8 405	15 610	17 933	20 276	22 148	25 063	28 739	31 864
4110 Households	0	0	0	0	0	0	0	0	0	0
4120 Others	0	4 753	8 405	15 610	17 933	20 276	22 148	25 063	28 739	31 864
Tax on rural land property (ITR)	0	234	288	421	485	571	614	764	900	1 105
Tax on urban land property (IPTU)	0	4 519	8 117	15 189	17 448	19 706	21 533	24 299	27 839	30 760
4200 Recurrent taxes on net wealth	0	0	0	0	0	0	0	0	0	0
4210 Individual	..	..	..	..	..	..	..	..	..	..
4220 Corporate	..	..	..	..	..	..	..	..	..	..
4300 Estate, inheritance and gift taxes	0	329	821	1 678	2 518	2 768	3 409	4 142	4 698	6 469
4310 Estate and inheritance taxes	0	329	821	1 678	2 518	2 768	3 409	4 142	4 698	6 469
4320 Gift taxes	0	0	0	0	0	0	0	0	0	0
4400 Taxes on financial and capital transactions	0	18 442	36 587	23 808	32 559	39 544	39 499	39 380	40 707	45 788
Tax on financial operations (IOF)	0	3 096	5 974	19 235	26 571	31 999	31 002	29 417	29 756	34 681
Real estate property transfers (ITBI)	0	950	1 593	4 610	6 005	7 466	8 497	9 963	10 950	11 107
Other	0	14 396	29 021	-36	-18	79	0	0	0	0
4500 Non-recurrent taxes	0	0	0	0	0	0	0	0	0	0
4510 On net wealth	..	..	..	..	..	..	..	..	..	..
4520 Other non-recurrent taxes	..	..	..	..	..	..	..	..	..	..
4600 Other recurrent taxes on property	0	5 294	10 460	20 107	21 367	24 112	27 030	29 232	32 453	36 257
5000 Taxes on goods and services	**2**	**164 144**	**317 875**	**449 338**	**542 259**	**617 617**	**665 106**	**736 786**	**767 868**	**793 382**
5100 Taxes on production, sale, transfer, etc	2	162 575	312 503	449 338	542 259	617 617	665 106	736 786	767 868	793 382
5110 General taxes	2	154 130	294 251	418 118	497 899	564 045	614 568	681 107	711 337	732 495
5111 Value added taxes	1	100 978	177 589	247 821	293 489	324 761	357 190	393 742	419 459	431 904
Tax on the circulation of goods and services (ICMS)	1	82 279	153 437	227 830	268 117	297 419	326 236	363 190	384 287	396 513
Tax on industrialised products (IPI)	0	18 699	24 153	19 991	25 372	27 342	30 954	30 552	35 172	35 391
5112 Sales tax	0	47 046	105 415	142 937	171 653	200 926	213 096	239 290	236 646	242 508
Contribution to financing social security (COFINS)	0	38 707	86 837	117 084	140 939	164 982	175 008	197 545	194 696	199 876
PIS contribution	0	8 339	18 578	25 853	30 714	35 944	38 088	41 745	41 950	42 632
5113 Other	0	6 106	11 247	27 360	32 757	38 358	44 282	48 074	55 232	58 084
5120 Taxes on specific goods and services	0	8 445	18 252	31 219	44 360	53 572	50 538	55 679	56 531	60 887
5121 Excises	..	0	7 683	12 656	19 681	22 845	14 587	13 105	14 055	15 929
5122 Profits of fiscal monopolies	..	0	0	0	0	0	0	0	0	0
5123 Customs and import duties	..	8 445	8 953	15 904	21 119	26 763	31 088	36 974	36 774	38 969

Table 5.6. Brazil / Brasil *(cont.)*

Details of tax revenue / Ingresos tributarios detallados

Million BRL

	1990	2000	2005	2009	2010	2011	2012	2013	2014	2015
5124 Taxes on exports	..	0	0	0	0	0	0	0	0	0
5125 Taxes on investment goods	..	0	0	0	0	0	0	0	0	0
5126 Taxes on specific services	..	0	983	1 511	2 349	2 457	2 883	3 367	3 204	3 005
5127 Other taxes on internat. trade and transactions	..	0	0	0	0	0	0	0	0	0
5128 Other taxes	..	0	633	1 147	1 212	1 507	1 979	2 233	2 499	2 983
5130 Unallocable between 5110 and 5120	..	0	0	0	0	0	0	0	0	0
5200 Taxes on use of goods and perform activities	0	1 569	5 372	0	0	0	0	0	0	0
5210 Recurrent taxes	0	1 569	5 372	..	..	..	..	..	..	..
5211 Paid by households: motor vehicles	0	1 569	5 372	..	..	..	..	..	..	..
5212 Paid by others: motor vehicles	0	0	0	..	..	..	..	..	..	..
5213 Paid in respect of other goods	0	0	0	..	..	..	..	..	..	..
5220 Non-recurrent taxes	0	0	0	..	..	..	..	..	..	..
5300 Unallocable between 5100 and 5200	0	0	0	0	0	0	0	0	0	0
6000 Other taxes	**0**	**2 913**	**4 993**	**30 831**	**33 041**	**41 459**	**46 152**	**51 720**	**56 281**	**59 870**
6100 Paid solely by business	0	0	277	0	0	0	0	0	0	0
Revenue service development fund (FUNDAF)	0	0	277	0	0	0	0	0	0	0
6200 Other	0	2 913	4 715	30 831	33 041	41 459	46 152	51 720	56 281	59 870 7
Other federal taxes	0	941	36	1 292	3 376	3 496	3 436	4 527	5 438	4 229
Other social contributions	0	1 273	1 725	6 752	4 124	8 661	9 491	10 438	11 293	12 519
Other state taxes	0	322	1 551	15 429	17 135	19 825	22 980	25 864	27 352	29 067
Other municipal taxes	0	377	1 404	7 359	8 406	9 476	10 245	10 891	12 198	14 054

Note: Year ending 31st December.

The data are on a cash basis.

Headings 3000, 5112 and 6200: For years prior to 2000 the PASEP (Program of Formation of the Patrimony of the Public Servants) contributions are combined with PIS (Social Integration Program) contributions in heading 5112.

Headings 5111 and 5121: From 2007 to 2011, a portion of the IPI (Industrial Products Tax) is levied separately as an excise tax on automobiles, beverages, and tobacco products.

Heading 6100: From 2008 FUNDAF (Special Fund for Development and Improvement of Auditing Activities) contributions are included in heading 6200.

Heading 5200: From 2009, taxes paid by households: motor vehicles are included in heading 6200.

Source: Secretaria da Receita Federal (Ministry of Finance) in Carga Tributária no Brasil.

StatLink http://dx.doi.org/10.1787/888933463233

Table 5.7. Chile
Details of tax revenue / Ingresos tributarios detallados

Million CLP

	1990	2000	2005	2009	2010	2011	2012	2013	2014	2015
Total tax revenue	**1 777 218**	**7 901 998**	**14 265 265**	**16 759 274**	**21 845 693**	**25 762 449**	**27 714 772**	**27 381 686**	**29 145 219**	**32 524 896**
1000 Taxes on income, profits and capital gains	**412 974**	**1 841 630**	**5 171 293**	**5 162 043**	**8 329 060**	**10 322 824**	**10 803 031**	**9 520 709**	**9 628 037**	**11 836 497**
1100 Of individuals	99 154	604 100	738 620	1 252 672	1 492 837	1 690 230	1 893 620	1 964 172	2 114 296	2 313 363
Second category tax	65 552	490 980	700 150	1 239 815	1 449 099	1 663 293	1 917 675	1 981 699	2 140 345	2 350 120
Global complementary tax	33 603	113 120	38 470	12 857	43 738	26 936	-24 055	-17 527	-26 050	-36 757
1110 On income and profits	..	..	..	..	..	..	..	..	..	..
1120 On capital gains	..	..	..	..	..	..	..	..	..	..
1200 Corporate	219 586	882 896	3 155 480	4 110 485	4 448 745	6 021 408	7 560 906	6 041 089	6 196 077	7 721 622
First category tax	200 891	815 747	3 040 875	3 729 488	3 913 870	5 254 907	6 770 329	5 473 355	5 182 214	7 071 943
Surtax on state owned enterprises	16 074	47 634	78 267	44 974	194 203	116 725	80 084	124 220	100 851	132 352
Mining tax	0	0	0	312 473	298 558	598 790	619 150	324 577	801 647	323 507
Other	2 621	19 516	36 338	23 550	42 114	50 987	91 343	118 937	111 365	193 820
1210 On profits	..	..	..	..	..	..	..	..	..	..
1220 On capital gains	..	..	..	..	..	..	..	..	..	..
1300 Unallocable between 1100 and 1200	94 233	354 634	1 277 193	-201 113	2 387 478	2 611 186	1 348 506	1 515 449	1 317 664	1 801 512
Additional tax	59 082	350 301	799 648	1 023 497	1 414 057	1 187 866	1 178 917	1 337 721	1 454 847	1 429 758
Other	35 151	4 332	477 545	-1 224 610	973 421	1 423 320	169 589	177 727	-137 183	371 755
2000 Social security contributions	**159 559**	**576 758**	**931 717**	**1 371 750**	**1 493 987**	**1 623 818**	**1 802 468**	**1 968 973**	**2 110 087**	**2 252 489**
2100 Employees	154 021	553 937	893 821	1 312 793	1 433 159	1 565 828	1 742 526	1 906 340	2 044 356	2 188 575
2110 On a payroll basis	154 021	553 937	893 821	1 312 793	1 433 159	1 565 828	1 742 526	1 906 340	2 044 356	2 188 575
2120 On an income tax basis	0	0	0	0	0	0	0	0	0	0
2200 Employers	5 538	22 821	37 896	58 957	60 828	57 990	59 942	62 633	65 731	63 914
2210 On a payroll basis	5 538	22 821	37 896	58 957	60 828	57 990	59 942	62 633	65 731	63 914
2220 On an income tax basis	0	0	0	0	0	0	0	0	0	0
2300 Self-employed or non-employed	0	0	0	0	0	0	0	0	0	0
2310 On a payroll basis	..	..	..	..	..	..	..	..	..	..
2320 On an income tax basis	..	..	..	..	..	..	..	..	..	..
2400 Unallocable between 2100, 2200 and 2300	0	0	0	0	0	0	0	0	0	0
2410 On a payroll basis	..	..	..	..	..	..	..	..	..	..
2420 On an income tax basis	..	..	..	..	..	..	..	..	..	..
3000 Taxes on payroll and workforce	**0**	**0**	**0**	**0**	**0**	**0**	**0**	**0**	**0**	**0**
4000 Taxes on property	**109 319**	**554 037**	**901 776**	**909 121**	**898 607**	**1 027 627**	**1 180 307**	**1 133 765**	**1 228 961**	**1 418 511**
4100 Recurrent taxes on immovable property	59 968	302 244	416 565	646 316	662 368	731 191	788 919	840 842	924 062	1 054 157
4110 Households	..	..	..	..	..	..	..	..	..	..
4120 Others	..	..	..	..	..	..	..	..	..	..
4200 Recurrent taxes on net wealth	0	0	0	0	0	0	0	0	0	0
4210 Individual	..	..	..	..	..	..	..	..	..	..
4220 Corporate	..	..	..	..	..	..	..	..	..	..
4300 Estate, inheritance and gift taxes	3 444	10 906	23 184	200 203	39 338	30 876	66 719	45 550	31 340	92 236
4310 Estate and inheritance taxes	..	..	..	..	..	..	..	..	..	..
4320 Gift taxes	..	..	..	..	..	..	..	..	..	..
4400 Taxes on financial and capital transactions	45 907	240 886	462 027	62 602	196 901	265 560	324 669	247 373	273 559	272 118
4500 Non-recurrent taxes	0	0	0	0	0	0	0	0	0	0
4510 On net wealth	..	..	..	..	..	..	..	..	..	..
4520 Other non-recurrent taxes	..	..	..	..	..	..	..	..	..	..
4600 Other recurrent taxes on property	0	0	0	0	0	0	0	0	0	0
5000 Taxes on goods and services	**1 118 722**	**5 041 769**	**7 346 434**	**9 321 798**	**11 185 156**	**12 700 180**	**13 873 611**	**14 779 915**	**16 127 841**	**17 562 132**
5100 Taxes on production, sale, transfer, etc	1 074 009	4 789 827	6 952 092	8 741 074	10 532 904	11 963 914	13 052 989	13 869 529	15 131 661	16 480 644
5110 General taxes	664 421	3 306 350	5 391 285	7 051 079	8 399 926	9 536 786	10 447 374	11 170 794	12 133 710	13 273 958
5111 Value added taxes	664 421	3 306 350	5 391 285	7 051 079	8 399 926	9 536 786	10 447 374	11 170 794	12 133 710	13 273 958
5112 Sales tax	0	0	0	0	0	0	0	0	0	0
5113 Other	0	0	0	0	0	0	0	0	0	0
5120 Taxes on specific goods and services	409 588	1 483 477	1 560 807	1 689 995	2 132 978	2 427 128	2 605 615	2 698 735	2 997 951	3 206 686
5121 Excises	166 050	816 160	1 107 703	1 248 243	1 561 205	1 750 916	1 892 713	1 987 475	2 224 209	2 378 198
Cigarettes and tobacco	60 604	283 275	382 690	556 651	647 637	744 302	783 995	815 991	856 595	981 422
Gasoline and diesel	105 445	532 885	724 803	684 698	913 568	1 006 614	1 108 718	1 171 483	1 361 724	1 388 218
Oil stabilisation fund	0	0	210	6 894	0	0	0	0	0	0
5122 Profits of fiscal monopolies	0	0	0	0	0	0	0	0	0	0
5123 Customs and import duties	222 486	548 571	286 044	162 987	267 331	301 828	314 441	303 393	337 839	343 491
5124 Taxes on exports	0	0	0	0	0	0	0	0	0	0
5125 Taxes on investment goods	0	0	0	0	0	0	0	0	0	0
5126 Taxes on specific services	21 052	118 746	167 060	278 765	304 442	374 384	398 461	407 867	435 903	484 997
5127 Other taxes on internat. trade and transactions	0	0	0	0	0	0	0	0	0	0
5128 Other taxes	0	0	0	0	0	0	0	0	0	0
5130 Unallocable between 5110 and 5120	0	0	0	0	0	0	0	0	0	0
5200 Taxes on use of goods and perform activities	44 714	251 942	394 343	580 724	652 252	736 266	820 622	910 386	996 180	1 081 488
5210 Recurrent taxes	44 714	251 942	394 343	580 724	652 252	736 266	820 622	910 386	996 180	1 081 488
Motor vehicles	24 469	93 880	139 174	187 569	218 219	267 116	301 895	330 754	365 316	397 297

Table 5.7. Chile *(cont.)*
Details of tax revenue / Ingresos tributarios detallados

Million CLP

	1990	2000	2005	2009	2010	2011	2012	2013	2014	2015
5211 Paid by households: motor vehicles	0	0	0	0	0	0	0	0	0	0
5212 Paid by others: motor vehicles	0	0	0	0	0	0	0	0	0	0
5213 Paid in respect of other goods	20 245	158 062	255 169	393 155	434 033	469 150	518 727	579 632	630 864	684 191
Municipal permits	18 401	136 138	234 460	359 730	396 944	425 138	468 938	527 955	578 671	630 852
Mining patents	3 374	34 730	20 094	32 690	36 213	42 944	47 899	50 094	50 448	51 767
Other	-1 530	-12 806	615	735	876	1 068	1 890	1 583	1 745	1 572
5220 Non-recurrent taxes	0	0	0	0	0	0	0	0	0	0
5300 Unallocable between 5100 and 5200	0	0	0	0	0	0	0	0	0	0
6000 Other taxes	**-23 356**	**-112 195**	**-85 954**	**-5 438**	**-61 117**	**88 000**	**55 355**	**-21 676**	**50 293**	**-544 733**
6100 Paid solely by business	0	0	0	0	0	0	0	0	0	0
6200 Other	-23 356	-112 195	-85 954	-5 438	-61 117	88 000	55 355	-21 676	50 293	-544 733

Note: Year ending 31st December.
The data are on a cash basis.
Heading 5121: In ECLAC data, figures from the Oil Prices Stabilisation Fund (FEPP) are considered as non-tax revenues.
Source: Servicio de Impuestos Internos (Chile's Tax Service).

StatLink http://dx.doi.org/10.1787/888933463245

Table 5.8. Colombia
Details of tax revenue / Ingresos tributarios detallados

Million COP

	1990	2000	2005	2009	2010	2011	2012	2013	2014	2015
Total tax revenue	**2 579 426**	**30 512 910**	**61 455 845**	**93 898 231**	**97 954 930**	**116 684 542**	**131 058 304**	**142 643 685**	**154 351 903**	**166 264 700**
1000 Taxes on income, profits and capital gains	**771 694**	**7 103 525**	**17 348 618**	**28 116 564**	**26 218 852**	**33 453 048**	**43 671 856**	**47 743 096**	**50 083 349**	**52 656 876**
1100 Of individuals	47 210	1 499 345	3 594 441	5 229 835	5 192 384	6 407 675	6 841 470	7 661 035	8 489 883	9 674 556
1110 On income and profits	47 210	1 499 345	3 594 441	5 229 835	5 192 384	6 407 675	6 841 470	7 661 035	8 489 883	9 674 556
1120 On capital gains	..	..	..	..	..	..	..	..	..	..
1200 Corporate	359 758	5 119 828	13 044 361	21 954 952	20 405 209	26 110 879	35 669 308	38 544 891	40 188 077	40 968 703
1210 On profits	359 758	5 119 828	13 044 361	21 954 952	20 405 209	26 110 879	35 669 308	38 544 891	40 188 077	40 968 703
Income tax	359 758	5 119 828	13 044 361	21 954 952	20 405 209	26 110 879	35 669 308	35 605 312	27 726 602	27 042 534
Pro Equity Income Tax - CREE	0	0	0	0	0	0	0	2 939 579	12 461 475	13 926 169
1220 On capital gains	..	..	..	..	..	..	..	..	..	..
1300 Unallocable between 1100 and 1200	364 726	484 352	709 816	931 777	621 258	934 494	1 161 078	1 537 170	1 405 388	2 013 617
Income tax	364 726	484 352	709 816	931 777	621 258	934 494	1 161 078	1 537 170	1 405 388	2 013 617
Pro Equity Income Tax - CREE	0	0	0	0	0	0	0	0	0	0
2000 Social security contributions	**203 596**	**4 989 000**	**7 845 000**	**10 335 748**	**11 478 085**	**10 303 830**	**11 815 723**	**16 645 000**	**19 272 000**	**20 169 000**
2100 Employees	..	..	..	..	..	..	..	..	..	..
2110 On a payroll basis	..	..	..	..	..	..	..	..	..	..
2120 On an income tax basis	..	..	..	..	..	..	..	..	..	..
2200 Employers	..	..	..	..	..	..	..	..	..	..
2210 On a payroll basis	..	..	..	..	..	..	..	..	..	..
2220 On an income tax basis	..	..	..	..	..	..	..	..	..	..
2300 Self-employed or non-employed	..	..	..	..	..	..	..	..	..	..
2310 On a payroll basis	..	..	..	..	..	..	..	..	..	..
2320 On an income tax basis	..	..	..	..	..	..	..	..	..	..
2400 Unallocable between 2100, 2200 and 2300	203 596	4 989 000	7 845 000	10 335 748	11 478 085	10 303 830	11 815 723	16 645 000	19 272 000	20 169 000
2410 On a payroll basis	203 596	4 989 000	7 845 000	10 335 748	11 478 085	10 303 830	11 815 723	16 645 000	19 272 000	20 169 000
2420 On an income tax basis	0	0	0	0	0	0	0	0	0	0
3000 Taxes on payroll and workforce	**0**	**1 286 803**	**2 179 842**	**3 587 147**	**4 022 503**	**4 479 886**	**4 775 034**	**3 527 459**	**2 627 958**	**2 797 308**
4000 Taxes on property	**56 160**	**2 027 654**	**4 838 158**	**8 220 499**	**8 535 238**	**13 017 193**	**13 668 964**	**15 018 163**	**16 119 573**	**18 306 740**
4100 Recurrent taxes on immovable property	56 160	991 070	1 974 213	3 076 434	3 338 935	3 707 075	4 016 861	4 845 576	5 559 528	6 212 601
4110 Households	0	0	0	0	0	0	0	0	0	0
4120 Others	56 160	991 070	1 974 213	3 076 434	3 338 935	3 707 075	4 016 861	4 845 576	5 559 528	6 212 601
4200 Recurrent taxes on net wealth	0	0	462 720	2 022 787	1 970 530	4 240 512	4 183 752	4 274 832	4 118 075	5 352 940
4210 Individual	..	..	462 720	2 022 787	1 970 530	4 240 512	4 183 752	4 274 832	4 118 075	5 352 940
4220 Corporate	..	..	0	0	0	0	0	0	0	0
4300 Estate, inheritance and gift taxes	0	0	0	0	0	0	0	0	0	0
4310 Estate and inheritance taxes	..	..	..	..	..	..	..	..	..	..
4320 Gift taxes	..	..	..	..	..	..	..	..	..	..
4400 Taxes on financial and capital transactions	0	1 036 584	2 401 226	3 121 278	3 225 773	5 069 606	5 468 351	5 897 755	6 441 969	6 741 200
4500 Non-recurrent taxes	0	0	0	0	0	0	0	0	0	0
4510 On net wealth	..	..	..	..	..	..	..	..	..	..
4520 Other non-recurrent taxes	..	..	..	..	..	..	..	..	..	..
4600 Other recurrent taxes on property	0	0	0	0	0	0	0	0	0	0
5000 Taxes on goods and services	**1 388 653**	**13 367 908**	**25 866 553**	**38 090 163**	**42 156 822**	**49 337 843**	**50 824 992**	**52 393 473**	**57 894 877**	**62 378 052**
5100 Taxes on production, sale, transfer, etc	1 388 653	13 367 908	25 866 553	38 090 163	42 156 822	49 337 843	50 824 992	52 393 473	57 894 877	62 378 052
5110 General taxes	672 368	9 585 866	19 934 400	30 185 624	33 333 802	40 138 667	41 862 732	40 598 702	45 330 387	48 721 833
5111 Value added taxes	583 078	8 445 776	17 427 948	25 910 469	28 811 682	35 093 071	36 324 330	34 642 822	38 749 869	41 553 967
5112 Sales tax	89 290	1 140 090	2 506 452	4 275 155	4 522 121	5 045 595	5 538 402	5 955 879	6 580 518	7 167 866
Industry and commerce tax (State)	89 290	1 140 090	2 506 452	4 275 155	4 522 121	5 045 595	5 538 402	5 955 879	6 580 518	7 167 866
5113 Other	0	0	0	0	0	0	0	0	0	0
5120 Taxes on specific goods and services	716 285	3 782 042	5 932 153	7 904 539	8 823 019	9 199 176	8 962 260	11 794 771	12 564 491	13 656 219
5121 Excises	404 699	2 037 944	3 109 633	3 903 697	4 171 020	5 118 461	5 438 940	7 897 588	8 577 767	9 065 288
Oil	141 270	833 004	1 143 308	1 291 493	1 418 766	1 603 227	1 735 062	2 883 410	2 980 883	3 297 392
Liquors (State)	52 898	213 410	287 379	317 317	390 472	499 531	486 283	508 089	493 868	524 357
Tobacco (State)	85 722	471 137	867 569	1 381 248	1 432 453	1 764 785	1 900 215	2 031 349	2 108 721	2 305 895
Beer (State)	124 808	520 393	811 377	913 640	929 328	1 250 918	1 317 381	1 292 742	1 345 827	1 253 466
Restaurant, vehicles sale and mobile telephony	0	0	0	0	0	0	0	1 181 998	1 648 467	1 684 179
5122 Profits of fiscal monopolies	0	0	0	0	0	0	0	0	0	0
5123 Customs and import duties	311 586	1 744 097	2 822 520	4 000 842	4 651 999	4 080 716	3 523 320	3 897 184	3 986 724	4 590 931
Custom duties	180 989	1 744 097	2 822 520	4 000 842	4 651 999	4 080 716	3 523 320	3 897 184	3 986 724	4 590 931
Imports surcharge	130 597	0	0	0	0	0	0	0	0	0
5124 Taxes on exports	0	0	0	0	0	0	0	0	0	0
5125 Taxes on investment goods	0	0	0	0	0	0	0	0	0	0
5126 Taxes on specific services	0	0	0	0	0	0	0	0	0	0
5127 Other taxes on internat. trade and transactions	0	0	0	0	0	0	0	0	0	0
5128 Other taxes	0	0	0	0	0	0	0	0	0	0
5130 Unallocable between 5110 and 5120	0	0	0	0	0	0	0	0	0	0
5200 Taxes on use of goods and perform activities	0	0	0	0	0	0	0	0	0	0
5210 Recurrent taxes	..	..	..	..	..	..	..	..	..	..

Table 5.8. Colombia (cont.)
Details of tax revenue / Ingresos tributarios detallados

Million COP

	1990	2000	2005	2009	2010	2011	2012	2013	2014	2015
5211 Paid by households: motor vehicles	..	..	..	..	..	..	..	..	..	..
5212 Paid by others: motor vehicles	..	..	..	..	..	..	..	..	..	..
5213 Paid in respect of other goods	..	..	..	..	..	..	..	..	..	..
5220 Non-recurrent taxes	..	..	..	..	..	..	..	..	..	..
5300 Unallocable between 5100 and 5200	0	0	0	0	0	0	0	0	0	0
6000 Other taxes	**159 323**	**1 738 020**	**3 377 674**	**5 548 110**	**5 543 430**	**6 092 742**	**6 301 735**	**7 316 494**	**8 354 147**	**9 956 724**
6100 Paid solely by business	0	0	0	0	0	0	0	0	0	0
6200 Other	159 323	1 738 020	3 377 674	5 548 110	5 543 430	6 092 742	6 301 735	7 316 494	8 354 147	9 956 724
Stamp tax	0	401 497	633 586	611 832	357 160	123 923	58 973	58 378	72 425	105 729
Other	78 306	79 287	48 498	120 721	126 602	143 770	174 845	200 465	260 721	318 271
Other (sub-national)	81 017	1 257 236	2 695 589	4 815 557	5 059 668	5 825 049	6 067 916	7 057 651	8 021 001	9 532 725

Note: Year ending 31st December.

The data are on a cash basis.

Includes the reported consolidated revenues of the territorial entities (departments and municipalities).

Heading 2000: Before 2013, social security contributions did not include all the contributions entering FOSYGA (Solidarity and Guarantee Fund). Only the portion of the contributions used to finance the subsidised regime (up to 1.5 pp of the 12.5% of the monthly wage paid by employers and employees as an obligatory health contribution) was included. The part of the contributions entering FOSYGA to finance the contributory regime was classified in the social security sector as "other incomes". From 2013 onwards, all of the health contributions entering FOSYGA are classified as Social Security Contributions. The portion of the contributions not entering FOSYGA that is both collected and spent by the health insurers – EPS - is not part of the fiscal accounts.

Headings 1100 and 1200: The data are estimated.

Source: Dirección de Impuestos y Aduanas Nacionales de Colombia, Ministerio de Hacienda y Crédito Público y Banco Central de Colombia. (National Tax and Customs Administration, Ministry of Finance and Public Credit and Central Bank of Colombia).

StatLink http://dx.doi.org/10.1787/888933463250

Table 5.9. Costa Rica
Details of tax revenue / Ingresos tributarios detallados

Million CRC

	1990	2000	2005	2009	2010	2011	2012	2013	2014	2015
Total tax revenue	**106 778**	**893 812**	**1 915 942**	**3 564 323**	**3 979 101**	**4 438 852**	**4 846 611**	**5 563 744**	**6 011 760**	**6 540 415**
1000 Taxes on income, profits and capital gains	**11 820**	**128 805**	**324 224**	**687 420**	**748 093**	**828 691**	**891 669**	**1 014 440**	**1 091 470**	**1 247 308**
1100 Of individuals	..	..	16 438	156 936	202 849	233 486	307 489	316 894	349 139	386 241
1110 On income and profits	..	..	16 438	156 936	202 849	233 486	307 489	316 894	349 139	386 241
1120 On capital gains	..	..	..	..	..	..	..	..	..	..
1200 Corporate	..	..	288 355	444 242	450 312	486 001	461 481	545 183	574 137	659 951
1210 On profits	..	..	288 355	444 242	450 312	486 001	461 481	545 183	574 137	659 951
1220 On capital gains	..	..	..	..	..	..	..	..	..	..
1300 Unallocable between 1100 and 1200	11 820	128 805	19 430	86 241	94 932	109 204	122 699	152 363	168 194	201 116
2000 Social security contributions	**29 065**	**249 886**	**528 132**	**1 044 617**	**1 204 995**	**1 354 199**	**1 482 847**	**1 874 010**	**2 045 389**	**2 218 719**
2100 Employees	..	3 405	5 354	8 777	9 649	11 014	12 936	12 774	22 151	31 120
2110 On a payroll basis	..	3 405	5 354	8 777	9 649	11 014	12 936	12 774	22 151	31 120
2120 On an income tax basis	..	0	0	0	0	0	0	0	0	0
2200 Employers	..	0	24 481	47 925	56 332	63 094	68 092	344 622	370 268	394 728
2210 On a payroll basis	..	..	..	..	..	..	..	..	..	..
2220 On an income tax basis	..	..	..	..	..	..	..	..	..	..
2300 Self-employed or non-employed	..	5 858	16 414	30 656	33 778	36 733	39 462	21 090	22 404	1 718
2310 On a payroll basis	..	5 858	16 414	30 656	33 778	36 733	39 462	21 090	22 404	1 718
2320 On an income tax basis	..	0	0	0	0	0	0	0	0	0
2400 Unallocable between 2100, 2200 and 2300	29 065	240 623	481 883	957 260	1 105 236	1 243 358	1 362 357	1 495 525	1 630 566	1 791 153
2410 On a payroll basis	..	..	..	..	..	..	..	..	..	..
2420 On an income tax basis	..	..	..	..	..	..	..	..	..	..
3000 Taxes on payroll and workforce	**7 054**	**41 918**	**81 290**	**163 991**	**182 529**	**201 667**	**226 575**	**247 775**	**270 834**	**268 775**
4000 Taxes on property	**366**	**12 681**	**25 110**	**48 040**	**63 663**	**70 927**	**81 868**	**99 771**	**115 174**	**122 506**
4100 Recurrent taxes on immovable property	0	5 310	14 245	34 233	47 607	50 279	60 918	71 526	82 474	89 248
Land tax	..	0	0	0	0	0	0	0	0	0
Additional land tax	..	0	0	0	0	0	0	0	0	0
Tax on sumptuary constructions	..	0	0	0	0	0	0	0	0	0
Immovable property tax	..	0	0	55	3 527	2 475	2 638	3 998	4 013	4 076
Municipal immovable property tax	..	5 310	14 245	34 178	44 080	47 804	58 280	67 528	78 461	85 172
4110 Households	..	..	..	..	..	..	..	..	..	..
4120 Others	..	..	..	..	..	..	..	..	..	..
4200 Recurrent taxes on net wealth	0	4 284	0	0	0	0	0	0	0	0
4210 Individual	..	0	..	..	..	..	..	..	..	..
4220 Corporate	..	4 284	..	..	..	..	..	..	..	..
Tax on corporate assets	..	4 284	..	..	..	..	..	..	..	..
4300 Estate, inheritance and gift taxes	0	0	0	0	0	0	0	0	0	0
4310 Estate and inheritance taxes	..	..	..	..	..	..	..	..	..	..
4320 Gift taxes	..	..	..	..	..	..	..	..	..	..
4400 Taxes on financial and capital transactions	366	3 007	10 846	12 734	14 743	19 053	20 950	28 245	32 700	33 258
4500 Non-recurrent taxes	0	0	0	0	0	0	0	0	0	0
4510 On net wealth	..	..	..	..	..	..	..	..	..	..
4520 Other non-recurrent taxes	..	..	..	..	..	..	..	..	..	..
4600 Other recurrent taxes on property	0	80	19	1 072	1 313	1 595	0	0	0	0
5000 Taxes on goods and services	**52 360**	**456 707**	**946 970**	**1 606 222**	**1 762 591**	**1 963 833**	**2 122 589**	**2 268 536**	**2 423 583**	**2 621 803**
5100 Taxes on production, sale, transfer, etc	49 980	437 334	914 200	1 524 363	1 664 652	1 872 449	2 015 909	2 149 169	2 288 435	2 470 900
5110 General taxes	21 326	222 775	485 168	830 538	920 298	1 029 811	1 122 978	1 176 758	1 266 798	1 336 075
5111 Value added taxes	21 326	222 775	485 168	830 538	920 298	1 029 811	1 122 978	1 176 758	1 266 798	1 336 075
5112 Sales tax	0	0	0	0	0	0	0	0	0	0
5113 Other	0	0	0	0	0	0	0	0	0	0
5120 Taxes on specific goods and services	28 654	213 499	423 486	688 697	739 494	837 573	813 013	880 232	916 915	1 020 292
5121 Excises	11 096	157 204	296 222	481 147	523 617	596 268	629 423	689 528	706 016	798 412
Fuels and energy	0	0	172 028	308 274	320 638	359 425	354 149	404 210	404 901	457 827
Alcohol beverages	0	8 229	20 219	29 639	28 035	32 936	35 620	35 254	36 293	43 095
Non alcoholic beverages	0	0	12 491	24 426	26 566	27 804	30 205	32 519	34 874	36 353
Soaps	0	0	573	1 110	1 317	1 425	1 487	1 989	1 493	2 562
Cement	0	0	0	253	227	250	247	291	340	304
Tobacco	0	0	0	0	0	0	19 852	38 860	32 277	33 681
Abolished specific taxes on production and consumption	0	31 756	0	0	0	0	0	0	0	0
Other specific taxes on consumption	11 096	117 219	90 913	117 444	146 834	174 428	187 863	176 405	195 838	224 590
5122 Profits of fiscal monopolies	0	0	0	0	0	0	0	0	0	0
5123 Customs and import duties	15 053	40 485	82 446	117 256	126 135	146 511	152 275	154 576	169 120	174 568
Import duties	13 977	32 336	66 598	97 001	103 851	122 355	128 358	130 634	142 226	148 666
Custom duties	1 076	8 149	15 848	20 255	22 284	24 156	23 917	23 942	26 894	25 902

Table 5.9. Costa Rica (*cont*)
Details of tax revenue / Ingresos tributarios detallados

Million CRC

	1990	2000	2005	2009	2010	2011	2012	2013	2014	2015
5124 Taxes on exports	2 226	2 238	969	4 677	3 973	3 990	3 823	4 877	4 853	4 468
Export duties	2 226	1 835	830	4 534	3 816	3 827	3 663	4 104	3 067	2 701
Export duties Law 133	0	0	0	0	0	0	0	0	0	0
Export duties Law 5519	0	253	0	0	0	0	0	0	0	0
Tax on banana exports	0	150	139	143	157	163	160	168	176	156
Export duties on ground transportation	0	0	0	0	0	0	0	605	1 610	1 611
5125 Taxes on investment goods	0	0	0	0	0	0	0	0	0	0
5126 Taxes on specific services	280	13 488	43 755	84 619	84 270	88 744	25 579	28 571	34 081	38 687
Casinos and gambling	0	225	519	411	445	288	213	1 000	897	1 392
Electronic betting business	0	0	0	0	0	0	0	19	43	63
Port cargo movements	0	6	13	12	0	0	0	0	0	0
Overseas departure tax	0	0	19 022	24 794	24 322	23 902	25 366	27 552	33 141	37 232
10% on public shows	0	26	0	0	0	0	0	0	0	0
Pro-national airport's stamp tax	0	6	0	0	0	0	0	0	0	0
Stamp tax on the use of borders and ports	280	2 697	0	0	0	0	0	0	0	0
Municipal licences and permits	0	8 692	19 974	52 492	52 637	55 606	0	0	0	0
Municipal tax on construction	0	1 836	4 226	6 910	6 866	8 948	0	0	0	0
5127 Other taxes on internat. trade and transactions	0	83	94	998	1 499	2 060	1 913	2 680	2 845	3 086
5128 Other taxes	0	0	0	0	0	0	0	0	0	1 071
5130 Unallocable between 5110 and 5120	0	1 061	5 546	5 128	4 860	5 065	79 913	92 179	104 723	114 533
5200 Taxes on use of goods and perform activities	2 380	19 357	32 758	81 705	97 803	91 266	106 557	119 235	135 005	150 755
5210 Recurrent taxes	2 380	19 357	32 758	81 705	97 803	91 266	106 557	119 235	135 005	150 755
5211 Paid by households: motor vehicles	0	0	0	0	0	0	0	0	0	0
5212 Paid by others: motor vehicles	1 425	15 487	30 918	77 924	94 101	85 152	101 903	113 727	130 000	145 894
Property tax on vehicles, aircraft and boats	1 425	15 374	30 918	77 924	94 101	85 152	101 903	113 727	130 000	145 894
Special tax on the use of public roads	0	113	0	0	0	0	0	0	0	0
5213 Paid in respect of other goods	955	3 870	1 841	3 781	3 702	6 114	4 654	5 508	5 005	4 861
Hunting and fishing licences	0	0	0	0	0	0	0	0	0	0
Hunting and fishing licences (Ministry of Natural Resources, Energy and Mines)	0	4	0	0	0	0	0	0	0	0
Spirits license	0	0	0	0	0	0	0	0	0	0
Revenue stamps	955	3 866	1 841	3 781	3 702	6 114	4 654	5 508	5 005	4 861
Sport stamp tax	0	0	0	0	0	0	0	0	0	0
5220 Non-recurrent taxes	0	0	0	0	0	0	0	0	0	0
5300 Unallocable between 5100 and 5200	0	15	12	153	136	118	123	132	142	148
6000 Other taxes	**6 113**	**3 816**	**10 216**	**14 034**	**17 230**	**19 535**	**41 063**	**59 212**	**65 311**	**61 303**
6100 Paid solely by business	0	15	624	521	459	526	22 724	36 125	39 542	33 117
6200 Other	6 113	3 801	9 592	13 513	16 771	19 009	18 339	23 087	25 769	28 186
Transfers of vehicles, aircraft and boats	497	2 530	6 357	9 612	12 311	13 672	12 947	17 177	19 099	20 999

Note: Year ending 31st December.

The data are on a cash basis.

The figures for years up to and including 1997 exclude local government tax revenues as the data are not available.

Heading 2000: In ECLAC data, social security contributions include INA (National Institute of Apprenticeship), IMAS (Joint Social Aid Institute), and FODESAF (Social Development and Family Allowances Fund).

Heading 3000: In ECLAC data, social security contributions from decentralised institutions are classified under heading 2000.

Heading 5121: In ECLAC data, the tax on transfers of vehicles is classified as a property tax (4000).

Heading 5212: In ECLAC data, tax on ownership of vehicles, aircraft and boats is classified in category 4000

Heading 6000: In ECLAC data, the tax on the transfer of used vehicles Law No. 7088 of 30/11/87 is classified as a property tax (4000).

Source: Secretaría Técnica de la Autoridad Presupuestaria, Ministerio de Finanzas y Contraloría General de la República (Technical Secretary of the Budgeting Authority, Ministry of Finance and National General Comptroller).

StatLink http://dx.doi.org/10.1787/888933463261

Table 5.10. Cuba
Details of tax revenue / Ingresos tributarios detallados

Million CUP

	1990	2000	2005	2009	2010	2011	2012	2013	2014	2015
Total tax revenue	**6 265**	**11 367**	**17 528**	**25 493**	**24 201**	**26 508**	**29 068**	**28 804**	**30 236**	**33 591**
1000 Taxes on income, profits and capital gains	**14**	**1 826**	**2 451**	**3 191**	**3 603**	**4 504**	**4 535**	**5 292**	**5 995**	**6 676**
1100 Of individuals	14	291	326	480	554	762	873	1 055	1 308	1 848
1110 On income and profits	..	..	..	..	..	..	..	..	..	..
1120 On capital gains	..	..	..	..	..	..	..	..	..	..
1200 Corporate	0	1 535	2 126	2 711	3 049	3 742	3 662	4 237	4 687	4 828
1210 On profits	..	..	..	..	..	..	..	..	..	..
1220 On capital gains	..	..	..	..	..	..	..	..	..	..
1300 Unallocable between 1100 and 1200	0	0	0	0	0	0	0	0	0	0
2000 Social security contributions	**691**	**1 181**	**1 778**	**2 774**	**2 974**	**2 996**	**3 043**	**3 123**	**3 622**	**4 322**
2100 Employees	..	..	..	..	..	..	..	..	..	..
2110 On a payroll basis	..	..	..	..	..	..	..	..	..	..
2120 On an income tax basis	0	0	0	0	0	0	0	0	0	0
2200 Employers	..	..	..	..	..	..	..	..	..	..
2210 On a payroll basis	..	..	..	..	..	..	..	..	..	..
2220 On an income tax basis	0	0	0	0	0	0	0	0	0	0
2300 Self-employed or non-employed	..	..	..	..	..	..	..	..	..	..
2310 On a payroll basis	..	..	..	..	..	..	..	..	..	..
2320 On an income tax basis	0	0	0	0	0	0	0	0	0	0
2400 Unallocable between 2100, 2200 and 2300	691	1 181	1 778	2 774	2 974	2 996	3 043	3 123	3 622	4 322
2410 On a payroll basis	691	1 181	1 778	2 774	2 974	2 996	3 043	3 123	3 622	4 322
2420 On an income tax basis	0	0	0	0	0	0	0	0	0	0
3000 Taxes on payroll and workforce	**0**	**970**	**2 962**	**4 246**	**4 414**	**4 235**	**4 108**	**3 424**	**2 939**	**2 753**
4000 Taxes on property	**0**	**0**	**0**	**0**	**0**	**0**	**0**	**0**	**0**	**0**
4100 Recurrent taxes on immovable property	..	..	..	..	..	..	..	..	..	..
4110 Households	..	..	..	..	..	..	..	..	..	..
4120 Others	..	..	..	..	..	..	..	..	..	..
4200 Recurrent taxes on net wealth	..	..	..	..	..	..	..	..	..	..
4210 Individual	..	..	..	..	..	..	..	..	..	..
4220 Corporate	..	..	..	..	..	..	..	..	..	..
4300 Estate, inheritance and gift taxes	..	..	..	..	..	..	..	..	..	..
4310 Estate and inheritance taxes	..	..	..	..	..	..	..	..	..	..
4320 Gift taxes	..	..	..	..	..	..	..	..	..	..
4400 Taxes on financial and capital transactions	..	..	..	..	..	..	..	..	..	..
4500 Non-recurrent taxes	..	..	..	..	..	..	..	..	..	..
4510 On net wealth	..	..	..	..	..	..	..	..	..	..
4520 Other non-recurrent taxes	..	..	..	..	..	..	..	..	..	..
4600 Other recurrent taxes on property	..	..	..	..	..	..	..	..	..	..
5000 Taxes on goods and services	**5 443**	**6 732**	**9 844**	**14 331**	**12 283**	**13 696**	**16 232**	**15 588**	**15 911**	**17 742**
5100 Taxes on production, sale, transfer, etc	5 443	6 732	9 844	14 331	12 283	13 696	16 232	15 588	15 911	17 742
5110 General taxes	5 017	6 131	9 036	12 768	10 525	11 819	14 511	14 057	14 171	15 611
5111 Value added taxes	..	..	..	..	..	..	..	..	..	..
5112 Sales tax	..	..	..	..	..	..	..	..	..	..
5113 Other	..	..	..	..	..	..	..	..	..	..
5120 Taxes on specific goods and services	426	602	808	1 564	1 758	1 876	1 721	1 531	1 740	2 131
5121 Excises	..	..	..	..	..	..	..	..	..	..
5122 Profits of fiscal monopolies	..	..	..	..	..	..	..	..	..	..
5123 Customs and import duties	..	..	..	..	..	..	..	..	..	..
5124 Taxes on exports	..	..	..	..	..	..	..	..	..	..
5125 Taxes on investment goods	..	..	..	..	..	..	..	..	..	..
5126 Taxes on specific services	..	..	..	..	..	..	..	..	..	..
5127 Other taxes on internat. trade and transactions	..	..	..	..	..	..	..	..	..	..
5128 Other taxes	..	..	..	..	..	..	..	..	..	..
5130 Unallocable between 5110 and 5120	..	..	..	..	..	..	..	..	..	..
5200 Taxes on use of goods and perform activities	0	0	0	0	0	0	0	0	0	0
5210 Recurrent taxes	..	..	..	..	..	..	..	..	..	..
5211 Paid by households: motor vehicles	..	..	..	..	..	..	..	..	..	..
5212 Paid by others: motor vehicles	..	..	..	..	..	..	..	..	..	..
5213 Paid in respect of other goods	..	..	..	..	..	..	..	..	..	..
5220 Non-recurrent taxes	..	..	..	..	..	..	..	..	..	..
5300 Unallocable between 5100 and 5200	..	..	..	..	..	..	..	..	..	..
6000 Other taxes	**117**	**657**	**493**	**951**	**927**	**1 078**	**1 150**	**1 378**	**1 769**	**2 098**
6100 Paid solely by business	..	..	..	..	..	..	..	..	..	..
6200 Other	..	..	..	..	..	..	..	..	..	..

Note: Year ending 31st December.
The data are on a cash basis.
The figures exclude local government tax revenues as the data are not available.
The figures for the sub-categories under headings 5110 and 5120 are not available.

Source: Oficina Nacional de Estadística e Información. Anuario Estadístico de Cuba. (National Office of Statistics and Information. Annual Statistical Review of Cuba.)

StatLink http://dx.doi.org/10.1787/888933463272

Table 5.11. Dominican Republic / República Dominicana
Details of tax revenue / Ingresos tributarios detallados

Million DOP

	1990	2000	2005	2009	2010	2011	2012	2013	2014	2015
Total tax revenue	**6 439**	**44 898**	**129 639**	**220 328**	**243 872**	**273 132**	**312 148**	**355 314**	**393 157**	**414 245**
1000 Taxes on income, profits and capital gains	**1 670**	**10 782**	**30 042**	**54 128**	**53 643**	**65 453**	**92 850**	**108 853**	**125 098**	**119 819**
1100 Of individuals	..	4 088	7 588	15 437	17 088	20 673	21 874	27 147	31 525	35 549
1110 On income and profits	..	4 070	7 509	15 200	16 901	20 220	21 575	26 723	31 119	35 187
1120 On capital gains	..	18	79	237	187	453	299	424	406	361
1200 Corporate	..	4 679	16 222	22 546	21 475	25 125	46 921	58 923	72 865	61 695
1210 On profits	..	4 605	16 147	22 414	21 325	24 913	46 582	58 597	72 628	61 455
1220 On capital gains	..	74	75	132	151	212	339	326	238	240
Casinos	..	59	73	132	151	182	213	187	173	184
Racetracks	..	15	2	0	0	0	0	0	0	0
Phone gaming	..	0	0	0	0	30	127	139	64	56
1300 Unallocable between 1100 and 1200	1 670	2 015	6 232	16 145	15 080	19 655	24 055	22 782	20 708	22 576
2000 Social security contributions	**53**	**490**	**35**	**1 009**	**1 845**	**1 328**	**1 250**	**1 552**	**1 515**	**1 483**
2100 Employees	..	..	..	..	..	..	..	..	..	..
2110 On a payroll basis	..	..	..	..	..	..	..	..	..	..
2120 On an income tax basis	..	..	..	..	..	..	..	..	..	..
2200 Employers	..	..	..	..	..	..	..	..	..	..
2210 On a payroll basis	..	..	..	..	..	..	..	..	..	..
2220 On an income tax basis	..	..	..	..	..	..	..	..	..	..
2300 Self-employed or non-employed	..	..	..	..	..	..	..	..	..	..
2310 On a payroll basis	..	..	..	..	..	..	..	..	..	..
2320 On an income tax basis	..	..	..	..	..	..	..	..	..	..
2400 Unallocable between 2100, 2200 and 2300	53	490	35	1 009	1 845	1 328	1 250	1 552	1 515	1 483
2410 On a payroll basis	53	490	35	1 009	1 845	1 328	1 250	1 552	1 515	1 483
2420 On an income tax basis	0	0	0	0	0	0	0	0	0	0
3000 Taxes on payroll and workforce	**0**	**0**	**0**	**0**	**0**	**0**	**0**	**0**	**0**	**0**
4000 Taxes on property	**56**	**529**	**6 579**	**11 177**	**12 782**	**15 356**	**18 924**	**22 123**	**17 285**	**18 097**
4100 Recurrent taxes on immovable property	9	115	1 710	2 702	3 004	5 235	8 351	10 183	5 037	5 200
4110 Households	9	115	1 710	473	555	629	686	1 518	1 579	1 755
4120 Others	0	0	0	2 230	2 449	4 605	7 665	8 666	3 458	3 445
Tax on assets	..	..	..	2 230	2 449	2 790	3 044	3 337	3 454	3 445
Tax on financial assets (Law 139-11)	..	..	..	0	0	1 816	4 620	5 329	4	0
4200 Recurrent taxes on net wealth	0	0	0	0	0	0	0	0	0	0
4210 Individual	..	..	..	..	..	..	..	..	..	..
4220 Corporate	..	..	..	..	..	..	..	..	..	..
4300 Estate, inheritance and gift taxes	11	96	84	199	231	237	227	315	325	418
4310 Estate and inheritance taxes	0	0	0	0	0	0	0	0	0	0
4320 Gift taxes	0	0	0	0	0	0	0	0	0	0
4400 Taxes on financial and capital transactions	22	217	4 546	7 181	8 125	8 255	8 723	10 404	10 496	11 120
Tax on checks	0	0	3 133	3 919	4 262	4 492	4 852	5 168	5 620	5 951
Real estate operations	22	217	1 413	3 262	3 864	3 763	3 872	5 236	4 876	5 169
4500 Non-recurrent taxes	3	32	89	282	488	578	609	412	677	591
4510 On net wealth	3	32	89	282	488	578	609	412	677	591
4520 Other non-recurrent taxes	0	0	0	0	0	0	0	0	0	0
4600 Other recurrent taxes on property	11	70	151	814	934	1 052	1 014	810	751	769
5000 Taxes on goods and services	**4 501**	**32 602**	**91 322**	**154 009**	**175 601**	**190 995**	**199 124**	**222 786**	**249 259**	**274 845**
5100 Taxes on production, sale, transfer, etc	4 432	31 884	89 604	151 796	173 337	188 561	196 556	219 940	246 107	271 372
5110 General taxes	970	9 912	40 983	69 401	81 226	88 892	92 205	112 731	130 447	147 039
5111 Value added taxes	970	9 912	40 983	69 401	81 226	88 892	92 205	112 731	130 447	147 039
5112 Sales tax	0	0	0	0	0	0	0	0	0	0
5113 Other	0	0	0	0	0	0	0	0	0	0
5120 Taxes on specific goods and services	3 462	21 972	48 621	82 395	92 111	99 669	104 351	107 209	115 660	124 333
5121 Excises	528	6 774	27 553	52 921	60 790	68 475	72 341	73 835	78 980	82 523
Vehicle registration	0	0	0	3 163	4 234	4 268	4 505	4 595	5 683	6 990
Transfer tax	18	160	170	507	533	572	682	805	898	947
Alcoholic beverages	251	2 451	8 142	13 343	15 054	16 240	17 089	17 969	19 779	22 371
Tobacco products	102	469	2 879	4 131	4 529	4 241	4 470	4 356	4 382	4 532
Petroleum products	105	3 143	14 712	30 373	34 598	40 303	42 460	42 222	44 335	43 315
Other	52	551	1 651	1 403	1 843	2 850	3 136	3 887	3 904	4 367
5122 Profits of fiscal monopolies	0	0	0	0	0	0	0	0	0	0
5123 Customs and import duties	1 548	13 459	14 403	18 265	19 455	18 801	18 891	19 043	21 315	25 212
Custom duties	615	13 456	14 293	18 264	19 455	18 801	18 776	18 916	21 238	24 378
Other	933	3	110	0	0	0	115	126	76	834
5124 Taxes on exports	6	4	46	132	146	181	264	34	12	8
5125 Taxes on investment goods	0	0	0	0	0	0	0	0	0	0

Table 5.11. Dominican Republic / República Dominicana *(cont.)*
Details of tax revenue / Ingresos tributarios detallados

Million DOP

	1990	2000	2005	2009	2010	2011	2012	2013	2014	2015
5126 Taxes on specific services	344	1 590	5 609	10 799	11 411	11 822	12 516	13 863	14 956	16 245
Telecommunications	85	0	3 193	4 592	4 886	4 947	5 124	5 897	6 129	6 375
Insurance premiums	33	584	0	2 978	3 088	3 238	3 437	3 674	3 965	4 301
Travel tickets	204	809	2 414	3 222	3 428	3 632	3 951	4 283	4 839	5 535
Hotels	22	191	0	0	0	0	0	0	0	0
Others	0	7	1	6	9	6	4	9	24	35
5127 Other taxes on internat. trade and transactions	1 037	145	1 010	279	309	389	338	436	397	346
Exchange commission	857	0	0	0	0	0	0	0	0	0
Consular fees	77	32	271	138	132	138	130	143	142	137
Other	103	112	738	141	176	251	209	293	256	209
5128 Other taxes	0	0	0	0	0	0	0	0	0	0
5130 Unallocable between 5110 and 5120	0	0	0	0	0	0	0	0	0	0
5200 Taxes on use of goods and perform activities	69	718	1 718	2 213	2 265	2 434	2 568	2 846	3 152	3 473
5210 Recurrent taxes	69	718	1 718	2 213	2 265	2 434	2 568	2 569	2 736	2 958
5211 Paid by households: motor vehicles	45	268	977	1 225	1 277	1 300	1 271	1 073	1 289	1 558
5212 Paid by others: motor vehicles	0	0	0	0	0	0	0	0	0	0
5213 Paid in respect of other goods	24	450	742	989	988	1 134	1 297	1 496	1 447	1 400
Licences to carry firearms	17	237	244	346	296	253	194	240	200	171
Licences to operate gambling houses	0	114	155	199	211	571	1 076	1 229	1 221	1 208
Licences to operate slot machines	4	60	102	409	458	287	0	0	0	0
Other	4	39	240	35	24	23	28	28	26	21
5220 Non-recurrent taxes	0	0	0	0	0	0	0	277	416	515
5300 Unallocable between 5100 and 5200	0	0	0	0	0	0	0	0	0	0
6000 Other taxes	**159**	**495**	**1 661**	**5**	**0**	**0**	**0**	**0**	**1**	**1**
6100 Paid solely by business	0	0	0	0	..	..	0	0	0	0
6200 Other	159	495	1 661	5	..	..	0	0	1	1

Note: Year ending 31st December.

The data are on a cash basis.

The figures exclude local government tax revenues as the data are not available.

Heading 2000: The data exclude social security contributions to general government managed by the private sector.

Heading 5121: In ECLAC data, the tax on transfer of movable goods is classified as a property tax (4000).

Heading 5123: The data corresponding to others under this heading has been revised.

Heading 5220: Data corresponds to the tax on CO_2 emissions which was previously classified as an excise tax under heading 5121, other.

Heading 6000: In ECLAC data, the vehicle transfer tax is classified as a property tax (4000).

Source: Ministerio de Hacienda (Ministry of Finance).

StatLink http://dx.doi.org/10.1787/888933463281

Table 5.12. Ecuador
Details of tax revenue / Ingresos tributarios detallados

Million USD

	1990	2000	2005	2009	2010	2011	2012	2013	2014	2015
Total tax revenue	**1 105**	**1 885**	**5 029**	**9 513**	**11 568**	**14 020**	**17 379**	**18 631**	**19 653**	**21 032**
1000 Taxes on income, profits and capital gains	**138**	**293**	**936**	**2 515**	**2 348**	**3 027**	**3 307**	**3 838**	**4 150**	**4 705**
1100 Of individuals	..	10	27	82	80	93	113	161	177	192
1110 On income and profits	..	..	..	..	..	..	..	..	..	..
1120 On capital gains	..	..	..	..	..	..	..	..	..	..
1200 Corporate	..	53	342	758	485	869	851	1 023	1 121	1 578
1210 On profits	..	..	..	..	..	..	..	..	..	..
1220 On capital gains	..	..	..	..	..	..	..	..	..	..
1300 Unallocable between 1100 and 1200	138	231	567	1 675	1 783	2 066	2 344	2 654	2 851	2 935
Unallocable income tax	138	204	854	1 709	1 858	2 148	2 422	2 740	2 965	3 034
Income tax refunds	0	27	-287	-34	-75	-82	-78	-86	-113	-99
2000 Social security contributions	**243**	**228**	**1 109**	**2 061**	**2 549**	**3 971**	**4 752**	**4 547**	**4 718**	**5 055**
2100 Employees	..	..	..	..	..	..	..	..	..	..
2110 On a payroll basis	..	..	..	..	..	..	..	..	..	..
2120 On an income tax basis	..	..	..	..	..	..	..	..	..	..
2200 Employers	..	..	..	..	..	..	..	..	..	..
2210 On a payroll basis	..	..	..	..	..	..	..	..	..	..
2220 On an income tax basis	..	..	..	..	..	..	..	..	..	..
2300 Self-employed or non-employed	..	..	..	..	..	..	..	..	..	..
2310 On a payroll basis	..	..	..	..	..	..	..	..	..	..
2320 On an income tax basis	..	..	..	..	..	..	..	..	..	..
2400 Unallocable between 2100, 2200 and 2300	243	228	1 109	2 061	2 549	3 971	4 752	4 547	4 718	5 055
2410 On a payroll basis	..	..	..	..	..	..	..	..	..	..
2420 On an income tax basis	..	..	..	..	..	..	..	..	..	..
3000 Taxes on payroll and workforce	**0**	**0**	**0**	**0**	**0**	**0**	**0**	**0**	**0**	**0**
4000 Taxes on property	**14**	**11**	**44**	**65**	**86**	**104**	**156**	**165**	**194**	**229**
4100 Recurrent taxes on immovable property	13	10	38	53	66	73	105	114	115	126
4110 Households	0	0	0	0	0	0	0	0	0	0
4120 Others	13	10	38	53	66	73	105	114	115	126
4200 Recurrent taxes on net wealth	0	0	0	0	0	0	0	0	0	0
4210 Individual	..	..	..	..	..	..	..	..	..	..
4220 Corporate	..	..	..	..	..	..	..	..	..	..
4300 Estate, inheritance and gift taxes	0	0	1	3	5	3	6	9	11	29
4310 Estate and inheritance taxes	..	..	1	3	5	3	6	9	11	29
4320 Gift taxes	..	..	0	0	0	0	0	0	0	0
4400 Taxes on financial and capital transactions	1	2	6	9	15	28	44	42	69	75
4500 Non-recurrent taxes	0	0	0	0	0	0	0	0	0	0
4510 On net wealth	..	..	..	..	..	..	..	..	..	..
4520 Other non-recurrent taxes	..	..	..	..	..	..	..	..	..	..
4600 Other recurrent taxes on property	0	0	0	0	0	0	0	0	0	0
5000 Taxes on goods and services	**682**	**1 350**	**2 887**	**4 639**	**6 295**	**6 889**	**9 052**	**9 950**	**10 462**	**10 907**
5100 Taxes on production, sale, transfer, etc	671	1 330	2 786	4 466	6 078	6 642	8 771	9 630	10 120	10 551
5110 General taxes	306	840	1 990	3 055	3 926	4 243	5 468	6 118	6 448	6 425
5111 Value added taxes	302	836	1 975	3 019	3 886	4 201	5 415	6 056	6 376	6 352
5112 Sales tax	0	0	0	0	0	0	0	0	0	0
5113 Other	4	4	15	36	39	42	53	62	72	73
5120 Taxes on specific goods and services	365	490	796	1 411	2 152	2 399	3 303	3 512	3 672	4 126
5121 Excises	90	75	221	448	530	618	685	744	804	698
Alcohol products	..	30	89	..	..	..	..	..	..	281
Soft drinks and mineral water	..	9	15	..	..	..	..	..	..	59
Cigarettes	..	24	71	..	..	..	..	..	..	195
Luxury goods and vehicles	..	11	46	..	..	..	..	..	..	163
Telecomunications	..	0	0	0	0	0	0	..	1	0
Pipeline tax	..	0	0	0	0	0	0	..	1	0
5122 Profits of fiscal monopolies	0	0	0	0	0	0	0	0	0	0
5123 Customs and import duties	227	217	547	923	1 152	1 156	1 261	1 352	1 357	2 026
5124 Taxes on exports	0	0	0	0	0	0	0	0	0	0
5125 Taxes on investment goods	0	0	0	0	0	0	0	0	0	0
5126 Taxes on specific services	8	23	29	39	470	625	1 358	1 417	1 511	1 402
Exit taxes	7	17	0	0	428	558	1 275	1 322	1 406	1 278
Public shows and events	1	2	3	5	6	8	8	8	7	8
Commercial, industrial and service patents	0	5	26	33	35	58	73	85	97	115
Construction contracts with the public sector	0	0	0	0	0	0	0	0	0	0
Disposal of livestock	0	0	0	1	1	1	1	1	1	1
Lotteries and gambling	0	0	0	0	0	0	0	0	0	0

Table 5.12. Ecuador *(cont.)*
Details of tax revenue / Ingresos tributarios detallados

Million USD

	1990	2000	2005	2009	2010	2011	2012	2013	2014	2015
5127 Other taxes on internat. trade and transactions	40	175	0	0	0	0	0	0	0	0
On capital movements	0	169	..	..	..	..	..	..	..	..
On purchase of foreign exchange	22	4	..	..	..	..	..	..	..	..
On credit operations in national currency	18	2	..	..	..	..	..	..	..	..
5128 Other taxes	0	0	0	0	0	0	0	0	0	0
5130 Unallocable between 5110 and 5120	0	0	0	0	0	0	0	0	0	0
5200 Taxes on use of goods and perform activities	8	13	69	127	168	191	220	245	260	265
5210 Recurrent taxes	8	13	69	127	168	191	220	245	260	265
5211 Paid by households: motor vehicles	2	0	0	0	0	0	0	0	0	0
5212 Paid by others: motor vehicles	5	11	69	127	168	188	209	231	248	245
Annual tax on motor vehicles	3	11	60	118	156	174	194	214	228	223
5213 Paid in respect of other goods	1	1	0	0	0	3	11	14	12	21
5220 Non-recurrent taxes	0	0	0	0	0	0	0	0	0	0
5300 Unallocable between 5100 and 5200	3	8	33	47	49	56	61	75	81	91
6000 Other taxes	**29**	**2**	**53**	**233**	**289**	**29**	**112**	**132**	**129**	**135**
6100 Paid solely by business	0	0	0	0	0	0	0	0	0	0
6200 Other	29	2	53	233	289	29	112	132	129	135

Note: Year ending 31st December.

The data are on a cash basis.

This edition includes for the first time local government tax revenues which affects headings 4000, 5000 and 6000 and their sub-headings.

Heading 1000: for this publication, it has been possible to allocate some revenue that was previously classified under 1300 (unallocable) in heading 1100 (of individuals) and 1200 (corporate).

Heading 2000: Social security data is recorded at the non-financial public sector level.

Heading 5212: In ECLAC data, the annual tax on motor vehicles is classified as a property tax (4000).

Source: Servicio de Rentas Internas (SRI) y Banco Central del Ecuador (Internal Revenue Service and Central Bank of Ecuador).

StatLink http://dx.doi.org/10.1787/888933463290

Table 5.13. El Salvador
Details of tax revenue / Ingresos tributarios detallados

Million USD

	1990	2000	2005	2009	2010	2011	2012	2013	2014	2015
Total tax revenue	**506**	**1 585**	**2 382**	**2 966**	**3 235**	**3 552**	**3 828**	**4 139**	**4 148**	**4 483**
1000 Taxes on income, profits and capital gains	**95**	**407**	**637**	**948**	**995**	**1 127**	**1 250**	**1 479**	**1 522**	**1 545**
1100 Of individuals	0	0	312	444	571	456	697	578	627	739
1110 On income and profits	..	..	312	444	571	456	697	578	627	739
1120 On capital gains	..	..	..	..	..	..	..	..	..	..
1200 Corporate	0	0	356	559	423	631	555	793	693	622
1210 On profits	..	..	356	559	423	631	555	793	693	622
1220 On capital gains	..	..	..	..	..	..	..	..	..	..
1300 Unallocable between 1100 and 1200	95	407	-31	-55	0	41	-2	108	201	183
Withholding income tax	95	429	0	0	55	107	66	135	204	213
Income tax refunds	0	-22	-31	-55	-55	-66	-68	-27	-3	-30
2000 Social security contributions	**67**	**263**	**282**	**358**	**369**	**382**	**404**	**425**	**445**	**488**
2100 Employees	..	75	76	96	99	100	106	112	117	130
2110 On a payroll basis	..	75	76	96	99	100	106	112	117	130
2120 On an income tax basis	..	0	0	0	0	0	0	0	0	0
2200 Employers	..	176	181	230	238	245	260	273	286	314
2210 On a payroll basis	..	176	181	230	238	245	260	273	286	314
2220 On an income tax basis	..	0	0	0	0	0	0	0	0	0
2300 Self-employed or non-employed	..	13	25	31	33	36	38	40	42	45
2310 On a payroll basis	..	13	25	31	33	36	38	40	42	45
2320 On an income tax basis	..	0	0	0	0	0	0	0	0	0
2400 Unallocable between 2100, 2200 and 2300	67	0	0	0	0	0	0	0	0	0
2410 On a payroll basis	67	..	..	..	..	..	..	..	..	..
2420 On an income tax basis	0	..	..	..	..	..	..	..	..	..
3000 Taxes on payroll and workforce	**0**	**0**	**0**	**0**	**0**	**0**	**0**	**0**	**0**	**0**
4000 Taxes on property	**26**	**12**	**16**	**13**	**16**	**16**	**20**	**21**	**24**	**107**
4100 Recurrent taxes on immovable property	0	0	0	0	0	0	0	0	0	0
4110 Households	..	..	..	..	..	..	..	..	..	..
4120 Others	..	..	..	..	..	..	..	..	..	..
4200 Recurrent taxes on net wealth	16	0	0	0	0	0	0	0	0	0
4210 Individual	16	..	..	..	..	..	..	..	..	..
4220 Corporate	0	..	..	..	..	..	..	..	..	..
4300 Estate, inheritance and gift taxes	0	0	0	0	0	0	0	0	0	0
4310 Estate and inheritance taxes	..	..	..	..	..	..	..	..	..	..
4320 Gift taxes	..	..	..	..	..	..	..	..	..	..
4400 Taxes on financial and capital transactions	10	12	16	13	16	16	20	21	24	107
Property transfers	..	..	..	..	..	..	..	..	..	20
Checks and electronic transfers of funds	..	..	..	..	..	..	..	..	..	55
Withholding for liquidity control	..	..	..	..	..	..	..	..	..	31
4500 Non-recurrent taxes	0	0	0	0	0	0	0	0	0	0
4510 On net wealth	..	..	..	..	..	..	..	..	..	..
4520 Other non-recurrent taxes	..	..	..	..	..	..	..	..	..	..
4600 Other recurrent taxes on property	0	0	0	0	0	0	0	0	0	0
5000 Taxes on goods and services	**259**	**903**	**1 447**	**1 646**	**1 855**	**2 027**	**2 155**	**2 213**	**2 158**	**2 266**
5100 Taxes on production, sale, transfer, etc	259	903	1 447	1 646	1 855	2 027	2 155	2 213	2 158	2 254
5110 General taxes	133	714	1 104	1 251	1 433	1 574	1 677	1 731	1 720	1 764
5111 Value added taxes	0	714	1 104	1 251	1 433	1 574	1 677	1 731	1 720	1 764
5112 Sales tax	0	0	0	0	0	0	0	0	0	0
5113 Other	133	0	0	0	0	0	0	0	0	0
5120 Taxes on specific goods and services	127	189	344	395	422	453	478	483	438	490
5121 Excises	65	49	162	202	218	238	262	249	234	285
Consumption of products	65	49	0	0	0	0	0	0	0	0
Alcoholic beverages	0	0	39	44	44	52	64	60	46	22
Cigarettes	0	0	23	31	31	38	40	27	22	29
Soft drinks	0	0	33	24	31	35	40	42	43	48
Beer	0	0	1	1	1	1	1	1	1	55
Weapons, ammunition and explosives	0	0	1	1	1	1	1	1	1	1
Ad-valorem on fuels	0	0	0	0	0	0	0	0	0	7
Special contribution- Sugar	0	0	0	34	35	35	36	36	37	1
Special contribution- Public transportation	0	0	66	68	69	69	71	72	74	40
Special contribution- FOVIAL	0	0	0	0	7	8	9	11	11	80
Special contribution- Public security	0	0	0	0	0	0	0	0	0	2
5122 Profits of fiscal monopolies	0	0	0	0	0	0	0	0	0	0
5123 Customs and import duties	61	141	181	138	148	167	180	199	181	194
5124 Taxes on exports	0	0	0	0	0	0	0	0	0	0
5125 Taxes on investment goods	0	0	0	0	0	0	0	0	0	0
5126 Taxes on specific services	0	0	0	55	56	48	36	34	22	11
5127 Other taxes on internat. trade and transactions	0	0	0	0	0	0	0	0	0	0

Table 5.13. El Salvador *(cont.)*

Details of tax revenue / Ingresos tributarios detallados

Million USD

	1990	2000	2005	2009	2010	2011	2012	2013	2014	2015
5128 Other taxes	0	0	0	0	0	0	0	0	0	0
5130 Unallocable between 5110 and 5120	0	0	0	0	0	0	0	0	0	0
5200 Taxes on use of goods and perform activities	0	0	0	0	0	0	0	0	0	12
5210 Recurrent taxes	..	..	..	..	..	..	..	..	..	0
5211 Paid by households: motor vehicles	..	..	..	..	..	..	..	..	..	..
5212 Paid by others: motor vehicles	..	..	..	..	..	..	..	..	..	..
5213 Paid in respect of other goods	..	..	..	..	..	..	..	..	..	..
5220 Non-recurrent taxes	..	..	..	..	..	..	..	..	..	12
5300 Unallocable between 5100 and 5200	0	0	0	0	0	0	0	0	0	0
6000 Other taxes	**58**	**0**	**0**	**0**	**0**	**0**	**0**	**0**	**0**	**77**
6100 Paid solely by business	0	0	..	..	..	..	..	..	..	0
6200 Other	58	0	..	..	..	..	..	..	..	77

Note: Year ending 31st December.

The data are on a cash basis.

Before 2015 the figures exclude local government tax revenues as the data are not available. For 2015 local government tax revenues are classified under 6200.

Heading 1000: For 2002 and from 2006 onwards sub-headings 1100 and 1200 are presented on a gross basis i.e. not including income tax refunds. The latter are classified under heading 1300.

Heading 2000: Corresponds to social security contributions paid to the Salvadoran Institute of Social Security and excludes payments to privately managed pension funds (AFPs).

Heading 5121: Special contributions to public security have been included for 2015.

Source: Dirección General de Tesorería, Ministerio de Hacienda. Banco Central de Reserva y el Instituto Salvadoreño del Seguro Social (General Treasury Directorate, Ministry of Finance, Central Reserve Bank and the Salvadoran Social Security Institute).

StatLink http://dx.doi.org/10.1787/888933463307

Table 5.14. Guatemala

Details of tax revenue / Ingresos tributarios detallados

Million GTQ

	1990	2000	2005	2009	2010	2011	2012	2013	2014	2015
Total tax revenue	**2 801**	**16 531**	**27 187**	**37 661**	**41 189**	**47 387**	**50 904**	**55 006**	**57 523**	**60 337**
1000 Taxes on income, profits and capital gains	**507**	**3 295**	**6 049**	**9 706**	**10 319**	**13 100**	**13 907**	**16 094**	**17 753**	**17 534**
1100 Of individuals	25	143	645	1 060	1 225	1 462	1 477	1 246	1 784	1 826
1110 On income and profits	25	143	645	1 060	1 225	1 462	1 477	1 246	1 784	1 826
Personal income tax	25	137	642	1 060	1 225	1 462	1 476	1 246	1 784	1 826
Income from financial products	0	6	4	0	0	0	1	0	0	0
1120 On capital gains	..	..	..	..	..	..	..	..	..	..
1200 Corporate	482	3 149	3 756	6 141	6 520	9 013	9 581	11 584	12 426	11 802
1210 On profits	482	3 149	3 756	6 141	6 520	9 013	9 581	11 584	12 426	11 802
Corporate income tax	482	1 610	3 495	5 768	6 132	8 601	9 118	11 529	12 423	11 801
Income from financial products	0	248	235	371	386	403	463	52	0	0
Commercial and agricultural enterprises	0	1 291	26	2	2	8	0	3	3	0
1220 On capital gains	..	..	..	..	..	..	..	..	..	..
1300 Unallocable between 1100 and 1200	0	2	1 647	2 505	2 574	2 625	2 849	3 263	3 543	3 907
Extraordinary and temporary solidarity tax in support of peace agreements	..	0	1 647	677	44	54	4	21	9	1
Solidarity tax	..	0	0	1 829	2 530	2 571	2 845	3 243	3 534	3 906
Extraordinary and temporary solidarity tax	..	2	0	0	0	0	0	0	0	0
2000 Social security contributions	**436**	**2 569**	**4 072**	**5 801**	**6 408**	**7 125**	**7 858**	**8 617**	**8 157**	**10 034**
2100 Employees	..	..	..	..	..	..	..	..	..	..
2110 On a payroll basis	..	..	..	..	..	..	..	..	..	..
2120 On an income tax basis	..	..	..	..	..	..	..	..	..	..
2200 Employers	..	..	..	..	..	..	..	..	..	..
2210 On a payroll basis	..	..	..	..	..	..	..	..	..	..
2220 On an income tax basis	..	..	..	..	..	..	..	..	..	..
2300 Self-employed or non-employed	..	..	..	..	..	..	..	..	..	..
2310 On a payroll basis	..	..	..	..	..	..	..	..	..	..
2320 On an income tax basis	..	..	..	..	..	..	..	..	..	..
2400 Unallocable between 2100, 2200 and 2300	436	2 569	4 072	5 801	6 408	7 125	7 858	8 617	8 157	10 034
2410 On a payroll basis	436	2 569	4 072	5 801	6 408	7 125	7 858	8 617	8 157	10 034
2420 On an income tax basis	0	0	0	0	0	0	0	0	0	0
3000 Taxes on payroll and workforce	**0**	**0**	**0**	**0**	**0**	**0**	**0**	**0**	**0**	**0**
4000 Taxes on property	**45**	**165**	**350**	**578**	**631**	**648**	**743**	**791**	**843**	**713**
4100 Recurrent taxes on immovable property	0	153	341	569	621	635	735	780	829	693
4110 Households	..	0	0	0	0	0	0	0	0	0
4120 Others	..	153	341	569	621	635	735	780	829	693
Property tax	..	6	1	1	1	1	1	1	1	1
Property tax (municipal)	..	147	341	568	620	634	734	779	827	692
4200 Recurrent taxes on net wealth	0	0	0	0	0	0	0	0	0	0
4210 Individual	..	..	..	..	..	..	..	..	..	..
4220 Corporate	..	..	..	..	..	..	..	..	..	..
4300 Estate, inheritance and gift taxes	0	0	0	0	0	0	0	0	0	0
4310 Estate and inheritance taxes	..	..	..	..	..	..	..	..	..	..
4320 Gift taxes	..	..	..	..	..	..	..	..	..	..
4400 Taxes on financial and capital transactions	45	12	8	9	10	13	8	10	15	20
4500 Non-recurrent taxes	0	0	0	0	0	0	0	0	0	0
4510 On net wealth	..	..	..	..	..	..	..	..	..	..
4520 Other non-recurrent taxes	..	..	..	..	..	..	..	..	..	..
4600 Other recurrent taxes on property	0	0	0	0	0	0	0	0	0	0
5000 Taxes on goods and services	**1 709**	**10 317**	**16 402**	**20 980**	**23 259**	**25 876**	**27 518**	**29 075**	**30 411**	**31 719**
5100 Taxes on production, sale, transfer, etc	1 681	10 131	16 083	20 513	22 754	25 317	26 614	27 545	29 092	30 088
5110 General taxes	762	6 259	10 753	15 015	16 980	19 472	20 913	21 874	23 153	23 271
5111 Value added taxes	762	6 259	10 753	15 015	16 980	19 472	20 913	21 874	23 153	23 271
5112 Sales tax	0	0	0	0	0	0	0	0	0	0
5113 Other	0	0	0	0	0	0	0	0	0	0
5120 Taxes on specific goods and services	919	3 872	5 330	5 497	5 773	5 845	5 701	5 671	5 939	6 816
5121 Excises	258	1 797	1 262	3 058	3 101	3 013	3 072	3 372	3 552	4 289
Tobacco and derivatives	76	205	312	340	347	259	312	385	405	369
Beer	0	97	122	143	159	176	191	217	243	293
Alcoholic beverages	0	77	76	90	98	101	100	90	56	88
Soft drinks	0	15	172	200	220	245	263	282	300	328
Other beverages	77	12	2	1	2	2	1	1	3	0
Cement	0	0	93	99	99	104	102	100	101	312
Oil and derivatives	105	1 389	485	2 184	2 179	2 125	2 103	2 297	2 445	2 899
5122 Profits of fiscal monopolies	0	0	0	0	0	0	0	0	0	0
5123 Customs and import duties	506	1 806	3 715	2 139	2 368	2 533	2 311	1 965	2 044	2 157
5124 Taxes on exports	0	0	0	0	0	0	0	0	0	0
5125 Taxes on investment goods	0	0	0	0	0	0	0	0	0	0

Table 5.14. Guatemala (cont.)
Details of tax revenue / Ingresos tributarios detallados

Million GTQ

	1990	2000	2005	2009	2010	2011	2012	2013	2014	2015
5126 Taxes on specific services	155	269	354	301	304	300	318	334	343	370
5127 Other taxes on internat. trade and transactions	0	0	0	0	0	0	0	0	0	0
5128 Other taxes	0	0	0	0	0	0	0	0	0	0
5130 Unallocable between 5110 and 5120	0	0	0	0	0	0	0	0	0	0
5200 Taxes on use of goods and perform activities	28	186	319	468	505	558	904	1 530	1 320	1 631
5210 Recurrent taxes	28	186	319	468	505	558	904	1 530	1 320	1 631
5211 Paid by households: motor vehicles	0	0	0	0	0	0	331	694	747	717
5212 Paid by others: motor vehicles	28	186	319	468	505	558	573	836	572	914
5213 Paid in respect of other goods	0	0	0	0	0	0	0	0	0	0
5220 Non-recurrent taxes	0	0	0	0	0	0	0	0	0	0
5300 Unallocable between 5100 and 5200	0	0	0	0	0	0	0	0	0	0
6000 Other taxes	**104**	**186**	**315**	**596**	**572**	**639**	**878**	**430**	**359**	**337**
6100 Paid solely by business	0	0	0	0	0	0	0	0	0	0
6200 Other	104	186	315	596	572	639	878	430	359	337
Revenue stamps and stamped paper	104	182	313	595	572	638	877	430	359	336
Other indirect taxes	0	4	1	1	1	1	1	1	0	0

Note: Year ending 31st December.

The data are on a cash basis.

The figures exclude some local government tax revenues as the data are not available. Revenues from the municipal property tax (IUSI) are included.

Heading 2000: Corresponds to social security contributions paid to the Guatemalan Social Security Institute (IGSS) and payments by public employees to the government's pension fund.

Headings 4120 and 4400: For years prior to 2000, the property tax under heading 4120 is included in the total under heading 4400.

Heading 5121: Up to 1999, "Other beverages" contains all alcoholic and non-alcoholic beverages.

Source: Dirección de Análisis de Política Fiscal del Ministerio de Hacienda, Instituto Guatemalteco del Seguro Social y Superintendencia de la Administración Tributaria (Fiscal Policy Analysis Directorate at the Ministry of Finance, the Guatemalan Institute of Social Security and the Tax Administration Superintendency).

StatLink http://dx.doi.org/10.1787/888933463316

Table 5.15. Honduras
Details of tax revenue / Ingresos tributarios detallados

Million HNL

	1990	2000	2005	2009	2010	2011	2012	2013	2014	2015
Total tax revenue	**2 122**	**17 307**	**32 973**	**49 041**	**54 060**	**58 763**	**66 357**	**71 653**	**83 702**	**95 724**
1000 Taxes on income, profits and capital gains	**431**	**2 985**	**7 498**	**12 658**	**13 972**	**16 979**	**17 540**	**19 611**	**21 736**	**25 178**
1100 Of individuals	157	991	2 312	4 067	4 528	5 232	5 745	6 478	7 312	8 451
1110 On income and profits	157	991	2 312	4 067	4 528	5 232	5 745	6 478	7 312	8 451
1120 On capital gains	..	..	..	..	..	..	..	..	..	..
1200 Corporate	274	1 916	4 725	8 424	8 705	11 437	11 564	12 888	14 034	16 392
1210 On profits	274	1 916	4 725	8 424	8 705	11 437	11 564	12 888	14 034	16 392
Corporate income tax	274	1 916	4 121	7 230	7 400	9 447	10 088	11 523	12 756	14 743
Income tax surcharge	0	0	604	1 194	1 305	1 990	1 468	1 352	1 265	1 637
Special contribution of the cooperative sector	0	0	0	0	0	0	8	14	13	13
1220 On capital gains	..	..	..	..	..	..	..	..	..	..
1300 Unallocable between 1100 and 1200	0	78	461	167	740	310	230	245	389	334
Tax on net assets	..	78	144	167	359	310	230	245	389	334
Revaluation of assets	..	0	316	0	381	0	0	0	0	0
2000 Social security contributions	**179**	**1 727**	**4 416**	**8 122**	**8 671**	**6 955**	**10 854**	**12 529**	**12 467**	**13 524**
2100 Employees	..	..	..	..	..	..	..	..	..	..
2110 On a payroll basis	..	..	..	..	..	..	..	..	..	..
2120 On an income tax basis	..	..	..	..	..	..	..	..	..	..
2200 Employers	..	..	..	..	..	..	..	..	..	..
2210 On a payroll basis	..	..	..	..	..	..	..	..	..	..
2220 On an income tax basis	..	..	..	..	..	..	..	..	..	..
2300 Self-employed or non-employed	..	..	..	..	..	..	..	..	..	..
2310 On a payroll basis	..	..	..	..	..	..	..	..	..	..
2320 On an income tax basis	..	..	..	..	..	..	..	..	..	..
2400 Unallocable between 2100, 2200 and 2300	179	1 727	4 416	8 122	8 671	6 955	10 854	12 529	12 467	13 524
2410 On a payroll basis	179	1 727	4 416	8 122	8 671	6 955	10 854	12 529	12 467	13 524
2420 On an income tax basis	0	0	0	0	0	0	0	0	0	0
3000 Taxes on payroll and workforce	**0**	**0**	**0**	**0**	**0**	**0**	**0**	**0**	**0**	**0**
4000 Taxes on property	**16**	**189**	**170**	**224**	**254**	**290**	**986**	**1 201**	**1 911**	**2 301**
4100 Recurrent taxes on immovable property	0	0	0	0	0	0	0	0	0	0
4110 Households	..	..	..	..	..	..	..	..	..	..
4120 Others	..	..	..	..	..	..	..	..	..	..
4200 Recurrent taxes on net wealth	0	0	0	0	0	0	0	0	0	0
4210 Individual	..	..	..	..	..	..	..	..	..	..
4220 Corporate	..	..	..	..	..	..	..	..	..	..
4300 Estate, inheritance and gift taxes	0	0	0	0	0	0	0	0	0	0
4310 Estate and inheritance taxes	..	..	..	..	..	..	..	..	..	..
4320 Gift taxes	..	..	..	..	..	..	..	..	..	..
4400 Taxes on financial and capital transactions	0	0	0	0	0	0	659	903	1 636	2 003
4500 Non-recurrent taxes	0	0	0	0	0	0	0	0	0	0
4510 On net wealth	..	..	..	..	..	..	..	..	..	..
4520 Other non-recurrent taxes	..	..	..	..	..	..	..	..	..	..
4600 Other recurrent taxes on property	16	189	170	224	254	290	327	298	275	299
5000 Taxes on goods and services	**1 405**	**11 445**	**19 032**	**26 141**	**28 937**	**32 266**	**34 764**	**35 908**	**44 945**	**52 217**
5100 Taxes on production, sale, transfer, etc	1 405	11 445	19 032	26 141	28 937	32 266	34 764	35 908	44 945	52 217
5110 General taxes	344	5 146	9 565	14 396	16 050	18 967	20 150	20 637	27 735	32 273
5111 Value added taxes	344	5 146	9 565	14 396	16 050	18 967	20 150	20 637	27 735	32 273
5112 Sales tax	0	0	0	0	0	0	0	0	0	0
5113 Other	0	0	0	0	0	0	0	0	0	0
5120 Taxes on specific goods and services	1 061	6 299	9 468	11 746	12 887	13 299	14 614	15 270	17 211	19 944
5121 Excises	256	3 600	6 322	8 022	8 458	8 670	9 490	10 119	11 588	13 349
Beer	71	376	338	344	376	466	503	503	525	668
Soft drinks	25	240	268	415	514	632	675	725	754	838
Liquors	32	48	69	76	121	164	165	165	188	195
Petroleum products	43	347	0	0	0	0	0	0	0	0
Cigarettes	57	369	437	646	607	660	633	495	610	598
Fuel tax	0	1 962	4 916	6 032	6 288	6 177	6 868	7 613	8 874	10 317
Other	28	258	295	509	551	572	646	618	638	735
5122 Profits of fiscal monopolies	0	0	0	0	0	0	0	0	0	0
5123 Customs and import duties	498	2 083	2 174	2 065	2 505	2 626	2 933	2 651	2 974	3 541
Petroleum	0	297	0	0	0	0	0	0	0	0
Other	498	1 786	2 174	2 065	2 505	2 626	2 933	2 651	2 974	3 541
5124 Taxes on exports	217	6	0	0	0	4	62	101	107	84
Bananas	39	5	..	..	..	0	0	0	0	0
Coffee	1	0	..	..	..	0	0	0	0	0
Temporary export tax	163	0	..	..	..	0	0	0	0	0
Special contribution of the mining sector	0	0	..	..	..	4	62	101	107	84
5125 Taxes on investment goods	0	0	0	0	0	0	0	0	0	0

Table 5.15. Honduras (*cont.*)
Details of tax revenue / Ingresos tributarios detallados

Million HNL

	1990	2000	2005	2009	2010	2011	2012	2013	2014	2015
5126 Taxes on specific services	0	0	0	0	0	16	92	87	90	91
Special contribution of mobile services	..	..	..	..	..	12	75	66	67	67
Special contribution of the food and services sector	..	..	..	..	..	3	14	18	20	21
Special contribution of casino games and slot machines	..	..	..	..	..	1	3	3	3	3
5127 Other taxes on internat. trade and transactions	0	0	0	0	0	0	0	0	0	0
5128 Other taxes	90	610	971	1 659	1 924	1 983	2 038	2 312	2 451	2 880
5130 Unallocable between 5110 and 5120	0	0	0	0	0	0	0	0	0	0
5200 Taxes on use of goods and perform activities	0	0	0	0	0	0	0	0	0	0
5210 Recurrent taxes	..	..	..	..	..	..	..	..	..	..
5211 Paid by households: motor vehicles	..	..	..	..	..	..	..	..	..	..
5212 Paid by others: motor vehicles	..	..	..	..	..	..	..	..	..	..
5213 Paid in respect of other goods	..	..	..	..	..	..	..	..	..	..
5220 Non-recurrent taxes	..	..	..	..	..	..	..	..	..	..
5300 Unallocable between 5100 and 5200	0	0	0	0	0	0	0	0	0	0
6000 Other taxes	**91**	**962**	**1 858**	**1 897**	**2 225**	**2 274**	**2 214**	**2 404**	**2 644**	**2 504**
6100 Paid solely by business	0	0	0	0	0	0	0	0	0	0
6200 Other	91	962	1 858	1 897	2 225	2 274	2 214	2 404	2 644	2 504

Note: Year ending 31st December.

The data are on a cash basis.

This edition includes for the first time local government tax revenues which affects headings 6000 and 6200.

Headings 1210, 4400, 5124 and 5126: For this publication, taxes from "tasa de seguridad poblacional" have been included. This includes: special contribution of the cooperative sector (1210), special contribution of the financial system (4400), special contribution of the mining sector (5124), special contribution of mobile services (5126), special contribution of the food and services sector (5126) and special contribution of casino games and slot machines (5126). These data were not available in the previous editions.

Heading 1300: In ECLAC data, the tax on net assets is classified as a property tax (4000).

Source: Secretaria de Finanzas (Ministry of Finance).

StatLink http://dx.doi.org/10.1787/888933463322

Table 5.16. Jamaica
Details of tax revenue / Ingresos tributarios detallados

Million JAM

	1990	2000	2005	2009	2010	2011	2012	2013	2014	2015
Total tax revenue	**7 748**	**87 713**	**163 291**	**264 936**	**287 139**	**303 983**	**322 299**	**356 956**	**380 942**	**427 404**
1000 Taxes on income, profits and capital gains	**3 944**	**39 277**	**69 894**	**124 475**	**118 708**	**122 752**	**126 441**	**129 951**	**134 083**	**149 460**
1100 Of individuals	1 687	17 441	36 043	62 043	54 798	62 792	64 315	66 282	70 867	74 537
1110 On income and profits	1 687	17 441	36 043	62 043	54 798	62 792	64 315	66 282	70 867	74 537
PAYE	1 489	16 515	34 223	58 577	50 828	58 851	60 637	62 172	66 645	70 075
Other individuals	198	926	1 820	3 466	3 969	3 940	3 678	4 111	4 223	4 463
1120 On capital gains	..	..	..	..	..	..	..	..	..	..
1200 Corporate	1 280	7 627	13 134	25 463	33 091	31 858	32 706	34 539	31 991	39 668
1210 On profits	1 280	7 627	13 134	25 463	33 091	31 858	32 706	34 539	31 991	39 668
Bauxite/alumina	134	430	446	19	866	0	1	0	0	0
Other companies	1 146	7 197	12 688	25 443	32 224	31 857	32 705	34 539	31 991	39 668
1220 On capital gains	..	..	..	..	..	..	..	..	..	..
1300 Unallocable between 1100 and 1200	977	14 209	20 718	36 969	30 820	28 103	29 419	29 130	31 224	35 254
Tax on dividends	68	854	248	230	1 059	1 028	1 080	1 175	1 904	980
Tax on interests	605	9 535	13 277	24 552	16 970	12 376	13 437	10 706	10 103	13 518
Education tax	305	3 821	7 193	12 187	12 792	14 699	14 903	17 249	19 217	20 756
2000 Social security contributions	**0**	**0**	**4 924**	**7 410**	**8 199**	**11 562**	**11 418**	**13 875**	**15 865**	**16 449**
2100 Employees	..	..	..	..	..	..	..	..	..	..
2110 On a payroll basis	..	..	..	..	..	..	..	..	..	..
2120 On an income tax basis	..	..	..	..	..	..	..	..	..	..
2200 Employers	..	..	..	..	..	..	..	..	..	..
2210 On a payroll basis	..	..	..	..	..	..	..	..	..	..
2220 On an income tax basis	..	..	..	..	..	..	..	..	..	..
2300 Self-employed or non-employed	..	..	..	..	..	..	..	..	..	..
2310 On a payroll basis	..	..	..	..	..	..	..	..	..	..
2320 On an income tax basis	..	..	..	..	..	..	..	..	..	..
2400 Unallocable between 2100, 2200 and 2300	..	..	4 924	7 410	8 199	11 562	11 418	13 875	15 865	16 449
National Insurance Scheme (NIS) contributions	..	..	4 924	7 410	8 199	11 562	11 418	13 875	15 865	16 449
2410 On a payroll basis	..	..	..	..	..	..	..	..	..	..
2420 On an income tax basis	..	..	..	..	..	..	..	..	..	..
3000 Taxes on payroll and workforce	**0**	**0**	**0**	**0**	**0**	**0**	**0**	**0**	**0**	**0**
4000 Taxes on property	**67**	**639**	**1 592**	**1 787**	**2 600**	**2 633**	**2 427**	**5 595**	**6 138**	**7 271**
4100 Recurrent taxes on immovable property	67	639	1 592	1 787	2 600	2 633	2 427	5 595	6 138	7 271
4110 Households	67	639	1 592	1 787	2 600	2 633	2 427	5 595	6 138	7 271
Property tax	67	0	0	0	0	0	0	0	0	0
Property tax (municipal)	0	639	1 592	1 787	2 600	2 633	2 427	5 595	6 138	7 271
4120 Others	0	0	0	0	0	0	0	0	0	0
4200 Recurrent taxes on net wealth	0	0	0	0	0	0	0	0	0	0
4210 Individual	..	..	..	..	..	..	..	..	..	..
4220 Corporate	..	..	..	..	..	..	..	..	..	..
4300 Estate, inheritance and gift taxes	0	0	0	0	0	0	0	0	0	0
4310 Estate and inheritance taxes	..	..	..	..	..	..	..	..	..	..
4320 Gift taxes	..	..	..	..	..	..	..	..	..	..
4400 Taxes on financial and capital transactions	0	0	0	0	0	0	0	0	0	0
4500 Non-recurrent taxes	0	0	0	0	0	0	0	0	0	0
4510 On net wealth	..	..	..	..	..	..	..	..	..	..
4520 Other non-recurrent taxes	..	..	..	..	..	..	..	..	..	..
4600 Other recurrent taxes on property	0	0	0	0	0	0	0	0	0	0
5000 Taxes on goods and services	**3 294**	**44 638**	**78 147**	**121 928**	**148 894**	**156 308**	**171 332**	**194 929**	**211 819**	**240 773**
5100 Taxes on production, sale, transfer, etc	3 230	43 838	77 036	119 749	146 850	154 208	168 940	192 166	208 885	237 566
5110 General taxes	4	13 059	27 274	40 825	45 152	47 788	50 963	57 474	62 023	70 648
5111 Value added taxes	0	13 059	27 274	40 825	45 152	47 788	50 963	57 474	62 023	70 523
5112 Sales tax	4	0	0	0	0	0	0	0	0	0
Sales tax on used cars	4	0	0	0	0	0	0	0	0	0
5113 Other	0	0	0	0	0	0	0	0	0	125
Environmental levy	0	0	0	0	0	0	0	0	0	125
5120 Taxes on specific goods and services	3 226	30 779	49 762	78 925	101 698	106 419	117 977	134 692	146 862	166 918
5121 Excises	1 158	5 344	3 536	5 272	9 168	9 403	11 216	12 149	10 991	13 104
Excise duty	44	0	0	0	0	0	0	0	0	0
Special consumption tax	1 115	5 344	3 536	5 272	9 168	9 403	11 216	12 149	10 991	13 104
5122 Profits of fiscal monopolies	0	0	0	0	0	0	0	0	0	0
5123 Customs and import duties	1 545	22 932	43 260	70 608	87 510	90 180	97 497	103 747	115 279	132 431
Custom duty	782	8 498	14 999	20 048	19 959	20 638	22 905	25 938	26 281	28 960
Stamp duty	470	731	1 083	1 284	1 352	1 444	1 635	1 945	1 910	1 957
General consumption tax (imports)	293	9 297	18 328	27 533	37 255	40 932	44 069	50 186	56 733	65 334
Special consumption tax (imports)	0	4 407	8 851	21 744	28 944	27 167	28 889	25 678	30 356	36 180
5124 Taxes on exports	0	0	0	0	0	0	0	0	0	0
5125 Taxes on investment goods	0	0	0	0	0	0	0	0	0	0

Table 5.16. Jamaica (*cont.*)
Details of tax revenue / Ingresos tributarios detallados

Million JAM

	1990	2000	2005	2009	2010	2011	2012	2013	2014	2015
5126 Taxes on specific services	523	2 503	2 966	3 044	5 020	6 837	9 264	18 796	20 592	21 384
Bank and trust	204	0	0	0	0	0	0	0	0	0
Entertainment tax	11	0	0	0	0	0	0	0	0	0
Betting, gaming and lottery	50	504	1 052	1 390	1 508	1 586	1 893	2 225	2 661	2 797
Accommodation tax	87	0	0	0	0	0	265	1 636	1 900	2 050
Telephone call tax	86	0	0	0	0	0	2 342	6 405	6 687	6 559
Travel tax	86	1 999	1 914	1 654	3 512	5 251	4 763	8 531	9 344	9 979
5127 Other taxes on internat. trade and transactions	0	0	0	0	0	0	0	0	0	0
5128 Other taxes	0	0	0	0	0	0	0	0	0	0
5130 Unallocable between 5110 and 5120	0	0	0	0	0	0	0	0	0	0
5200 Taxes on use of goods and perform activities	64	800	1 111	2 179	2 045	2 100	2 393	2 763	2 934	3 206
5210 Recurrent taxes	64	800	1 111	2 179	2 045	2 100	2 393	2 763	2 934	3 206
5211 Paid by households: motor vehicles	47	751	935	1 734	1 775	1 748	2 043	2 493	2 666	2 901
5212 Paid by others: motor vehicles	0	0	0	0	0	0	0	0	0	0
5213 Paid in respect of other goods	17	49	176	445	270	352	350	270	268	305
5220 Non-recurrent taxes	0	0	0	0	0	0	0	0	0	0
5300 Unallocable between 5100 and 5200	0	0	0	0	0	0	0	0	0	0
6000 Other taxes	**444**	**3 159**	**8 733**	**9 336**	**8 738**	**10 729**	**10 680**	**12 606**	**13 037**	**13 450**
6100 Paid solely by business	0	0	0	0	0	0	0	0	0	0
6200 Other	444	3 159	8 733	9 336	8 738	10 729	10 680	12 606	13 037	13 450
Environmental levy	0	0	0	2 147	2 002	2 217	2 103	2 159	2 200	2 240
Contractors levy	16	266	475	812	748	1 139	1 198	1 091	909	994
Stamp duty (domestic)	428	2 893	8 259	6 378	5 987	7 372	7 380	9 356	9 928	10 217

Note: Data collected by fiscal year (1st April - 31st March) for 1990-2003, then by calendar year (year ending 31st December).

The data are on a cash basis.

The figures exclude local government tax revenues as the data are not available.

Heading 5113: For this publication, the environmental levy on consumption has been added. These data were not available in the previous editions.

Heading 6200: The data for the environmental levy are estimated for 2014 and 2015.

Source: Ministry of Finance and Planning.

StatLink http://dx.doi.org/10.1787/888933463333

Table 5.17. Mexico / México
Details of tax revenue / Ingresos tributarios detallados

Million MXN

	1990	2000	2005	2009	2010	2011	2012	2013	2014	2015
Total tax revenue	**102 005**	**833 275**	**1 192 089**	**1 639 243**	**1 872 613**	**2 038 462**	**2 171 389**	**2 349 963**	**2 607 696**	**2 962 235**
1000 Taxes on income, profits and capital gains	**34 673**	**276 548**	**402 036**	**591 942**	**683 604**	**772 704**	**803 071**	**957 213**	**979 251**	**1 230 555**
1100 Of individuals	..	..	195 869	280 230	313 473	352 386	397 701	425 621	514 208	609 384
Tax on income of individuals	..	..	195 869	280 230	313 473	352 386	397 701	425 621	514 208	609 384
1110 On income and profits	..	..	..	..	..	..	..	..	..	..
1120 On capital gains	..	..	..	..	..	..	..	..	..	..
1200 Corporate	..	..	135 840	191 685	246 745	303 176	288 360	392 199	441 317	592 443
Tax on income of corporations	..	..	135 840	191 685	246 745	303 176	288 360	392 199	441 317	592 443
1210 On profits	..	..	..	..	..	..	..	..	..	..
1220 On capital gains	..	..	..	..	..	..	..	..	..	..
1300 Unallocable between 1100 and 1200	34 673	276 548	70 327	120 027	123 386	117 143	117 010	139 393	23 726	28 728
Tax on income of other individuals and corporations	..	244 841	40 780	64 816	66 937	66 004	74 042	89 028	31 076	36 268
Tax on asset	..	13 913	12 033	-2 540	-624	-1 120	-1 192	-1 325	-735	-502
Credit on salary	..	17 794	17 514	12 113	9 708	2 076	1 387	1 274	2 423	993
Oil yields tax	..	0	0	921	2 296	3 019	573	3 210	4 669	0
IETU	..	0	0	44 718	45 069	47 165	42 199	47 205	-13 707	-11 777
Imposed by Activity Exploration and extraction of hydrocarbon	..	0	0	0	0	0	0	0	0	3 746
2000 Social security contributions	**17 165**	**167 292**	**261 673**	**346 031**	**378 006**	**411 289**	**454 778**	**490 918**	**538 213**	**588 280**
2100 Employees	..	..	..	..	..	..	..	..	..	..
2110 On a payroll basis	..	..	..	..	..	..	..	..	..	..
2120 On an income tax basis	..	..	..	..	..	..	..	..	..	..
2200 Employers	..	..	..	..	..	..	..	..	..	..
2210 On a payroll basis	..	..	..	..	..	..	..	..	..	..
2220 On an income tax basis	..	..	..	..	..	..	..	..	..	..
2300 Self-employed or non-employed	..	..	..	..	..	..	..	..	..	..
2310 On a payroll basis	..	..	..	..	..	..	..	..	..	..
2320 On an income tax basis	..	..	..	..	..	..	..	..	..	..
2400 Unallocable between 2100, 2200 and 2300	17 165	167 292	261 673	346 031	378 006	411 289	454 778	490 918	538 213	588 280
2410 On a payroll basis	..	167 292	261 673	346 031	378 006	411 289	454 778	490 918	538 213	588 280
2420 On an income tax basis	..	0	0	0	0	0	0	0	0	0
3000 Taxes on payroll and workforce	**1 797**	**11 217**	**20 461**	**31 965**	**36 911**	**41 980**	**48 033**	**53 042**	**64 713**	**0**
Substitute tax on salary	..	0	0	0	0	0	0	0	0	..
Payroll tax	..	11 101	15 746	23 530	27 813	31 817	35 480	41 184	64 581	..
Tax on remuneration to the personal work	..	65	4 562	8 180	8 841	9 990	12 333	11 645	0	..
Tax on professions and fees	..	36	53	70	71	58	48	50	51	..
Tax on operations by contract	..	15	100	186	186	116	173	163	81	..
4000 Taxes on property	**1 914**	**13 964**	**26 796**	**35 484**	**38 955**	**41 186**	**45 186**	**46 238**	**54 920**	**0**
4100 Recurrent taxes on immovable property	1 036	9 948	16 641	22 862	25 724	28 728	31 544	31 338	37 693	..
4110 Households	0	0	0	0	0	0	0	0	0	..
4120 Others	1 036	9 948	16 641	22 862	25 724	28 728	31 544	31 338	37 693	..
Property tax	..	9 948	16 641	22 862	25 724	28 728	31 544	31 338	37 693	..
4200 Recurrent taxes on net wealth	0	0	0	0	0	0	0	0	0	..
4210 Individual	..	..	..	..	..	..	..	..	..	..
4220 Corporate	..	..	..	..	..	..	..	..	..	..
4300 Estate, inheritance and gift taxes	8	0	0	0	0	0	0	0	0	..
4310 Estate and inheritance taxes	8	..	..	..	..	..	..	..	..	..
4320 Gift taxes	0	..	..	..	..	..	..	..	..	..
4400 Taxes on financial and capital transactions	870	4 017	10 155	12 622	13 231	12 458	13 642	14 900	17 227	..
Alienation of immovable property	..	1 763	984	1 163	1 122	1 379	1 341	1 271	1 308	..
Transfer of ownership of real estate	..	2 236	5 528	5 005	5 027	3 923	4 575	4 518	5 008	..
Purchasing property	..	18	3 643	6 454	7 082	7 157	7 725	9 110	10 911	..
4500 Non-recurrent taxes	0	0	0	0	0	0	0	0	0	..
4510 On net wealth	..	..	..	..	..	..	..	..	..	..
4520 Other non-recurrent taxes	..	..	..	..	..	..	..	..	..	..
4600 Other recurrent taxes on property	0	0	0	0	0	0	0	0	0	..
5000 Taxes on goods and services	**44 837**	**356 603**	**469 430**	**606 742**	**707 739**	**738 891**	**783 241**	**761 349**	**933 832**	**1 116 021**
5100 Taxes on production, sale, transfer, etc	44 171	310 325	403 158	529 540	630 129	658 962	720 052	695 675	854 189	1 115 520
5110 General taxes	26 635	189 606	318 432	407 795	504 509	537 143	579 988	556 794	667 085	707 213
5111 Value added taxes	26 635	189 606	318 432	407 795	504 509	537 143	579 988	556 794	667 085	707 213
5112 Sales tax	0	0	0	0	0	0	0	0	0	0
5113 Other	0	0	0	0	0	0	0	0	0	0
5120 Taxes on specific goods and services	17 519	120 720	84 726	121 745	125 620	121 819	140 064	138 881	187 104	408 307
5121 Excises	10 072	86 163	55 286	69 770	86 098	94 623	98 490	104 111	155 764	361 538
Special tax on production and services	..	81 544	49 627	65 708	81 427	89 544	92 620	97 860	149 337	354 294
Tax on new automobiles	..	4 619	5 659	4 063	4 671	5 079	5 870	6 252	6 427	7 244
Tax on luxury goods and services	..	0	0	0	0	0	0	0	0	0
5122 Profits of fiscal monopolies	0	0	0	0	0	0	0	0	0	0

Table 5.17. Mexico / México (cont.)
Details of tax revenue / Ingresos tributarios detallados

Million MXN

	1990	2000	2005	2009	2010	2011	2012	2013	2014	2015
5123 Customs and import duties	6 998	33 285	27 512	31 732	26 602	29 946	31 161	32 324	36 841	45 361
Step customs officer	..	423	692	1 535	2 071	3 065	3 255	3 065	2 913	1 265
Import taxes	..	32 861	26 820	30 196	24 531	26 881	27 906	29 260	33 928	44 096
5124 Taxes on exports	75	4	0	1	0	2	1	1	1	1
Tax on exports	..	4	0	1	0	2	1	1	1	1
5125 Taxes on investment goods	0	0	0	0	0	0	0	0	0	0
5126 Taxes on specific services	132	1 042	1 578	18 461	10 958	-5 610	7 169	-1 441	-7 541	-3 323
IDE	..	0	0	15 888	8 022	-8 442	2 786	-5 988	-12 322	-3 323
Tax on lodging	..	504	798	1 147	1 384	1 375	1 702	1 890	2 067	0
Public entertainment tax	..	240	349	486	462	360	625	566	543	0
Tax on lotteries, raffles and gambling	..	267	417	789	923	952	1 329	1 213	1 218	0
Tax on commercials	..	4	15	150	166	145	16	203	216	0
Various indirect taxes	..	28	0	0	1	0	711	674	738	0
5127 Other taxes on internat. trade and transactions	0	0	0	0	0	0	0	0	0	0
5128 Other taxes	242	226	350	1 782	1 962	2 858	3 243	3 886	2 040	4 730
Mining fees	..	226	350	1 782	1 962	2 858	3 243	3 886	2 040	4 730
5130 Unallocable between 5110 and 5120	17	0	0	0	0	0	0	0	0	0
5200 Taxes on use of goods and perform activities	666	46 278	66 272	77 202	77 609	79 930	63 189	65 674	79 643	501
5210 Recurrent taxes	666	46 278	66 272	77 202	77 609	79 930	63 189	65 674	79 643	501
5211 Paid by households: motor vehicles	567	8 878	15 237	21 301	21 319	22 186	16 464	19 174	20 370	0
Tax on motor vehicules	..	8 878	15 237	21 301	21 319	22 186	16 464	19 174	20 370	0
5212 Paid by others: motor vehicles	0	301	357	270	281	296	370	357	367	439
Tax on federal auto transport	..	301	357	270	281	296	370	357	367	439
5213 Paid in respect of other goods	99	37 099	50 678	55 631	56 010	57 447	46 355	46 143	58 906	62
Sport fishing	..	40	80	68	76	50	55	50	65	62
Sport hunting	..	3	0	0	51	0	0	0	0	0
Tax on commercial activities	..	63	113	42	50	66	42	26	33	0
Trade in books and magazines	..	0	0	0	0	0	0	3	1	0
Tax on industrial activities	..	2	0	35	82	38	145	49	13	0
Mining	..	0	0	1	1	0	0	1	2	0
Fee on use of public assets	..	36 991	50 485	55 485	55 749	57 292	46 113	46 013	58 792	0
5220 Non-recurrent taxes	0	0	0	0	0	0	0	0	0	0
5300 Unallocable between 5100 and 5200	0	0	0	0	0	0	0	0	0	0
6000 Other taxes	**1 619**	**7 651**	**11 693**	**27 078**	**27 398**	**32 412**	**37 080**	**41 204**	**36 767**	**27 379**
6100 Paid solely by business	0	0	0	0	0	0	0	0	0	0
6200 Other	1 619	7 651	11 693	27 078	27 398	32 412	37 080	41 204	36 767	27 379
Accessories	..	5 504	9 543	21 710	22 206	24 059	24 077	25 301	23 717	23 211
Unallocable between 1000 and 5000 caused in exercices fiscal previous liquidation slopes or of payment	..	374	-927	7	30	-118	2 260	1 618	504	4 168
Additional state and local taxes	..	1 773	3 077	5 361	5 162	8 471	10 743	14 285	12 546	0

Note: Year ending 31st December.
The data are on a cash basis.
The 2015 data for tax revenues of the state and local levels of government are not available. They comprise revenues in categories 3000, 4000, 5000 and 6000.
Heading 1000: In ECLAC data, income taxes are presented net of credit on salary figures.
Heading 2000: In ECLAC data, social security contributions are presented net of transfers from the Federal government for the payment of IMSS (Mexican Social Security Institute) pensions.
Heading 5128: Revenue Statistics in Latin America and the Caribbean and Revenue Statistics in OECD countries included fees levied on hydrocarbon production in 5128. From the data provided for Revenue Statistics in OECD countries (2016) and for this publication, revenues from hydrocarbon production have been separated from tax revenues and are instead treated as non-tax revenues net of these fees.
Source: Secretaría de Hacienda y Crédito Público, Departamento económico (Ministry of Finance, Economic Department).

StatLink http://dx.doi.org/10.1787/888933463342

Table 5.18. Nicaragua
Details of tax revenue / Ingresos tributarios detallados

Million NIO

	1990	2000	2005	2009	2010	2011	2012	2013	2014	2015
Total tax revenue	..	**8 418**	**17 009**	**28 863**	**33 620**	**41 185**	**48 131**	**53 486**	**62 330**	**72 322**
1000 Taxes on income, profits and capital gains	..	**1 144**	**3 902**	**7 818**	**8 351**	**11 144**	**13 107**	**14 521**	**17 658**	**20 800**
1100 Of individuals	..	..	..	..	..	..	..	..	..	..
1110 On income and profits	..	..	..	..	..	..	..	..	..	..
1120 On capital gains	..	..	..	..	..	..	..	..	..	..
1200 Corporate	..	..	..	..	..	..	..	..	..	..
1210 On profits	..	..	..	..	..	..	..	..	..	..
1220 On capital gains	..	..	..	..	..	..	..	..	..	..
1300 Unallocable between 1100 and 1200	..	1 144	3 902	7 818	8 351	11 144	13 107	14 521	17 658	20 800
Income tax	..	1 144	3 902	7 818	8 351	11 144	13 107	14 521	17 658	20 800
2000 Social security contributions	..	**1 678**	**3 363**	**6 804**	**8 090**	**9 433**	**11 007**	**12 805**	**15 161**	**18 194**
2100 Employees	..	..	..	..	..	..	..	..	..	..
2110 On a payroll basis	..	..	..	..	..	..	..	..	..	..
2120 On an income tax basis	..	..	..	..	..	..	..	..	..	..
2200 Employers	..	..	..	..	..	..	..	..	..	..
2210 On a payroll basis	..	..	..	..	..	..	..	..	..	..
2220 On an income tax basis	..	..	..	..	..	..	..	..	..	..
2300 Self-employed or non-employed	..	..	..	..	..	..	..	..	..	..
2310 On a payroll basis	..	..	..	..	..	..	..	..	..	..
2320 On an income tax basis	..	..	..	..	..	..	..	..	..	..
2400 Unallocable between 2100, 2200 and 2300	..	1 678	3 363	6 804	8 090	9 433	11 007	12 805	15 161	18 194
2410 On a payroll basis	..	1 678	3 363	6 804	8 090	9 433	11 007	12 805	15 161	18 194
2420 On an income tax basis	..	0	0	0	0	0	0	0	0	0
3000 Taxes on payroll and workforce	..	**0**	**0**	**0**	**0**	**0**	**0**	**0**	**0**	**0**
4000 Taxes on property	..	**0**	**2**	**48**	**130**	**191**	**239**	**311**	**374**	**513**
4100 Recurrent taxes on immovable property	..	..	0	0	0	0	0	0	0	0
4110 Households	..	..	..	..	..	..	..	..	..	..
4120 Others	..	..	..	..	..	..	..	..	..	..
4200 Recurrent taxes on net wealth	..	..	2	48	130	191	239	311	374	513
4210 Individual	..	..	2	48	130	191	239	311	374	513
4220 Corporate	..	..	0	0	0	0	0	0	0	0
4300 Estate, inheritance and gift taxes	..	..	0	0	0	0	0	0	0	0
4310 Estate and inheritance taxes	..	..	..	..	..	..	..	..	..	..
4320 Gift taxes	..	..	..	..	..	..	..	..	..	..
4400 Taxes on financial and capital transactions	..	..	0	0	0	0	0	0	0	0
4500 Non-recurrent taxes	..	..	0	0	0	0	0	0	0	0
4510 On net wealth	..	..	..	..	..	..	..	..	..	..
4520 Other non-recurrent taxes	..	..	..	..	..	..	..	..	..	..
4600 Other recurrent taxes on property	..	..	0	0	0	0	0	0	0	0
5000 Taxes on goods and services	..	**5 584**	**9 725**	**14 170**	**17 029**	**20 395**	**23 754**	**25 771**	**29 050**	**32 725**
5100 Taxes on production, sale, transfer, etc	..	5 584	9 725	14 170	17 029	20 395	23 754	25 771	29 050	32 725
5110 General taxes	..	2 931	5 599	8 871	10 353	12 876	15 151	16 736	19 385	20 714
5111 Value added taxes	..	2 931	5 599	8 871	10 353	12 876	15 151	16 736	19 385	20 714
5112 Sales tax	..	0	0	0	0	0	0	0	0	0
5113 Other	..	0	0	0	0	0	0	0	0	0
5120 Taxes on specific goods and services	..	2 653	4 126	5 299	6 676	7 519	8 603	9 035	9 665	12 011
5121 Excises	..	2 034	3 227	4 392	5 541	6 070	6 884	7 254	7 761	9 773
Liquor	..	84	102	147	198	240	214	253	230	264
Beer	..	203	340	556	645	781	915	1 047	1 184	1 370
Cigarettes	..	70	143	171	45	0	0	174	1	0
Soft drinks	..	123	128	188	248	292	351	389	423	501
Petroleum products	..	1 359	1 756	2 277	2 699	2 700	3 045	3 418	3 938	4 396
Excise taxes on imports	..	196	734	975	1 559	1 901	2 233	1 924	1 908	3 105
Other specific excises on consumption	..	-1	25	77	148	156	126	49	78	136
5122 Profits of fiscal monopolies	..	0	0	0	0	0	0	0	0	0
5123 Customs and import duties	..	619	856	908	1 135	1 449	1 719	1 782	1 904	2 238
Custom duties	..	452	837	870	1 094	1 400	1 661	1 717	1 828	2 155
Temporary protection duty	..	96	0	0	0	0	0	0	0	0
On products originating in Colombia or Honduras	..	72	18	38	41	49	58	64	76	83
5124 Taxes on exports	..	0	0	0	0	0	0	0	0	0
5125 Taxes on investment goods	..	0	0	0	0	0	0	0	0	0
5126 Taxes on specific services	..	0	0	0	0	0	0	0	0	0
5127 Other taxes on internat. trade and transactions	..	0	43	0	0	0	0	0	0	0
5128 Other taxes	..	0	0	0	0	0	0	0	0	0
5130 Unallocable between 5110 and 5120	..	0	0	0	0	0	0	0	0	0
5200 Taxes on use of goods and perform activities	..	0	0	0	0	0	0	0	0	0
5210 Recurrent taxes	..	..	..	..	..	..	..	..	..	..
5211 Paid by households: motor vehicles	..	..	..	..	..	..	..	..	..	..

Table 5.18. Nicaragua *(cont.)*
Details of tax revenue / Ingresos tributarios detallados

Million NIO

	1990	2000	2005	2009	2010	2011	2012	2013	2014	2015
5212 Paid by others: motor vehicles	..	..	..	..	..	..	..	..	..	..
5213 Paid in respect of other goods	..	..	..	..	..	..	..	..	..	..
5220 Non-recurrent taxes	..	..	..	..	..	..	..	..	..	..
5300 Unallocable between 5100 and 5200	..	0	0	0	0	0	0	0	0	0
6000 Other taxes	**..**	**11**	**17**	**24**	**20**	**22**	**24**	**77**	**87**	**90**
6100 Paid solely by business	..	0	0	0	0	0	0	0	0	0
6200 Other	..	11	17	24	20	22	24	77	87	90
Stamp tax	..	11	17	24	20	22	24	77	87	90

Note: Year ending 31st December.
The data are on a cash basis.
Comparable statistics for 1990 cannot be shown due to the devaluation of the Nicaraguan cordoba.

Source: Banco Central de Nicaragua y Ministerio de Hacienda y Crédito Público (Central Bank of Nicaragua and Ministry of Finance and Public Credit).

StatLink http://dx.doi.org/10.1787/888933463358

Table 5.19. Panama / Panamá
Details of tax revenue / Ingresos tributarios detallados

Thousand PAB

	1990	2000	2005	2009	2010	2011	2012	2013	2014	2015
Total tax revenue	**892 837**	**2 018 072**	**2 354 542**	**4 351 502**	**5 012 449**	**5 832 848**	**6 971 352**	**7 822 416**	**7 939 049**	**8 446 536**
1000 Taxes on income, profits and capital gains	**216 950**	**484 872**	**562 852**	**1 285 649**	**1 317 028**	**1 349 792**	**1 985 220**	**2 199 534**	**1 997 811**	**2 154 061**
1100 Of individuals	139 518	295 142	303 283	495 774	440 404	514 246	553 624	678 949	721 965	798 914
1110 On income and profits	139 518	295 142	303 283	495 774	440 404	514 246	553 624	678 949	721 965	798 914
Payroll	115 138	222 025	226 563	394 854	352 550	420 411	455 553	568 026	602 339	688 576
Panama Canal commission	10 225	52 774	52 325	62 109	52 398	65 377	60 246	59 325	61 936	65 024
1120 On capital gains	..	..	..	..	..	..	..	..	..	..
1200 Corporate	66 194	158 535	212 624	658 704	603 428	538 920	1 068 090	970 183	895 789	937 944
1210 On profits	66 194	158 535	212 624	658 704	603 428	538 920	1 068 090	970 183	895 789	937 944
Colón Free Zone	5 019	3 379	4 496	17 855	19 666	24 074	50 735	38 903	43 266	36 397
1220 On capital gains	..	..	..	..	..	..	..	..	..	..
1300 Unallocable between 1100 and 1200	11 238	31 195	46 945	131 171	273 196	296 626	363 505	550 402	380 057	417 203
Dividends and complimentary tax	11 238	31 195	46 945	90 644	166 056	186 518	239 823	251 094	242 603	266 041
2000 Social security contributions	**271 300**	**742 000**	**827 300**	**1 383 300**	**1 637 100**	**2 041 500**	**2 168 500**	**2 676 700**	**2 794 000**	**3 048 500**
2100 Employees	..	..	..	..	..	..	..	..	..	..
2110 On a payroll basis	..	..	..	..	..	..	..	..	..	..
2120 On an income tax basis	..	..	..	..	..	..	..	..	..	..
2200 Employers	..	..	..	..	..	..	..	..	..	..
2210 On a payroll basis	..	..	..	..	..	..	..	..	..	..
2220 On an income tax basis	..	..	..	..	..	..	..	..	..	..
2300 Self-employed or non-employed	..	..	..	..	..	..	..	..	..	..
2310 On a payroll basis	..	..	..	..	..	..	..	..	..	..
2320 On an income tax basis	..	..	..	..	..	..	..	..	..	..
2400 Unallocable between 2100, 2200 and 2300	271 300	742 000	827 300	1 383 300	1 637 100	2 041 500	2 168 500	2 676 700	2 794 000	3 048 500
2410 On a payroll basis	..	..	..	..	..	..	..	..	..	..
2420 On an income tax basis	..	..	..	..	..	..	..	..	..	..
3000 Taxes on payroll and workforce	**0**	**36 400**	**36 243**	**50 962**	**58 844**	**65 200**	**70 400**	**82 400**	**134 100**	**111 295**
Education insurance	0	36 400	36 243	50 962	58 844	65 200	70 400	82 400	134 100	111 295
4000 Taxes on property	**43 443**	**62 090**	**109 086**	**175 370**	**212 194**	**229 398**	**261 033**	**337 721**	**336 903**	**319 247**
4100 Recurrent taxes on immovable property	28 330	33 898	56 424	104 522	107 791	109 986	119 964	180 621	175 627	151 229
4110 Households	28 330	33 898	56 424	104 522	107 791	109 986	119 964	180 621	175 627	151 229
4120 Others	0	0	0	0	0	0	0	0	0	0
4200 Recurrent taxes on net wealth	0	0	0	0	0	0	0	0	0	0
4210 Individual	..	..	..	..	..	..	..	..	..	..
4220 Corporate	..	..	..	..	..	..	..	..	..	..
4300 Estate, inheritance and gift taxes	154	0	0	0	0	0	0	0	0	0
4310 Estate and inheritance taxes	..	..	..	..	..	..	..	..	..	..
4320 Gift taxes	..	..	..	..	..	..	..	..	..	..
4400 Taxes on financial and capital transactions	3 419	9 343	21 049	24 456	29 810	36 195	40 998	49 391	44 800	48 037
4500 Non-recurrent taxes	0	0	0	0	0	0	0	0	0	0
4510 On net wealth	..	..	..	..	..	..	..	..	..	..
4520 Other non-recurrent taxes	..	..	..	..	..	..	..	..	..	..
4600 Other recurrent taxes on property	11 540	18 849	31 613	46 392	74 593	83 218	100 071	107 709	116 476	119 981
Commercial licences	11 540	18 849	31 613	46 392	74 593	83 218	100 071	107 709	116 476	119 981
5000 Taxes on goods and services	**335 470**	**573 374**	**692 339**	**1 261 432**	**1 513 066**	**1 893 533**	**2 124 349**	**2 253 283**	**2 384 202**	**2 539 122**
5100 Taxes on production, sale, transfer, etc	331 758	530 329	641 713	1 191 097	1 472 515	1 845 207	2 067 189	2 193 466	2 318 584	2 466 638
5110 General taxes	80 303	69 013	137 585	557 166	766 154	1 042 213	1 183 878	1 269 055	1 351 246	1 359 344
5111 Value added taxes	80 303	69 013	137 585	557 166	766 154	1 042 213	1 183 878	1 269 055	1 351 246	1 359 344
5112 Sales tax	0	0	0	0	0	0	0	0	0	0
5113 Other	0	0	0	0	0	0	0	0	0	0
5120 Taxes on specific goods and services	138 623	461 316	504 128	633 931	706 360	802 993	883 311	924 411	967 338	1 107 293
5121 Excises	0	141 348	106 469	188 411	238 728	310 441	355 717	397 066	452 299	580 760
Gasoline products	..	108 783	69 400	111 404	96 518	90 136	100 903	117 377	133 266	242 221
Beer	..	18 249	22 317	30 635	31 025	32 715	34 572	35 641	41 882	47 816
Wine and liquor	..	11 971	10 741	11 071	10 775	10 769	10 486	15 751	22 689	15 293
Soft drinks	..	2 292	2 935	4 951	5 646	6 207	6 622	6 773	6 736	7 289
Various products	..	0	821	30 302	94 726	170 595	45 285	53 248	47 960	53 297
Automobiles	..	0	0	0	0	0	132 880	141 220	175 560	182 401
Other	..	53	255	48	38	19	24 969	27 056	24 207	32 443
5122 Profits of fiscal monopolies	0	0	0	0	0	0	0	0	0	0
5123 Customs and import duties	124 914	298 323	363 687	390 129	390 024	393 668	420 448	408 901	381 382	390 672
5124 Taxes on exports	12 621	158	0	104	104	0	0	0	0	0
5125 Taxes on investment goods	0	0	0	0	0	0	0	0	0	0
5126 Taxes on specific services	0	16 637	26 554	45 323	65 110	80 484	86 146	96 144	109 158	110 797
Insurance premiums	..	16 637	19 482	34 514	47 056	51 664	54 188	60 483	62 840	48 297
Cable and telecommunications	..	0	5 987	9 870	17 015	27 827	30 507	33 729	44 805	39 046
Gambling	..	0	1 085	939	1 039	993	1 451	1 932	1 512	23 455

Table 5.19. Panama / Panamá (cont.)
Details of tax revenue / Ingresos tributarios detallados

Thousand PAB

	1990	2000	2005	2009	2010	2011	2012	2013	2014	2015
5127 Other taxes on internat. trade and transactions	1 088	4 850	7 418	9 964	12 395	18 400	21 000	22 300	24 500	25 064
Banks, financial institutions, and currency exchange	0	2 005	7 418	9 964	12 395	18 400	21 000	22 300	24 500	25 064
Other	1 088	2 845	0	0	0	0	0	0	0	0
5128 Other taxes	0	0	0	0	0	0	0	0	0	0
5130 Unallocable between 5110 and 5120	112 832	0	0	0	0	0	0	0	0	0
5200 Taxes on use of goods and perform activities	3 712	43 045	50 626	70 335	40 551	48 327	57 160	59 817	65 618	72 485
5210 Recurrent taxes	0	38 758	43 177	55 807	40 551	48 327	57 160	59 817	65 618	72 485
5211 Paid by households: motor vehicles	..	7 042	8 423	11 332	0	0	0	0	0	0
5212 Paid by others: motor vehicles	..	4 682	4 387	5 173	0	0	0	0	0	0
5213 Paid in respect of other goods	..	27 033	30 367	39 302	40 551	48 327	57 160	59 817	65 618	72 485
On commercial activities	..	25 405	28 685	37 184	38 367	45 723	54 382	56 739	62 485	69 058
On industrial activities	..	1 628	1 682	2 118	2 184	2 604	2 778	3 078	3 132	3 426
5220 Non-recurrent taxes	3 712	4 287	7 449	14 528	0	0	0	0	0	0
Building and construction	0	4 287	7 449	14 528	..	..	..	..	..	..
Ship registration	3 712	0	0	0	..	..	..	..	..	..
5300 Unallocable between 5100 and 5200	0	0	0	0	0	0	0	0	0	0
6000 Other taxes	**25 674**	**119 336**	**126 722**	**194 789**	**274 217**	**253 424**	**361 851**	**272 778**	**292 033**	**274 310**
6100 Paid solely by business	0	11	0	0	0	0	0	0	0	0
6200 Other	25 674	119 325	126 722	194 789	274 217	253 424	361 851	272 778	292 033	274 310
Legal services	16 691	42 330	27 684	36 278	41 064	47 000	44 900	46 200	41 450	37 185
Fiscal documents	0	76 449	97 938	158 454	197 620	167 210	268 253	172 012	198 672	178 459
Others	8 983	546	1 100	58	35 533	39 214	48 698	54 566	51 911	58 665

Note: Year ending 31st December.

The data are on a cash basis.

Heading 1110: Payroll taxes and Panama Canal commission have been included under this category, previously in 1300.

Heading 1210: Colón Free zone has been included under this category, previously 1300.

Heading 1300: Dividends and complimentary tax were included in this category, dividends where previously in 1210.

Heading 3000: In ECLAC data, education insurance is classified as "Other taxes" (6000).

Heading 5127: In CIAT and ECLAC data, the tax on banks, financial institutions and currency exchange is classified as a property tax (4000).

Heading 6200: Includes for this publication revenue from fiscal documents.

Source: Contraloría General de la República (General Comptroller of the Republic of Panama).

StatLink http://dx.doi.org/10.1787/888933463362

Table 5.20. Paraguay
Details of tax revenue / Ingresos tributarios detallados

Million PYG

	1990	2000	2005	2009	2010	2011	2012	2013	2014	2015
Total tax revenue	**348 889**	**3 587 451**	**7 434 024**	**12 725 017**	**15 637 675**	**17 727 016**	**19 261 951**	**20 540 296**	**24 472 900**	**25 833 690**
1000 Taxes on income, profits and capital gains	**73 726**	**470 388**	**938 886**	**2 187 607**	**2 096 498**	**2 607 282**	**2 902 725**	**3 100 223**	**3 678 392**	**3 922 384**
1100 Of individuals	..	41 021	82 086	192 037	184 361	228 802	254 965	283 915	398 570	457 693
1110 On income and profits	..	41 021	82 086	192 037	184 361	228 802	254 965	283 915	398 570	457 693
IRACIS - IRAGRO	..	41 021	82 086	191 463	183 211	228 648	254 458	270 540	314 649	331 856
1120 On capital gains	..	..	..	..	..	..	..	..	..	..
1200 Corporate	..	429 367	856 800	1 995 570	1 912 137	2 378 480	2 647 760	2 816 308	3 279 822	3 464 691
1210 On profits	..	429 367	856 800	1 995 570	1 912 137	2 378 480	2 647 760	2 816 308	3 279 822	3 464 691
Income tax on small businesses	..	0	0	8 838	9 380	5 129	5 764	7 831	9 063	14 563
Single tax	..	4 238	5 802	644	715	544	317	32	72	5
Single tax on maquiladoras	..	0	289	1 833	3 310	3 182	4 570	4 669	9 783	10 892
IRACIS - IRAGRO	..	425 129	850 709	1 984 255	1 898 732	2 369 625	2 637 109	2 803 776	3 260 905	3 439 232
1220 On capital gains	0	0	0	0	0	0	0	0	0	0
1300 Unallocable between 1100 and 1200	73 726	0	0	0	0	0	0	0	0	0
Others	73 726	0	0	0	0	0	0	0	0	0
2000 Social security contributions	**28 882**	**919 533**	**1 591 980**	**3 118 645**	**3 552 640**	**3 979 252**	**4 844 110**	**5 158 072**	**6 336 260**	**7 044 316**
2100 Employees	..	..	..	..	..	..	..	..	..	..
2110 On a payroll basis	..	..	..	..	..	..	..	..	..	..
2120 On an income tax basis	..	..	..	..	..	..	..	..	..	..
2200 Employers	..	..	..	..	..	..	..	..	..	..
2210 On a payroll basis	..	..	..	..	..	..	..	..	..	..
2220 On an income tax basis	..	..	..	..	..	..	..	..	..	..
2300 Self-employed or non-employed	..	..	..	..	..	..	..	..	..	..
2310 On a payroll basis	..	..	..	..	..	..	..	..	..	..
2320 On an income tax basis	..	..	..	..	..	..	..	..	..	..
2400 Unallocable between 2100, 2200 and 2300	28 882	919 533	1 591 980	3 118 645	3 552 640	3 979 252	4 844 110	5 158 072	6 336 260	7 044 316
2410 On a payroll basis	28 882	919 533	1 591 980	3 118 645	3 552 640	3 979 252	4 844 110	5 158 072	6 336 260	7 044 316
2420 On an income tax basis	0	0	0	0	0	0	0	0	0	0
3000 Taxes on payroll and workforce	**0**	**0**	**0**	**0**	**0**	**0**	**0**	**0**	**0**	**0**
4000 Taxes on property	**17 162**	**0**	**0**	**253 821**	**272 385**	**289 456**	**310 237**	**350 169**	**390 102**	**430 034**
4100 Recurrent taxes on immovable property	17 162	..	..	240 217	254 306	266 371	289 493	..	..	398 251
4110 Households	17 162	..	..	240 217	254 306	266 371	289 493	..	..	398 251
Real estate tax	0	..	..	233 423	249 697	261 051	285 034	..	..	390 772
Tax on vacant lots	0	..	..	2 953	2 925	3 212	3 472	..	..	4 818
Other	17 162	..	..	3 841	1 684	2 109	987	..	..	2 661
4120 Others	0	..	..	0	0	0	0	..	..	0
4200 Recurrent taxes on net wealth	0	..	..	0	0	0	0	..	..	0
4210 Individual	..	..	..	..	..	..	..	..	..	..
4220 Corporate	..	..	..	..	..	..	..	..	..	..
4300 Estate, inheritance and gift taxes	0	..	..	0	0	0	0	..	..	0
4310 Estate and inheritance taxes	..	..	..	..	..	..	..	..	..	..
4320 Gift taxes	..	..	..	..	..	..	..	..	..	..
4400 Taxes on financial and capital transactions	0	..	..	13 391	16 316	22 406	20 061	..	..	30 987
Real estate transfer tax	..	..	..	9 675	11 766	16 362	14 704	..	..	22 406
Other	..	..	..	3 716	4 551	6 044	5 357	..	..	8 581
4500 Non-recurrent taxes	0	..	..	0	0	0	0	..	..	0
4510 On net wealth	..	..	..	..	..	..	..	..	..	..
4520 Other non-recurrent taxes	..	..	..	..	..	..	..	..	..	..
4600 Other recurrent taxes on property	0	..	..	213	1 762	679	682	..	..	796
5000 Taxes on goods and services	**179 312**	**2 080 878**	**4 309 832**	**7 068 556**	**9 460 962**	**10 749 735**	**11 081 105**	**11 808 277**	**13 919 885**	**14 416 197**
5100 Taxes on production, sale, transfer, etc	179 312	2 080 878	4 309 832	6 928 055	9 249 698	10 501 464	10 849 519	11 524 523	13 583 267	13 982 529
5110 General taxes	0	1 150 496	2 478 998	4 399 503	5 991 694	6 887 685	7 126 623	7 843 002	9 363 648	9 768 800
5111 Value added taxes	..	1 150 496	2 478 998	4 399 503	5 991 694	6 887 685	7 126 623	7 843 002	9 363 648	9 768 800
5112 Sales tax	..	0	0	0	0	0	0	0	0	0
5113 Other	..	0	0	0	0	0	0	0	0	0
5120 Taxes on specific goods and services	179 312	930 382	1 830 834	2 528 552	3 258 004	3 613 779	3 722 896	3 681 521	4 219 619	4 213 729
5121 Excises	41 087	456 561	949 962	1 532 365	1 710 531	1 892 587	2 063 020	2 048 143	2 442 895	2 391 628
Fuels	41 087	316 694	688 773	1 093 058	1 126 143	1 328 213	1 455 820	1 427 769	1 787 112	1 775 286
Other excises	0	136 194	249 239	399 940	537 887	564 374	607 200	620 374	655 783	616 342
Animal health and quality service	0	3 673	11 950	39 367	46 501	0	0	0	0	0
Livestock trade	0	0	0	0	0	0	0	0	0	0
5122 Profits of fiscal monopolies	0	0	0	0	0	0	0	0	0	0
5123 Customs and import duties	138 225	473 821	880 872	975 487	1 524 252	1 696 945	1 637 588	1 633 378	1 776 724	1 659 535
5124 Taxes on exports	0	0	0	0	0	0	0	0	0	0
5125 Taxes on investment goods	0	0	0	0	0	0	0	0	0	0

Table 5.20. Paraguay *(cont.)*
Details of tax revenue / Ingresos tributarios detallados

Million PYG

	1990	2000	2005	2009	2010	2011	2012	2013	2014	2015
5126 Taxes on specific services	0	0	0	20 700	23 221	24 247	22 288	0	0	162 566
Advertising	..	..	..	4 555	5 249	6 047	6 560	..	..	7 428
Public transport	..	..	..	4 245	4 363	4 649	4 121	..	..	4 297
Gambling	..	..	..	0	0	0	0	..	..	804
Other	..	..	..	11 900	13 609	13 551	11 607	..	..	150 037
5127 Other taxes on internat. trade and transactions	0	0	0	0	0	0	0	0	0	0
5128 Other taxes	0	0	0	0	0	0	0	0	0	0
5130 Unallocable between 5110 and 5120	0	0	0	0	0	0	0	0	0	0
5200 Taxes on use of goods and perform activities	0	0	0	140 466	211 027	208 542	230 890	283 754	336 618	389 482
5210 Recurrent taxes	0	0	0	140 466	211 027	208 542	230 890	283 754	336 618	389 482
5211 Paid by households: motor vehicles	..	..	..	0	0	0	0	0	0	0
5212 Paid by others: motor vehicles	..	..	..	41 701	52 365	64 667	67 399	..	..	94 393
Motor vehicle licences	..	..	..	41 701	52 365	64 667	67 399	..	..	..
5213 Paid in respect of other goods	..	..	..	98 765	158 662	143 875	163 491	..	..	295 090
Tax on construction	..	..	..	24 476	31 696	38 891	50 337	..	..	65 403
Licencing fees	..	..	..	74 289	126 965	104 983	113 153	..	..	229 686
5220 Non-recurrent taxes	..	..	..	0	0	0	0	0	0	0
5300 Unallocable between 5100 and 5200	0	0	0	35	237	39 730	696	0	0	44 186
6000 Other taxes	**49 807**	**116 652**	**593 326**	**96 388**	**255 190**	**101 291**	**123 774**	**123 554**	**148 260**	**20 758**
6100 Paid solely by business	0	0	0	0	0	0	0	0	0	0
6200 Other	49 807	116 652	593 326	96 388	255 190	101 291	123 774	123 554	148 260	20 758
Registration and stamp duties	0	71 777	192 393	319	332	159	168	179	106	91
Luxury automobile tax	0	0	3 897	118	91	129	153	218	57	54
Other	49 807	44 875	397 036	95 951	254 767	101 003	123 453	123 157	148 098	20 613

Note: Year ending 31st December.

The data are on a cash basis.

The figures for years up to and including 2004, as well as for 2013 and 2014, exclude local government tax revenues as the data are not available. This affects data in categories 4000, 5000 and 6000.

Heading 2000: Data on social security contributions collected by decentralised institutions are not available for 2011 to 2014, with the exception of the contributions made to the Instituto de Previsión Social (Social Security Institute).

Heading 1110: Data for the income tax on agricultural activities (IRAGRO) and the tax on industrial, commercial and service activities (IRACIS) have been included in this category, which were previously in 1300. The proportion of data included in this category has been estimated from 1999 to 2014 based on the disaggregation provided in 2015.

Heading 1210: Data for the income tax on agricultural activities (IRAGRO) and the tax on industrial, commercial and service activities (IRACIS) have been included in this category, which were previously in 1300. The proportion of data included in this category has been estimated from 1999 to 2014 based on the disaggregation provided in 2015.

Heading 5121: Data for animal health and quality service are not available from 2011.

Source: Subsecretaría de Estado de Tributación, Ministerio de Hacienda del Paraguay (Tax Undersecretary, Ministry of Finance of Paraguay).

StatLink http://dx.doi.org/10.1787/888933463379

Table 5.21. Peru / Perú
Details of tax revenue / Ingresos tributarios detallados

Million PEN

	1990	2000	2005	2009	2010	2011	2012	2013	2014	2015
Total tax revenue	**645**	**26 106**	**40 732**	**61 930**	**74 758**	**86 632**	**95 969**	**100 651**	**108 333**	**104 692**
1000 Taxes on income, profits and capital gains	**37**	**5 078**	**11 950**	**21 686**	**27 317**	**35 341**	**39 720**	**39 357**	**43 577**	**37 772**
1100 Of individuals	3	2 117	3 327	5 861	6 518	8 208	9 462	10 570	11 423	11 137
First category	..	167	181	145	160	196	253	310	374	443
Second category	..	7	250	661	869	1 291	1 136	1 275	1 214	1 287
Fourth category	..	234	395	473	521	567	637	744	834	783
Fifth category	..	1 641	2 369	4 329	4 735	5 877	7 054	7 820	8 473	8 044
Tax debt payments	..	68	130	254	233	277	382	421	529	581
1110 On income and profits	..	..	..	..	..	..	..	..	..	..
1120 On capital gains	..	..	..	..	..	..	..	..	..	..
1200 Corporate	32	2 526	8 391	14 816	19 561	26 036	28 453	26 207	26 593	24 266
1210 On profits	32	2 526	8 391	14 816	19 561	26 036	28 453	26 207	26 593	24 266
Third category	..	2 023	5 316	10 691	14 652	19 321	20 744	19 633	18 536	16 817
Income tax on mining	..	0	0	0	0	59	442	337	372	208
Income tax special regime	..	47	55	89	118	153	202	246	275	310
Other incomes corporate	..	18	41	98	148	224	229	187	193	167
Tax debt payments	..	438	1 908	2 216	2 856	3 987	4 397	3 029	3 703	3 066
Temporary tax on net assets	..	0	1 073	1 722	1 788	2 293	2 439	2 776	3 513	3 697
1220 On capital gains	..	..	..	..	..	..	..	..	..	..
1300 Unallocable between 1100 and 1200	1	436	232	1 009	1 239	1 097	1 804	2 579	5 561	2 369
Income tax on non-residents	1	487	542	1 391	1 511	1 735	2 244	2 848	6 027	3 248
Income tax refunds	0	-51	-310	-382	-272	-638	-439	-269	-466	-879
2000 Social security contributions	**50**	**3 184**	**4 023**	**7 244**	**7 957**	**8 979**	**10 185**	**11 303**	**11 893**	**12 935**
2100 Employees	..	541	667	1 978	2 385	2 657	2 879	3 143	3 139	3 424
2110 On a payroll basis	..	541	644	1 401	1 618	1 997	2 389	2 786	3 027	3 287
2120 On an income tax basis	..	0	23	577	768	661	491	357	112	137
Solidarity contribution for pension plan	..	..	23	577	768	661	491	357	112	137
2200 Employers	..	2 447	3 207	5 015	5 283	6 099	7 075	7 928	8 524	9 250
2210 On a payroll basis	..	2 447	3 207	5 015	5 283	6 099	7 075	7 928	8 524	9 250
2220 On an income tax basis	..	0	0	0	0	0	0	0	0	0
2300 Self-employed or non-employed	..	95	36	38	42	46	51	55	58	60
2310 On a payroll basis	..	95	36	38	42	46	51	55	58	60
2320 On an income tax basis	..	..	..	..	..	..	..	..	..	..
2400 Unallocable between 2100, 2200 and 2300	50	102	113	213	246	177	179	177	172	202
2410 On a payroll basis	50	102	113	213	246	177	179	177	172	202
2420 On an income tax basis	0	0	0	0	0	0	0	0	0	0
3000 Taxes on payroll and workforce	**0**	**1 149**	**7**	**5**	**1**	**0**	**2**	**0**	**-82**	**4**
4000 Taxes on property	**99**	**0**	**1 340**	**2 042**	**2 236**	**1 876**	**1 897**	**2 130**	**2 159**	**2 399**
4100 Recurrent taxes on immovable property	0	0	460	676	731	856	958	1 126	1 234	1 444
4110 Households	..	..	..	..	..	..	..	..	..	..
4120 Others	..	..	..	..	..	..	..	..	..	..
4200 Recurrent taxes on net wealth	61	0	0	0	0	0	0	0	0	0
4210 Individual	60	0	0	..	..	..	..	..	..	..
4220 Corporate	1	0	0	..	..	..	..	..	..	..
Revaluation of fixed assets	1	..	..	..	..	..	..	..	..	..
4300 Estate, inheritance and gift taxes	0	0	0	0	0	0	0	0	0	0
4310 Estate and inheritance taxes	..	..	..	..	..	..	..	..	..	..
4320 Gift taxes	..	..	..	..	..	..	..	..	..	..
4400 Taxes on financial and capital transactions	38	0	803	1 366	1 505	1 020	939	1 004	925	955
Financial transactions tax	0	..	706	968	944	395	126	134	153	161
Real estate transfer tax	0	..	97	398	561	625	813	870	772	795
Tax Law Decree 519	38	..	0	0	0	0	0	0	0	0
4500 Non-recurrent taxes	0	0	0	0	0	0	0	0	0	0
4510 On net wealth	..	..	..	..	..	..	..	..	..	..
4520 Other non-recurrent taxes	..	..	..	..	..	..	..	..	..	..
4600 Other recurrent taxes on property	0	0	76	0	0	0	0	0	0	0
5000 Taxes on goods and services	**423**	**15 952**	**22 203**	**29 105**	**35 330**	**38 621**	**41 666**	**45 401**	**48 843**	**50 196**
5100 Taxes on production, sale, transfer, etc	423	15 952	22 203	29 105	35 330	38 621	41 666	45 401	48 843	50 196
5110 General taxes	78	9 694	15 156	23 837	29 094	32 455	35 078	37 953	41 779	42 612
5111 Value added taxes	78	9 646	15 109	23 837	29 094	32 455	35 078	37 953	41 779	42 612
5112 Sales tax	0	0	0	0	0	0	0	0	0	0
5113 Other	0	47	47	0	0	0	0	0	0	0
5120 Taxes on specific goods and services	345	6 259	7 047	5 269	6 236	6 166	6 588	7 448	7 064	7 583
5121 Excises	232	3 518	4 193	4 287	4 875	4 965	5 212	5 787	5 488	5 796
Fuels	151	2 145	2 607	2 255	2 410	2 231	2 149	2 502	2 041	2 211
Gasoline sales tax	3	97	140	143	210	282	325	335	380	332
Other	78	1 304	1 459	1 890	2 258	2 487	2 769	2 978	3 094	3 284
Refunds on excise taxes	0	-28	-12	-1	-4	-36	-31	-28	-27	-31

Table 5.21. Peru / Perú *(cont.)*
Details of tax revenue / Ingresos tributarios detallados

Million PEN

	1990	2000	2005	2009	2010	2011	2012	2013	2014	2015
5122 Profits of fiscal monopolies	0	0	0	0	0	0	0	0	0	0
5123 Customs and import duties	64	2 741	2 681	591	933	741	880	1 077	963	1 153
5124 Taxes on exports	2	0	0	0	0	0	0	0	0	0
5125 Taxes on investment goods	0	0	0	0	0	0	0	0	0	0
5126 Taxes on specific services	0	0	173	390	428	460	496	585	614	634
Casinos and slot machines	..	..	49	163	187	195	219	269	279	279
Tourism tax	..	..	74	104	105	116	115	118	127	144
Municipal taxes on services	..	..	50	123	136	149	162	198	208	211
5127 Other taxes on internat. trade and transactions	48	0	0	0	0	0	0	0	0	0
5128 Other taxes	0	0	0	0	0	0	0	0	0	0
5130 Unallocable between 5110 and 5120	0	0	0	0	0	0	0	0	0	0
5200 Taxes on use of goods and perform activities	0	0	0	0	0	0	0	0	0	0
5210 Recurrent taxes	..	..	..	..	..	..	..	..	..	..
5211 Paid by households: motor vehicles	..	..	..	..	..	..	..	..	..	..
5212 Paid by others: motor vehicles	..	..	..	..	..	..	..	..	..	..
5213 Paid in respect of other goods	..	..	..	..	..	..	..	..	..	..
5220 Non-recurrent taxes	..	..	..	..	..	..	..	..	..	..
5300 Unallocable between 5100 and 5200	0	0	0	0	0	0	0	0	0	0
6000 Other taxes	**36**	**741**	**1 209**	**1 847**	**1 916**	**1 814**	**2 500**	**2 459**	**1 944**	**1 387**
6100 Paid solely by business	0	84	73	98	108	118	133	147	158	179
Single simplified regime	..	84	73	98	108	118	133	147	158	179
University Development Fund	..	0	0	0	0	0	0	0	0	0
6200 Other	36	658	1 136	1 749	1 808	1 697	2 367	2 312	1 786	1 208
Tax debt payments	9	543	397	735	714	709	857	893	814	922
Penalties	0	114	159	287	330	453	937	1 001	831	559
Municipal fees	0	0	450	643	672	704	798	568	527	461
Other national level	28	20	171	234	238	0	0	0	0	0
Other local level	0	0	36	80	54	72	76	82	74	73
Other tax refund	0	-20	-77	-230	-199	-241	-300	-232	-461	-807

Note: Year ending 31st December.

The data are on a cash basis.

The figures for years up to and including 2004 exclude local government tax revenues as the data are not available.

The figures for tax refunds have been updated using data from refunds on the date of issuance date instead of the date of request.

Heading 2120: The solidarity contribution for pension plan has been reclassified under heading 2120. In previous publications, this tax was classified under heading 1100 (Taxes on income of individuals).

Source: Superintendencia Nacional de Aduanas y de Administración Tributaria y Banco Central de Reserva del Perú (National Superintendency for Customs and Tax Administrations and Central Reserve Bank of Peru).

StatLink http://dx.doi.org/10.1787/888933463387

Table 5.22. Trinidad and Tobago / Trinidad y Tobago
Details of tax revenue / Ingresos tributarios detallados

Million TTD

	1990	2000	2005	2009	2010	2011	2012	2013	2014	2015
Total tax revenue	**4 932**	**10 853**	**26 698**	**34 215**	**38 610**	**43 356**	**45 302**	**47 003**	**50 302**	**46 384**
1000 Taxes on income, profits and capital gains	**2 497**	**5 912**	**18 904**	**22 695**	**26 017**	**31 423**	**31 285**	**31 725**	**34 892**	**28 721**
1100 Of individuals	571	2 169	4 250	4 267	4 467	4 961	5 435	6 207	6 620	7 445
1110 On income and profits	571	2 169	4 250	4 267	4 467	4 961	5 435	6 207	6 620	7 445
Health surcharge	92	149	187	186	185	216	187	218	210	264
Insurance surrender tax	6	7	15	22	22	21	27	33	29	42
1120 On capital gains	..	..	..	..	..	..	..	..	..	..
1200 Corporate	1 856	3 547	14 118	17 250	20 670	25 265	24 767	24 633	27 330	20 209
1210 On profits	1 856	3 547	14 118	17 250	20 670	25 265	24 767	24 633	27 330	20 209
Oil companies	1 439	2 441	10 806	11 881	13 834	16 023	15 827	14 772	16 970	10 513
Other companies	383	1 041	3 166	5 170	6 630	9 034	8 647	9 675	10 151	9 481
Business levy	0	65	146	199	206	209	294	187	210	215
National recovery impost	34	0	0	0	0	0	0	0	0	0
1220 On capital gains	..	..	..	..	..	..	..	..	..	..
1300 Unallocable between 1100 and 1200	70	195	536	1 178	881	1 197	1 084	885	942	1 067
2000 Social security contributions	**183**	**702**	**1 173**	**2 549**	**2 645**	**2 723**	**3 086**	**3 514**	**4 137**	**4 639**
2100 Employees	..	..	..	..	..	..	..	..	..	..
2110 On a payroll basis	..	..	..	..	..	..	..	..	..	..
2120 On an income tax basis	..	..	..	..	..	..	..	..	..	..
2200 Employers	..	..	..	..	..	..	..	..	..	..
2210 On a payroll basis	..	..	..	..	..	..	..	..	..	..
2220 On an income tax basis	..	..	..	..	..	..	..	..	..	..
2300 Self-employed or non-employed	..	..	..	..	..	..	..	..	..	..
2310 On a payroll basis	..	..	..	..	..	..	..	..	..	..
2320 On an income tax basis	..	..	..	..	..	..	..	..	..	..
2400 Unallocable between 2100, 2200 and 2300	183	702	1 173	2 549	2 645	2 723	3 086	3 514	4 137	4 639
2410 On a payroll basis	..	..	..	..	..	..	..	..	..	..
2420 On an income tax basis	..	..	..	..	..	..	..	..	..	..
3000 Taxes on payroll and workforce	**0**	**0**	**0**	**0**	**0**	**0**	**0**	**0**	**0**	**0**
4000 Taxes on property	**148**	**277**	**389**	**523**	**433**	**470**	**472**	**635**	**742**	**703**
4100 Recurrent taxes on immovable property	147	277	389	523	433	470	472	635	742	703
Lands and building taxes	39	64	63	71	22	11	5	4	3	3
House rate tax	108	213	326	452	411	459	468	631	738	700
4110 Households	..	..	..	..	..	..	..	..	..	..
4120 Others	..	..	..	..	..	..	..	..	..	..
4200 Recurrent taxes on net wealth	0	0	0	0	0	0	0	0	0	0
4210 Individual	..	..	..	..	..	..	..	..	..	..
4220 Corporate	..	..	..	..	..	..	..	..	..	..
4300 Estate, inheritance and gift taxes	1	0	0	0	0	0	0	0	0	0
4310 Estate and inheritance taxes	1	..	..	..	..	..	..	..	..	..
4320 Gift taxes	0	..	..	..	..	..	..	..	..	..
4400 Taxes on financial and capital transactions	0	0	0	0	0	0	0	0	0	0
4500 Non-recurrent taxes	0	0	0	0	0	0	0	0	0	0
4510 On net wealth	..	..	..	..	..	..	..	..	..	..
4520 Other non-recurrent taxes	..	..	..	..	..	..	..	..	..	..
4600 Other recurrent taxes on property	0	0	0	0	0	0	0	0	0	0
5000 Taxes on goods and services	**2 055**	**3 852**	**5 988**	**8 258**	**9 342**	**8 556**	**10 245**	**10 883**	**10 246**	**11 918**
5100 Taxes on production, sale, transfer, etc	1 928	3 559	5 690	7 880	8 924	8 077	9 663	10 273	9 614	11 271
5110 General taxes	980	1 890	2 963	5 147	6 032	4 917	6 337	6 658	5 745	7 223
5111 Value added taxes	927	1 890	2 963	5 147	6 032	4 917	6 337	6 657	5 745	7 223
5112 Sales tax	54	0	0	0	0	0	0	0	0	0
5113 Other	0	0	0	0	0	0	0	0	0	0
5120 Taxes on specific goods and services	948	1 669	2 727	2 733	2 891	3 160	3 326	3 616	3 869	4 048
5121 Excises	481	801	1 072	629	708	708	729	707	680	703
Excise duties	473	801	1 071	627	705	705	725	704	676	695
Alcohol and tobacco taxes	9	0	1	2	2	3	3	3	4	8
5122 Profits of fiscal monopolies	0	0	0	0	0	0	0	0	0	0
5123 Customs and import duties	260	748	1 473	1 828	1 905	2 168	2 319	2 588	2 861	3 014
5124 Taxes on exports	0	0	0	0	0	0	0	0	0	0
5125 Taxes on investment goods	0	0	0	0	0	0	0	0	0	0
5126 Taxes on specific services	4	120	182	275	278	284	278	322	328	330
Insurance premium tax	0	56	98	146	167	172	174	194	197	191
Transaction tax on financial services	0	23	33	53	53	55	57	64	75	75
Hotel room tax	0	23	42	52	46	43	46	50	56	64
Betting and entertainment taxes	4	17	9	24	12	14	0	13	0	0
5127 Other taxes on internat. trade and transactions	202	0	0	0	1	0	0	0	0	0
5128 Other taxes	0	0	0	0	0	0	0	0	0	0
5130 Unallocable between 5110 and 5120	0	0	0	0	0	0	0	0	0	0

Table 5.22. Trinidad and Tobago / Trinidad y Tobago (cont.)
Details of tax revenue / Ingresos tributarios detallados

Million TTD

	1990	2000	2005	2009	2010	2011	2012	2013	2014	2015
5200 Taxes on use of goods and perform activities	127	293	299	378	418	479	582	610	632	647
5210 Recurrent taxes	127	293	299	378	418	479	582	610	632	647
Motor vehicle taxes and duties	76	239	217	327	375	429	524	552	569	575
5211 Paid by households: motor vehicles	0	0	0	0	0	0	0	0	0	0
5212 Paid by others: motor vehicles	0	0	0	0	0	0	0	0	0	0
5213 Paid in respect of other goods	51	53	82	50	43	50	57	58	63	71
Liquor and miscellaneous business license fees	5	10	10	10	10	11	10	11	11	11
Other taxes on the use of goods	45	44	72	40	33	39	47	47	52	61
5220 Non-recurrent taxes	0	0	0	0	0	0	0	0	0	0
5300 Unallocable between 5100 and 5200	0	0	0	0	0	0	0	0	0	0
6000 Other taxes	**49**	**111**	**245**	**190**	**172**	**185**	**214**	**246**	**285**	**403**
6100 Paid solely by business	0	0	0	0	0	0	0	0	0	0
6200 Other	49	111	245	190	172	185	214	246	285	403
Stamp duties	49	111	245	190	172	185	214	246	285	403

Note: Fiscal year ending on 30th September.

The data are on a cash basis.

Heading 4100: The data are estimated for 2015 at the local level.

Source: Ministry of Finance and BID-CIAT (2015), *Equivalent Fiscal Pressure for Latin America and the Caribbean.*

StatLink http://dx.doi.org/10.1787/888933463398

Table 5.23. Uruguay
Details of tax revenue / Ingresos tributarios detallados

Million UYU

	1990	2000	2005	2009	2010	2011	2012	2013	2014	2015
Total tax revenue	**2 351**	**59 703**	**101 442**	**183 929**	**210 869**	**245 045**	**278 720**	**322 351**	**361 950**	**393 704**
1000 Taxes on income, profits and capital gains	**114**	**5 620**	**11 969**	**38 126**	**44 068**	**50 323**	**57 336**	**70 132**	**75 269**	**86 404**
1100 Of individuals	0	0	44	16 101	19 148	23 795	29 116	33 378	40 334	45 451
1110 On income and profits	..	..	44	3 660	4 505	5 374	6 583	7 330	8 969	10 571
First category	..	..	..	1 921	2 358	2 946	3 764	4 278	4 967	5 838
Social security assistance	..	..	..	2 066	2 651	3 061	3 773	4 285	5 518	6 576
Tax refund	..	..	..	-327	-504	-634	-955	-1 233	-1 517	-1 844
1120 On capital gains	..	..	..	12 441	14 643	18 422	22 534	26 048	31 365	34 881
Second category	..	..	..	12 441	14 643	18 422	22 534	26 048	31 365	34 881
1200 Corporate	114	5 620	11 925	20 240	23 257	23 940	26 166	34 075	31 698	37 078
1210 On profits	114	5 620	11 925	20 240	23 257	23 940	26 166	34 075	31 698	37 078
Corporate income tax (IRAE)	0	0	0	16 512	21 280	21 719	23 937	31 812	29 152	34 375
Corporate income tax (IRIC)	97	5 096	10 516	2 355	491	469	414	387	396	439
Small firms (minimum VAT)	0	296	457	596	586	600	631	686	741	796
Other	17	228	952	777	900	1 151	1 185	1 190	1 408	1 467
1220 On capital gains	..	..	..	..	..	..	..	..	..	..
1300 Unallocable between 1100 and 1200	0	0	0	1 785	1 662	2 588	2 053	2 679	3 237	3 875
Non resident taxpayers	0	0	0	1 785	1 662	2 588	2 053	2 679	3 237	3 875
2000 Social security contributions	**717**	**17 679**	**21 425**	**42 922**	**49 742**	**59 930**	**72 601**	**86 012**	**100 993**	**108 742**
2100 Employees	..	..	..	..	..	..	..	..	..	..
2110 On a payroll basis	..	..	..	..	..	..	..	..	..	..
2120 On an income tax basis	..	..	..	..	..	..	..	..	..	..
2200 Employers	..	..	..	..	..	..	..	..	..	..
2210 On a payroll basis	..	..	..	..	..	..	..	..	..	..
2220 On an income tax basis	..	..	..	..	..	..	..	..	..	..
2300 Self-employed or non-employed	..	..	..	..	..	..	..	..	..	..
2310 On a payroll basis	..	..	..	..	..	..	..	..	..	..
2320 On an income tax basis	..	..	..	..	..	..	..	..	..	..
2400 Unallocable between 2100, 2200 and 2300	717	17 679	21 425	42 922	49 742	59 930	72 601	86 012	100 993	108 742
2410 On a payroll basis	717	17 679	21 425	42 922	49 742	59 930	72 601	86 012	100 993	108 742
2420 On an income tax basis	0	0	0	0	0	0	0	0	0	0
3000 Taxes on payroll and workforce	**0**	**0**	**0**	**0**	**0**	**0**	**0**	**0**	**0**	**0**
4000 Taxes on property	**196**	**6 123**	**12 176**	**16 294**	**18 118**	**20 206**	**21 940**	**24 198**	**27 357**	**30 369**
4100 Recurrent taxes on immovable property	71	2 567	4 776	6 334	7 491	8 187	8 993	10 310	11 698	13 471
4110 Households	0	0	0	0	0	0	0	0	0	0
4120 Others	71	2 567	4 776	6 334	7 491	8 187	8 993	10 310	11 698	13 471
4200 Recurrent taxes on net wealth	94	2 076	4 943	8 634	8 948	10 030	11 067	11 892	13 714	14 776
4210 Individual	64	108	336	371	382	422	445	491	629	606
4220 Corporate	30	1 968	4 607	8 263	8 567	9 607	10 622	11 401	13 085	14 170
Corporate wealth	28	1 661	4 383	8 056	8 354	9 413	10 609	11 390	13 079	14 167
Other	1	307	224	207	213	194	13	11	6	3
4300 Estate, inheritance and gift taxes	0	0	0	0	0	0	0	0	0	0
4310 Estate and inheritance taxes	..	..	..	..	..	..	..	..	..	..
4320 Gift taxes	..	..	..	..	..	..	..	..	..	..
4400 Taxes on financial and capital transactions	0	372	886	1 027	1 347	1 545	1 413	1 516	1 442	1 601
Capital transfers	..	372	886	1 027	1 347	1 545	1 413	1 516	1 442	1 601
Capital transfers (additional)	..	0	0	0	0	0	0	0	0	0
4500 Non-recurrent taxes	0	0	0	0	0	0	0	0	0	0
4510 On net wealth	..	..	..	..	..	..	..	..	..	..
4520 Other non-recurrent taxes	..	..	..	..	..	..	..	..	..	..
4600 Other recurrent taxes on property	31	1 107	1 571	299	331	445	466	480	503	522
5000 Taxes on goods and services	**1 334**	**30 877**	**55 798**	**86 505**	**98 942**	**114 586**	**126 844**	**141 794**	**157 790**	**167 686**
5100 Taxes on production, sale, transfer, etc	1 270	28 301	52 727	82 657	94 990	110 473	122 310	136 035	151 001	160 146
5110 General taxes	660	18 009	34 641	61 469	69 365	79 672	88 338	98 758	108 260	113 651
5111 Value added taxes	660	17 995	34 601	61 469	69 365	79 672	88 338	98 758	108 260	113 651
5112 Sales tax	1	14	40	0	0	0	0	0	0	0
5113 Other	0	0	0	0	0	0	0	0	0	0
5120 Taxes on specific goods and services	610	10 291	18 086	21 188	25 625	30 801	33 972	37 278	42 741	46 495
5121 Excises	393	7 673	10 524	13 312	16 401	19 401	21 417	23 365	26 362	29 710
Fuels	203	4 067	4 900	5 462	6 551	8 447	9 147	10 269	11 816	14 096
Tobacco products	80	1 741	2 705	3 248	4 236	4 925	4 768	4 755	4 913	5 778
Alcoholic beverages	24	229	375	657	602	622	800	840	918	811
Beer	8	205	308	480	602	895	895	1 024	1 035	1 102
Non-alcoholic beverages	19	464	532	1 240	1 172	1 451	1 518	1 718	1 926	2 131
Motor vehicles	20	656	977	1 662	2 289	2 710	3 025	3 388	3 924	4 017
Sales of agricultural goods (MEVIR and INIA)	4	76	260	414	451	538	648	681	736	736
Other	35	235	468	148	497	-188	616	689	1 094	1 039
5122 Profits of fiscal monopolies	0	0	0	0	0	0	0	0	0	0

Table 5.23. Uruguay *(cont.)*
Details of tax revenue / Ingresos tributarios detallados

Million UYU

	1990	2000	2005	2009	2010	2011	2012	2013	2014	2015
5123 Customs and import duties	214	1 967	5 195	7 042	8 478	10 543	11 670	13 020	15 167	15 440
5124 Taxes on exports	1	92	287	349	371	446	432	422	520	582
5125 Taxes on investment goods	0	0	0	0	0	0	0	0	0	0
5126 Taxes on specific services	3	293	1 590	484	376	411	454	470	691	763
5127 Other taxes on internat. trade and transactions	0	265	489	0	0	0	0	0	0	0
5128 Other taxes	0	0	0	0	0	0	0	0	0	0
5130 Unallocable between 5110 and 5120	0	0	0	0	0	0	0	0	0	0
5200 Taxes on use of goods and perform activities	64	2 576	3 071	3 848	3 952	4 113	4 534	5 759	6 789	7 540
5210 Recurrent taxes	64	2 576	3 071	3 848	3 952	4 113	4 534	5 759	6 789	7 540
5211 Paid by households: motor vehicles	0	0	0	0	0	0	0	0	0	0
5212 Paid by others: motor vehicles	64	2 576	3 071	3 848	3 952	4 113	4 534	5 759	6 789	7 540
5213 Paid in respect of other goods	0	0	0	0	0	0	0	0	0	0
5220 Non-recurrent taxes	0	0	0	0	0	0	0	0	0	0
5300 Unallocable between 5100 and 5200	0	0	0	0	0	0	0	0	0	0
6000 Other taxes	**-10**	**-596**	**76**	**82**	**0**	**0**	**0**	**214**	**541**	**503**
6100 Paid solely by business	-10	-596	76	82	0	0	0	214	541	503
6200 Other	0	0	0	0	0	0	0	0	0	0

Note: Year ending 31st December.

The data are on a cash basis.

Heading 2000: Figures for 1990-98 are estimated by the Direction General of Taxes as the methodology they use to calculate social security contributions was not employed until 1999.

Heading 4120: The data have been revised from 1990.

Headings 4000 and 5000: In ECLAC data, the tax on sales in public auctions is classified in category 4000.

Heading 5112: In ECLAC data, the tax on the sale of goods by public auctions is classified in category 4000

Source: Dirección General Impositiva, Banco de Previsión Social e Instituto Nacional de Estadísticas (General Tax Directorate, Social Security Bank and National Statistics Institute).

StatLink http://dx.doi.org/10.1787/888933463409

Table 5.24. Venezuela
Details of tax revenue / Ingresos tributarios detallados

Million VEF

	1990	2000	2005	2009	2010	2011	2012	2013	2014	2015
Total tax revenue	**412**	**10 849**	**48 285**	**101 014**	**120 455**	**183 748**	**232 106**	**325 472**	**574 426**	**1 260 083**
1000 Taxes on income, profits and capital gains	**344**	**4 686**	**18 529**	**38 966**	**36 836**	**53 280**	**70 739**	**93 694**	**187 884**	**284 786**
1100 Of individuals	..	..	..	..	..	..	..	..	..	..
1110 On income and profits	..	..	..	..	..	..	..	..	..	..
1120 On capital gains	..	..	..	..	..	..	..	..	..	..
1200 Corporate	315	3 368	11 184	12 944	8 700	16 510	22 879	25 270	67 601	47 388
1210 On profits	315	3 368	11 184	12 944	8 700	16 510	22 879	25 270	67 601	47 388
Oil	315	3 368	11 184	12 944	8 700	16 510	22 879	25 270	67 601	47 388
1220 On capital gains	..	..	..	..	..	..	..	..	..	..
1300 Unallocable between 1100 and 1200	30	1 317	7 345	26 022	28 137	36 770	47 859	68 424	120 283	237 399
2000 Social security contributions	**20**	**591**	**1 890**	**6 740**	**9 690**	**12 936**	**15 585**	**21 422**	**28 600**	**38 200**
2100 Employees	..	..	..	..	..	..	..	..	..	..
2110 On a payroll basis	..	..	..	..	..	..	..	..	..	..
2120 On an income tax basis	..	..	..	..	..	..	..	..	..	..
2200 Employers	..	..	..	..	..	..	..	..	..	..
2210 On a payroll basis	..	..	..	..	..	..	..	..	..	..
2220 On an income tax basis	..	..	..	..	..	..	..	..	..	..
2300 Self-employed or non-employed	..	..	..	..	..	..	..	..	..	..
2310 On a payroll basis	..	..	..	..	..	..	..	..	..	..
2320 On an income tax basis	..	..	..	..	..	..	..	..	..	..
2400 Unallocable between 2100, 2200 and 2300	20	591	1 890	6 740	9 690	12 936	15 585	21 422	28 600	38 200
2410 On a payroll basis	..	..	..	..	..	..	..	..	..	..
2420 On an income tax basis	..	..	..	..	..	..	..	..	..	..
3000 Taxes on payroll and workforce	**0**	**0**	**0**	**0**	**0**	**0**	**0**	**0**	**0**	**0**
4000 Taxes on property	**1**	**400**	**2 834**	**175**	**222**	**273**	**346**	**530**	**1 044**	**2 946**
4100 Recurrent taxes on immovable property	0	0	0	0	0	0	0	0	0	0
4110 Households	..	..	..	..	..	..	..	..	..	..
4120 Others	..	..	..	..	..	..	..	..	..	..
4200 Recurrent taxes on net wealth	0	0	0	0	0	0	0	0	0	0
4210 Individual	..	..	..	..	..	..	..	..	..	..
4220 Corporate	..	..	..	..	..	..	..	..	..	..
4300 Estate, inheritance and gift taxes	1	19	55	175	222	273	346	530	1 044	2 946
4310 Estate and inheritance taxes	..	..	..	..	..	..	..	..	..	..
4320 Gift taxes	..	..	..	..	..	..	..	..	..	..
4400 Taxes on financial and capital transactions	0	381	2 779	0	0	0	0	0	0	0
Bank debits	..	292	2 743	..	..	..	..	..	..	..
Registration of immovable property rights	..	89	36	..	..	..	..	..	..	..
4500 Non-recurrent taxes	0	0	0	0	0	0	0	0	0	0
4510 On net wealth	..	..	..	..	..	..	..	..	..	..
4520 Other non-recurrent taxes	..	..	..	..	..	..	..	..	..	..
4600 Other recurrent taxes on property	0	0	0	0	0	0	0	0	0	0
5000 Taxes on goods and services	**46**	**5 173**	**25 032**	**55 134**	**73 707**	**108 268**	**141 505**	**205 423**	**348 872**	**918 317**
5100 Taxes on production, sale, transfer, etc	46	5 173	25 032	55 134	73 707	108 268	141 505	205 423	348 872	918 317
5110 General taxes	0	3 272	19 513	41 611	56 101	84 348	111 102	164 737	272 187	702 743
5111 Value added taxes	..	3 272	19 513	41 611	56 101	84 348	111 102	164 737	272 187	702 743
5112 Sales tax	..	0	0	0	0	0	0	0	0	0
5113 Other	..	0	0	0	0	0	0	0	0	0
5120 Taxes on specific goods and services	46	1 901	5 519	13 523	17 606	23 920	30 403	40 686	76 685	215 575
5121 Excises	16	774	1 604	6 727	8 872	8 774	11 247	16 371	30 525	116 575
Oil	6	468	472	756	1 280	0	0	0	0	0
Alcoholic beverages	6	85	427	1 765	2 192	2 762	3 542	5 975	10 888	44 498
Tobacco	4	220	704	4 205	5 401	6 011	7 706	10 397	19 636	72 077
Matches	0	1	1	2	0	0	0	0	0	0
5122 Profits of fiscal monopolies	0	0	0	0	0	0	0	0	0	0
5123 Customs and import duties	30	972	3 652	6 409	8 504	15 017	19 052	24 185	45 998	98 757
5124 Taxes on exports	0	0	0	0	0	0	0	0	0	0
5125 Taxes on investment goods	0	0	0	0	0	0	0	0	0	0
5126 Taxes on specific services	0	155	263	386	230	129	104	130	162	242
Telecommunications	0	151	237	183	0	0	0	0	0	0
Casinos, bingo and slot machines	0	5	26	203	230	129	104	130	162	242
5127 Other taxes on internat. trade and transactions	0	0	0	0	0	0	0	0	0	0
5128 Other taxes	0	0	0	0	0	0	0	0	0	0
5130 Unallocable between 5110 and 5120	0	0	0	0	0	0	0	0	0	0
5200 Taxes on use of goods and perform activities	0	0	0	0	0	0	0	0	0	0
5210 Recurrent taxes	..	..	..	..	..	..	..	..	..	..
5211 Paid by households: motor vehicles	..	..	..	..	..	..	..	..	..	..
5212 Paid by others: motor vehicles	..	..	..	..	..	..	..	..	..	..
5213 Paid in respect of other goods	..	..	..	..	..	..	..	..	..	..

Table 5.24. Venezuela (cont.)
Details of tax revenue / Ingresos tributarios detallados

Million VEF

	1990	2000	2005	2009	2010	2011	2012	2013	2014	2015
5220 Non-recurrent taxes	..	..	..	..	..	..	..	..	..	..
5300 Unallocable between 5100 and 5200	0	0	0	0	0	0	0	0	0	0
6000 Other taxes	**0**	**0**	**0**	**0**	**0**	**8 991**	**3 931**	**4 403**	**8 026**	**15 833**
6100 Paid solely by business	..	..	..	..	..	0	0	0	0	0
6200 Other	..	..	..	..	..	8 991	3 931	4 403	8 026	15 833

Note: The figures for 2015 should be interpreted with caution as they have been affected by the high rate of inflation over this period.
Year ending 31st December.
The data are on a cash basis.
The figures exclude state and local government tax revenues as the data are not available.
Heading 1210: The data on oil profits for 2015 are estimated by Oficina Nacional de Presupuesto (Onapre) and Oficina Nacional del Tesoro (ONT).
Heading 2000: The data on social security contributions are estimated from 2011.
Heading 5121: Data on oil excises are not available from 2011.

Source: Servicio Nacional Integrado de Administración Aduanera y Tributaria, Ministerio de Finanzas (National Integrated Service of Customs and Tax Administration, Ministry of Finance).

StatLink http://dx.doi.org/10.1787/888933463419

CHAPTER 6

TAX REVENUES BY SUB-SECTORS OF GENERAL GOVERNMENT

Revenues of both the Latin American and the OECD countries have been attributed to the different levels of government according to the revised guidelines set out in to the final version of the 2008 System of National Accounts (SNA). Under this, revenues are generally attributed to the level of government that exercises the authority to impose the tax or has the final discretion to set and vary the tax rate.

CAPÍTULO 6

INGRESOS TRIBUTARIOS POR SUB-SECTORES DE GOBIERNO GENERAL

Los ingresos de los países latinoamericanos y de los países de la OCDE se han atribuido a los diferentes niveles de gobierno de acuerdo con lo recogido en la versión final 2008 del Sistema de Cuentas Nacionales (SCN), según el cual, los ingresos se atribuyen por lo general al nivel de gobierno que ejerce la facultad de aplicar el impuesto o que puede a su discreción establecer y modificar la tasa del impuesto.

Table 6.1. Argentina, tax revenues by sub-sectors of government

Million ARS

	Federal government					State/Regional				
	1990	2000	2005	2010	2015	1990	2000	2005	2010	2015
1000 Taxes on income, profits and capital gains	**542**	**11 303**	**29 203**	**78 427**	**384 536**	**0**	**0**	**0**	**0**	**0**
1100 Of individuals	141	3 937	8 192	23 980	188 218	..	..	..	..	..
1200 Corporate	357	6 575	19 602	50 664	185 725	..	..	..	..	..
1300 Unallocable between 1100 and 1200	43	792	1 409	3 783	10 593	..	..	..	..	..
2000 Social security contributions	**0**	**0**	**0**	**0**	**0**	**0**	**0**	**0**	**0**	**0**
2100 Employees	..	..	..	..	..	..	..	..	..	..
2200 Employers	..	..	..	..	..	..	..	..	..	..
2300 Self-employed or non-employed	..	..	..	..	..	..	..	..	..	..
2400 Unallocable between 2100, 2200 and 2300	..	..	..	..	..	..	..	..	..	..
3000 Taxes on payroll and workforce	**0**	**0**	**0**	**0**	**0**	**0**	**0**	**0**	**0**	**0**
4000 Taxes on property	**616**	**1 254**	**11 439**	**32 674**	**117 274**	**549**	**2 614**	**4 558**	**10 864**	**48 908**
4100 Recurrent taxes on immovable property	0	0	0	0	0	419	1 809	2 837	5 035	21 738
4200 Recurrent taxes on net wealth	246	1 084	1 867	5 248	18 538	0	0	0	0	0
4300 Estate, inheritance and gift taxes	0	0	0	0	0	0	0	0	0	0
4400 Taxes on financial and capital transactions	330	100	9 550	27 423	98 736	130	804	1 722	5 829	27 170
4500 Non-recurrent taxes	40	70	21	3	0	0	0	0	0	0
4600 Other recurrent taxes on property	0	0	0	0	0	0	0	0	0	0
5000 Taxes on goods and services	**4 669**	**27 592**	**62 056**	**198 346**	**634 068**	**967**	**6 947**	**15 903**	**54 746**	**255 256**
5100 Taxes on production, sale, transfer, etc	4 671	28 174	63 941	201 402	642 899	791	6 114	14 613	51 148	238 221
5110 General taxes	1 594	19 009	36 853	116 386	433 076	791	6 114	14 613	51 148	238 221
5120 Taxes on specific goods and services	3 077	9 166	27 088	85 016	209 822	0	0	0	0	0
5130 Unallocable between 5110 and 5120	0	0	0	0	0	0	0	0	0	0
5200 Taxes on use of goods and perform activities[1]	0	0	0	0	0	177	833	1 289	3 598	17 035
5300 Unallocable between 5100 and 5200	-3	-583	-1 885	-3 056	-8 831	0	0	0	0	0
6000 Other taxes	**214**	**395**	**877**	**2 386**	**6 931**	**78**	**1 309**	**1 469**	**3 110**	**10 533**
6100 Paid solely by business	0	354	757	2 093	5 624	0	0	0	0	0
6200 Other	214	41	120	294	1 306	78	1 309	1 469	3 110	10 533
Total tax revenue	**6 040**	**40 544**	**103 575**	**311 834**	**1 142 808**	**1 594**	**10 870**	**21 931**	**68 720**	**314 697**

Million ARS

	Local government[2]					Social Security Funds				
	1990	2000	2005	2010	2015	1990	2000	2005	2010	2015
1000 Taxes on income, profits and capital gains	..	..	..	..	..	**0**	**0**	**0**	**0**	**0**
1100 Of individuals	..	..	..	..	..	..	..	..	..	..
1200 Corporate	..	..	..	..	..	..	..	..	..	..
1300 Unallocable between 1100 and 1200	..	..	..	..	..	..	..	..	..	..
2000 Social security contributions	..	..	..	..	..	**2 583**	**9 670**	**17 400**	**102 460**	**415 410**
2100 Employees	..	..	..	..	..	0	2 486	3 690	37 990	163 590
2200 Employers	..	..	..	..	..	0	6 069	12 557	54 713	235 610
2300 Self-employed or non-employed	..	..	..	..	..	98	1 115	1 153	9 757	16 210
2400 Unallocable between 2100, 2200 and 2300	..	..	..	..	..	2 485	0	0	0	0
3000 Taxes on payroll and workforce	..	..	..	..	..	**0**	**0**	**0**	**0**	**0**
4000 Taxes on property	..	..	..	..	..	**0**	**0**	**0**	**0**	**0**
4100 Recurrent taxes on immovable property	..	..	..	..	..	..	..	..	..	..
4200 Recurrent taxes on net wealth	..	..	..	..	..	..	..	..	..	..
4300 Estate, inheritance and gift taxes	..	..	..	..	..	..	..	..	..	..
4400 Taxes on financial and capital transactions	..	..	..	..	..	..	..	..	..	..
4500 Non-recurrent taxes	..	..	..	..	..	..	..	..	..	..
4600 Other recurrent taxes on property	..	..	..	..	..	..	..	..	..	..
5000 Taxes on goods and services	..	..	..	..	..	**0**	**0**	**0**	**0**	**0**
5100 Taxes on production, sale, transfer, etc	..	..	..	..	..	..	..	..	..	..
5110 General taxes	..	..	..	..	..	..	..	..	..	..
5120 Taxes on specific goods and services	..	..	..	..	..	..	..	..	..	..
5130 Unallocable between 5110 and 5120	..	..	..	..	..	..	..	..	..	..
5200 Taxes on use of goods and perform activities[1]	..	..	..	..	..	..	..	..	..	..
5300 Unallocable between 5100 and 5200	..	..	..	..	..	..	..	..	..	..
6000 Other taxes	..	..	..	..	..	**0**	**0**	**0**	**0**	**0**
6100 Paid solely by business	..	..	..	..	..	..	..	..	..	..
6200 Other	..	..	..	..	..	..	..	..	..	..
Total tax revenue	..	..	..	..	..	**2 583**	**9 670**	**17 400**	**102 460**	**415 410**

1. In ECLAC data, tax on ownership of motor vehicles is classified in category 4000.
2. The figures exclude local government tax revenues as the data are not available.

StatLink http://dx.doi.org/10.1787/888933463420

Table 6.2. Bahamas, tax revenues by sub-sectors of government

Million BSD

	Federal government					State/Regional				
	1990	2000	2005	2010	2015	1990	2000	2005	2010	2015
1000 Taxes on income, profits and capital gains	**0**	**0**	**0**	**0**	**0**	..	..	..	..	..
1100 Of individuals	..	..	..	..	..	..	..	..	..	..
1200 Corporate	..	..	..	..	..	..	..	..	..	..
1300 Unallocable between 1100 and 1200	..	..	..	..	..	..	..	..	..	..
2000 Social security contributions	**0**	**0**	**0**	**0**	**0**	..	..	..	..	..
2100 Employees	..	..	..	..	..	..	..	..	..	..
2200 Employers	..	..	..	..	..	..	..	..	..	..
2300 Self-employed or non-employed	..	..	..	..	..	..	..	..	..	..
2400 Unallocable between 2100, 2200 and 2300	..	..	..	..	..	..	..	..	..	..
3000 Taxes on payroll and workforce	**0**	**0**	**0**	**0**	**0**	..	..	..	..	..
4000 Taxes on property	**19**	**32**	**54**	**92**	**107**	..	..	..	..	..
4100 Recurrent taxes on immovable property	19	32	54	92	107	..	..	..	..	..
4200 Recurrent taxes on net wealth	0	0	0	0	0	..	..	..	..	..
4300 Estate, inheritance and gift taxes	0	0	0	0	0	..	..	..	..	..
4400 Taxes on financial and capital transactions	0	0	0	0	0	..	..	..	..	..
4500 Non-recurrent taxes	0	0	0	0	0	..	..	..	..	..
4600 Other recurrent taxes on property	0	0	0	0	0	..	..	..	..	..
5000 Taxes on goods and services	**386**	**723**	**736**	**795**	**1 203**	..	..	..	..	..
5100 Taxes on production, sale, transfer, etc	354	654	657	672	993	..	..	..	..	..
5110 General taxes	0	0	0	0	219	..	..	..	..	..
5120 Taxes on specific goods and services	354	654	657	672	775	..	..	..	..	..
5130 Unallocable between 5110 and 5120	0	0	0	0	0	..	..	..	..	..
5200 Taxes on use of goods and perform activities	32	69	78	123	209	..	..	..	..	..
5300 Unallocable between 5100 and 5200	0	0	0	0	0	..	..	..	..	..
6000 Other taxes	**33**	**95**	**135**	**223**	**191**	..	..	..	..	..
6100 Paid solely by business	0	0	0	0	0	..	..	..	..	..
6200 Other	33	95	135	223	191	..	..	..	..	..
Total tax revenue	**438**	**849**	**924**	**1 109**	**1 500**	..	..	..	..	..

Million BSD

	Local government[2]					Social Security Funds				
	1990	2000	2005	2010	2015	1990	2000	2005	2010	2015
1000 Taxes on income, profits and capital gains	..	..	..	..	..	**0**	**0**	**0**	**0**	**0**
1100 Of individuals	..	..	..	..	..	..	..	..	..	..
1200 Corporate	..	..	..	..	..	..	..	..	..	..
1300 Unallocable between 1100 and 1200	..	..	..	..	..	..	..	..	..	..
2000 Social security contributions[1]	..	..	..	..	..	**66**	**115**	**136**	**167**	**260**
2100 Employees	..	..	..	..	..	..	..	..	..	..
2200 Employers	..	..	..	..	..	..	..	..	..	..
2300 Self-employed or non-employed	..	..	..	..	..	..	..	..	..	..
2400 Unallocable between 2100, 2200 and 2300	..	..	..	..	..	66	115	136	167	260
3000 Taxes on payroll and workforce	..	..	..	..	..	**0**	**0**	**0**	**0**	**0**
4000 Taxes on property	..	..	..	..	..	**0**	**0**	**0**	**0**	**0**
4100 Recurrent taxes on immovable property	..	..	..	..	..	..	..	..	..	..
4200 Recurrent taxes on net wealth	..	..	..	..	..	..	..	..	..	..
4300 Estate, inheritance and gift taxes	..	..	..	..	..	..	..	..	..	..
4400 Taxes on financial and capital transactions	..	..	..	..	..	..	..	..	..	..
4500 Non-recurrent taxes	..	..	..	..	..	..	..	..	..	..
4600 Other recurrent taxes on property	..	..	..	..	..	..	..	..	..	..
5000 Taxes on goods and services	..	..	..	..	..	**0**	**0**	**0**	**0**	**0**
5100 Taxes on production, sale, transfer, etc	..	..	..	..	..	..	..	..	..	..
5110 General taxes	..	..	..	..	..	..	..	..	..	..
5120 Taxes on specific goods and services	..	..	..	..	..	..	..	..	..	..
5130 Unallocable between 5110 and 5120	..	..	..	..	..	..	..	..	..	..
5200 Taxes on use of goods and perform activities	..	..	..	..	..	..	..	..	..	..
5300 Unallocable between 5100 and 5200	..	..	..	..	..	..	..	..	..	..
6000 Other taxes	..	..	..	..	..	**0**	**0**	**0**	**0**	**0**
6100 Paid solely by business	..	..	..	..	..	..	..	..	..	..
6200 Other	..	..	..	..	..	..	..	..	..	..
Total tax revenue	..	..	..	..	..	**66**	**115**	**136**	**167**	**260**

1. The data for social security contributions are estimated for 2015.
2. The figures exclude local government tax revenues as the data are not available.

StatLink http://dx.doi.org/10.1787/888933463432

Table 6.3. Barbados, tax revenues by sub-sectors of government

Thousand BAR

	Federal government					State/Regional				
	1990	2000	2005	2010	2015	1990	2000	2005	2010	2015
1000 Taxes on income, profits and capital gains	**254 016**	**573 920**	**639 432**	**762 340**	**727 047**	..	..	..	..	..
1100 Of individuals	128 857	288 692	295 737	388 177	451 578	..	..	..	..	..
1200 Corporate	111 111	252 291	294 320	327 471	209 959	..	..	..	..	..
1300 Unallocable between 1100 and 1200	14 048	32 937	49 375	46 692	65 510	..	..	..	..	..
2000 Social security contributions	**0**	**0**	**0**	**0**	**0**	..	..	..	..	..
2100 Employees	..	..	..	..	..	..	..	..	..	..
2200 Employers	..	..	..	..	..	..	..	..	..	..
2300 Self-employed or non-employed	..	..	..	..	..	..	..	..	..	..
2400 Unallocable between 2100, 2200 and 2300	..	..	..	..	..	..	..	..	..	..
3000 Taxes on payroll and workforce	**0**	**0**	**0**	**0**	**0**	..	..	..	..	..
4000 Taxes on property	**39 117**	**91 928**	**127 362**	**113 533**	**149 963**	..	..	..	..	..
4100 Recurrent taxes on immovable property	25 991	60 216	76 247	97 595	134 424	..	..	..	..	..
4200 Recurrent taxes on net wealth	0	0	0	0	0	..	..	..	..	..
4300 Estate, inheritance and gift taxes	0	0	0	0	0	..	..	..	..	..
4400 Taxes on financial and capital transactions	0	0	0	0	0	..	..	..	..	..
4500 Non-recurrent taxes	13 126	31 712	51 115	15 938	15 539	..	..	..	..	..
4600 Other recurrent taxes on property	0	0	0	0	0	..	..	..	..	..
5000 Taxes on goods and services	**422 259**	**897 092**	**1 101 319**	**1 242 416**	**1 303 210**	..	..	..	..	..
5100 Taxes on production, sale, transfer, etc	422 259	793 469	973 944	1 092 106	1 177 680	..	..	..	..	..
5110 General taxes	196 817	501 399	609 915	753 003	810 593	..	..	..	..	..
5120 Taxes on specific goods and services	225 442	292 069	364 029	339 103	367 087	..	..	..	..	..
5130 Unallocable between 5110 and 5120	0	0	0	0	0	..	..	..	..	..
5200 Taxes on use of goods and perform activities	0	103 623	127 375	150 310	125 530	..	..	..	..	..
5300 Unallocable between 5100 and 5200	0	0	0	0	0	..	..	..	..	..
6000 Other taxes	**93 077**	**26 105**	**20 787**	**75 546**	**12 143**	..	..	..	..	..
6100 Paid solely by business	0	0	0	0	0	..	..	..	..	..
6200 Other	93 077	26 105	20 787	75 546	12 143	..	..	..	..	..
Total tax revenue	**808 469**	**1 589 045**	**1 888 901**	**2 193 835**	**2 192 363**	..	..	..	..	..

Thousand BAR

	Local government[2]					Social Security Funds				
	1990	2000	2005	2010	2015	1990	2000	2005	2010	2015
1000 Taxes on income, profits and capital gains	..	..	..	..	..	**0**	**0**	**0**	**0**	**0**
1100 Of individuals	..	..	..	..	..	..	..	..	..	..
1200 Corporate	..	..	..	..	..	..	..	..	..	..
1300 Unallocable between 1100 and 1200	..	..	..	..	..	..	..	..	..	..
2000 Social security contributions[1]	..	..	..	..	..	**133 866**	**295 268**	**408 109**	**525 467**	**552 000**
2100 Employees	..	..	..	..	..	..	..	..	..	..
2200 Employers	..	..	..	..	..	..	..	..	..	..
2300 Self-employed or non-employed	..	..	..	..	..	..	..	..	..	..
2400 Unallocable between 2100, 2200 and 2300	..	..	..	..	..	133 866	295 268	408 109	525 467	552 000
3000 Taxes on payroll and workforce	..	..	..	..	..	**0**	**0**	**0**	**0**	**0**
4000 Taxes on property	..	..	..	..	..	**0**	**0**	**0**	**0**	**0**
4100 Recurrent taxes on immovable property	..	..	..	..	..	..	..	..	..	..
4200 Recurrent taxes on net wealth	..	..	..	..	..	..	..	..	..	..
4300 Estate, inheritance and gift taxes	..	..	..	..	..	..	..	..	..	..
4400 Taxes on financial and capital transactions	..	..	..	..	..	..	..	..	..	..
4500 Non-recurrent taxes	..	..	..	..	..	..	..	..	..	..
4600 Other recurrent taxes on property	..	..	..	..	..	..	..	..	..	..
5000 Taxes on goods and services	..	..	..	..	..	**0**	**0**	**0**	**0**	**0**
5100 Taxes on production, sale, transfer, etc	..	..	..	..	..	..	..	..	..	..
5110 General taxes	..	..	..	..	..	..	..	..	..	..
5120 Taxes on specific goods and services	..	..	..	..	..	..	..	..	..	..
5130 Unallocable between 5110 and 5120	..	..	..	..	..	..	..	..	..	..
5200 Taxes on use of goods and perform activities	..	..	..	..	..	..	..	..	..	..
5300 Unallocable between 5100 and 5200	..	..	..	..	..	..	..	..	..	..
6000 Other taxes	..	..	..	..	..	**0**	**0**	**0**	**0**	**0**
6100 Paid solely by business	..	..	..	..	..	..	..	..	..	..
6200 Other	..	..	..	..	..	..	..	..	..	..
Total tax revenue	..	..	..	..	..	**133 866**	**295 268**	**408 109**	**525 467**	**552 000**

1. The data for social security contributions are estimated for 2015.
2. The figures exclude local government tax revenues as the data are not available.

StatLink http://dx.doi.org/10.1787/888933463447

Table 6.4. Belize, tax revenues by sub-sectors of government

Million BZD

	Federal government					State/Regional				
	1990	2000	2005	2010	2015	1990	2000	2005	2010	2015
1000 Taxes on income, profits and capital gains	**37**	**76**	**129**	**248**	**261**	..	..	..	..	..
1100 Of individuals	21	19	35	52	71	..	..	..	..	..
1200 Corporate	12	51	90	189	175	..	..	..	..	..
1300 Unallocable between 1100 and 1200	4	6	4	7	14	..	..	..	..	..
2000 Social security contributions	**0**	**0**	**0**	**0**	**0**	..	..	..	..	..
2100 Employees	..	..	..	..	..	..	..	..	..	..
2200 Employers	..	..	..	..	..	..	..	..	..	..
2300 Self-employed or non-employed	..	..	..	..	..	..	..	..	..	..
2400 Unallocable between 2100, 2200 and 2300	..	..	..	..	..	..	..	..	..	..
3000 Taxes on payroll and workforce	**0**	**0**	**0**	**0**	**0**	..	..	..	..	..
4000 Taxes on property	**5**	**11**	**22**	**16**	**29**	..	..	..	..	..
4100 Recurrent taxes on immovable property	0	0	0	0	0	..	..	..	..	..
4200 Recurrent taxes on net wealth	0	0	0	0	0	..	..	..	..	..
4300 Estate, inheritance and gift taxes	0	0	0	0	0	..	..	..	..	..
4400 Taxes on financial and capital transactions	5	11	22	16	29	..	..	..	..	..
4500 Non-recurrent taxes	0	0	0	0	0	..	..	..	..	..
4600 Other recurrent taxes on property	0	0	0	0	0	..	..	..	..	..
5000 Taxes on goods and services	**126**	**211**	**289**	**412**	**531**	..	..	..	..	..
5100 Taxes on production, sale, transfer, etc	122	207	282	400	521	..	..	..	..	..
5110 General taxes	0	82	131	199	263	..	..	..	..	..
5120 Taxes on specific goods and services	122	124	151	200	258	..	..	..	..	..
5130 Unallocable between 5110 and 5120	0	0	0	0	0	..	..	..	..	..
5200 Taxes on use of goods and perform activities	4	4	7	13	10	..	..	..	..	..
5300 Unallocable between 5100 and 5200	0	0	0	0	0	..	..	..	..	..
6000 Other taxes	**0**	**0**	**0**	**0**	**0**	..	..	..	..	..
6100 Paid solely by business	..	..	..	..	..	..	..	..	..	..
6200 Other	..	..	..	..	..	..	..	..	..	..
Total tax revenue	**168**	**298**	**441**	**677**	**820**	..	..	..	..	..

Million BZD

	Local government					Social Security Funds				
	1990	2000	2005	2010	2015	1990	2000	2005	2010	2015
1000 Taxes on income, profits and capital gains	**0**	**0**	**0**	**0**	**0**	**0**	**0**	**0**	**0**	**0**
1100 Of individuals	..	..	..	..	..	..	..	..	..	..
1200 Corporate	..	..	..	..	..	..	..	..	..	..
1300 Unallocable between 1100 and 1200	..	..	..	..	..	..	..	..	..	..
2000 Social security contributions[1]	**0**	**0**	**0**	**0**	**0**	**10**	**18**	**50**	**60**	**70**
2100 Employees	..	..	..	..	..	..	..	..	..	..
2200 Employers	..	..	..	..	..	..	..	..	..	..
2300 Self-employed or non-employed	..	..	..	..	..	..	..	..	..	..
2400 Unallocable between 2100, 2200 and 2300	..	..	..	..	..	10	18	50	60	70
3000 Taxes on payroll and workforce	**0**	**0**	**0**	**0**	**0**	**0**	**0**	**0**	**0**	**0**
4000 Taxes on property	**1**	**2**	**6**	**7**	**5**	**0**	**0**	**0**	**0**	**0**
4100 Recurrent taxes on immovable property	1	2	6	7	5	..	..	..	..	..
4200 Recurrent taxes on net wealth	0	0	0	0	0	..	..	..	..	..
4300 Estate, inheritance and gift taxes	0	0	0	0	0	..	..	..	..	..
4400 Taxes on financial and capital transactions	0	0	0	0	0	..	..	..	..	..
4500 Non-recurrent taxes	0	0	0	0	0	..	..	..	..	..
4600 Other recurrent taxes on property	0	0	0	0	0	..	..	..	..	..
5000 Taxes on goods and services	**0**	**0**	**0**	**0**	**0**	**0**	**0**	**0**	**0**	**0**
5100 Taxes on production, sale, transfer, etc	..	..	..	..	..	..	..	..	..	..
5110 General taxes	..	..	..	..	..	..	..	..	..	..
5120 Taxes on specific goods and services	..	..	..	..	..	..	..	..	..	..
5130 Unallocable between 5110 and 5120	..	..	..	..	..	..	..	..	..	..
5200 Taxes on use of goods and perform activities	..	..	..	..	..	..	..	..	..	..
5300 Unallocable between 5100 and 5200	..	..	..	..	..	..	..	..	..	..
6000 Other taxes	**0**	**0**	**0**	**0**	**0**	**0**	**0**	**0**	**0**	**0**
6100 Paid solely by business	..	..	..	..	..	..	..	..	..	..
6200 Other	..	..	..	..	..	..	..	..	..	..
Total tax revenue	**1**	**2**	**6**	**7**	**5**	**10**	**18**	**50**	**60**	**70**

1. The data for social security contributions are estimated for the period 2013-2015.

StatLink http://dx.doi.org/10.1787/888933463451

Table 6.5. Bolivia, tax revenues by sub-sectors of government

Million BOB

	Federal government					State/Regional				
	1990	2000	2005	2010	2015	1990	2000	2005	2010	2015
1000 Taxes on income, profits and capital gains	**68**	**1 209**	**2 383**	**6 294**	**12 809**	..	..	..	..	..
1100 Of individuals	68	214	214	263	508	..	..	..	..	..
1200 Corporate	0	995	2 169	6 031	12 302	..	..	..	..	..
1300 Unallocable between 1100 and 1200	0	0	0	0	0	..	..	..	..	..
2000 Social security contributions	**0**	**0**	**0**	**0**	**0**	..	..	..	..	..
2100 Employees	..	..	..	..	..	..	..	..	..	..
2200 Employers	..	..	..	..	..	..	..	..	..	..
2300 Self-employed or non-employed	..	..	..	..	..	..	..	..	..	..
2400 Unallocable between 2100, 2200 and 2300	..	..	..	..	..	..	..	..	..	..
3000 Taxes on payroll and workforce	**0**	**0**	**0**	**0**	**0**	..	..	..	..	..
4000 Taxes on property	**1**	**3**	**640**	**367**	**424**	..	..	..	..	..
4100 Recurrent taxes on immovable property	0	0	0	0	0	..	..	..	..	..
4200 Recurrent taxes on net wealth	0	0	0	0	0	..	..	..	..	..
4300 Estate, inheritance and gift taxes	1	3	7	20	36	..	..	..	..	..
4400 Taxes on financial and capital transactions	0	0	633	347	388	..	..	..	..	..
4500 Non-recurrent taxes	0	0	0	0	0	..	..	..	..	..
4600 Other recurrent taxes on property	0	0	0	0	0	..	..	..	..	..
5000 Taxes on goods and services	**875**	**5 651**	**8 753**	**15 509**	**30 268**	..	..	..	..	..
5100 Taxes on production, sale, transfer, etc	875	5 651	8 753	15 509	30 268	..	..	..	..	..
5110 General taxes	551	2 949	5 314	10 259	20 757	..	..	..	..	..
5120 Taxes on specific goods and services[1]	324	2 702	3 439	5 250	9 511	..	..	..	..	..
5130 Unallocable between 5110 and 5120	0	0	0	0	0	..	..	..	..	..
5200 Taxes on use of goods and perform activities	0	0	0	0	0	..	..	..	..	..
5300 Unallocable between 5100 and 5200	0	0	0	0	0	..	..	..	..	..
6000 Other taxes	**334**	**1 051**	**1 896**	**2 733**	**6 943**	..	..	..	..	..
6100 Paid solely by business	4	6	5	12	26	..	..	..	..	..
6200 Other	330	1 045	1 892	2 720	6 917	..	..	..	..	..
Total tax revenue	**1 277**	**7 913**	**13 671**	**24 903**	**50 444**	..	..	..	..	..

Million BOB

	Local government[3]					Social Security Funds				
	1990	2000	2005	2010	2015	1990	2000	2005	2010	2015
1000 Taxes on income, profits and capital gains	..	..	..	..	..	..	**0**	**0**	**0**	**0**
1100 Of individuals	..	..	..	..	..	..	..	..	..	..
1200 Corporate	..	..	..	..	..	..	..	..	..	..
1300 Unallocable between 1100 and 1200	..	..	..	..	..	..	..	..	..	..
2000 Social security contributions[2]	..	..	..	..	..	..	**666**	**936**	**1 645**	**3 200**
2100 Employees	..	..	..	..	..	..	..	..	..	..
2200 Employers	..	..	..	..	..	..	..	..	..	..
2300 Self-employed or non-employed	..	..	..	..	..	..	..	..	..	..
2400 Unallocable between 2100, 2200 and 2300	..	..	..	..	..	..	666	936	1 645	3 200
3000 Taxes on payroll and workforce	..	..	..	..	..	..	**0**	**0**	**0**	**0**
4000 Taxes on property	..	..	..	..	..	..	**0**	**0**	**0**	**0**
4100 Recurrent taxes on immovable property	..	..	..	..	..	..	..	..	..	..
4200 Recurrent taxes on net wealth	..	..	..	..	..	..	..	..	..	..
4300 Estate, inheritance and gift taxes	..	..	..	..	..	..	..	..	..	..
4400 Taxes on financial and capital transactions	..	..	..	..	..	..	..	..	..	..
4500 Non-recurrent taxes	..	..	..	..	..	..	..	..	..	..
4600 Other recurrent taxes on property	..	..	..	..	..	..	..	..	..	..
5000 Taxes on goods and services	..	..	..	..	..	..	**0**	**0**	**0**	**0**
5100 Taxes on production, sale, transfer, etc	..	..	..	..	..	..	..	..	..	..
5110 General taxes	..	..	..	..	..	..	..	..	..	..
5120 Taxes on specific goods and services	..	..	..	..	..	..	..	..	..	..
5130 Unallocable between 5110 and 5120	..	..	..	..	..	..	..	..	..	..
5200 Taxes on use of goods and perform activities	..	..	..	..	..	..	..	..	..	..
5300 Unallocable between 5100 and 5200	..	..	..	..	..	..	..	..	..	..
6000 Other taxes	..	**575**	**762**	**1 381**	**2 585**	..	**0**	**0**	**0**	**0**
6100 Paid solely by business	..	0	0	0	0	..	..	..	..	..
6200 Other	..	575	762	1 381	2 585	..	..	..	..	..
Total tax revenue	..	**575**	**762**	**1 381**	**2 585**	..	**666**	**936**	**1 645**	**3 200**

1. Previous editions of Revenue Statistics in Latin America and the Caribbean included fees levied on hydrocarbon production at the federal level. For this publication, revenues from hydrocarbon production have been excluded from tax revenues and are instead treated as non-tax revenues.
2. The data for social security contributions are available from the year 2000 only and are estimated for the period 2013-2015.
3. The figures exclude local government tax revenues for the period 1990–1993 as the data are not available.

StatLink http://dx.doi.org/10.1787/888933463466

Table 6.6. Brazil, tax revenues by sub-sectors of government

Million BRL

	Federal government					State/Regional				
	1990	2000	2005	2010	2015	1990	2000	2005	2010	2015
1000 Taxes on income, profits and capital gains	**1**	**68 667**	**149 309**	**236 631**	**355 264**	**0**	**0**	**0**	**16 499**	**33 202**
1100 Of individuals	0	3 406	6 981	65 721	103 010	..	..	..	16 499	33 202
1200 Corporate	0	25 430	73 071	128 255	164 057	..	..	..	0	0
1300 Unallocable between 1100 and 1200	0	39 831	69 257	42 656	88 196	..	..	..	0	0
2000 Social security contributions	**0**	**0**	**0**	**0**	**0**	**0**	**0**	**0**	**0**	**0**
2100 Employees	..	..	..	..	..	..	..	..	..	..
2200 Employers	..	..	..	..	..	..	..	..	..	..
2300 Self-employed or non-employed	..	..	..	..	..	..	..	..	..	..
2400 Unallocable between 2100, 2200 and 2300	..	..	..	..	..	..	..	..	..	..
3000 Taxes on payroll and workforce[1]	**0**	**6 749**	**14 468**	**33 090**	**50 399**	**0**	**0**	**0**	**0**	**0**
4000 Taxes on property	**0**	**17 726**	**35 282**	**27 038**	**35 786**	**0**	**5 623**	**11 282**	**23 885**	**42 726**
4100 Recurrent taxes on immovable property	0	234	288	485	1 105	0	0	0	0	0
4200 Recurrent taxes on net wealth	0	0	0	0	0	0	0	0	0	0
4300 Estate, inheritance and gift taxes	0	0	0	0	0	0	329	821	2 518	6 469
4400 Taxes on financial and capital transactions	0	17 492	34 994	26 553	34 681	0	0	0	0	0
4500 Non-recurrent taxes	0	0	0	0	0	0	0	0	0	0
4600 Other recurrent taxes on property	0	0	0	0	0	0	5 294	10 460	21 367	36 257
5000 Taxes on goods and services	**1**	**74 190**	**147 819**	**241 385**	**338 785**	**1**	**83 848**	**158 809**	**268 117**	**396 513**
5100 Taxes on production, sale, transfer, etc	1	74 190	147 819	241 385	338 785	1	82 279	153 437	268 117	396 513
5110 General taxes[1]	1	65 745	129 567	197 025	277 898	1	82 279	153 437	268 117	396 513
5120 Taxes on specific goods and services	0	8 445	18 252	44 360	60 887	0	0	0	0	0
5130 Unallocable between 5110 and 5120	0	0	0	0	0	0	0	0	0	0
5200 Taxes on use of goods and perform activities	0	0	0	0	0	0	1 569	5 372	0	0
5300 Unallocable between 5100 and 5200	0	0	0	0	0	0	0	0	0	0
6000 Other taxes[2]	**0**	**2 214**	**2 039**	**7 500**	**16 748**	**0**	**322**	**1 551**	**17 135**	**29 067**
6100 Paid solely by business	0	0	277	0	0	0	0	0	0	0
6200 Other[1]	0	2 214	1 761	7 500	16 748	0	322	1 551	17 135	29 067
Total tax revenue	**1**	**169 546**	**348 917**	**545 644**	**796 982**	**1**	**89 793**	**171 641**	**325 636**	**501 508**

Million BRL

	Local government					Social Security Funds				
	1990	2000	2005	2010	2015	1990	2000	2005	2010	2015
1000 Taxes on income, profits and capital gains	**0**	**0**	**0**	**5 608**	**12 583**	**0**	**0**	**0**	**0**	**0**
1100 Of individuals	..	..	..	5 608	12 583	..	..	..	..	..
1200 Corporate	..	..	..	0	0	..	..	..	..	..
1300 Unallocable between 1100 and 1200	..	..	..	0	0	..	..	..	..	..
2000 Social security contributions	**0**	**0**	**0**	**0**	**0**	**1**	**83 469**	**168 226**	**313 949**	**497 791**
2100 Employees	..	..	..	..	..	..	..	..	..	..
2200 Employers	..	..	..	..	..	0	18 709	32 248	64 271	118 323
2300 Self-employed or non-employed	..	..	..	..	..	..	..	..	..	..
2400 Unallocable between 2100, 2200 and 2300	..	..	..	..	..	1	64 760	135 978	249 679	379 469
3000 Taxes on payroll and workforce[1]	**0**	**0**	**0**	**0**	**0**	**0**	**0**	**0**	**0**	**0**
4000 Taxes on property	**0**	**5 469**	**9 710**	**23 454**	**41 866**	**0**	**0**	**0**	**0**	**0**
4100 Recurrent taxes on immovable property	0	4 519	8 117	17 448	30 760	..	..	..	..	..
4200 Recurrent taxes on net wealth	0	0	0	0	0	..	..	..	..	..
4300 Estate, inheritance and gift taxes	0	0	0	0	0	..	..	..	..	..
4400 Taxes on financial and capital transactions	0	950	1 593	6 005	11 107	..	..	..	..	..
4500 Non-recurrent taxes	0	0	0	0	0	..	..	..	..	..
4600 Other recurrent taxes on property	0	0	0	0	0	..	..	..	..	..
5000 Taxes on goods and services	**0**	**6 106**	**11 247**	**32 757**	**58 084**	**0**	**0**	**0**	**0**	**0**
5100 Taxes on production, sale, transfer, etc	0	6 106	11 247	32 757	58 084	..	..	..	..	..
5110 General taxes[1]	0	6 106	11 247	32 757	58 084	..	..	..	..	..
5120 Taxes on specific goods and services	0	0	0	0	0	..	..	..	..	..
5130 Unallocable between 5110 and 5120	0	0	0	0	0	..	..	..	..	..
5200 Taxes on use of goods and perform activities	0	0	0	0	0	..	..	..	..	..
5300 Unallocable between 5100 and 5200	0	0	0	0	0	..	..	..	..	..
6000 Other taxes[2]	**0**	**377**	**1 404**	**8 406**	**14 054**	**0**	**0**	**0**	**0**	**0**
6100 Paid solely by business	0	0	0	0	0	..	..	..	..	..
6200 Other[1]	0	377	1 404	8 406	14 054	..	..	..	..	..
Total tax revenue	**0**	**11 952**	**22 360**	**70 225**	**126 587**	**1**	**83 469**	**168 226**	**313 949**	**497 791**

1. The PASEP (Program of Formation of the Patrimony of the Public Servants) contributions are added to the PIS (Social Integration Program) contributions in heading 5110 for the years prior to 2000.
2. The FUNDAF (Special Fund for Development and Improvement of Auditing Activities) contributions are included in heading 6200 from 2008.

StatLink http://dx.doi.org/10.1787/888933463477

Table 6.7. Chile, tax revenues by sub-sectors of government

Million CLP

	Federal government					State/Regional				
	1990	2000	2005	2010	2015	1990	2000	2005	2010	2015
1000 Taxes on income, profits and capital gains	**412 974**	**1 841 630**	**5 171 293**	**8 329 060**	**11 836 497**	..	..	..	..	..
1100 Of individuals	99 154	604 100	738 620	1 492 837	2 313 363	..	..	..	..	..
1200 Corporate	219 586	882 896	3 155 480	4 448 745	7 721 622	..	..	..	..	..
1300 Unallocable between 1100 and 1200	94 233	354 634	1 277 193	2 387 478	1 801 512	..	..	..	..	..
2000 Social security contributions	**66 738**	**232 728**	**287 422**	**371 386**	**434 658**	..	..	..	..	..
2100 Employees	61 200	209 907	249 526	310 558	370 744	..	..	..	..	..
2200 Employers	5 538	22 821	37 896	60 828	63 914	..	..	..	..	..
2300 Self-employed or non-employed	0	0	0	0	0	..	..	..	..	..
2400 Unallocable between 2100, 2200 and 2300	0	0	0	0	0	..	..	..	..	..
3000 Taxes on payroll and workforce	**0**	**0**	**0**	**0**	**0**	..	..	..	..	..
4000 Taxes on property	**59 682**	**255 371**	**490 120**	**245 044**	**379 603**	..	..	..	..	..
4100 Recurrent taxes on immovable property	10 331	3 578	4 909	8 805	15 249	..	..	..	..	..
4200 Recurrent taxes on net wealth	0	0	0	0	0	..	..	..	..	..
4300 Estate, inheritance and gift taxes	3 444	10 906	23 184	39 338	92 236	..	..	..	..	..
4400 Taxes on financial and capital transactions	45 907	240 886	462 027	196 901	272 118	..	..	..	..	..
4500 Non-recurrent taxes	0	0	0	0	0	..	..	..	..	..
4600 Other recurrent taxes on property	0	0	0	0	0	..	..	..	..	..
5000 Taxes on goods and services	**1 063 677**	**4 719 255**	**6 831 482**	**10 330 378**	**16 147 145**	..	..	..	..	..
5100 Taxes on production, sale, transfer, etc	1 060 304	4 684 525	6 811 389	10 294 165	16 095 378	..	..	..	..	..
5110 General taxes	664 421	3 306 350	5 391 285	8 399 926	13 273 958	..	..	..	..	..
5120 Taxes on specific goods and services[1]	395 883	1 378 175	1 420 104	1 894 239	2 821 420	..	..	..	..	..
5130 Unallocable between 5110 and 5120	0	0	0	0	0	..	..	..	..	..
5200 Taxes on use of goods and perform activities	3 374	34 730	20 094	36 213	51 767	..	..	..	..	..
5300 Unallocable between 5100 and 5200	0	0	0	0	0	..	..	..	..	..
6000 Other taxes	**-23 356**	**-112 195**	**-85 954**	**-61 117**	**-544 733**	..	..	..	..	..
6100 Paid solely by business	0	0	0	0	0	..	..	..	..	..
6200 Other	-23 356	-112 195	-85 954	-61 117	-544 733	..	..	..	..	..
Total tax revenue	**1 579 715**	**6 936 788**	**12 694 362**	**19 214 751**	**28 253 170**	..	..	..	..	..

Million CLP

	Local government					Social Security Funds				
	1990	2000	2005	2010	2015	1990	2000	2005	2010	2015
1000 Taxes on income, profits and capital gains	**0**	**0**	**0**	**0**	**0**	**0**	**0**	**0**	**0**	**0**
1100 Of individuals	0	0	0	0	0	0	0	0	0	0
1200 Corporate	0	0	0	0	0	0	0	0	0	0
1300 Unallocable between 1100 and 1200	0	0	0	0	0	0	0	0	0	0
2000 Social security contributions	**0**	**0**	**0**	**0**	**0**	**92 821**	**344 030**	**644 295**	**1 122 601**	**1 817 831**
2100 Employees	..	..	..	..	..	92 821	344 030	644 295	1 122 601	1 817 831
2200 Employers	..	..	..	..	..	0	0	0	0	0
2300 Self-employed or non-employed	..	..	..	..	..	0	0	0	0	0
2400 Unallocable between 2100, 2200 and 2300	..	..	..	..	..	0	0	0	0	0
3000 Taxes on payroll and workforce	**0**	**0**	**0**	**0**	**0**	**0**	**0**	**0**	**0**	**0**
4000 Taxes on property	**49 637**	**298 666**	**411 656**	**653 563**	**1 038 908**	**0**	**0**	**0**	**0**	**0**
4100 Recurrent taxes on immovable property	49 637	298 666	411 656	653 563	1 038 908	..	..	..	..	..
4200 Recurrent taxes on net wealth	0	0	0	0	0	..	..	..	..	..
4300 Estate, inheritance and gift taxes	0	0	0	0	0	..	..	..	..	..
4400 Taxes on financial and capital transactions	0	0	0	0	0	..	..	..	..	..
4500 Non-recurrent taxes	0	0	0	0	0	..	..	..	..	..
4600 Other recurrent taxes on property	0	0	0	0	0	..	..	..	..	..
5000 Taxes on goods and services	**55 045**	**322 514**	**514 952**	**854 778**	**1 414 987**	**0**	**0**	**0**	**0**	**0**
5100 Taxes on production, sale, transfer, etc	13 705	105 302	140 703	238 739	385 266	..	..	..	..	..
5110 General taxes	0	0	0	0	0	..	..	..	..	..
5120 Taxes on specific goods and services[1]	13 705	105 302	140 703	238 739	385 266	..	..	..	..	..
5130 Unallocable between 5110 and 5120	0	0	0	0	0	..	..	..	..	..
5200 Taxes on use of goods and perform activities	41 340	217 212	374 249	616 039	1 029 721	..	..	..	..	..
5300 Unallocable between 5100 and 5200	0	0	0	0	0	..	..	..	..	..
6000 Other taxes	**0**	**0**	**0**	**0**	**0**	**0**	**0**	**0**	**0**	**0**
6100 Paid solely by business	..	..	..	..	..	..	..	..	..	..
6200 Other	..	..	..	..	..	..	..	..	..	..
Total tax revenue	**104 682**	**621 180**	**926 608**	**1 508 341**	**2 453 895**	**92 821**	**344 030**	**644 295**	**1 122 601**	**1 817 831**

1. ECLAC classifies Oil Prices Stabilisation Fund (FEPP) revenues as non-tax revenues.

StatLink http://dx.doi.org/10.1787/888933463482

Table 6.8. Colombia, tax revenues by sub-sectors of government

Million COP

	Federal government					State/Regional[1]				
	1990	2000	2005	2010	2015	1990	2000	2005	2010	2015
1000 Taxes on income, profits and capital gains	**771 694**	**7 103 525**	**17 348 618**	**26 218 852**	**52 656 876**	**0**	**0**	**0**	**0**	**0**
1100 Of individuals	47 210	1 499 345	3 594 441	5 192 384	9 674 556	..	..	..	..	..
1200 Corporate	359 758	5 119 828	13 044 361	20 405 209	40 968 703	..	..	..	..	..
1300 Unallocable between 1100 and 1200	364 726	484 352	709 816	621 258	2 013 617	..	..	..	..	..
2000 Social security contributions	**0**	**0**	**0**	**0**	**0**	**0**	**0**	**0**	**0**	**0**
2100 Employees	..	..	..	..	..	..	..	..	..	..
2200 Employers	..	..	..	..	..	..	..	..	..	..
2300 Self-employed or non-employed	..	..	..	..	..	..	..	..	..	..
2400 Unallocable between 2100, 2200 and 2300	..	..	..	..	..	..	..	..	..	..
3000 Taxes on payroll and workforce	**0**	**1 286 803**	**2 179 842**	**4 022 503**	**2 797 308**	**0**	**0**	**0**	**0**	**0**
4000 Taxes on property	**0**	**1 036 584**	**2 863 946**	**5 196 303**	**12 094 140**	**0**	**0**	**0**	**0**	**0**
4100 Recurrent taxes on immovable property	..	0	0	0	0	..	..	..	..	..
4200 Recurrent taxes on net wealth	..	0	462 720	1 970 530	5 352 940	..	..	..	..	..
4300 Estate, inheritance and gift taxes	..	0	0	0	0	..	..	..	..	..
4400 Taxes on financial and capital transactions	..	1 036 584	2 401 226	3 225 773	6 741 200	..	..	..	..	..
4500 Non-recurrent taxes	..	0	0	0	0	..	..	..	..	..
4600 Other recurrent taxes on property	..	0	0	0	0	..	..	..	..	..
5000 Taxes on goods and services	**1 035 934**	**11 022 878**	**21 393 776**	**34 882 447**	**51 126 468**	**263 429**	**1 204 940**	**1 966 325**	**2 752 254**	**4 083 718**
5100 Taxes on production, sale, transfer, etc	1 035 934	11 022 878	21 393 776	34 882 447	51 126 468	263 429	1 204 940	1 966 325	2 752 254	4 083 718
5110 General taxes	583 078	8 445 776	17 427 948	28 811 682	41 553 967	0	0	0	0	0
5120 Taxes on specific goods and services	452 856	2 577 102	3 965 828	6 070 765	9 572 501	263 429	1 204 940	1 966 325	2 752 254	4 083 718
5130 Unallocable between 5110 and 5120	0	0	0	0	0	0	0	0	0	0
5200 Taxes on use of goods and perform activities	0	0	0	0	0	0	0	0	0	0
5300 Unallocable between 5100 and 5200	0	0	0	0	0	0	0	0	0	0
6000 Other taxes	**78 306**	**480 784**	**682 084**	**483 762**	**424 000**	**0**	**518 253**	**1 117 016**	**2 029 017**	**3 533 010**
6100 Paid solely by business	0	0	0	0	0	..	0	0	0	0
6200 Other	78 306	480 784	682 084	483 762	424 000	..	518 253	1 117 016	2 029 017	3 533 010
Total tax revenue	**1 885 934**	**20 930 574**	**44 468 266**	**70 803 867**	**119 098 791**	**263 429**	**1 723 193**	**3 083 341**	**4 781 271**	**7 616 728**

Million COP

	Local government[1]					Social Security Funds[2]				
	1990	2000	2005	2010	2015	1990	2000	2005	2010	2015
1000 Taxes on income, profits and capital gains	**0**	**0**	**0**	**0**	**0**	**0**	**0**	**0**	**0**	**0**
1100 Of individuals	..	..	..	..	..	..	..	..	..	..
1200 Corporate	..	..	..	..	..	..	..	..	..	..
1300 Unallocable between 1100 and 1200	..	..	..	..	..	..	..	..	..	..
2000 Social security contributions	**0**	**0**	**0**	**0**	**0**	**203 596**	**4 989 000**	**7 845 000**	**11 478 085**	**20 169 000**
2100 Employees	..	..	..	..	..	..	..	..	..	..
2200 Employers	..	..	..	..	..	..	..	..	..	..
2300 Self-employed or non-employed	..	..	..	..	..	..	..	..	..	..
2400 Unallocable between 2100, 2200 and 2300	..	..	..	..	..	203 596	4 989 000	7 845 000	11 478 085	20 169 000
3000 Taxes on payroll and workforce	**0**	**0**	**0**	**0**	**0**	**0**	**0**	**0**	**0**	**0**
4000 Taxes on property	**56 160**	**991 070**	**1 974 213**	**3 338 935**	**6 212 601**	**0**	**0**	**0**	**0**	**0**
4100 Recurrent taxes on immovable property	56 160	991 070	1 974 213	3 338 935	6 212 601	..	..	..	..	..
4200 Recurrent taxes on net wealth	0	0	0	0	0	..	..	..	..	..
4300 Estate, inheritance and gift taxes	0	0	0	0	0	..	..	..	..	..
4400 Taxes on financial and capital transactions	0	0	0	0	0	..	..	..	..	..
4500 Non-recurrent taxes	0	0	0	0	0	..	..	..	..	..
4600 Other recurrent taxes on property	0	0	0	0	0	..	..	..	..	..
5000 Taxes on goods and services	**89 290**	**1 140 090**	**2 506 452**	**4 522 121**	**7 167 866**	**0**	**0**	**0**	**0**	**0**
5100 Taxes on production, sale, transfer, etc	89 290	1 140 090	2 506 452	4 522 121	7 167 866	..	..	..	..	..
5110 General taxes	89 290	1 140 090	2 506 452	4 522 121	7 167 866	..	..	..	..	..
5120 Taxes on specific goods and services	0	0	0	0	0	..	..	..	..	..
5130 Unallocable between 5110 and 5120	0	0	0	0	0	..	..	..	..	..
5200 Taxes on use of goods and perform activities	0	0	0	0	0	..	..	..	..	..
5300 Unallocable between 5100 and 5200	0	0	0	0	0	..	..	..	..	..
6000 Other taxes	**81 017**	**738 983**	**1 578 573**	**3 030 650**	**5 999 714**	**0**	**0**	**0**	**0**	**0**
6100 Paid solely by business	0	0	0	0	0	..	..	..	..	..
6200 Other	81 017	738 983	1 578 573	3 030 650	5 999 714	..	..	..	..	..
Total tax revenue	**226 467**	**2 870 144**	**6 059 238**	**10 891 707**	**19 380 181**	**203 596**	**4 989 000**	**7 845 000**	**11 478 085**	**20 169 000**

1. The data corresponds to the reported consolidated revenues of the territorial entities (departments and municipalities).
2. All of the health contributions pertaining to FOSYGA (Solidarity and Guarantee Fund) are classified as social security contributions from 2013. Prior to 2013, only the portion of the contributions used to finance the subsidised regime was included and the part to finance the contributory regime was classified in the social security sector as "other incomes".

StatLink http://dx.doi.org/10.1787/888933463491

Table 6.9. Costa Rica, tax revenues by sub-sectors of government

Million CRC

	Federal government					State/Regional				
	1990	2000	2005	2010	2015	1990	2000	2005	2010	2015
1000 Taxes on income, profits and capital gains	**11 820**	**128 805**	**324 224**	**748 093**	**1 247 308**	..	..	..	..	..
1100 Of individuals	..	..	16 438	202 849	386 241	..	..	..	..	..
1200 Corporate	..	..	288 355	450 312	659 951	..	..	..	..	..
1300 Unallocable between 1100 and 1200	11 820	128 805	19 430	94 932	201 116	..	..	..	..	..
2000 Social security contributions[1]	**0**	**18 677**	**30 854**	**61 193**	**63 458**	..	..	..	..	..
2100 Employees	..	3 405	5 354	9 649	31 120	..	..	..	..	..
2200 Employers	..	..	..	..	..	..	..	..	..	..
2300 Self-employed or non-employed	..	5 858	16 414	33 778	1 718	..	..	..	..	..
2400 Unallocable between 2100, 2200 and 2300	..	9 413	9 086	17 766	30 620	..	..	..	..	..
3000 Taxes on payroll and workforce	**0**	**0**	**0**	**0**	**0**	..	..	..	..	..
4000 Taxes on property	**366**	**7 291**	**10 846**	**18 270**	**37 334**	..	..	..	..	..
4100 Recurrent taxes on immovable property	0	0	0	3 527	4 076	..	..	..	..	..
4200 Recurrent taxes on net wealth	0	4 284	0	0	0	..	..	..	..	..
4300 Estate, inheritance and gift taxes	0	0	0	0	0	..	..	..	..	..
4400 Taxes on financial and capital transactions	366	3 007	10 846	14 743	33 258	..	..	..	..	..
4500 Non-recurrent taxes	0	0	0	0	0	..	..	..	..	..
4600 Other recurrent taxes on property	0	0	0	0	0	..	..	..	..	..
5000 Taxes on goods and services	**52 360**	**444 726**	**920 160**	**1 696 729**	**2 504 184**	..	..	..	..	..
5100 Taxes on production, sale, transfer, etc	49 980	425 353	887 390	1 598 790	2 353 281	..	..	..	..	..
5110 General taxes	21 326	222 775	485 168	920 298	1 336 075	..	..	..	..	..
5120 Taxes on specific goods and services[2]	28 654	202 887	399 192	678 492	1 017 206	..	..	..	..	..
5130 Unallocable between 5110 and 5120	0	-308	3 031	0	0	..	..	..	..	..
5200 Taxes on use of goods and perform activities	2 380	19 357	32 758	97 803	150 755	..	..	..	..	..
5300 Unallocable between 5100 and 5200	0	15	12	136	148	..	..	..	..	..
6000 Other taxes[3]	**6 113**	**2 573**	**7 009**	**12 864**	**54 182**	..	..	..	..	..
6100 Paid solely by business	0	15	624	459	33 117	..	..	..	..	..
6200 Other	6 113	2 558	6 385	12 405	21 065	..	..	..	..	..
Total tax revenue	**70 660**	**602 072**	**1 293 094**	**2 537 149**	**3 906 466**	..	..	..	..	..

Million CRC

	Local government[4]					Social Security Funds				
	1990	2000	2005	2010	2015	1990	2000	2005	2010	2015
1000 Taxes on income, profits and capital gains	..	**0**	**0**	**0**	**0**	**0**	**0**	**0**	**0**	**0**
1100 Of individuals	..	..	..	..	..	..	..	..	..	..
1200 Corporate	..	..	..	..	..	..	..	..	..	..
1300 Unallocable between 1100 and 1200	..	..	..	..	..	..	..	..	..	..
2000 Social security contributions[1]	..	**0**	**0**	**0**	**0**	**29 065**	**231 209**	**497 279**	**1 143 802**	**2 155 261**
2100 Employees	..	..	..	..	..	..	..	..	..	..
2200 Employers	..	..	..	..	..	..	..	24 481	56 332	394 728
2300 Self-employed or non-employed	..	..	..	..	..	..	..	..	..	..
2400 Unallocable between 2100, 2200 and 2300	..	..	..	..	..	29 065	231 209	472 797	1 087 470	1 760 533
3000 Taxes on payroll and workforce	..	**0**	**0**	**0**	**0**	**7 054**	**41 918**	**81 290**	**182 529**	**268 775**
4000 Taxes on property	..	**5 390**	**14 264**	**45 393**	**85 172**	**0**	**0**	**0**	**0**	**0**
4100 Recurrent taxes on immovable property	..	5 310	14 245	44 080	85 172	..	..	..	..	..
4200 Recurrent taxes on net wealth	..	0	0	0	0	..	..	..	..	..
4300 Estate, inheritance and gift taxes	..	0	0	0	0	..	..	..	..	..
4400 Taxes on financial and capital transactions	..	0	0	0	0	..	..	..	..	..
4500 Non-recurrent taxes	..	0	0	0	0	..	..	..	..	..
4600 Other recurrent taxes on property	..	80	19	1 313	0	..	..	..	..	..
5000 Taxes on goods and services	..	**11 981**	**26 810**	**65 862**	**117 619**	**0**	**0**	**0**	**0**	**0**
5100 Taxes on production, sale, transfer, etc	..	11 981	26 810	65 862	117 619	..	..	..	..	..
5110 General taxes	..	0	0	0	0	..	..	..	..	..
5120 Taxes on specific goods and services[2]	..	10 612	24 294	61 002	3 086	..	..	..	..	..
5130 Unallocable between 5110 and 5120	..	1 369	2 515	4 860	114 533	..	..	..	..	..
5200 Taxes on use of goods and perform activities	..	0	0	0	0	..	..	..	..	..
5300 Unallocable between 5100 and 5200	..	0	0	0	0	..	..	..	..	..
6000 Other taxes[3]	..	**1 242**	**3 207**	**4 366**	**7 121**	**0**	**0**	**0**	**0**	**0**
6100 Paid solely by business	..	0	0	0	0	..	..	..	..	..
6200 Other	..	1 242	3 207	4 366	7 121	..	..	..	..	..
Total tax revenue	..	**18 613**	**44 280**	**115 621**	**209 912**	**36 119**	**273 127**	**578 568**	**1 326 331**	**2 424 036**

1. Social security contributions data presented by ECLAC include INA (National Institute of Apprenticeship), IMAS (Joint Social Aid Institute), and FODESAF (Social Development and Family Allowances Fund).
2. In ECLAC data, the tax on ownership of vehicles, aircraft and boats is classified in category 4000.
3. In ECLAC data, the tax on the transfer of used vehicles Law No. 7088 of 30/11/87 is classified as a property tax (4000).
4. The figures for years up to and including 1997 exclude local government tax revenues as the data are not available.

StatLink http://dx.doi.org/10.1787/888933463504

Table 6.10. Cuba, tax revenues by sub-sectors of government

Million CUP

	Federal government					State/Regional				
	1990	2000	2005	2010	2015	1990	2000	2005	2010	2015
1000 Taxes on income, profits and capital gains	**14**	**1 826**	**2 451**	**3 603**	**6 676**	..	..	..	..	..
1100 Of individuals	14	291	326	554	1 848	..	..	..	..	..
1200 Corporate	0	1 535	2 126	3 049	4 828	..	..	..	..	..
1300 Unallocable between 1100 and 1200	0	0	0	0	0	..	..	..	..	..
2000 Social security contributions	**0**	**0**	**0**	**0**	**0**	..	..	..	..	..
2100 Employees	..	..	..	..	..	..	..	..	..	..
2200 Employers	..	..	..	..	..	..	..	..	..	..
2300 Self-employed or non-employed	..	..	..	..	..	..	..	..	..	..
2400 Unallocable between 2100, 2200 and 2300	..	..	..	..	..	..	..	..	..	..
3000 Taxes on payroll and workforce	**0**	**970**	**2 962**	**4 414**	**2 753**	..	..	..	..	..
4000 Taxes on property	**0**	**0**	**0**	**0**	**0**	..	..	..	..	..
4100 Recurrent taxes on immovable property	..	..	..	..	..	..	..	..	..	..
4200 Recurrent taxes on net wealth	..	..	..	..	..	..	..	..	..	..
4300 Estate, inheritance and gift taxes	..	..	..	..	..	..	..	..	..	..
4400 Taxes on financial and capital transactions	..	..	..	..	..	..	..	..	..	..
4500 Non-recurrent taxes	..	..	..	..	..	..	..	..	..	..
4600 Other recurrent taxes on property	..	..	..	..	..	..	..	..	..	..
5000 Taxes on goods and services	**5 443**	**6 732**	**9 844**	**12 283**	**17 742**	..	..	..	..	..
5100 Taxes on production, sale, transfer, etc	5 443	6 732	9 844	12 283	17 742	..	..	..	..	..
5110 General taxes	5 017	6 131	9 036	10 525	15 611	..	..	..	..	..
5120 Taxes on specific goods and services	426	602	808	1 758	2 131	..	..	..	..	..
5130 Unallocable between 5110 and 5120	0	0	0	0	0	..	..	..	..	..
5200 Taxes on use of goods and perform activities	0	0	0	0	0	..	..	..	..	..
5300 Unallocable between 5100 and 5200	0	0	0	0	0	..	..	..	..	..
6000 Other taxes	**117**	**657**	**493**	**927**	**2 098**	..	..	..	..	..
6100 Paid solely by business	..	..	..	..	..	..	..	..	..	..
6200 Other	..	..	..	..	..	..	..	..	..	..
Total tax revenue	**5 574**	**10 185**	**15 750**	**21 227**	**29 269**	..	..	..	..	..

Million CUP

	Local government[1]					Social Security Funds				
	1990	2000	2005	2010	2015	1990	2000	2005	2010	2015
1000 Taxes on income, profits and capital gains	..	..	..	..	..	**0**	**0**	**0**	**0**	**0**
1100 Of individuals	..	..	..	..	..	..	..	..	..	..
1200 Corporate	..	..	..	..	..	..	..	..	..	..
1300 Unallocable between 1100 and 1200	..	..	..	..	..	..	..	..	..	..
2000 Social security contributions	..	..	..	..	..	**691**	**1 181**	**1 778**	**2 974**	**4 322**
2100 Employees	..	..	..	..	..	..	..	..	..	..
2200 Employers	..	..	..	..	..	..	..	..	..	..
2300 Self-employed or non-employed	..	..	..	..	..	..	..	..	..	..
2400 Unallocable between 2100, 2200 and 2300	..	..	..	..	..	691	1 181	1 778	2 974	4 322
3000 Taxes on payroll and workforce	..	..	..	..	..	**0**	**0**	**0**	**0**	**0**
4000 Taxes on property	..	..	..	..	..	**0**	**0**	**0**	**0**	**0**
4100 Recurrent taxes on immovable property	..	..	..	..	..	..	..	..	..	..
4200 Recurrent taxes on net wealth	..	..	..	..	..	..	..	..	..	..
4300 Estate, inheritance and gift taxes	..	..	..	..	..	..	..	..	..	..
4400 Taxes on financial and capital transactions	..	..	..	..	..	..	..	..	..	..
4500 Non-recurrent taxes	..	..	..	..	..	..	..	..	..	..
4600 Other recurrent taxes on property	..	..	..	..	..	..	..	..	..	..
5000 Taxes on goods and services	..	..	..	..	..	**0**	**0**	**0**	**0**	**0**
5100 Taxes on production, sale, transfer, etc	..	..	..	..	..	..	..	..	..	..
5110 General taxes	..	..	..	..	..	..	..	..	..	..
5120 Taxes on specific goods and services	..	..	..	..	..	..	..	..	..	..
5130 Unallocable between 5110 and 5120	..	..	..	..	..	..	..	..	..	..
5200 Taxes on use of goods and perform activities	..	..	..	..	..	..	..	..	..	..
5300 Unallocable between 5100 and 5200	..	..	..	..	..	..	..	..	..	..
6000 Other taxes	..	..	..	..	..	**0**	**0**	**0**	**0**	**0**
6100 Paid solely by business	..	..	..	..	..	..	..	..	..	..
6200 Other	..	..	..	..	..	..	..	..	..	..
Total tax revenue	..	..	..	..	..	**691**	**1 181**	**1 778**	**2 974**	**4 322**

1. The figures exclude local government tax revenues as the data are not available.

StatLink http://dx.doi.org/10.1787/888933463515

Table 6.11. Dominican Republic, tax revenues by sub-sectors of government

Million DOP

	Federal government					State/Regional				
	1990	2000	2005	2010	2015	1990	2000	2005	2010	2015
1000 Taxes on income, profits and capital gains	**1 670**	**10 782**	**30 042**	**53 643**	**119 819**	..	..	..	..	..
1100 Of individuals	..	4 088	7 588	17 088	35 549	..	..	..	..	..
1200 Corporate	..	4 679	16 222	21 475	61 695	..	..	..	..	..
1300 Unallocable between 1100 and 1200	1 670	2 015	6 232	15 080	22 576	..	..	..	..	..
2000 Social security contributions	**0**	**0**	**0**	**0**	**0**	..	..	..	..	..
2100 Employees	..	..	..	..	..	..	..	..	..	..
2200 Employers	..	..	..	..	..	..	..	..	..	..
2300 Self-employed or non-employed	..	..	..	..	..	..	..	..	..	..
2400 Unallocable between 2100, 2200 and 2300	..	..	..	..	..	..	..	..	..	..
3000 Taxes on payroll and workforce	**0**	**0**	**0**	**0**	**0**	..	..	..	..	..
4000 Taxes on property	**56**	**529**	**6 579**	**12 782**	**18 097**	..	..	..	..	..
4100 Recurrent taxes on immovable property	9	115	1 710	3 004	5 200	..	..	..	..	..
4200 Recurrent taxes on net wealth	0	0	0	0	0	..	..	..	..	..
4300 Estate, inheritance and gift taxes	11	96	84	231	418	..	..	..	..	..
4400 Taxes on financial and capital transactions	22	217	4 546	8 125	11 120	..	..	..	..	..
4500 Non-recurrent taxes	3	32	89	488	591	..	..	..	..	..
4600 Other recurrent taxes on property	11	70	151	934	769	..	..	..	..	..
5000 Taxes on goods and services	**4 501**	**32 602**	**91 322**	**175 601**	**274 845**	..	..	..	..	..
5100 Taxes on production, sale, transfer, etc	4 432	31 884	89 604	173 337	271 372	..	..	..	..	..
5110 General taxes	970	9 912	40 983	81 226	147 039	..	..	..	..	..
5120 Taxes on specific goods and services[1]	3 462	21 972	48 621	92 111	124 333	..	..	..	..	..
5130 Unallocable between 5110 and 5120	0	0	0	0	0	..	..	..	..	..
5200 Taxes on use of goods and perform activities	69	718	1 718	2 265	3 473	..	..	..	..	..
5300 Unallocable between 5100 and 5200	0	0	0	0	0	..	..	..	..	..
6000 Other taxes[2]	**159**	**495**	**1 661**	**0**	**1**	..	..	..	..	..
6100 Paid solely by business	0	0	0	..	0	..	..	..	..	..
6200 Other	159	495	1 661	..	1	..	..	..	..	..
Total tax revenue	**6 386**	**44 408**	**129 604**	**242 027**	**412 762**	..	..	..	..	..

Million DOP

	Local government[3]					Social Security Funds[4]				
	1990	2000	2005	2010	2015	1990	2000	2005	2010	2015
1000 Taxes on income, profits and capital gains	..	..	..	..	..	**0**	**0**	**0**	**0**	**0**
1100 Of individuals	..	..	..	..	..	..	..	..	..	..
1200 Corporate	..	..	..	..	..	..	..	..	..	..
1300 Unallocable between 1100 and 1200	..	..	..	..	..	..	..	..	..	..
2000 Social security contributions	..	..	..	..	..	**53**	**490**	**35**	**1 845**	**1 483**
2100 Employees	..	..	..	..	..	..	..	..	..	..
2200 Employers	..	..	..	..	..	..	..	..	..	..
2300 Self-employed or non-employed	..	..	..	..	..	..	..	..	..	..
2400 Unallocable between 2100, 2200 and 2300	..	..	..	..	..	53	490	35	1 845	1 483
3000 Taxes on payroll and workforce	..	..	..	..	..	**0**	**0**	**0**	**0**	**0**
4000 Taxes on property	..	..	..	..	..	**0**	**0**	**0**	**0**	**0**
4100 Recurrent taxes on immovable property	..	..	..	..	..	..	..	..	..	..
4200 Recurrent taxes on net wealth	..	..	..	..	..	..	..	..	..	..
4300 Estate, inheritance and gift taxes	..	..	..	..	..	..	..	..	..	..
4400 Taxes on financial and capital transactions	..	..	..	..	..	..	..	..	..	..
4500 Non-recurrent taxes	..	..	..	..	..	..	..	..	..	..
4600 Other recurrent taxes on property	..	..	..	..	..	..	..	..	..	..
5000 Taxes on goods and services	..	..	..	..	..	**0**	**0**	**0**	**0**	**0**
5100 Taxes on production, sale, transfer, etc	..	..	..	..	..	..	..	..	..	..
5110 General taxes	..	..	..	..	..	..	..	..	..	..
5120 Taxes on specific goods and services[1]	..	..	..	..	..	..	..	..	..	..
5130 Unallocable between 5110 and 5120	..	..	..	..	..	..	..	..	..	..
5200 Taxes on use of goods and perform activities	..	..	..	..	..	..	..	..	..	..
5300 Unallocable between 5100 and 5200	..	..	..	..	..	..	..	..	..	..
6000 Other taxes[2]	..	..	..	..	..	**0**	**0**	**0**	**0**	**0**
6100 Paid solely by business	..	..	..	..	..	..	..	..	..	..
6200 Other	..	..	..	..	..	..	..	..	..	..
Total tax revenue	..	..	..	..	..	**53**	**490**	**35**	**1 845**	**1 483**

1. In ECLAC data, the tax on transfer of movable goods is classified as a property tax (4000).
2. In ECLAC data, the vehicle transfer tax is classified as a property tax (4000).
3. The figures exclude local government tax revenues as the data are not available.
4. The figures exclude social security contributions to general government managed by the private sector.

StatLink http://dx.doi.org/10.1787/888933463528

Table 6.12. Ecuador, tax revenues by sub-sectors of government

Million USD

	Federal government					State/Regional				
	1990	2000	2005	2010	2015	1990	2000	2005	2010	2015
1000 Taxes on income, profits and capital gains	**138**	**293**	**936**	**2 348**	**4 705**	..	..	..	..	..
1100 Of individuals	0	10	27	80	192	..	..	..	..	..
1200 Corporate	0	53	342	485	1 578	..	..	..	..	..
1300 Unallocable between 1100 and 1200	138	231	567	1 783	2 935	..	..	..	..	..
2000 Social security contributions	**0**	**0**	**0**	**0**	**0**	..	..	..	..	..
2100 Employees	..	..	..	..	..	..	..	..	..	..
2200 Employers	..	..	..	..	..	..	..	..	..	..
2300 Self-employed or non-employed	..	..	..	..	..	..	..	..	..	..
2400 Unallocable between 2100, 2200 and 2300	..	..	..	..	..	..	..	..	..	..
3000 Taxes on payroll and workforce	**0**	**0**	**0**	**0**	**0**	..	..	..	..	..
4000 Taxes on property	**0**	**0**	**1**	**5**	**29**	..	..	..	..	..
4100 Recurrent taxes on immovable property	..	..	0	0	0	..	..	..	..	..
4200 Recurrent taxes on net wealth	..	..	0	0	0	..	..	..	..	..
4300 Estate, inheritance and gift taxes	..	..	1	5	29	..	..	..	..	..
4400 Taxes on financial and capital transactions	..	..	0	0	0	..	..	..	..	..
4500 Non-recurrent taxes	..	..	0	0	0	..	..	..	..	..
4600 Other recurrent taxes on property	..	..	0	0	0	..	..	..	..	..
5000 Taxes on goods and services	**668**	**1 330**	**2 802**	**6 152**	**10 577**	..	..	..	..	..
5100 Taxes on production, sale, transfer, etc	665	1 319	2 742	5 997	10 354	..	..	..	..	..
5110 General taxes	302	836	1 975	3 886	6 352	..	..	..	..	..
5120 Taxes on specific goods and services	363	483	767	2 110	4 001	..	..	..	..	..
5130 Unallocable between 5110 and 5120	0	0	0	0	0	..	..	..	..	..
5200 Taxes on use of goods and perform activities[1]	3	11	60	156	223	..	..	..	..	..
5300 Unallocable between 5100 and 5200	0	0	0	0	0	..	..	..	..	..
6000 Other taxes	**27**	**0**	**2**	**289**	**135**	..	..	..	..	..
6100 Paid solely by business	0	..	0	0	0	..	..	..	..	..
6200 Other	27	..	2	289	135	..	..	..	..	..
Total tax revenue	**833**	**1 623**	**3 741**	**8 794**	**15 446**	..	..	..	..	..

Million USD

	Local government					Social Security Funds				
	1990	2000	2005	2010	2015	1990	2000	2005	2010	2015
1000 Taxes on income, profits and capital gains	**0**	**0**	**0**	**0**	**0**	**0**	**0**	**0**	**0**	**0**
1100 Of individuals	..	..	..	..	..	..	..	..	..	..
1200 Corporate	..	..	..	..	..	..	..	..	..	..
1300 Unallocable between 1100 and 1200	..	..	..	..	..	..	..	..	..	..
2000 Social security contributions	**0**	**0**	**0**	**0**	**0**	**243**	**228**	**1 109**	**2 549**	**5 055**
2100 Employees	..	..	..	..	..	..	..	..	..	..
2200 Employers	..	..	..	..	..	..	..	..	..	..
2300 Self-employed or non-employed	..	..	..	..	..	..	..	..	..	..
2400 Unallocable between 2100, 2200 and 2300	..	..	..	..	..	243	228	1 109	2 549	5 055
3000 Taxes on payroll and workforce	**0**	**0**	**0**	**0**	**0**	**0**	**0**	**0**	**0**	**0**
4000 Taxes on property	**14**	**11**	**44**	**82**	**200**	**0**	**0**	**0**	**0**	**0**
4100 Recurrent taxes on immovable property	13	10	38	66	126	..	..	..	..	..
4200 Recurrent taxes on net wealth	0	0	0	0	0	..	..	..	..	..
4300 Estate, inheritance and gift taxes	0	0	0	0	0	..	..	..	..	..
4400 Taxes on financial and capital transactions	1	2	6	15	75	..	..	..	..	..
4500 Non-recurrent taxes	0	0	0	0	0	..	..	..	..	..
4600 Other recurrent taxes on property	0	0	0	0	0	..	..	..	..	..
5000 Taxes on goods and services	**14**	**20**	**85**	**143**	**330**	**0**	**0**	**0**	**0**	**0**
5100 Taxes on production, sale, transfer, etc	6	11	43	81	197	..	..	..	..	..
5110 General taxes	4	4	15	39	73	..	..	..	..	..
5120 Taxes on specific goods and services	1	6	29	42	124	..	..	..	..	..
5130 Unallocable between 5110 and 5120	0	0	0	0	0	..	..	..	..	..
5200 Taxes on use of goods and perform activities[1]	5	2	9	12	42	..	..	..	..	..
5300 Unallocable between 5100 and 5200	3	8	33	49	91	..	..	..	..	..
6000 Other taxes	**2**	**2**	**50**	**1**	**0**	**0**	**0**	**0**	**0**	**0**
6100 Paid solely by business	0	0	0	0	0	..	..	..	..	..
6200 Other	2	2	50	1	0	..	..	..	..	..
Total tax revenue	**29**	**33**	**179**	**225**	**530**	**243**	**228**	**1 109**	**2 549**	**5 055**

1. In ECLAC data, the annual tax on motor vehicles is classified as a property tax (4000).

StatLink http://dx.doi.org/10.1787/888933463534

Table 6.13. El Salvador, tax revenues by sub-sectors of government

Million USD

	Federal government					State/Regional				
	1990	2000	2005	2010	2015	1990	2000	2005	2010	2015
1000 Taxes on income, profits and capital gains	**95**	**407**	**637**	**995**	**1 545**	..	..	..	..	..
1100 Of individuals	..	..	312	571	739	..	..	..	..	..
1200 Corporate	..	..	356	423	622	..	..	..	..	..
1300 Unallocable between 1100 and 1200	95	407	-31	0	183	..	..	..	..	..
2000 Social security contributions	**0**	**0**	**0**	**0**	**0**	..	..	..	..	..
2100 Employees	..	..	..	..	..	..	..	..	..	..
2200 Employers	..	..	..	..	..	..	..	..	..	..
2300 Self-employed or non-employed	..	..	..	..	..	..	..	..	..	..
2400 Unallocable between 2100, 2200 and 2300	..	..	..	..	..	..	..	..	..	..
3000 Taxes on payroll and workforce	**0**	**0**	**0**	**0**	**0**	..	..	..	..	..
4000 Taxes on property	**26**	**12**	**16**	**16**	**107**	..	..	..	..	..
4100 Recurrent taxes on immovable property	0	0	0	0	0	..	..	..	..	..
4200 Recurrent taxes on net wealth	16	0	0	0	0	..	..	..	..	..
4300 Estate, inheritance and gift taxes	0	0	0	0	0	..	..	..	..	..
4400 Taxes on financial and capital transactions	10	12	16	16	107	..	..	..	..	..
4500 Non-recurrent taxes	0	0	0	0	0	..	..	..	..	..
4600 Other recurrent taxes on property	0	0	0	0	0	..	..	..	..	..
5000 Taxes on goods and services	**259**	**903**	**1 447**	**1 855**	**2 266**	..	..	..	..	..
5100 Taxes on production, sale, transfer, etc	259	903	1 447	1 855	2 254	..	..	..	..	..
5110 General taxes	133	714	1 104	1 433	1 764	..	..	..	..	..
5120 Taxes on specific goods and services	127	189	344	422	490	..	..	..	..	..
5130 Unallocable between 5110 and 5120	0	0	0	0	0	..	..	..	..	..
5200 Taxes on use of goods and perform activities	0	0	0	0	12	..	..	..	..	..
5300 Unallocable between 5100 and 5200	0	0	0	0	0	..	..	..	..	..
6000 Other taxes	**58**	**0**	**0**	**0**	**0**	..	..	..	..	..
6100 Paid solely by business	0	0	..	..	..	..	..	..	..	..
6200 Other	58	0	..	..	..	..	..	..	..	..
Total tax revenue	**438**	**1 322**	**2 100**	**2 865**	**3 918**	..	..	..	..	..

Million USD

	Local government[1]					Social Security Funds[2]				
	1990	2000	2005	2010	2015	1990	2000	2005	2010	2015
1000 Taxes on income, profits and capital gains	..	..	..	..	**0**	**0**	**0**	**0**	**0**	**0**
1100 Of individuals	..	..	..	..	..	..	..	..	..	..
1200 Corporate	..	..	..	..	..	..	..	..	..	..
1300 Unallocable between 1100 and 1200	..	..	..	..	..	..	..	..	..	..
2000 Social security contributions	..	..	..	..	**0**	**67**	**263**	**282**	**369**	**488**
2100 Employees	..	..	..	..	..	..	75	76	99	130
2200 Employers	..	..	..	..	..	..	176	181	238	314
2300 Self-employed or non-employed	..	..	..	..	..	..	13	25	33	45
2400 Unallocable between 2100, 2200 and 2300	..	..	..	..	..	67	0	0	0	0
3000 Taxes on payroll and workforce	..	..	..	..	**0**	**0**	**0**	**0**	**0**	**0**
4000 Taxes on property	..	..	..	..	**0**	**0**	**0**	**0**	**0**	**0**
4100 Recurrent taxes on immovable property	..	..	..	..	..	..	..	..	..	..
4200 Recurrent taxes on net wealth	..	..	..	..	..	..	..	..	..	..
4300 Estate, inheritance and gift taxes	..	..	..	..	..	..	..	..	..	..
4400 Taxes on financial and capital transactions	..	..	..	..	..	..	..	..	..	..
4500 Non-recurrent taxes	..	..	..	..	..	..	..	..	..	..
4600 Other recurrent taxes on property	..	..	..	..	..	..	..	..	..	..
5000 Taxes on goods and services	..	..	..	..	**0**	**0**	**0**	**0**	**0**	**0**
5100 Taxes on production, sale, transfer, etc	..	..	..	..	..	..	..	..	..	..
5110 General taxes	..	..	..	..	..	..	..	..	..	..
5120 Taxes on specific goods and services	..	..	..	..	..	..	..	..	..	..
5130 Unallocable between 5110 and 5120	..	..	..	..	..	..	..	..	..	..
5200 Taxes on use of goods and perform activities	..	..	..	..	..	..	..	..	..	..
5300 Unallocable between 5100 and 5200	..	..	..	..	..	..	..	..	..	..
6000 Other taxes	..	..	..	..	**77**	**0**	**0**	**0**	**0**	**0**
6100 Paid solely by business	..	..	..	..	0	..	..	..	..	..
6200 Other	..	..	..	..	77	..	..	..	..	..
Total tax revenue	..	..	..	..	**77**	**67**	**263**	**282**	**369**	**488**

1. Local government tax revenues are only available for 2015.
2. Social security contributions are those paid to the Salvadoran Institute of Social Security (ISSS).

StatLink http://dx.doi.org/10.1787/888933463547

Table 6.14. Guatemala, tax revenues by sub-sectors of government

Million GTQ

	Federal government					State/Regional				
	1990	2000	2005	2010	2015	1990	2000	2005	2010	2015
1000 Taxes on income, profits and capital gains	**507**	**3 295**	**6 049**	**10 319**	**17 534**	..	..	..	..	..
1100 Of individuals	25	143	645	1 225	1 826	..	..	..	..	..
1200 Corporate	482	3 149	3 756	6 520	11 802	..	..	..	..	..
1300 Unallocable between 1100 and 1200	0	2	1 647	2 574	3 907	..	..	..	..	..
2000 Social security contributions	**0**	**0**	**0**	**0**	**0**	..	..	..	..	..
2100 Employees	..	..	..	..	..	..	..	..	..	..
2200 Employers	..	..	..	..	..	..	..	..	..	..
2300 Self-employed or non-employed	..	..	..	..	..	..	..	..	..	..
2400 Unallocable between 2100, 2200 and 2300	..	..	..	..	..	..	..	..	..	..
3000 Taxes on payroll and workforce	**0**	**0**	**0**	**0**	**0**	..	..	..	..	..
4000 Taxes on property	**45**	**17**	**9**	**11**	**21**	..	..	..	..	..
4100 Recurrent taxes on immovable property	0	6	1	1	1	..	..	..	..	..
4200 Recurrent taxes on net wealth	0	0	0	0	0	..	..	..	..	..
4300 Estate, inheritance and gift taxes	0	0	0	0	0	..	..	..	..	..
4400 Taxes on financial and capital transactions	45	12	8	10	20	..	..	..	..	..
4500 Non-recurrent taxes	0	0	0	0	0	..	..	..	..	..
4600 Other recurrent taxes on property	0	0	0	0	0	..	..	..	..	..
5000 Taxes on goods and services	**1 709**	**10 317**	**16 402**	**23 259**	**31 719**	..	..	..	..	..
5100 Taxes on production, sale, transfer, etc	1 681	10 131	16 083	22 754	30 083	..	..	..	..	..
5110 General taxes	762	6 259	10 753	16 980	23 271	..	..	..	..	..
5120 Taxes on specific goods and services	919	3 872	5 330	5 773	6 816	..	..	..	..	..
5130 Unallocable between 5110 and 5120	0	0	0	0	0	..	..	..	..	..
5200 Taxes on use of goods and perform activities	28	186	319	505	1 631	..	..	..	..	..
5300 Unallocable between 5100 and 5200	0	0	0	0	0	..	..	..	..	..
6000 Other taxes	**104**	**186**	**315**	**572**	**337**	..	..	..	..	..
6100 Paid solely by business	0	0	0	0	0	..	..	..	..	..
6200 Other	104	186	315	572	337	..	..	..	..	..
Total tax revenue	**2 365**	**13 816**	**22 775**	**34 161**	**49 611**	..	..	..	..	..

Million GTQ

	Local government[1]					Social Security Funds[2]				
	1990	2000	2005	2010	2015	1990	2000	2005	2010	2015
1000 Taxes on income, profits and capital gains	..	**0**	**0**	**0**	**0**	**0**	**0**	**0**	**0**	**0**
1100 Of individuals	..	..	..	..	..	..	..	..	..	..
1200 Corporate	..	..	..	..	..	..	..	..	..	..
1300 Unallocable between 1100 and 1200	..	..	..	..	..	..	..	..	..	..
2000 Social security contributions	..	**0**	**0**	**0**	**0**	**436**	**2 569**	**4 072**	**6 408**	**10 034**
2100 Employees	..	..	..	..	..	..	..	..	..	..
2200 Employers	..	..	..	..	..	..	..	..	..	..
2300 Self-employed or non-employed	..	..	..	..	..	..	..	..	..	..
2400 Unallocable between 2100, 2200 and 2300	..	..	..	..	..	436	2 569	4 072	6 408	10 034
3000 Taxes on payroll and workforce	..	**0**	**0**	**0**	**0**	**0**	**0**	**0**	**0**	**0**
4000 Taxes on property	..	**147**	**341**	**620**	**692**	**0**	**0**	**0**	**0**	**0**
4100 Recurrent taxes on immovable property	..	147	341	620	692	..	..	..	..	..
4200 Recurrent taxes on net wealth	..	0	0	0	0	..	..	..	..	..
4300 Estate, inheritance and gift taxes	..	0	0	0	0	..	..	..	..	..
4400 Taxes on financial and capital transactions	..	0	0	0	0	..	..	..	..	..
4500 Non-recurrent taxes	..	0	0	0	0	..	..	..	..	..
4600 Other recurrent taxes on property	..	0	0	0	0	..	..	..	..	..
5000 Taxes on goods and services	..	**0**	**0**	**0**	**0**	**0**	**0**	**0**	**0**	**0**
5100 Taxes on production, sale, transfer, etc	..	..	..	..	..	..	..	..	..	..
5110 General taxes	..	..	..	..	..	..	..	..	..	..
5120 Taxes on specific goods and services	..	..	..	..	..	..	..	..	..	..
5130 Unallocable between 5110 and 5120	..	..	..	..	..	..	..	..	..	..
5200 Taxes on use of goods and perform activities	..	..	..	..	..	..	..	..	..	..
5300 Unallocable between 5100 and 5200	..	..	..	..	..	..	..	..	..	..
6000 Other taxes	..	**0**	**0**	**0**	**0**	**0**	**0**	**0**	**0**	**0**
6100 Paid solely by business	..	..	..	..	..	..	..	..	..	..
6200 Other	..	..	..	..	..	..	..	..	..	..
Total tax revenue	..	**147**	**341**	**620**	**692**	**436**	**2 569**	**4 072**	**6 408**	**10 034**

1. The figures exclude some local government tax revenues as the data are not available. Revenues from the municipal property tax (IUSI) are included.
2. Corresponds to social security contributions to the Guatemalan Social Security Institute (IGSS) and payments by public employees to the government's pension fund.

StatLink http://dx.doi.org/10.1787/888933463558

Table 6.15. Honduras, tax revenues by sub-sectors of government

Million HNL

	Federal government					State/Regional				
	1990	2000	2005	2010	2015	1990	2000	2005	2010	2015
1000 Taxes on income, profits and capital gains	**431**	**2 985**	**7 498**	**13 972**	**25 178**	..	..	..	..	..
1100 Of individuals	157	991	2 312	4 528	8 451	..	..	..	..	..
1200 Corporate	274	1 916	4 725	8 705	16 392	..	..	..	..	..
1300 Unallocable between 1100 and 1200	0	78	461	740	334	..	..	..	..	..
2000 Social security contributions	**0**	**0**	**0**	**0**	**0**	..	..	..	..	..
2100 Employees	..	..	..	..	..	..	..	..	..	..
2200 Employers	..	..	..	..	..	..	..	..	..	..
2300 Self-employed or non-employed	..	..	..	..	..	..	..	..	..	..
2400 Unallocable between 2100, 2200 and 2300	..	..	..	..	..	..	..	..	..	..
3000 Taxes on payroll and workforce	**0**	**0**	**0**	**0**	**0**	..	..	..	..	..
4000 Taxes on property	**16**	**189**	**170**	**254**	**2 301**	..	..	..	..	..
4100 Recurrent taxes on immovable property	0	0	0	0	0	..	..	..	..	..
4200 Recurrent taxes on net wealth	0	0	0	0	0	..	..	..	..	..
4300 Estate, inheritance and gift taxes	0	0	0	0	0	..	..	..	..	..
4400 Taxes on financial and capital transactions	0	0	0	0	2 003	..	..	..	..	..
4500 Non-recurrent taxes	0	0	0	0	0	..	..	..	..	..
4600 Other recurrent taxes on property	16	189	170	254	299	..	..	..	..	..
5000 Taxes on goods and services	**1 405**	**11 445**	**19 032**	**28 937**	**52 217**	..	..	..	..	..
5100 Taxes on production, sale, transfer, etc	1 405	11 445	19 032	28 937	52 217	..	..	..	..	..
5110 General taxes	344	5 146	9 565	16 050	32 273	..	..	..	..	..
5120 Taxes on specific goods and services	1 061	6 299	9 468	12 887	19 944	..	..	..	..	..
5130 Unallocable between 5110 and 5120	0	0	0	0	0	..	..	..	..	..
5200 Taxes on use of goods and perform activities	0	0	0	0	0	..	..	..	..	..
5300 Unallocable between 5100 and 5200	0	0	0	0	0	..	..	..	..	..
6000 Other taxes	**1**	**2**	**7**	**9**	**8**	..	..	..	..	..
6100 Paid solely by business	0	0	0	0	0	..	..	..	..	..
6200 Other	1	2	7	9	8	..	..	..	..	..
Total tax revenue	**1 853**	**14 620**	**26 708**	**43 173**	**79 704**	..	..	..	..	..

Million HNL

	Local government					Social Security Funds				
	1990	2000	2005	2010	2015	1990	2000	2005	2010	2015
1000 Taxes on income, profits and capital gains	**0**	**0**	**0**	**0**	**0**	**0**	**0**	**0**	**0**	**0**
1100 Of individuals	..	..	..	..	..	..	..	..	..	..
1200 Corporate	..	..	..	..	..	..	..	..	..	..
1300 Unallocable between 1100 and 1200	..	..	..	..	..	..	..	..	..	..
2000 Social security contributions	**0**	**0**	**0**	**0**	**0**	**179**	**1 727**	**4 416**	**8 671**	**13 524**
2100 Employees	..	..	..	..	..	..	..	..	..	..
2200 Employers	..	..	..	..	..	..	..	..	..	..
2300 Self-employed or non-employed	..	..	..	..	..	..	..	..	..	..
2400 Unallocable between 2100, 2200 and 2300	..	..	..	..	..	179	1 727	4 416	8 671	13 524
3000 Taxes on payroll and workforce	**0**	**0**	**0**	**0**	**0**	**0**	**0**	**0**	**0**	**0**
4000 Taxes on property	**0**	**0**	**0**	**0**	**0**	**0**	**0**	**0**	**0**	**0**
4100 Recurrent taxes on immovable property	..	..	..	..	..	..	..	..	..	..
4200 Recurrent taxes on net wealth	..	..	..	..	..	..	..	..	..	..
4300 Estate, inheritance and gift taxes	..	..	..	..	..	..	..	..	..	..
4400 Taxes on financial and capital transactions	..	..	..	..	..	..	..	..	..	..
4500 Non-recurrent taxes	..	..	..	..	..	..	..	..	..	..
4600 Other recurrent taxes on property	..	..	..	..	..	..	..	..	..	..
5000 Taxes on goods and services	**0**	**0**	**0**	**0**	**0**	**0**	**0**	**0**	**0**	**0**
5100 Taxes on production, sale, transfer, etc	..	..	..	..	..	..	..	..	..	..
5110 General taxes	..	..	..	..	..	..	..	..	..	..
5120 Taxes on specific goods and services	..	..	..	..	..	..	..	..	..	..
5130 Unallocable between 5110 and 5120	..	..	..	..	..	..	..	..	..	..
5200 Taxes on use of goods and perform activities	..	..	..	..	..	..	..	..	..	..
5300 Unallocable between 5100 and 5200	..	..	..	..	..	..	..	..	..	..
6000 Other taxes	**90**	**960**	**1 850**	**2 216**	**2 496**	**0**	**0**	**0**	**0**	**0**
6100 Paid solely by business	0	0	0	0	0	..	..	..	..	..
6200 Other	90	960	1 850	2 216	2 496	..	..	..	..	..
Total tax revenue	**90**	**960**	**1 850**	**2 216**	**2 496**	**179**	**1 727**	**4 416**	**8 671**	**13 524**

StatLink http://dx.doi.org/10.1787/888933463568

Table 6.16. Jamaica, tax revenues by sub-sectors of government

Million JAM

	Federal government					State/Regional[2]				
	1990	2000	2005	2010	2015	1990	2000	2005	2010	2015
1000 Taxes on income, profits and capital gains	**3 944**	**39 277**	**69 894**	**118 708**	**149 460**	..	..	..	..	..
1100 Of individuals	1 687	17 441	36 043	54 798	74 537	..	..	..	..	..
1200 Corporate	1 280	7 627	13 134	33 091	39 668	..	..	..	..	..
1300 Unallocable between 1100 and 1200	977	14 209	20 718	30 820	35 254	..	..	..	..	..
2000 Social security contributions[1]	**0**	**0**	**0**	**0**	**0**	..	..	..	..	..
2100 Employees	..	..	..	..	..	..	..	..	..	..
2200 Employers	..	..	..	..	..	..	..	..	..	..
2300 Self-employed or non-employed	..	..	..	..	..	..	..	..	..	..
2400 Unallocable between 2100, 2200 and 2300	..	..	..	..	..	..	..	..	..	..
3000 Taxes on payroll and workforce	**0**	**0**	**0**	**0**	**0**	..	..	..	..	..
4000 Taxes on property	**67**	**0**	**0**	**0**	**0**	..	..	..	..	..
4100 Recurrent taxes on immovable property[1]	67	..	..	..	..	..	..	..	..	..
4200 Recurrent taxes on net wealth	0	..	..	..	..	..	..	..	..	..
4300 Estate, inheritance and gift taxes	0	..	..	..	..	..	..	..	..	..
4400 Taxes on financial and capital transactions	0	..	..	..	..	..	..	..	..	..
4500 Non-recurrent taxes	0	..	..	..	..	..	..	..	..	..
4600 Other recurrent taxes on property	0	..	..	..	..	..	..	..	..	..
5000 Taxes on goods and services	**3 294**	**44 638**	**78 147**	**148 894**	**240 773**	..	..	..	..	..
5100 Taxes on production, sale, transfer, etc	3 230	43 838	77 036	146 850	237 566	..	..	..	..	..
5110 General taxes	4	13 059	27 274	45 152	70 648	..	..	..	..	..
5120 Taxes on specific goods and services	3 226	30 779	49 762	101 698	166 918	..	..	..	..	..
5130 Unallocable between 5110 and 5120	0	0	0	0	0	..	..	..	..	..
5200 Taxes on use of goods and perform activities	64	800	1 111	2 045	3 206	..	..	..	..	..
5300 Unallocable between 5100 and 5200	0	0	0	0	0	..	..	..	..	..
6000 Other taxes	**444**	**3 159**	**8 733**	**8 738**	**13 450**	..	..	..	..	..
6100 Paid solely by business	0	0	0	0	0	..	..	..	..	..
6200 Other[1]	444	3 159	8 733	8 738	13 450	..	..	..	..	..
Total tax revenue	**7 748**	**87 074**	**156 775**	**276 340**	**403 683**	..	..	..	..	..

Million JAM

	Local government					Social Security Funds				
	1990	2000	2005	2010	2015	1990	2000	2005	2010	2015
1000 Taxes on income, profits and capital gains	**0**	**0**	**0**	**0**	**0**	**0**	**0**	**0**	**0**	**0**
1100 Of individuals	..	..	..	..	..	..	..	..	..	..
1200 Corporate	..	..	..	..	..	..	..	..	..	..
1300 Unallocable between 1100 and 1200	..	..	..	..	..	..	..	..	..	..
2000 Social security contributions[1]	**0**	**0**	**0**	**0**	**0**	**0**	**0**	**4 924**	**8 199**	**16 449**
2100 Employees	..	..	..	..	..	..	..	..	..	..
2200 Employers	..	..	..	..	..	..	..	..	..	..
2300 Self-employed or non-employed	..	..	..	..	..	..	..	..	..	..
2400 Unallocable between 2100, 2200 and 2300	..	..	..	..	..	..	..	4 924	8 199	16 449
3000 Taxes on payroll and workforce	**0**	**0**	**0**	**0**	**0**	**0**	**0**	**0**	**0**	**0**
4000 Taxes on property	**0**	**639**	**1 592**	**2 600**	**7 271**	**0**	**0**	**0**	**0**	**0**
4100 Recurrent taxes on immovable property[1]	..	639	1 592	2 600	7 271	..	..	..	..	..
4200 Recurrent taxes on net wealth	..	0	0	0	0	..	..	..	..	..
4300 Estate, inheritance and gift taxes	..	0	0	0	0	..	..	..	..	..
4400 Taxes on financial and capital transactions	..	0	0	0	0	..	..	..	..	..
4500 Non-recurrent taxes	..	0	0	0	0	..	..	..	..	..
4600 Other recurrent taxes on property	..	0	0	0	0	..	..	..	..	..
5000 Taxes on goods and services	**0**	**0**	**0**	**0**	**0**	**0**	**0**	**0**	**0**	**0**
5100 Taxes on production, sale, transfer, etc	..	..	..	..	..	..	..	..	..	..
5110 General taxes	..	..	..	..	..	..	..	..	..	..
5120 Taxes on specific goods and services	..	..	..	..	..	..	..	..	..	..
5130 Unallocable between 5110 and 5120	..	..	..	..	..	..	..	..	..	..
5200 Taxes on use of goods and perform activities	..	..	..	..	..	..	..	..	..	..
5300 Unallocable between 5100 and 5200	..	..	..	..	..	..	..	..	..	..
6000 Other taxes	**0**	**0**	**0**	**0**	**0**	**0**	**0**	**0**	**0**	**0**
6100 Paid solely by business	..	..	..	..	..	..	..	..	..	..
6200 Other	..	..	..	..	..	..	..	..	..	..
Total tax revenue	**0**	**639**	**1 592**	**2 600**	**7 271**	**0**	**0**	**4 924**	**8 199**	**16 449**

1. Data are estimated for 2014 and 2015.
2. The figures exclude state/regional government tax revenues as the data are not available.

StatLink http://dx.doi.org/10.1787/888933463573

Table 6.17. Mexico, tax revenues by sub-sectors of government

Million MXN

	Federal government					State/Regional				
	1990	2000	2005	2010	2015	1990	2000	2005	2010	2015
1000 Taxes on income, profits and capital gains[1]	**34 668**	**276 548**	**402 036**	**683 604**	**1 230 555**	**3**	**0**	**0**	**0**	..
1100 Of individuals	..	..	195 869	313 473	609 384	..	..	..	..	..
1200 Corporate	..	..	135 840	246 745	592 443	..	..	..	..	..
1300 Unallocable between 1100 and 1200	34 668	276 548	70 327	123 386	28 728	3	..	..	..	..
2000 Social security contributions[2]	**0**	**0**	**0**	**0**	**0**	**0**	**0**	**0**	**0**	..
2100 Employees	..	..	..	..	..	..	..	..	..	..
2200 Employers	..	..	..	..	..	..	..	..	..	..
2300 Self-employed or non-employed	..	..	..	..	..	..	..	..	..	..
2400 Unallocable between 2100, 2200 and 2300	..	..	..	..	..	..	..	..	..	..
3000 Taxes on payroll and workforce	**818**	**0**	**0**	**0**	**0**	**972**	**11 215**	**20 429**	**36 818**	..
4000 Taxes on property	**3**	**0**	**0**	**0**	**0**	**894**	**7 018**	**10 905**	**13 137**	..
4100 Recurrent taxes on immovable property	0	..	..	..	..	482	5 238	6 544	8 522	..
4200 Recurrent taxes on net wealth	0	..	..	..	..	0	0	0	0	..
4300 Estate, inheritance and gift taxes	0	..	..	..	..	7	0	0	0	..
4400 Taxes on financial and capital transactions	3	..	..	..	..	405	1 781	4 361	4 615	..
4500 Non-recurrent taxes	0	..	..	..	..	0	0	0	0	..
4600 Other recurrent taxes on property	0	..	..	..	..	0	0	0	0	..
5000 Taxes on goods and services	**44 605**	**355 056**	**467 019**	**701 446**	**1 116 021**	**118**	**1 346**	**2 124**	**5 805**	..
5100 Taxes on production, sale, transfer, etc	44 029	309 283	401 580	627 193	1 115 520	45	910	1 364	2 470	..
5110 General taxes	26 635	189 606	318 432	504 509	707 213	0	0	0	0	..
5120 Taxes on specific goods and services[3]	17 394	119 677	83 148	122 684	408 307	30	910	1 364	2 470	..
5130 Unallocable between 5110 and 5120	0	0	0	0	0	15	0	0	0	..
5200 Taxes on use of goods and perform activities	576	45 773	65 439	74 253	501	73	436	760	3 335	..
5300 Unallocable between 5100 and 5200	0	0	0	0	0	0	0	0	0	..
6000 Other taxes	**1 340**	**5 878**	**8 616**	**22 236**	**27 379**	**165**	**907**	**1 537**	**2 546**	..
6100 Paid solely by business	0	0	0	0	0	0	0	0	0	..
6200 Other	1 340	5 878	8 616	22 236	27 379	165	907	1 537	2 546	..
Total tax revenue	**81 434**	**637 482**	**877 671**	**1 407 286**	**2 373 955**	**2 152**	**20 485**	**34 995**	**58 307**	..

Million MXN

	Local government					Social Security Funds				
	1990	2000	2005	2010	2015	1990	2000	2005	2010	2015
1000 Taxes on income, profits and capital gains[1]	**2**	**0**	**0**	**0**	..	**0**	**0**	**0**	**0**	**0**
1100 Of individuals	..	..	..	..	..	..	..	..	..	..
1200 Corporate	..	..	..	..	..	..	..	..	..	..
1300 Unallocable between 1100 and 1200	2	..	..	..	..	..	..	..	..	..
2000 Social security contributions[2]	**0**	**0**	**0**	**0**	..	**17 165**	**167 292**	**261 673**	**378 006**	**588 280**
2100 Employees	..	..	..	..	..	..	..	..	..	..
2200 Employers	..	..	..	..	..	..	..	..	..	..
2300 Self-employed or non-employed	..	..	..	..	..	..	..	..	..	..
2400 Unallocable between 2100, 2200 and 2300	..	..	..	..	..	17 165	167 292	261 673	378 006	588 280
3000 Taxes on payroll and workforce	**7**	**2**	**32**	**93**	..	**0**	**0**	**0**	**0**	**0**
4000 Taxes on property	**1 017**	**6 946**	**15 891**	**25 818**	..	**0**	**0**	**0**	**0**	**0**
4100 Recurrent taxes on immovable property	554	4 710	10 098	17 202	..	..	..	..	..	..
4200 Recurrent taxes on net wealth	0	0	0	0	..	..	..	..	..	..
4300 Estate, inheritance and gift taxes	1	0	0	0	..	..	..	..	..	..
4400 Taxes on financial and capital transactions	462	2 236	5 793	8 616	..	..	..	..	..	..
4500 Non-recurrent taxes	0	0	0	0	..	..	..	..	..	..
4600 Other recurrent taxes on property	0	0	0	0	..	..	..	..	..	..
5000 Taxes on goods and services	**114**	**202**	**288**	**487**	..	**0**	**0**	**0**	**0**	**0**
5100 Taxes on production, sale, transfer, etc	97	133	214	466	..	..	..	..	..	..
5110 General taxes	0	0	0	0	..	..	..	..	..	..
5120 Taxes on specific goods and services	95	133	214	466	..	..	..	..	..	..
5130 Unallocable between 5110 and 5120	2	0	0	0	..	..	..	..	..	..
5200 Taxes on use of goods and perform activities	17	69	74	21	..	..	..	..	..	..
5300 Unallocable between 5100 and 5200	0	0	0	0	..	..	..	..	..	..
6000 Other taxes	**114**	**866**	**1 539**	**2 616**	..	**0**	**0**	**0**	**0**	**0**
6100 Paid solely by business	0	0	0	0	..	..	..	..	..	..
6200 Other	114	866	1 539	2 616	..	..	..	..	..	..
Total tax revenue	**1 254**	**8 016**	**17 750**	**29 014**	..	**17 165**	**167 292**	**261 673**	**378 006**	**588 280**

Note: The 2015 data for tax revenues of the State and Local levels of government are not available. They comprise revenues in categories 3000, 4000, 5000 and 6000.

1. In ECLAC data, income taxes are presented net of credit on salary figures.
2. In ECLAC data, social security contributions are presented net of transfers from the Federal government for the payment of IMSS (Mexican Social Security Institute) pensions.
3. Revenue Statistics in Latin America and the Caribbean and Revenue Statistics in OECD countries included fees levied on hydrocarbon production at the federal level. From the data provided for Revenue Statistics in OECD countries (2016) and for this publication, revenues from hydrocarbon production have been excluded from tax revenues and are instead treated as non-tax revenues.

StatLink http://dx.doi.org/10.1787/888933463580

Table 6.18. Nicaragua, tax revenues by sub-sectors of government

Million NIO

	Federal government					State/Regional				
	1990	2000	2005	2010	2015	1990	2000	2005	2010	2015
1000 Taxes on income, profits and capital gains	..	**1 144**	**3 902**	**8 351**	**20 800**	..	..	..	..	..
1100 Of individuals	..	..	..	..	..	..	..	..	..	..
1200 Corporate	..	..	..	..	..	..	..	..	..	..
1300 Unallocable between 1100 and 1200	..	1 144	3 902	8 351	20 800	..	..	..	..	..
2000 Social security contributions	..	**0**	**0**	**0**	**0**	..	..	..	..	..
2100 Employees	..	..	..	..	..	..	..	..	..	..
2200 Employers	..	..	..	..	..	..	..	..	..	..
2300 Self-employed or non-employed	..	..	..	..	..	..	..	..	..	..
2400 Unallocable between 2100, 2200 and 2300	..	..	..	..	..	..	..	..	..	..
3000 Taxes on payroll and workforce	..	**0**	**0**	**0**	**0**	..	..	..	..	..
4000 Taxes on property	..	**0**	**2**	**130**	**513**	..	..	..	..	..
4100 Recurrent taxes on immovable property	..	..	0	0	0	..	..	..	..	..
4200 Recurrent taxes on net wealth	..	..	2	130	513	..	..	..	..	..
4300 Estate, inheritance and gift taxes	..	..	0	0	0	..	..	..	..	..
4400 Taxes on financial and capital transactions	..	..	0	0	0	..	..	..	..	..
4500 Non-recurrent taxes	..	..	0	0	0	..	..	..	..	..
4600 Other recurrent taxes on property	..	..	0	0	0	..	..	..	..	..
5000 Taxes on goods and services	..	**5 584**	**9 725**	**17 029**	**32 725**	..	..	..	..	..
5100 Taxes on production, sale, transfer, etc	..	5 584	9 725	17 029	32 725	..	..	..	..	..
5110 General taxes	..	2 931	5 599	10 353	20 714	..	..	..	..	..
5120 Taxes on specific goods and services	..	2 653	4 126	6 676	12 011	..	..	..	..	..
5130 Unallocable between 5110 and 5120	..	0	0	0	0	..	..	..	..	..
5200 Taxes on use of goods and perform activities	..	0	0	0	0	..	..	..	..	..
5300 Unallocable between 5100 and 5200	..	0	0	0	0	..	..	..	..	..
6000 Other taxes	..	**11**	**17**	**20**	**90**	..	..	..	..	..
6100 Paid solely by business	..	0	0	0	0	..	..	..	..	..
6200 Other	..	11	17	20	90	..	..	..	..	..
Total tax revenue	..	**6 739**	**13 646**	**25 530**	**54 128**	..	..	..	..	..

Million NIO

	Local government[1]					Social Security Funds				
	1990	2000	2005	2010	2015	1990	2000	2005	2010	2015
1000 Taxes on income, profits and capital gains	..	..	..	..	..	..	**0**	**0**	**0**	**0**
1100 Of individuals	..	..	..	..	..	..	..	..	..	..
1200 Corporate	..	..	..	..	..	..	..	..	..	..
1300 Unallocable between 1100 and 1200	..	..	..	..	..	..	..	..	..	..
2000 Social security contributions	..	..	..	..	..	..	**1 678**	**3 363**	**8 090**	**18 194**
2100 Employees	..	..	..	..	..	..	..	..	..	..
2200 Employers	..	..	..	..	..	..	..	..	..	..
2300 Self-employed or non-employed	..	..	..	..	..	..	..	..	..	..
2400 Unallocable between 2100, 2200 and 2300	..	..	..	..	..	..	1 678	3 363	8 090	18 194
3000 Taxes on payroll and workforce	..	..	..	..	..	..	**0**	**0**	**0**	**0**
4000 Taxes on property	..	..	..	..	..	..	**0**	**0**	**0**	**0**
4100 Recurrent taxes on immovable property	..	..	..	..	..	..	..	..	..	..
4200 Recurrent taxes on net wealth	..	..	..	..	..	..	..	..	..	..
4300 Estate, inheritance and gift taxes	..	..	..	..	..	..	..	..	..	..
4400 Taxes on financial and capital transactions	..	..	..	..	..	..	..	..	..	..
4500 Non-recurrent taxes	..	..	..	..	..	..	..	..	..	..
4600 Other recurrent taxes on property	..	..	..	..	..	..	..	..	..	..
5000 Taxes on goods and services	..	..	..	..	..	..	**0**	**0**	**0**	**0**
5100 Taxes on production, sale, transfer, etc	..	..	..	..	..	..	..	..	..	..
5110 General taxes	..	..	..	..	..	..	..	..	..	..
5120 Taxes on specific goods and services	..	..	..	..	..	..	..	..	..	..
5130 Unallocable between 5110 and 5120	..	..	..	..	..	..	..	..	..	..
5200 Taxes on use of goods and perform activities	..	..	..	..	..	..	..	..	..	..
5300 Unallocable between 5100 and 5200	..	..	..	..	..	..	..	..	..	..
6000 Other taxes	..	..	..	..	..	..	**0**	**0**	**0**	**0**
6100 Paid solely by business	..	..	..	..	..	..	..	..	..	..
6200 Other	..	..	..	..	..	..	..	..	..	..
Total tax revenue	..	..	..	..	..	..	**1 678**	**3 363**	**8 090**	**18 194**

Note: Comparable statistics for 1990 cannot be shown due to the devaluation of the Nicaraguan cordoba.

1. The figures exclude local government tax revenues as the data are not available.

StatLink http://dx.doi.org/10.1787/888933463597

Table 6.19. Panama, tax revenues by sub-sectors of government

Thousand PAB

	Federal government					State/Regional				
	1990	2000	2005	2010	2015	1990	2000	2005	2010	2015
1000 Taxes on income, profits and capital gains	**216 950**	**484 872**	**562 852**	**1 317 028**	**2 154 061**	..	..	..	..	..
1100 Of individuals	139 518	295 142	303 283	440 404	798 914	..	..	..	..	..
1200 Corporate	66 194	158 535	212 624	603 428	937 944	..	..	..	..	..
1300 Unallocable between 1100 and 1200	11 238	31 195	46 945	273 196	417 203	..	..	..	..	..
2000 Social security contributions	**0**	**0**	**0**	**0**	**0**	..	..	..	..	..
2100 Employees	..	..	..	..	..	..	..	..	..	..
2200 Employers	..	..	..	..	..	..	..	..	..	..
2300 Self-employed or non-employed	..	..	..	..	..	..	..	..	..	..
2400 Unallocable between 2100, 2200 and 2300	..	..	..	..	..	..	..	..	..	..
3000 Taxes on payroll and workforce[1]	**0**	**36 400**	**36 243**	**58 844**	**111 295**	..	..	..	..	..
4000 Taxes on property	**43 443**	**62 090**	**109 086**	**212 194**	**319 247**	..	..	..	..	..
4100 Recurrent taxes on immovable property	28 330	33 898	56 424	107 791	151 229	..	..	..	..	..
4200 Recurrent taxes on net wealth	0	0	0	0	0	..	..	..	..	..
4300 Estate, inheritance and gift taxes	154	0	0	0	0	..	..	..	..	..
4400 Taxes on financial and capital transactions	3 419	9 343	21 049	29 810	48 037	..	..	..	..	..
4500 Non-recurrent taxes	0	0	0	0	0	..	..	..	..	..
4600 Other recurrent taxes on property	11 540	18 849	31 613	74 593	119 981	..	..	..	..	..
5000 Taxes on goods and services	**335 470**	**530 276**	**641 708**	**1 472 515**	**2 466 638**	..	..	..	..	..
5100 Taxes on production, sale, transfer, etc	331 758	530 276	641 708	1 472 515	2 466 638	..	..	..	..	..
5110 General taxes	80 303	69 013	137 585	766 154	1 359 344	..	..	..	..	..
5120 Taxes on specific goods and services[2]	138 623	461 263	504 123	706 360	1 107 293	..	..	..	..	..
5130 Unallocable between 5110 and 5120	112 832	0	0	0	0	..	..	..	..	..
5200 Taxes on use of goods and perform activities	3 712	0	0	0	0	..	..	..	..	..
5300 Unallocable between 5100 and 5200	0	0	0	0	0	..	..	..	..	..
6000 Other taxes	**25 674**	**119 336**	**126 722**	**238 684**	**215 644**	..	..	..	..	..
6100 Paid solely by business	0	11	0	0	0	..	..	..	..	..
6200 Other	25 674	119 325	126 722	238 684	215 644	..	..	..	..	..
Total tax revenue	**621 537**	**1 232 974**	**1 476 611**	**3 299 265**	**5 266 885**	..	..	..	..	..

Thousand PAB

	Local government					Social Security Funds				
	1990	2000	2005	2010	2015	1990	2000	2005	2010	2015
1000 Taxes on income, profits and capital gains	**0**	**0**	**0**	**0**	**0**	**0**	**0**	**0**	**0**	**0**
1100 Of individuals	..	..	..	..	..	..	..	..	..	..
1200 Corporate	..	..	..	..	..	..	..	..	..	..
1300 Unallocable between 1100 and 1200	..	..	..	..	..	..	..	..	..	..
2000 Social security contributions	**0**	**0**	**0**	**0**	**0**	**271 300**	**742 000**	**827 300**	**1 637 100**	**3 048 500**
2100 Employees	..	..	..	..	..	..	..	..	..	..
2200 Employers	..	..	..	..	..	..	..	..	..	..
2300 Self-employed or non-employed	..	..	..	..	..	..	..	..	..	..
2400 Unallocable between 2100, 2200 and 2300	..	..	..	..	..	271 300	742 000	827 300	1 637 100	3 048 500
3000 Taxes on payroll and workforce[1]	**0**	**0**	**0**	**0**	**0**	**0**	**0**	**0**	**0**	**0**
4000 Taxes on property	**0**	**0**	**0**	**0**	**0**	**0**	**0**	**0**	**0**	**0**
4100 Recurrent taxes on immovable property	..	0	0	..	..	..	..	..	..	..
4200 Recurrent taxes on net wealth	..	0	0	..	..	..	..	..	..	..
4300 Estate, inheritance and gift taxes	..	0	0	..	..	..	..	..	..	..
4400 Taxes on financial and capital transactions	..	0	0	..	..	..	..	..	..	..
4500 Non-recurrent taxes	..	0	0	..	..	..	..	..	..	..
4600 Other recurrent taxes on property	..	0	0	..	..	..	..	..	..	..
5000 Taxes on goods and services	**0**	**43 098**	**50 631**	**40 551**	**72 435**	**0**	**0**	**0**	**0**	**0**
5100 Taxes on production, sale, transfer, etc	..	53	5	0	0	..	..	..	..	..
5110 General taxes	..	0	0	0	0	..	..	..	..	..
5120 Taxes on specific goods and services[2]	..	53	5	0	0	..	..	..	..	..
5130 Unallocable between 5110 and 5120	..	0	0	0	0	..	..	..	..	..
5200 Taxes on use of goods and perform activities	..	43 045	50 626	40 551	72 435	..	..	..	..	..
5300 Unallocable between 5100 and 5200	..	0	0	0	0	..	..	..	..	..
6000 Other taxes	**0**	**11**	**0**	**35 533**	**58 655**	**0**	**0**	**0**	**0**	**0**
6100 Paid solely by business	..	0	0	0	0	..	..	..	..	..
6200 Other	..	11	0	35 533	58 655	..	..	..	..	..
Total tax revenue	**0**	**43 109**	**50 631**	**76 085**	**131 150**	**271 300**	**742 000**	**827 300**	**1 637 100**	**3 048 500**

1. In ECLAC data, education insurance is classified as "Other taxes" (6000).
2. In CIAT and ECLAC data, the tax on banks, financial institutions and currency exchange is classified as a property tax (4000).

StatLink http://dx.doi.org/10.1787/888933463606

Table 6.20. Paraguay, tax revenues by sub-sectors of government

Million PYG

	Federal government					State/Regional				
	1990	2000	2005	2010	2015	1990	2000	2005	2010	2015
1000 Taxes on income, profits and capital gains	**73 726**	**470 388**	**938 886**	**2 096 498**	**3 922 384**	**..**	**..**	**..**	**..**	**..**
1100 Of individuals	..	41 021	82 086	184 361	457 693	..	..	..	..	..
1200 Corporate	..	429 367	856 800	1 912 137	3 464 691	..	..	..	..	..
1300 Unallocable between 1100 and 1200	73 726	0	0	0	0	..	..	..	..	..
2000 Social security contributions[1]	**28 882**	**300 451**	**541 310**	**1 140 654**	**1 987 988**	**..**	**..**	**..**	**..**	**..**
2100 Employees	..	..	..	..	..	..	..	..	..	..
2200 Employers	..	..	..	..	..	..	..	..	..	..
2300 Self-employed or non-employed	..	..	..	..	..	..	..	..	..	..
2400 Unallocable between 2100, 2200 and 2300	28 882	300 451	541 310	1 140 654	1 987 988	..	..	..	..	..
3000 Taxes on payroll and workforce	**0**	**0**	**0**	**0**	**0**	**..**	**..**	**..**	**..**	**..**
4000 Taxes on property	**17 162**	**0**	**0**	**0**	**0**	**..**	**..**	**..**	**..**	**..**
4100 Recurrent taxes on immovable property	17 162	..	..	..	..	..	..	..	..	..
4200 Recurrent taxes on net wealth	0	..	..	..	..	..	..	..	..	..
4300 Estate, inheritance and gift taxes	0	..	..	..	..	..	..	..	..	..
4400 Taxes on financial and capital transactions	0	..	..	..	..	..	..	..	..	..
4500 Non-recurrent taxes	0	..	..	..	..	..	..	..	..	..
4600 Other recurrent taxes on property	0	..	..	..	..	..	..	..	..	..
5000 Taxes on goods and services	**179 312**	**2 080 878**	**4 309 832**	**9 226 477**	**13 820 767**	**..**	**..**	**..**	**..**	**..**
5100 Taxes on production, sale, transfer, etc	179 312	2 080 878	4 309 832	9 226 477	13 820 767	..	..	..	..	..
5110 General taxes	0	1 150 496	2 478 998	5 991 694	9 768 800	..	..	..	..	..
5120 Taxes on specific goods and services	179 312	930 382	1 830 834	3 234 783	4 051 967	..	..	..	..	..
5130 Unallocable between 5110 and 5120	0	0	0	0	0	..	..	..	..	..
5200 Taxes on use of goods and perform activities	0	0	0	0	0	..	..	..	..	..
5300 Unallocable between 5100 and 5200	0	0	0	0	0	..	..	..	..	..
6000 Other taxes	**49 807**	**116 652**	**238 134**	**109 424**	**12 547**	**..**	**..**	**..**	**..**	**..**
6100 Paid solely by business	0	0	0	0	0	..	..	..	..	..
6200 Other	49 807	116 652	238 134	109 424	12 547	..	..	..	..	..
Total tax revenue	**348 889**	**2 968 370**	**6 028 162**	**12 573 052**	**19 743 686**	**..**	**..**	**..**	**..**	**..**

Million PYG

	Local government[2]					Social Security Funds[3]				
	1990	2000	2005	2010	2015	1990	2000	2005	2010	2015
1000 Taxes on income, profits and capital gains	**..**	**..**	**0**	**0**	**0**	**..**	**0**	**0**	**0**	**0**
1100 Of individuals	..	..	..	..	..	..	..	..	..	..
1200 Corporate	..	..	..	..	..	..	..	..	..	..
1300 Unallocable between 1100 and 1200	..	..	..	..	..	..	..	..	..	..
2000 Social security contributions[1]	**..**	**..**	**0**	**0**	**0**	**..**	**619 082**	**1 050 670**	**2 411 987**	**5 056 327**
2100 Employees	..	..	..	..	..	..	..	..	..	..
2200 Employers	..	..	..	..	..	..	..	..	..	..
2300 Self-employed or non-employed	..	..	..	..	..	..	..	..	..	..
2400 Unallocable between 2100, 2200 and 2300	..	..	..	..	..	..	619 082	1 050 670	2 411 987	5 056 327
3000 Taxes on payroll and workforce	**..**	**..**	**0**	**0**	**0**	**..**	**0**	**0**	**0**	**0**
4000 Taxes on property	**..**	**..**	**0**	**272 385**	**430 034**	**..**	**0**	**0**	**0**	**0**
4100 Recurrent taxes on immovable property	..	..	..	254 306	398 251	..	..	..	..	..
4200 Recurrent taxes on net wealth	..	..	..	0	0	..	..	..	..	..
4300 Estate, inheritance and gift taxes	..	..	..	0	0	..	..	..	..	..
4400 Taxes on financial and capital transactions	..	..	..	16 316	30 987	..	..	..	..	..
4500 Non-recurrent taxes	..	..	..	0	0	..	..	..	..	..
4600 Other recurrent taxes on property	..	..	..	1 762	796	..	..	..	..	..
5000 Taxes on goods and services	**..**	**..**	**0**	**234 485**	**595 430**	**..**	**0**	**0**	**0**	**0**
5100 Taxes on production, sale, transfer, etc	..	..	..	23 221	161 762	..	..	..	..	..
5110 General taxes	..	..	..	0	0	..	..	..	..	..
5120 Taxes on specific goods and services	..	..	..	23 221	161 762	..	..	..	..	..
5130 Unallocable between 5110 and 5120	..	..	..	0	0	..	..	..	..	..
5200 Taxes on use of goods and perform activities	..	..	..	211 027	389 482	..	..	..	..	..
5300 Unallocable between 5100 and 5200	..	..	..	237	44 186	..	..	..	..	..
6000 Other taxes	**..**	**..**	**355 192**	**145 766**	**8 211**	**..**	**0**	**0**	**0**	**0**
6100 Paid solely by business	..	..	0	0	0	..	..	..	..	..
6200 Other	..	..	355 192	145 766	8 211	..	..	..	..	..
Total tax revenue	**..**	**..**	**355 192**	**652 636**	**1 033 676**	**..**	**619 082**	**1 050 670**	**2 411 987**	**5 056 327**

1. Data on social security contributions collected by decentralised institutions are not available from 2011, with the exception of the contributions made to the Instituto de Previsión Social (Social Security Institute).
2. The figures for years up to and including 2004, as well as for 2013 and 2014, exclude local government tax revenues as the data are not available.
3. The figures for years up to and including 1998 exclude decentralised institutions as the data are not available.

StatLink http://dx.doi.org/10.1787/888933463619

Table 6.21. Peru, tax revenues by sub-sectors of government

Million PEN

	Federal government					State/Regional				
	1990	2000	2005	2010	2015	1990	2000	2005	2010	2015
1000 Taxes on income, profits and capital gains	**37**	**5 078**	**11 950**	**27 317**	**37 772**	..	..	..	..	..
1100 Of individuals	3	2 117	3 327	6 518	11 137	..	..	..	..	..
1200 Corporate	32	2 526	8 391	19 561	24 266	..	..	..	..	..
1300 Unallocable between 1100 and 1200	1	436	232	1 239	2 369	..	..	..	..	..
2000 Social security contributions	**0**	**0**	**0**	**0**	**0**	..	..	..	..	..
2100 Employees	..	..	..	..	..	..	..	..	..	..
2200 Employers	..	..	..	..	..	..	..	..	..	..
2300 Self-employed or non-employed	..	..	..	..	..	..	..	..	..	..
2400 Unallocable between 2100, 2200 and 2300	..	..	..	..	..	..	..	..	..	..
3000 Taxes on payroll and workforce	**0**	**1 149**	**7**	**1**	**4**	..	..	..	..	..
4000 Taxes on property	**99**	**0**	**783**	**944**	**161**	..	..	..	..	..
4100 Recurrent taxes on immovable property	0	0	0	0	0	..	..	..	..	..
4200 Recurrent taxes on net wealth	61	0	0	0	0	..	..	..	..	..
4300 Estate, inheritance and gift taxes	0	0	0	0	0	..	..	..	..	..
4400 Taxes on financial and capital transactions	38	0	706	944	161	..	..	..	..	..
4500 Non-recurrent taxes	0	0	0	0	0	..	..	..	..	..
4600 Other recurrent taxes on property	0	0	76	0	0	..	..	..	..	..
5000 Taxes on goods and services	**423**	**15 952**	**22 098**	**35 040**	**49 703**	..	..	..	..	..
5100 Taxes on production, sale, transfer, etc	423	15 952	22 098	35 040	49 703	..	..	..	..	..
5110 General taxes	78	9 694	15 156	29 094	42 612	..	..	..	..	..
5120 Taxes on specific goods and services	345	6 259	6 942	5 946	7 090	..	..	..	..	..
5130 Unallocable between 5110 and 5120	0	0	0	0	0	..	..	..	..	..
5200 Taxes on use of goods and perform activities	0	0	0	0	0	..	..	..	..	..
5300 Unallocable between 5100 and 5200	0	0	0	0	0	..	..	..	..	..
6000 Other taxes	**36**	**741**	**723**	**1 190**	**852**	..	..	..	..	..
6100 Paid solely by business	0	84	73	108	179	..	..	..	..	..
6200 Other	36	658	650	1 083	673	..	..	..	..	..
Total tax revenue	**595**	**22 922**	**35 561**	**64 493**	**88 492**	..	..	..	..	..

Million PEN

	Local government[1]					Social Security Funds				
	1990	2000	2005	2010	2015	1990	2000	2005	2010	2015
1000 Taxes on income, profits and capital gains	..	..	**0**	**0**	**0**	**0**	**0**	**0**	**0**	**0**
1100 Of individuals	..	..	..	..	..	..	..	..	..	..
1200 Corporate	..	..	..	..	..	..	..	..	..	..
1300 Unallocable between 1100 and 1200	..	..	..	..	..	..	..	..	..	..
2000 Social security contributions	..	..	**0**	**0**	**0**	**50**	**3 184**	**4 023**	**7 957**	**12 935**
2100 Employees	..	..	..	..	..	..	541	667	2 385	3 424
2200 Employers	..	..	..	..	..	..	2 447	3 207	5 283	9 250
2300 Self-employed or non-employed	..	..	..	..	..	..	95	36	42	60
2400 Unallocable between 2100, 2200 and 2300	..	..	..	..	..	50	102	113	246	202
3000 Taxes on payroll and workforce	..	..	**0**	**0**	**0**	**0**	**0**	**0**	**0**	**0**
4000 Taxes on property	..	..	**557**	**1 292**	**2 238**	**0**	**0**	**0**	**0**	**0**
4100 Recurrent taxes on immovable property	..	..	460	731	1 444	..	..	..	..	..
4200 Recurrent taxes on net wealth	..	..	0	0	0	..	..	..	..	..
4300 Estate, inheritance and gift taxes	..	..	0	0	0	..	..	..	..	..
4400 Taxes on financial and capital transactions	..	..	97	561	795	..	..	..	..	..
4500 Non-recurrent taxes	..	..	0	0	0	..	..	..	..	..
4600 Other recurrent taxes on property	..	..	0	0	0	..	..	..	..	..
5000 Taxes on goods and services	..	..	**105**	**290**	**493**	**0**	**0**	**0**	**0**	**0**
5100 Taxes on production, sale, transfer, etc	..	..	105	290	493	..	..	..	..	..
5110 General taxes	..	..	0	0	0	..	..	..	..	..
5120 Taxes on specific goods and services	..	..	105	290	493	..	..	..	..	..
5130 Unallocable between 5110 and 5120	..	..	0	0	0	..	..	..	..	..
5200 Taxes on use of goods and perform activities	..	..	0	0	0	..	..	..	..	..
5300 Unallocable between 5100 and 5200	..	..	0	0	0	..	..	..	..	..
6000 Other taxes	..	..	**486**	**726**	**534**	**0**	**0**	**0**	**0**	**0**
6100 Paid solely by business	..	..	0	0	0	..	..	..	..	..
6200 Other	..	..	486	726	534	..	..	..	..	..
Total tax revenue	..	..	**1 148**	**2 308**	**3 265**	**50**	**3 184**	**4 023**	**7 957**	**12 935**

1. The figures for years up to and including 2001 exclude local government tax revenues as the data are not available.

StatLink http://dx.doi.org/10.1787/888933463625

Table 6.22. Trinidad and Tobago, tax revenues by sub-sectors of government

Million TTD

	Federal government					State/Regional				
	1990	2000	2005	2010	2015	1990	2000	2005	2010	2015
1000 Taxes on income, profits and capital gains	**2 497**	**5 912**	**18 904**	**26 017**	**28 721**	..	..	..	..	..
1100 Of individuals	571	2 169	4 250	4 467	7 445	..	..	..	..	..
1200 Corporate	1 856	3 547	14 118	20 670	20 209	..	..	..	..	..
1300 Unallocable between 1100 and 1200	70	195	536	881	1 067	..	..	..	..	..
2000 Social security contributions	**0**	**0**	**0**	**0**	**0**	..	..	..	..	..
2100 Employees	..	..	..	..	..	..	..	..	..	..
2200 Employers	..	..	..	..	..	..	..	..	..	..
2300 Self-employed or non-employed	..	..	..	..	..	..	..	..	..	..
2400 Unallocable between 2100, 2200 and 2300	..	..	..	..	..	..	..	..	..	..
3000 Taxes on payroll and workforce	**0**	**0**	**0**	**0**	**0**	..	..	..	..	..
4000 Taxes on property	**41**	**64**	**63**	**22**	**3**	..	..	..	..	..
4100 Recurrent taxes on immovable property	39	64	63	22	3	..	..	..	..	..
4200 Recurrent taxes on net wealth	0	0	0	0	0	..	..	..	..	..
4300 Estate, inheritance and gift taxes	1	0	0	0	0	..	..	..	..	..
4400 Taxes on financial and capital transactions	0	0	0	0	0	..	..	..	..	..
4500 Non-recurrent taxes	0	0	0	0	0	..	..	..	..	..
4600 Other recurrent taxes on property	0	0	0	0	0	..	..	..	..	..
5000 Taxes on goods and services	**2 055**	**3 852**	**5 988**	**9 342**	**11 918**	..	..	..	..	..
5100 Taxes on production, sale, transfer, etc	1 928	3 559	5 690	8 924	11 271	..	..	..	..	..
5110 General taxes	980	1 890	2 963	6 032	7 223	..	..	..	..	..
5120 Taxes on specific goods and services	948	1 669	2 727	2 891	4 048	..	..	..	..	..
5130 Unallocable between 5110 and 5120	0	0	0	0	0	..	..	..	..	..
5200 Taxes on use of goods and perform activities	127	293	299	418	647	..	..	..	..	..
5300 Unallocable between 5100 and 5200	0	0	0	0	0	..	..	..	..	..
6000 Other taxes	**49**	**111**	**245**	**172**	**403**	..	..	..	..	..
6100 Paid solely by business	0	0	0	0	0	..	..	..	..	..
6200 Other	49	111	245	172	403	..	..	..	..	..
Total tax revenue	**4 641**	**9 938**	**25 199**	**35 553**	**41 045**	..	..	..	..	..

Million TTD

	Local government					Social Security Funds				
	1990	2000	2005	2010	2015	1990	2000	2005	2010	2015
1000 Taxes on income, profits and capital gains	**0**	**0**	**0**	**0**	**0**	**0**	**0**	**0**	**0**	**0**
1100 Of individuals	..	..	..	..	..	..	..	..	..	..
1200 Corporate	..	..	..	..	..	..	..	..	..	..
1300 Unallocable between 1100 and 1200	..	..	..	..	..	..	..	..	..	..
2000 Social security contributions	**0**	**0**	**0**	**0**	**0**	**183**	**702**	**1 173**	**2 645**	**4 639**
2100 Employees	..	..	..	..	..	..	..	..	..	..
2200 Employers	..	..	..	..	..	..	..	..	..	..
2300 Self-employed or non-employed	..	..	..	..	..	..	..	..	..	..
2400 Unallocable between 2100, 2200 and 2300	..	..	..	..	..	183	702	1 173	2 645	4 639
3000 Taxes on payroll and workforce	**0**	**0**	**0**	**0**	**0**	**0**	**0**	**0**	**0**	**0**
4000 Taxes on property	**108**	**213**	**326**	**411**	**700**	**0**	**0**	**0**	**0**	**0**
4100 Recurrent taxes on immovable property[1]	108	213	326	411	700	..	..	..	..	..
4200 Recurrent taxes on net wealth	0	0	0	0	0	..	..	..	..	..
4300 Estate, inheritance and gift taxes	0	0	0	0	0	..	..	..	..	..
4400 Taxes on financial and capital transactions	0	0	0	0	0	..	..	..	..	..
4500 Non-recurrent taxes	0	0	0	0	0	..	..	..	..	..
4600 Other recurrent taxes on property	0	0	0	0	0	..	..	..	..	..
5000 Taxes on goods and services	**0**	**0**	**0**	**0**	**0**	**0**	**0**	**0**	**0**	..
5100 Taxes on production, sale, transfer, etc	..	..	..	..	..	..	..	..	..	..
5110 General taxes	..	..	..	..	..	..	..	..	..	..
5120 Taxes on specific goods and services	..	..	..	..	..	..	..	..	..	..
5130 Unallocable between 5110 and 5120	..	..	..	..	..	..	..	..	..	..
5200 Taxes on use of goods and perform activities	..	..	..	..	..	..	..	..	..	..
5300 Unallocable between 5100 and 5200	..	..	..	..	..	..	..	..	..	..
6000 Other taxes	**0**	**0**	**0**	**0**	**0**	**0**	**0**	**0**	**0**	**0**
6100 Paid solely by business	..	..	..	..	..	..	..	..	..	..
6200 Other	..	..	..	..	..	..	..	..	..	..
Total tax revenue	**108**	**213**	**326**	**411**	**700**	**183**	**702**	**1 173**	**2 645**	**4 639**

1. Data are estimated for 2015.

StatLink http://dx.doi.org/10.1787/888933463635

Table 6.23. Uruguay, tax revenues by sub-sectors of government

Million UYU

	Federal government					State/Regional				
	1990	2000	2005	2010	2015	1990	2000	2005	2010	2015
1000 Taxes on income, profits and capital gains	**114**	**5 620**	**11 969**	**44 068**	**86 404**	..	..	..	..	..
1100 Of individuals	0	0	44	19 148	45 451	..	..	..	..	..
1200 Corporate	114	5 620	11 925	23 257	37 078	..	..	..	..	..
1300 Unallocable between 1100 and 1200	0	0	0	1 662	3 875	..	..	..	..	..
2000 Social security contributions[1]	**0**	**0**	**0**	**0**	**0**	..	..	..	..	..
2100 Employees	..	..	..	..	..	..	..	..	..	..
2200 Employers	..	..	..	..	..	..	..	..	..	..
2300 Self-employed or non-employed	..	..	..	..	..	..	..	..	..	..
2400 Unallocable between 2100, 2200 and 2300	..	..	..	..	..	..	..	..	..	..
3000 Taxes on payroll and workforce	**0**	**0**	**0**	**0**	**0**	..	..	..	..	..
4000 Taxes on property[2]	**125**	**3 709**	**7 400**	**10 627**	**17 784**	..	..	..	..	..
4100 Recurrent taxes on immovable property	0	153	0	0	886	..	..	..	..	..
4200 Recurrent taxes on net wealth	94	2 076	4 943	8 948	14 776	..	..	..	..	..
4300 Estate, inheritance and gift taxes	0	0	0	0	0	..	..	..	..	..
4400 Taxes on financial and capital transactions	0	372	886	1 347	1 601	..	..	..	..	..
4500 Non-recurrent taxes	0	0	0	0	0	..	..	..	..	..
4600 Other recurrent taxes on property	31	1 107	1 571	331	522	..	..	..	..	..
5000 Taxes on goods and services[2]	**1 270**	**28 301**	**52 727**	**94 990**	**160 146**	..	..	..	..	..
5100 Taxes on production, sale, transfer, etc	1 270	28 301	52 727	94 990	160 146	..	..	..	..	..
5110 General taxes[2]	660	18 009	34 641	69 365	113 651	..	..	..	..	..
5120 Taxes on specific goods and services	610	10 291	18 086	25 625	46 495	..	..	..	..	..
5130 Unallocable between 5110 and 5120	0	0	0	0	0	..	..	..	..	..
5200 Taxes on use of goods and perform activities	0	0	0	0	0	..	..	..	..	..
5300 Unallocable between 5100 and 5200	0	0	0	0	0	..	..	..	..	..
6000 Other taxes	**-10**	**-596**	**76**	**0**	**503**	..	..	..	..	..
6100 Paid solely by business	-10	-596	76	0	503	..	..	..	..	..
6200 Other	0	0	0	0	0	..	..	..	..	..
Total tax revenue	**1 500**	**37 034**	**72 171**	**149 684**	**264 838**	..	..	..	..	..

Million UYU

	Local government					Social Security Funds				
	1990	2000	2005	2010	2015	1990	2000	2005	2010	2015
1000 Taxes on income, profits and capital gains	**0**	**0**	**0**	**0**	**0**	**0**	**0**	**0**	**0**	**0**
1100 Of individuals	..	..	..	..	..	..	..	..	..	..
1200 Corporate	..	..	..	..	..	..	..	..	..	..
1300 Unallocable between 1100 and 1200	..	..	..	..	..	..	..	..	..	..
2000 Social security contributions[1]	**0**	**0**	**0**	**0**	**0**	**717**	**17 679**	**21 425**	**49 742**	**108 742**
2100 Employees	..	..	..	..	..	..	..	..	..	..
2200 Employers	..	..	..	..	..	..	..	..	..	..
2300 Self-employed or non-employed	..	..	..	..	..	..	..	..	..	..
2400 Unallocable between 2100, 2200 and 2300	..	..	..	..	..	717	17 679	21 425	49 742	108 742
3000 Taxes on payroll and workforce	**0**	**0**	**0**	**0**	**0**	**0**	**0**	**0**	**0**	**0**
4000 Taxes on property[2]	**71**	**2 414**	**4 776**	**7 491**	**12 585**	**0**	**0**	**0**	**0**	**0**
4100 Recurrent taxes on immovable property	71	2 414	4 776	7 491	12 585	..	..	..	..	..
4200 Recurrent taxes on net wealth	0	0	0	0	0	..	..	..	..	..
4300 Estate, inheritance and gift taxes	0	0	0	0	0	..	..	..	..	..
4400 Taxes on financial and capital transactions	0	0	0	0	0	..	..	..	..	..
4500 Non-recurrent taxes	0	0	0	0	0	..	..	..	..	..
4600 Other recurrent taxes on property	0	0	0	0	0	..	..	..	..	..
5000 Taxes on goods and services[2]	**64**	**2 576**	**3 071**	**3 952**	**7 540**	**0**	**0**	**0**	**0**	**0**
5100 Taxes on production, sale, transfer, etc	0	0	0	0	0	..	..	..	..	..
5110 General taxes[2]	0	0	0	0	0	..	..	..	..	..
5120 Taxes on specific goods and services	0	0	0	0	0	..	..	..	..	..
5130 Unallocable between 5110 and 5120	0	0	0	0	0	..	..	..	..	..
5200 Taxes on use of goods and perform activities	64	2 576	3 071	3 952	7 540	..	..	..	..	..
5300 Unallocable between 5100 and 5200	0	0	0	0	0	..	..	..	..	..
6000 Other taxes	**0**	**0**	**0**	**0**	**0**	**0**	**0**	**0**	**0**	**0**
6100 Paid solely by business	..	..	..	..	..	..	..	..	..	..
6200 Other	..	..	..	..	..	..	..	..	..	..
Total tax revenue	**135**	**4 990**	**7 846**	**11 443**	**20 125**	**717**	**17 679**	**21 425**	**49 742**	**108 742**

1. Figures for 1990-98 are estimated by the Direction General of Taxes as the methodology they use to calculate social security contributions was not employed until 1999.
2. In ECLAC data, the tax on the sale of goods by public auction is classified in category 4000.

StatLink http://dx.doi.org/10.1787/888933463643

Table 6.24. Venezuela, tax revenues by sub-sectors of government

Million VEF

	Federal government					State/Regional[2]				
	1990	2000	2005	2010	2015	1990	2000	2005	2010	2015
1000 Taxes on income, profits and capital gains	**344**	**4 686**	**18 529**	**36 836**	**284 786**	..	..	..	..	..
1100 Of individuals	..	..	..	..	..	..	..	..	..	..
1200 Corporate	315	3 368	11 184	8 700	47 388	..	..	..	..	..
1300 Unallocable between 1100 and 1200	30	1 317	7 345	28 137	237 399	..	..	..	..	..
2000 Social security contributions[1]	**0**	**0**	**0**	**0**	**0**	..	..	..	..	..
2100 Employees	..	..	..	..	..	..	..	..	..	..
2200 Employers	..	..	..	..	..	..	..	..	..	..
2300 Self-employed or non-employed	..	..	..	..	..	..	..	..	..	..
2400 Unallocable between 2100, 2200 and 2300	..	..	..	..	..	..	..	..	..	..
3000 Taxes on payroll and workforce	**0**	**0**	**0**	**0**	**0**	..	..	..	..	..
4000 Taxes on property	**1**	**400**	**2 834**	**222**	**2 946**	..	..	..	..	..
4100 Recurrent taxes on immovable property	0	0	0	0	0	..	..	..	..	..
4200 Recurrent taxes on net wealth	0	0	0	0	0	..	..	..	..	..
4300 Estate, inheritance and gift taxes	1	19	55	222	2 946	..	..	..	..	..
4400 Taxes on financial and capital transactions	0	381	2 779	0	0	..	..	..	..	..
4500 Non-recurrent taxes	0	0	0	0	0	..	..	..	..	..
4600 Other recurrent taxes on property	0	0	0	0	0	..	..	..	..	..
5000 Taxes on goods and services	**46**	**5 173**	**25 032**	**73 707**	**918 317**	..	..	..	..	..
5100 Taxes on production, sale, transfer, etc	46	5 173	25 032	73 707	918 317	..	..	..	..	..
5110 General taxes	0	3 272	19 513	56 101	702 743	..	..	..	..	..
5120 Taxes on specific goods and services	46	1 901	5 519	17 606	215 575	..	..	..	..	..
5130 Unallocable between 5110 and 5120	0	0	0	0	0	..	..	..	..	..
5200 Taxes on use of goods and perform activities	0	0	0	0	0	..	..	..	..	..
5300 Unallocable between 5100 and 5200	0	0	0	0	0	..	..	..	..	..
6000 Other taxes	**0**	**0**	**0**	**0**	**15 833**	..	..	..	..	..
6100 Paid solely by business	..	..	..	..	0	..	..	..	..	..
6200 Other	..	..	..	..	15 833	..	..	..	..	..
Total tax revenue	**391**	**10 258**	**46 395**	**110 765**	**1 221 883**	..	..	..	..	..

Million VEF

	Local government[2]					Social Security Funds				
	1990	2000	2005	2010	2015	1990	2000	2005	2010	2015
1000 Taxes on income, profits and capital gains	..	..	..	..	..	**0**	**0**	**0**	**0**	**0**
1100 Of individuals	..	..	..	..	..	..	..	..	..	..
1200 Corporate	..	..	..	..	..	..	..	..	..	..
1300 Unallocable between 1100 and 1200	..	..	..	..	..	..	..	..	..	..
2000 Social security contributions[1]	..	..	..	..	..	**20**	**591**	**1 890**	**9 690**	**38 200**
2100 Employees	..	..	..	..	..	..	..	..	..	..
2200 Employers	..	..	..	..	..	..	..	..	..	..
2300 Self-employed or non-employed	..	..	..	..	..	..	..	..	..	..
2400 Unallocable between 2100, 2200 and 2300	..	..	..	..	..	20	591	1 890	9 690	38 200
3000 Taxes on payroll and workforce	..	..	..	..	..	**0**	**0**	**0**	**0**	**0**
4000 Taxes on property	..	..	..	..	..	**0**	**0**	**0**	**0**	**0**
4100 Recurrent taxes on immovable property	..	..	..	..	..	..	..	..	..	..
4200 Recurrent taxes on net wealth	..	..	..	..	..	..	..	..	..	..
4300 Estate, inheritance and gift taxes	..	..	..	..	..	..	..	..	..	..
4400 Taxes on financial and capital transactions	..	..	..	..	..	..	..	..	..	..
4500 Non-recurrent taxes	..	..	..	..	..	..	..	..	..	..
4600 Other recurrent taxes on property	..	..	..	..	..	..	..	..	..	..
5000 Taxes on goods and services	..	..	..	..	..	**0**	**0**	**0**	**0**	**0**
5100 Taxes on production, sale, transfer, etc	..	..	..	..	..	..	..	..	..	..
5110 General taxes	..	..	..	..	..	..	..	..	..	..
5120 Taxes on specific goods and services	..	..	..	..	..	..	..	..	..	..
5130 Unallocable between 5110 and 5120	..	..	..	..	..	..	..	..	..	..
5200 Taxes on use of goods and perform activities	..	..	..	..	..	..	..	..	..	..
5300 Unallocable between 5100 and 5200	..	..	..	..	..	..	..	..	..	..
6000 Other taxes	..	..	..	..	..	**0**	**0**	**0**	**0**	**0**
6100 Paid solely by business	..	..	..	..	..	..	..	..	..	..
6200 Other	..	..	..	..	..	..	..	..	..	..
Total tax revenue	..	..	..	..	..	**20**	**591**	**1 890**	**9 690**	**38 200**

1. The data on social security contributions are estimated from 2011 to 2015.
2. The figures exclude state and local government tax revenues as the data are not available.

StatLink http://dx.doi.org/10.1787/888933463651

ANNEX A

The OECD Interpretative Guide[1]

Table of contents

A.1. The OECD classification of taxes

1000 *Taxes on income, profits and capital gains*

- 1100 Taxes on income, profits and capital gains of individuals
  - 1110 On income and profits
  - 1120 On capital gains
- 1200 Corporate taxes on income, profits and capital gains
  - 1210 On income and profits
  - 1220 On capital gains
- 1300 Unallocable as between 1100 and 1200

2000 *Social security contributions*

- 2100 Employees
  - 2110 On a payroll basis
  - 2120 On an income tax bas
- 2200 Employers
  - 2210 On a payroll basis
  - 2220 On an income tax basis
- 2300 Self-employed, non-employed
  - 2310 On a payroll basis
  - 2320 On an income tax basis
- 2400 Unallocable as between 2100, 2200 and 2300
  - 2410 On a payroll basis
  - 2420 On an income tax basis

3000 *Taxes on payroll and workforce*

4000 *Taxes on property*

- 4100 Recurrent taxes on immovable property
  - 4110 Households
  - 4120 Other
- 4200 Recurrent taxes on net wealth
  - 4210 Individual
  - 4220 Corporate
- 4300 Estate, inheritance and gift taxes
  - 4310 Estate and inheritance taxes
  - 4320 Gift taxes
- 4400 Taxes on financial and capital transactions

4500 Other non-recurrent taxes on property

4510 On net wealth

4520 Other non-recurrent taxes

4600 Other recurrent taxes on property

5000 *Taxes on goods and services*

5100 Taxes on production, sale, transfer, leasing and delivery of goods and rendering of services

5110 General taxes

5111 Value-added taxes

5112 Sales taxes

5113 Other general taxes on goods and services

5120 Taxes on specific goods and services

5121 Excises

5122 Profits of fiscal monopolies

5123 Customs and import duties

5124 Taxes on exports

5125 Taxes on investment goods

5126 Taxes on specific services

5127 Other taxes on international trade and transactions

5128 Other taxes on specific goods and services

5130 Unallocable as between 5110 and 5120

5200 Taxes on use of goods, or on permission to use goods or perform activities

5210 Recurrent taxes

5211 Paid by households in respect of motor vehicles

5212 Paid by others in respect of motor vehicles

5213 Other recurrent taxes

5220 Non-recurrent taxes

5300 Unallocable as between 5100 and 5200

6000 *Other taxes*

6100 Paid solely by business

6200 Paid by other than business, or unidentifiable

The OECD Interpretative Guide[1]

A.2. Coverage

General criteria

1. In the OECD classification the term "taxes" is confined to compulsory unrequited payments to general government. Taxes are unrequited in the sense that benefits provided by government to taxpayers are not normally in proportion to their payments.

2. The term 'tax' does not include fines, penalties and compulsory loans paid to government. Borderline cases between tax and non-tax revenues in relation to certain fees and charges are discussed in §9–12.

3. General government consists of the central administration, agencies whose operations are under its effective control, state and local governments and their administrations, certain social security schemes and autonomous governmental entities, excluding public enterprises. This definition of government follows that of the 2008 System of National Accounts (SNA).[2] In that publication, the general government sector and its sub-sectors are defined in chapter 4, section F, pages 80-84.

4. Compulsory payments to supra-national bodies and their agencies are no longer included as taxes as from 1998, with some exceptions. However, custom duties collected by EU member states on behalf of the European Union are still identified as memorandum items and included in overall tax revenue amounts in the country tables (Chapter 5) of the country in which they are collected. (See §94). In countries where the church forms part of general government church taxes are included, provided they meet the criteria set out in §1 above. As the data refer to receipts of general government, levies paid to non-government bodies, welfare agencies or social insurance schemes outside general government, trade unions or trade associations, even where such levies are compulsory, are excluded. Compulsory payments to general government earmarked for such bodies are, however, included, provided that the government is not simply acting in an agency capacity.[3] Profits from fiscal monopolies are distinguished from those of other public enterprises and are treated as taxes because they reflect the exercise of the taxing power of the state by the use of monopoly powers (see §61–63), as are profits received by the government from the purchase and sale of foreign exchange at different rates (see §69).

5. Taxes paid by governments (e.g. social security contributions and payroll taxes paid by governments in their capacity as an employer, consumption taxes on their purchases or taxes on their property) are not excluded from the data provided. However, where it is possible to identify the amounts of revenue involved,[4] they are shown in Chapter 4.3 of this Report.

6. The relationship between this classification and that of the System of National Accounts (SNA) is set out in Sections A.9 and A.11 below. Because of the differences between the two classifications, the data shown in national accounts are sometimes calculated or classified differently from the practice set out in this guide. These and other differences are mentioned where appropriate (e.g. in §25 below) but it is not possible to refer to all of them. There may also be some differences between this classification and that employed domestically by certain national administrations (e.g. see §10 below), so that OECD and national statistics data may not always be consistent: any such differences, however, are likely to be very slight in terms of amounts of revenues involved.

Social security contributions

7. Compulsory social security contributions, as defined in §34 below, paid to general government, are treated here as tax revenues. Being compulsory payments to general government they clearly resemble taxes. They may, however, differ from other taxes in that the receipt of social security benefits depends, in most countries, upon appropriate contributions having been made, although the size of the benefits is not necessarily related to the amount of the contributions. Better comparability between countries is obtained by treating social security contributions as taxes, but they are listed under a separate heading so that they can be distinguished in any analysis.

8. Social security contributions which are either voluntary or not payable to general government (see §1) are not treated as taxes, though in some countries, as indicated in the country footnotes, there are difficulties in eliminating voluntary contributions and certain compulsory payments to the private sector. Imputed social security contributions are also not treated as taxes.

Fees, user charges and licence fees

9. Apart from vehicle licence fees, which are universally regarded as taxes, it is not easy to distinguish between those fees and user charges which are to be treated as taxes and those which are not, since, whilst a fee or charge is levied in connection with a specific service or activity, the strength of the link between the fee and the service provided may vary considerably, as may the relation between the amount of the fee and the cost of providing the service. Where the recipient of a service pays a fee clearly related to the cost of providing the service, the levy may be regarded as requited and under the definition of §1 would not be considered as a tax. In the following cases, however, a levy could be considered as 'unrequited':

a) where the charge greatly exceeds the cost of providing the service;

b) where the payer of the levy is not the receiver of the benefit (e.g. a fee collected from slaughterhouses to finance a service which is provided to farmers);

c) where government is not providing a specific service in return for the levy which it receives even though a licence may be issued to the payer (e.g. where the government grants a hunting, fishing or shooting licence which is not accompanied by the right to use a specific area of government land);

d) where benefits are received only by those paying the levy but the benefits received by each individual are not necessarily in proportion to his payments (e.g. a milk marketing levy paid by dairy farmers and used to promote the consumption of milk).

10. In marginal cases, however, the application of the criteria set out in §1 can be particularly difficult. The solution adopted – given the desirability of international uniformity and the relatively small amounts of revenue usually involved – is to follow the predominant practice among tax administrations rather than to allow each country to adopt its own view as to whether such levies are regarded as taxes or as non-tax revenue.[5]

11. A list of the main fees and charges in question and their normal[6] treatment in this publication is as follows:

Non-tax revenues:	court fees; driving licence fees; harbour fees; passport fees; radio and television licence fees where public authorities provide the service.
Taxes within heading 5200:	permission to perform such activities as distributing films; hunting, fishing and shooting; providing entertainment or gambling facilities; selling alcohol or tobacco; permission to own dogs or to use or own motor vehicles or guns; severance taxes.

12. In practice it may not always be possible to isolate tax receipts from non-tax revenue receipts when they are recorded together. If it is estimated that the bulk of the receipts derive from non-tax revenues, the whole amount involved is treated as a non-tax revenue; otherwise, such government receipts are included and classified according to the rules provided in §27 below.

Royalties

13. Royalty payments for the right to extract oil and gas or to exploit other mineral resources are normally regarded as non-tax revenues since they are property income from government-owned land or resources.

Fines and penalties

14. In principle, fines and penalties charged on overdue taxes or penalties imposed for the attempted evasion of taxes should not be recorded as tax revenues. However it may not be possible to separate payments of fines or other penalties from the revenues from the taxes to which they relate. In this case the fines and penalties relating to a particular tax are recorded together with the revenues from that tax and fines and penalties paid with revenue from unidentifiable taxes are classified as other taxes in Category 6000. Fines not relating to tax offences (e.g. for parking offences), or not identifiable as relating to tax offences, are also not treated as tax revenues.

A.3. Basis of reporting

Accrual reporting

15. The data reported in this publication for recent years are predominantly recorded on an accrual basis, i.e. recorded at the time that the tax liability was created. Further information is provided in the footnotes to the country table in Chapter 4 of the Report.

16. However, data for earlier years are still predominantly recorded on a cash basis, i.e. at the time at which the payment was received by government. Thus, for example, taxes withheld by employers in one year but paid to the government in the following year and taxes due in one year but actually paid in the following year are both included in the receipts of the second year. Corrective transactions, such as refunds, repayments and drawbacks, are deducted from gross revenues of the period in which they are made.

17. Data on tax revenues are recorded without offsets for the administrative expenses connected with tax collection. Similarly, where the proceeds of tax are used to subsidise particular members of the community, the subsidy is not deducted from the yield of the tax, though the tax may be shown net of subsidies in the national records of some countries.

18. As regards fiscal monopolies (heading 5122), only the amount actually transferred to the government is included in government revenues. However, if any expenditures of fiscal monopolies are considered to be government expenditures (e.g. social expenditures undertaken by fiscal monopolies at the direction of the government) they are added back for the purpose of arriving at tax revenue figures (see §61 below).

The distinction between tax and expenditure provisions[7]

19. Because this publication is concerned only with the revenue side of government operations, no account being taken of the expenditure side, a distinction has to be made between tax and expenditure provisions. Normally there is no difficulty in making this distinction as expenditures are made outside the tax system and the tax accounts and under legislation separate from the tax legislation. In borderline cases, cash flow is used

to distinguish between tax provisions and expenditure provisions. Insofar as a provision affects the flow of tax payments from the taxpayer to the government, it is regarded as a tax provision and is taken into account in the data shown in this publication. A provision which does not affect this flow is seen as an expenditure provision and is disregarded in the data recorded in this publication.

20. Tax allowances, exemptions and deductions against the tax base clearly affect the amount of tax paid to the government and are therefore considered as tax provisions. At the other extreme, those subsidies which cannot be offset against tax liability and which are clearly not connected with the assessment process, do not reduce tax revenues as recorded in this publication. Tax credits are amounts deductible from tax payable (as distinct from deductions from the tax base). Two types of tax credits are distinguished, those (referred to here as wastable tax credits) which are limited to the amount of the tax liability and therefore cannot give rise to a payment by the authorities to the taxpayer, and those (referred to as non-wastable tax credits) which are not so limited, so that the excess of the credit over the tax liability can be paid to the taxpayer.[8] A wastable tax credit, like a tax allowance, clearly affects the amount of tax paid to the government, and is therefore considered as a tax provision. The practice followed for non-wastable tax credits[9] is to distinguish between the "tax expenditure component",[10] which is that portion of the credit that is used to reduce or eliminate a taxpayer's liability, and the 'transfer component', which is the portion that exceeds the taxpayer's liability and is paid to that taxpayer. Reported tax revenues should be reduced by the amount of the tax expenditure component but not by the amount of the transfer component. In addition, the amounts of the tax expenditure and transfer components should be reported as memorandum items in the country tables. Countries that are unable to distinguish between the tax expenditure and transfer components should indicate whether or not the tax revenues have been reduced by the total of these components, and provide any available estimates of the amounts of the two components. Further information is given in Chapter 2 of the Report, which illustrates the effect of alternative treatments of non-wastable tax credits on Tax to GDP.

Calendar and fiscal years

21. National authorities whose fiscal years do not correspond to the calendar year show data, where possible, on a calendar year basis to permit maximum comparability with the data of other countries. There remain a few countries where data refer to fiscal years. For these the GDP data used in the comparative tables also correspond to the fiscal years.

A.4. General classification criteria

The main classification criteria

22. The classification of receipts among the main headings (1000, 2000, 3000, 4000, 5000 and 6000) is generally governed by the base on which the tax is levied: 1000 income, profits and capital gains; 2000 and 3000 earnings, payroll or number of employees; 4000 property; 5000 goods and services; 6000 multiple bases, other bases or unidentifiable bases. Where a tax is calculated on more than one base, the receipts are, where possible, split among the various headings (see §27 and §77). The headings 4000 and 5000 cover not only taxes where the tax base is the property, goods or services themselves but also certain related taxes. Thus, taxes on the transfer of property are included in 4400[11] and taxes on the use of goods or on permission to perform activities in 5200. In headings 4000 and 5000 a distinction is made in certain sub-headings between recurrent and non-recurrent taxes: recurrent taxes are defined as those levied at regular intervals (usually annually) and non-recurrent taxes are levied once and for all (see also §42 to §45, §48, §49 and §75 for particular applications of this distinction).

23. Earmarking of a tax for specific purposes does not affect the classification of tax receipts. However, as explained in §34 on the classification of social security contributions, the conferment of an entitlement to social benefits is crucial to the definition of the 2000 main heading.

24. The way that a tax is levied or collected (e.g. by use of stamps) does not affect classification.

Classification of taxpayers

25. In certain sub-headings distinctions are made between different categories of taxpayers. These distinctions vary from tax to tax:

a) Between individuals and corporations in relation to income and net wealth taxes

The basic distinction is that corporation income taxes, as distinct from individual income taxes, are levied on the corporation as an entity, not on the individuals who own it, and without regard to the personal circumstances of these individuals. The same distinction applies to net wealth taxes on corporations and those on individuals. Taxes paid on the profits of partnerships and the income of institutions, such as life insurance or pension funds, are classified according to the same rule. They are classified as corporate taxes (1200) if they are charged on the partnership or institution as an entity without regard to the personal circumstances of the owners. Otherwise, they are treated as individual taxes (1100). Usually, there is different legislation for the corporation taxes and for the individual taxes.[12] The distinction made here between individuals and corporations does not follow the sector classification between households, enterprises, and so on of the System of National Accounts for income and outlay accounts. The SNA classification requires certain unincorporated businesses[13] to be excluded from the household sector and included with non-financial enterprises and financial institutions. The tax on the profits of these businesses, however, cannot always be separated from the tax on the other income of their owners, or can be separated only on an arbitrary basis. No attempt at this separation is made here and the whole of the individual income tax is shown together without regard to the nature of the income chargeable.

b) Between households and others in relation to taxes on immovable property

Here the distinction is that adopted by the SNA for the production and consumption expenditure accounts. The distinction is between households as consumers (i.e. excluding non-incorporated business) on the one hand and producers on the other hand. However, taxes on dwellings occupied by households, whether paid by owner-occupiers, tenants or landlords, are classified under households. This follows the common distinction made between taxes on domestic property versus taxes on business property. Some countries are not, however, in a position to make this distinction.

c) Between households and others in relation to motor vehicle licences

Here the distinction is between households as consumers on the one hand and producers on the other, as in the production and consumption expenditure accounts of the SNA.

d) Between business and others in relation to the residual taxes (6000)

The distinction is the same as in c) above between producers on the one hand and households as consumers on the other hand. Taxes which are included under the heading 6000 because they involve more than one tax base or because the tax base does not fall within any of the previous categories but which are identifiable as levyable only on producers and not on households are included under 'business'. The rest of the taxes which are included under the heading 6000 are shown as 'other' or non-identified.

Surcharges

26. Receipts from surcharges in respect of particular taxes are usually classified with the receipts from the relevant tax whether or not the surcharge is temporary. If, however, the surcharge has a characteristic which would render it classifiable in a different heading of the OECD list, receipts from the surcharge are classified under that heading separately from the relevant tax.

Unidentifiable tax receipts and residual sub-headings

27. A number of cases arise where taxes cannot be identified as belonging entirely to a heading or sub-heading of the OECD classification and the following practices are applied in such cases:

a) The heading is known, but it is not known how receipts should be allocated between sub-headings: receipts are classified in the appropriate residual sub-heading (1300, 2400, 4520, 4600, 5130, 5300 or 6200).

b) It is known that the bulk of receipts from a group of taxes (usually local taxes) is derived from taxes within a particular heading or sub-heading, but some of the taxes in the group whose amount cannot be precisely ascertained may be classifiable in other headings or sub-headings: receipts are shown in the heading or sub-heading under which most of the receipts fall.

c) Neither the heading nor sub-heading of a tax (usually local) can be identified: the tax is classified in 6200 unless it is known that it is a tax on business in which case it is classified in 6100.

A.5. Commentaries on items of the list

1000 – *Taxes on income, profits and capital gains*

28. This heading covers taxes levied on the net income or profits (i.e. gross income minus allowable tax reliefs) of individuals and enterprises. Also covered are taxes levied on the capital gains of individuals and enterprises, and gains from gambling.

29. Included in the heading are:

a) taxes levied predominantly on income or profits, though partially on other bases. Taxes on various bases which are not predominantly income or profits are classified according to the principles laid down in §27 and §77;

b) taxes on property, which are levied on a presumed or estimated income as part of an income tax (see also §42(a), (c) and (d));

c) compulsory payments to social security fund contributions that are levied on income but do not confer an entitlement to social benefits. When such contributions do confer an entitlement to social benefits, they are included in heading 2000 (see §34);

d) receipts from integrated scheduler income tax systems are classified as a whole in this heading, even though certain of the scheduler taxes may be based upon gross income and may not take into account the personal circumstances of the taxpayer.

30. The main subdivision of this heading is between levies on individuals (1100) and those on corporate enterprises (1200). Under each subdivision a distinction is made between taxes on income and profits (1110 and 1210), and taxes on capital gains (1120 and 1220). If certain receipts cannot be identified as appropriate to either 1100 or 1200, or if in practice this distinction cannot be made (e.g. because there are no reliable data on the recipients of payments from which withholding taxes are deducted) they are classified in 1300 as not-allocable.

Treatment of credits under imputation systems

31. Under imputation systems of corporate income tax, a company's shareholders are wholly or partly relieved of their liability to income tax on dividends paid by the company out of income or profits liable to corporate income tax. In countries with such systems,[14] part of the tax on the company's profits is available to provide relief against the shareholders' own tax liability. The relief to the shareholder takes the form of a tax credit, the amount of which may be less than, equal to, or more than the shareholder's overall tax liability. If the tax credit exceeds this tax liability the excess may be payable to the shareholder. As this type of tax credit is an integral part of the imputation system of corporate income tax, any payment to the shareholders is treated as a repayment of tax and not as expenditure (compare the treatment of other tax credits described in §20).

32. As the tax credit under imputation systems (even when exceeding tax liability) is to be regarded as a tax provision, the question arises whether it should be deducted from individual income tax receipts (1110) or corporate income tax receipts (1210). In this Report, the full amount of corporate income tax paid is shown under 1210 and no imputed tax is included under 1110. Thus, the full amount of the credit reduces the amount of 1110 whether the credit results in a reduction of personal income tax liability or whether an actual refund is made because the credit exceeds the income tax liability. (Where, however, such tax credits are deducted from corporation tax in respect of dividends paid to corporations the amounts are deducted from the receipts of 1210.)

1120 and 1220 – *Taxes on capital gains*

33. These sub-headings comprise taxes imposed on capital gains, 1120 covering those levied on the gains of individuals and 1220 those levied on the gains of corporate enterprises, where receipts from such taxes can be separately identified. In many countries this is not the case and the receipts from such taxes are then classified with those from the income tax. Heading 1120 also includes taxes on gains from gambling.

2000 – *Social security contributions*

34. Classified here are all compulsory payments that confer an entitlement to receive a (contingent) future social benefit. Such payments are usually earmarked to finance social benefits and are often paid to institutions of general government that provide such benefits. However, such earmarking is not part of the definition of social security contributions and is not required for a tax to be classified here. However, conferment of an entitlement is required for a tax to be classified under this heading. So, levies on income or payroll that are earmarked for social security funds but do not confer an entitlement to benefit are excluded from this heading and shown under personal income taxes (1100) or taxes on payroll and workforce (3000). Taxes on other bases, such as goods and services, which are earmarked for social security benefits are not shown here but are classified according to their respective bases because they generally confer no entitlement to social security benefits.

35. Contributions for the following types of social security benefits would, *inter alia*, be included: unemployment insurance benefits and supplements, accident, injury and sickness benefits, old-age, disability and survivors' pensions, family allowances, reimbursements for medical and hospital expenses or provision of hospital or medical services. Contributions may be levied on both employees and employers.

36. Contributions may be based on earnings or payroll ('on a payroll basis') or on net income after deductions and exemptions for personal circumstances ('on an income tax basis'), and the revenues from the two bases should be separately identified if possible. However, where contributions to a general social security scheme are on a payroll basis, but the contributions of particular groups (such as the self-employed) cannot be assessed

on this basis and net income is used as a proxy for gross earnings, the receipts may still be classified as being on a payroll basis. In principle, this heading excludes voluntary contributions paid to social security schemes. When separately identifiable these are shown in the memorandum item on the financing of social security benefits. In practice, however, they cannot always be separately identified from compulsory contributions, in which case they are included in this heading.

37. Contributions to social insurance schemes which are not institutions of general government and to other types of insurance schemes, provident funds, pension funds, friendly societies or other saving schemes are not considered as social security contributions. Provident funds are arrangements under which the contributions of each employee and of the corresponding employer on his/her behalf are kept in a separate account earning interest and withdrawable under specific circumstances. Pension funds are separately organised schemes negotiated between employees and employers and carry provisions for different contributions and benefits, sometimes more directly tied to salary levels and length of service than under social security schemes. When contributions to these schemes are compulsory or quasi-compulsory (e.g. by virtue of agreement with professional and union organisations) they are shown in the memorandum item (refer to Chapter 4.2 of the Report).

38. Contributions by government employees and by governments in respect of their employees, to social security schemes classified within general government are included in this heading. Contributions to separate schemes for government employees, which can be regarded as replacing general social security schemes, are also regarded as taxes.[15] Where, however, a separate scheme is not seen as replacing a general scheme and has been negotiated between the government, in its role as an employer, and its employees, it is not regarded as social security and contributions to it are not regarded as taxes, even though the scheme may have been established by legislation.

39. This heading excludes 'imputed' contributions, which correspond to social benefits paid directly by employers to their employees or former employees or to their representatives (e.g. when employers are legally obliged to pay sickness benefits for a certain period).

40. Contributions are divided into those of employees (2100), employers (2200), and self-employed or non-employed (2300), and then further sub-divided according to the basis on which they are levied. Employees are defined for this purpose as all persons engaged in activities of business units, government bodies, private non-profit institutions, or other paid employment, except the proprietors and their unpaid family members in the case of unincorporated businesses. Members of the armed forces are included, irrespective of the duration and type of their service, if they contribute to social security schemes. The contributions of employers are defined as their payments on account of their employees to social security schemes. Where employees or employers are required to continue the payment of social security contributions when the employee becomes unemployed these contributions, data permitting, are shown in 2100 and 2200 respectively. Accordingly, the sub-heading 2300 is confined to contributions paid by the self-employed and by those outside of the labour force (e.g. disabled or retired individuals).

3000 – *Taxes on payroll and workforce*

41. This heading covers taxes paid by employers, employees or the self-employed either as a proportion of payroll or as a fixed amount per person, and which do not confer entitlement to social benefits. Examples of taxes classified here are the United Kingdom national insurance surcharge (introduced in 1977), the Swedish payroll tax (1969–1979), and the Austrian Contribution to the Family Burden Equalisation Fund and Community Tax.

4000 – *Taxes on property*

42. This heading covers recurrent and non-recurrent taxes on the use, ownership or transfer of property. These include taxes on immovable property or net wealth, taxes on the change of ownership of property through inheritance or gift and taxes on financial and capital transactions. The following kinds of tax are excluded from this heading:

a) taxes on capital gains resulting from the sale of a property (1120 or 1220);

b) taxes on the use of goods or on permission to use goods or perform activities (5200); see §72;

c) taxes on immovable property levied on the basis of a presumed net income which take into account the personal circumstances of the taxpayer. They are classified as income taxes along with taxes on income and capital gains derived from property (1100);

d) taxes on the use of property for residence, where the tax is payable by either proprietor or tenant and the amount payable is a function of the user's personal circumstances (pay, dependants, and so on). They are classified as taxes on income (1100);

e) taxes on building in excess of permitted maximum density, taxes on the enlargement, construction or alteration of certain buildings beyond a permitted value and taxes on building construction. They are classified as taxes on permission to perform activities (5200);

f) taxes on the use of one's own property for special trading purposes like selling alcohol, tobacco, meat or for exploitation of land resources (e.g. United States severance taxes). They are classified as taxes on permission to perform activities (5200).

4100 – *Recurrent taxes on immovable property*

43. This sub-heading covers taxes levied regularly in respect of the use or ownership of immovable property.

- these taxes are levied on land and buildings;
- they can be in the form of a percentage of an assessed property value based on a national rental income, sales price, or capitalised yield; or in terms of other characteristics of real property, (for example size or location) from which a presumed rent or capital value can be derived.
- such taxes can be levied on proprietors, tenants, or both. They can also be paid by one level of government to another level of government in respect of property under the jurisdiction of the latter.
- debts are not taken into account in the assessment of these taxes, and they differ from taxes on net wealth in this respect.

44. Taxes on immovable property are further sub-divided into those paid by households (4110) and those paid by other entities (4120), according to the criteria set out in §25(b) above.

4200 – *Recurrent taxes on net wealth*

45. This sub-heading covers taxes levied regularly (in most cases annually) on net wealth, i.e. taxes on a wide range of movable and immovable property, net of debt. It is sub-divided into taxes paid by individuals (4210) and taxes paid by corporate enterprises (4220) according to the criteria set out in §25(a) above. If separate figures exist for receipts paid by institutions, the tax payments involved are added to those paid by corporations.

4300 – *Estate, inheritance and gift taxes*

46. This sub-heading is divided into taxes on estates and inheritances (4310) and taxes on gifts (4320).[16] Estate taxes are charged on the amount of the total estate whereas inheritance taxes are charged on the shares of the individual recipients; in addition the latter may take into account the relationship of the individual recipients to the deceased.

4400 – *Taxes on financial and capital transactions*

47. This sub-heading comprises, inter alia, taxes on the issue, transfer, purchase and sale of securities, taxes on cheques, and taxes levied on specific legal transactions such as validation of contracts and the sale of immovable property. The heading does not include:

a) taxes on the use of goods or property or permission to perform certain activities (5200);

b) fees paid to cover court charges, charges for birth, marriage or death certificates, which are normally regarded as non-tax revenues (see §9);

c) taxes on capital gains (1000);

d) recurrent taxes on immovable property (4100);

e) recurrent taxes on net wealth (4200);

f) once-and-for-all levies on property or wealth (4500).

4500 – *Other non-recurrent taxes on property*[16]

48. This sub-heading covers once-and-for-all, as distinct from recurrent, levies on property. It is divided into taxes on net wealth (4510) and other non-recurrent taxes on property (4520). Heading 4510 would include taxes levied to meet emergency expenditures, or for redistribution purposes. Heading 4520 would cover taxes levied to take account of increases in land value due to permission given to develop or provision of additional local facilities by general government, any taxes on the revaluation of capital and once-and-for-all taxes on particular items of property.

4600 – *Other recurrent taxes on property*

49. These rarely exist in OECD member countries, but the heading would include taxes on goods such as cattle, jewellery, windows, and other external signs of wealth.

5000 – *Taxes on goods and services*

50. All taxes and duties levied on the production, extraction, sale, transfer, leasing or delivery of goods, and the rendering of services (5100), or in respect of the use of goods or permission to use goods or to perform activities (5200) are included here. The heading thus covers:

a) multi-stage cumulative taxes;

b) general sales taxes – whether levied at manufacture/production, wholesale or retail level;

c) value-added taxes;

d) excises;

e) taxes levied on the import and export of goods;

f) taxes levied in respect of the use of goods and taxes on permission to use goods, or perform certain activities;

g) taxes on the extraction, processing or production of minerals and other products.

51. Borderline cases between this heading and heading 4000 (taxes on property) and 6100 (other taxes on business) are referred to in §42, §47 and §74. Residual sub-headings (5300) and (5130) cover tax receipts which cannot be allocated between 5100 and 5200 and between 5110 and 5120, respectively; see §27.

5100 – *Taxes on the production, sale, transfer, leasing and delivery of goods and rendering of services*

52. This sub-heading consists of all taxes, levied on transactions in goods and services on the basis of their intrinsic characteristics (e.g. value, weight of tobacco, strength of alcohol, and so on) as distinct from taxes imposed on the use of goods, or permission to use goods or perform activities, which fall under 5200.

5110 – *General taxes on goods and services*

53. This sub-heading includes all taxes, other than import and export duties (5123 and 5124), levied on the production, leasing, transfer, delivery or sales of a wide range of goods and/or the rendering of a wide range of services, irrespective of whether they are domestically produced or imported and irrespective of the stage of production or distribution at which they are levied. It thus covers value-added taxes, sales taxes and multi-stage cumulative taxes. Receipts from border adjustments in respect of such taxes when goods are imported are added to gross receipts for this category, and repayments of such taxes when goods are exported are deducted. These taxes are subdivided into 5111 value-added taxes, 5112 sales taxes, 5113 other general taxes on goods and services.

54. Borderline cases arise between this heading and taxes on specific goods (5120) when taxes are levied on a large number of goods, for example, the United Kingdom purchase tax (repealed in 1973) and the Japanese commodity tax (repealed in 1988). In conformity with national views, the former United Kingdom purchase tax is classified as a general tax (5112) and the former Japanese commodity tax as excises (5121).

5111 – *Value-added taxes*

55. All general consumption taxes charged on value-added are classified in this sub-heading, irrespective of the method of deduction and the stages at which the taxes are levied. In practice, all OECD countries with value-added taxes normally allow immediate deduction of taxes on purchases by all but the final consumer and impose tax at all stages. In some countries the heading may include certain taxes, such as those on financial and insurance activities, either because receipts from them cannot be identified separately from those from the value-added tax, or because they are regarded as an integral part of the value-added tax, even though similar taxes in other countries might be classified elsewhere (e.g. 5126 as taxes on services or 4400 as taxes on financial and capital transactions).

5112 – *Sales taxes*

56. All general taxes levied at one stage only, whether at manufacturing or production, wholesale or retail stage are classified here.

5113 – *Other general taxes on goods and services*

57. This sub-heading covers multi-stage cumulative taxes (also know as ‘cascade taxes’) where tax is levied each time a transaction takes place without deduction for tax paid on inputs, and also those general consumption taxes where elements of value-added, sales or cascade taxes are combined.

5120 – *Taxes on specific goods and services*

58. Excises, profits generated and transferred from fiscal monopolies, and customs and imports duties as well as taxes on exports, foreign exchange transactions, investment goods and betting stakes and special taxes on services, which do not form part of a general tax of 5110, are included in this category.

5121 – *Excises*

59. Excises are taxes levied on particular products, or on a limited range of products, which are not classifiable under 5110 (general taxes), 5123 (import duties) and 5124 (export duties). They may be imposed at any stage of production or distribution and are usually assessed by reference to the weight or strength or quantity of the product, but sometimes by reference to value. Thus, special taxes on, for example, sugar, beetroot, matches, chocolates, and taxes at varying rates on a certain range of goods, as well as those levied in most countries on tobacco goods, alcoholic drinks and hydrocarbon oils and other energy sources, are included in this sub-heading.

60. Excises are distinguished from:

a) 5110 (general taxes). This is discussed in §53-54;

b) 5123 (import duties). If a tax collected principally on imported goods also applies, or would apply, under the law by which the tax is imposed to comparable home-produced goods, the receipts there from would be classified as excises (5121). This principle applies even if there is no comparable home production or no possibility of it (see also §64);

c) 5126 (taxes on services). The problem here arises in respect of taxes on electricity, gas and energy. All of these are regarded as taxes on goods and are included under 5121.

5122 – *Profits of fiscal monopolies*

61. This sub-heading covers that part of the profits of fiscal monopolies which is transferred to general government or which is used to finance any expenditures considered to be government expenditures (see §18). Amounts are shown when they are transferred to general government or used to make expenditures considered to be government expenditures.

62. Fiscal monopolies reflect the exercise of the taxing power of government by the use of monopoly powers. Fiscal monopolies are non-financial public enterprises exercising a monopoly in most cases over the production or distribution of tobacco, alcoholic beverages, salt, matches, playing cards and petroleum or agricultural products (i.e. on the kind of products which are likely to be, alternatively or additionally, subject to the excises of 5121), to raise the government revenues which in other countries are gathered through taxes on dealings in such commodities by private business units. The government monopoly may be at the production stage or, as in the case of government-owned and controlled liquor stores, at the distribution stage.

63. Fiscal monopolies are distinguished from public utilities such as rail transport, electricity, post offices, and other communications, which may enjoy a monopoly or quasi-monopoly position but where the primary purpose is normally to provide basic services rather than to raise revenue for government. Transfers from such other public enterprises to the government are considered as non-tax revenues. The traditional concept of fiscal monopoly is not generally extended to include state lotteries, the profits of which are usually accordingly regarded as non-tax revenues. However, they can be included as tax revenues if the prime reason for their operation is to raise revenues to finance government expenditure. Fiscal monopoly profits are distinguished from export and import monopoly profits (5127) transferred from marketing boards or other enterprises dealing with international trade.

5123 – *Customs and other import duties*

64. Taxes, stamp duties and surcharges restricted by law to imported products are included here. Also included are levies on imported agricultural products which are imposed in member countries of the European Union and amounts paid by certain of these countries under the Monetary Compensation Accounts (MCA) system.[17] Starting from 1998, customs duties collected by European Union member states on behalf of the European Union are no longer reported under this heading in the country tables (in Chapter 4 of the Report). Excluded here are taxes collected on imports as part of a general tax on goods and services, or an excise applicable to both imported and domestically produced goods.

5124 – *Taxes on exports*

65. In the 1970s, export duties were levied in Australia, Canada and Portugal as a regular measure and they have been used in Finland for counter-cyclical purposes. Some member countries of the European Union pay, as part of the MCA system, a levy on exports (see note 16 to §64). Where these amounts are identifiable, they are shown in this heading. This heading does not include repayments of general consumption taxes or excises or customs duties on exported goods, which should be deducted from the gross receipts under 5110, 5121 or 5123, as appropriate.

5125 – *Taxes on investment goods*

66. This sub-heading covers taxes on investment goods, such as machinery. These taxes may be imposed for a number of years or temporarily for counter-cyclical purposes. Taxes on industrial inputs which are also levied on consumers [e.g. the Swedish energy tax which is classified under (5121)] are not included here.

5126 – *Taxes on specific services*

67. All taxes assessed on the payment for specific services, such as taxes on insurance premiums, banking services, gambling and betting stakes (e.g. from horse races, football pools, lottery tickets), transport, entertainment, restaurant and advertising charges, fall into this category. Taxes levied on the gross income of companies providing the service (e.g. gross insurance premiums or gambling stakes received by the company) are also classified under this heading. Tax revenues from bank levies and payments to deposit insurance and financial stability schemes are provisionally included here for the 2012 edition. The detailed classification is set out in paragraph 104.

68. Excluded from this sub-heading are:

a) taxes on services forming part of a general tax on goods and services (5110);

b) taxes on electricity, gas and energy (5121 as excises);

c) taxes on individual gains from gambling (1120 as taxes on capital gains of individuals and non-corporate enterprises) and lump-sum taxes on the transfer of private lotteries or on the permission to set up lotteries (5200);[18]

d) taxes on cheques and on the issue, transfer or redemption of securities (4400 as taxes on financial and capital transactions).

5127 – *Other taxes on international trade and transactions*

69. This sub-heading covers revenue received by the government from the purchase and sale of foreign exchange at different rates. When the government exercises monopoly powers to extract a margin between the purchase and sales price of foreign exchange, other than to cover administrative costs, the revenue derived constitutes a compulsory levy exacted in indeterminate proportions from both purchaser and seller of foreign exchange.

It is the common equivalent of an import duty and export duty levied in a single exchange rate system or of a tax on the sale or purchase of foreign exchange Like the profits of fiscal monopolies and import or export monopolies transferred to government, it represents the exercise of monopoly powers for tax purposes and is included in tax revenues.

70. The sub-heading covers also the profits of export or import monopolies, which do not however exist in OECD countries, taxes on purchase or sale of foreign exchange, and any other taxes levied specifically on international trade or transactions.

5128 – *Other taxes on specific goods and services*

71. This item includes taxes on the extraction of minerals, fossil fuels and other exhaustible resources from deposits owned privately or by another government together with any other unidentifiable receipts from taxes on specific goods and services. Taxes on the extraction of exhaustible resources are usually a fixed amount per unit of quality or weight, but can be a percentage of value. The taxes are recorded when the resources are extracted. Payments from the extraction of exhaustible resources from deposits owned by the government unit receiving the payment are classified as rent.

5200 – *Taxes on use of goods or on permission to use goods or perform activities*

72. This sub-heading covers taxes which are levied in respect of the use of goods as distinct from taxes on the goods themselves. Unlike the latter taxes – reported under 5100 –, they are not assessed on the value of the goods but usually as fixed amounts. Taxes on permission to use goods or to perform activities are also included here, as are pollution taxes not based upon the value of particular goods. It is sometimes difficult to distinguish between compulsory user charges and licence fees which are regarded as taxes and those which are excluded as non-tax revenues. The criteria which are employed are noted in §9–10.

73. Although the sub-heading refers to the 'use' of goods, registration of ownership rather than use may be what generates liability to tax, so that the taxes of this heading may apply to the ownership of animals or goods rather than their use (e.g. race horses, dogs and motor vehicles) and may apply even to unusable goods (e.g. unusable motor vehicles or guns).

74. Borderline cases arise with:

a) taxes on the permission to perform business activities which are levied on a combined income, payroll or turnover base and, accordingly, are classified following the rules in §77;

b) taxes on the ownership or use of property of headings 4100, 4200 and 4600. The heading 4100 is confined to taxes on the ownership or tenancy of immovable property and – unlike the taxes of 5200 – they are related to the value of the property. The net wealth taxes and taxes on chattels of 4200 and 4600 respectively are confined to the ownership rather than the use of assets, apply to groups of assets rather than particular goods and again are related to the value of the assets.

5210 – *Recurrent taxes on use of goods and on permission to use goods or perform activities*

75. The principal characteristic of taxes classified here is that they are levied at regular intervals and that they are usually fixed amounts. The most important item in terms of revenue receipts is vehicle licence taxes. This sub-heading also covers taxes on permission to hunt, shoot, fish or to sell certain products and taxes on the ownership of dogs and on the performance of certain services, provided that they meet the criteria set out in §9–10. The sub-divisions of 5210 are user taxes on motor vehicles paid by households (5211) and those paid by others (5212).[19] Sub-heading 5213 covers dog licences and user charges for permission to perform activities such as selling meat or liquor when

the levies are on a recurring basis. It also covers recurrent general licences for hunting, shooting and fishing where the right to carry out these activities is not granted as part of a normal commercial transaction (e.g. the granting of the licence is not accompanied by the right to use a specific area which is owned by government).

5220 – *Non-recurrent taxes on use of goods and on permission to use goods or perform activities*

76. This section covers non-recurrent taxes levied on the use of goods or on permission to use goods or perform activities and taxes levied each time goods are used. It includes taxes levied on the emission or discharge into the environment of noxious gases, liquids or other harmful substances.

- Payments for tradable emission permits issued by governments under cap and trade schemes should be recorded here at the time the emissions occur. No revenue should be recorded for permits that governments issue free of charge. The accrual basis of recording means that there can be a timing difference between the cash being received by government for the permits and the time the emission occurs. In the national accounts, this timing gives rise to a financial liability for government during the period.
- Payments made for the collection and disposal of waste or noxious substances by public authorities should be excluded as they constitute a sale of services to enterprises.

77. Other taxes falling under heading 5200 that are not levied recurrently are also included here. Thus, once-and-for-all payments for permission to sell liquor or tobacco or to set up betting shops are included provided they meet the criteria set out in §9–10.

6000 – *Other taxes*

78. Taxes levied on a base, or bases, other than those described under headings 1000, 3000, 4000 and 5000, or on bases of which none could be regarded as being predominantly the same as that of any one of these headings, are covered here. As regards taxes levied on a multiple base, if it is possible to estimate receipts related to each base (e.g. the Austrian and German 'Gewerbesteuer') this is done and the separate amounts included under the appropriate headings. If the separate amounts cannot be estimated, but it is known that most of the receipts are derived from one base, the whole of the receipts are classified according to that base. If neither of these procedures can be followed, they are classified here. The sub-headings may also include receipts from taxes which governments are unable to identify or isolate (see §27). Included here also are fines and penalties paid for infringement of regulations relating to taxes but not identifiable as relating to a particular category of taxes (see §14). A subdivision is made between taxes levied wholly or predominantly on business (6100) and those levied on others (6200).

A.6. Conciliation with National Accounts

79. This section of the tables provides a re-conciliation between the OECD calculation of total tax revenues and the total of all taxes and social contributions paid to general government as recorded in the country's National Accounts. Where the country is a member of the European Union (EU), the comparison is between the OECD calculation of total tax revenues and the sum of tax revenues and social contributions recorded in the combination of the general government and the institutions of the EU sectors of the National Accounts.

A.7. Memorandum item on the financing of social security benefits

80. In view of the varying relationship between taxation and social security contributions and the cases referred to in §34 to §40, a memorandum item collects together all payments earmarked for social security-type benefits, other than voluntary payments to the private sector. Data are presented as follows (refer Chapter 4.2 of the Report):

a) Taxes of 2000 series.

b) Taxes earmarked for social security benefits.

c) Voluntary contributions to the government.

d) Compulsory contributions to the private sector.

Guidance on the breakdown of (a) to (d) above is provided in §34 to §40.

A.8. Memorandum item on identifiable taxes paid by government

81. Identifiable taxes actually paid by government are presented in a memorandum item classified by the main headings of the OECD classification of taxes. In the vast majority of countries, only social security contributions and payroll taxes paid by government can be identified. These are, however, usually the most important taxes paid by governments (refer to Chapter 4.3 of the Report).

A.9. Relation of OECD classification of taxes to national accounting systems

82. A system of national accounts (SNA) seeks to provide a coherent framework for recording and presenting the main flows relating respectively to production, consumption, accumulation and external transactions of a given economic area, usually a country or a major region within a country. Government revenues are an important part of the transactions recorded in SNA. The final version of the 2008 SNA was jointly published by five international organisations: the United Nations, the International Monetary Fund, the European Union, the Organisation for Economic Co-operation and Development, and the World Bank in August 2009. The System is a comprehensive, consistent and flexible set of macroeconomic accounts. It is designed for use in countries with market economies, whatever their stage of economic development, and also in countries in transition to market economies. The important parts of the SNA's conceptual framework and its definitions of the various sectors of the economy have been reflected in the OECD's classification of taxes.

83. There are, however, some differences between the OECD classification of taxes and SNA concepts that are listed below. They arise because the aim of the former is to provide the maximum disaggregation of statistical data on what are generally regarded as taxes by tax administrations.

a) OECD includes compulsory social security contributions paid to general government in total tax revenues. Imputed and voluntary contributions plus those paid to private funds are not treated as taxes (§7 and §8 above);

b) there are different points of view on whether or not some levies and fees are classified as taxes (§9 and §10 above);

c) OECD excludes imputed taxes or subsidies resulting from the operation of official multiple exchange rates or from the central bank paying a rate of interest on required reserves that is different from other market rates;

d) there are differences in the treatment of non-wastable tax credits.

84. As noted in §1 and §2, headings 1000 to 6000 of the OECD list of taxes cover all unrequited payments to general government, other than compulsory loans and fines. Such unrequited payments including fines, but excluding compulsory loans can be obtained from adding together the following figures in the 2008 SNA

- value-added type taxes (D.211);
- taxes and duties on imports, excluding VAT (D.212);
- export taxes (D.213);
- taxes on products, excluding VAT, import and export taxes (D.214);
- other taxes on production (D.29);
- taxes on income (D.51);
- other current taxes (D.59);
- social contributions (D.61), excluding voluntary contributions;
- capital taxes (D.91).

A.10. Relation of OECD classification of taxes to the International Monetary Fund system

85. The coverage and valuation of tax revenues in the GFS system and the 2008 SNA are very similar. Therefore, the differences between the OECD classification and that of the 2008 SNA (see §83 above) also apply to the GFS. In addition the International Monetary Fund subdivides the OECD 5000 heading into section IV (Domestic Taxes on Goods and Services) and section V (Taxes on International Trade and Transactions). This reflects the fact that while the latter usually yield insignificant amounts of revenue in OECD countries, this is not the case in many non-OECD countries.

A.11. Comparison of the OECD classification of taxes with other international classifications

86. The table below describes an item by item comparison of the OECD classification of taxes and the classifications used in the following:

i) System of National Accounts (2008 SNA);

ii) European System of Accounts (1995 ESA);

iii) IMF *Government Finance Statistics Manual* (GFSM2001).

87. These comparisons represent those that would be expected to apply in the majority of cases. However in practice some flexibility should be used in their application. This is because in particular cases, countries can adopt varying approaches to the classification of revenues in National Accounts.

OECD Classification		2008 SNA	2010 ESA	GFSM 2014
1000	Taxes on income, profits and capital gains			
	1100 Individuals			
	1110 Income/profits	D51-8.61a	D51A	1111
	1120 Capital gains	D51-8.61c,d	D51C,D	1111
	1200 Corporations			
	1210 Income/profits	D51-8.61b	D51B	1112
	1220 Capital gains	D51-8.61c	D51C	1112
	1300 Unallocable as between 1100 and 1200			1113
2000	Social security contributions			
	2100 Employees	D613-8.85	D613	1211
	2200 Employers	D611-8.83	D611	1212
	2300 Self-employed, non-employed	D613-8.85	D613	1213
	2400 Unallocable as between 2100, 2200 and 2300			1214
3000	Taxes on payroll and workforce	D29-7.97a	D29C	112
4000	Taxes on property			
	4100 Recurrent taxes on immovable property			
	4110 Households	D59-8.63a	D59A	1131
	4120 Other	D29-7.97b	D29A	1131
	4200 Recurrent net wealth taxes			
	4210 Individual	D59-8.63b	D59A	1132
	4220 Corporations	D59-8.63b	D59A	1132
	4300 Estate, inheritance and gift taxes			
	4310 Estate and inheritance taxes	D91-10.207b	D91A	1133
	4320 Gift taxes	D91-10.207b	D91A	1133
	4400 Taxes on financial and capital transactions	D59-7.96d; D29-7.97e	D214B,C	114114; 1161
	4500 Other non-recurrent taxes on property	D91-10.207a	D91B	1135
	4600 Other recurrent taxes on property	D59-8.63c	D59A	1136
5000	Taxes on goods and services			
	5100 Taxes on production, sale and transfer of goods and services			
	5110 General taxes on goods and services			
	5111 Value-added taxes	D211-7.89	D211; D29G	11411
	5112 Sales taxes	D2122-7.94a; D214-7.96a	D21224; D214I	11412
	5113 Other general taxes on goods and services	D214-7.96a	D214I	11413
	5120 Taxes on specific goods and services			
	5121 Excises	D2122-7.94b; D214-7.96b	D21223; D214A,B D	1142
	5122 Profits of fiscal monopolies	D214-7.96e	D214J	1143
	5123 Customs/import duties	D2121-7.93	D2121; D2122A,B	1151
	5124 On exports	D213-7.95a	D214K	1152-4
	5125 On investment goods			
	5126 On specific services	D2122-7.94c; D214-7.96c	D21225; D214E,F,G; D29F	1144; 1156
	5127 Other taxes on international trade and transactions	D2122-7.94d D29-7.95b D29-7.97g D59-8.64d	D21226; D29D; D59E	1153 1155-6
	5128 Other taxes on specific goods and services			1146
	5130 Unallocable as between 5110 and 5120			
	5200 Taxes on use of goods and on permission to use goods or perform activities			
	5210 Recurrent taxes on use of goods and on permission to use goods or perform activities			
	5211 Motor vehicle taxes households	D59-8.64c	D59D	11451
	5212 Motor vehicles taxes others	D29-7.97d	D214D; D29B	11451
	5213 Other recurrent taxes on use of goods and on permission to use goods or perform activities	D29-7.97c,d,f D59-8.64c	D29B,E,F; D59D	11452
	5220 Non-recurrent taxes on permission to use goods or perform activities			
	5300 Unallocable as between 5100 and 5200			
6000	Other taxes			
	6100 Payable solely by business			1161
	6200 Payable by other than business, or unidentifiable	D59-8.64a,b	D59B,C	1162

A.12. Attribution of tax revenues by sub-sectors of general government

88. The OECD classification requires a breakdown of tax revenues by sub-sectors of government. The definition of each sub-sector and the criteria to be used to attribute tax revenues between these sub-sectors are set out below. They follow the guidance of the 2008 SNA and GFSM 2014.

Sub-sectors of general government to be identified

a) Central government

89. The central government sub-sector includes all governmental departments, offices, establishments and other bodies which are agencies or instruments of the central authority whose competence extends over the whole territory, with the exception of the administration of social security funds. Central government therefore has the authority to impose taxes on all resident and non-resident units engaged in economic activities within the country.

b) State, provincial or regional government

90. This sub-sector consists of intermediate units of government exercising a competence at a level below that of central government. It includes all such units operating independently of central government in a part of a country's territory encompassing a number of smaller localities, with the exception of the administration of social security funds. In unitary countries, regional governments may be considered to have a separate existence where they have substantial autonomy to raise a significant proportion of their revenues from sources within their control and their officers are independent of external administrative control in the actual operation of the unit's activities.

91. At present, federal countries comprise the majority of cases where revenues attributed to intermediate units of government are identified separately. Spain is the only unitary country in this position. In the remaining unitary countries, regional revenues are included with those of local governments.

c) Local government

92. This sub-sector includes all other units of government exercising an independent competence in part of the territory of a country, with the exception of the administration of social security funds. It encompasses various urban and/or rural jurisdictions (e.g. local authorities, municipalities, cities, boroughs, districts).

d) Social security funds

93. Social security funds form a separate sub-sector of general government. The social security sub-sector is defined in the 2008 SNA by the following extracts from paragraphs 4.124 to 4.126 and 4.147:

"Social security schemes are social insurance schemes covering the community as a whole or large section of the community that are imposed and controlled by government units. The schemes cover a wide variety of programmes, providing benefits in cash or in kind for old age, invalidity or death, survivors, sickness and maternity, work injury, unemployment, family allowance, health care, etc. There is not necessarily a direct link between the amount of the contribution paid by an individual and the benefits he or she may receive." (Paragraph 4.124).

"When social security schemes are separately organised from the other activities of government units and hold their assets and liabilities separately from the latter and engage in financial transactions on their own account they qualify as institutional units that are described as social security funds." (Paragraph 4.125).

"The amounts raised, and paid out, in social security contributions and benefits may be deliberately varied in order to achieve objectives of government policy that have no direct connection with the concept of social security as a scheme to provide social benefits to members of the community. They may be raised or lowered in order to influence the level of aggregate demand in the economy, for example. Nevertheless, so long as they remain separately constituted funds, they must be treated as separate institutional units in the SNA." (Paragraph 4.126).

"The social security funds sub-sector (of general government) consists of the social security funds operating at all levels of government. Such funds are social insurance schemes covering the community as a whole or large section of the community that are imposed by government units." (Paragraph 4.147).

94. This definition of social security funds is followed in the OECD classification with the two following exceptions which are excluded:

- Schemes imposed by government and operated by bodies outside the general government sector, as defined in §3 of this manual; and
- Schemes to which all contributions are voluntary.

Supra-national authorities

95. This sub-sector covers the revenue-raising operations of supra-national authorities within a country. In practice, the only relevant supra-national authority in the OECD area is that of the institutions of the European Union (EU). As from 1998, supra-national authorities are no longer included in the *Revenue Statistics*, to achieve consistency with the SNA definition of general government which excludes them. For example, income taxes and social security contributions collected by European Institutions and paid by European civil servants who are resident of EU member countries should not be included. However the specific levies paid by the member states of the EU continue to be included in total tax revenues and they are shown under this heading.

Criteria to be used for the attribution of tax revenues

96. When a government collects taxes and pays them over in whole or in part to other governments, it is necessary to determine whether the revenues should be considered to be those of the collecting government which it distributes to others as grants, or those of the beneficiary governments which the collecting government receives and passes on only as their agent. The criteria to be used in the attribution of revenues are set out in §97 to §100 which replicate paragraphs 3.70 to 3.73 from the 2008 SNA.

97. In general, a tax is attributed to the government unit that:

a) exercises the authority to impose the tax (either as a principal or through the delegated authority of the principal);

b) has final discretion to set and vary the rate of the tax.

98. Where an amount is collected by one government for and on behalf of another government, and the latter government has the authority to impose the tax, and set and vary its rate, then the former is acting as an agent for the latter and the tax is reassigned. Any amount retained by the collecting government as a collection charge should be treated as a payment for a service. Any other amount retained by the collecting government, such as under a tax-sharing arrangement, should be treated as a current grant. If the collecting government was delegated the authority to set and vary the rate, then the amount collected should be treated as tax revenue of this government.

99. Where different governments jointly and equally set the rate of a tax and jointly and equally decide on the distribution of the proceeds, with no individual government having ultimate overriding authority, then the tax revenues are attributed to each government according to its respective share of the proceeds. If an arrangement allows one government unit to exercise ultimate overriding authority, then all of the tax revenue is attributed to that unit.

100. There may also be the circumstance where a tax is imposed under the constitutional or other authority of one government, but other governments individually set the tax rate in their jurisdictions. The proceeds of the tax generated in each respective government's jurisdiction are attributed as tax revenues of that government.

Levies paid by member states of the European Union

101. The levies paid by the member states of the EU take the form of special levies which include:

a) custom duties and levies on agricultural goods (5123);

b) gross monetary compensation accounts (5123 if relating to imports and 5124 if relating to exports); and

c) Steel, coal, sugar and milk levies (5128).

102. The custom duties collected by member states on behalf of the EU are recorded:

- on a gross of collection fee basis;
- using figures adjusted so that duties are shown on a 'final destination' as opposed to a 'country of first entry' basis where such adjustments can be made. These adjustments concern in particular duties collected at important (sea) ports. Although the EU duties are collected by the authorities of the country of first entry, when possible these duties should be excluded from the revenue of the collecting country and be included in the revenue of the country of final destination.

103. This is the specific EU levy that most clearly conforms to the attribution criterion described in §95 above. Consequently as from 1998, these amounts are footnoted as a memorandum item to the EU member state country tables (in Chapter 4) and no longer shown under heading 5123. However the figures are included in the total tax revenue figures on the top line for all the relevant years shown in the tables.

A.13. Provisional classification of revenues from bank levies and payments to deposit insurance and financial stability schemes

104. The OECD have adopted the following interim approach to reporting revenue from bank levies plus deposit insurance and stability fees for the 2012 and subsequent editions of *OECD Revenue Statistics*. It is recommended that the amounts should be recorded under category 5126.

- Compulsory payments of stability fees, bank levies and deposit insurance should generally be treated as tax revenues where the payments are made to General Government and allocated to the governments' consolidated or general funds so that the Government is free to make immediate use of the money for the purposes that it chooses. This principle would apply regardless of whether the Government is promising to make payments to guarantee the banks' customer deposits in some future contingency.

- If the compulsory payments are made to general government and placed in funds that are earmarked to be entirely channelled back to the sector of the economy that comprises the companies that are subject to the payment, they would still generally be treated as tax revenues on the grounds that the funds would be available for the government and would reduce its budget deficit, the fee is unrequited for an individual entity and the amounts raised could be unrelated to any eventual pay out to depositors or expenditure on wider support for the financial sector.
- Payments to made to the smaller long-standing schemes for insuring 'retail' deposits, where the payment levels are consistent with the costs of insurance should be classified as fee for service.
- Any payments which involve governments realising the assets of a failed institution or receiving a priority claim on its assets in liquidation in order to fund payments of compensation to customers for their lost deposits would be treated as a fee for a service as opposed to tax revenues.
- Compulsory payments that are made to funds operated outside the government sector and non-state institutions backed by the deposit takers and all payments to voluntary schemes should not be treated as tax revenues.

Notes

1. References in this OECD Interpretative Guide to Sections or Parts of "this Report" refer to OECD (2016), *Revenue Statistics 2016*, OECD Publishing, Paris.
2. All references to SNA are to the 2008 edition.
3. See section A.12 of this guide for a discussion of the concept of agency capacity.
4. It is usually possible to identify amounts of social security contributions and payroll taxes, but not other taxes paid by government.
5. If, however, a levy which is considered as non-tax revenue by most countries is regarded as a tax – or raises substantial revenue – in one or more countries, the amounts collected are footnoted at the end of the relevant country tables, even though the amounts are not included in total tax revenues.
6. Names, however, can frequently be misleading. For example, though a passport fee would normally be considered a non-tax revenue, if a supplementary levy on passports (as is the case in Portugal) were imposed in order to raise substantial amounts of revenue relative to the cost of providing the passport, the levy would be regarded as a tax under 5200.
7. A more detailed explanation of this distinction can be found in the special feature, "Current issues in reporting tax revenues", in the 2001 edition of the *Revenue Statistics*.
8. Sometimes the terms "non-refundable" and "refundable" are used, but it may be considered illogical to talk of "refundable" when nothing has been paid.
9. A different treatment, however, is accorded to non-wastable tax credits under imputation systems of corporate income tax (§31–33).
10. This is not strictly a true tax expenditure in the formal sense. Such tax expenditures require identification of a benchmark tax system for each country or, preferably, a common international benchmark. In practice it has not been possible to reach agreement on a common international benchmark.
11. Unless based on the profit made on a sale, in which case they would be classified as capital gains taxes under 1120 or 1220.
12. In some countries the same legislation applies to both individual and corporate enterprises for particular taxes on income.However, the receipts from such taxes are usually allocable between individuals and enterprises and can therefore be shown in the appropriate sub-heading.
13. For example, "...sufficiently self-contained and independent that they behave in the same way as corporations.......(including) keeping a complete set of accounts" (2008 SNA, section 4.44).
14. In Canada – a country also referred to as having an imputation system – the (wastable) tax credit for the shareholder is in respect of domestic corporation tax deemed to have been paid whether or not a corporation tax liability has arisen.As there is no integral connection between the corporation tax liability and the credit given against income tax under such systems, these credits for dividends are treated, along with other tax credits, on the lines described in §20.
15. This may also apply where a scheme for government employees existed prior to the introduction of a general social security scheme.
16. In the 2008 SNA these are regarded as capital transfers and not as taxes (see section A.8).
17. This is the system by which the European Union adjusts for differences between the exchange rates used to determine prices under the Common Market Agricultural Policy and actual exchange rates. Payments under the system may relate to imports or exports and where these amounts are separately identifiable they are shown under the appropriate heading (5123 or 5124). In this Report, these amounts are shown gross (i.e. without deducting any subsidies paid out under the MCA system).
18. Transfers of profits of State lotteries are regarded as non-tax revenues (see also §63).
19. See §25(c) as regards this distinction.

ANEXO A

Guía de interpretación de la OCDE

Índice

A.1. Clasificación de impuestos de la OCDE

1000 *Impuestos sobre la renta, las utilidades y las ganancias de capital*

1100 físicasImpuestos sobre la renta, utilidades y ganancias de capital de personas físicas

1110 Renta y utilidades

1120 Ganancias de capital

1200 Impuesto sobre la renta, utilidades y ganancias de capital de sociedades

1210 Renta y utilidades

1220 Ganancias de capital

1300 No clasificables entre 1100 y 1200

2000 *Contribuciones a la seguridad social*

2100 Empleados

2110 Sobre la base de la nómina

2120 Sobre la base del impuesto sobre la renta

2200 Empleadores

2210 Sobre la base de la nómina

2220 Sobre los ingresos gravables

2300 Trabajadores por cuenta propia o no empleados

2310 Sobre la base de la nómina

2320 Sobre los ingresos gravables

2400 No clasificables entre 2100, 2200 y 2300

2410 Sobre la base de la nómina

2420 Sobre los ingresos gravables

3000 *Impuestos sobre la nómina y la fuerza de trabajo*

4000 *Impuestos sobre la propiedad*

4100 Impuestos recurrentes sobre la propiedad inmueble

4110 Hogares

4120 Otros

4200 Impuestos recurrentes sobre la riqueza neta

4210 Personas físicas

4220 Sociedades

4300 Impuestos sobre sucesiones, herencias y donaciones

4310 Impuestos sobre sucesiones y herencias

4320 Impuestos sobre donaciones

4400 Impuestos sobre transacciones financieras y de capital

4500 Otros impuestos no recurrentes sobre la propiedad

4510 Sobre el patrimonio neto

4520 Otros impuestos no recurrentes

4600 Otros impuestos recurrentes sobre la propiedad

5000 *Impuestos sobre los bienes y servicios*

5100 Impuestos sobre la producción, venta, transferencia, arrendamiento y entrega de bienes y prestación de servicios

5110 Impuestos generales

5111 Impuestos sobre el valor agregado

5112 Impuestos sobre las ventas

5113 Otros impuestos generales sobre los bienes y servicios

5120 Impuestos sobre bienes y servicios específicos

5121 Impuestos selectivos

5122 Utilidades de los monopolios fiscales

5123 Derechos de aduanas y otros derechos de importación

5124 Impuestos sobre las exportaciones

5125 Impuestos sobre los bienes de inversión

5126 Impuestos sobre servicios específicos

5127 Otros impuestos sobre el comercio y las transacciones internacionales

5128 Otros impuestos sobre bienes y servicios específicos

5130 No clasificables entre 5110 y 5120

5200 Impuestos sobre el uso de bienes y sobre el permiso para usar bienes y realizar actividades

5210 Impuestos recurrentes

5211 Pagados por los hogares sobre vehículos automotores

5212 Pagados por otros sobre vehículos automotores

5213 Otros impuestos recurrentes

5220 Impuestos no recurrentes

5300 No clasificables entre 5100 y 5200

6000 *Otros impuestos*

6100 Pagados únicamente por empresas

6200 Pagados por otros distintos de las empresas o no identificables

Guía de interpretación de la OCDE[1]

A.2. Cobertura

Criterios generales

1. En la clasificación de la OCDE, el término "impuestos" se circunscribe exclusivamente a los pagos sin contraprestación efectuados al gobierno general. Los impuestos carecen de contraprestación en el sentido en que, normalmente, las prestaciones proporcionadas por el gobierno a los contribuyentes no guardan relación directa con los pagos realizados por estos.

2. El término "impuestos" no incluye las multas, sanciones pecuniarias, ni préstamos obligatorios pagados al gobierno. La delimitación entre ingresos tributarios y no tributarios en relación con ciertas tasas y cargos se abordan en los §§ 9–12.

3. El gobierno general comprende la Administración central y los organismos que se hallan bajo su control efectivo, los gobiernos estatales y locales y sus respectivas administraciones, y ciertos regímenes de seguridad social y entidades gubernamentales autónomas, excluidas las empresas públicas. Esta definición del gobierno proviene del Sistema de Cuentas Nacionales (SCN) 2008;[2] en esa publicación, el sector del gobierno general y sus subsectores se hallan definidos en el capítulo 4, sección F, páginas 80-84 de la versión inglesa.

4. Los pagos obligatorios a autoridades supranacionales y a los organismos vinculados a ellas no se incluyen como impuestos desde 1998, con contadas excepciones; sin embargo, los derechos de aduana recaudados por los estados miembros de la Unión Europea en nombre de esta siguen registrándose como partidas informativas y se incluyen en los cuadros de países (Capítulo 4 de la publicación Revenue Statistics de la OCDE), concretamente en la recaudación tributaria total del país en el que se cobran (véase el § 94). Por otra parte, en los países en los que la Iglesia forma parte del gobierno general, se computan los impuestos eclesiásticos, siempre que reúnan los criterios establecidos en el § 1. Además, habida cuenta de que los datos hacen referencia a las entradas que recibe el gobierno general, quedan excluidos los gravámenes abonados a órganos no gubernamentales, organismos de bienestar o regímenes de seguro social externos al gobierno general, y sindicatos u organizaciones profesionales, aun cuando dichos gravámenes sean obligatorios; sin embargo, los pagos obligatorios al gobierno general asignados a esos entes sí están incluidos aquí siempre que el gobierno no actúe como mero agente de estos.[3] Las utilidades de los monopolios fiscales se diferencian de las de otras empresas públicas, y se tratan como impuestos porque reflejan el ejercicio del poder tributario del Estado mediante el uso de prerrogativas monopolísticas (véanse los §§ 61–63), al igual que las utilidades percibidas por el gobierno por la compra y la venta de divisas a diferentes tipos de cambio (véase el § 69).

5. Los impuestos pagados por el gobierno (p. ej., contribuciones a la seguridad social e impuestos sobre la nómina pagados por el gobierno en su calidad de empleador, impuestos sobre el consumo en sus compras o impuestos sobre sus propiedades) no se han excluido de los datos presentados. Sin embargo, cuando ha sido posible identificar las cantidades de ingreso implicadas,[4] se han mostrado en el Capítulo 4.3 de la publicación *Estadísticas Tributarias en países de la OCDE.*

6. La relación entre esta clasificación y la del Sistema de Cuentas Nacionales (SCN) se aclara en los apartados A.9 y A.11 infra.; dado que estas dos clasificaciones no coinciden en todos sus aspectos, en ocasiones, los datos presentados en las cuentas nacionales se

calculan o clasifican de forma diferente a lo establecido en la presente guía y, aunque esas y otras diferencias se han mencionado en determinados casos (p. ej., en el § 25 *infra*), no ha sido posible hacer referencia a todas ellas. Por otra parte, pueden darse asimismo ciertas disparidades entre la presente clasificación y la empleada internamente por algunas administraciones nacionales (véase el § 10), por lo que quizá las estadísticas de la OCDE y las nacionales no siempre concuerden; sin embargo, es más que probable que esas diferencias sean mínimas en lo que a la cuantía de ingresos se refiere.

Contribuciones a la seguridad social

7. Las contribuciones obligatorias a la seguridad social, tal y como se definen en el § 34, abonadas al gobierno general, se tratan aquí como ingresos tributarios, ya que, al tratarse de pagos preceptivos al gobierno general, se asemejan claramente a los impuestos. No obstante, pueden diferir de otros impuestos por el hecho de que la recepción de prestaciones de la seguridad social depende, en numerosos países, de que se hayan aportado las debidas contribuciones, aunque la magnitud de dichas prestaciones no tiene por qué estar supeditada obligatoriamente al importe de las contribuciones. Al tratar las contribuciones sociales como impuestos, se obtiene un mayor grado de comparabilidad entre países, aunque se han consignado en una categoría separada para poder distinguirlas en cualquier análisis.

8. Por el contrario, las contribuciones a la seguridad social voluntarias o no pagaderas al gobierno general (véase el § 1) no se tratan como impuestos, aunque en ciertos países, tal y como se indica debidamente en cada caso en las notas que figuran al pie de los cuadros, plantea dificultades el eliminar tanto las contribuciones voluntarias como algunos pagos obligatorios al sector privado. Las contribuciones a la seguridad social imputadas tampoco son considerados impuestos.

Tasas, cargos a usuarios y licencias

9. Aparte de las tasas por licencia de vehículos, universalmente consideradas como impuestos, no resulta fácil distinguir entre las tasas y cargos a usuarios que deben tratarse como impuestos y las que no, ya que, aunque toda tasa o cargo se impone en conexión con un servicio o una actividad específicos, la intensidad del vínculo entre el derecho cobrado y el servicio prestado puede variar considerablemente, al igual que puede hacerlo la relación entre la cuantía de la tasa y el costo que supone proporcionar el servicio en cuestión. En todo caso, cuando el beneficiario del servicio pague una tasa claramente relacionada con el costo que supone prestar un servicio, puede inferirse que el gravamen tiene contraprestación y, de acuerdo con la definición reseñada en el § 1, no se considerará como impuesto. En sentido contrario, puede estimarse que el gravamen "carece de contraprestación" cuando:

a) el cargo exceda con creces el costo que supone prestar el servicio;

b) el pagador o sujeto pasivo del gravamen no sea el beneficiario del servicio (p. ej., tasas recaudadas de los mataderos para financiar un servicio proporcionado a los titulares de explotaciones agropecuarias);

c) el gobierno no proporcione un servicio específico a cambio del pago del gravamen, aun y cuando se emita un permiso en beneficio del sujeto pasivo (p. ej., cuando el gobierno concede licencias de caza, pesca o tiro que no otorgan el derecho a usar una zona específica propiedad del gobierno);

d) los servicios beneficien únicamente a los pagadores del gravamen, pero las utilidades recibidas por cada persona no guarden necesariamente proporción con sus pagos (p. ej., el gravamen sobre la comercialización de la leche que recae en los criadores de ganado lechero y que se utiliza para fomentar el consumo de la leche).

10. Pese a las anteriores consideraciones, en ciertos casos excepcionales la aplicación de los criterios plasmados en el § 1 puede resultar particularmente compleja. La solución adoptada –dada la conveniencia de uniformidad internacional y las cantidades de ingreso relativamente bajas implicadas por lo general– ha consistido en seguir la práctica dominante en la mayoría de las administraciones, en lugar de permitir que cada país aplique su propia visión sobre si estos gravámenes deben considerarse como ingresos tributarios o no tributarios.[5]

11. Seguidamente, se ofrece una lista de las principales tasas y cargos en cuestión, y su tratamiento normal[6] en esta publicación:

Ingresos no tributarios:	tasas procesales, permisos de conducir, tasas portuarias, tasas por expedición de pasaportes, licencias de radio y televisión cuando las autoridades públicas proporcionan el servicio de difusión.
Impuestos de la partida 5200:	permiso para realizar actividades tales como distribución cinematográfica; caza, pesca o tiro; suministro de instalaciones para actividades recreativas o de ocio o juegos de azar; venta de bebidas alcohólicas o tabaco; posesión de animales domésticos o uso de vehículos automotores; derechos sobre la extracción.

12. En la práctica, puede que no siempre resulte posible aislar las entradas tributarias de las no tributarias cuando estas se registran conjuntamente. En ese caso, si se considera que la mayoría de las entradas proviene de ingresos no tributarios, se tratará el importe total como tal; de lo contrario, esas entradas del gobierno se incluirán y clasificarán según las normas recogidas en el § 27.

Regalías

13. Las regalías percibidas por el derecho a extraer petróleo o gas, o a explotar otros recursos minerales, se consideran normalmente ingresos no tributarios, ya que son rentas de la propiedad procedentes de tierras o recursos del gobierno.

Multas y sanciones pecuniarias

14. En principio, las multas y sanciones pecuniarias impuestas por el pago tardio de los impuestos o por el intento de evasión de los impuestos no deben registrarse como ingresos tributarios. Sin embargo, en ocasiones no es posible distinguir y separar los pagos por multas y penalidades del recaudo del impuesto a los que estos están relacionados. En este caso, las multas y sanciones pecuniarias vinculadas a un determinado impuesto se registran con los ingresos de ese impuesto. Las multas y penalidades pagadas sobre el recaudo de impuestos no identificados se clasifican como otros impuestos en la partida 6000. Las multas que no están relacionadas con delitos tributarios (por ejemplo, las infracciones por estacionamiento indebido), o que no puedan ser identificadas como ofensas tributarias, no serán tratadas como ingresos tributarios.

A.3. Principios de registro

Criterio de devengo

15. Los datos recogidos en esta publicación relativos a los últimos años se han registrado predominantemente según el criterio de devengo, esto es, se han computado en el momento en que nace la obligación. Se ofrece más información al respecto en las notas que figuran al pie de los cuadros de países en el Capítulo 4 del informe.

16. Sin embargo, los datos relativos a años anteriores han seguido registrándose principalmente según el criterio de caja, es decir, en el momento en que el gobierno recibió el pago. Por lo tanto, por ejemplo, los impuestos descontados por los empleadores en un año pero pagados al gobierno al año siguiente y los impuestos debidos un año pero liquidados el año después constan ambos en las entradas del segundo año. Las transacciones correctoras, tales como devoluciones, reembolsos y reintegros, se deducen de los ingresos brutos del periodo en que se realizan.

17. Los datos sobre ingresos tributarios se registran sin deducción de los gastos administrativos propios de la recaudación impositiva. De igual modo, cuando los recursos generados por un impuesto se emplean para subvencionar a miembros particulares de la comunidad, el subsidio no se descuenta del producto impositivo, aunque puede que el impuesto aparezca sin los subsidios en los registros nacionales de algunos países.

18. En lo que a los monopolios fiscales se refiere (5122), únicamente se incluye en los ingresos del gobierno el importe realmente transferido a este. Sin embargo, si cualquier gasto de los monopolios fiscales se considera gasto del gobierno (p. ej., gastos sociales emprendidos por los monopolios fiscales en beneficio del gobierno), se añadirán posteriormente con el fin de llegar a cifras de ingreso tributario (véase el § 61 infra.).

Distinción entre disposiciones tributarias y disposiciones relativas al gasto[8]

19. Dado que la presente publicación aborda únicamente la actividad del gobierno desde el punto de vista del ingreso, sin tener en cuenta los aspectos relacionados con el gasto, resulta preciso realizar una distinción entre las disposiciones que rigen estos dos elementos. Por lo general, no existe dificultad alguna en diferenciar ambos aspectos, ya que los gastos operan en un ámbito externo al sistema tributario y sus cuentas, y se rigen por una legislación separada de la impositiva. En los casos de difícil delimitación, se emplea el flujo de caja para distinguir entre disposiciones tributarias y disposiciones relativas al gasto. En la medida en que una disposición incida en el flujo de pagos tributarios del contribuyente al gobierno, se entenderá que reviste un carácter tributario y se tendrá en cuenta en los datos recogidos en esta publicación. Cualquier disposición que no afecte a ese flujo se reputará como relativa al gasto y no se tendrá en consideración en la información plasmada en la publicación.

20. Las desgravaciones, exenciones y deducciones tributarias sobre la base imponible afectan claramente a la cantidad transferida al gobierno y, por ende, se consideran disposiciones de naturaleza tributaria. En el extremo opuesto, los subsidios o exoneraciones que no compensen la obligación tributaria y que estén claramente desvinculados del proceso de evaluación, no reducen los ingresos tributarios consignados en esta publicación. De particular interés en este ámbito resultan los créditos fiscales, que son cantidades deducibles del impuesto liquidable (lo que los diferencia de las deducciones sobre la base imponible). Cabe distinguir dos tipos de créditos fiscales: los créditos fiscales no exigibles (a veces denominados desaprovechables), limitados al importe de la obligación tributaria y que, por ende, no pueden generar un pago de las autoridades al contribuyente; y los créditos fiscales exigibles (o no desaprovechables), que no están sometidos a dicho límite, de forma que toda cantidad que exceda la obligación tributaria puede abonarse al contribuyente.[9] Al igual que las desgravaciones, un crédito fiscal no exigible afecta claramente a la cantidad transferida al gobierno y, por ende, se considerará como tributario. La práctica seguida para los créditos fiscales exigibles[10] consiste en distinguir entre "el componente de gasto tributario"[11] que es la porción del crédito empleada en reducir o eliminar la obligación del contribuyente" y el "componente de transferencia", constituido por la parte que excede la obligación del contribuyente y que se paga a este. Al registrar los ingresos tributarios deberá restarse la parte equivalente al componente de gasto tributario, pero no la correspondiente al

componente de transferencia. Además, las cantidades de ambos componentes deberán figurar como partidas informativas en los cuadros de países. Los países que no puedan diferenciar entre estos dos componentes deberán indicar si se ha restado de los ingresos tributarios el total de ellos y presentar las evaluaciones disponibles del valor que ambos representan. Para mayor información, consúltese el Capítulo 2 de la publicación *Revenue Statistics* de la OCDE, que examina el efecto de los diversos tratamientos de los créditos fiscales exigibles en la relación impuestos sobre PIB.

Calendario y ejercicio fiscal

21. Las autoridades nacionales cuyos ejercicios fiscales no coinciden con el año calendario deben presentar los datos, siempre que sea posible, sobre la base del año calendario, a fin de permitir el mayor grado posible de comparación con la información de otros países. Subsisten algunos países en los que los datos hacen referencia a los ejercicios fiscales; para ellos, los datos relativos al PIB utilizados en los cuadros comparativos corresponden igualmente a los ejercicios fiscales.

A.4. Criterios generales de clasificación

Principales criterios de clasificación

22. El desglose de las entradas fiscales en las diversas categorías (1000, 2000, 3000, 4000, 5000 y 6000) se rige en general por la base sobre la cual recae el impuesto: 1000, renta, utilidades y ganancias de capital; 2000 y 3000, remuneraciones, nómina o número de empleados (fuerza de trabajo); 4000, propiedad; 5000, bienes y servicios; 6000, bases múltiples, otras bases o bases no identificables. Cuando un impuesto se calcula sobre más de una base, las entradas que genera se distribuyen, en la medida de lo posible, entre las diversas categorías (véanse los §§ 27 y 77). Las categorías 4000 y 5000 no sólo cubren aquellos impuestos en los que la base tributaria está constituida por la propiedad, los bienes o los servicios en sí mismos, sino también ciertos impuestos afines; y así, por ejemplo, los impuestos sobre transmisiones patrimoniales se incluyen en la partida 4400,[12] y los impuestos sobre el uso de bienes y sobre el permiso para realizar actividades, en la 5200. En las categorías 4000 y 5000, se distingue en ocasiones entre impuestos recurrentes y no recurrentes: son impuestos recurrentes los que se recaudan a intervalos regulares (por lo general, anualmente), y no recurrentes, los que se imponen una sola vez (véanse los §§ 42-45, 48, 49 y 75 para profundizar en las aplicaciones particulares de esta distinción).

23. La asignación de un impuesto a fines específicos no afecta a la clasificación de las entradas fiscales que genera. Sin embargo, tal y como se explica en el § 34 en relación con la clasificación de las contribuciones a la seguridad social, el hecho de que estas confieran un derecho a recibir prestaciones sociales es decisivo para la definición de la categoría 2000.

24. La forma en que se establece o recauda un impuesto (p.ej., mediante el uso de timbres) no afecta a su clasificación.

Clasificación de los contribuyentes

25. En ocasiones, se distingue entre diversas clases de contribuyentes. Esas distinciones dependen de cada impuesto.

a) Entre personas físicas y sociedades en relación con los impuestos sobre la renta y sobre la riqueza neta

La distinción básica aquí es que los impuestos sobre la renta de las sociedades (impuesto de sociedades), a diferencia de los impuestos sobre la renta de las personas físicas, gravan a la sociedad como entidad y no a sus propietarios, independientemente de las circunstancias personales de estos; la misma distinción se aplica a los impuestos sobre la riqueza neta de las sociedades y de las personas físicas. Los impuestos liquidados sobre las utilidades de las asociaciones y sobre la renta de las instituciones, tales como seguros de vida o fondos de pensiones, se clasifican siguiendo la misma regla, y así, se considerarán impuestos sobre las sociedades (1200) si se cargan a la asociación o institución como persona jurídica sin tener en cuenta las circunstancias personales de sus propietarios, o impuestos sobre las personas físicas en el caso contrario (1100). Por lo general, los impuestos aplicados a las sociedades y a las personas físicas se rigen por legislaciones diferentes.[13] La distinción realizada aquí entre personas físicas y sociedades no sigue la categorización por sectores entre hogares, empresas, etcétera, del Sistema de Cuentas Nacionales para las cuentas de ingresos y desembolsos. La clasificación del SCN requiere que ciertas empresas no constituidas en sociedad[14] se excluyan del sector de los hogares y vengan a sumarse a las empresas no financieras y las instituciones financieras. Sin embargo, el impuesto sobre las utilidades de esos negocios no siempre puede separarse del impuesto sobre la renta de sus propietarios o, como mucho, puede deslindarse sólo arbitrariamente. Por ello, no se ha intentado reproducir aquí esa separación, y la totalidad del impuesto sobre la renta de las personas físicas se ha recogido en un solo bloque, independientemente de la naturaleza del ingreso imponible.

b) Entre hogares y otros en relación con los impuestos sobre la propiedad inmueble

Esta distinción es la misma que la adoptada por el SCN para las cuentas de gasto del consumo final de los hogares y de producción. Se trata pues de diferenciar a los hogares como consumidores (esto es, excluidas las empresas no constituidas en sociedad), por una parte, y a los productores, por otra. Los impuestos sobre las viviendas ocupadas por los hogares, tanto a cargo de los propietarios-ocupantes como de los arrendatarios o de los arrendadores, se incluyen en los hogares, lo que coincide con la diferenciación que suele hacerse comúnmente entre los impuestos sobre la propiedad doméstica y los impuestos sobre la propiedad empresarial. No obstante, algunos países no se hallan en situación de operar esta distinción.

c) Entre hogares y otros en relación con las licencias de vehículos automotores

Se distingue aquí entre los hogares como consumidores, por una parte, y los productores, por otra, al igual que en las cuentas de gasto del consumo final de los hogares y de producción del SCN.

d) Entre empresas y otros en relación con los impuestos residuales (6000)

La distinción es la misma que en c), esta vez, entre los productores, por una parte, y los hogares como consumidores, por otra. Los impuestos recogidos en la categoría 6000 bien porque gravan más de una base tributaria, o bien porque su base no entra dentro del ámbito de ninguna de las categorías anteriores pero es identificable como imponible sobre los productores, y no sobre los hogares, se incluyen en 'empresas'. El resto de los impuestos de la categoría 6000 se imputan a 'otros' o no identificables.

Recargos

26. Las entradas procedentes de recargos relacionados con impuestos particulares se clasifican por lo general en base al impuesto correspondiente, ya sea el recargo temporal o no. Pero si el recargo posee una característica que lo califica para ser clasificada en una categoría diferente de la lista de la OCDE, las entradas generadas por el recargo se recogen en dicha categoría, separadas de las del correspondiente impuesto.

Entradas tributarias no identificables y partidas residuales

27. En un cierto número de casos, no logra determinarse que los impuestos pertenezcan enteramente a una categoría o partida de la clasificación de la OCDE y, en esos casos, se aplican las siguientes pautas:

a) Se conoce la categoría, pero no la forma de distribuir las entradas entre las diversas subdivisiones: las entradas se clasifican en la correspondiente partida o subpartida residual (1300, 2400, 4520, 4600, 5130, 5300 o 6200).

b) Se sabe que la mayor parte de las entradas procedentes de un grupo de impuestos (normalmente, impuestos locales) proviene de impuestos de una categoría o una partida particulares, pero algunos de los impuestos del grupo cuya cuantía no puede determinarse con exactitud pueden clasificarse en otras categorías o partidas: las entradas se consignan en la categoría o partida a la que pertenezca la mayoría de ellas.

c) No puede identificarse ni la categoría ni la partida correspondiente al impuesto (normalmente, local): el impuesto se incorpora a la partida 6200, a menos que se conozca que se trata de un impuesto sobre las empresas, en cuyo caso se incluye en la partida 6100.

A.5. Comentarios sobre ítems de la lista

1000 – *Impuestos sobre la renta, las utilidades y las ganancias de capital*

28. Esta categoría cubre los impuestos aplicados a la renta o a las utilidades netas (esto es, la renta bruta menos las deducciones permitidas) de las personas físicas y las sociedades, así como los impuestos a los que se someten las ganancias de capital de esos mismos sujetos pasivos, y las ganancias obtenidas en juegos de azar.

29. Se incluyen en esta categoría:

a) los impuestos que gravan predominantemente la renta o las utilidades, aunque recaigan parcialmente sobre otras bases; los impuestos aplicados a varias bases que no sean mayoritariamente la renta o las utilidades se clasifican de acuerdo con los principios establecidos en los §§ 27 y 77;

b) los impuestos sobre la propiedad aplicados a un ingreso presunto o estimado como parte de un impuesto sobre la renta (véase el § 42(a), (c) y (d));

c) los pagos obligatorios al fondo de contribuciones de la seguridad social impuestos sobre la renta que no confieran un derecho a prestaciones sociales; si esas contribuciones otorgan derecho a prestaciones sociales, se incluyen en la categoría 2000 (véase el § 34);

d) el producto de los sistemas integrados de impuestos sobre la renta de régimen cedular se clasifican como un todo en esta categoría, aunque algunos de los impuestos cedulares puedan basarse en la renta bruta y no tener en cuenta las circunstancias personales del contribuyente.

30. La principal división de esta categoría se efectúa entre los gravámenes a personas físicas (1100) y aquellos a sociedades (1200). A su vez, en cada partida, se separa entre impuestos sobre la renta y las utilidades (1110 y 1210) e impuestos sobre las ganancias de capital (1120 y 1220). Si algunas entradas no pueden atribuirse pertinentemente a la partida 1100 o a la 1200, o si no puede realizarse esta distinción en la práctica (p. ej., por falta de datos fiables sobre los receptores de los pagos de los que se deducen los impuestos con retención en la fuente), las entradas se incorporan a la partida 1300 como "no clasificables".

Tratamiento de los créditos fiscales en los sistemas de imputación

31. En los sistemas de imputación del impuesto de sociedades, los accionistas están exentos, total o parcialmente, de responder en concepto del impuesto sobre la renta por los dividendos abonados por la compañía a partir de la renta o de las utilidades sometidas al impuesto de sociedades. En los países con este sistema,[15] una parte del impuesto sobre las utilidades de la sociedad está disponible para exonerar a los accionistas de su propia obligación tributaria. La exoneración del accionista reviste la forma de un crédito fiscal, cuyo importe puede ser inferior, igual o superior al pasivo tributario total del accionista. Si el crédito fiscal excede al pasivo tributario, puede que ese exceso sea pagadero al accionista. Dado que este tipo de crédito fiscal es parte integrante del sistema de imputación del impuesto sobre la renta de las sociedades, cualquier pago a los accionistas se trata como devolución tributaria, y no como gasto (compárese con el tratamiento de otros créditos fiscales descrito en el § 20).

32. Puesto que en los sistemas de imputación el crédito fiscal (incluso cuando excede la obligación tributaria) debe considerarse como disposición tributaria, se plantea la cuestión de determinar si deberá deducirse de las entradas en concepto de impuesto sobre la renta de las personas físicas (1110) o de las entradas atribuibles al impuesto sobre la renta de las sociedades (1210). En este informe, la cantidad total pagada a título del impuesto sobre la renta de las sociedades se recoge en la subpartida 1210, y el impuesto no imputado en la subpartida 1110. Por lo tanto, la cuantía total del crédito se resta de esta última subpartida, tanto si el crédito da lugar a una reducción de la obligación tributaria por renta personal, como si se realiza un reembolso porque el crédito fiscal excede el pasivo tributario por este concepto. (No obstante, si los créditos fiscales se deducen del impuesto de sociedades por dividendos repartidos a otras sociedades, las correspondientes cantidades se descuentan de las entradas registradas en la subpartida 1210.)

1120 y 1220 – *Impuestos sobre las ganancias de capital*

33. Como su nombre indica, estas subpartidas engloban los impuestos sobre las ganancias de capital, ya de las personas físicas (1120), ya de las sociedades (1220), siempre que las entradas procedentes de estos impuestos puedan identificarse por separado. Ese no es el caso en numerosos países, y las entradas de estos impuestos se clasifican junto con las del impuesto sobre la renta. La subpartida 1120 contiene asimismo los impuestos sobre las ganancias obtenidas en juegos de azar.

2000 – *Contribuciones a la seguridad social*

34. Entran en esta categoría todos los pagos obligatorios que confieran un derecho a recibir una prestación social futura (contingente). Esos pagos suelen estar asignados al financiamiento de prestaciones sociales y, a menudo, se pagan a las instituciones del gobierno general que proporcionan dichas prestaciones. Sin embargo, esa asignación no forma parte de la definición de las contribuciones a la seguridad social y no es necesaria para que un impuesto sea clasificado en esta categoría, pero, para que un impuesto se incluya aquí, sí será preciso que confiera un derecho. Y así, los gravámenes sobre la renta o la nómina asignados a los fondos de seguridad social pero que no confieran el derecho a recibir prestaciones sociales quedan excluidos de la presente categoría y se registran bien entre los impuestos sobre la renta de las personas físicas (1100), bien junto con los impuestos sobre la nómina y la fuerza de trabajo (3000). Los impuestos aplicados sobre otras bases, como los bienes y servicios, no se consignarán aquí aunque estén asignados a prestaciones de la seguridad social, sino que se catalogarán según sus respectivas bases, ya que por lo general no otorgarán derecho alguno a prestaciones sociales.

35. Entre otras, se incluirán aquí las contribuciones a los siguientes tipos de prestaciones de la seguridad social: prestaciones y suplementos por seguro de desempleo; prestaciones por accidente, lesión o enfermedad; pensiones por jubilación, invalidez y supervivencia; ayudas familiares; reembolsos de gastos médicos u hospitalarios o prestación de servicios médicos u hospitalarios. Las contribuciones pueden recaudarse tanto de los empleados como de los empleadores.

36. Las contribuciones pueden tener como base bien las remuneraciones o la nómina ('sobre la base de la nómina'), bien la renta neta tras deducciones y exenciones por circunstancias personales ('sobre la base del impuesto sobre la renta'), y el producto de ambas bases deberá identificarse separadamente en la medida de lo posible. Cuando las contribuciones al régimen general de la seguridad social se basen en la nómina, pero las de grupos particulares (tales como los trabajadores por cuenta propia) no puedan evaluarse en función de esta base y se emplee en ese caso la renta neta como una aproximación de las remuneraciones brutas, las entradas seguirán clasificándose sobre la base de la nómina. En principio, esta categoría excluye las contribuciones voluntarias aportadas a los regímenes de seguridad social, que, cuando sea posible identificarlas de forma separada, se recogerán en la partida informativa sobre el financiamiento de las prestaciones sociales; sin embargo, en la práctica, estas aportaciones no siempre pueden desvincularse de las contribuciones obligatorias, en cuyo caso se incluirán igualmente en esta categoría.

37. Las contribuciones a los regímenes de seguro social no vinculados a instituciones del gobierno general, así como las aportaciones a otros tipos de sistemas de seguro, tales como planes de previsión o planes de pensiones, mutualidades u otros planes de ahorro, no se consideran contribuciones a la seguridad social. Los planes de previsión son acuerdos por los que las contribuciones de cada empleado y la parte correspondiente del empleador en nombre de aquél se conservan en una cuenta separada que genera interés, de la que pueden retirarse en circunstancias específicas. Por su parte, los planes de pensiones son regímenes organizados separadamente, negociados entres empleados y empleadores, que conllevan disposiciones sobre diversas contribuciones y prestaciones, a veces más directamente vinculadas a los niveles salariales y a la duración del servicio que en otros esquemas sociales. Cuando las contribuciones a esos regímenes son obligatorias o cuasiobligatorias (p. ej., en virtud de un acuerdo con sindicatos u organizaciones profesionales), se hacen constar en la partida informativa (véase el Capítulo 4.2 de este Reporte).

38. Las contribuciones de los empleados del gobierno y de este con respecto a sus empleados a los regímenes de seguridad social incluidos en el gobierno general se clasifican en esta categoría. También se consideran impuestos las contribuciones de los empleados del gobierno a regímenes diferentes que puedan reputarse sustitutivos de los regímenes generales de seguridad social.[16] Por el contrario, cuando un régimen diferente no pueda considerarse sustitutivo de uno general y haya sido negociado entre el gobierno, en su papel de empleador, y sus empleados, no se estimará como régimen de seguridad social y, por lo tanto, las contribuciones a él no se tendrán como impuestos, aunque el régimen haya sido instaurado por la legislación.

39. Esta categoría excluye las contribuciones "imputadas", que corresponden a las prestaciones sociales pagadas directamente por los empleadores a sus empleados, antiguos empleados o personas a cargo de estos (p. ej., cuando los empleadores están legalmente obligados a correr con las prestaciones por enfermedad durante cierto tiempo).

40. Las contribuciones se dividen en tres partidas principales –empleados (2100), empleadores (2200) y trabajadores por cuenta propia o no empleados (2300)– y se subdividen posteriormente en función de la base que gravan. A efectos de la presente

publicación, se entiende por empleados todas las personas contratadas en actividades de unidades empresariales, órganos gubernamentales, instituciones privadas sin ánimo de lucro u otro tipo de empleo remunerado, con excepción de los dueños de empresas no constituidas en sociedad y de los miembros no remunerados de sus familias. También se consideran empleados los miembros de las Fuerzas Armadas, independientemente de la duración y del tipo de su servicio, siempre que coticen a regímenes de la seguridad social. Por su parte, las contribuciones de los empleadores se definen como las aportaciones que estos realizan por cuenta de sus empleados a los sistemas de seguridad social. Si los empleados o los empleadores tienen la obligación de continuar cotizando a la seguridad social en el caso de desempleo de un empleado, esas contribuciones se muestran en las partidas 2100 y 2200, respectivamente, siempre que los datos lo permitan. En consecuencia, la partida 2300 queda reservada a las contribuciones abonadas por los trabajadores por cuenta propia y por quienes no se hallan incluidos en la población activa (p. ej., incapacitados o jubilados).

3000 – *Impuestos sobre la nómina y la fuerza de trabajo*

41. Esta categoría cubre los impuestos satisfechos por los empleadores, los empleados o los trabajadores por cuenta propia, ya como una proporción de la nómina, ya como una cantidad fija por persona, que no confieren derecho a prestaciones sociales. Como ejemplos de impuestos integrados en esta categoría, cabe citar la aportación al seguro nacional del Reino Unido (introducido en 1977), el impuesto sobre la nómina de Suecia (1969–1979) o la contribución al fondo de equiparación de la carga familiar e impuesto comunitario de Austria.

4000 – *Impuestos sobre la propiedad*

42. Esta categoría engloba los impuestos, recurrentes y no recurrentes, sobre el uso, la titularidad o la transmisión de la propiedad, lo que incluye impuestos sobre la propiedad inmueble y la riqueza neta, sobre el cambio de titularidad en la propiedad por herencia o donación, y sobre transacciones financieras y de capital. Quedan excluidas de esta categoría los siguientes tipos de impuestos:

a) los impuestos sobre las ganancias de capital procedentes de la venta de propiedad (1120 o 1220);

b) los impuestos sobre el uso de bienes y sobre el permiso para usar bienes o realizar actividades (5200): véase el § 72;

c) los impuestos sobre los bienes inmuebles gravados sobre la base de un ingreso neto presunto que tiene en cuenta las circunstancias personales del contribuyente: se clasifican como impuestos sobre la renta junto con los impuestos sobre la renta y sobre las ganancias de capital derivadas de la propiedad (1100);

d) los impuestos sobre el uso de la propiedad con fines residenciales, tanto si debe responder del impuesto el propietario como el arrendatario, siempre que la cantidad debida tenga en cuenta las circunstancias personales del usuario (ingresos, personas a cargo, etcétera): se integran en los impuestos sobre la renta (1100);

e) los impuestos sobre los edificios con una densidad máxima superior a la permitida; sobre la ampliación, construcción o modificación de ciertos edificios más allá de un valor umbral; y sobre la construcción de edificios: todos ellos se integran en los impuestos sobre el permiso para realizar actividades (5200);

f) los impuestos sobre el uso de la propiedad propia para fines comerciales especiales, tales como la venta de bebidas alcohólicas, tabaco o carne, o para la explotación de tierras (p. ej., impuestos sobre la extracción en Estados Unidos): se integran en los impuestos sobre el permiso para realizar actividades (5200).

4100 – *Impuestos recurrentes sobre la propiedad inmueble*

43. Esta partida comprende los impuestos con que se grava de forma regular el uso o la titularidad de bienes inmuebles.

- Estos impuestos gravan las tierras y los edificios.
- Pueden consistir en un porcentaje del valor tasado de una propiedad, basado a su vez en un ingreso por alquiler hipotético, en el precio de venta, en un rendimiento capitalizado o en otras características de la propiedad inmueble (por ejemplo, el tamaño o la ubicación) de las que quepa inferir un alquiler o un valor de capital hipotéticos.
- Estos impuestos pueden aplicarse a los propietarios, a los arrendatarios o a ambos. También pueden pagarse de un nivel de gobierno a otro en relación con los bienes bajo jurisdicción de este último.
- Para la evaluación de estos impuestos, no se tienen en cuenta las deudas y, en ese sentido, difieren de los impuestos sobre la riqueza neta.

44. Los impuestos recurrentes sobre la propiedad inmueble se subdividen a su vez en los pagados por los hogares (4110) y los abonados por otros sujetos pasivos (4120), de acuerdo con los criterios establecidos en el § 25(b) supra.

4200 – *Impuestos recurrentes sobre la riqueza neta*

45. Esta partida abarca los impuestos con que se grava periódicamente (por lo general, anualmente) la riqueza neta, esto es, los impuestos sobre un amplio abanico de bienes muebles e inmuebles, descontadas sus deudas. Esta partida se subdivide a su vez en los impuestos pagados por las personas físicas (4210) y los abonados por las sociedades (4220), de acuerdo con los criterios establecidos en el § 25(a) supra. Si existen cifras separadas para las entradas correspondientes a pagos realizados por instituciones, se añaden a la subpartida de las sociedades.

4300 – *Impuestos sobre sucesiones, herencias y donaciones*

46. Esta partida se divide entre impuestos sobre sucesiones o herencias (4310) e impuestos sobre donaciones (4320).[17] Los impuestos sobre sucesiones gravan el valor total de la sucesión o del caudal hereditario, mientras los impuestos sobre herencias se aplican a las cuotas recibidas por los causahabientes individualmente considerados o en función de la relación de estos con el difunto.

4400 – *Impuestos sobre transacciones financieras y de capital*

47. Esta partida incluye, entre otros, los impuestos sobre la emisión, transmisión, compra y venta de valores, sobre los cheques, y sobre transacciones legales específicas, tales como la validación de contratos o la venta de bienes inmuebles. La partida no incluye:

a) los impuestos sobre el uso de bienes y sobre el permiso para realizar ciertas actividades (5200);

b) las tasas abonadas en concepto de costos procesales o expedición de actas de nacimiento, matrimonio o defunción, que suelen considerarse como ingresos no tributarios (véase el § 9);

c) los impuestos sobre ganancias de capital (1000);

d) los impuestos recurrentes sobre la propiedad inmueble (4100);

e) los impuestos recurrentes sobre la riqueza neta (4200);

f) otros impuestos no recurrentes sobre la propiedad o la riqueza (4500).

4500 – *Otros impuestos no recurrentes sobre la propiedad*[17]

48. Esta partida cubre los gravámenes sobre la propiedad que, a diferencia de los impuestos recurrentes, se recaudan una sola vez. Se divide en impuestos no recurrentes sobre la riqueza neta (4510) y otros impuestos no recurrentes sobre la propiedad (4520). La subpartida 4510 contiene los impuestos que se recaudan a fin de hacer frente a gastos excepcionales o de redistribuir la riqueza. Por su parte, la subpartida 4520 comprende los impuestos que gravan los incrementos de valor de la tierra, debido, por ejemplo, a permisos para su desarrollo concedidos por el gobierno general o a la provisión por parte de este de instalaciones locales adicionales; cualesquiera impuestos sobre la reevaluación del capital; y aquellos impuestos gravados una sola vez sobre determinados tipos de propiedad.

4600 – *Otros impuestos recurrentes sobre la propiedad*

49. Aunque este tipo de impuestos rara vez se dan en los países miembros de la OCDE, esta partida incluye los impuestos sobre bienes tales como ganado bovino, joyas, ventanas y otros signos externos de riqueza.

5000 – *Impuestos sobre los bienes y servicios*

50. Se incluyen en esta categoría todos los impuestos y derechos sobre la producción, extracción, venta, transmisión, arrendamiento y entrega de bienes, así como sobre la prestación de servicios (5100), y también los impuestos aplicados al uso de bienes y al permiso para usar bienes o realizar actividades (5200). Por lo tanto, esta categoría comprende:

a) los impuestos acumulativos de etapas múltiples;

b) los impuestos generales sobre las ventas aplicados, ya sea en la fabricación/producción, ya sea en la venta al por mayor o al por menor;

c) los impuestos sobre el valor agregado;

d) los impuestos selectivos;

e) los impuestos sobre las importaciones y exportaciones de bienes;

f) los impuestos sobre el uso de bienes y sobre el permiso para usar bienes o realizar ciertas actividades;

g) los impuestos sobre la extracción, el procesamiento o la producción de minerales y otros productos.

51. Los casos de difícil delimitación entre esta categoría y la categoría 4000 (impuestos sobre la propiedad) o la partida 6100 (otros impuestos pagados únicamente por empresas) se tratan en los §§ 42, 47 y 74. La partida 5300 y la subpartida 5130, ambas residuales, incluyen, respectivamente, las entradas tributarias que no hayan podido clasificarse entre las partidas 5100 y 5200 o entre las subpartidas 5110 y 5120, respectivamente, veáse §27.

5100 – *Impuestos sobre la producción, venta, transmisión, arrendamiento y entrega de bienes, y la prestación de servicios*

52. Esta partida comprende todos los impuestos aplicados a transacciones de bienes y servicios por las características intrínsecas de estos (p. ej., valor, peso del tabaco, graduación de las bebidas alcohólicas, etcétera) a diferencia de los impuestos determinados por el uso de bienes o por el permiso para usar bienes o realizar actividades, que entran dentro del ámbito de la partida 5200.

5110 – *Impuestos generales*

53. En esta subpartida, se incluyen todos los impuestos, aparte de los derechos de importación y exportación (5123 y 5124, respectivamente), que gravan la producción, el arrendamiento, la transmisión, la entrega o la venta de un amplio abanico de bienes o la prestación de una gran variedad de servicios, independientemente de que sean de producción nacional o importados, o de la etapa de producción o de distribución en la que recaigan. Por ende, comprende los impuestos sobre el valor agregado, los impuestos sobre las ventas y los impuestos acumulativos de etapas múltiples. A las entradas brutas generadas, se añaden las entradas por ajustes fronterizos en concepto de esos impuestos cuando se importan bienes, y se restan las devoluciones de dichos impuestos cuando se exportan bienes. Esta subpartida se divide a su vez en los epígrafes 5111, impuestos sobre el valor agregado; 5112, impuestos sobre las ventas; y 5113, otros impuestos generales sobre los bienes y servicios.

54. Suelen plantearse dificultades de delimitación entre esta subpartida y la dedicada a los impuestos sobre bienes y servicios específicos (5120) cuando los impuestos se aplican a un gran número de bienes, como, por ejemplo, en el caso del impuesto sobre las compras del Reino Unido (abolido en 1973) o el impuesto sobre mercancías de Japón (abolido en 1988). De acuerdo con las respectivas perspectivas nacionales, el antiguo impuesto sobre las compras británico se ha clasificado como impuesto general (5112), mientras el desaparecido impuesto sobre mercancías japonés se ha incluido entre los impuestos selectivos (5121).

5111 – *Impuestos sobre el valor agregado*

55. Todos los impuestos generales al consumo cargados sobre el valor agregado entran dentro de este epígrafe, independientemente del método de deducción y de las etapas en las que recaiga el impuesto. En la práctica, todos los países de la OCDE con este tipo de impuestos permiten que todos los intermediarios, excepto el consumidor final, se deduzcan inmediatamente los impuestos sobre las compras e imponen tributación en todas las etapas. Para algunos países, puede que se incluyan en este epígrafe otros impuestos, tales como los aplicados sobre actividades financieras y de seguros, o bien porque las entradas que generan no pueden identificarse separadamente de las procedentes del impuesto sobre el valor agregado, o bien porque se considera que forman parte de este último, aunque esos mismos impuestos puedan clasificarse diferentemente en terceros países (p. ej., como impuestos sobre servicios específicos (5126) o impuestos sobre transacciones financieras y de capital (4400).

5112 – *Impuestos sobre las ventas*

56. Se clasifican aquí todos los impuestos generales aplicados a una sola etapa, ya sea en la fabricación/producción, o en la venta al por mayor o al por menor.

5113 – *Otros impuestos generales sobre los bienes y servicios*

57. Este epígrafe comprende los impuestos acumulativos de etapas múltiples (también conocidos como "impuestos en cascada"), en los que el impuesto se aplica cada vez que se realiza una transacción sin deducción del valor del impuesto pagado sobre los insumos, así como los impuestos generales al consumo cuando estos combinan elementos de los impuestos sobre el valor agregado, sobre las ventas o en cascada.

5120 – *Impuestos sobre bienes y servicios específicos*

58. Se incluyen en esta subpartida los impuestos selectivos, las utilidades generadas y transferidas por los monopolios fiscales, y los derechos de aduana y otros derechos de importación, así como los impuestos sobre las exportaciones, las transacciones de divisas, los bienes de inversión y las apuestas, y los impuestos especiales sobre los servicios que no formen parte de uno de los impuestos generales de la subpartida 5110.

5121 – *Impuestos selectivos*

59. Los impuestos selectivos son impuestos que se aplican a productos particulares o a un abanico limitado de productos, que no pueden clasificarse ni en 5110 (impuestos generales) ni en 5123 (derechos de aduana y otros derechos de importación) ni en 5124 (impuestos sobre las exportaciones). Pueden imponerse en cualquier etapa de la producción o la distribución, y suelen determinarse por referencia al peso, la graduación o la cantidad del producto, aunque, en ocasiones, también en función del valor de éste. Se incluyen, por lo tanto, en este epígrafe, los impuestos especiales sobre, por ejemplo, el azúcar, la remolacha, los fósforos o el chocolate; los impuestos a tasas impositivas variables sobre una cierta gama de bienes; y los impuestos que gravan en la mayoría de los países los productos derivados del tabaco, las bebidas alcohólicas, y los aceites de hidrocarburos y otras fuentes de energía.

60. Los impuestos selectivos se distinguen de:

a) los impuestos generales (5110): abordado en los §§ 53 y 54;

b) los derechos de aduana y otros derechos de importación (5123): si un impuesto recaudado principalmente sobre los bienes importados también se aplica, o podría aplicarse, de conformidad con la misma ley que establece el impuesto, a bienes comparables producidos en el país, las entradas de dicho impuesto se clasifican como impuestos selectivos (5121); este principio rige incluso cuando no existan productos nacionales comparables ni la posibilidad de que se produzcan (véase el § 64);

c) los impuestos sobre servicios específicos (5126): el problema se plantea en relación con los impuestos sobre la electricidad, el gas y la energía, que se consideran impuestos sobre los bienes y se incluyen en el epígrafe 5121.

5122 – *Utilidades de los monopolios fiscales*

61. Este epígrafe comprende la parte de las utilidades de los monopolios fiscales transferida al gobierno general o usada para financiar gastos considerados como gastos del gobierno (véase el § 18). Las cantidades implicadas se registran cuando se transfieren al gobierno general o cuando se usan para gastos considerados como gastos del gobierno.

62. Los monopolios fiscales reflejan el ejercicio del poder tributario del gobierno mediante el uso de prerrogativas monopolísticas. Se trata de empresas públicas no financieras que ejercen un monopolio, en la mayoría de los casos sobre la producción o la distribución de tabaco, bebidas alcohólicas, sal, fósforos, cartas de juego, productos derivados del petróleo y productos agrícolas (es decir, sobre el tipo de productos susceptibles de estar sometidos, alternativa o adicionalmente, a los impuestos selectivos del epígrafe 5121), con el fin de recaudar ingresos para el gobierno que en otros países se obtienen gravando las operaciones que sobre dichos bienes efectúan las unidades empresariales privadas. El monopolio del gobierno puede intervenir en la etapa de producción o, en el caso de los establecimientos de licores propiedad del gobierno o bajo control de éste, en la etapa de distribución.

63. Cabe distinguir los monopolios fiscales de los servicios públicos, tales como el transporte ferroviario, la electricidad, los servicios de correos y otras comunicaciones, que pueden gozar también de una posición monopolística o cuasimonopolística, pero cuyo fin primero suele ser la prestación de servicios básicos y no la obtención de ingresos para el gobierno; las transferencias de esas otras empresas públicas al gobierno se consideran ingresos no tributarios. Generalmente, el concepto tradicional de monopolio fiscal no abarca a las loterías estatales, cuyas utilidades usualmente se consideran, en consecuencia, ingresos no tributarios. No obstante, se pueden considerar como ingresos tributarios si su función principal es la de recaudar para financiar gasto gubernamental.

Las utilidades de los monopolios fiscales se han separado de las de los monopolios de importación y exportación (5127) transferidas de juntas de comercialización u otras empresas dedicadas al comercio internacional.

5123 – *Derechos de aduana y otros derechos de importación*

64. Se incluyen aquí los impuestos, derechos de timbre y sobrecargas limitados por ley a los productos importados, así como los gravámenes sobre los productos agrícolas importados impuestos en los países miembros de la Unión Europea y las cantidades satisfechas por algunos de esos países a tenor del sistema de montantes compensatorios monetarios (MCM).[18] Desde 1998, los derechos de aduana recaudados por los Estados miembros de la Unión Europea en nombre de ésta ya no se registran en este epígrafe en los cuadros de países (Capítulo 4 de la publicación *Revenue Statistics* de la OCDE). Quedan excluidos aquí los impuestos recaudados de las importaciones como parte de un impuesto general sobre los bienes y servicios, así como los impuestos selectivos aplicables tanto a bienes importados como a bienes de producción nacional.

5124 – *Impuestos sobre las exportaciones*

65. En los años 1970, los derechos de exportación se aplicaban en Australia, Canadá y Portugal como una medida de carácter regular, y en Finlandia se han utilizado con fines contracíclicos. Algunos países miembros de la Unión Europea pagan un gravamen sobre las exportaciones, en el marco del sistema MCM (véase la nota a pie de página 16 en el § 64). Cuando las cantidades recaudadas son identificables, se integran en este epígrafe, que no incluye, sin embargo, las devoluciones de impuestos generales al consumo, de impuestos selectivos o de derechos de aduana sobre los bienes exportados, que se deducirán de las entradas brutas de 5110, 5121 o 5123, según corresponda.

5125 – *Impuestos sobre los bienes de inversión*

66. Este epígrafe cubre los impuestos sobre los bienes de inversión, tales como la maquinaria. Estos impuestos pueden cargarse por un cierto número de años o temporalmente con fines contracíclicos. No se incluyen aquí aquellos impuestos sobre los insumos industriales que recaen también en los consumidores (p. ej., el impuesto sobre la energía en Suecia, que se clasifica en 5121).

5126 – *Impuestos sobre servicios específicos*

67. Todos los impuestos sobre el pago por servicios específicos, tales como los impuestos sobre las primas de seguro, los servicios bancarios, los juegos de azar y las apuestas (p. ej., carreras de caballos, quinielas de fútbol, lotería), el transporte, las actividades recreativas o de ocio, los restaurantes y la publicidad, entran dentro de este epígrafe. También se clasifican aquí los impuestos sobre el ingreso bruto de las empresas que prestan el servicio (p. ej., primas de seguro o apuestas brutas recibidas por una empresa). Los ingresos tributarios procedentes de gravámenes bancarios y pagos a sistemas de seguro de depósitos y de estabilidad financiera se han incluido provisionalmente en este epígrafe para la edición de 2012. La clasificación detallada figura en el párrafo 104.

68. Se excluyen de este epígrafe:

a) los impuestos sobre servicios que formen parte de un impuesto general sobre los bienes y servicios (5110);

b) los impuestos sobre la electricidad, el gas y la energía (5121, impuestos selectivos);

c) los impuestos sobre las ganancias de las personas físicas en los juegos de azar (1120, impuestos sobre las ganancias de capital de las personas físicas o de las empresas no constituidas en sociedad) y los impuestos fijos sobre la transferencia de loterías privadas o sobre el permiso para crear loterías (5200);[19]

d) los impuestos sobre los cheques y sobre la emisión, transmisión o compra y venta de valores (4400, impuestos sobre transacciones financieras y de capital).

5127 – *Otros impuestos sobre el comercio y las transacciones internacionales*

69. Este epígrafe abarca los ingresos percibidos por el gobierno por la compra y la venta de divisas a diferentes tipos de cambio. Cuando el gobierno ejerce poderes monopolísticos para obtener un margen entre los precios de compra y de venta de divisas superior al que sería necesario para cubrir los costos administrativos, el ingreso generado constituye un gravamen obligatorio impuesto en proporciones indeterminadas tanto sobre el comprador como sobre el vendedor de divisas. Es un equivalente común de los derechos de importación y exportación cargados en un sistema con tipo de cambio único o de un impuesto sobre la compraventa de divisas. Al igual que las utilidades de los monopolios fiscales o de los monopolios de importación y exportación transferidas al gobierno, representa el ejercicio de las prerrogativas monopolísticas con fines fiscales y, por lo tanto, se incluye en los ingresos tributarios.

70. El epígrafe engloba asimismo las utilidades de los monopolios de importación y exportación, que, sin embargo, son inexistentes en los países de la OCDE; los impuestos sobre la compraventa de divisas; y cualesquiera otros impuestos que recaigan sobre el comercio o las transacciones internacionales.

5128 – *Otros impuestos sobre bienes y servicios específicos*

71. Este epígrafe incluye los impuestos sobre la extracción de minerales, combustibles fósiles y otros recursos agotables de yacimientos de propiedad privada o de otro nivel de gobierno, así como cualesquiera otras entradas no identificables procedentes de impuestos sobre bienes y servicios específicos. Los impuestos sobre la extracción de recursos agotables suelen traducirse en un importe fijo por cantidad o peso, pero también pueden adoptar un valor porcentual. Los impuestos se registran en el momento de extracción de los recursos. Los pagos por extracción de recursos agotables de yacimientos propiedad de la unidad de gobierno que recibe el pago se clasifican como alquiler.

5200 – *Impuestos sobre el uso de bienes y sobre el permiso para usar bienes o realizar actividades*

72. Esta partida incluye los impuestos aplicados al uso de bienes a diferencia de los impuestos sobre los propios bienes. Al contrario que los impuestos de este último tipo (registrados en la partida 5100), los impuestos considerados aquí no se basan en el valor de los bienes, sino que suelen revestir la forma de importes fijos. Los impuestos sobre el permiso para usar bienes o realizar actividades entran asimismo en esta partida, como, por ejemplo, los impuestos sobre la contaminación que no se basan en el valor de bienes particulares. En ocasiones, resulta complejo distinguir entre cargos obligatorios a los usuarios y tasas de licencia que se consideran como impuestos y aquellos que quedan excluidos por reputarse como ingresos no tributarios; los criterios de deslinde empleados se explican en los §§ 9 y 10.

73. Aunque el título de esta partida menciona el "uso" de bienes, es posible que sea el registro de la propiedad, y no el uso, lo que dé lugar a la obligación tributaria, y que los impuestos contenidos aquí se apliquen más al hecho de ser titular de ciertos animales o bienes (p. ej., caballos de carreras, perros y vehículos automotores) que al uso que se hace de ellos, o que recaigan incluso en bienes inutilizables (p. ej., vehículos automotores o armas inservibles).

74. Se plantean casos de difícil delimitación con respecto a:

a) los impuestos sobre el permiso para realizar actividades empresariales que parten de una base combinada de renta, nómina o volumen de ventas, que se clasifican de acuerdo con las normas del § 77;

b) los impuestos sobre la propiedad o el uso de la propiedad de las partidas 4100, 4200 y 4600; la partida 4100 se dedica exclusivamente a los impuestos sobre la titularidad o la posesión de bienes inmuebles y, a diferencia de los impuestos de la partida 5200, recaen siempre sobre el valor de la propiedad; los impuestos sobre la riqueza neta (4200) y otros impuestos recurrentes sobre la propiedad (4600) se circunscriben al hecho de ser titular de propiedades, y no al uso de activos; se aplican a grupos de activos, y no a bienes particulares; y están en todo caso relacionados con el valor de los activos en cuestión.

5210 – *Impuestos recurrentes*

75. La principal característica de los impuestos consignados aquí es que se recaudan a intervalos regulares y se cobran por lo general según una cantidad fija. En términos de ingresos, el elemento más importante está constituido por los impuestos por licencia de vehículos, aunque también integran esta subpartida los impuestos sobre los permisos de caza, pesca o tiro o sobre la venta de ciertos productos, así como los impuestos sobre la propiedad de animales domésticos y sobre la prestación de ciertos servicios siempre que estos reúnan los criterios establecidos en los §§ 9 y 10. Los epígrafes en que se divide la partida 5210 son: los impuestos sobre vehículos automotores pagados por los hogares (5211) y los satisfechos por otros sujetos pasivos (5212);[20] por su parte, el epígrafe 5213 abarca las licencias a propietarios de animales domésticos y los cargos a usuarios por el permiso de realizar actividades, tales como la venta de carne o de bebidas alcohólica cuando los gravámenes se imponen de forma recurrente, así como las licencias generales periódicas de caza, pesca y tiro cuando el derecho a emprender esas actividades no se otorga como parte de una transacción comercial normal (p. ej., la concesión de la licencia no implica el derecho a usar una zona específica propiedad del gobierno).

5220 – *Impuestos no recurrentes*

76. Se incluyen aquí los impuestos no recurrentes aplicados sobre el uso de bienes y sobre el permiso para utilizar bienes o realizar actividades, así como los impuestos aplicados cada vez que se utilizan los bienes.

- Entran en esta subpartida los impuestos sobre la emisión o liberación en el medio ambiente de gases y líquidos nocivos y otras sustancias peligrosas. Los pagos por permisos negociables de emisión expedidos por los gobiernos en el marco de programas de límites máximos y comercio de emisiones deberán registrarse aquí en la fecha en que se produzcan las emisiones. No se computarán ingresos por los permisos que los gobiernos expidan a título gratuito.
- El registro según el criterio de devengo implica que habrá una diferencia temporal entre el momento en que el gobierno reciba el pago por los permisos y el momento en que se produzca la emisión. En las cuentas nacionales, esta diferencia genera un pasivo para el gobierno durante ese periodo.
- Se excluirán los pagos efectuados por la recogida y eliminación de desechos o sustancias nocivas por parte de los poderes públicos, ya que constituyen una venta de servicios a las empresas.

77. También se incluyen aquí otros impuestos que entren dentro del ámbito de aplicación de la partida 5200 y que no se recauden recurrentemente. Por lo tanto, quedarán comprendidos los pagos únicos por permisos para la venta de alcohol o tabaco o para la creación de centros de apuestas, siempre que cumplan los criterios de los §§ 9 y 10.

6000 – *Otros impuestos*

78. Esta categoría recoge los impuestos que reposan en una o varias bases diferentes de las descritas en las categorías 1000, 3000, 4000 y 5000, o en bases que no puedan considerarse predominantemente las mismas que las incluidas en esas categorías. En relación con los impuestos de base múltiple, si es posible estimar las entradas relacionadas con cada base (p. ej., el impuesto Gewerbesteuer en Alemania y Austria), las cantidades desglosadas se repartirán en las correspondientes categorías. Si no pueden calcularse los valores por separado, pero se sabe que la mayoría de las entradas proceden de una base determinada, el total de estas se atribuirán de acuerdo con dicha base. Si no puede seguirse ninguno de estos procedimientos, las entradas se clasificarán aquí. Las diversas partidas de esta categoría podrán incluir asimismo el producto de impuestos que los gobiernos no puedan identificar o aislar (véase el § 27). Se incorporan asimismo aquí las multas y sanciones pecuniarias pagadas por el incumplimiento de normas tributarias, pero no imputables a una categoría particular de impuestos (véase el § 14). Esta categoría se subdivide entre los impuestos pagados completa o principalmente por las empresas (6100) y los abonados por otros sujetos pasivos (6200).

A.6. Conciliación con las cuentas nacionales

79. Esta sección de los cuadros reconcilia el cálculo de la recaudación tributaria total realizado por la OCDE y el total de todos los impuestos y contribuciones sociales pagados al gobierno general tal y como figuran en el registro de las cuentas nacionales de cada país. Cuando el país es miembro de la Unión Europea (UE), la comparación se establece entre el cálculo de la recaudación tributaria total realizado por la OCDE y la suma de los ingresos tributarios y contribuciones sociales registrado en la combinación del gobierno general y de las instituciones de los sectores de la UE de las cuentas nacionales.

A.7. Partida informativa sobre el financiamiento de las prestaciones sociales

80. A la vista de la variedad de relaciones entre la tributación y las contribuciones a la seguridad social y de los casos mencionados en los §§ 34–40, se ha previsto una partida informativa que recopile todos los pagos asignados a las prestaciones tipo de la seguridad social, aparte de los pagos voluntarios al sector privado. Los datos se presentan de la forma siguiente (véase el Capítulo 4.2 de este Reporte):

a) Impuestos de la categoría 2000.

b) Impuestos asignados a las prestaciones de la seguridad social.

c) Contribuciones voluntarias al gobierno.

d) Contribuciones obligatorias al sector privado.

Los §§ 34–40 ofrecen las debidas orientaciones para efectuar el desglose entre las rúbricas (a) a (d).

A.8. Partida informativa sobre impuestos identificables pagados por el gobierno

81. Los impuestos identificables realmente pagados por el gobierno se presentan en una partida informativa, desglosados según las principales categorías de la clasificación de impuestos de la OCDE. En la vasta mayoría de los países, sólo pueden identificarse las contribuciones a la seguridad social y los impuestos sobre la nómina satisfechos por el gobierno, que, sin embargo, suelen ser los gravámenes más importantes liquidados por los gobiernos (véase el Capítulo 4.3 de este Reporte).

A.9. Relación de la clasificación de impuestos de la OCDE con el Sistema de Cuentas Nacionales

82. El Sistema de Cuentas Nacionales (SCN) pretende proporcionar un marco coherente para registrar y presentar los principales flujos relacionados con la producción, el consumo, la acumulación y las transacciones con el exterior de una determinada zona económica, por lo general, un país o una región destacada de un país, y, en este sentido, los ingresos del gobierno constituyen una importante parte de las transacciones registradas en todo sistema de cuentas nacionales. En agosto de 2009, la versión final del SCN 2008 se publicó conjuntamente por cinco organizaciones internacionales: la Organización de las Naciones Unidas, el Fondo Monetario Internacional, la Unión Europea, la Organización para la Cooperación y el Desarrollo Económicos, y el Banco Mundial. La publicación está diseñada para ser empleada en países con economías de mercado, sea cual sea su estadio de desarrollo económico, así como en países en transición hacia economías de mercado. Las principales partes del marco conceptual y las definiciones de los diversos sectores económicos del SCN se han plasmado en la clasificación de impuestos de la OCDE.

83. Sin embargo, existen ciertas diferencias, reseñadas seguidamente, entre la clasificación de impuestos de la OCDE y los conceptos del SCN, debidas a que la finalidad de la clasificación de la OCDE consiste en lograr la máxima desagregación posible de los datos estadísticos en relación con lo que, por lo general, las Administraciones tributarias consideran como impuestos. Y así:

a) la OCDE incluye las contribuciones a la seguridad social obligatorias, pagadas al gobierno general en la recaudación tributaria total. No se consideran como impuestos las contribuciones imputadas y voluntarias, además de aquellas pagadas a fondos privados (véase los §§ 7 y 8 *supra*.);

b) los puntos de vista sobre la calificación de algunos gravámenes y tasas como impuestos son diferentes (§§ 9 y 10 *supra*.);

c) la OCDE excluye los impuestos imputados o los subsidios procedentes de la aplicación de múltiples tipos de cambio oficiales, o del pago de una tasa diferente a otras del mercado sobre reservas requeridas que pueda hacer el banco central;

d) los créditos fiscales exigibles se tratan de forma diferente.

84. Tal y como se ha apuntado en los §§ 1 y 2, las categorías 1000 a 6000 de la lista de impuestos de la OCDE cubren todos los pagos sin contraprestación al gobierno general, aparte de las multas y los préstamos obligatorios. Esos pagos sin contraprestación, incluidas las multas pero excluidos los préstamos obligatorios, pueden obtenerse añadiendo los siguientes valores del SCN 2008:

- impuestos sobre el valor agregado (D211);
- impuestos y derechos sobre las importaciones, IVA no incluido (D212);
- impuestos sobre las exportaciones (D213);
- impuestos sobre los productos, IVA e impuestos sobre las importaciones y exportaciones no incluidos (D214);
- otros impuestos sobre la producción (D29);
- impuestos sobre la renta (D51);
- otros impuestos corrientes (D59);
- contribuciones sociales (D61), excluidas las contribuciones voluntarias;
- impuestos sobre el capital (D91).

A.10. Relación de la clasificación de impuestos de la OCDE con el sistema de estadísticas de finanzas públicas del Fondo Monetario Internacional

85. La cobertura y la valoración de los ingresos tributarios en el sistema de estadísticas de finanzas públicas (EFP) y en el SCN 2008 son muy similares. Por lo tanto, a excepción del tratamiento dado a los créditos fiscales exigibles, las diferencias entre la clasificación de la OCDE y la del SCN 2008 (véase el § 83 *supra.*) son de aplicación igualmente al sistema de EFP. Además, el Fondo Monetario Internacional (FMI) escinde la categoría única 5000 de la OCDE en dos categorías distintas dedicadas a los impuestos nacionales sobre bienes y servicios (114) y a los impuestos sobre el comercio y las transacciones internacionales (115). Esto refleja el hecho de que, mientras estos últimos impuestos suelen generar insignificantes cantidades de ingresos en la zona de la OCDE, ese no es el caso en la mayoría de los países no pertenecientes a la Organización.

A.11. Comparación de la clasificación de impuestos de la OCDE con otras clasificaciones internacionales

86. El cuadro siguiente recoge una comparación ítem por ítem entre la clasificación de impuestos de la OCDE y las clasificaciones empleadas en:

i) el Sistema de Cuentas Nacionales (SCN 2008);

ii) el Sistema Europeo de Cuentas (SEC 1995);

iii) el *Manual de estadísticas de finanzas públicas* del FMI (MEFP 2001).

87. Estas comparaciones representan equivalencias que podrán aplicarse en la mayoría de los casos. Con todo, deberán emplearse con cierta flexibilidad, ya que, en casos particulares, los países pueden adoptar enfoques diferentes para la clasificación de los ingresos en las cuentas nacionales.

Clasificación de la OCDE		SCN 2008	SEC 2010	MEFP 2014
1000	Impuestos sobre la renta, las utilidades y las ganancias de capital			
	1100 Personas físicas			
	1110 Renta/utilidades	D51-8.61a	D51A	1111
	1120 Ganancias de capital	D51-8.61c,d	D51C,D	1111
	1200 Sociedades			
	1210 Renta/utilidades	D51-8.61b	D51B	1112
	1220 Ganancias de capital	D51-8.61c	D51C	1112
	1300 No clasificables entre 1100 y 1200			1113
2000	Contribuciones a la seguridad social			
	2100 Empleados	D613-8.85	D613	1211
	2200 Empleadores	D611-8.83	D611	1212
	2300 Trabajadores por cuenta propia o no empleados	D613-8.85	D613	1213
	2400 No clasificables entre 2100, 2200 y 2300			1214
3000	Impuestos sobre la nómina y la fuerza de trabajo	D29-7.97a	D29C	112
4000	Impuestos sobre la propiedad			
	4100 Impuestos recurrentes sobre la propiedad inmueble			
	4110 Hogares	D59-8.63a	D59A	1131
	4120 Otros	D29-7.97b	D29A	1131
	4200 Impuestos recurrentes sobre la riqueza neta			
	4210 Personas físicas	D59-8.63b	D59A	1132
	4220 Sociedades	D59-8.63b	D59A	1132
	4300 Impuestos sobre sucesiones, herencias y donaciones			
	4310 Impuestos sobre sucesiones y herencias	D91-10.207b	D91A	1133
	4320 Impuestos sobre donaciones	D91-10.207b	D91A	1133
	4400 Impuestos sobre transacciones financieras y de capital	D59-7.96d; D29-7.97e	D214B,C	1134:1161
	4500 Otros impuestos no recurrentes sobre la propiedad	D91-10.207a	D91B	1135
	4600 Otros impuestos recurrentes sobre la propiedad	D59-8.63c	D59A	1136
5000	Impuestos sobre los bienes y servicios			
	5100 Impuestos sobre la producción, venta y transmisión de bienes y prestación de servicios			
	5110 Impuestos generales sobre bienes y servicios			
	5111 Impuestos sobre el valor agregado	D211-7.89	D211; D29G	11411
	5112 Impuestos sobre las ventas	D2122-7.94a; D214-7.96a	D21224; D214I	11412
	5113 Otros impuestos generales sobre los bienes y servicios	D214-7.96a	D214I	11413
	5120 Impuestos sobre bienes y servicios específicos			
	5121 Impuestos selectivos	D2122-7.94b; D214-7.96b	D21223; D214A,B,D	1142
	5122 Utilidades de los monopolios fiscales	D214-7.65e	D214J	1143
	5123 Derechos de aduanas y otros derechos de importación	D2121-7.93	D2121; D2122A,B	1151
	5124 Sobre las exportaciones	D213-7.95a	D214K	1152-4
	5125 Sobre los bienes de inversión			
	5126 Sobre servicios específicos	D2122-7.94c; D214-7.96c	D21225; D214E,F,G; D29F	1144; 1156
	5127 Otros impuestos sobre el comercio y las transacciones internacionales	D2122-7.94d D29-7.95b D29-7.97g D59-8.64d	D21226; D29D D59E	1153 1155-6
	5128 Otros impuestos sobre bienes y servicios específicos			1146
	5130 No clasificables entre 5110 y 5120			
	5200 Impuestos sobre el uso de bienes y sobre el permiso para usar bienes y realizar actividades			
	5210 Impuestos recurrentes			
	5211 Sobre vehículos automotores: hogares	D59-8.64c	D59D	11451
	5212 Sobre vehículos automotores: otros	D29-7.97d	D214D; D29B	11451
	5213 Otros impuestos recurrentes	D29-7.97c,d,f D59-8.64c	D29B,E,F; D59D	11452
	5220 Impuestos no recurrentes			
	5300 No clasificables entre 5100 y 5200			
6000	Otros impuestos			
	6100 Pagados únicamente por empresas			1161
	6200 Pagados por otros distintos de las empresas o no identificables	D59-8.64a,b	D59B,C	1162

A.12. Atribución de ingresos tributarios por subsectores del gobierno general

88. La clasificación de la OCDE requiere un desglose de los ingresos tributarios por subsectores del gobierno general. Seguidamente, se establecen la definición de cada subsector y los criterios que deben emplearse para atribuir los ingresos tributarios entre ellos, que siguen las orientaciones del SCN 2008 y del MEFP 2014.

Identificación de los subsectores del gobierno general

a) Gobierno central

89. El subsector del gobierno central incluye todos los departamentos, oficinas y establecimientos del gobierno, así como otros órganos que constituyen organismos o instrumentos de la autoridad central, cuya competencia se extiende a todo el territorio, con excepción de la administración de los fondos de seguridad social. En consecuencia, el gobierno central tiene la facultad de someter a tributación a todas las unidades residentes y no residentes que emprendan actividades económicas en el país.

b) Gobierno estatal, provincial o regional

90. Este subsector está compuesto por unidades intermedias del gobierno que ejercen su competencia a un nivel inferior al del gobierno central. Incluye a todas las unidades que operan independientemente del gobierno central en una parte del territorio de un país que engloba numerosas pequeñas localidades, con la excepción de la administración de los fondos de seguridad social. En los países unitarios, puede considerarse que los gobiernos regionales tienen una existencia separada, en la que cuentan con la suficiente autonomía como para recaudar sus ingresos de fuentes bajo su control, y sus funcionarios son independientes del control administrativo externo en el ejercicio de las actividades de la unidad.

91. En la actualidad, los países federales representan la mayoría de los casos en los que los ingresos atribuidos a unidades intermedias del gobierno se identifican de forma separada. España es el único país unitario en ese caso; en el resto de los países unitarios, los ingresos regionales se computan junto con los de los gobiernos locales.

c) Gobierno local

92. Este subsector incluye todas las demás unidades del gobierno que ejercen una competencia independiente en parte del territorio de un país, con excepción de la administración de los fondos de seguridad social. Engloba varios entes urbanos o rurales (p. ej., autoridades locales, municipios, ciudades, delegaciones, distritos).

d) Fondos de seguridad social

93. Los fondos de seguridad social forman un subsector separado del gobierno general. El SCN 2008 define el subsector de la seguridad social según lo expuesto en sus párrafos 4.124 a 4.126 y 4.147, citados seguidamente:

> "Los regímenes de seguridad social son sistemas de seguros sociales que cubren a la comunidad en su conjunto o a amplios sectores de la misma, y que son impuestos y controlados por unidades del gobierno. Los sistemas abarcan una gran variedad de programas, y ofrecen prestaciones en dinero o en especie por vejez, invalidez o muerte, supervivencia, enfermedad y maternidad, accidentes de trabajo, desempleo, ayudas familiares, asistencia sanitaria, etc. No existe necesariamente una relación directa entre la cuantía de la contribución pagada por un individuo y las prestaciones que este pueda recibir." (Párrafo 4.124)

"Cuando los sistemas de seguridad social se organizan por separado de las demás actividades de las unidades del gobierno, mantienen sus activos y pasivos separados de estas últimas, y realizan operaciones financieras por cuenta propia, se califican de unidades institucionales, que reciben el nombre de fondos de seguridad social." (Párrafo 4.125)

"Las cantidades recaudadas y pagadas por contribuciones y prestaciones de la seguridad social pueden modificarse deliberadamente con el fin de alcanzar determinados objetivos de la política del gobierno que no tengan relación directa con el concepto de la seguridad social como sistema destinado a ofrecer prestaciones sociales a los miembros de la comunidad. Pueden aumentarse o disminuirse, por ejemplo, con el fin de influir en el nivel de la demanda agregada de la economía. No obstante, mientras se mantengan como fondos constituidos por separado, han de ser tratados, en el SCN, como unidades institucionales diferentes." (Párrafo 4.126)

"El subsector de los fondos de seguridad social [del gobierno general] está conformado por los fondos de seguridad social que operan en todos los niveles del gobierno. Dichos fondos son sistemas de seguros sociales que cubren a la comunidad en su conjunto o a amplios sectores de la misma, y que son impuestos por unidades del gobierno." (Párrafo 4.147)

94. La clasificación de la OCDE sigue esta definición de los fondos de seguridad social con las dos siguientes excepciones, por las se excluyen:

- os sistemas impuestos por el gobierno pero administrados por órganos externos al sector del gobierno general, tal y como se ha definido en el § 3 de este manual, y
- los sistemas en los que todas las contribuciones son voluntarias.

Autoridades supranacionales

95. Este subsector engloba las operaciones de recaudación fiscal de autoridades supranacionales dentro de un país. En la práctica, la única autoridad supranacional que cabe tener en cuenta en la zona de la OCDE es la que conforman las instituciones de la Unión Europea (UE). Desde 1998, las autoridades supranacionales no se incluyen en *Revenue Statistics*, a fin de ser coherentes con la definición que el SCN da del gobierno general, que las excluye. Por ejemplo, los impuestos sobre la renta y las contribuciones a la seguridad social recaudados por instituciones europeas y pagados a empleados públicos europeos que residen en países miembros de la OCDE no deberían incluirse. Pese a todo, ciertos gravámenes específicos pagados por los Estados miembros de la UE siguen incorporándose a la recaudación tributaria total y, en ese caso, se muestran bajo esta denominación.

Criterios de atribución de los ingresos tributarios

96. Cuando un gobierno recauda impuestos y los transfiere, en todo o en parte, a otros gobiernos, es necesario determinar si esos ingresos se imputarán al gobierno recaudador que los distribuye a otros en forma de donaciones, o si se atribuirán a los gobiernos beneficiarios para los que el gobierno recaudador actúa como mero agente, recibiendo el producto de los impuestos y transfiriéndolos posteriormente. Los criterios de atribución de los ingresos se establecen en los §§ 97–100 siguientes, y siguen lo dispuesto en los puntos 3.70 a 3.73 del SCN 2008.

97. Por regla general, un impuesto se atribuye a la unidad de gobierno que:

a) ejerce la facultad de aplicar el impuesto (como entidad principal o a través de la autoridad delegada por la entidad principal), y

b) puede a su discreción establecer y modificar la tasa del impuesto.

98. Cuando un gobierno recauda impuestos para y en nombre de otro, y este último tiene la facultad de aplicar el impuesto y establecer y modificar su tasa impositiva, entonces el gobierno recaudador actúa como agente de este, y el impuesto se reasigna. Cualquier cantidad retenida por el gobierno recaudador como cargo por la recaudación deberá tratarse como pago por un servicio. Cualquier otra cantidad retenida por el gobierno recaudador, por ejemplo, en el marco de un arreglo de coparticipación de impuestos, deberá tratarse como una donación corriente. Si se delegó al gobierno recaudador la autoridad para establecer y modificar la tasa impositiva entonces las cantidades recaudadas deberán tratarse como ingresos tributarios de este gobierno.

99. Cuando diferentes gobiernos establecen conjuntamente y por igual la tasa de un impuesto y el uso de los recursos, sin que ninguno de ellos tengan la autoridad final y exclusiva, entonces los ingresos tributarios se atribuyen a cada gobierno según la proporción de recursos que le corresponda; si el acuerdo permite a una unidad del gobierno ejercer el control final y exclusivo, entonces todos los ingresos tributarios se atribuirán a dicha unidad.

100. También puede ocurrir que un gobierno tenga la autoridad constitucional o de otra índole de aplicar un impuesto, pero que otros gobiernos establezcan individualmente la tasa de ese impuesto en sus jurisdicciones; los recursos generados por el impuesto en cuestión en la jurisdicción de cada gobierno se atribuirán como ingresos tributarios a los respectivos gobiernos.

Gravámenes satisfechos por los Estados miembros de la Unión Europea

101. Los gravámenes satisfechos por los Estados miembros de la Unión Europea (UE) revisten la forma de:

a) derechos de aduana y gravámenes sobre los bienes agrícolas (5123),

b) cuentas de compensación monetaria brutas (5123 en relación con las importaciones y 5124 en relación con las exportaciones), y

c) gravámenes sobre el acero, el carbón, el azúcar y la leche (5128).

102. Los derechos de aduana recaudados por los Estados miembros de la UE en nombre de esta se registran de la siguiente forma:

- sobre la base de un coeficiente de recaudación bruta;
- ajustando los resultados, siempre que sea posible, de forma que esos derechos se muestren en relación con una base de "destino final", por oposición a la base de "país de primera entrada"; estos ajustes atañen particularmente a los derechos colectados en importantes puertos (marítimos); aunque los derechos de la UE se perciben por las autoridades del país de primera entrada, siempre que sea posible cabrá excluir esos derechos del ingreso del país recaudador e incluirlos en el ingreso del país de destino final.

103. Este es el gravamen específico de la UE que más claramente se ciñe al criterio de atribución consignado en el § 95. En consecuencia, desde 1998, las cantidades en relación con este gravamen se registran como partida informativa en los cuadros de países de los Estados miembros de la UE (en el Capítulo 4 de la publicación *Revenue Statistics* de la OCDE) y no se integran ya en la partida 5123. Sin embargo, se incluyen en las cifras de recaudación tributaria total de la línea superior para los años correspondientes mostrados en los cuadros.

A.13. Clasificación provisional de los ingresos tributarios procedentes de gravámenes bancarios y pagos a sistemas de seguro de depósitos y de estabilidad financiera

104. La OCDE ha adoptado el siguiente enfoque provisional para el registro de los ingresos procedentes de gravámenes bancarios, así como de seguro de depósitos y tasas de estabilidad para la edición 2012 de la publicación *Revenue Statistics* de la OCDE. Los importes deberán consignarse en la subpartida 5126.

- Los pagos obligatorios de tasas de estabilidad, gravámenes bancarios y primas de seguro de depósitos se tratarán por lo general como ingresos tributarios cuando se abonen al gobierno general y se asignen a los fondos consolidados o generales de este, de forma que el gobierno pueda utilizar libre e inmediatamente el dinero para los fines que elija. Este principio se aplicará independientemente de que el gobierno prometa revertir esos pagos para garantizar los depósitos de los clientes de los bancos en caso de necesidad futura.
- Si los pagos obligatorios se abonan al gobierno general y se destinan a fondos afectados exclusivamente a volver al sector de la economía que engloba a las sociedades sujetas a dichos pagos, éstos seguirán considerándose ingresos tributarios dado que los fondos estarán disponibles para el gobierno y podrán reducir su déficit presupuestario, que la tasa no conlleva contraprestación para una entidad individual y que las cantidades recaudadas no tienen relación con cualquier pago posterior a los depositantes o cualquier gasto realizado como medio de respaldo más amplio al sector financiero.
- Se clasificarán como tasa por servicio los pagos que deban aportarse a sistemas permanentes más reducidos para garantizar los depósitos de "particulares" cuando los niveles de pago concuerden con el coste del seguro.
- También se clasificarán como tasa por servicio, y no como ingreso tributario, los pagos que impliquen que el gobierno ejecute los activos de una institución en quiebra o tenga un derecho prioritario sobre la liquidación de activos de esta con objeto de financiar los pagos de compensación a los clientes por la pérdida de sus depósitos.

No se tratarán como ingresos tributarios los pagos obligatorios destinados a fondos externos al sector de gobierno y a instituciones no estatales respaldadas por los tomadores de depósitos, ni los pagos hechos a sistemas voluntarios.

Notas

1. Las referencias en la Guía de interpretación de la OCDE a las secciones o partes de "este reporte" se refieren a OCDE (2016), *Revenue Statistics 2016* (Estadísticas tributarias 2016), Publicaciones de la OCDE, París.
2. Todas las referencias al SCN deberán entenderse hechas a la edición de 2008.
3. Véase el apartado A.12 de la presente guía para el análisis del concepto de agente.
4. Por lo general, es posible identificar la cuantía de las contribuciones a la seguridad social y de los impuestos sobre la nómina, pero no otros impuestos asumidos por el gobierno.
5. Sin embargo, si un gravamen considerado como ingreso no tributario en la mayoría de los países se califica de tributario – o permite recaudar sustanciales ingresos – en uno o más países, las entradas en concepto de dicho gravamen se indican en las notas que figuran al pie de los cuadros de países, pero no se incluyen en la recaudación tributaria total.
6. Obsérvese, no obstante, que los nombres pueden dar lugar a confusión. Por ejemplo, aunque una tasa sobre los pasaportes se trataría normalmente como ingreso no tributario, si se impone un gravamen suplementario sobre los pasaportes (como en el caso de Portugal) con el fin de conseguir un ingreso sustancialmente mayor que el costo que supone proporcionar el pasaporte, dicho gravamen deberá considerarse como un impuesto sobre el uso de bienes (5200).
7. Para una explicación más detallada de esta distinción, consúltese el estudio especial sobre cuestiones de actualidad en relación con el registro de los ingresos tributarios Current issues in reporting tax revenues, en la edición 2001 de Revenue Statistics.
8. En ocasiones, se emplean asimismo los términos "no reembolsable" y "reembolsable", pero puede parecer ilógico hablar de "reembolsable" cuando no se ha pagado nada.
9. Con la excepción del diferente tratamiento dado a los créditos fiscales exigibles en los sistemas de imputación del impuesto sobre sociedades (§§ 31–33).
10. No se trata aquí de verdaderos gastos tributarios en sentido formal, ya que tales gastos requieren que se identifique un sistema tributario de referencia para cada país o, mejor si cabe, una referencia internacional común y, en la práctica, no se ha logrado acuerdo sobre esta última.
11. A menos que se basen en la plusvalía obtenida con la venta, en cuyo caso se clasificarían como impuestos sobre las ganancias de capital, en las subpartidas 1120 o 1220.
12. Con todo, algunos países aplican la misma legislación a ambos en impuestos particulares sobre la renta, aunque las entradas procedentes de dichos impuestos suelen ser fácilmente atribuibles a uno u otro caso y pueden, por lo tanto, consignarse en la debida partida.
13. Por ejemplo, "[...] que son suficientemente autónomas e independientes y se comportan como si fueran sociedades [...] (incluido en el hecho de llevar) conjuntos completos de cuentas" (SCN 2008, 4.44).
14. En Canadá, país en el que se considera que rige un sistema de imputación, el crédito fiscal (no exigible) para el accionista nace en relación con el impuesto nacional sobre sociedades que se reputa haber pagado, tanto si ha surgido una obligación tributaria para la sociedad como si no. Habida cuenta de que no existe una conexión íntegra entre la obligación tributaria de la sociedad y el crédito concedido en relación con el impuesto sobre la renta en esos sistemas, los créditos por dividendos se tratan, junto con otros créditos fiscales, según lo descrito en el § 20.
15. Esto puede darse, por ejemplo, cuando ya existía un régimen para los empleados del gobierno previo a la introducción de un régimen general de seguridad social.
16. En el SCN 2008, se consideran transferencias de capital y no impuestos (véase el apartado A.8).
17. Mediante este sistema, la Unión Europea ajusta las diferencias entre los tipos de cambio empleados para determinar los precios de la política agrícola común (PAC) y los tipos de cambio reales. Los pagos realizados en este sistema pueden estar relacionados con importaciones o exportaciones y, cuando ha sido posible identificar por separado las respectivas cantidades, se han mostrado en el correspondiente epígrafe (5123 o 5124). En el presente informe, esas cantidades se han consignado en valores brutos (esto es, sin deducir ningún subsidio otorgado en el marco del sistema MCM).
18. Las transferencias de las utilidades de las loterías del Estado se consideran ingresos no tributarios (véase el § 63).
19. Véase el § 25(c) en relación con esta distinción.

OECD PUBLISHING, 2, rue André-Pascal, 75775 PARIS CEDEX 16
(23 2017 05 3 P) ISBN 978-92-64-27289-7 – 2017

www.ingramcontent.com/pod-product-compliance
Lightning Source LLC
Chambersburg PA
CBHW061201240926
51846CB00006B/1086
9789264272897